INDONESIA
Law and Society

INDONESIA
Law and Society

Editor

Timothy Lindsey

The Federation Press
1999

For Lanita Idrus, as always,
and for the two other women in my life,
Miriam and Samira Idrus Lindsey

Published in Sydney by

The Federation Press
71 John St, Leichhardt, NSW, 2040
PO Box 45, Annandale, NSW, 2038
Ph: (02) 9552 2200 Fax: (02) 9552 1681

National Library of Australia Cataloguing-in-Publication data:
    Indonesia Law and Society

    Includes index.
    ISBN 1 86287 311 9

    1. Law – Indonesia. 2. Law – Social aspects – Indonesia. 3. Law and politics – Indonesia.
    4. Islamic law – Indonesia. I. Lindsey, Timothy.

349.598

Typeset by The Federation Press, Leichhardt, NSW.
Printed by Ligare Pty Ltd, Riverwood, NSW.

Foreword

Arief Budiman

Many Indonesians do not believe in the rule of law, because they have virtually no experience of such a thing. Under the New Order government led by General Soeharto, law was manipulated to serve politics and the expression 'law of the ruler' was more often heard than 'rule of law'.

This notion that law must serve politics goes back to the pre-New Order period, however, when Indonesia was ruled directly by Soekarno after his Political Manifesto of 1959 (Manipol) led to the introduction of Guided Democracy. Declaring that 'the revolution has not finished', Soekarno added that one could not talk about revolution with lawyers because lawyers were inherently conservative. Soekarno's preference was for his radical and unpredictable 'law of the revolution'.

In studying the practice of law one must read it in the context of the socio-political dynamics of the society in question. One must study both the 'text' and the 'context' of the existing legal system. It is the same as studying religion: one cannot fully understand Islam or Christianity simply by reading the *Qur'an* or the Bible as texts. And one cannot understand the political system of a country just by studying its Constitution. One has to study also the society in which the religious text or the Constitution is being implemented. In this respect, religion, politics and law have similarities. All have 'texts,' consisting of rules to be followed. All have a 'context ' in which these rules are interpreted and implemented – and adjusted to social, political and economic needs and interests.

Indonesia: Law and Society uses a combination of textual and contextual approaches to the study of Indonesian law. Many of the contributions to this volume deal with the practices of law to analyse the dynamics of Indonesian society under the New Order government. Under Soeharto, law was bent by the powerful state functionaries and high military officers working together with the powerful business people. This meant that the political context of law was actually more important than any existing legal text.

Of course law in Indonesia is more than just a tool of the government. Complex value systems deriving from ancient local traditions and religions (Islam in most cases) have also influenced the writing of the text and continue to play a part in its implementation. In fact, the inherent conflict between state 'texts' and 'contexts' and alternatives deriving from popular traditions, often sources of resistance, must be a key theme in any reading of Indonesian law.

This book discusses this interaction between 'text' and 'context' in the Indonesian law, covering current debate on legal aspects of pluralism and syncretism; Islam; tradition and modernity; constitutionalism and ideology; judges and lawyers; trade and globalisation; and human rights to name a few. In fact, so much is covered that some readers will feel that this diversity of information has made them aware of the richness of the problems discussed but fails to offer a comprehensive conclusion. In my opinion, this is more the result of the complexity of the problem rather any shortcoming of the book. The fact that this is an edited

Foreword

book with a broad range of contributions – some previously published but revised and updated in a single volume for the first time – by a diverse range of authors with many different interests makes it impossible for the collection to offer a unified comprehensive conclusion. In some ways, this reflects the current circumstances of Indonesia itself. Problems are easily identified but solutions seem more elusive.

At a time of dramatic and unpredictable change in Indonesia the publication of a book that identifies the agenda for legal change is to be welcomed. It is to be hoped that *Indonesia: Law and Society* may play some part in both creating a better understanding of the Indonesian legal system and encouraging its reform.

Melbourne
July 1998

Contents

Foreword   v
   Arief Budiman

Acknowledgments   x
Sources   xi
Contributors   xii
Using this book   xiv
Table of Statutes   xv
Glossary   xxiii

Introduction: An Overview of Indonesian Law   1
   Timothy Lindsey

PART I
Locating Indonesian Law

1. From Rule of Law to Law of the Rulers – to Reformation?   11
   Timothy Lindsey

2. The Rule of Law, Economic Development & Indonesia   21
   Gary Goodpaster

PART II
Pluralism & Syncretism: *Adat* and *Syariah*

3. The Indonesian Chinese as 'Foreign Orientals' in the Netherlands Indies   33
   Charles A Coppel

4. *Hak Ulayat* and the State: Land Reform in Indonesia   42
   Rachel Haverfield

5. Beyond Dualism: Land Acquisition and Law in Indonesia   74
   Daniel Fitzpatrick

6. The State and *Syariah* in Indonesia 1945-1995   94
   MB Hooker

PART III
Tradition and Modernity: Sexuality, Marriage and the Law

7. Between Crime and Custom: Extra-Marital Sex in Modern Indonesian Law   111
   Sebastiaan Pompe

8. Polygamy and Mixed Marriage in Indonesia: The Application of the Marriage Law in the Courts   122
   Simon Butt

9. Murder, Gender and the Media: Sexualising Politics and Violence   145
   Saraswati Sunindyo

10. Islam and Medical Science: Evidence from Indonesian *Fatawa*: 1960-1995   158
   MB Hooker

Contents

PART IV
Constitution & Ideology: *Negara Hukum* & the Politics of Government

11. The *Rechsstaat* and Human Rights   171
    Mulya Lubis

12. Positivism and Romanticism in Indonesian Legal Thought   186
    David Bourchier

13. Not your Local Member   197
    Sugeng Permana

14. Regional Government and Central Authority in Indonesia   200
    Peter Holland

15. Decentralisation versus Administrative Courts: Which path holds greater promise?   221
    David Linnan

PART V
Law in Action: Judges, Lawyers and the State

16. Between State and Society: Professional Lawyers and Reform in Indonesia   227
    Daniel S Lev

17. The *Eksekusi* of the *Negara Hukum*: Implementing Judicial Decisions in Indonesia   247
    Simon Butt

18. Indonesia: Patrimonial or Legal State? The Law on Administrative Justice of 1986 in Socio-Political Context   258
    Bernard Quinn

19. The Tempo Case: Indonesia's Press Laws, the *Pengadilan Tata Usaha Negara* and the Indonesian *Negara Hukum*   269
    Julian Millie

PART VI
Nationalism and Globalisation: Commercial Regulation

20. The Transformation of Indonesian Commercial Contracts and Legal Advisers   279
    Veronica Taylor

21. Arbitration: A Viable Alternative for Resolving Commercial Disputes in Indonesia?   291
    Stephen B Green

22. Intellectual Property Law Reform in Indonesia   304
    Christoph Antons

23. Indonesian Islamic Banking in Historical and Legal Context   323
    Abdullah Saeed

Contents

PART VII
Deconstructing the Rule of Law: Human Rights

24. Culture, Ideology and Human Rights: The Case of Indonesia's Code
    of Criminal Procedure   339
    Daniel Fitzpatrick

25. 'But a Shadow of Justice': Political Trials in Indonesia   355
    Spencer Zifcak

26. Unionism and Workers' Rights in Indonesia – The Future   367
    Ian Fehring

27. Overlapping Sovereigns: Some Reflections on the Case Concerning
    East Timor   381
    Gerry J Simpson

Index   400

Acknowledgments

This book would never have been completed without the research and editing assistance of Simon Butt of the Australian National University, who brought enthusiasm, intelligence and hard work to our task of transforming 28 very different papers into a single book.

The idea for 'Indonesia: Law and Society' arose from a conference, 'Indonesian Law: The First 50 Years'. Convened by the Asian Law Centre at the University of Melbourne in 1995 and supported by a grant from the Australia Indonesia Institute, the conference commemorated the half-century since Indonesian independence. This was, to the best of my knowledge, the first Australian conference exclusively devoted to Indonesian law. In the course of the conference it became obvious that although many scholars were actively involved in researching Indonesian law and many had published widely on the specific subjects that interested them, the absence of a general text in English on Indonesian law was an obstacle to scholarship in this area. This book aims to fill that gap.

Accordingly, although this book contains revised versions of some papers presented for the first time at the Asian Law Centre conference (for example, Fitzpatrick on land, Hooker on *syariah*, Taylor on contracts, Antons on intellectual property and Simpson on East Timor) other scholars were invited to submit chapters in their area of expertise with aim of providing analysis of a representative selection of current issues in Indonesian law. In some cases this involved re-printing influential articles in an updated form. Of course, in almost all cases updating was required again when the incredible happened and President Soeharto stepped down. Acknowledgment of the specific sources of reprinted or adapted chapters appears overleaf.

It is hoped the book will be a useful resource for both research and teaching and will be used by lawyers as well as scholars working on Indonesia.

I am grateful to my colleagues at the Asian Law Centre and, in particular, Veronica Taylor and Malcolm Smith, for making available the research funding needed to finalise the editing of this book. My thanks also go to Stacey Steele, Anne Vouzellard and Andy Schmulow, Research Assistants at the Asian Law Centre, for the assistance they gave me in the editing process. Both Barry Hooker and Dan Lev also gave moral support and generous advice without which this project would have been incomplete.

Learning about Indonesia is a lifetime's journey. I am forever indebted to my parents, Jenny and Paul, who started me on it; and to Lanita, my wife, who showed me the way.

Tim Lindsey
October 1998

Acknowledgment of Sources

Sebastiaan Pompe first published his chapter under the same title in (1994) 150-1 *Bijdragen tot de Taal-, Land- en Volkenkunde*, pp 110-122. It is republished with the kind permission of the publishers of that journal.

Saraswati Sunindyo's chapter was first published under the same title by Duke University Press (Durham and London) in *Fantasizing the Feminine in Indonesia*, edited by Laurie J Sears, 1996, pp 120-139. It is republished with the kind permission of Duke University Press.

An extended version of MB Hooker's chapter on *fatawa* and medical science dealing also with Malaysia was previously published as 'Islam & Medical Science: Evidence from Malaysian and Indonesian *Fatawa*: 1960-1995', *Studia Islamica*, Dec 1997, vol 4: 1, 1-33.

Todung Mulya Lubis's chapter is an adapted version of Chapter 5 of his *In Search of Human Rights: Legal-Political Dilemmas of Indonesia's New Order, 1966-1990*, Gramedia, Jakarta, SPES, 1993.

Sugeng Permana's chapter first appeared in *Istiqlal*, 8 October 1997. It was reprinted in David Williams' translation in *Inside Indonesia*, January-March 1998: 3-4, and appears with the kind permission of the translator and the editors of that magazine.

Daniel Lev's chapter appeared previously in a much truncated version, delivered as a lecture and published as Working Paper no 2 (November 1992) by the Law Department of the School of Oriental and African Studies of the University of London.

Veronica Taylor's chapter draws on material that appeared in her '"Asian" Contracts: An Indonesian Case Study' in Milner, A and Quilty, M (eds), 1998, *Australia in Asia: Episodes*, Oxford University Press, Melbourne.

A version of Stephen Green's chapter was published as "Commercial Arbitration in Indonesia: Implications for Australia-Indonesia Trade and Investment", *Commercial Dispute Resolution Journal*, 1996 vol 3: 142-155.

A shorter version of Spencer Zifcak's Chapter was published in *Eureka Street*, Volume 8, No 6, 1998.

Ian Fehring's Chapter was developed from a paper written with Timothy Lindsey, 'Indonesian Labour Law Under the New Order: The Military and Prospects for Change', Working Paper No 7, Centre for Employment and Labour Relations, Faculty of Law, University of Melbourne, 1995

The analysis of self-determination in Gerry Simpson's chapter is largely drawn from his 1993 paper, "Judging the East Timor Dispute: Self-Determination at the World Court", *Hastings International and Comparative Law Review*, vol 17, no 3: 323-347 and from his article "Indispensable Sovereigns: Third and Fourth Parties in the Timor Gap Treaty Case at the World Court", *ILA, Marin House Papers* 1993 vol 4: 75-92. A shorter version of the chapter appeared in "The Timor Gap Treaty Case at the World Court", 28 *International Law News*: 1995, 43-49; and under the same title as part of a collection of International Law Association Occasional Papers in *ILA, Marin House Papers* vol 4: 75-92.

Contributors

Christoph Antons is a Lecturer in the School of Law and Legal Studies, La Trobe University, Melbourne, Australia.

David Bourchier graduated from Monash University with a Doctoral degree in 1996 and now lectures at the University of Western Australia. He has written widely on Indonesian politics.

Arief Budiman is the foundation Professor of Indonesian at the University of Melbourne, Australia and well-known reform activist in Indonesia. He is the author of *State and Civil Society in Indonesia*.

Simon Butt studied law at Gadjah Mada University, Yogyakarta and is completing his degree at the Australian National University. He was awarded the ANU University Medal for Asian Studies for his Honours Thesis on the *Mahkamah Agung* in 1996.

Charles Coppel is Associate Professor in the Department of History at the University of Melbourne, Australia. His Doctoral thesis was published as *Indonesian Chinese in Crisis*.

Ian Fehring is a barrister at the Victorian Bar with an interest in industrial and employment law.

Daniel Fitzpatrick is a Lecturer at the Faculty of Law, Australian National University. In 1996 he was granted a Merdeka Fellowship to research Indonesian commercial law.

Garry Goodpaster is a Professor of Law at the University of California, Davis. He is also former Chief of Party, The ELIPS Project, a USAID-Government of Indonesia joint law development program in Indonesia.

Stephen Green obtained his Masters degree in Law from Kyushu University, Japan, and is an Australian Barrister and Solicitor.

Rachel Haverfield studied law at Gadjah Mada University, Yogyakarta. She is a graduate of the University of Melbourne and now works as a solicitor with the firm of Arthur Robinson & Hedderwicks in Melbourne, Australia.

Peter Holland is Principal Lecturer, Swinburne University of Technology, Melbourne, Australia.

MB Hooker is Adjunct Professor of Law at the Australian National University and at Northern Territory University, Australia. He was formerly Professor of Comparative Law at Kent University, Canterbury, United Kingdom. He has written widely on Islamic and traditional laws in Southeast Asia and is the author of *Legal Pluralism: An Introduction to Colonial & Neo-colonial Law* and *A Concise Legal History of Southeast Asia*, to name a few.

Daniel Lev is Professor of Political Science at the University of Washington, Seattle, and the author of *The Transition to Guided Democracy* and *Islamic Courts in Indonesia* among many essays, books and articles about Indonesian and Malaysian politics and law.

Timothy Lindsey is Associate Director (South East Asia) in the Asian Law Centre and a Senior Associate of the Faculty of Law, both at the University of Melbourne, Australia. He is also a Barrister-at-Law and convenor of the Indonesia Forum at the University of Melbourne. His Doctoral thesis was published as *The Romance of K'tut Tantri & Indonesia*.

Acknowledgments

David Linnan is Associate Professor of Law holding appointments at the University of South Carolina, USA in the School of Law and the School of the Environment. A legal comparativist, he has performed extensive empirical research in Germany and Indonesia.

Todung Mulya Lubis is a prominent Indonesian human rights lawyer. He holds the degree of Master of Laws from Harvard and another from Boalt Law School, University of California, where he also obtained his SJD. He is a partner in the firm Lubis, Santosa & Maulana and a former chair of the Indonesia Legal Aid Foundation (Yayasan Lembaga Bantuan Hukum – LBH). He also teaches at the University of Indonesia.

Julian Millie is a postgraduate student with the Centre for Southeast Asian Studies at Monash University, Australia.

Sugeng Permana is the pen-name of an Indonesian activist who wishes to remain anonymous.

Sebastiaan Pompe is Lecturer in Indonesian law at the University of Leiden, The Netherlands. He holds degrees from the School of Oriental and African Studies in London and the Universities of Cambridge and Leiden.

Bernard Quinn is a graduate in Law and Asian Studies from the Australian National University and now works as a solicitor with the firm of Arthur Robinson & Hedderwicks in Melbourne, Australia.

Abdullah Saeed is Head of Islamic Studies in the Melbourne Institute of Asian Languages and Societies at the University of Melbourne, Australia. He has published widely on Islamic law and, in particular, on banking and *riba*.

Gerry Simpson is a Senior Lecturer in the Faculty of Law at the Australian National University; and a Doctoral candidate at the University of Michigan Law School.

Saraswati Sunindyo is an Assistant Professor in Women's Studies at the University of Washington, Seattle and holds the Jane Watson Irwin Chair in Women's Studies at Hamilton College, New York. Her poetry has been published in the Indonesian literary magazine, *Horison*, in Indonesian newspapers and widely in translation in English-language journals.

Veronica Taylor is Associate Director (Japan) in the Asian Law Centre and a Senior Lecturer in the Faculty of Law, both at the University of Melbourne, Australia. She is also an Associate of the Australia-Japan Research Centre, Australian National University. She is the editor of *Asian Laws Through Australian Eyes*.

Spencer Zifcak is Associate Professor of Law and Legal Studies at La Trobe University in Melbourne. He chairs the Victorian Section of the International Commission of Jurists.

Using This Book

An introduction to the themes explored in this book cross-referenced to individual chapters can be found in Chapter 1, 'From Rule of Law to Law of the Rulers – to Reformation' on page 11.

A brief summary of Indonesian legal history and the structure of the Indonesian legal system designed for the reader with no prior knowledge of Indonesia appears in the Introduction, 'An Overview of Indonesian Law' on page 1.

This book has been designed so that each chapter can be understood on its own by a reader with no prior knowledge of Indonesia. For this reason, Indonesian language words are redefined as they are first used in each chapter. In addition, a glossary of non-English language terms appears on p xxiii.

The modern Indonesian standard orthography determined by the Indonesian Ministry of Education since 17 August 1972 is used for all Indonesian words except where *ejaan lama* (old spelling) is used in quotation. In the case of names, the spelling used by the person named has been preferred where it is known, thus 'Soeharto', rather than 'Suharto'.

For simplicity the 'Law' has been preferred to 'Basic Law' or 'Act' in translating the term *undang-undang*. Likewise, 'Elucidation' has been preferred to 'Explanatory Memorandum' for *penjelasaan* when used in the context of legislation.

A table of statutes appears on p xv and a general index on p 400.

Table of Statutes

Decided cases and international conventions appear in the Index on p 400.

Colonial Laws

Civil Procedure Code for Europeans (BRV)
  Art 436: 293, 294
  Art 436(2): 293
  Arts 615-651: 295
  Art 643: 300
(Dutch) Civil Code
  Art 1365: 223
  Art 1401: 223
Constitutional Regulation (*Regeerings Reglement*) of 1854: 34
  Art 75: 4, 36, 37
  Art 109: 34, 35, 36, 37
Indies State Regulation or Indies Constitution *(Indische Staatsregeling)* of 1925: 38-41
  Art 131: 4
  Art 163: 4, 35-41
(Dutch) Law on Judicial Organisation
  Art 2: 223
Marriage Law of 1929: 106
Marriage Ordinance for Indonesian Christians of 1933 No 74: 125
(Dutch) Nationality Law of 1892: 38
Rechtsreglement buiten gewesten (Rbg)
  Art 206(1): 248
  Art 207(1): 248
  Art 208: 248
  Art 215(1): 248
  Art 259(1): 248
Reglemen Acara Pedata (HIR)
  Art 195(1): 248
  Art 192(2): 248
  Art 197(1): 248
  Art 200(1): 248
  Art 225(1): 248
Wet Administratiere Rechtspraak Overheidsbeslissingen
  Art 8(1): 224

Constitutions

Constitutional Regulation (*Regeerings Reglement*) of 1854: 34
  Art 75: 4, 36-37
  Art 109: 34-37
Indies State Regulation or Indies Constitution *(Indische Staatsregeling)* of 1925: 38-41
  Art 131: 4
  Art 163: 4, 35-41

Indonesian Constitution of 1945: 6-7, 14-15, 17, 100-104, 106, 109, 126, 130, 171-174, 176, 179, 181-183, 186-187, 189, 193-195, 197-199, 201, 206, 211, 222-223, 232-233, 259, 273-274, 283, 292-293, 304, 357, 368
  General Elucidation: 247
  Elucidation: 173, 201, 237, 269
  Elucidation Art IV: 191
  Art II: 191, 293, 304
  Art 1(2): 197, 275
  Art 2: 173
  Art 2(1): 199
  Art 2(3): 191
  Art 3: 173
  Art 4(1): 107
  Art 17: 107
  Art 17(1): 107
  Art 17(3): 107
  Art 18: 201
  Art 24: 176, 179
  Art 25: 176
  Art 27: 16, 124, 138, 198
  Art 28: 371
  Art 29: 103
  Art 29(2): 138
  Art 33: 18, 19, 52, 55, 283
  Art 33(3): 53, 86
Indonesian Constitution of 1949: 182, 201, 233, 304
  Art 233: 304
Indonesian Constitution of 1950: 6-7, 14-15, 192, 201, 206, 221, 233, 304

Statutes

Criminal Code
  Art 279: 128
  Art 281: 114
  Art 285: 114-115
  Art 286: 115
  Art 378: 113
  Art 1467: 61
  Art 1678: 61
Law No 18 of 1870 (Agrarian Law of 1870): 34, 53
Law No 22 of 1946 concerning Registration of Marriages, Reconciliation and Divorces: 100
  Art 1: 123

Law No 22 of 1948: 202-203
    Art 3(4): 202
    Art 13(1): 202
    Art 18(1): 202
    Art 23: 202
    Art 24: 202
    Art 25: 202
    Art 33: 202
    Art 36: 202
    Art 36(1): 202
    Art 42: 202
Law of 1950 concerning the Supreme Court: 300
Law No 44 of 1950: 202
Emergency Law No 1 of 1951: 112, 114-115
Law No 7 of 1955 concerning Economic Crimes: 349
Law No 18 of 1956: 371
Law No 32 of 1956: 205
Law No 1 of 1957: 204-207
    Art 6: 204
    Art 7: 205
    Art 19: 205
    Art 23: 205
    Art 23(1): 205
    Art 24(1): 205
    Art 31: 205
    Art 36: 204
    Art 44: 205
    Art 64: 205
    Art 65: 205
Law No 1 of 1958 concerning All Ex-Foreign Plantation Land: 53
Law No 68 of 1958: 124
Law No 5 of 1960 (Agrarian Law): 7, 15, 42, 47, 49-51, 54, 57, 61-63, 65-75, 82-83, 86-89, 91, 132
    Elucidation Part A (III)(2): 52
    Elucidation (Chapter II): 76
    Art IV: 52
    Art 2: 52
    Art 2(1): 53
    Art 2(4): 47, 49
    Art 3: 47, 51, 86
    Art 5: 42, 51, 75
    Art 5(3): 52
    Art 6: 52-53, 76
    Art 7: 52
    Art 10: 52
    Art 11(2): 48, 49
    Art 13: 75
    Art 15: 52
    Art 17: 52
    Art 18: 76
    Art 19: 75
    Art 20(2): 75
    Art 23: 75

    Art 24: 75
    Art 25: 75
    Art 27: 75-76, 88
    Art 27(3): 53
    Art 33: 52
    Art 34: 76
    Art 40: 76
    Art 46: 63
    Art 49(3): 75
    Art 56: 88
Law No 51 of 1960 concerning Prohibition on Using Land without Permission: 63
Law No 56 of 1960 concerning Maximum Land Holdings: 53, 253
Law of 1961 concerning the Revocation of Titles: 81, 83-84, 93
    Elucidation Art 2: 77
    Elucidation part 3: 77
    Art 3: 77
    Art 4(b): 77
    Art 6(1): 77
    Art 6(2): 77
    Art 8: 77
    Art 9: 77
Law No 21 of 1961 concerning Trademarks: 304, 315
Law No 11/PNPS/1963 (Anti-Subversion Law): 19, 183, 349, 356-359, 362
    Art 1(a): 357
    Art 1(b): 357
    Art 1(c): 357
    Art 7: 350
Law No 19 of 1964 concerning Judicial Power: 14, 174, 176, 193, 234
    Art 19: 176
Law No 13 of 1965 on the Organisation of the Civil Judiciary: 14, 174, 176, 234
    Art 23(1): 176
Law No 19 of 1965: 209
Law No 11 of 1966 concerning the Press: 270
    Art 4: 270, 275
    Art 7: 271
    Art 20(1)(a): 270
Law No 5 of 1967 concerning Forestry: 53, 62
    Art 5(2): 53
    Art 17: 47, 86
Law No 5 of 1969: 349, 356, 357
Law No 14 of 1969: 371
    Art 11: 371
Law No 14 of 1970 concerning Judicial Power: 14, 18, 48, 99, 103-104, 174-177, 238, 274
    Elucidation to Art 1: 176
    Art 2(1): 247, 252
    Elucidation to Art 3(1): 295

Art 4(3): 254
Art 10(3): 128
Art 11: 14, 175, 178
Art 26: 262, 274
Art 26(1): 259
Art 33(3): 248
Arts 67-72: 85
Law No 3 of 1971 on Combating Corruption: 349
Law No 1 of 1974 concerning Marriage: 104-105, 122-137, 140
General Elucidation: 106
General Elucidation part 2(a): 125
General Elucidation part 2(b): 125
General Elucidation part 2(c): 125
General Elucidation part 2(d): 125
General Elucidation part 2(e): 125
General Elucidation part 2(f): 125
General Elucidation part 3: 137
General Elucidation part 4(c): 127
General Elucidation part 4(2): 131
Art 1: 135
Art 2(c): 125
Art 2(d): 125
Art 2(e): 125
Art 2(f): 125
Elucidation of Art 2(1): 134
Art 2(1): 134-136
Art 3: 126
Elucidation para 4: 127
Art 3(2): 127
Art 4(1): 127
Art 4(2): 127
Art 5: 108
Art 5(1): 127
Art 8: 108
Art 8(f): 134
Arts 57-62: 134
Art 66: 135, 136
Art 68: 108
Art 69: 108
Law No 5 of 1974 on the Principles of Regional Government: 200, 209-210, 215-216, 218
Elucidation: 209
Art 13: 210
Art 14: 211-212
Art 15(1): 212
Art 17: 211
Art 22(1): 210
Art 22(3): 210
Art 23(1): 252
Art 35: 211
Art 38: 210
Art 39(1): 210
Art 39(2): 210
Art 39(3): 210
Art 88: 208

Law No 3 of 1975 concerning Political Organisations: 208
Law No 9 of 1976 concerning Narcotics: 349
Law No 5 of 1979 concerning Village Government: 56, 60-61, 80, 209
Art 1: 209
Art 2: 56
Art 3: 208
Arts 4-10: 209
Art 23(i): 252
Art 24: 209
Arts 27-30: 211
Art 28: 218
Art 31: 209
Arts 47-48: 211
Art 61: 218
Law No 8 of 1981: Code of Criminal Procedure of 1981 (KUHAP): 238
Art 1: 349
Art 2: 349
Arts 16-31: 180
Art 17: 345
Art 18: 344
Art 18(1): 344
Art 18(3): 344
Art 19: 345
Art 19(2): 344
Art 21(1): 345
Art 21(2)(3): 345
Art 21(4): 345
Art 24(1): 345
Art 24(2): 345
Art 24(4): 345
Art 25(2): 345
Art 26(1): 345
Art 26(2): 345
Art 31: 345
Art 50: 347-348
Art 51: 347
Art 52: 347
Art 55: 347
Art 56: 347
Art 62: 348
Art 66: 348-349
Art 69: 347
Art 70: 347-348
Art 71(2): 348
Arts 77-83: 346
Art 79: 346
Art 82: 345
Art 82(3): 346
Art 83: 346
Art 102(1): 344
Art 106: 344
Art 115(1): 347
Art 117: 347
Art 117(2): 347

Table of Statutes

Law No 8 of 1981: Code of Criminal
  Procedure of 1981 (KUHAP) (cont)
  Art 118(1): 347
  Art 118(2): 347
  Art 124: 346
  Art 134: 357
  Art 137: 344
  Art 141: 349
  Art 142: 349
  Art 152: 348
  Art 153: 348
  Art 154: 348, 357, 372
  Art 155: 357
  Art 175: 349
  Art 183: 349
  Art 184: 349
  Art 188(1): 349
  Art 188(2): 340
  Art 270: 344
  Art 284(2): 350
Law No 6 of 1982 concerning Copyright:
  304-311
  Elucidation to Art 1(1): 309
  Elucidation to Art 11: 310
  Art 1(1): 308-309
  Art 1(2): 308
  Art 5: 309
  Art 6: 309
  Art 6(2)(d): 310
  Art 7: 309
  Art 8: 309, 310
  Art 8(1a): 310
  Art 9: 309
  Art 9(1): 310
  Art 10: 306, 310
  Art 10(1): 309-310
  Art 10(2): 310
  Art 10(2)(b): 311
  Art 10(3): 310
  Art 10(4): 310
  Art 11: 307, 308
  Art 11(1)(a): 309
  Art 11(1)(e): 310
  Art 11(1)(h): 310
  Art 11(1)(k): 310
  Art 12: 308
  Art 15: 311
  Art 15(a): 311
  Art 15(1)(b): 311
  Art 15(1)(c): 311
  Art 16: 311
  Art 17: 311
  Art 26(1): 308
  Art 27(1): 308
  Art 36(1): 309
  Art 36(2): 309
  part IIA: 307
  part VA: 307
  part IV: 310

Law No 21 of 1982 concerning the Press:
  270
  Art 4: 270, 272
  Art 13(5): 270
  Art 33(h): 275
Law of 1984 concerning Trade and Tariff:
  375
Law No 8 of 1985 concerning Social Or-
  ganisations: 12, 126, 351, 369, 126
Law No 14 of 1985 concerning the Mah-
  kamah Agung: 17, 104, 172, 174,
  176, 243, 300
  Art 32: 249, 252
  Art 34: 250
Law No 2 of 1986 concerning the General
  Courts: 17, 172, 174-176, 243, 274
  Art 5: 178
  Art 13: 175
  Art 14(1)(e): 130, 254
  Art 16: 175
  Art 54(4): 243
Law No 5 of 1986 concerning Adminis-
  trative Justice: 223-226, 250, 258,
  260-267, 273-274, 276
  General Elucidation, para 1: 273
  Preamble: 260, 261
  Art 13(1): 276
  Art 16(1): 276
  Art 53(1): 273
  Art 53(2): 261
Law No 6 of 1986 on the Administrative
  Courts: 172, 174-175
Law No 7 of 1987 on Amendments to Law
  No 6 of 1982 on Copyright: 304, 307
Law No 2 of 1989
  Art 5: 346
Law No 6 of 1989 on Patents: 304, 312-315
  Art 1(1): 313
  Art 2(1): 312
  Art 3: 312
  Art 5: 312
  Art 6: 315
  Art 7: 312
  Art 8: 313
  Art 9(1): 315
  Art 10: 315
  Art 11(1): 313
  Art 13: 313
  Art 14: 313
  Art 15: 313
  Art 16: 313
  Art 17: 314
  Art 17(2): 314
  Art 20: 314
  Art 21: 314
  Art 21(2): 314
  Art 22: 313
  Art 42: 315

Art 62(2): 314
Art 62(3): 314
Art 65(3): 314
Art 68: 314
Elucidation to Art 68(3): 314
Art 71(1): 314
Art 71(2): 314
Art 78: 319
Arts 81-93: 314
Art 83(1)(a)(3): 314
Art 88(1): 314
Art 88(2): 314
Art 88(2a)(a): 314
Art 89(1): 314, 315
Art 89(1)(a): 314
Elucidation to 89(1)(a): 314
Arts 104-108: 315
Art 104(1): 315
Art 105(3): 315
Art 106(2): 315
Elucidation to Art 106(2): 315
Art 107: 315
Arts 109-113: 315
Art 131: 312
Law No 7 of 1989 concerning Religious
    Justice: 103, 129
Art 5(1): 104
Art 5(2): 104
Art 12(1): 104
Art 13(1): 130
Art 15(1): 104
Art 19(3): 104
Art 21(1): 104
Art 49(2): 104
Art 50: 105
Art 54: 105
Art 62: 105
Art 66(1): 105
Art 67(6): 105
Art 68(2): 105
Art 70: 105
Art 70(2): 105
Art 73: 105
Art 78: 105
Art 81(2): 105
Art 107(1): 106
Law No 10 of 1992 concerning Population
    and Prosperous Families: 51
Elucidation to 6(b): 51
Art 6(b): 51
Elucidation to 6(c): 51
Art 6(c): 51
Law No 19 of 1992 concerning Trade
    Marks: 304, 309-310, 315-319
Art 1: 316
Art 1(1): 316
Art 5: 316, 318
Art 5(a): 316

Art 5(b): 316
Art 5(c): 316
Art 6: 316, 318
Art 6(1): 317
Art 6(2)(a): 317-318
Art 6(2)(b): 317
Art 6(2)(c): 317
Art 6(2)(d): 317
Art 6(3): 318
Art 6(4): 318
Art 25(2): 316
Art 34(2): 318
Art 48: 319
Art 56(3): 318
Law of 1995 concerning Customs: 319
Law No 12 of 1997 on the Amendment of
    Law No 6 of 1982 concerning Copy-
    right: 307
Law No 13 of 1997 on the Amendment of
    Law No 6 of 1989 concerning Patents:
    312
Labour Law of 1997: 374

Draft Laws

Criminal Code Bill
Art 1(4): 118
Art 285: 114-115
Art 286: 115
Art 378: 113
Art 279: 128
Art 281: 114
Art 76: 120
Marriage Bill
Art 3: 123
Art 11: 135
Art 11(2): 123
Art 49: 123

Instructions

Instruction of Minister for Home Affairs No
    593/5707/SJ of 22 May 1984: 56
Presidential Instruction No 1 of 1991 (Com-
    pilation of Islamic Law): 106-9, 130
Introductory Consideration: 130
General Elucidation: 130
    General Elucidation part 1: 130
    General Elucidation part 5: 130
    Elucidation Art 1: 106
    Elucidation Art 3: 106
    Elucidation Art 4: 106
    Art 4: 108
    Elucidation Art 5: 106
    Art 56(3): 108
    Art 57: 116
    Art 58(1): 108
    Art 59: 114
    Art 189: 107

Government Regulations

Government Regulation No 2 of 10 October 1945: 7
Para II, 191
Government Regulation No 8 of 1953 concerning Control of State Lands: 63
Government Regulation No 10 of 1961: 42, 57, 58, 61
Art 7: 61
Art 25: 61
Government Regulation No 224 of 1961 concerning Division of Land: 53, 57
Government Regulation No 2 of 1962 concerning Conversion and Registration of Ex-Indonesian Rights to Land: 66
Government Regulation No 6 of 1970: 214
Government Regulation No 21 of 1970 concerning Forest Enterprise
Art 6: 56
Government Regulation No 9 of 1975: 128
Art 40: 127, 128
Art 41(b): 127
Art 41(c): 127
Government Regulation No 20 of 1976: 214
Art 2: 214
Government Regulation No 30 of 1980 concerning Disciplining Civil Servants: 130, 254
Government Regulation No 10 of 1983
Art 4: 127
Art 4(2): 127
Government Regulation No 27 of 1983
Art 12: 346
Government Regulation No 14 of 1986 on the Copyright Council: 305
Government Regulation No 1 of 1989 on Translation and/or Reproduction of Copyright Protected for Works of Education, Science, Research and Development: 305
Art 3: 311
Government Regulation No 45 of 1990 concerning Marriages Regulations for Civil Servants: 118, 131
Government Regulation No 7 of 1991: 250
Government Regulation No 32 of 1991 on the Importation of Raw Materials or Certain Patented Products for Domestic Pharmaceutical Products: 305, 314
Government Regulation No 33 of 1991 on Registration of Patent Attorneys: 305
Government Regulation No 34 of 1991 on Procedures for Application for Patent Registration: 305
Government Regulation No 3 of 1992 (Workers Social Security Law): 376
Government Regulation No 77 of 1992: 139

Government Regulation No 23 of 1993 on Procedures for Application for Trade Mark Registration: 305
Government Regulation No 8 of 1995: 216, 225
Government Regulation No 16 of 1997: 286
Government Regulation No 24 of 1997 concerning Registration of Land: 42, 53, 57, 59-61
General Explanation, Elucidation: 58
Art 1(5): 59
Art 7: 66
Art 9(1): 59
Art 18(3): 66
Art 24(2)(b): 47
Art 37: 61

Ministerial Regulations

Minister of Agrarian Affairs Regulation No 2 of 1962: 57
Art 8: 87
Minister of Internal Affairs Regulation No 6 of 1972
Art 11: 61
Minister of Internal Affairs Regulation No 11 of 1984 concerning Supervision and Development of Adat at Village Level
Art 3: 56
Art 5: 56
Minister of Justice Regulation No M.02-UM.09.08 of 1980: 348
Minister of Justice Regulation No M.14.-PW.07.03 of 1983
Art 17: 348
Minister of Justice Regulation No M.02.-UM.09.08 of 1983
Art 17: 348
Minister of Information Regulation No 1 of 1984: 271, 272, 274, 275, 276
Art 16: 271
Art 33: 271
Art 33(h): 272, 275
Minister of Justice Regulation No M.01-HC.03.01 of 1987 on the Regulation of Copyright: 305
Minister of Labour Regulation No 131 of 1970: 374
Minister of Labour Regulation No 20 of 1971: 374
Minister of Labour Regulation No 3 of 1993: 370
Art 2(a): 370
Art 2(b): 370
Art 2(c): 370
Minister of Labour Regulation No 62 of 1993: 373

Decrees

Decree No 39 of 1978: 297
Decree No 34 of 1981: 296
Government Decree No 1 of 1989
  Arts 6-7: 311
  Art 15(1)(c): 311
  Art 17: 311
  Art 18: 311
  Art 131: 311
Ministry of Labour Decree No 72 of 1984: 376
Ministry of Labour Decree No 4 of 1986: 373
Ministry of Labour Decree No 1108 of 1986: 373
Ministry of Labour Decree No 5 of 1987: 369-370
Ministry of Labour Decree No 50 of 1992: 376
Ministry of Labour Decree No 1 of 1994: 370
  Art 4: 370
Minister of Industry and Trade Decree No 259/MPP/Kep 7/1997 of 1997: 286
Minister of Internal Affairs Decree No 15 of 1975: 84
Minister of Internal Affairs Decree of 1976: 78-79
Ministry of Justice Decree of 1953: 312
Minister of Justice Decree No M.02-HC.01.01.1987: 316
Minister of Justice Decree No M.03-HC.02.01 of 2 May 1991: 316
Ministerial Decree No 2 of 1962 concerning Conversion and Regulation
  Art 8: 53
  Art 9: 66
Ministerial Decree 1975: 77-78.
  Art 1(3): 78
  Art 6(1): 78
  Art 6(2)(a): 78
  Art 6(2)(b): 78
  Art 6(3): 78
  Art 8(1): 78
  Art 8(2): 78
MPR Decree No XX/MPRS/1966: 137
  part II(A) para (3): 269
MPR Decree No IV/MPR/1973: 183
MPR Decree No II/MPR/1978
  Art 11: 254
MPR Decree No III/MPR/1978
  Art 11(3): 183
MPR Decree No II/MPR/1983: 174
MPR Decree No II/MPR/1988: 174
MPRS Decree No XX/MPRS/1966: 136, 269

MPRS Decree No II/MPRS/1960
  Appendix A, para 402: 50
Presidential Decree No 6 of 1959: 206, 207
  Art 4(4): 206
  Art 14: 206
  Art 14(2): 206
  Art 14(3): 206
  Art 15: 206
  Art 18: 206
  Art 19: 207
Presidential Decree No 150 of 1959: 193, 292
Presidential Decree No 5 of 1963: 356
Presidential Decree No 11 of 1963 concerning Combating Subversion: 349, 357
Presidential Decree No 1 of 1964: 134
Presidential Decree No 43 of 1971: 297
Presidential Decree No 82 of 1971 concerning KORPRI: 130, 254
Presidential Decree No 34 of 1981: 288, 295
Presidential Decree No 26 of 1988: 54
Presidential Decree No 53 of 1989 concerning Regional Industry: 49
Presidential Decree No 21 of 1991
  Art 3(1): 286
Presidential Decree No 55 of 1992 concerning Land Acquisition: 51
Presidential Decree No 55 of 1993 concerning Interests of Development: 53
Presidential Decree No 97 of 1993 concerning Permission for Foreign Investors regarding Rights to Land: 49
Presidential Decree No 15 of 1997: 305
Regeling Opdegemengde Huwelijikens 98-158 of 1896 (GHR)
  Art 7: 133

Decisions

Governor of East Java Decision of 15 September 1980 (GNRStab1898 No 158): 135
Head of the Jakarta Civil Registry Decision No 2158/-1.755.2/CS/1986: 135
Minister of Internal Affairs Decision No SK26/DDA/1970
  Art 9: 66
Minister of Justice Decision No M.04-PW.07.03 of 1988 on Copyright Investigators: 305
Ministerial Decision No 18 of 1975: 107
Ministerial Decision No 75 of 1984: 107
Presidential Decision No 82 of 1971: 179
Presidential Decision No 44 of 1974: 107
Presidential Decision No 15 of 1984: 107
Presidential Decision No 5 of 1993: 77

Presidential Decision No 55 of 1993: 77-80, 84
  Art 6: 78
  Art 8: 78
  Art 1: 79
  Art 2: 79
  Art 9: 79
  Art 10: 79
  Art 13: 79
  Art 14: 79
  Art 15: 79
  Art 19: 79

Miscellaneous

BANI Rules
  Art 4(2): 299
  Art 5: 300
  Art 11: 300
  Art 12: 300
  Art 12(2): 300
  Art 12(5): 300
  Art 17: 301

  Art 18: 301
  Art 19: 301
Estatuto das Sociedades Indigenas 1994 (Brazil)
  Art 14: 64
  Art 15: 64
Foreign Judgment Act (Australia)
  Art 7(2)(a)(xi): 293
  Art 7(2)(a)(iv): 293
  Art 7(5): 293
International Court of Justice Rules of Court
  Art 31: 386
International Court of Justice Statute
  Art 59: 385
  Art 62: 385
Indian Law 1973 No 6001 (Brazil): 64
Philippines Constitution of 1987
  Art 5(XII): 65
  Art 6(XIII): 65
  Art 22(II): 65
United Nations Charter
  Art 2(4): 395
  Art 2(7): 394-395
  Art 25: 392
  Art 75(e): 391

Glossary

abangan	nominal adherent to Islam, usually Javanese
ABRI (*Angkatan Bersenjata Republik Indonesia*)	Armed Forces of the Republic of Indonesia
adat	traditional or customary 'law'
adatrechtpolitiek	adat law policy
adatrechtskring	adat law area (literally, adat circle)
administratief beroep	administrative appeal
AHM (*Akademi Hukum Militer*)	Academy of Military Law
anak daerah	native son; a local (literally, a child of the area)
apel	appeal (of a judicial decision)
asas kekeluargaan	the family principle
asas tunggal	sole principle
Astek	worker's insurance
ayam goreng	fried chicken
badan hukum	legal entity
Badan Peradilan Semu	A quasi-judicial body
Bakorstanas (*Badan Koordinasi Bantuan Pemantapan Stabilitas Nasional*)	Coordinating Board for Assisting the Consolidation of National Stability
Bakosurtanal	National Coordinating Agency for Surveying and Mapping
banding	appeal (of a judicial decision)
BANI (*Badan Arbitrase Nasional Indonesia*)	Indonesian National Arbitration Body
bapak	father, an honorific equivalent to 'Mr'
Bappeda (*Badan Pembangunan Daerah*)	Provincial Development Planning Board
Bappenas (*Badan Perancangan Pembangunan Nasional*)	Government Development Planning Board
batal	void
beamtenstaat	bureaucratic state
benda	object
beschenn	dispose
bewusteloosheid	unconsciousness
Bhinneka Tunggal Ika	Unity in Diversity, literally 'many remain one' (Indonesia's national motto)
Biro Keuangan	Bureau of Finance
Biro Pembangunan	Development Bureau
BPH (*Badan Pemerintah Harian*)	Daily Government Board
BPHN (*Badan Pembinaan Hukum Nasional*)	Institute for National Legal Development
BPN (*Badan Pertanahan Nasional*)	National Land Affairs Body
bupati	regent
camat	sub-district head
catur tunggal	Soekarno's version of *Mahkejapol* (qv)
cupang	love bite
daerah tingkat I	level I region
daerah tingkat II	level II region

Darul Islam	'the abode of Islam'; the name of an armed movement seeking to establish an Islamic state in Indonesia in the 1950s
dasar negara	basis of the state
Demokrasi Terpimpin	Guided Democracy 1959-1966)
dengan kekerasan	with the use of force
dengan paksa	to compel
desa	village
Dewan Kekaryaan	Functional Service Board
Dewan Perwakilan Rakyat	See DPR
Dharma Wanita	'Women's Way' (the Association of Wives of Civil Servants)
dhukuh	hamlet
dikuasai	controlled
dimiliki	owned
dinas	government office
domeinverklaring	domain principle
DPPD (*Dewan Penelitian Pengupahan Daerah*)	Local Wage Research Council
DPD (*Dewan Pemerintah Daerah*)	Local Government Council
DPR (*Dewan Perwakilan Raykat*)	People's Representative Council
DPRD (*Dewan Perwakilan Raykat Daerah*)	Regional People's Representative Council
dukun	spiritual healer
dwi fungsi	'dual function', the formal ideology by which ABRI (qv) claims a socio-political role as well as a military role
egalite des armes	equality between the parties
eksepsi	demurrer (defence on legal grounds)
eigendom	a right of ownership of land, similar to the fee simple, under the Dutch Civil code
erfpacht	proprietary usufructuary right under the Dutch Civil Code
fasah	judicial process
fatwa (pl *fatawa*)	ruling(s) on a point of Islamic law
FBSI (*Federasi Buruh Seluruh Indonesia*)	All-Indonesia Worker's Federation
fikh/fiqh	rules or prescripts of Islamic law
finanzverfassung	local government share in national government revenue
fuehrer	leader
GOLKAR (*golongan karya*)	Functional Group (the Indonesian government's electoral vehicle)
gotong royong	mutual cooperation
guru	teacher
haji	returned pilgrim
hak	a right
hak menguasai negara	state right of control
hak milik	ownership right
hak panyampeto	communal *adat* land right (Kalimantan)
hak ulayat	communal *adat* land right
hak uji	The power to review the legality of a law
hakam	arbitrator
hakim	judge
harga catut	profiteering price

Glossary

harga umum setempat	local public price
HATI (*Hapus Hukum Mati*)	Abolish the Death Penalty
hibah	to grant or bequeath
HIP (*Hubungan Industrial Pancasila*)	Pancasila Industrial Relations
HIR (*Herziene Indonesisch Reglement*)	(Colonial) Revised Indonesian Regulation
Hoge Raad	High Court
HPHI (*Himpunan Nasehat Hukum Indonesia*)	Indonesian Legal Counsellors Association
hukum	law
hukum internasional	international law
hukum perdata	civil law
hukum pidana	criminal law
hukuman	punishment
ibu	mother, honorific equivalent to 'Mrs' or 'Ms'.
ICCPR	International Covenant on Civil and Political Rights
ICJ	International Commission of Jurists; International Court of Justice
ILO	International Labour Organisation
IPHI (*Ikatan Penasehat Hukum Indonesia*)	Indonesian Legal Advisors Association
ijma	scholarly consensus
ijtihad	individual opinion/interpretation
Ikadin (*Ikatan Advokat Indonesia*)	Indonesian Bar Association
Ikahi (*Ikatan Hakim Indonesia*)	Indonesian Judges' Association
iklim pembangunan	development climate
in forma pauperis	'in the form of a pauper' a term associated with voluntary unpaid legal assistance by advocates
Indische Staatsregeling	Colonial 'Indies State Regulation'
Instruksi Presiden	Presidential Instruction
integralistic staatsidee	integralist state concept
integralisticstaat	integralist state
Intel	Military intelligence service
jaksa	public prosecutor/district attorney
jaksa agung	attorney general/chief public prosecutor
jer basuki mawa beyo	sacrifice for the glory of the nation
jual	sell
jual-beli	trade
juru sita	bailiff
Kadin (*Kamar Dagang dan Industri*)	Chamber of Commerce and Industry
kabupaten	regency
Kanwil (*kantor wilayah*)	Regional office
kasasi	cassation (appeal on a point of law)
kasepuhan	council of village elders
kawula-gusti	lord/subject
keadilan	justice
Keadilan Sosial Bagi Seluruh Rakyat Indonesia	Social Justice for all Indonesian People
kebatinan	inner self/spiritualism/mysticism
kebijaksanaan	discretion, policy
kecamatan	sub-district
kernbegriff	supreme leader
kekosongan hukum	legal vacuum
Kelompok Tani Hutan	Jungle Farmers Group

kelurahan	area under administrative control of a *lurah*, or village chief
Kemanusiaan Yang Adil dan Beradab	A Just and Civilised Humanity
kepala desa	village head
keputusan	decision
Keraykatan Yang Dipimpin Oleh Hikmat Kebijaksanaan dalam Pemusyawaratan/Perwakilan	Leadership of the People by Wise Policies Arrived at through a Process of Consultation and Consensus
keterbukaan	openness
ketertiban	order
Ketuhanan yang Maha Esa	Supreme Being
kewewenangan	authority
KFM (*Kebutuhan Fisik Minimum*)	Minimum Physical Needs
khitab	(sacred) text
khitabiyyah	'woman of the book', usually Jewish, Muslim or Christian
Kodim (*Komando Distrik Militer*)	District Military Command
kompilasi	compilation
Kongres Perempuan Indonesia	Indonesian Women's Congress
Konstituante	Constituent Assembly
Kopkamtib (*Komando Operasi Pemulihan Keamanan dan Ketertiban*)	Operational Command for the Restoration of Security and Order
Koramil (*Komando Rayon Militer*)	Subdistrict Military Headquarters
KORPRI (*Korps Pegawai Republik Indonesia*)	Indonesian Civil Service Corps
kotamadya	municipality
KUA (*Kantor Urusan Agama*)	Office of Religious Affairs
KUHP (*Kitab Undang-undang Hukum Pidana*)	Criminal Code
KUHAP (*Kitab Undang-undang Hukum Acara Pidana*)	Code of Criminal Procedure
kumpul kebo	cohabitation
kyai	religious sage (Islamic)
Laksuda	See *Bakorstanas*
Landraad	'Native Court', the colonial Court of Law for indigenous Indonesians
Landraden	Plural of 'Landraad'
LAP	Land Administration Project
layak	appropriate
LBH (Lembaga Bantuan Hukum)	Indonesian Institute of Legal Aid
lembaga masyarakat desa	village council
lian	infidelity
LKMD (*Lembaga Ketahanan Masyarakat Desa)*	Village Public Security Council
LMD (*Lembaga Musyawarah Desa*)	Village Consultative Council
lurah	village head
machtsstaat	state based on power
madzhab	school of (Islamic) thought
Mahkejapol	Council of senior officials of the *Mahkamah Agung, Kehakiman* (Justice Department), *Jaksa* (prosecutor) and *Polisi* (police)
Mahkamah Agung	Supreme Court, the highest court in Indonesia
Mahkamah Islam Tinggi	Islamic Appellate Court

Majelis Pertimbangan Pajak	Tax Review Board
Manunggaling kawula lan gusti	the unity of authority and people
masyarakat hukum adat	*adat* law community
Masyumi (Majlis Syuro Muslimin Indonesia)	Modernist Islamic party (banned in 1960)
mempunyai kekuatan hukum yang tetap	has 'certainty status'
menteri	minister
met geweld	with the use of force
MPR *(Majelis Permusyawaratan Rakyat)*	People's Consultative Assembly, Indonesia's supreme sovereign body
MPRS *(Majelis Permusyawaratan Rakyat Sementara)*	Provisional People's Consultative Assembly
MPPH *(Majelis Pertimbangan Penelitian Hakim)*	Council for the Examination and Evaluation of Judges
mudaraba	A particular form of Islamic financial arrangement designed to avoid *riba*
mufakat	consensus/agreement
murah	cheap/inexpensive
Murba	common/proletariat *also* a minor Indonesian communist party
musyawarah/t	deliberation/discussion
nagari/negeri	country/state
notaris	notary
ne bis in idem	a crime cannot result in punishment twice
negara	state
negara hukum	law state, rule of law, state based on the rule of law
negara hukum berdasarkan Pancasila	law stated based on Pancasila
negara Islam	Islamic state
NEI	Netherlands East Indies
NGO	Non-Government Organisation
NU *(Nahdlatul Ulama)*	Association of Islamic scholars (Islamic organisation).
onrechtmatig	unlawful
operasi tertib	operation order (operation to establish order)
organisasi perjuang	struggle organisation
otonomi yang nyata dan bertanggung jawab	real and responsible (local) authority
P4P *(Panitian Penyelesaian Perburuhan Pusat)*	Central Labour Dispute Arbitration Committee.
pamong praja	civil service/government bureaucracy
Pancasila	Indonesia's National Ideology
pangreh praja	civil service/government bureaucracy
panitera	court clerk
panyanturi	communal *adat* land right (Kalimantan)
pasal	article (of a law)
patuanan	communal *adat* land right (East Sumatra)
paer/payer	communal *adat* land right (Bali)
PDI *(Partai Demokrasi Indonesia)*	Indonesian Democracy Party
pegawai negeri	civil servant
pelaksanaan eksekusi putusan	implementing the execution of a decision
pemali	wrath of the gods or spirits
pembangunan	development
pembebasan	release
pembreidelan	banning or cancelling

pemerintah	government
pemerintahan yang baik	good government
pembinaan	building up, development
pencabutan	revocation
pencatat	registrar
penduduk	inhabitant/occupant
penegak hukum	upholder of law
penetapan	decision/decree/ communal *adat* land right (Kalimantan)
pengacara	lawyer
pengacara praktek	practical lawyer
pengadilan	court
pengadilan agama	religious court
pengadilan militer	military court
pengadilan negeri	state court, district court, court of first instance
pengadilan tinggi	high court, court of appeal
pengadilan tata usaha negeri (PTUN)	Administrative Law Court
penghulu	Islamic priest
pengurus adat	adat leader
peninjauan kembali	Review of the facts of a case by the *Mahkamah Agung*, sometimes used to mean judicial review of legislation
pejabat	office holder, official
penjelasan	Elucidation, the explanatory memorandum that forms part of Indonesian statutes
Peradin (*Persatuan Advokat Indonesia*)	Indonesian Advocates Association
peraturan	regulation
perkawinan	marriage
perkawinan antar agama	interreligious marriage
perkawinan campur	mixed marriage
perkara	case
permusyawarahan	deliberation/discussion
Persahi (*Persatuan Sarjana Hukum Indonesia*)	Indonesian Lawyers Association
persatuan Indonesia	Indonesian unity
pesantren	local Islamic schools
petrus (penembak misterius)	mysterious gunmen
pertuanan	upper class/ landlord
perwakilan	representation
piagam Jakarta	Jakarta Charter
PKI (*Partai Komunis Indonesia*)	Indonesian Communist Party
PKK (*Pembinaan Kesejahteraan Keluarga*)	Organisation for Family Welfare
PNI (*Partai Nasionalis Indonesia*)	Indonesian Nationalist Party
pokrol bambu	bush lawyer
Polres (*Polisi Resort*)	district police
Polsek (*Polisi sektor*)	sub-district police
PPAT	Notarial Deed Official
PPP (*Partai Persatuan Pembangunan*)	United Development Party
prabumian	communal *adat* land right (Bali)
pra-peradilan	pre-trial
priyayi	upper class (Javanese)
propinsi	province
PRRI (Pemerintah Revolusioner Republik Indonesia)	Revolutionary Government of the Republic of Indonesia

PTHM	College of Military Law
PTUN (*Pengadilan Tata Usaha Negara*)	Administrative Law Court
Raden van Justitie	Colonial Court of Justice
Repelita (Rencana Pembangunan Lima Tahun)	Five Year Development Plan
rechtsstaat	rule of law, state based on law
rechtsgemeenschappen	adat law area
rechtsstam	adat law area
riba	forbidden interest payment, usury (Islam)
rukun tetangga	neighbourhood association
rukun warga	administrative unit
rumah tangga	household
santri	orthodox adherent to Islam
SBM (*Serikat Merdeka Buruh*)	Independent Workers' Union
SBSI (*Serikat Buruh Sejahtera Indonesia*)	Indonesian Workers Prosperity Union
secara sukarela	voluntarily
sekretariat daerah	regional secretariat
shikak	serious disagreement
sistem pemerintahan	system of government
sjiqaq	serious disagreement
SK (*Surat Keputusan*)	written decision
SOBSI (*Sentral Organisasi Buruh Seluruh Indonesia*)	All-Indonesian Central Labour Organisation
SPSI (*Serikat Pekerja Seluruh Indonesia*)	All Indonesian Employees Union
stabilitas	stability
State *Ibuism*	Indonesian state ideology whereby women are viewed and treated only as mothers and wives
suku	clan
sunna	traditions of the prophet in Islam
surat nikah	marriage certificate
surat sakti	immutable or sacred letter
syariah	The whole corpus of Islamic jurisprudence
syigag	irreconcilable difference
tajdi	Islamic revivalism
talak	unilateral divorce initiated by the husband
tanah	land
tanah kas desa	village's land assets
tanah negara	state land
tanah titisari	*hak ulayat* land in Cimaca, West Java
taqwa	obedience
temenggung	title of regent or high ranking royal official
Tennoo	Emperor of Japan
terdakwa	the accused in criminal proceedings
Tim Koordinasi Pengelolaan Tata Ruang Nasional	Coordinating Team for National Spatial Management
toetsingrecht	judicial review
transmigrasi	transmigration
tuan tanah	landlord
UDHR	Universal Declaration of Human Rights
UGM (Universitas Gadjah Mada)	Gadjah Mada University
ulama	Islamic scholar
undang-undang	statute

undang-undang dasar	constitution
UUPK (*Undang-undang Pokok Kehutanan*)	Basic Forestry Law
wadah tunggal	unified organisation
Walhi (Wahana Lingkungan Hidup Indonesia)	Indonesian environmental NGO
wahyu	divine radiance; spiritual aura
wakaf	religious foundation
Walikota	mayor
Wetboek van Koophandel	Dutch Commercial Code
Wetboek van Strafrecht	Dutch Criminal Code
wewengkon	communal *adat* land right (Java)
wilayah	region
yasan	individual right to land that accrues when forest land is cleared and cultivated
YLBHI (*Yayasan Lembaga Bantuan Hukum Indonesia*)	Indonesian Institute of Legal Aid Foundation
yurisprudensi	jurisprudence (judicial decisions)
zaak	object; business; (law) case
zina/zinah	adultery

Introduction

An Overview of Indonesian Law

Timothy Lindsey

This introduction aims to provide a broad overview of the development of the Indonesian legal system, aimed at the reader with no prior knowledge. The issues addressed here in general terms are considered in detail elsewhere in this book.

Indonesian law is often described as a member of the 'civil law' group of systems found in European countries such as France and Holland, as opposed to 'common law' systems such as those in the United Kingdom and its former colonies. This description is true to the extent that much of Indonesia's legal system is derived from Dutch models inherited from the archipelago's former colonial master. Government sources claim that 400 pieces of Dutch legislation remain in force today (Pakpahan, 1995) and in many ways the modern Indonesian state has continued to rely on the coercively backed bureaucratic method of rule developed under colonial rule. It would be wrong, however, to assume that Indonesia has simply adopted the Dutch legal system.

Indonesia's history has been characterised not only by successive waves of influence from overseas but also by its people's ability to absorb those influences and make them part of their own systems. This process is often emphasised in sociological, anthropological and historical studies of the region but it is equally applicable to a legal analysis.

It is therefore misleading to speak of an Indonesian legal system. In fact, as in many other former colonies, the law that emerged after independence is made up of several legal systems interwoven with each other and operating simultaneously.[1] To understand how these systems now operate, it is necessary to understand some of the basic themes of Indonesian legal history. What follows is a generalised summary of the development of modern Indonesian law divided into four periods: the 'traditional' period (up to the early 19th century); the 'colonial' period (from the early 19th century to 1945); the Old Order (from 1945 to March 1966);[2] and the New Order, under Soeharto from March 1966 to 21 May 1998 when he resigned, to

---

1   For a discussion of the implications of legal pluralism and its links to colonialism, see Hooker (1975).

2   I date the New Order from the 11 March 1966, when President Soekarno was coerced into granting the *Supersemar* Decree (*Surat Perintah Sebelas Maret* – Letter of Instruction of 11 March) by which he transferred presidential authority for the restoration of security – and effective control of the government – to General Soeharto. Soeharto was not formally installed as President until 1968.

be replaced by his former deputy, President BJ Habibie. These delineations are made for convenience of analysis and the periods should not be seen as discrete. Each has influenced those that it succeeds and will continue to do so in the foreseeable future.

Traditional Laws and Early European Presence

Indonesian society has long been made up of a diverse range of ethnic groups. Some observers argue that as many as 300 discrete cultures can still be identified although most scholars agree that they can be grouped into 19 main categories.[3]

In rural areas, village communities were the norm and this was traditionally the basic unit of Indonesian societies. When urbanised centres developed, they took the form of simple city-states. The classic kingdoms of pre-colonial Indonesia were small inland principalities based on wet rice, or *padi*, cultivation. Others controlled sea ports and become entrepots, acting as trading links between inland agricultural societies and the multicultural sea traders of Southeast Asia.

Whether located on the coast or in the hinterland, the rulers of these traditional city states were closely identified with their metropoles, the focus of the rituals and structures by which their power was defined and articulated. They ruled through a constantly shifting web of regional allegiances; and relied upon aristocratic bureaucracies to administer the state and provide military support. Outside their urban centres, these states were loosely defined and characterised by their constant rivalry with other small states for control of the widely distributed village communities in which lived the majority of the population. Significantly, the ruler and the bureaucratic hierarchy also administered law which in the urban context was chiefly concerned with ownership of land, inheritance and marriage and, of course, social control – as reflected in a preponderance of criminal provisions in early legal codes. To the extent that the law of this period was codified, it often reflected influences from Indic Hindu and Buddhist cultures. From the 14th century onwards, however, *syariah,* or Islamic law, came increasingly to determine the content of both public law and some aspects of private law. This was particularly the case in the coastal principalities where Islam came as a religion of trade, providing an ideological justification for breaking with Hindu-Buddhist inland overlords. Both Indic and Islamic cultures were, however, always mediated through pre-existing indigenous cultures, usually focused on animism and the spirit world.

As influential as the urban cultures in the development of traditional Indonesian ideas of law were the cultures of the rural hinterland. Village communities living in a traditional style had often only limited contact with the principalities which commanded their nominal allegiance. Diverse ethnic groups observed laws which were indistinguishable from their traditional customs and religious beliefs. These laws were typically concerned with the agricultural cycle and the stages of life from birth, through adolescence and marriage to death. They typically show strong

---

3 Aceh; Gayo, Alas and Batak islands; Minagkabau; South Sumatra; East Sumatra, Malaya and West Borneo; Bangka and Billiton; Borneo; Minahasa; Gorontolo; Toraja; South Sulawesi; Ternate archipelago; Ambon and the Moluccas, Irian Jaya; Timor archipelago; Bali and Lombok; Central and East Java; the Sultanates of Solo and Yogyakarta; and West Java (Sunda).

influence from animist and pre-Indic folk beliefs, as well as an overlay of the combination of Hindu, Buddhist and Islamic ideas previously identified as typical of traditional urban societies.

As traditional jurisprudence continued to evolve across the archipelago, it developed into a complex fusion of parochial pre-Indic magico-religious legal ideas, linked to animism, and spirit and ancestor worship; Hindu-Buddhist concepts of universal law; and Islamic notions of sacred authority. This idiosyncratic amalgam formed the basis of Indonesia's pre-colonial legal systems but its content varied radically from place to place. So, for example, while Balinese legal culture remained dominated by Hindu-Buddhist influences, Aceh in Northern Sumatra became a stronghold of Islamic thought and the tribal peoples of West New Guinea (now Irian Jaya) continued as animists, without significant influence from other cultures or religions. In many parts of Indonesia, particularly in the outer islands and more isolated regions, these traditional customary forms of law or *adat,* continue today to be a major source of law for everyday life.

While European influence began to interrupt indigenous political control of the archipelago from the mid-17th century onwards, it was not until the early 19th century that Dutch interests expanded significantly beyond Java and a fully developed colonial state was established.

In the early period of Dutch involvement, the Dutch showed little interest in interfering with traditional laws. They were interested more in protecting their commercial trading interests. At first, the Dutch Law of the Sea applied to Europeans in Dutch settlements (from 1596 to 1609). From 1609, VOC regulations applied. The Dutch VOC, the *Vereenigde Oost-Indische Compagnie* or United East India Company, exercised a policy of minimal social legal intervention and maximum economic interference from around 1600 until the late 1700s. Supplanting indigenous rulers at the top of the traditional social, economic and legal pyramids, the Dutch used the existing bureaucratic state to administer the indigenous peoples. Outside the Dutch trading bases, the urban laws of the indigenous princes and, in agrarian areas, traditional *adat* – both frequently entwined with *syariah*, or Islamic law – continued largely undisturbed, save where these systems interfered with Dutch commercial interests and trade.

Dutch Colonialism

The occupation of the Netherlands by the French in 1795 was to bring major changes to the administration of Dutch possessions in the East Indies. The early decades of the 19th century were marked by extensive reforms under Herman Willem Daendels, the Napoleonic Governor-General. He began a process by which the colonial presence was reinvented in terms of the assumption of sovereignty and administrative authority by the colonising state. In 1811, however, the consequences of the European war between Britain and France were felt in Southeast Asia. In that year Thomas Stamford Raffles, later famous as the founder of Singapore, extended English legal jurisdiction over what had briefly been 'Napoleonic' Java.

This interregnum did not, however, bring an end to the processes initiated by Daendels. Raffles' five-year rule as Lieutenant-Governor was also marked by a program of change, adopting much of his predecessor's model. Although many of the ideas of these two reformers were never fully implemented, they were originators of a 'colonial revolution', replacing or appropriating indigenous institutions as it suited the purposes of the colonial state they were bringing into being, albeit for different European masters (Ricklefs, 1993: Chapter 10).

Accordingly, by the time most of the archipelago was returned to the Netherlands in 1816 as part of the general reconstruction of European interests following Napoleon's defeat, the colonial administration of the Indies had moved from the trading outpost model to a more imperial style. Within a few decades, the Dutch had defeated the Diponegoro uprising in Java (1825-30) and were consolidating their hold in Sumatra and other outer islands where wars of conquest were being fought. While the Dutch still maintained a policy of only limited interference in 'native' affairs, it was clear that rationalisation of the parallel European and indigenous legal systems was required to reflect the vastly expanded nature of their colonial interests.

The essentially 'apartheid' structure of colonial jurisprudence was embodied in Art 75 of the *Regerings Reglement* of 1854, the de facto colonial Constitution, which divided the population of the Netherlands East Indies into Europeans; and *inlanders* or non-Christian natives. This latter category theoretically included indigenous Indonesians as well as Chinese, Arabs and Indians, although in practice indigenes were treated as a discrete group. This distinction was later confirmed in Arts 163 and 131 of the *Indische Staatsregeling* (as amended) of 1925 which defined three racial groups (Europeans – including the Japanese as 'honorary Europeans'; 'foreign orientals' – Chinese, Indians and Arabs; and 'natives'). The effect of these regulations was to create three legal systems such that different laws applied to each racial group. Although these provisions had the effect of confirming that *adat* remained the law applicable to most of the indigenous population (Gautama & Hornick, 1974: Chapter 2) the commercial and political imperative of securing and protecting Dutch commercial interests meant that exceptions existed in the case of criminal law and state security. In these areas, Dutch law applied to all individuals, regardless of their ethnic background. Likewise, in the case of commercial law, any person dealing with a European came under European law for the purposes of that transaction, thus securing the mercantile dominance of the colonisers.

In time a complex jurisprudence developed to deal with legal problems involving persons of different racial groups. Known as *hukum antargolongan,* or 'intergroup law', sophisticated rules arose to deal with transfer of individuals between racial and legal groups and to define the status of persons of mixed race. Racial division manifested itself even in the structure of the judicial system. As with the colonial system of dual bureaucracies in which European officers 'shadowed' native officials, so dual court systems arose. With the Japanese occupation of the archipelago from 1942 to 1945 this judicial duality was formally abolished but the Dutch plural legal system that underpinned it continued in force, save where Japanese security, 'war economy' and censorship decrees supervened. The Japanese preferred a modified version of the complex colonial legal system to the chaos they expected would result from its removal.

Since the turn of the century Indonesian nationalists had struggled for national rejuvenation and independence. The 'Ethical Policy' implemented in the first three decades of the 20th century was an attempt by the Dutch government to correct the social consequences of their systematic economic exploitation of the colony in the

19th century. A new educational liberalisation brought *inlanders* of all ethnic groups together in centres of learning in Batavia and Bandung and for the first time created an educated and politicised 'native' intelligentsia. Exposed to radical Western political ideas, an articulate, energetic nationalist movement soon evolved. This was to find its first expression in organisations devoted to the cultural rejuvenation of particular ethnic groups, such as *Budi Utomo*, a Javanese organisation founded in 1908. By 1912, however, a pan-Indonesian political radicalism linked to Islam had become an alternative to regionalist culturally-oriented chauvinism, a change exemplified by the founding of *Sarekat Islam* (Islamic Association). Originally intended to defend the interests of indigenous Islamic traders against European and Chinese competitors, it rapidly became a nationalist political movement, often expressing radical ideas in traditional forms. It in turn spawned major political parties such as the *Partai Komunis Indonesia* (PKI) or Indonesian Communist Party and the *Partai Nasional Indonesia (*PNI*)* or Indonesian Nationalist Party, led by the charismatic Soekarno.

By the time World War II began in 1939, however, most nationalist leaders had been jailed, exiled or silenced. There seemed little real prospect of independence, whether through negotiation or force of arms. Ironically, it was another conquest of the Indies that was ultimately to deliver freedom to Indonesia. Hailed as fellow-Asian liberators in 1942, the Japanese gained cooperation from nationalist leaders with thin promises of independence backed with threats of imprisonment or worse.

Only when it became clear that Japan would lose the war in the Pacific were nationalists able to call in their occupiers' promise. On 17 August 1945, two days after the Japanese surrender, Soekarno and Hatta (the two key leaders of the nationalist movement) obtained covert Japanese approval and proclaimed the independence of Indonesia to a small group of supporters in Batavia, soon to be renamed Jakarta – the city of Victory. It would take five years of armed revolution and negotiation before the world community accepted their claim. It would take even longer before Indonesia's new rulers could begin to deal with the problem that had so occupied the Dutch and defeated the Japanese: what legal system could replace colonial law; service a vast and complex state adequately; take into account diverse traditional cultures and the region's many religions; fit the needs of a modernising society; and be somehow 'Indonesian'?

The declaration of Indonesian independence was to be the start of a process by which the laws and systems of a new state evolved, rather than the moment of their creation.

The Old Order: 1945 – 1966

For five years following the declaration of independence on 17 August 1945 Indonesians fought a bloody war of independence against the Dutch. At times it seemed that the embattled, ill-equipped and inexperienced Republic would be overwhelmed by well-armed Dutch forces, fresh from the Allied defeat of the Axis forces in Europe and the Pacific. A hard-fought guerrilla campaign was sustained, however, by *pemuda* (youths). Often armed only with bamboo poles and knives they were led effectively by a small corps of soldiers previously trained by the Japanese and, ironically, the Dutch colonial military. Indonesia's youth were supported in their armed struggle by the astute diplomacy of gifted politicians such as Sjahrir, Soekarno and Hatta who had learnt both their craft and the value of persistence in long years of protest, exile and imprisonment under the Dutch.

Eventually, popular opinion in the West – and, in particular, the United States – turned against colonialism. The Dutch claim on the Indies was increasingly seen as morally unjustifiable in light of the war just won against what was seen as German and Japanese imperialism. Post-war reconstruction aid to the Netherlands became a key bargaining chip. Eventually a settlement was negotiated under the auspices of United Nations, through the 'good offices' of America, Australia and Belgium who acted as facilitators of talks. In December 1949, sovereignty was formally transferred to the Republic of the United States of Indonesia, an essentially Dutchcreated and United Nations-sponsored state with a federal Constitution, loosely based on Western models. This federal system, seen by many Indonesians as an attempt by the departing Dutch to set up 'puppet states', soon collapsed. It was replaced by a provisional unitary parliamentary Constitution largely identical to its predecessor but without a federal structure. This new system was always regarded as temporary and a Constituent Assembly – the *Konstituante* – was established to draft a permanent Constitution. The fundamental question therefore remained unresolved: just what sort of legal structure should the new state of Indonesia have?

Both the federal and parliamentary constitutions faced a continued challenge from the skeletal revolutionary Constitution of 1945 which had been briefly in force in Republican-controlled areas during the revolution. All constitutions shared a similar approach to one issue, however – the basic structure of the legal system. The framers of all three Constitutions, like the Japanese and Dutch before them, saw the prospect of abolishing the colonial plural system by replacing colonial statutes and *adat* and *syariah* with new statutes as an impossibly large and time-consuming project. Accordingly, transitional provisions stated that all existing institutions and regulations valid at the date of independence would continue to be valid pending the enactment of new legislation in conformity with the Constitution. Their effect was to add the legislation and other laws produced by the government of independent Indonesia to the existing, essentially colonial, mixture of interacting *adat, syariah* and Dutch jurisprudence. As it was to be many years before the Indonesian political system was sufficiently stable to allow a comprehensive and coordinated legislative program, the end result of the transitional provisions was, effectively, the survival of the colonial legal status quo. The great problem of Indonesian jurisprudence – what laws for the new state? – remained unresolved.

In Indonesia today legal pluralism continues. In the rural sector, many Indonesians continue to live out their lives under the laws that have applied to their ethnic group for centuries before Europeans arrived. At the same time, however, Islamic law, once so important in the coastal principalities, is in decline, its jurisdiction restricted to limited areas of family and inheritance law.

Indonesia's experiment with parliamentary democracy under the 1950 Constitution was marred by instability as parties jostled for dominance in a frequently-splintered parliament. Rivalry between parties and political crises as the military intervened to put down regional rebellions meant that there was little opportunity for law reform. Indonesia's legal system remained largely the same as that which the Dutch had established before the Japanese invasion of 1942, save for the unified court system introduced by the Japanese and the democratic parliamentary system of the 1950 Constitution. Political turmoil meant there was little real opportunity for sustained consideration of the broader legal issues underpinning the tumultuous operation of the new state, other than in the *Konstiuante*. Here debate raged but, as in the parliament, agreement seemed elusive. Indonesia's political factions returned to the agendas they had temporarily abandoned to fight the revolution against their common enemy. For many, even the fundamentals remained unresolved. A key issue remained the question of what sort of a state Indonesia was to be – democratic, Islamic, communist, socialist, military or authoritarian?

In 1959, President Soekarno, with the support of the armed forces, dissolved the *Konstituante* and unilaterally declared a return to the 1945 Constitution. This coup allowed him to do away with both the parliamentary party system and secured him great personal power. With resurrection of the revolutionary, wartime Constitution, Indonesia returned to an authoritarian system similar in some ways to the colonial and traditional models of a ruler exercising control through a patrimonial bureaucracy backed by military force.

The analogy with the colonial system has it limits, however. The period of presidential rule from 1959 to 1965 (which came to be known as 'Guided Democracy') was also a period of radical revolutionary legal culture. Law became secondary to policy and the 'revolutionary' politics espoused by the charismatic 'President for Life' and 'Great Leader of the Revolution'. From a theoretical point of view, Government Regulation No 2 of 10 October 1945 was important in this subordination of law by policy. This regulation provided that Dutch law could only survive in accordance with the transitional provisions of the 1945 Constitution, if it was not contrary to that Constitution. This meant that Dutch law which was not in accordance with Soekarno's leftist revolutionary policies (considered to embody the 'spirit' of that Constitution) was unenforceable.

In effect, the question of whether law was sufficiently 'revolutionary' was a matter for the President, who thereby became the de facto source of legal legitimacy. His interference in the judicial process led to the judiciary being increasingly seen as a mere arm of the executive (Lev, 1972: 246-318). The legal profession, and in particular the judiciary, became degraded and demoralised. The consequences for legal certainty and commercial confidence are obvious but the results were more far-reaching and subtle in jurisprudential terms.

These developments were also part of an old and continuing debate about the 'Indonesian-ness' of law. Led by the prominent jurist Soepomo, the chief drafter of the 1945 Constitution, Indonesian lawyers began a search for an intrinsically 'Indonesian' law, based on principles derived from *adat*. A direct product of this process was declaration in a Circular Letter (*surat edaran*) issued by the Supreme Court in the 1960s that key provisions of the Dutch Commercial and Civil Codes were to be considered 'guidelines' rather than enforceable law. Another example were the ultimately unsuccessful attempts to preserve the role of *adat* land through the Agrarian Law of 1960.

The New Order 1966 – 1998

Hukum revolusi or 'revolutionary law' and the search for an 'Indonesianised' law came to a dramatic end with the political swing from left to right that occurred when General Soeharto, backed by the military and Islamic groups, obliterated the

Indonesian Communist Party, then the world's largest, following an attempted coup in 1965. The killing of around 500,000 suspected communists and sympathisers and the imprisonments of thousands of others left the armed forces with no significant rival for power.

Ironically, although the rhetoric of Soeharto's 'New Order' emphasised the importance of *negara hukum,* or the Rule of Law, the New Order essentially continued the Dutch-derived legal and political model of Guided Democracy but abandoned Soekarno's left-wing rhetoric. In other words, the Indonesian political system continued to be dominated by the executive with the legislature and the judicature firmly under its control.

The New Order took rapid steps to re-integrate the Indonesian economy with the West, following the advice of American-trained technocrats known as the 'Berkeley Mafia'. Development was spectacular, with Indonesia becoming one of the Asian 'tiger' economies with growth consistent at around 8% (and as high as 11% in the industrial sector) by the 1990s. This process was accompanied by a nominal emphasis on 'black letter' reform but Indonesian law continued to be notable chiefly for its uncertainty and the political nature of judicial decision-making. Ingrained judicial corruption and structural limits on judges' independence meant that the courts proved unable to recover from the degradation visited upon them by Soekarno.

In fact, real reform was strongly resisted by the Soeharto group, which relied on the exercise of far-reaching executive authority and the grant of commercial monopolies to military and ethnic Chinese associates closely linked to the President's inner circle and family to secure support.[4] This resistance began to diminish after the mid-1980s as the collapse in oil prices made Indonesia vulnerable to foreign demands for the opening of the economy. The early 1990s saw a gradual trickle of legal deregulation, mostly focused on the commercial sector and designed to allow Indonesia to compete with other Asian economies for foreign investment. The government was able, however, to resist pressure for deeper or more widespread change.

As mentioned, the New Order's focus on commercial and security regulation can be seen as continuation of the approach of Indonesia's formal colonial masters, as can its reliance on a coercively-backed bureaucratic system. There was real irony in the reliance of the New Order on the same anti-subversion provisions that were once used by the Dutch to jail nationalist leaders, including Soekarno, and which Soekarno himself used in the Guided Democracy period to crush dissent. This approach is also reflected in the continued expansion of the security apparatus under the New Order; and systematic human rights abuses by the military and other security organisations, most obvious in connection with the annexation of East Timor. Indeed, New Order Indonesia has been described as an intelligence state (Tanter, 1990) and most forms of state control relied on the descendants of the extra-constitutional intelligence organisations that were developed during the brutal purge of communists in the mid-1960s.

---

4   For discussion of the Soeharto group's business activities and their political implications, see Jenkins (1984) and Robison (1986).

Reformation? 1998 –

Foreign influences were not the only source of pressure for economic and legal reform of the New Order system. They echoed an increasingly vocal middle class which by the late 1980s had increased its socio-political influence and began to demand political freedom as the benefits of economic growth 'trickled down'. Demands for greater openness or *keterbukaan* led to some relaxation of state control but failed to significantly alter the repressive New Order political and legal system. Despite growing opposition, the New Order system seemed invulnerable to criticism until the Asian economic crisis began to bite in late 1997.

By May 1998 Indonesia had slumped to 7% negative growth, unemployment had hit 12%, interest rates had climbed to 75% and the rupiah had dropped from 6000 to the US dollar to a catastrophic 18,000. Student and middle-class protest had given way to rioting and looting in urban centres across the archipelago. The breakdown of law and order in the capital finally forced the replacement of President Soeharto with his deputy and intimate, Dr Baharuddin Jusuf Habibie, the former Minister for Research and Technology.

Habibie was widely expected to do little more than continue the policies of his mentor, Soeharto. In his first three weeks in office, however, Habibie initiated more reform than was delivered by Soeharto in his three decades of rule. The release of political prisoners was accompanied by promises to scrap the anti-subversion law, to remove bans on political party activity, to legitimise opposition trade unions, to reform the electoral system, to create an insolvency system, to introduce anti-monopoly legislation and to hold fresh democratic elections in May 1999.

There can be no doubt that this radical new agenda was driven by political necessity and by the dictates of the International Monetary Fund which Indonesia then saw as providing its only hope for economic recovery. This does not, however, diminish the significance of Habibie's 'reformation'. If implemented fully, the reforms will re-invent Indonesia's political and economic systems – and of course the legal system as well. At the time of writing Indonesia was waiting for the promised introduction into parliament in November 1998 of legislative confirmation of the reforms promised. The question remained: after a half century of independence could Indonesia at last create a legal system relevant to the needs of a modern state?

References

Gautama, Sudargo & Hornick, Robert N, 1974, *An Introduction to Indonesian Law: Unity in Diversity*, Alumni, Bandung.

Hooker, MB, 1975, *Legal Pluralism: An Introduction to Colonial and Neo-Colonial Law*, Clarendon, Oxford.

Jenkins, David, 1984, *Suharto and His Generals: Indonesian Military Politics, 1975-1983*, Modern Indonesia Project, Cornell University, Ithaca.

Lev, Daniel, 1972, 'Judicial Institutions and Legal Culture in Indonesia' in Holt, C (ed), *Culture and Politics in Indonesia*, Cornell University Press, Ithaca and London.

Pakpahan, Normin, 1995, *Commercial Law Reform in Indonesia*, paper given at the Asian Law Centre conference, 'Indonesian Law: The First 50 Years', University of Melbourne, 28 September.

Ricklefs, MC, 1993, *A History of Modern Indonesia*, 2nd ed, Macmillan, Houndmills and London.

Robison, Richard, 1986, *Indonesia: The Rise of Capital*, Allen & Unwin for the Asian Studies Association of Australia, Sydney.

Tanter, Richard, 1990, 'The Totalitarian Ambition: Intelligence Organisations in the Indonesian State' in Budiman, A (ed), *State and Civil Society in Indonesia*, Monash Papers on Southeast Asia No 22, Melbourne: 213-84.

1. From Rule of Law to Law of the Rulers – to Reformation?

Timothy Lindsey

This chapter summarises the themes of this book and directs the reader to chapters which examine specific issues in more detail.

In popular perceptions, Indonesia is a country without a real legal system. Indonesian law is either primitive or is entirely coopted by the military-business elite, or both.

There is some truth in this but not enough. Indonesia has a complex legal system which, although dysfunctional, is at the heart of debate about how Indonesia might be reformed as it enters the first of the post-Soeharto years. Consequently, most political, social and economic controversies have always found expression in legal terms. Likewise most political, economic and social change is mediated through law. This has never been clearer than in the rigid legalism of President Soeharto's carefully constitutional transfer of power to his Vice-President, Dr Baharuddin Jusuf Habibie, an event forced, ironically, by popular dissatisfaction with his regime's manipulation and subversion of the law.

An Imagined Community

Anderson has described the modern nation state as an 'imagined community' (Anderson, 1983: 6-7); an abstract political entity whose members may have nothing in common with one another other than acceptance that that they are unified by membership of that entity.

By any measure Indonesia is one of the world's largest and most complex 'imagined communities'. It comprises more than 200 million people from over 200 different ethnic groups, scattered over hundreds of islands. There is no ethnic, social or economic logic to the state's boundaries – East Timor aside, the modern Indonesian state has simply adopted the former limits of Dutch colonial power in the region (see Simpson). Government is carried out by a tiny elite through a gigantic and complex bureaucracy centred on the capital, Jakarta, a modern megalopolis with a daytime population of over 18 million. This city alone holds almost as many as live in either of Indonesia's near neighbours, Malaysia and Australia. Outside the cities, tens of millions still live in much the same way as their ancestors did for centuries. Religion is another source of division as Islam contests other faiths and government ambivalence to define its role (see Hooker, both chapters; Butt, Chapter 8 and Saeed). Power in this community has been mediated by the coercive authority of the military. Since the armed revolution against the Dutch from 1945 to 1949, the armed forces have maintained a right of socio-political intervention where they consider the integrity of the state to be threatened. In the mid-1960s this well-articulated doctrine resulted in the killing of at least 500,000 leftists and the violent extermination of communism in the archipelago.

Since independence was declared in 1945, Indonesian governments have tried to control this extraordinary economic, social and political diversity, and their community's consequent tendency to fragmentation, by developing a massive, highly-centralised and authoritarian bureaucratic system (see Holland and Linnan) and by aggressively promoting the means of imagining unity to achieve consensual acceptance of this system. This 'means of imagining' took the form of dissemination of a pervasive and cliched ideology of central authority that combined the rhetoric of the state motto 'unity in diversity' with a cult of 'development' (see Haverfield, Lubis and Bourchier). It created what has been described as virtually a state religion based on the vague and protean state ideology, the *Pancasila* (Geertz, 1990).

Obviously, this system could not survive without a sophisticated legal framework. The Dutch colonial plural legal model inherited in 1945 combined *adat* (traditional customary law), *syariah* (Islamic law) and an incomplete permutation of the legal system of the Netherlands (see Coppel, Haverfield, Fitzpatrick and Hooker in Part II; and Butt, Chapter 17). This system has since been significantly modified to create a web of legislation embodying state *Pancasila*-ism and the authoritarian model of power behind it. The apogee of this process was Law No 8 of 1985 on Social Organisations. This statute required all organisations to adopt the Pancasila, as their 'sole foundation' and allowed the government to formally marginalise alternative imaginings of the Indonesian community, including political Islam and socialism.

The result is paradox: a society of extraordinary diversity that has remained more or less cohesive for half a century; and a system of government exceptional for the simplicity of its structure but bewildering in the obscurity of its operation. Indonesia's legal system has been a key to both building this contrived unity and the labyrinthine system by which it is regulated. It too has therefore become a paradox. On the one hand the conflict between the demand that it support the state 'religion' of enforced unity and 'stability' led the legal system to become little more than a tool of the elite who comprise the government. To that extent it caused the legislature and the judicature to become blatantly dysfunctional and allowed the Soeharto regime to monopolise power for three decades (see Lev, Butt, Quinn, and Millie, Part V). On the other hand, it has remained the source of the powerful ideas of egalitarianism and justice that motivate the government's critics and ultimately led to both the fall of Soeharto and the rise of the *reformasi* (reformation) movement (see Zifcak).

The problem Indonesia now faces is whether the sources of dysfunction in its legal system are so profound that it is incapable of dealing with the challenges of reform, with the result that it will collapse; or whether it can remake itself as more than an exercise in legalism.

Negara Hukum

This book is an attempt to build a framework for understanding the role of the legal system in the imagining of the Indonesian state by reference to disciplines active in Indonesian studies, such as politics, anthropology, sociology and historiography. In doing so, the contributors to this book have focused on the concept of the *negara hukum*. The term, 'a nation of law', literally is used in Indonesia as an equivalent of the Western notion of the 'rule of law' (see Goodpaster, Lubis and Bourchier). This is a highly charged notion that has played a central role in Indonesian political and legal thinking. Its precise meaning has been contested since 1945 when it was written into the Indonesian Constitution as the basic foundation of the state by reference to the Dutch notion of the *rechtsstaat* as opposed to *maachtstaat*, that is, a state based on right rather than might (see Lubis and Bourchier).

The formal nadir of the *negara hukum* was reached during the final decade of Soekarno's presidency when he presided as President-for-life and virtual dictator over Indonesia's radical leftist Guided Democracy polity (see Lev). *Hukum revolusi* or 'revolutionary law' was the fundamental legal principle of Guided Democracy and was best summed up with the aphorism of Liebknecht quoted by Soekarno 'You cannot make a revolution with lawyers'.[1] He was as good as Liebknecht's word. Lev (1972) has shown how under the Old Order lawyers were degraded and the very practice of law frowned upon as inherently neo-colonial and thus anti-Indonesian. The legislative process was effectively replaced by executive instruction and legal legitimacy lay in ideology as defined by the President rather than in written statute or a formal jurisprudence. This, combined with executive intervention in the judicial process and a culture of contempt for the rule of law, led to widespread legal uncertainty and the collapse of the legal process. The result was a system in which the citizen was vulnerable to, and defenceless against, the instrumentalities of state, where policy was the supreme source of legitimacy.

After 1966, Soeharto's New Order government sought political legitimacy as it moved to replace Soekarno. It was quick to emphasise *negara hukum* as its central legal principle. A new generation of *pemuda*, revolutionary youth, supported Soeharto's rise with an energy comparable to that of their revolutionary predecessors 20 years earlier. They saw the New Order as an opportunity to correct the failings of Soekarno's system.[2] Indeed, many believed that the New Order they supported in the streets and in the press would deliver an end to 'revolutionary law'. Their hope was for a system in which lawyers, or more particularly, the law, could reclaim a role as the normative machinery of social equilibrium, mediating between citizen and citizen and between citizen and state, rather than continuing as the coercive tool of the executive (see Lev).

These would-be reformers were, of course, to be disappointed. The killings that accompanied the fall of the Old Order[3] were a high price for regime change and they make the failure of the reformist aspirations of many New Order supporters all the more tragic. Rather than engineering a reformed polity in which rights were

---

1   Quoted by Soekarno at a national conference of Indonesian lawyers in 1961 and published in 'Hukum & Masjarakat', Jakarta, Djambatan, 1962 (Lev, 1972: 261).

2   Many leaders of the Generation of 1945 shared their vision. Soetomo, famous for his role in the early years of the revolution as the impassioned leader of Surabaya's revolutionary *Pemberontakan* (rebellion) movement, is one example (Soetomo, 1965; Lindsey, 1997: 289)

3   For detailed accounts of these killings, see Cribb (1991).

determined by law, the Soeharto government maintained the subordination of law to executive policy that Soekarno had imposed in the late 1950s, notwithstanding the New Order's violent repudiation of the radical socialist ideology that had under-pinned that policy. In this sense, the New Order legal system did not begin in 1966 but rather can be traced to Soekarno's 1959 decree replacing the parliamentary Constitution of 1950 with the revolutionary and top-heavy Constitution of 1945 and ushering in Guided Democracy.

An example of continuity in anti-legalism between Old and New Orders is the practice of presidential interference in the judicial process. The right enjoyed by Soekarno under Law No 19 of 1964 and No 13 of 1965 to intervene directly in court decisions was formally repealed by Soeharto's Law No 14 of 1970 but executive intervention continued. The same law authorised the Minister of Justice to determine judicial appointment, promotion, salary and dismissal (Art 11), creating the so-called 'two-hat' controversy, whereby judges are seen as owing conflicting duties to both government and the courts (see Lev, Quinn and Millie). One of the most blatant examples of this was the Kedung Ombo case where, after a meeting between the Chief Justice and the President, the *Mahkamah Agung*, or Supreme Court, reversed its own decision to increase compensation for farmers whose land had been taken to allow construction of the Kedung Ombo dam (see Fitzpatrick, Chapter 5).

In this sense, Soeharto was able to be as effective with intervention in the judicial process as was Soekarno with an express legal authority to do so. The difference was that Soeharto's method was informal. He claimed merit for repealing Soekarno's law but enjoyed the same benefit Soekarno obtained from the method embodied in that law. Legalism is given lip service by repeal of bad law but the 'mischief' continues. This trait of recourse to informal means of achieving executive control of legal process while presenting that process as formally independent can be found throughout the New Order system, most notably through the technique of legislatively preserving executive discretion to overrule even the most sophisticated legislative schema (see Fitzpatrick, Chapter 5; Millie and Green).

Culture as Law

So, to determine what conduct is formally acceptable and what is unacceptable in modern Indonesia one must therefore understand not so much its statutes but rather state policy and executive guidelines. In other words, political culture is effectively law. In Nasution's words on democratisation, legal certainty, social justice and human rights, 'The … government is of the opinion that these are domestic problems that can be solved by … culture' (Nasution, 1966: 157). If the Old Order notion of legality was 'law without lawyers', then the New Order system can be described in June and Ronald Katz's phrase as 'law without law' (Katz & Katz, 1975). This raises the problem of the role of statutes. In a civil law system like Indonesia which has no formal system of precedent, statutes constitute the entirety of 'law', *adat* aside. If statutes are replaced by culture, and often do not operate as formal 'law', what role is left for them? To answer this another question must first be answered: if in Indonesia state political culture is effectively law, what is the content of that culture?

Pemberton (1994) and Geertz (1990) have analysed New Order official culture as a construction of 'Javanese cultural tradition'. 'Culture' here is an officially-approved reductionist appropriation of Javanese tradition which absorbs and trivialises regional and marginalised aspirations and critiques in the same way that Pemberton analyses regional house styles as being absorbed as political statements of nationalist homogeneity in that masterpiece of pan-Indonesian hyperbole, *Taman Mini Indonesia Indah* ('Beautiful Indonesia in Miniature Park'). This theme park of Indonesian nationalism is a project that constitutes a concrete expression of the implicit imperialist ambitions of New Order 'Javanism' (Lindsey, 1995: 172) and embodies the stylised nature of the political ideology that has defined the imagining of the Indonesian state. Geertz describes this ideology as a muffling and pervasive 'Javanising' of Indonesian cultures which stifles regional impulses and the critical expression of politics and religion. He traces the political expression in the arts of this 'official Javanism' linked to an elite culture based around the circle of wealth controlled by the New Order *pembesar* or VIPs.

This process is also present in law and, in fact, determined its content until Soeharto's fall. It appears perhaps not often in an overtly 'Javanese' form but it is certainly present in the ascendancy of (Javanese-dominated) government policy. It has the same muffling, stifling and monolithic effect in the law as in other areas of culture. Policy subsumes regionalist or dissenting expressions that might be legitimised in a system subject to the rule of law (see Holland and Linnan). Ultimately it creates a fundamental inegalitarian social system predicated on bad faith that is manifest in the way the legal system deals with marginal or minority groups, including women (see Pompe and Sunindyo).

The National Interest

A key mechanism in this process is the notion of 'national interest'. The Katz's Indonesian tradition of 'law without law' can encompass laws that are ignored, such as the land redistribution prescribed in the Agrarian Law of 1960[4] (see Haverfield and Fitzpatrick, Chapter 5). It can also be a reference to the government's ability to 'legally' waive the application of its own laws to suit executive interests. The requirement that law conform with the 'national interest' is the key here. It is a saving provision that allows the government to 'legally' ignore its own legislation. At the last minute it can pull the rug out from the lawyer and allow elite interests – the sole determinant of national interest in realpolitik terms – to replace law.

In this sense, Indonesian law reflects its constitutional source, the 1945 Constitution,[5] a document often described as based on obligations, rather than

---

4   PKI (*Partai Komunis Indonesia* or Indonesian Communist Party) attempts to enforce these provisions through unilateral land seizures were one of the triggers for the confrontation between Islamic land-owners and the left that led to the coup of 1965 and the killings thereafter.

5   Indonesia has experienced three constitutions since it declared independence in 1945. The 1945 Constitution applied until 1949 when sovereignty was transferred by the Dutch to a federation under UN auspices. The constituent states of that Republic of the United States of Indonesia voluntarily ceded their rights to the unitary Republic of Indonesia in early 1950. A provisional Constitution developed from the Federal Constitution based on a Westminster-style parliamentary system was in force until President Soekarno unilaterally decreed a return to the 1945 Constitution in 1959.

rights. This is seen nowhere more clearly than in Art 27 of the Constitution which provides that:

> Without any exception, all citizens shall have equal positions in law and government and shall be obliged to uphold that law and government.

Like government policy, the notion of 'national interest' is vague and protean, precisely because it has no content other than elite policy. It is held up to legitimise that policy but it is, in fact, not different from that which it purports to legitimise. 'National interest' may thus best described by what it clearly does not include. It does not legitimise regional dissent but it may encourage that regionalism where it can be co-opted (see Holland and Linnan). It does not legitimise radical Islam but it may encourage Islamic politics where tactically convenient (see Hooker, Chapter 6; and Saeed). It does not legitimise foreign involvement in 'internal Indonesian affairs' but it does encourage massive foreign investment (see Green and Antons). It does not legitimise real political opposition but it does tolerate the limited dissidence necessary to establish legitimacy as a 'legalist' regime – such as the closely-controlled opposition parties and 'yellow' trade unionism under Soeharto (see Fehring).

This is not to say that the elite's manipulation of 'national interest' has ever been simple in its execution or even consistency. It has always been complicated by the tension between protectionism and internationalism in state policy and thus law. For example, 'national interest' has often been read by the government to mean protection of the elite business interests. In this mode it defeats 'national interest' as defined to mean the need to encourage foreign investment and thus deregulation which at other times may suit elite interests (see Taylor, Green and Antons). The question of how elite interests can best be protected has thus been a source of great tension even in the government itself. Culture in the sense of elite political culture may be real law but a consequence of this is that law in Indonesia is often as unclear and uncertain as are elite politics.[6] Legal certainty, in the sense of predictable policy, gives way under the mantra of 'national interest' to unexpected decisions privileging particular members of the inner circle at the expense of others. Policy becomes confused, unpredictable and puzzling. Legalism, in the sense of transparency and predictability, is muffled and obscured. The centre, the predominantly Javanese elite, benefit; the margins – and the diverse groups who inhabit them – are baffled and excluded again (see Haverfield and Sunindyo).

This tussle between pressure to protect elite interests and the need for a rational and predictable business environment for foreigners has been won for the time being by the foreigners. The Habibie government's desperate need for foreign aid to extricate Indonesia from its *krismon* or monetary crisis gives it little choice but to accept the dictates of aid organisations such as the IMF (International Monetary Fund). These are essentially driven by the needs of the creditor/investor nations they represent, most notably the United States. It is reasonable to expect, however, that this policy tension will re-emerge as Indonesia's economy recovers.

Proposals for a competition – read 'anti-monopoly' – law are an example of these problems. Experiences elsewhere in Asia have proved that effective competition regulation can lead to the dismantling of previously entrenched political

---

6   The 'Timor' national car debacle is an excellent example of the uncertainty generated by this tension. See van Klinken, 1996.

and economic elites.[7] An effective anti-monopoly law would be more likely to force a dramatic restructuring of Indonesia's political economy than any other single measure. It is therefore obvious why Indonesia's political elite – synonymous with its business elites – has long resisted the introduction of such a law.[8] The IMF has now made it a condition of its rescue package that such a statute be introduced before the end of 1998. There can be no doubt that the question of how far elite interests can ensure that the real law will not be located in the legislation but reserved for executive discretion 'in the national interest' will play a major part in the future location of political power in Indonesia. Popular anger at so-called 'KKN'[9] (corruption, collusion and nepotism) has focused on the Soeharto family's enrichment through the grant of nepotistic monopolies. This will make it hard for the government of President Habibie to water down any proposed new anti-monopoly legislation in the usual way.

The Integralist State

What then is the basic source of the failure of the rule of law in contemporary Indonesia since the return to the 1945 Constitution in 1959? One answer lies in the Constitution itself which has proved capable of functioning as the 'grundnorm' for both Soekarno's leftist 'Guided Democracy' polity and the right-wing New Order state. This constitutional flexibility comes from its simplicity. Created in the interregnum between impending Japanese collapse and establishment of the first Republican government in August 1945 it is the shortest Constitution in the world, notable more for what it does not state than for what it does. The hurried debate in mid-1945 between proponents of liberal democracy and supporters of an integralist or organicist state – the authoritarian model – was lost to the supporters of the *negara hukum* on a vote but it is clear that it is the integralist system that has prevailed until now. This is largely because the working out of the notion of *negara hukum* in the Constitution is itself problematic. The essence of the *negara hukum* is said to be *trias politika*, the 'political triad'. This is a concept interpreted by New Order opponents as implying separation of powers but interpreted by orthodox Indonesian constitutionalists as creating a unified, 'integrated' state – the *integralistic staatsidee*, based not on separation, but on distribution, of power, through the President (see Lubis, Bourchier and Permana).[10]

On this analysis, power stems from Indonesia's supreme sovereign body, the *Majelis Permusyawaratan Rakyat*[11] or MPR. The President, as its 'mandatory' is answerable only to the MPR. It is therefore proper for the President to influence decisions of the subordinate bodies to which that power is distributed – the judiciary and the legislature. There is no constitutional court or any other court that can

---

7   The *chaebol*, or conglomerates of South Korea, for example, were forced to divest 2 trillion Won between 1980 and 1993 following the introduction of the Monopoly Regulation and Fair Trade Act (OECD, 1995: 342).

8   For a discussion of the application of competition theory to developing countries, see Gray & Davis, 1993.

9   *Korupsi, kolusi, nepotisme.*

10   See also Law No 14, 1985 on the Supreme Court; Law No 2, 1986 on the General Courts.

11   *Majelis Permusyawaratan Rakyat*, People's Consultative (sometimes translated as 'Deliberative') Assembly.

review legislation in Indonesia (see Lubis and Quinn) as, on the orthodox integralist reading of the Constitution established in 1945 by Soepomo, its chief drafter, only the MPR has the right to review the legislation: Law No 14 of 1970.

Interestingly, when considering the integralist model for Indonesia, Soepomo's expressly stated points of reference were Nazi Germany and wartime imperial Japan (Lubis, 1993: 92 and see Chapter 11). He saw these states as embodying the principle of *kekeluargaan*, or 'family-ness', which for him was the proper basis of the new Indonesian Republic. The new state was to function on paternalistic terms, with the children, the *rakyat* or people, following the will of the father, the executive, and accepting punishment by him when their actions displease (see Bourchier). There was no place in this system for 'answering back', or judicial review. In the absence of judicial review, and because it controls the MPR and DPR, the executive can therefore control the interpretation of state ideology and, consequently, legal meaning.

In this way, the principle of *kekeluargaan* allows what is, in effect, a return to Soepomo's integralist state. Suggestions of separation of powers in the Constitution drawn from American precedent are overwhelmed by political orthodoxy to rationalise precisely the opposite result, the concentration of powers in the hands of the executive at the expense of the other limbs of government.

Law as Memory

So, to return to the question raised earlier, if culture is law what role is left for laws? With law deflected where it touches the power of the state it has been marginalised and is left to those who inhabit the margins. Law, and in particular the Constitution and statutes, have also operated as a form of memory, a reminder of alternatives. Indonesia's abandoned democratic course of the 1950s, and in particular the deliberations of the *Konstituante*, Indonesia's Constituent Assembly, dissolved by Soekarno in 1959, saw the development of the typically wide range of alternative and sometimes divisive visions that appear whenever Indonesia's diverse groups have the opportunity to express themselves freely. The New Order has been able to marginalise the democratic tradition of the pre-Guided Democracy 1950s through its ideological program and, more particularly, by reinventing accounts of that period (Bourchier, 1994: 50-62). One provision of the Constitution remains, however, as a reliquary for alternative and now marginalised visions. Article 33 of the 1945 Constitution:

(1) The economy shall be organised as a common endeavour based upon the principle of the family system.
(2) Branches of production which are important for the State and which affect the life of most people shall be controlled by the State.
(3) Land and water and the natural riches contained therein shall be controlled by the State and shall be made use of for the people.

These provisions theoretically require a 'social economy' and they have long been the basis for dissident criticism of the failure of New Order claims to the rule of law. Proponents of a competition law, for example, rely on Art 33 to argue not only a justification for such law but even its absolute constitutional necessity. Opponents of conglomerates and the New Order Chinese-military-business complex argue that their anti-competitive practices are in breach of Art 33. When reformers criticise the government in its own, legitimised forums, for example, the DPR[12] or parliament, it has been often done on the basis of Art 33.

Of course, Art 33 has not been the only legal avenue relied upon to legitimise critiques of the New Order system. Indonesia's corrupt judiciary has long been the focus of protest. Reformist judges like Adi Andojo and, before him, Benyamin Mangkoedilaga who were prepared to decide against the government (see Lev, Butt, Quinn and Millie in Part V), have found themselves popular heroes because law has now been enlisted in the broader political debate about what Indonesia should be like in the post-Soeharto era.

Subversion trials, however, have been the most dramatic legal forum for the expression of alternative imaginings of the Indonesian community. The trials of dissidents such as Muchtar Pakpahan,[13] Ratna Sarumpaet[14] and Sri Bintang Pamungkas[15] became set pieces where arguments on democracy and the rule of law were regularly and aggressively aired (see Zifcak), in a tradition established by Soekarno's trial by the Dutch under similar provisions in 1930. Their inevitable convictions were in fact political victories because they focused attention on the illegitimacy of the final result, rather than the subject of the dispute. This was demonstrated by the speed with which President Habibie announced within days of taking office that the Anti-Subversion Law would be repealed and then released most prisoners convicted under this statute, including Pakpahan, Sarumpaet and Pamungkas.

In fact it was precisely these attempts to re-locate law at the centre of debate on how Indonesia is to be ruled that have forced President Habibie to look to legal reform to find legitimacy. Indonesia's catastrophic economic crisis has been widely perceived as stemming from the failure of the New Order regime to provide transparent, just and predictable administration – in other words, the *negara hukum* (see Goodpaster). The popular anger this generated contributed to the breakdown of law and order that led to Soeharto's fall on 21 May 1998 amidst rioting unknown in Indonesia since the mid-1960s, when Soekarno's Old Order collapsed. Consequent popular demands for *reformasi* coupled with the highly specific list of reforms insisted upon by the IMF as a precondition of economic assistance have made the introduction of a series of packages of major legal reform – on elections, commercial law, competition and the judicial system among others – inevitable.

What is not inevitable, however, is the form new laws will take. Will the Indonesian system of Guided Democracy and the New Order slip through loopholes of discretion and cracks of formalism to emerge intact? Will Habibie's reformasi be as disappointing as Soeharto's *negara hukum*? Perhaps not. The student activists of 1965 have outlived Soeharto's generation of 1945 who turned the Soekarnoist system into New Order sleight of hand. The generation of '65 are now among the intellectual leaders and the senior government figures who will have a role in shaping the new laws demanded by their children and the international financial bureaucracy. Together they may give Indonesia the change to resurrect the

---

12   *Dewan Perwakilan Rakyat*, People's Representative Assembly.

13   The leader of the formerly banned trade union, SBSI (*Serikat Buruh Sejahtera Indonesia*) or 'Prosperity Labour Union of Indonesia'.

14   A well known Indonesian dramatist.

15   A former parliamentarian and staunch critic of the Soeharto who has established his own opposition party.

alternative political and legal imaginings abandoned by the state in 1959 – to re-imagine again a true *negara hukum*.

References

Anderson, Benedict, 1983 (revised edition, 1991), *Imagined Communities: reflections on the origin and spread of nationalism*, Verso, London.

Bourchier, David, 1994, 'The 1950s in New Order Ideology & Politics' in Bourchier, B and Legge, J, *Democracy in Indonesia: 1950s and 1990s*, Centre of Southeast Asian Studies, Monash University, Clayton: 50-62.

Cribb, Robert (ed), 1991, *The Indonesian Killings 1965-1966: Stories from Java and Bali*, 2nd ed, Monash Papers on Southeast Asia No 21, Monash University, Melbourne.

Geertz, Clifford, 1990, ' "Popular Art" and the Javanese Tradition', *Indonesia*, 50: 77-94.

Gray, Clive and Davis, Anthony, 1993, 'Competition Policy in Developing Countries Pursuing Structural Adjustment', *The Antitrust Bulletin*, Summer: 425-67.

IRIP News Service, 1997, 'Courting Corruption', *Inside Indonesia* (January-March 1997): 49.

Katz, June and Ronald, 1975, 'The New Indonesian Marriage Law: a Mirror of Indonesia's Political, Cultural & Legal Systems' [1975] *AJCL* 653.

van Klinken, Gerry, 1996, 'Clash of Interests', *Inside Indonesia*, March issue.

Lev, Daniel, 1972, 'Judicial Institutions and Legal Culture in Indonesia' in Holt, C (ed), *Culture and Politics in Indonesia*, Cornell University Press, Ithaca and London.

Lindsey, Timothy, 1995, 'Concrete Ideology: Taste, Tradition, and the Javanese Past in New Order Public Space' in Virginia Hooker, *Culture & Society in New Order Indonesia*, Oxford, Kuala Lumpur.

Lindsey, Timothy, 1997, *The Romance of K'tut Tantri and Indonesia*, Oxford University Press, New York.

Lubis, Todung Mulya, 1993, *In Search of Human Rights*, PT Gramedia Pers, Jakarta.

Nasution, Adnan Buyung, 1996, *Culture, Human Rights and Diplomacy* in Brown, C (ed), *Indonesia: dealing with a neighbour*, Allen & Unwin in association with the Australian Institute of International Affairs, Sydney.

OECD, 1995, *Competition Policy in OECD Countries 1992-1993*, paper in the possession of the author.

Pemberton, John, 1994, *On the Subject of 'Java'*, Cornell University Press, Ithaca & London.

Soetomo, 1965, 'Kerikil Tadjam'. *Harian Kami*, 7 October.

2. The Rule of Law, Economic Development & Indonesia

Gary Goodpaster

I.

Good governments provide public goods, secure peace, social harmony and national security, and assist citizens in their collective efforts to achieve better lives. Law is an essential public good in modern societies and economies interacting and competing on a global level (World Bank, 1997b: 26-28). Law and the institutions and systems that make it effective comprise institutional frameworks that governments can use to steer, guide, and manage societies and economies, and to secure social order, human well-being and justice. They are not the only such frameworks: the command and control system of former and current socialist economies is a different framework, as is ordering through kinship networks and patronage. Such frameworks can be efficient or inefficient in the sense that they enhance or retard economically productive activity and social development (Scully, 1992: 56).[1] The choice of the institutional framework for an economy and society has great impacts on personal incentives, the development of institutions intermediate between the state and citizen, and an economy's efficiency and growth (Scully, 1992: 169, 183; North, 1990).

Basic to modern rule of law systems are the ideas that governments and citizens both obey the laws and use them to guide their activities. Laws embody legislative policy choices that provide officials with directives and inform people what to expect if they do or fail to do certain things. Effective law creates structures of expectation that guide official behaviour and citizens can learn and use to make decisions and guide their own activities.

Rule of law systems of social control require cultures that support regulating the state, economy, and society, and the rights and duties of persons, according to publicly known, broadly accepted principles and rules, applied fairly and in a non-discriminatory way. Rule of law systems, at least in ideal form, are characterised by widespread, general obedience to reasonably clear, enacted rules or authoritative interpretations of rules; in other words, rule-based behaviour.

Rule of law systems of social ordering are not the only systems of social ordering. In fact, they are rather the exception than the rule. I would not even claim that they are the best systems of social ordering for all purposes and under all conditions. Indeed, one can imagine nations where the preconditions of rule of law

---

1   See generally North (1990).

do not exist or exist only weakly. Haiti appears to be a clear case but one can even question whether Russia and the former Soviet Republics are yet rule of law states.

In the absence of rule of law as a basis for social and economic ordering, governments devise other means, usually culturally based, often personalistic but sometimes based on imported ideologies. The nations that – after colonialism and possibly in reaction to it – turned to communist socialism, adopted command and control systems of governance and economic regulation that were sometimes culturally quite alien. Whatever system a nation adopts, or has adopted, all well-intentioned systems – excluding from consideration predatory states (World Bank, 1997b: 149) kleptocracies and fiercely ideological theocracies – face common problems of governance: provision for the masses, maintenance of order, some effort toward progress, external security and the like. Non-rule of law systems can sometimes manage these matters with considerable success.

For those who believe that rule of law and rule-based behaviour are essential to any modern polity and economy, some Asian states, including Indonesia, have, at least until the occurrence of the Asian financial crisis, presented a serious problem. The problem arises because, effectively, these states have had astonishing success, as measured by many social indicators, without relying on rule of law and rule-based behaviour as principal means of social ordering, direction and control. The current crisis, which some pundits claim proves the 'Asian' version of capitalism has failed, suggests that while it is possible to operate modern economies on some basis other than rule of law for a time, they cannot sustain themselves in the face of global markets.

But Indonesia's story before the unfolding of its recent economic crisis is useful to relate, for it appears, at least on the surface, to show how much can be done economically without rule of law. Within five decades, Indonesia has advanced from being an assortment of colonially-administered islands with a large, and largely poor, uneducated and unmodern population to a coherent and regionally powerful nation-state with an increasingly aware and increasingly educated population. Within the past three decades, Indonesia metamorphosed from a dismal failure as a governable entity and an economic failure, comparable to the worst of the African states, into a unified, effective state, most of whose people feel a common identity; and into an extraordinary economic success, recent problems notwithstanding. In other words, it has succeeded in transforming itself from a chaotic, colonial collectivity of dubious provenance into an economically successful, modernising state that has already greatly advanced the welfare and well-being of its citizens. By many, although certainly not all, international standards used to measure the progress of developing nations, Indonesia has been an extraordinary success (Hill, 1995: 3-8; World Bank, 1997a: 92, 108).

Indonesia created its phenomenal success without the use of rule of law (at least in the complete Western sense of that term). It succeeded through political centralisation aimed at the integration and stability of an extremely heterogeneous, potentially fractious state, and through economic liberalisation aimed at economic growth. Political control, and patronage (which included corruption and bribery) as a method of governance, kept the country together while moving it forward; and economic growth provided the real benefits essential to maintaining citizens' allegiance.

Rule of law and legalistic rule-based behaviour were not fundamental bases of social and political order in Indonesia. In Indonesia order flowed not from a convergence of expectations based on commonly understood and enforced legal rules, but from a system of hierarchical relationships – from state power, control and authority, allied with powerful cultural values of harmony, indirectness and hierarchical deference to authority.

> Today this mentality [of great respect toward superiors in a hierarchy] … is especially well-developed in the circle of white-collar civil servants, the military, and the educated middle class. … The behaviour of these social strata is conditioned by the maxim that 'men behave best when they pattern their actions on the conduct of their superiors' and that everyone 'should honour and serve his superiors, high ranking persons, and elders.'. … 'The social order is a moral order of derived patrimonial leadership.' Subordinates have no business to measure their superiors or other senior people against moral guidelines, to criticise them or call them to acknowledge their responsibilities. The opposite is the case: the actual behaviour of the superior is justified and becomes the standard which the subordinate strives to imitate (Magnis-Suseno, 1997: 68).

Rule of persons and authority, patronage as a method of securing loyalty and control and tight control of interest groups and potentially competing power centres – not rule of law – have been normative in Indonesia. The system is a patrimonial system of vertically-structured patron-client relationships 'in which orders flow down from the top' with little input from the bottom (Mackie & MacIntyre, 1994: 6, 21).

Systems of social ordering create incentive structures that motivate, reward, and punish people, and '[i]ncentives are the underlying determinants of economic performance' (North, 1990: 135). Incentives, depending on what they are and on how they solidify and endure in institutions, can be hospitable to economic growth and social development, or hostile and retarding. Patronage, as a system of incentives, profits both patron and patronised; it provides rewards and generates dependency, personal loyalty, trust, executive capacity and control. Indeed, to a certain degree, all governance systems use patronage as a tool of governance. Similarly, controlling interest groups and competing power centres is a rational strategy for a potentially fractious society attempting to avoid destabilising social conflict and transform itself into a unified nation-state.

After a certain point, however, patronage and control of intermediate groups create a seriously distorted incentive structure; and lead to major economic inefficiencies by creating a political market for income-shifting and redistribution services or excessive rent-seeking. They therefore entail unproductive activity and unproductive use of resources; and may also lead to extensive corruption, not least by tempting parties to gain brokerage fees for distributional services. They also create envy and resentment, as most recently evidenced and expressed in the extensive rioting and social disorder that occurred in Indonesia in May 1998 and in the subsequent political consensus prompting President Soeharto's resignation. Furthermore,

> increasing returns characteristic of an initial set of institutions that provide disincentives to productive activity will create organisations and interest groups with a stake in the existing constraints. They will shape the polity in their interests. Such institutions provide incentives that may encourage military domination of the polity and economy, religious fanaticism, or plain, simple redistributive organisations, but they provide few rewards from increases in the stock and dissemination of economically useful knowledge. The subjective mental constructs of participants will evolve an ideology that not only rationalises the society's structure but accounts for its poor performance (North, 1990: 99).

When access to wealth through services to a regime is more important for many actors than wealth maximisation through the efficient exchange of resources, products and services in the market, the economy will suffer. Similarly, restraining the development of institutions intermediate between citizens and the state suppresses initiative and the growth of competing, organised economic interests that appear to contribute to the fashioning of an efficient market economy.

This Indonesian system, however deplorable some might find it, was not a rule of law system but was quite successful, both economically and politically, for almost 30 years. Given the circumstances in which Indonesia found itself after overthrowing colonial rule, at least once the revolutionary fervour settled, one could argue that rule of law governance was not then appropriate. The conditions essential for rule of law were simply not there. One could credit those who ruled the country for the adoption of a system that worked quite well to solve both the immediate and medium-term problems of governance. The sense now, however, is that the existing method of governance has run its course and is not as successful as it once was, and that Indonesia now needs to turn to new methods of governance.

This, indeed, is the burden of this chapter, but it is not to deride what Indonesia has accomplished without full rule of law, even though it is too soon to determine what remains of its accomplishment. At the very least, and as much in collapse as in operation, Indonesia's alternative method of governance has succeeded in creating the conditions essential to rule of law. It is also to claim that Indonesia now needs a rule of law system of governance in order to advance its society and economy for the benefit of all its peoples.

II

Indonesia achieved its success and its central goals of political stability and economic growth with little regard to the state of its laws and legal system. Indonesia did not wholly ignore law. Because Indonesia increasingly followed a path of generating economic growth through private markets, it learned to use law-like directives as tools to facilitate, increase and direct economic growth in those markets. Indonesia also had, and continues to have, clearly a legal system that is useful for some purposes. Nonetheless, law, legal institutions and legal system reform had not been development priorities under the Soeharto regime. Indeed, Indonesia by and large is not a polity where law-based behaviour is a norm. As one would expect, old methods of management and governance maintain their grip: culture and custom, old belief systems and norms continue to reign; special interests, while confronted with and extraordinarily new and different political situation, have not lost their interest; expertise in the old system, and memories of past profit, remain; temptations to corruption increase as the economy declines.

Given Indonesia's success without complete rule of law, what are the arguments that Indonesia will not continue to succeed without moving to a system of rule of law? The answer has to do with societal management and the roles played by institutional incentive creation, the management of risk and uncertainty, and transaction costs.[2] Simply put, Indonesia will find that it cannot manage and

---

2   For an illuminating description of the transaction costs that an antiquated and unresponsive legal system and set of laws can impose on productive activity, see De Soto (1989: 131-86).

function effectively in the global economy nor continue strong economic growth without rule of law and widespread rule-based behaviour. This, in fact, may be one of the lessons of the recent series of financial crises that Asian countries have experienced.

Rule of law is a public good, essential both for the operation of free market economies and for a citizen-enabling governance. Because rule of law is a commons, it is a resource all may use. But like a commons it has few defenders: while all may use it, no particular individual has any incentive to provide, or protect, it for all. For this reason, it is a public good only governments can supply (although there may be various ways in which governments can supply it.)

One major feature of large modern societies and economies is their incredible complexity, fluidity, interdependency and changeability, features calling for sophisticated, sensitive and effective management devices. These features make societal management so difficult that the resources of any political authority are inadequate to manage effectively through purely hierarchical means – the decisions of top power holders. Managing the complexity requires coordinated decision-making throughout the system; but even the most efficient and effective bureaucracy cannot adequately and responsively manage complexity through directives from the top. In particular, patronage systems cannot succeed because they require too much deference to the top and offer too little to stir individual initiative, creativity, private energy, industry and responsibility (Scully, 1992: 135). To increase system capacity and ability it is essential to find some other way to create coordination and consistency within the system; a way to enlist all relevant system actors in coordinated action. Free markets, operating within well-defined and well-enforced rules do exactly this.

This is familiar to economists. For example, the free economic market operates as a system for coordinating decision-making. It creates a system of order that coordinates many disparate activities and actions without any centralised control. It is the nature of the market and the rules for its operation, known to players, that allows participants to coordinate their actions and decisions. In other words, the rules of the market create a structure of expectations that engages the energies and creativity of persons eager to make a good living, or better. It allows people to make considered decisions, take calculated risks and learn how to make money while efficiently providing goods and services that have value for others. Indeed, there appears to be good empirical evidence that societies operating within a framework of enforceable economic liberties are far more productive, economically, than countries without such a framework.

> Politically open societies, which bind themselves to the rule of law, to private property, and to the market allocation of resources grow at three times ... the rate of and are two and one half times as efficient as societies where these freedoms are circumscribed or proscribed (Scully, 1992: 183).

It also appears that societies having the greatest economic liberty also have less income inequality (Scully, 1992: 188-94) and that much of the income redistribution goes to the middle classes (Scully, 1992: 194).

Laws of property and contract, and the legal systems and institutions that make them effective, form the foundation for free markets. Even further, and in less grand ways, in some countries, legal institutions and particular bodies of laws establish something like 'mini-markets' where participating parties can, through relying on the rules of those markets, stabilise their expectations, coordinate activities and achieve desired results.

Take as an example a secured transactions law. Such a law allows lenders to register a so-called 'security interest' in collateral, to know the entire set of security interests attached to any particular piece of collateral; and to know the priority of their own security interest and what will happen should the debtor default. This permits lenders to make risk assessments and calculations, and to make decisions regarding loans and interest rates, and so on. Securing loans in this way to a certain extent relieves a lender of the need to make risk assessments based on the party to whom the loan is made. And that allows both an expansion of the market for making loans and a lowering of the transaction costs involved in making a loan. In this sense, in a highly complex, interdependent and contingent world, good legal institutions and laws operate as risk management tools.

Modern laws facilitate business, economic and other activities through creating calculable 'structures of expectation' (Luhmann, 1985: 73). Law does not eliminate all contingencies and doubts, but it does operate to reduce decision-making variables to a manageable number and scope. Laws do this through a form of 'conditional programming' (Luhmann, 1985: 174-79). The law simply says, normatively, that if certain conditions are fulfilled, then certain consequences follow. Such a program shapes, guides and limits expectations about what might occur, and allows parties to make educated decisions about what is likely to occur. This results in creating a kind of coordinated system of action facilitated by law and the way it defines the playing field and permissible moves: all actors know, at least within a reasonable range, what decisions and actions follow from the existence of the defined conditions. There is no need for direction from the top; system management arises through the operations of the legal program.

For this form of conditional programming to work in ordering society and managing complexity, several things are required. First, the law itself must be known and reasonably clear so that actors can know the if-then programs of the law. Laws and regulations must be sufficiently clear to inform intelligent people, either on their own or with the assistance of legal professionals, what the law requires. Vague and ambiguous laws increase, rather than reduce, risk and contingency, and *disempower*, rather than empower, citizens' ability to make reasonable predictions and judgments. Such laws, when administered and interpreted by a 'gatekeeper', a bureaucrat in some Ministry, for example, also provide opportunities for rent-seeking.

Secondly, there must be fairly free access to information so that actors can determine whether or not the conditions defined in the law are met. These two information items together, clear and reasonably specific laws and free information flows, partly comprise what is generally referred to as transparency.

Finally, governmental decision-makers must follow and enforce the rules, that is, decide as the rules require regardless of the effects and consequences of the decision on particular persons. This means both that decision-makers must be accountable, in the sense that they must decide and be known to have done so; and that they must be independent, in the sense that they base their decisions on law and nothing else. The decision-maker, whether bureaucrat or judge, must determine what the law requires, whether the conditions laid down in the law exist, and decide solely on that basis. One must assume that the law-makers who laid down the law's conditional 'if-then' decision matrix considered possible consequences and effects when creating it.

Most emphatically this means that, in enforcing the law, decision-makers cannot take into account the consequences of enforcement on particular individuals, no matter who they are (Luhmann, 1985: 177). The only issue is: what decision does the law require, not whom the decision will affect, nor how it will affect them. This too is a part of legal transparency, but also involves reliability, that is, the ability of people to rely on the law. Finally, it is what makes the principle of judicial independence and equality before the law meaningful (Luhmann, 1985: 177).

These elements – clear, known laws; widespread information concerning whatever it is the law treats; and decision-maker-accountability for, and independence from, *decisional* results – comprise *predictability* and form the foundation for rule-based behaviour throughout a society. Social ordering through rule-based behaviour comprises a relatively high stage of legal development. It facilitates all sorts of decisions, particularly economic decisions, by allowing people to make predictions reasonably accurate within a range. It allows officials and citizens to manage the contingencies and risks of complexity, allows planning, and generates the undirected, unsupervised coordination of the behaviour and decisions of many actors.

Such rule-based social ordering systems contribute to social stability, economic growth, harmony, enhanced personal freedom and even democratisation. They clarify for citizens what is expected of them and their institutions, facilitate voluntary citizen compliance with law, and enhance law enforcement and effectiveness. In effect, because such systems both assure citizens that officials will obey and carry out the law and direct citizens what to consider in making decisions and taking actions, they enlist citizens to carry out the policies embodied in the law. By contrast, in non-rule-based social ordering systems, parties attempting to figure out what is *expectable* so that they can navigate their futures are immensely disadvantaged. They cannot calculate, they cannot predict, they cannot fairly estimate either until some party with authority decides or until they know decision-makers sufficiently well to be able to anticipate, and calibrate, a superior's possible decision.

III

A legalistic social ordering system of rule-based behaviour, or rule of law, is not a simple matter easily instituted, but consists of a complex system of coordinated behaviours difficult to put in place. At a minimum it requires properly trained and socialised officials, judicial personnel, and legal professionals; a system of educational indoctrination; and all sorts of institutional, political and social supports. Given these requirements, and the natural inclinations of human beings, we should understand that rule of law in any society is a truly extraordinary and highly improbable revolutionary achievement (Luhmann, 1985: 58-59, 88, 105-109). Familiarity should not mislead those who come from countries where rule of law is both normative and effective: rule of law is the exceptional, not the usual, method of social ordering. If you doubt this, consider for a moment the countries of the world and ask yourself where rule of law is truly normative – or consider the great difficulties the former Soviet republics are experiencing in trying to create functioning legal systems.

As mentioned, Indonesia has not yet reached the stage of legal development where rule of law is normative. Their decision-making remains personalised and patronage based, rather than being rule-based as I have defined it. Indonesia, of course, does have law, and, in the past decade or so, has adopted many new laws, most of them modelled on provisions on Western codes. But the experience in Indonesia, like the experience in numerous other formerly colonised countries, is that legal transplants have not worked well. When there is a substantial difference between cultures, legal transplants do not 'take'; the body politic and social simply rejects or ignores them (Seidman, 1978: 34-36).[3] Transplanted laws and regulatory systems assume a framework of institutions, incentive structures, customs, practices, attitudes and a complex of other laws – a rule of law culture – that simply does not exist in these countries. Furthermore, as a country with a Muslim tradition, Indonesia appears to find elements of Western-style rule of law, for example, the ideas of separation of powers, an independent judiciary and an at least quasi-independent bureaucracy somewhat alien (Scully, 1992: 155). Indonesia has specifically rejected the doctrine of separation of powers and does not have an independent judiciary (Mackie and MacIntyre, 1994: 23, 28).

In Indonesia, the cultural ground for Western style rule of law is not yet fertile, although it is too soon to predict how much compost the current crisis will deliver. Furthermore, although Indonesia has followed economic growth policies in order to develop and to benefit its peoples, 'unrestrained capitalist competition and the supremacy of markets' are also not yet culturally accepted (Mackie and MacIntyre, 1994: 36). Even with political will, therefore, Indonesia's transition to a rule-based, free-market oriented system of social ordering will be difficult. It is not a simple thing to introduce true rule of law and market competition in a country where the governance and cultural infrastructure generally does not support the norms and where the advantages they would bring are not self-evident. There are many, many problems to overcome.

Nations, that is, the elite who rule nations, like the people composing them, are generally loss-averse: they will take much greater risks to avoid a loss – fight harder – than they will to secure a gain (Kahnemann and Tversky, 1979: 263, 273, 277; 1981: 453, 456). The same is surely true for all those who have profited from an existing system, where rent-seeking through connections is substantial. Those now profiting from government-sponsored economic inefficiencies are not only not likely to endorse changes but rather to fight them vigorously.

We should expect then that it would be very hard to ask those who govern Indonesia, and those tied to them, to give up a known and effective system of political control and social ordering in favour of a system that is both mostly unknown and also seems to import all sorts of losses and risks. Indonesia is a society in which authority and patronage-based decisions are culturally validated, and have produced what appear to be excellent results. There was order, progress and proud nationhood; and while the economy grew, all were better off – unequally better off to be sure but the tide raised both the poor fisherman's *prahu* and the taipan's yacht.

---

3   'Most of the constraints and resources within which individuals choose, however, are of course not a function of the law. Custom, geography, history, technology and a host of other non-legal factors affect my behaviour directly and indirectly by structuring the choice and thus channelling the behaviour of others. These other, non-legal constraints and resources are the reason for the failure of legal transplants' (Seidman, 1978: 35).

Giving up, or at least, relaxing, patronage must seem a deep threat not only to the economic and status benefits the system presently confers, but also to the very tools of management, social control, and security heretofore used to govern effectively. It is always most difficult to persuade anyone to give up immediate benefits in exchange for long-run benefits with immediate costs. How much more difficult to persuade those who need persuading that their ways of viewing the world, politics and making a living need to be changed.

The present crisis, of course, may form a most powerful persuasion, but even with a will the transition and transformation would take a monumental and long sustained effort. Notwithstanding all the experts who might declaim about the appropriate path for Indonesia to take, and adapt itself to – rule of law ordering – in truth no one quite knows how to get from here to there. Furthermore, it is doubtful whether Indonesia presently has the human resources and skills to effect and sustain the necessary changes.

Clearly, a shift from the existing system of governance to a rule-of-law based system, even with wholehearted effort, will be an immensely difficult and long-term reform. It involves changing minds, many minds, systems, ways of being and doing; re-education, retooling, on a grand scale. We might expect that incrementalism is the only way to proceed.

Beyond relying upon the present economic and political crisis to supply motives for reform, it is also important to make an extraordinarily persuasive case that using a system of rule-based decision-making and behaviour would both maintain order and also lead to considerably better social and economic results than does the existing system. Or it may arrive, as increasingly appears to be the case, that Indonesia's involvement in the global economy creates a selection pressure that will impel it to adapt, or – put it this way – Indonesia will discover that its dependency on global markets makes moving to a system of social ordering through rule of law imperative.

The argument that it is advantageous is that, in terms of social progress, wealth maximisation, equity, competitive success and the ability to manage social complexity, rule of law is a superior form of social organisation. Rule of law leads to 'adaptive efficiency', which is concerned

> with the willingness of a society to acquire knowledge and learning, to induce innovation, to undertake risk and creative activity of all sorts, as well as to resolve problems and bottlenecks of the society through time. ... Adaptive efficiency, therefore, provides the incentives to encourage the development of decentralised decision-making processes that will allow societies to maximise the efforts required to explore alternative ways of solving problems (North, 1990: 80-81).

Economically speaking, rule of law is also greatly more efficient than a tradition or patronage-based system. Governing through law means giving up hierarchical decision-making control but does not mean giving up control. In fact, governing through law provides more system control, albeit of a different kind, and far better system results, than governing through fiat decree.

General argument, and more importantly, the current crisis may help convince Indonesia to move rapidly toward a rule of law system of governance. But it would also help to have convincing, specific demonstrations of the superiority of rule of law. Here is where economics, and lawyers in alliance, enter the rule of law effort. Because of the Indonesian government's continuing commitment to economic growth, it is essential always to make the economic case for general and particular legal system changes and law reforms, but lawyers are not particularly good at that. I know that, generally speaking, economists do support law reform, rule-based behaviour and transparency of decision-making. Economists have also enlightened everyone regarding transaction costs and the importance of reducing them. Recent economic literature supports the claim that rule of law as a fundamental feature of social organisation and social ordering is a superior way of achieving collective social aims, economic growth and equity by comparison to a system of patronage and fiat decrees (North, 1990; Scully, 1992).

What has been lacking for Indonesia, however, are studies of the economic and social effects of existing ways of decision-making and the incentive structures thereby created, and what economic and social ordering differences genuine legal reforms would make. There are as yet few persuasive demonstrations that wholesale and retail legal, and legal institutional, changes are necessary to advance the Indonesian economy and the aspirations of its peoples.

For example, I think it is important to demonstrate, empirically and concretely in the Indonesian context that social ordering through rule of law is in fact economically more efficient than other forms of ordering; and to show just how current incentive structures affect economic performance and social development. On a less grand scale, and to be more specific with regard to particular legal reforms, it would be useful to have studies investigating how much credit extension and possible productive economic activity is lost because it is difficult to *collateralise* moveables in Indonesia. A study, say for Jakarta alone, concerning the transactions costs particular industries experience because the Indonesian legal system performs the way it does would also be beneficial. How much legal services income is lost to Indonesia because its lawyers are inadequately trained to handle sophisticated international commercial transactions? How much foreign investment, and in what sectors, does Indonesia lose because of its legal, judicial and other decision-making systems? Presently, most foreign investment has fled Indonesia. While it was there, however, there were important, unanswered questions as to how much foreign investment, and in what sectors, Indonesia lost because of its legal, judicial and other decision-making systems. Now I suppose the appropriate question is: what specific changes in Indonesia's legal, judicial and administrative decision-making systems are necessary to help restore foreign investor confidence?

Frankly, even with the best of legal-economic analyses supporting legal system and law reform, Indonesia does not appear ready for a global change to a rule of law system. There are now, of course, great pressures on Indonesia to move in that direction. I think, however, this shift – a cultural transformation actually – if it is ever to be made, will be made incrementally over a long period of time. And it will take place in response to economic and other pressures, and, initially, in discrete areas or segments of activity rather than system-wide. Eventually, an 'ink blot' strategy may work to make rule of law generally normative in Indonesia. By 'ink blot' strategy, I mean locating and analysing those areas of economic activity where rule of law is a kind of precondition for real success, where it is in the interests of private parties to have and obey rules and then directing reform and law development support efforts. The capital and commodities markets, banking and the operations of other credit institutions are examples. In this respect, it is important to remember that commercial, business, and trade laws originally developed privately and were only later nationalised by states. Consider *lex mercatoria*:

It evolved. Good customs that worked, and good ways of settling disputes, drove out bad by natural selection. By the mid twelfth century, merchants travelling abroad had substantial protection in disputes with local merchants under the merchant law. The only and final sanction against a transgressor was ostracism ... A merchant with a reputation as a cheat could not carry on his trade. Merchants formed their own courts, which were more efficient and uniform than the royal and state courts. A set of standardised customs about how bills should be settled, interest paid and disputes resolved obtained all across the continent – and all without the slightest direction from above (Ridley, 1996: 203).

In general, law development should seek out those private arenas or economic 'games' where rule-based behaviour makes a significant institutional performance and economic difference, and support the efforts of those attempting to introduce such ordering. Such a strategy should also focus on facilitating the creation of private institutions intermediate between the citizens and the state and support the development of group and social norms that can later be codified into law, a sensible bottom-up approach to law-making.[4] Eventually, performance will constitute proof and provide models that Indonesia will find useful to follow throughout the society.

References

Cooter, Robert D, 1997, 'The Rule of State Law Versus the Rule-of-Law State' in Buscaglia, E, Ratliff, W and Cooter, R (eds), *The Law and Economics of Development*, JAI Press, Greenwich, Conn: 101-40.

De Soto, Hernando, 1989, *The Other Path: the invisible revolution in the Third World* (trans June Abbott), Harper & Row, New York.

Hill, Hal, 1995, *The Indonesian Economy Since 1966: South East Asia's emerging giant*, Cambridge University Press, Melbourne.

Kahnemann, Daniel and Tversky, Amos, 1979, 'Prospect Theory: An Analysis of Decision under Risk', *Econometrica*, vol 47(2): 263-91.

Luhmann, Niklas, 1985, *A Sociological Theory of Law*, trans Elizabeth King and Martin Albrow (ed), Martin Albrow, Routledge & Kegan Paul, London.

Mackie, Jamie and MacIntyre, Andrew, 1994, 'Politics' in Hill, Hal (ed), *Indonesia's New Order: The Dynamics of Socio-Economic Transformation*, Allen & Unwin, Sydney: 1-53.

Magnis-Suseno, Franz, 1997, *Javanese Ethics and World View*, PT Gramedia Pustaka Utama, Jakarta.

North, Douglass C, 1990, *Institutions, Institutional Change and Economic Performance*, Cambridge University Press, Cambridge.

Ridley, Matt, 1996, *The Origins of Virtue*, Penguin Books, USA.

Scully, Gerald W, 1992, *Constitutional Environments and Economic Growth*, Princeton University Press, Princeton.

Seidman, Robert B, 1978, *The State, Law, and Development*, Croom Helm, London.

---

4 'Technical assistance should not focus primarily on large documents that provide new codes and more up-to-date regulations. Counting the number of new [statutes] and regulations is a kind of 'commodity fetishism,' which cannot measure legal modernisation. The rule of law cannot come from top-down planning, because central officials do not have enough information or the right motivation. Without the support of private citizens and intermediate institutions land [sic] a community of judges, lawyers, and scholars who can shape law to reality' (Cooter, 1997: 140).

Tversky, Amos & Kahnemann, Daniel, 1981, 'The Framing of Decisions and the Psychology of Choice', *Science*, vol 211: 453-58.

World Bank, 1997a, *Global Economic Prospects and the Developing Countries 92*, World Bank, Washington, DC.

World Bank, 1997b, *World Development Report*: *The State in a Changing World*, Oxford University Press, New York.

3. The Indonesian Chinese as 'Foreign Orientals' in the Netherlands Indies

Charles A Coppel

It is one of the lesser-known curiosities of legal history that the planned introduction by the Republic of China around 1930 of a new Civil Code for China was the direct cause of the recruitment of a group of 75 young Dutch law graduates for service in the Netherlands Indies judiciary. The reason for this was the belief in some official quarters that the Code, which was to include a new system of family law, might have the effect of automatically redefining the status of all Chinese in the Netherlands Indies so that they were classified as 'Europeans' rather than 'Foreign Orientals'. This would in turn require a massive increase in the number of European judges employed in the colony because criminal cases involving Chinese would thenceforth have to be heard by the *Raad van Justitie* (European Court of Justice) rather than the *Landraad* (Native Court).[1]

Europeans, Natives and Foreign Orientals

When I first started to study Indonesian history about 35 years ago, it was a commonplace observation that the colonial government had classified the population of the Netherlands Indies into three groups (*bevolkingsgroepen*), namely Europeans, Natives (*Inlanders*) and Foreign Orientals (*Vreemde Oosterlingen*). You could read that in standard texts such as Wertheim's *Indonesian Society in Transition* or Furnivall's *Netherlands India* (Wertheim, 1959; Furnivall, 1944).

What was not clear to me then (and I think many others were similarly ignorant) was just how recently it was that this fully fledged threefold classification

---

1   Professor Wim Wertheim, who was one of the lawyers recruited in 1930, first alerted me to the story in his comments on a paper which I presented to a seminar of the Centre for Asian Studies Amsterdam in early 1996, later published as Coppel (1997). We agreed that the issue deserved closer scholarly scrutiny, and he later published his version in Wertheim (1997a) and Wertheim (1997b). The present paper is heavily indebted to these publications (and to his kindness in sending them to me); and to the discussion in Cees Fasseur's excellent essay (1992b). I am grateful for Prof Wertheim's assistance and for that of Faye Chan and Rosy Antons-Susanto for respectively finding and commenting on relevant archival material. I also acknowledge the assistance of the Faculty of Arts at the University of Melbourne for its financial support.

had come into existence. To take the same two books, Wertheim passes over this point in silence; and Furnivall, while mentioning that the Chinese 'were placed under the same legal footing as natives' by the Constitutional Regulation (*Regeerings Reglement*) of 1854, does not make clear when the threefold classification came into being. The same is true of many comparative or historical studies of Indonesian law (Hooker, 1975; Hooker, 1988). The treatment in such 'big picture' works of a concept like that of the category 'Foreign Oriental' in Netherlands Indies law is of necessity so abbreviated that we lose all the complexity and contestation that went with it; and are left with a kind of snapshot or even a stereotype.

Indonesian nationalists – like nationalists elsewhere – often use the catchcry that colonialists built their empires on the principle of 'divide and rule' (*divide et impera*). The tripartite racial classification in the Netherlands Indies is often cited in this context. Although this notion contains more than a grain of truth, of course, it also obscures the uncomfortable truth that the colonialists were often divided amongst themselves about how best to rule their colonies. Not only did the British in India and the Dutch in Indonesia have quite different ideas about the way in which the different peoples under their rule should be treated by the law but the Dutch differed amongst themselves about whether all 'races' should be treated equally under the law; or whether they should each be treated in accordance with their own customs.

Article 109 of the Constitutional Regulation of 1854 made a basic legal separation between 'lords and subjects', as Wertheim (1997b, 1) nicely puts it. On the one hand there were those identified as 'Europeans and those equated (*gelijkgestelde*) with Europeans'. On the other hand, there were the Natives and those equated (*gelijkgestelde*) with them. Those equated with the Natives were Chinese, Arabs, Japanese and other – '*what would later be called*' – Foreign Orientals (*Vreemde Oosterlingen*) (Fasseur, 1992b, my emphasis).[2]

The more closely one examines it, the more complicated this concept of 'equating' (*gelijkstelling*) becomes, however. The 1854 Constitutional Regulation conferred power on the government to make exceptions to the classification just referred to. Within a year, the government was to exercise that power by passing an ordinance which 'applied to all Foreign Orientals in Java the European Civil and Commercial Code while leaving them under the customary law [*adat*] in other matters' (Furnivall, 1944: 241). The exception was designed to protect European business interests against insolvent Chinese, not to raise the status of the Chinese as a group. Various other pieces of legislation muddied the waters further, as in the case of the Agrarian Law of 1870 which prohibited the sale or permanent transfer of land from 'natives' to Europeans or other 'foreigners' like the Chinese. The Chinese were also required to reside in designated districts (*wijken*) and were not permitted to travel from one part of the colony to another unless they obtained a government pass.

Despite these and other departures from the dualistic classification set out in 1854, at the end of the century the category of 'Foreign Orientals' was still legally a subset of those equated to 'Natives' rather than a third category intermediate to

---

2   According to Professor Wertheim, Fasseur erred in stating that indigenous Christians (*inheemsche christenen*) were equated with Europeans. A provision to that effect was suspended by the Governor General and they remained subject to *adat* law until the end of colonial law.

those of 'Europeans' and 'Natives'. According to an 1890 Malay-language booklet on the legal position of the Chinese in the Netherlands Indies written by JE Albrecht, a former President of the *Weeskamer* (Orphanage Board), Chinese comprised the majority of those equated (*di samaken*) with the natives (*anak negri*), together with Arabs, Indians (Chodja and Kling) and 'other foreigners below the winds' (*orang asing di bawah angin*) and all Muslims and unbelievers (*kafir*) (Albrecht, 1890: 3).

Determining those who were to be 'equated' with the Europeans became a complicated business. In 1871 it became possible for individual Indonesians or other non-Europeans like the Chinese to be equated with Europeans by decree of the Governor-General published in the *Indisch Staatsblad*. Such people became known as *Staatsblad-Europeanen* or 'Government Gazette Europeans'. Illegitimate children of a non-European mother could become European through acknowledgment by the father; and where a European man married a non-European woman, she and their children acquired European status. It has been estimated that more than one-third of the increase in the European population between 1881 and 1940 (excluding immigration) can be attributed to such sources as opposed to births arising out of marriages between Europeans (Fasseur (1992b: 224), citing Marle (1951-52: 500)).

The Case of the Japanese

By the end of the 1890s, another important group of those 'equated' with Europeans suddenly appeared. The Netherlands government implemented a treaty with Japan by legislating that all Japanese nationals in the Netherlands Indies (including ethnic Chinese originating from Formosa (Taiwan)) should be equated with Europeans. For the next half-century, there were to be Chinese agitating for the colonial government to 'equate' *all* Chinese in the Indies with Europeans. Chinese found it particularly offensive that, say, a Japanese prostitute or fisherman charged with a criminal offence should have the right to be tried by a European court (*Raad van Justitie*), whereas they, no matter what their education or social standing, would have to be tried by a native court (*Landraad*). This was not simply a matter of social discrimination. Defendants tried by the European court were protected by the provisions of the European criminal code with respect to arbitrary arrest and jail conditions, and they faced a legally qualified tribunal, whereas trials in the native court were conducted under the *Indisch Reglement* where only the presiding chairman was legally qualified.

The discrepancy between its treatment of the Japanese and Chinese – which had been brought about by the Japanese victory over China in the 1894 Sino-Japanese war – was one for which the government was never able to find a ready and persuasive explanation other than one of political convenience. Lurking behind its refusal to equalise all Chinese with Europeans was the problem of what should then be done in the case of indigenous Indonesians. No matter what measures the government took to mitigate the legal discrimination between the different races or population groups (and there were a number of these), there were serious political and budgetary difficulties which stood in the way of creating equality of the races before the law as was the case in British India or the American Philippines.[3]

---

3   These mitigations included the application of the Civil Code (*Burgerlijk Wetboek*) with respect to their family law and succession (*familie- en erfrecht*) to the Chinese of Java in 1917 and of the Outer Islands in 1925.

This 1899 'Japanese law' (*Japannerwet*) contributed to an amendment to Art 109 of the Constitutional Regulation which was adopted by the Netherlands parliament in 1906 but only came into effect in 1920. By admitting all Japanese to European status, regardless of their religion or connection with European society, the government had 'robbed Article 109 of its foundations', according to one later commentator (Prins, 1933: 679). A new rationale for equalisation had to be found. This amended Art 109, with minor changes, was renumbered as Art 163 of the Indies Constitution of 1925, which replaced the former Constitutional Regulation. Fasseur (1994: 40) has pointed out that this amended legislation had three significant features:

> First, the principle of racial classification in the new article was made conditional ('If other legal provisions distinguish between Europeans, Natives and Foreign Orientals …') Second, the Foreign Orientals were classified as a separate group and no longer 'equated' with Indonesians. Third, the definition of Europeans was enlarged. Henceforth it covered not only Dutchmen and other persons originating from Europe (Japanese included) but everyone who *in his country of origin* was subjected to a family and marriage law 'mainly' based on the same principles as had been adopted in Dutch law. This last addition opened the door for Turks, Siamese and other Asians whose governments had incorporated European principles of family law in their *national* legislation or did so at any time in the future.[4]

The amendments which made their way into Art 163 of the Indies Constitution thus not only introduced the threefold classification of population groups into the basic law but also in effect made family and marriage laws enshrining monogamy the test of Europeanness for this purpose. A projected change in the Chinese Civil Code in the late 1920s under which Chinese family law was to be reformed thus would have constitutional implications for the position of the Chinese in the Netherlands Indies – or at least so some in the colonial administration believed.

Unification vs *Adat* Law

Before discussing this, however, there are more complexities in the Netherlands Indies legal system to be addressed. Dualism had been a feature of the legal system in the Indies for a long time and it was apparent in Art 75 as well as Art 109 of the Constitutional Regulation of 1854.[5] Article 75 provided that jurisdiction, legislation and legal procedures for Dutchmen and other 'Europeans' must be based upon regulations and ordinances as much as possible in conformity with the laws and procedures in the Netherlands. 'Natives', by contrast, were subjected to their own 'religious laws, institutions and customs' in so far as they were 'not in conflict with generally recognised principles of equity and justice' (unless they had accepted or were deemed to have accepted European law). The Chinese, who were equated with the natives, were subject to the same provisions, although the colonial government could, and often did, declare that the native population (or a part of it, such as the Chinese) was to be subject to particular provisions.

In the early years of the 20th century, there were two contradictory trends in the development of law in the colony. On the one hand, there were those who wanted to abandon the pluralism in law and judicial administration and to develop instead a

---

4   Emphasis in original. This is an abridged version of Fasseur (1992b).
5   This and the following two paragraphs are indebted to Fasseur (1992a).

modern, unified legal system. In this camp could be found those who saw a need for legal certainty as well as those proponents of the so-called Ethical Policy who believed that the indigenous population could only be emancipated or elevated on the basis of Western law. Cees Fasseur quotes the Ethicus C Th van Deventer, famous for his formulation of the notion of the Netherlands' 'debt of honour' to the native population of Indonesia, as saying that 'one must recognise that the natural development for Orientals in a colony administered by a Western power is that they, albeit slowly, will have to conform to Western law' (Fasseur, 1992a: 249).[6] In opposition to them stood the champions of the newly discovered adat law (*adatrecht*) under the vigorous leadership of the young Leiden University professor of adat law of the Netherlands Indies, Cornelis van Vollenhoven.

The conflict between the two camps came to a head over a Bill which was introduced into the Dutch parliament in 1904. The intent of the Bill was to apply European law to native society unless 'the different needs' of the indigenous people made it necessary to use *adat* law. Somewhat surprisingly, the Bill was amended by its opponents after two years of debate, to such effect that its thrust was reversed. Article 75 of the revised Constitutional Regulation was now to have the effect that European law would only apply to natives if the needs of native society required it. According to Fasseur, the outcome of the long debates was a stalemate. The 'movement for unification ... gradually lost its momentum and finally petered out' (Fasseur, 1992a: 251). In his view, the only success for its proponents was the adoption of a unified penal code for the Netherlands Indies in 1918, in which the separate codes for Europeans and natives (which had differed little anyway) were amalgamated. But their attempts to introduce a uniform code of criminal procedure for all groups of the population broke down in 1919.

Equalisation for the Chinese?

In the case of the Chinese, however, there was another move toward *gelijkstelling* on a group basis in the late 1920s. Even before it took its place in the Indies Constitution in 1925, influential people in the colonial administration were arguing that Art 163, with its system of racial classification, should be repealed. This was the recommendation of the *Herzieningscommissie* (Revision Committee) set up by Governor-General Van Limburg Stirum at the end of 1918 (and which reported in 1920) and was chaired by the president of the Supreme Court (*Hooggerechtshof*) in Batavia, JH Carpentier Alting. It was also the view of another small committee within the Justice Department, chaired by W Sonneveld, a member of the Council of the Indies (*Raad van Nederlandsch-Indië*), which rejected the partial solution of equating Chinese with Europeans in favour of revoking what was then still Art 109 of the Constitutional Regulation (as amended). This was also the view expressed in 1922 by the eminent lawyer and friend of the Indies Chinese, Mr PH Fromberg. Governor-General Van Limburg Stirum adopted the proposals of the Sonneveld Committee in January 1921 but the conservative Minister of Colonies, S de Graaff, refused to entertain them (Fasseur, 1994: 43-48; Wertheim, 1997a: 9, citing Fromberg, 1926: 793).

The contradictions of discrimination on the basis of race kept cropping up, next in the context of an electoral bill in the *Volksraad* (People's Council). This new law,

---

6   Another leading Ethicus advocate of equalising the Chinese was the lawyer PH Fromberg.

applied first in 1925, discriminated formally speaking on the basis of nationality (though in practice on the basis of race) by distinguishing between 'Netherlanders'; 'indigenous' Netherlands subjects (non-Netherlanders); and 'foreign' Netherlands subjects (non-Netherlanders). Its author, JJ Schrieke, was then Government Deputy for General Affairs (Fasseur, 1994: 49).[7]

The Chinese and others kept the issue alive in the major Dutch newspapers in the Indies and the Netherlands; in the Malay press in the Indies; and through speeches in the *Volksraad* with demands for the 'odious Article' to be repealed. But although indigenous Indonesians had not objected to the Japanese or the Siamese being given European status, the numbers of Japanese and Siamese in the Indies were very small compared with the number of Chinese; and there were those like MH Thamrin who opposed the equalisation of the Chinese if the consequence was to be that the indigenous Indonesians would be left behind.[8] The political implications of the latter, and the prohibitive cost of extending the European system of justice to the whole population, were to be recurrent themes in the debates of succeeding years.

In 1927 Schrieke produced another Bill (after three years in the making) in which 'Netherlanders' and 'Netherlands subjects, non-Netherlanders' ('indigenous' and 'foreign') were differentiated. This was dismissed by the Director of the Batavia Department of Justice, D Rutgers (Fasseur, 1994: 49-50; Wertheim, 1997a: 9). Governor-General ACD de Graeff then appointed a committee of three professors (JHA Logemann, B ter Haar, and RD Kollewijn) of the newly founded Batavia Faculty of Law (*Rechtshoogeschool*) to find a solution. Their 1927 report rejected Schrieke's proposal but also recommended the repeal of Art 163. Rather than the criterion of nationality favoured by Schrieke, they preferred to introduce a system in which the 'social needs' of any group of the population should form the criteria for differential treatment under the law. The influence of the *adat* law school was clearly evident in this approach. Rutgers, apparently an advocate of full legal unification, was equally opposed to this proposal (Fasseur, 1994: 50-51; Wertheim, 1997a: 9-10).

The Council of the Netherlands Indies (*Raad van Nederlandsch-Indië*) opted for yet another course. It proposed that Art 163 should be repealed and Chinese (but not other Foreign Orientals) merged with Europeans. This bundle of contradictory proposals was sent for decision to the Minister of Colonies in The Hague in late 1928 (Fasseur, 1994: 51).

In the meantime news had reached the Dutch government from its embassy in Peking that the government of the Republic of China was to introduce a system of

---

7   This distinction drew on a different classification of the population which has a history too complex to pursue in depth here. In 1892 a Dutch Nationality Law was passed which made it clear that only Netherlanders (but not Natives or those equated to them) held Dutch citizenship. It was not until 1910 that a law was passed which clarified the national status of Natives (and Foreign Orientals born in the Netherlands Indies) to be 'Netherlands subjects, non-Netherlanders'. This legislation was passed to counter the effect of the 1909 Chinese Nationality law on the locally-born Chinese population in the Indies. See Willmott (1961: Chapter 2).

8   See, for example, PLG (Phoa Liong Gie), 1926, 'De rechtstoestand der Chineezen in Indonesië', *Chung Hwa Hui Tsa Chih*, vol 5, no 2, October-November 1926; KTH [Kwee Tek Hoay], 1927, 'Gelijkstelling bagi bangsa Tionghoa', *Panorama*, vol 29. 2 July 1927: 1-3; KTH (Kwee Tek Hoay), 1927, 'Boemipoetra dan gelijkstelling Tionghoa', *Panorama*, vol 32, 23 July: 1-4; CT Bertling, 1927, 'Gelijkstelling van Chineezen met Europeanen', *Koloniale Studien*, vol 11, no 2: 44-71.

European family law on 1 January 1930. This implied, as previously indicated, that the Chinese in the Indies would automatically achieve the status of Europeans unless Art 163 was to be further amended. The Netherlands government thus faced the spectre of having the quite small ranks of the European population in the Indies swelled by the much larger number of Chinese with the certain prospect of further demands for equality of status from indigenous Indonesians – and all as a consequence of a change of the family law in China (Fasseur, 1994: 51; Wertheim, 1997a: 10)!

On 23 February 1929, the deputy Director of Justice, HJ Spit, proposed to the Governor-General through the Supreme Court that the budget allocation should be increased to take account of an extra fifty jurists to be recruited in the Netherlands to meet 'the possibility … that within the foreseeable future the Chinese will have to be treated on an equal footing with the Europeans, with all its consequences, among others with respect to jurisdiction'. The Governor-General cabled his adoption of this proposal to the Minister for Colonies on 7 May 1929 (Wertheim, 1997a: 11).

In July 1929 the Dutch envoy in Nanking, WJ Oudendijk, reported back to The Hague that it was very likely that Western family law would not in fact be adopted by the Chinese people for many years to come but that the Chinese government would do what it could to promulgate a new Civil Code within the year. Meanwhile Governor General de Graeff in Batavia expected that Western family law would come into effect on 1 January 1930, and he publicly broached the implications of this in his address to the *Volksraad* in August 1929. 'If this plan is realised', he said, 'all Chinese in this country will be subjected to the law valid for Europeans'. If the native population wanted this extended to them, he said, the government would welcome it if it were possible but it could not be introduced overnight. But members of the *Volksraad* might well consider that this was a reform which should be implemented with all due haste, and the government would systematically pursue a general unified criminal procedure and the like (Wertheim, 1997a: 12-13).

By the end of 1929 it had become apparent to the colonial administration that the new Chinese family law would not, after all, come into effect by 1 January 1930, but it now announced that '[a]s already promised, the Government would, at short notice, of its own accord, realise equalization of the Chinese with Europeans, substantially in the realm of criminal procedure'. It acknowledged that it could not delay this (pending legal unification for all ethnic groups) without breaking its word. The plan to equalise the Chinese with Europeans first, and then to equalise all native Indonesians as soon as possible thereafter, was generally welcomed in the *Volksraad* (Wertheim, 1997a: 13-14).

From Equalisation to Equivalence

So what went wrong? A shift seems to have occurred in the course of 1930. On the one hand, envoy Oudendijk wrote from China to the ministry of foreign affairs in The Hague casting doubt on whether the new Chinese Civil Code would after all satisfy Western norms with respect to family and succession law. Illegitimate children who were brought up in their father's household would thereby enjoy the same status as his legitimate children. In his view this constituted a legitimation of concubinage and the supposedly monogamous intent of the legislation was likely to be received as advisory rather than mandatory (Wertheim, 1997a: 17). Meanwhile, Professor Kollewijn published an article on 'The Modern Chinese Codification' in the *Indisch Tijdschrift van het Recht* (Wertheim, 1997a: 17-18; Kollewijn, 1930: 323-40). In his opinion, the question of whether the new Chinese legislation accorded with Art 163 should be submitted for determination by the Supreme Court as a test case, preferably through a criminal prosecution at the instance of the Attorney-General. After the books of the new Chinese Civil Code concerning family law and succession had come into effect on 5 May 1931, Kollewijn wrote a further article entitled 'The Modern Chinese Family Law', in which he concluded that although monogamy had been officially introduced and bigamy was punishable as a crime, the marriage law, for technical reasons, 'could not possibly be called "Western"' (Wertheim, 1997a: 18; Kollewijn, 1931: 107-11).

Meanwhile the wind had changed again in Batavia. From 17 October 1930, the *Raad van Indië* had taken a view opposing Schrieke (who was by now the Director of Justice). They wanted to put aside his proposal in support of equalisation, and not to permit any formal declaration of equalisation of the Chinese. They now adopted the idea of a general criminal procedure for *all* ethnic groups. This shift may well have been influenced, as Wertheim suggests, by the admission of two Indonesians (Koesoemo Joedo and Achmad Djajadiningrat) to the *Raad* that year (Wertheim, 1997a: 19).

Despite continuing opposition by Schrieke, the *Raad*'s position gained support from another quarter. This was the report of the Vonk Commission, which formulated a draft emergency ordinance on the simplification of criminal procedure (which was published on behalf of the Netherlands Indies Government) but proposed that it should also apply, as a first step, to the Chinese pending the preparation of a unified criminal procedure for all ethnic groups. This in turn was challenged by ter Haar (Professor of *Adat* Law) who warned of the dangers to the quality of the native criminal jurisdiction if a unified criminal procedure was introduced in the way proposed because of the number of judges required. The effect of an ordinance designed to simplify criminal procedure was therefore watered down in response to his representations so as to apply only to Europeans (Wertheim, 1997a: 19-20).

Ultimately, the government in The Hague in the person of the Minister for Colonies made a decision. Essentially, it seems to have been a decision to sit on its hands, so far as Art 163 was concerned. Kollewijn's argument that the effect of the Chinese law should be determined by the Supreme Court was adopted, but without taking any proceedings to elicit such a determination. The Minister, like ter Haar, was opposed on the grounds of its expense to a two-stage process in which European criminal procedure would be extended to the Chinese with the later institution of an improved *Landraad* (Wertheim, 1997a: 23-25).

For the rest of the colonial period, the Government retreated from its promised aim of a unified criminal procedure. It now spoke of aiming for *gelijkwaardigheid* ('equivalence') rather than *gelijkheid* ('equality') of jurisdiction for all ethnic groups. No more was heard of the views of the Chinese Government or of the effect of the new Chinese Civil Code on the operation of Art 163. Presumably, as Wertheim suggests, they were too busy trying to cope with the Japanese aggression in Manchuria. The Visman Commission, which was set up on the eve of the Japanese occupation of Indonesia to study political reforms, discovered that the notion of 'equivalence' had no appeal to the Chinese, whatever its attractions to the indigenous Indonesian population (Wertheim, 1997a: 27-28; Verslag..., 1942: 60-61).

Thus it was that the well-known division of Netherlands Indies society into three population groups – Europeans, 'Foreign Orientals' and 'Natives' – remained in existence to the end of the colonial period. But the recentness of its introduction and the continuous challenges to its existence in Art 163 of the Indies Constitution seem to have slipped from the collective memory of Indonesians and even of legal historians. The history of the divided views of the Dutch ruling elite on this subject might be thought to give a new meaning to the old saying 'divide and rule'.

References

Albrecht, JE, 1890, *Soerat Ketrangan dari pada hal Kaadaan Bangsa Tjina di Negri Hindia Olanda*, Albrecht & Rusche, Batavia.

Coppel, Charles A, 1997, 'Revisiting Furnivall's "plural society": Colonial Java as a mestizo society?' *Ethnic and Racial Studies*, vol 20, no 3 July: 562-79.

Fasseur, C, 1992a, 'Colonial dilemma: van Vollenhoven and the struggle between adat law and Western law in Indonesia' in Mommsen, WJ and Moor, JA de (eds), *European Expansion and Law: The Encounter of European and Indigenous Law in 19th- and 20th-Century Africa and Asia*, Berg, Oxford and New York: 237-56.

Fasseur, C, 1992b, 'Hoeksteen en struikelblok. Rasonderscheid en overheidsbeleid in Nederlands-Indië', *Tijdschrift voor Geschiedenis* vol 105 no 2: 218-42.

Fasseur, C, 1994, 'Cornerstone and stumbling block: Racial classification and the late colonial state in Indonesia' in Cribb, Robert (ed), *The Late Colonial State in Indonesia: Political and Economic Foundations of the Netherlands Indies 1880-1942*, KITLV Press, Leiden.

Fromberg, PH, 1926, *Verspreide Geschriften*, Leidsche Uitgeversmaatschappij, Leiden.

Furnivall, JS, 1944, *Netherlands India: A Study of Plural Economy*, Cambridge University Press, Cambridge.

Hooker, MB, 1975, *Legal Pluralism: An Introduction to Colonial and Neo-Colonial Laws*, Clarendon Press, Oxford.

Hooker, MB (ed), 1988, *Laws of South-East Asia, Volume II European Laws in South-East Asia*, Butterworths, Singapore.

Kollewijn, 1930, 'De Moderne Chinese Kodifikatie', *Indisch Tijdschrift van het Recht*, 132: 323-40.

Kollewijn, 1931, 'Het moderne Chinese familierecht', *Indisch Tijdschrift van het Recht*, 134: 107-111.

Marle, A van, 1951-52, 'De groep der Europeanen in Nederlands-Indië, iets over onststaan en groei', *Indonesië*, vol 5: 500.

Prins, WF, 1933, 'De bevolkingsgroepen in het Nederlandsch-Indische recht', *Koloniale Studiën* vol 17, no 2: 679.

Verslag van de Commissie tot Bestudeering van Staatsrechtelijke Hervormingen..: Deel II Indië's Wenschen, 1942, Landsdrukkerij, Batavia (2nd printing).

Wertheim, WF, 1959, *Indonesian Society in Transition: A Study of Social Change*, 2nd ed, Van Hoeve, The Hague and Bandung.

Wertheim, WF, 1997a, *De Status van de Chinezen in Vooroorlogs Nederlands-Indië: Zeer geheime documenten uit de jaren 1928-1932*, Research Report no 97/1, van Vollenhoven Institute for Law and Administration in Non-Western Countries, Leiden.

Wertheim, 1997b, 'Political status of the Chinese in Pre-War Netherlands-Indies: Secret Documents from 1928-1932', *Indonesian Law and Administration Review*, vol 3, no 2.

Willmott, Donald, E, 1961, *The National Status of the Chinese in Indonesia 1900-1958*, revised edition, Cornell Modern Indonesia Project Monograph Series, Cornell University.

4. *Hak Ulayat* and the State: Land Reform in Indonesia

Rachel Haverfield

In 1945 Indonesia's founders were deeply committed to implementing the Revolution's ideal of 'unity in diversity' (*Bhinneka Tunggal Ika*). However, rather than recognising *adat*[1] rights of communities over their ancestral lands in a pluralist legal framework, the policy of the government has been uncertain, inconsistent and, ultimately, unjust. Since 1945 land regulation has been marked by a pattern of ever-increasing state centralism at the expense of regional traditional interests.

The problems associated with traditional land and its administration have proved to be juridically difficult and politically delicate. Successive governments have made failed attempts to unify land tenure, first under the Agrarian Law of 1960; related land registration regulations (Government Regulation No 10 of 1961 and Government Regulation No 24 of 1997 on the Registration of Land); and by the systematic registration of land under the World Bank's Land Administration Project (LAP). Unfortunately, these efforts have not reconciled the aspirations of the thousands of ethnolinguistic communities in Indonesia with the developmentalist programs of the Jakarta government.[2] The result is that Indonesian land law has become a volatile brew of mutually antagonistic aims, legal principles and ideologies.

In government rhetoric the customs of the various *adat* (traditional customary) groups have been incorporated into the legal system. The Agrarian Law is expressed to be 'based upon' *adat* law (Art 5), emphasising the needs of the community over individual rights. In reality their experience has been one of systematic demise.

The LAP also acknowledges *adat* rights to land, by insisting upon investigation of the history of such rights before registration. In practice, however, the overwhelming policy has been acculturation and assimilation to the dominant position, ignoring the existing legal pluralism. This has ultimately led to the failure of the national land management system.

---

1   *Adat* is an Arabic term meaning 'custom', 'usage', 'rule', 'proper behaviour', 'propriety' or 'law'. *Adat* and 'custom' are used in this chapter for the basic way of life of a community originating from traditions and customs understood and adhered to concerning what is appropriate and just behaviour.

2   For Indonesia's high cultural and biological diversity, see Durning (1992: 17).

The Nature of *Adat*

Establishing the form and content of *adat* is made difficult by the heterogeneity of the archipelagic nation and the fact that Indonesian *adat* systems have been exposed to a succession of influences: Hindu, Chinese, Islamic, European (Portugese, English, Dutch). It is clear, however, that autochthonous institutions (such as folk patterns, religious values, cultivation and land tenure methods) have remained an important part of the matrix (Kroef, 1960: 414). This diversity of influences have made *adat*'s legal evolution a free and unconscious growth rather than the product of deliberate decisions.

> *Adat* law is living law, because it is the incarnation of the legal feeling among society. According to its natural character, *adat* law is continuously in a state of growth and development, like life itself (Soepomo, 1962: 6).

Underlying the analysis in this chapter is the assumption that 'law' is not a clearly separate social phenomenon easily distinguishable from 'custom'. *Adat* law in most cases is inextricably bound up with history, mythology and the institutional behaviour of each ethnic or cultural unit; and so the various usages of 'legal' terms are not fixed and certain between communities. It was the Dutch scholar van Vollenhoven who popularised use of the term *adat* among colonial jurists, as it did not imply an unworkably stringent distinction between 'law' and popular customs. In particular, van Vollenhoven warned against assuming that 'legal' terms were transferable between cultures or even between individual communities (Hooker, 1978: 144).

The positivist division between law and custom, however, sees the two entities as entirely distinct in character (Burns, 1989: 4; Radcliffe-Brown, 1952: 203-11). 'Law' is a product of the emergence of a sovereign state where social control is achieved through the systematic application of force or imposition of sanctions, by a constituted authority.[3] The positivist asserts that coercion and the authority of a leader of the community are the pillars on which the order of law depends. This definition becomes problematic when applied to *adat* which often contains equally important positive sanctions which contribute to the binding quality of obligations in the absence of a coercive authority. In general, it is not the threat of judicial or administrative force that achieves compliance but rather compliance has become habit for a variety of reasons: for example, because the community fears its ancestors, because violation would not serve their best interests or because of the force of oral tradition (Holleman, 1981: 216). Ideally, coercion is tempered by peaceful consultation and patient mediation in which religion, myth and tradition all play an important part.

Historically, *adat* 'law' was suffused with familial and religious significance bound to eternal orders of the family, locality, religion and status. Community leaders were followed because they were natural parts of the cosmic order of things, acting as the representatives of the community's ancestors or the spirit world. The power relationship between the governor and the governed was determined by charismatic characteristics of the leader, such as his ability to think, spiritual powers (*wahyu*)[4] and physical strength. The ideal ruler is conservative, incorruptible and

---

3   Originally, this was van Vollenhoven's stance which he changed as he found it was impossible to divorce legal institutions from the non-legal elements of popular customs and beliefs (Holleman, 1981: xlii).

4   There are numerous versions of the concept of *wahyu*. For the Javanese versions, see Magnis-Suseno (1993: 98-100).

passionless. The concept of justice is paternalistic based on familial principles and the role of a ruler is to give guidance in the observance of *adat* without there necessarily being any question of dispute resolution or enforcement action. This 'attested law observance'[5] is natural because a leader's word is a manifestation of the 'voice of God' (Tsuchiya, 1987: 203-15). The idea of challenging such a person is not part of this view of social power (Anderson, 1972: 13-19).

Thus, positivist categories used to separate 'legal' and 'moral' considerations create:

> a wild oversimplification of the historical relationship between the *adat* laws and state organisation at all periods of Indonesian history (Hooker, 1978: 147).

Thus, a better approach to artificially dividing law from custom is to regard as 'legal' all factors that contribute to the maintenance of rights and obligations in a given society.[6]

Adat Concepts of Land

Some general characteristics of *adat* land rights can be identified. Before the 20th century, villages were largely isolated by Indonesia's high mountains and impenetrable jungles. There was little mobility, whether physical (due to poor infrastructure) or social (due to unrest between villages). This, in turn, led to unique variations in custom and developments in customary law (Slaats & Portier, 1992: 97). Land was abundant relative to the low density population and the overall pattern of Indonesian society was largely agrarian, creating a deep and enduring relationship with the land. Land had little economic value because there was no need to sell or purchase it and because it was the basic intergenerational bond for the community.

Under English common law, 'land' in its legal meaning is immovable property and a definite portion of the earth's surface. It denotes the quantity and character of the interest or estate which a person may own in land. Thus it comprehends both legal and equitable interests in land. Trees, crops and permanent fixtures are deemed to be a part of the land. In traditional Indonesia, however, the importance accorded to the land transcends its market value.

At *adat* law, land is not simply an asset which can be used for economic production or traded for cash. It is the basis of a community's existence and an essential part of its social, economic and political life (Soekanto, 1985: 67) because it provides security for a community and future descendants. Land cannot be owned by an individual or individuals but only by a lineage or other group, such as a clan or tribe. Crops, trees and other improvements on the land can, however, be claimed or owned by individuals but their rights will be subject to the community's overriding claim in perpetuity. Even the Western concept of 'rights to land' is often

---

5   Van Vollenhoven, quoted in Holleman (1981: 222).

6   Van Vollenhoven argued that *adat* law was to be found by 'careful inquiry into how, in a given area, matters of consequence for the legal order are usually done or tolerated as being normal ... and how in cases of deviation, fellow villagers or *adat* heads, or occasionally the courts react ... Even approbation and disapprobation, if inextricably associated with precept and prohibition in popular thinking and conduct, are law and not mere morality'. Such a view would include moral, religious, traditional, spiritual and childhood socialisation considerations (van Vollenhoven, 1909: 258).

not understood in the clan or tribe view. The availability of land as a resource is simply a 'reality' and has little to do with rights (Abdurrahman, 1984: 2). Dodson's description of Australian indigenous perceptions of land as the 'generational point of existence' (1983: 5) applies equally well to traditional communities in Indonesia.

In Indonesia, there is no 'owner-less' or 'vacant' land. Under *adat* law, it is possible for a group to hold land that it does not occupy or that it may use for only certain purposes. In many traditional communities shifting cultivation meant that land was only cleared when necessary. Alternatively, the group would hunt and collect forest materials on parts of the land; or claim it as part of the legends connecting their community to that land. The existence of communal notions of tenure under *adat*, which are completely beyond the scope of market mechanisms based on absolute individualised ownership, indicates the insufficiency of Western concepts of the market for distributing and managing land in Indonesia.

Hak Ulayat

The most common form of *adat* land tenure is a communal right over land shared by all members of an *adat* society (Kroef, 1960: 415; ter Haar, 1948: 81). For it to exist, there must be a definable community, a designated leader and a territory controlled by the community. This right is widely described in Indonesia as *hak ulayat*. *Hak* means 'right' and *ulayat* is an Arabic word meaning a 'controlled or ruled area, territory or jurisdiction'. Various terms are used by the different *adat* communities to describe their communal *adat* land rights. The examples are limitless: *totabuan* in Bolaang Mongodow (Abdurrahman, 1990: 3); *patuanan* in Ambon; *pertuanan* in East Sumatra; *panyanturi, penetapan, hak panyampeto* in Kalimantan; *wewengkon* in Java; *payer, paer* and *prabumian* in Bali; and *hak ulayat* in West Sumatra (Soedarso, 1976: 68). These were collectively described as *hak ulayat* or *beschikkingsrecht* by van Vollenhoven, which loosely translates as the 'right of disposition' or the 'right of avail'.[7] Despite increasing urbanisation in Indonesia, manifestations of *hak ulayat* persevere in even the major cities of Java such as Yogyakarta, Malang and Jakarta.[8] It is widespread in most of the outer islands.

As a general principle, under *hak ulayat* the community retains the authority to manage land use and ownership, both internally and externally. Internally, *hak ulayat* gives the community's members the ability to use, cultivate and derive benefit from the land for themselves and their families; but not for trading purposes or individual enrichment. Certain areas are set aside for particular communal needs, such as grazing areas, cemeteries and places of worship. Externally, the community has the power to ban non-members from being on the land. In certain circumstances, non-members will be allowed to use land but permission must be granted by the community and a recognition fee paid.

Hak ulayat points to the legal relationship between the people (subjects of the rights) and the land (object of the rights). Communocentricity is the dominant trait,

---

7   *Beschenn* literally means 'dispose', which in Dutch and German law does not necessarily include the right of alienation (van Vollenhoven, 1909, cited in Holleman, 1981: xxxvi).

8   Personal information from an interview with the local government member, Jakarta, February 1996.

whereby the group interacts with the environment and safeguards the natural resources which comprise the group's primary material possessions.

Etymologically, the usual English translation of *beschikkingsrecht* as a 'right of disposition' is therefore inaccurate. Under *hak ulayat,* the individual is not the normative point of reference for the purposes of the law (Soepomo, 1963: 10) and theoretically neither the community nor any of its members can dispose of the land in perpetuity. A better term would therefore be 'right of allocation' (Burns, 1989: 109). *Hak ulayat* is conceived as the basic communal source of a whole range of discrete, individualised user rights. The community allocates the land to its members and it is a member's labour on the land which then establishes his or her legal connection with the land that will decrease the relative right of the community to that plot. If improvements are made to the land, the individual responsible for improvements will retain rights to them. If the individual subsequently neglects the plot, the communal right of assignment revives and the rights of use will be reallocated. The community's right is also manifest in other powers, including continuous rights of passage over property; rights to hold purification and other rituals; rights to recover land upon the death of the individual, upon the conviction for criminal offences or departure of the individual from the territory; and the imposition of maximum limits on land holdings to maintain equitable distribution.[9]

The separation between proprietary and usufructuary rights of an individual is also unclear. The English law concepts of 'ownership' and 'right of use' are mere approximations of their *adat* equivalents. If one interprets 'ownership' as an individual right to freely use the land (with limited public law interference), then 'ownership' in Indonesia only existed in very few areas, such as Aceh, Madura, West Java and Bali. If, however, one accepts 'ownership' as a person's preferential right to a certain parcel of land for a period of time where the 'owner' accepts that he is bound by certain traditional restrictions, then 'ownership' is acknowledged throughout most of the archipelago.

Adat Law Communities

Van Vollenhoven's definition of *adat* was based predominantly on his notion of the 'law clan' or 'jural community'. He believed that law is sociologically dependent and could only be known through examination of the community to which it applies. Van Vollenhoven found that each jural community in existence in the archipelago was based on a different structure and he concluded that it could not simply be assumed that the differences between the Indonesian *adat* law areas were confined merely to differences of rule and precept within identical legal frameworks.

Van Vollenhoven grouped the *adat* jural communities into four generic types. First, genealogical groups, based on descent from common ancestors;[10] secondly, territorial communities with an autonomous governing body and common property, embracing various genealogical jural communities;[11] thirdly, territorial groupings

---

9   Equitable access to members would also be guaranteed when external pressures, such as taxes, constitute pressure on the community to resume and reallocate land. Ecological factors, such as infertile soil may also cause redistribution.

10   For example, the Gayo people of Irian Jaya (Bowen, 1988: 274-93).

11   An example of this is the Minangkabau people of West Sumatra. A family lives together in one house. A section of the clan (*suku*) lives in one village. The territorial village itself (*nagari*) consists of two or more *suku*. Often a federation of villages occurs and sometimes, a confederation of village federations will arise (Kato, 1979).

without subordinate genealogical communities;[12] and fourthly, voluntary corporate associations.[13] The process by which communities occur is spontaneous. They are coordinating vessels to organise and implement legal relationships within and without the territorial or genealogical boundaries (Soesangobeng, 1975: 14).

In modern Indonesia, the term *masyarakat hukum adat* or *adat* law society is found in many laws and regulations, yet in none of them is it defined in detail. It is found in the Agrarian Law[14] and is defined as the 'subject' which practises traditional land rights, including *hak ulayat* (Arts 2(4) and 3, Agrarian Law).[15] In practice, the government definition of a jural community is based on purely administrative criteria[16] which means that often the political boundaries asserted by the government will not coincide with the social reality of the people. Definite administrative boundaries do not sit easily with many of the traditional under-standings of *adat* law community where the nature of the community's attachment with its territory is magico-religious, that is, the community as abode of ancestral spirits and deities (ter Haar, 1950: 15).

Attitudes to *Adat*

In this context, it becomes clear why successive regimes have been averse to the wholesale acknowledgment of *adat* law. *Adat* communities, in fact, practice an inchoate form of autonomy. If allowed to develop, this autonomy might eventually find expression in a proclamation of territorial independence.

Critics of *adat* assert that over the course of the past century the individualisation of rights to land has advanced as the processes of monetarisation and individuation in economic behaviour have become more widespread (Lekkerkerker, 1938: 565-70). Indeed in some places, collectivised tenure is largely unknown.[17] However, the processes of individuation are by no means uniform across the archipelago. In other areas, communal and individual rights have achieved an ad hoc balance, such that adjacent plots of land can be governed by different tenure principles.[18] Even in some areas where individualised ownership is the norm, it is difficult to draw distinctions between 'individual' rights and 'communal' rights.[19]

---

12 For example, in Java, the basic territorial unit is the *dhukuh* (hamlet), which is subordinate to the village (*desa*), which is, in turn, part of the chiefdom (*kalurahan*) and the federation of chiefdoms (*kacamatan*) (Koentjaraningrat, 1967).

13 For example, societies such as irrigation corporations and other recreational groups in Bali and Lombok.

14 The term is used to in Art 3 of the Agrarian Law, Art 17 of the Law on Forestry Law No 5 of 1967 and Art 24(2)(b) of Government Regulation No 24 of 1997 on Registration of Land.

15 See also Art 17, Law on Forestry No 5 1967; Art 24(2)(b) Government Regulation No 24 of 1997 on Registration of Land.

16 (i) A distinct community of persons (*penduduk*); (ii) a community source of wealth (*kekayaan ekonomi*) separate from individualised ownership (*kekayaan perorangan*); (iii) a leader (*sistem pemerintahan*); (iv) an ascertainable territory (*wilayah*); (v) and ascertainable authority (*kewenangan*) within those territorial boundaries towards both members and outsiders who come into their area (Sumardjono, 1993: 4).

17 For example, Probolinggo, Pasuruan, Besuki. See Kroef (1960: 416).

18 For example, the Baduy people of West Java (Garna, 1990: 89).

19 For example, the land holders of the Karo Batak people in North Sumatra will still consult their community before they sell the land and rarely sell to outsiders. Likewise in 1960, 99% of arable lands in the Cirebon region of Java were communally controlled with fixed individual shares in the common area (Kroef, 1960: 417).

It is commonly assumed – and argued by the state – that *adat* communities are inherently anti-development.

> If we still sometimes hear some modern Asian intellectual praising customary law, it must be considered the expression of a confused mind in the face of the tremendous spirit and material change which is taking place in Asia and elsewhere. If he is a man of the modern world, very often his adulation of *adat* law is the expression of the nostalgia of a tired man for a more peaceful archaic society (Alisjahbana, 1968: 6).

This view illustrates the common misconception that traditional laws dictate rights which are simple and static.[20] In fact a major premise of *adat* is that legal and social structures are organic entities. As long as there is a connection or some relevance to the old way of life, new ways and beliefs can be incorporated in the legal and social systems. Any proposal for extensive land management, therefore, must take into account sociological, political and historical issues, rather than mere legalities (Seidman & Seidman, 1994: 131). It must concurrently implement a system of culturally appropriate dispute resolution mechanisms to resolve the strains caused by acknowledgment of a multitude of laws.

> It is not *adat* regulations that are an obstacle to development, but rather it is our pigeon-holed thinking. If it is true that we have had difficulty in obtaining *adat* land for development, then this should not be seen as the fault or the lacking of *adat*, but the result of excessive tunnel vision which has destroyed a system for the development of values, influencing the behaviour of its people, the compact between grandparents and grandchildren and hence between the government and the people (Anas, 1972: 22).

In many *adat* systems, an outsider wishing to work on land held under *hak ulayat* can, in fact, do so via *adat* commercial law mechanisms. The mechanism is negotiation and the making of a contract with the entire community.[21] *Adat* contracts are recognised by the formal laws which stipulate that judges must take into account every law which is effective in society in order to make just and justifiable decisions.[22]

However, vested interests seek marginalisation of traditional communities from the decision-making process for resource development of their homelands. This is done by pre-emptive alienation of community lands; legislative definitions of indigenous peoples as backward and in need of paternal development;[23] and a

---

20 As an example, for a discussion of the complexity of traditional laws of Minangkabau community, see Benda-Beckmann (1984).

21 Choice of law rules in Indonesia are intricate and convoluted but the basic principles determining whether a commercial transaction will be covered by *adat* include: (i) the intention of the parties (whether there has been an explicit statement that *adat* law is determinative); (ii) the *milieu* (that is, if the transaction takes place in a village *milieu*, then *adat* will apply); (iii) the law sphere (for example, if the foreign investor enters a village then *adat* will apply. If a villager goes to a European owned store, he or she has entered the Western law sphere); (iv) public offer (if someone makes a public offer, the offeror's law sphere will apply); (v) overpowering economic and social position of one party (the overwhelming party can more or less dictate its own terms) (Himawan, 1973: 1-2).

22 See the Law on the Judicial Powers No 14 of 1970.

23 The closest thing to recognition of such groups is under the Social Department's definition of 'isolated persons': 'Isolated persons are peoples who have limited capacity to communicate with other, more developed, societies. Because of this, they are characteristically backward having been left behind in the economic, political, socio-cultural, religious and ideological development' (Departemen Sosial, 1989: 1; Koentjaraningrat, 1993: 10). In Art 11(2) of the Agrarian Law, there is also mention of an 'economically weak' class who may have special rights.

confusing diversity of statutes dealing with land rights excision.[24] The position is similar to colonial policies aimed at the elimination of ethnic groups as primitive or barbaric, for the sake of civilisation (Vlist, 1994: 35). Because of this view, the term 'village' has become a pejorative term, as have the terms 'indigene', 'native' and 'villager'.[25] National unity, assimilation and acculturation to the dominant position have become the key themes of state policy for *adat* groups.

Nationalism and the Agrarian Law

The Agrarian Law of 1960 was passed to provide a system of land law that would abolish the racially inequitable land system set up by the Dutch and reflect the legal and cultural pluralism of the Indonesian people as expressed through *adat* (Art 11(2)). The legislation did not explain whether it referred to *adat* in general or to specific local rules, nor did it explicitly synthesise *adat* land tenure with the Western forms of interest provided under the Law. The very vagueness of its terms has left the Agrarian Law largely devoid of content as many of the provisions are stated to depend upon subordinate legislation for implementation – and this has, in most cases, never materialised.[26]

A significant feature of the rights established under the Agrarian Law is that they are closer in nature to Western land rights and have few counterparts, even as individual rights, under *adat* law (Depdagri, 1978). For example, the primary right recognised by the Agrarian Law is 'ownership' *(hak milik),* which is individual, unlimited in time; and is registrable, mortgageable and transferable by an owner. This conflicts with fundamental *adat* concepts relating to communally held land by which the right to allocate the land remains with the leader of the clan at all times. Under such a system there is no real distinction between ownership and usufruct.

One often-proposed solution to Indonesia's chaotic land law regime, the wholesale abolition of *adat* rights, would be untenable in areas where Western rights are simply non-existent. It would be 'too great a quantum leap to gain acceptance at this time' (Badan Pertanahan Nasional, 1993: 275). However, there has been no real attempt to create a working mixture of the *adat* laws and the codes. What arises, therefore, is the existence of two only slightly related systems of law: a formal one, and a real one. The 'living law of actual practice' (Lev, 1965: 304) operates through an intricate network of personal and familial relationships; local concepts of justice; and countless other uncertainties in the civil relations of a developing society.

Originally, *adat* as a positive source of agrarian law was motivated by ideological considerations, the very term *adat* serving to legitimise the new law and

---

24 For example, (i) Presidential Decree No 53 of 1989 on Regional Industry which allowed the procurement of 51,744 hectares of land in Java, Sumatra, Sulawesi, Kalimantan and Irian since 1955; (ii) Presidential Decree No 97 of 1993 on Permission for Foreign Investors regarding rights to land; and (iii) BPN Regulation No 2 of 1993 which authorised the allocation of 81,203 hectares in Botabek, West Java (Kasim & Suhendar, 1996: 15).

25 For example, in Javanese, the term *desa* (village) is often used as an adjective to connote a simple, backward or uncivilised person (Kartodirdjo, 1972: 84). In *bahasa Indonesia*, the pejorative term *kampongan*, 'of the village', implies crudeness and even stupidity.

26 For example, although Art 2(4) of the Agrarian Law allows part of state control over land to be delegated to semi-autonomous regions and traditional *adat* communities, no such delegation has ever taken place (World Bank 1994: 45).

quell dissent. *Adat* was a powerful ideological weapon for the nationalists in their struggle for independence as an unadulterated expression of the Indonesian character, which could be set up in opposition to the incompatible and alien laws and systems of Dutch colonialism.[27] In reality, however, the leaders of the newly independent Indonesia were distinctly ambivalent to *adat*. For many of them *adat* represented something primitive, connotative of the 'feudal' for anti-colonialists. As a result, much of the Agrarian Law imported foreign legal concepts, undermining the assertion of a nationalistic impulse to create law which was specifically Indonesian (Nasution, 1992: 2). The Agrarian Law and accompanying land reform, while asserting its basis in *adat,* also takes a major step towards the abolition of *adat* land rights by declaring all land subject to the national interests and aims of national unity. The Agrarian Law is consequently a confusing miscellany of articles with no clear purpose or unifying ambition. It is a good example of characteristically Indonesian legislation 'which defines a social battle without settling it' (Lev, 1965: 290).

There have been three main, and quite distinct, views as to the utility of *adat* as a positive source of law. The late *Mahkamah Agung* (Supreme Court) Judge, Malikoel Adil, believed that the civil law needs of modern Indonesian society could be served by tacking on European legal concepts, as long as these did not violate particular *adat* sensitivities. *Adat* was to be used merely as the basic yardstick of what constituted justice. Therefore, the law-maker would somehow need to discover the sense of justice of the whole people before framing a rule. A second view saw *adat* as the main source of law. The reception of European rules was therefore to be determined by whether a rule has been accepted by the people as *adat*. The Soekarno government asserted a third view, whereby *adat* as a 'source' did not exclude the use of other sources to complete the law. On this view, the 'simplistic' law of *adat* was full of inadequacies and needed to be 'cleansed' and 'perfected' (Djumialdji, 1995). *Adat* was useful only if it did not 'obstruct the development of a just and prosperous society' by undermining nationalism and unification (MPRS No II/MPRS/1960 Appendix A, para 402; Harsono, 1994; Gouwgioksiong, 1960: 306).

> The course of legal development since the revolution ... has begun to break down the law myths of the colony in favour of the new myths of the independent state. 'Myth' is used here in the sense of symbols of legitimacy which, for all the loose thinking and hypocrisy they often conceal, are nevertheless major bonds of social, political, economic and therefore legal life (Lev, 1965: 306).

Following this view, Soekarno Old Order coopted certain principles of *adat* law which were seen as capable of contributing to the political stability of the state,[28] such *gotong-royong* or 'mutual help' based on communalism and familism,[29] manifested in traditional societies by communal work on building temples, stables and harvesting crops and so on. The emphasis on the individual as part of a more

---

27 Burns (1989: 2) argues that 'the myth of *adat*' was used as the nationalising instrument which embraced the entire area of the former Dutch colony, marking it off from the rest of the world as an entity, whilst at the same time, internally integrated.

28 Interview with Herman Soesangobeng at BPN Central Office Jakarta, February 1996. See also Bourchier, Chapter 12.

29 This has been described as a solidarity between individuals in the community, whereby the individual's interests are subsumed by those of the community. Deferral to the community is not seen as a burden but part of a 'sub-conscious understanding of the people' that this is the correct way to live (Soerojo Wignjodipoero, 1982: 41).

significant community inherent in this idea became a justification for authoritarian rule under Soekarno's Guided Democracy regime.

A second element of *adat* utilised by the government was that people have a social responsibility to their society. For example, villagers are responsible for using their skills to protect the village from danger, that is, by building weirs in monsoon season, taking turns to be the village night-watchman or reporting subversive or socially unacceptable behaviour. This responsibility extends to private ownership. In the same vein, the Javanese philosophy of *jer basuki mawa beyo* (sacrifice for the glory of the nation) is often used to justify self-sacrifice and rallying to the cause by not asking for compensation (Soestrisno, 1995: 46).

The third element of *adat* which was emphasised was the *adat* hierarchy as the basis of public authority and dispute resolution. The traditional head was often called the 'People's Head', who was duty-bound not to act without the consultation and consensus of his people. This is characterised by the social and political processes which are carried out in the spirit of *musyarawah* (consensus, compromise) rather than the supposedly Western-type of partisanship characterised by majority rule. All arguments are smoothed out before the (unanimous) vote is taken (Roeder, 1971: 29). The high priority of peace and consensus in the Indonesian legal process, over and above the satisfaction of rights in, means that compromise is the ideal method of dispute settlement. In no context is conflict considered functional (Lubis, 1993: 106).

Yet this political advocacy of *adat* principles was not reflected in substantive legal content. The only *adat* land right not converted to a Western-style statutory right was *hak ulayat*; however, laws to clearly define the extent and status of *hak ulayat* were never forthcoming (Art 3, Agrarian Law).[30] This has allowed the state to further turn communal title on itself, to become a paradoxical rationale for its own obliteration, by positing a 'national *hak ulayat*'. This form of *hak ulayat* subsumes local power and control, displacing the authority of the local chief to that of the state leader (the President). On this analysis, the community (the state) has ultimate power to revoke or annul rights of Indonesians who have communal 'usufructuary' rights to land, when this is desirable in the interests of the wider community. This has proved open to abuse at all levels.

Limits on *Adat* Rights

The existence of the following significant caveats on the recognition of *adat* rights under Art 5 of the Agrarian Law has also contributed to the prevailing uncertainty of traditional land rights in Indonesia.

1.   *Adat must not be Contrary to the National Interest*

Hak ulayat as described in the Agrarian Law is the law of 'traditional communities' acting under their individual *adat* laws (Art 5). However, rather than encouraging

---

30   *Hak ulayat* has continued to receive recognition in recent legislation, for example Law No 10 of 1992 on Population and Prosperous Families, in Arts 6(b) and (c) as well as the official Elucidation to these sections; and Presidential Decree No 55 of 1992 on Land Acquisition. However, again, these laws only contain statements and fail to provide practical guidelines or instructions as to implementation.

the development of these local laws, the government has constructed the separate and distinct interests of *adat* communities in land as divisive and working against national unity. The concept of 'national interest' has been interpreted by the power holders such that

> The 'global' in the dominant discourse is the political space in which the dominant local seeks global control. The global in this sense does not represent the universal human interest; it represents a particular local and parochial interest which has been globalised through its reach and control (Shiva, 1993: 60)

Under the rubric of national interest, the wholesale expropriation of land for the purpose of development has been legitimised. National interest, which is synonymous with the government's interests, has been raised to a form of religio-political significance providing legitimacy for anything the government wishes to do (Fakih, 1995: 28).

2.   Adat must not be Contrary to 'Indonesian socialism'

The term 'Indonesian socialism'(Arts 6 & 15, Agrarian Law) is an abstract term which asserts that all land has a 'social function'. It is the formal legislative manifestation of the *gotong royong* principle (Art 6, Agrarian Law); and draws on the 'social economy' provisions of Art 33 of the 1945 Constitution. Here, 'social function' means that the use of the land and exploitation of its produce must be in harmony with the general interests of achieving justice and equality for the greater society. At the time the Agrarian Law was drafted, this meant a failed attempt to abolish the class of land-owners and reduce the number of landless peasants by granting real property only to those who cultivated the land (Elucidation Agrarian Law Part A (III)(2)).[31]

'Social function' is a potentially powerful counterweight to the widespread individualisation of rights to land. It has the potential to support the communalism of *adat*. It is here that the principle of balance in relation to the use of land is acknowledged. By 'balance' is meant that the use of land must be in accordance with its character and function. A balance must also be maintained between rights and obligations – read 'interests' – more important than the owners, must be taken into account even if this causes the owner financial loss. Under the New Order, however 'social function' has been defined in terms of the 'national interest', making *adat* rights subordinate to elite commercial interests.

3.   Adat must not be Contrary to the Principles of the Agrarian Law or to other Government Laws

The clearest explanation of what is meant by this statement is found in the provisions for the conversion of *adat* rights into 'new rights' under the Law (Arts 2, II and IV). Only the new rights set out under the law – that is, ownership,

---

31   Article 7 prohibits unlimited land ownership; Art 10 provides that each occupier must cultivate his own land; and Art 17 provides for maximum and minimum land holdings. Absentee landlordism is prohibited and the government cannot authorise exceptions to this: Art 5(3). Government failure to implement these provisions led in the early 'sixties to the *aksi sephihak* or 'unilateral action' of the PKI (*Partai Komunis Indonesia* – Indonesian Communist Party) in which peasants attempted to seize land from landlords by force.

exploitation, building and use – can be registered. Therefore, to acquire legal certainty, *adat* laws must be subsumed under, or converted into, one of these rights.

The status of old *adat* rights which have not been converted under the Agrarian Law remains unclear. Although, theoretically under the Agrarian Law, registered and certified ownership (*hak milik*) is legally the same as *adat* 'ownership' (*hak milik adat*), in practice they are given different status by government officials, at the expense of *adat* rights. There is also controversy over the status of 'new' *adat* rights created after the enactment of the Agrarian Law. The conversion provisions of the Agrarian Law only regulate conversion of rights existing *at the time* the Agrarian Law was promulgated. Converted or not, it would appear that these newer rights are equally valid although unregistrable (Parlindungan, 1987: 104).[32]

4. State land – 'Tanah Negara'

The most pervasive attack on *adat* rights stems from the definition of 'state land'.[33] Upon Independence, the new national government continued the concessions that had been granted as Crown land by the Dutch at the expense of large tracts of uninhabited *hak ulayat* land under the colonial 'domain principle' (*domeinverklaring*).[34] Under this principle, all land considered to be 'unoccupied' or which could not be proved to be owned under the formal law was deemed to be Crown land. *Hak ulayat* land which was left uncleared for hunting and gathering, cleared land which was left fallow or land used as common pasture all became the 'domain' of the Colonial state.[35] These colonial principles were sanctioned by Art 33(3) of the 1945 Constitution which stated that the state was the successor to the (semi) autonomous powers of *adat* societies and local rulers and reinforced the absolute authority of the state over sea and water as well as the land and all in or on it.

The policy of the Agrarian Law is clear in this regard. All land is considered 'controlled by the state' as an entity empowered by the whole of the people. The state determines the proper use of land, the relationship between the land and individuals and consequences of legal actions involving the land. This control extends even to privately held land. Privately owned land can revert to the state if it remains unused or is left lying fallow (Art 27(3)), as the owner is considered to have violated the 'social function' of the land (Art 6).[36]

The controversial definition of state land has meant that any land not subject to registration or *adat* title comes under unfettered state control. The powers of control are limited only by executive interpretation. Any land that is subject to registration under the Agrarian Law and has not been so affirmed can be deemed to be held under mere usufructuary rights for a maximum of five years. Upon expiration of this period it will revert to state control.[37]

---

32 See also Government Regulation No 24 of 1997.

33 Article 2(1) Agrarian Law; Art 5(2) of the Law on Forestry, No 5 of 1967

34 Agrarian Law 1870 (*Agrarische Besluit*), No 118.

35 Ter Haar argued that the domain principle was legally flawed for two reasons: first, the colonial state as successor to the power over land of the sultanates and principalities wrongly assumed that this power was absolute; and, secondly, because succession, even if by conquest, does not automatically invalidate existing laws (ter Haar, 1950).

36 See also Law No 1 of 1958, on All Ex-Foreign Plantation Land; Presidential Decree No 55 of 1993 on the Interests of Development; Law No 56 of 1960 regarding Maximum Land Holdings (under which any excess hectarage reverts to the state); Government Regulation No 224 of 1961 on Division of Land (absentee land will revert to the state); and the Law on Forestry No 5 of 1967 (forest land may not be alienated to citizens).

37 Article 8, Ministerial Decree No 2 of 1962. See Kameo (1994: 4).

The effect of these caveats have been that the Agrarian Law is merely 'hortatory and symbolic' (Gautama & Hornick, 1974: 78-79) in its attempts to establish a useful land law system. Although it declares the *adat* principle of communal ownership to be a fundamental principle, it modifies it to such an extent that any 'basis in *adat*' cannot be entertained as a serious working principle (Katz & Katz, 1975: 667).

Developmentalism and the Decline of *Adat*

The pro-interventionist stance of Soeharto's New Order government demonstrated a somewhat different set of priorities from the populist agrarian strategies of the Old Order. Soon after its establishment in 1966 the New Order sought to develop capitalist development strategies in the industrial sector, funded by external as well as internal investment. The result has been that 'development;' has prevailed over most other interests.

Yet, perhaps surprisingly, given that New Order society has been tightly controlled, land issues have proven to be one of the areas of most open discontent and dissatisfaction. The incidence of poverty, urbanisation, landlessness[38] and the political repression of farmers and indigenous communities has risen dramatically. Open conflicts are increasingly occurring throughout the archipelago, for example, between the Sugapa people in North Sumatra and PT Indorayon Utama; the Moi, Amungme and Kamoro people and PT Freeport in Irian Jaya; the Sou people and forest concession holders in Wanokwari, Irian Jaya (Kompas, 1993); the traditional communities in Bentian against the PT Klahod in East Kalimantan; and the Dayak people in Sandai Ketapang against PT Teja Lingga Wana in West Kalimantan, to name but a few (Masruchah, 1995: 2).

Although the Indonesian Government has recognised the significance of land issues in its policy – witness, for example, the creation of BPN, the National Land Affairs Body,[39] the commitment to the LAP and the elevation of the head of BPN to State Minister – there is no clear focal point of authoritative policy-making within the government. This is mainly because there is no single entity with unambiguous responsibility for coordinating land management policies and initiatives. A plethora of regulations and regulating bodies exists, ranging from specialist bodies to departments, each with its own perspective and agenda.[40] There is not even agreement among the bodies involved in land management about what the key issues are.

---

38 In 1963, 73% of village families owned more than 0.1 hectares of land. By 1983, the number had decreased to 57%. Typically, farmers sell their land to rich farmers, agricultural enterprises or development projects and move to Jakarta to join the masses of itinerant labour for the industrial sector (Fakih, 1995: 12).

39 *Badan Pertanahan Nasional.* Under Presidential Decree No 26 of 1988, BPN was created to replace the Director General of Agrarian Affairs in the Department of Domestic Affairs.

40 A non-exhaustive list of the agencies, involved in various aspects of formulating and implementing land management policy at all levels of government, includes National Development Planning Board (*Bappenas*); State Ministry for the Environment; BPN; Ministry of Home Affairs; Ministry of Public Works (Land Management Policy); Ministry of Transmigration and Forest Encroachment; Ministry of Forestry; Ministry of Agriculture; Ministry of Mining; Ministry of Transport (land acquisition for in public sector projects); Ministry of Finance; Directorate of Land and Property Tax (government revenue and land tax); National Coordinating Agency for Surveying and Mapping (*Bakosurtanal*); National Institute of Aeronautics and Space; and *Lapan* (land use planning)

The constitutional rhetoric of 'prosperity for all'[41] is meaningless in the face of the government's command-capitalist interpretation of 'national interest'. The general paradigm for the displacement of traditional communities is in efforts to use their lands for development purposes (Cycon, 1991: 761). This has been described as 'internal colonialism', as it is the extension of wealth creation in modern Western capitalism's economic vision but is based on the exploitation and degradation of the natural environment and the exploitation and erosion of other cultures (ILO, 1988: 65). The drive for economic growth has created tensions between the collectivism that many see as the heart of Indonesian society; and Western-style neo-classical economics.

Transmigration and forest exploitation projects are particularly striking examples of this conflict of systems and have had a noticeably detrimental effect on the environment and *adat* land tenure systems of the outer islands.[42] Individual settlement plots are granted indefeasible title by the state, with resulting conflict with local *adat* landholders. *Adat* communities are left with a stark choice: to refuse to negotiate and face the full force of the political system; or to accept that they have been beaten and try to get the best deal they can. In the absence of any effective forum for debate, where communities have sought to overcome their relative weakness, they have faced the full force of the dominant legal and political system.[43]

Centralised Control: 'Administrative' Communities

There have been blunt attacks by the central and provincial governments on *adat* leadership structures. For example, in Sanggau, East Kalimantan, each tribal community was traditionally headed by an *adat* leader. The government has attempted to simplify (and control) the power structures of these communities by restructuring leadership. The previously complex leadership hierarchy[44] was effectively rationalised by central government edict to include only the *Temenggung* (leader or chief) and a *Pengurus Adat* (*adat* head). Promotion of a person as *Temenggung* now occurs via Gubernatorial Decree after a public election, bringing traditional authority within the formal system. This back-handed 'acknowledgment' of *adat* authority was seen as a way of adjusting traditional power to synchronise with rapid agricultural industrialisation and the planning of new villages. At the same time that traditional leaders were nominally admitted into the official power

---

41   Article 33, 1945 Constitution.

42   There is debate as to whether agricultural practices utilised by the transmigrants are appropriate or not, as much of this settlement takes place on land ecologically, agronomically or economically unsuitable to usual foodcrops with soils that are low on nutrients and often acidic (Dove, 1986: 121-140).

43   These people also suffer at the hands of extra-constitutional forces, that is, vandalisation of their houses and physical attacks by hired thugs and security operatives (Kompas, 1995b); Forum Keadilan (1996); Kompas (1995a); and Kompas (1995d).

44   Titles for Dayak traditional leaders include, *Temenggung, Singa, Patiraja, Macan, Panggawa* and *Panglima* (Sumardjono, 1996) although it should be noted that differing power structures exist in almost all the different Dayak tribes. In the Dayak Atas group, for example, the hierarchical order includes *Temenggung – Menteri – Patih – Pengurus Adat*. Among the Dayak Menyuke the leaders include *Temenggung – Panjeneng – Pengurus Adat*. In other areas of Sanggau, the hierarchy is even more complex: *Temenggung – Mangku – Kepala Kampong – Kebayan – Pengurus Adat* (Sumardjono, 1996).

structures, however, their real power was in effect curtailed. So, for example, where traditionally each *Temenggung* was responsible for only one district, their jurisdictions have now been merged to include members from two or more neighbouring tribes. Likewise, if a *Temenggung* dies, the authority he holds will no longer be passed on to a new traditional leader but will revert to the government

Similarly, in Java, where the linkage between the land and communal sovereignty is based on a collective of familial units called *dhukuh* (hamlet), the formalisation of village (*desa*) authority as the lowest level in the Indonesian local government system has meant that administrative boundaries of villages no longer coincide with the traditional territorial hierarchies.[45]

The Law on Village Government has also coopted the *dhukuh* in a more insidious way by integrating *adat* functionaries in the local government system alongside state employees. Village government is now headed by the state-employed village head, supported by the powerful *adat* leaders such as *kyai* (religious sage), *haji* (returned pilgrim), *guru* (spiritual teacher) and *dukun* (spiritual healer). Age also elicits power, as is reflected in the existence alongside the official structure of local government of a powerful council of village elders (*kasepuhan*) (Koentjaraningrat, 1967: 244-80). The village council (*lembaga masyarakat desa*) as a conglomerate of *adat* functionaries and state employees is given the authority to manage the day-to-day running of the society 'in the field of government'.[46] The problem lies in the delineation of authority over issues of *adat* law which remains unclear.[47]

For example, under the Law on Village Government, every village is permitted to own substantial land holdings as part of the village's land assets (*tanah kas desa*). There have been attempts to convert communal *adat* lands to form part of the *tanah kas desa* with the right of ownership then vested in the state-delineated village rather than the *adat* jural community whose members may be quite different.

Another example relates to the rights of *adat* communities to collect forest produce. These rights are frozen notwithstanding that for generations they have been entitled to collect forest produce to fulfil their needs. It is stated that *adat* communities hunting and collecting produce in forests must do so without interfering with forest concessions and enterprises.[48] The *adat* leader's function of allowing the opening of new forest land has been removed and villagers may only do so with permission from the government.[49]

---

45   This was formalised under Law No 5 of 1979 on Village Government.

46   Article 2, Law No 5 of 1979 concerning Village Government.

47   See, for example, Art 5, Regulation of the Minister for Internal Affairs No 11 of 1984 regarding the Supervision and Development of *Adat* at Village Level, which states that 'the (state-employed) *Camat* (district head) together with the village head are responsible for the construction and development of the living traditions and customs of the communities within their area'. This is to be done 'in accordance with the need for continued stability, in the areas of ideology, politics, economics and socio-cultural as well as national security' (Art 3).

48   Article 6, Government Regulation No 21 of 1970 on Forest Enterprise. For example, the Dayak Bentian people of East Kalimantan have a sophisticated system of rotational forest cropping which has been practised through the generations. However, without their knowledge or input, 90,000 hectares of their traditional forest land was granted to timber concessions (YBLHI, 1992: 20).

49   See, for example, Instruction of Minister for Home Affairs No 593 / 5707/SJ, 22 May 1984 which revokes the right of *adat* chiefs to open new land in Kalimantan.

The Land Registration System

The registration of titles is often considered a necessary part of land reform programs as it facilitates orderly land management in the face of population growth and increased urbanisation. Government rhetoric states that registration delivers socio-economic benefits to all, whereas in reality, it works in Indonesia to facilitate development at the expense of the rural class and as an instrument for the transformation of tribal and traditional forms of tenure (Dorner, 1972: 18).[50]

Although registration of individual title was instituted over 35 years ago by the Agrarian Law, it is thought that only 22% of the estimated 58 million land parcels in Indonesia have ever been registered (Badan Pertanahan Nasional, 1993: 10). At this rate, given the size of Indonesia, the number of land parcels and the resources available, it is estimated that even an accelerated registration program would take 100 years to complete (USAID, 1992). The failure to register and the consequent continued prevalence of indigenous tenure systems is largely a product of the dysfunction of the registration system itself. At the same time, however, lack of registration has left *adat* communities without security of title and therefore vulnerable to land speculators.

Under the registration regime set out in the LAP, *adat* right holders lose both ways. If they convert their rights to rights acknowledged under the Agrarian Law and register their land on an individual basis, there is an increased prospect of monetarisation and dissolution of communities whose very existence integrally depends on communalism. If they do not register, they lose their land to the state, transmigrants or developers who will obtain superior title.[51]

More significant yet, no provision has been made for the legal registration of communally held land. The titles issued under Government Regulation No 10 of 1961 and Government Regulation No 24 of 1997 are individual titles and give the holder rights of absolute ownership and rights of alienation, which excludes *hak ulayat*. Furthermore, the object of land registration is specifically identified as village units regulated by the Law on Village Administration, reflecting the state's agenda of individualising tenure and removing the autonomy of *adat* communities.

A variety of other obstacles to registration exist. The current framework for registration is unnecessarily intricate with a plethora of complex regulations governing the process. There are, in fact, over 2000 guiding regulations and this increases transfer costs, time and scope for mistakes. It also means that the process for registration is extremely long winded and expensive.[52] Administrative inefficiencies are, in fact, epidemic within the BPN.

---

50 For example, as support for transmigration projects, public works projects, industrialisation, luxury housing and by setting up more efficient land markets encouraging foreign investment (Dorner, 1972: 18).

51 Holders of *adat* rights that have not been converted can request confirmation if there is requisite proof of their rights (although this rarely exists in a tangible form). These rights would then be converted into (individual) rights under the Agrarian Law: Minister of Agrarian Affairs Regulation No 2 of 1962. As mentioned, unconverted *adat* rights are deemed to revert to 'state land' under Government Regulation No 224 of 1961 (Parlindungan, 1994: 37-53).

52 For *adat* land, there are a number of steps required which discourage small land holders from attempting to title their land. When an applicant files for land title the application must include information on the chronological status of the land certified by the village head; a rough sketch map showing the boundaries; information on the land ownership verified by the subdistrict head; and certification of tax payment, verified by the subdistrict head. The BPN

Under the bureaucratic authoritarian system that prevails in Indonesia, bureaucrats see their role as 'rent-seekers'. Business is run by involving powerful state bureaucrats as business partners, who obtain benefits (rent) from their clients. Petty corruption is widespread, with informal payments charged in excess of the official fees. Bogus certificates are given and certified land is often fraudulently re-registered and some officials actively work to sabotage efficiencies within the system to ensure their access to corrupt payments.[53] At an operational level, the registration system also suffers from a serious lack of funding and established infrastructure. Likewise, BPN lacks qualified personnel, especially those who are willing to work in remote areas (World Bank, 1993b, 395). This is another cause of delay.

The Indonesian titling system has been described as a 'negative system with positive tendencies' (Harsono, 1971: 5),[54] as the registration certificate issued only confers defeasible title upon the holder. The notion of it being a 'negative system' stems from the fact that the certificate does not constitute conclusive proof of title but merely creates a prima facie assumption that the registered proprietor is the true owner, that is, it serves as 'strong evidence of ownership' (Sumardjono, 1982: 24). The government does not guarantee the accuracy of the register and only impliedly suggests that best efforts will be made to provide guaranteed legal certainty. The title is open to challenge; and where the contesting party can 'prove' a stronger claim to the land, the court will direct for rectification of the Register. There is no assurance fund to compensate for faults in the system, for example, where a purchaser who acquires his interest in good faith finds his or her registered title is void. the result is that the state and its allies can often effectively ignore even registered title.

Nowhere are the deficiencies in the titling system more obvious than in the case of *hak ulayat*, which, as mentioned, is unregistrable. An example of the practical problems the current system creates for *adat* communities is the case of Cimacan in Cianjur, West Java. The land was originally held under *erfpacht* (proprietary usufructuary rights under the Dutch Civil Code) in 1937. The Japanese occupation and the revolution intervened and the land was declared state land in 1954, based on the Governor's Decree No GB.21/BA. In 1961, the land was given to the people of Cimacan by the Minister of Agraria as *hak ulayat* land (*tanah titisari*). In early 1970, the people requested certification of their land via the village head. In 1980, they made a written request to the Governor of Jabar and the Director General of

---

(*cont*)

District Office then carries out a field check to identify any adverse claims. Next the land is officially surveyed and a map prepared. Upon completion, the map and the documents are posted to the office of the village head and the subdistrict to permit complainants. BPN then prepares a letter of recommendation if there are no complaints; the letter of recommendation is sent to the provincial office of the Ministry for a letter of decision; and the applicant is informed of the decision and required to pay fees for the completion of the process. Finally, the certificate of title is issued and a copy provided to the applicant. This process can take anywhere from six months to three years.

53 There is a prevailing attitude amongst BPN bureaucrats that if systematic registration is implemented their source of funds will quickly dry up, as there is a limit to the number of land parcels which can be registered. This view obviously ignores future income from transactions on registered land: personal information from a land law official, Central BPN Office, Jakarta, 23 February 1996.

54 Quoting Muntoha, the drafter of Government Regulation No 10 of 1961. See also, General Explanation, Elucidation to Government Regulation No 24 of 1997.

BPN. In 1984, the village head once again entreated the head of the Cianjur land office to give each farmer a certificate of his holding. Nothing was achieved. In 1987, PT Bandung Asri Mulia put forward a proposal for the development of a golf course in the area. They were awarded a lease in 1988. Meanwhile, the Cimacan people had been awarded usufructuary rights as long as the land was used for farming. Although the 1500 farmers had cultivated the land since the war, they were given Rp 3000 (AUS$00.40 in June 1998) per metre for their land as compensation. Those who refused compensation were intimidated physically and mentally, by being labelled as anti-Indonesian and communist (YLBHI & Jarim, 1991). The World Bank made government recognition of *hak ulayat* a key part of its Land Administration Project. The Indonesian government, however, has achieved precisely the reverse with Government Regulation No 24 of 1997. Specifically, it continues not to recognise communal title as a registrable right[55] and has refused to exempt *hak ulayat* from the definition of state land. The furthest the government has been willing to compromise is by making issues of evidence relating to registration and conversion more lenient. Previously, proof of title to land for the purposes of registration necessitated the production of documentary evidence. Under Government Regulation No 24 of 1997, convincing oral testimonies (that is, of *adat* leaders) will be relevant, although not conclusive. In the absence of conclusive proof, 20 years of uninterrupted possession, without other claims made on the land, will be 'strong evidence' of ownership. Before this, farmers in Indonesia, who have cultivated *adat* land for many years and had even paid land tax were still considered trespassers. This new acknowledgment of the relevance of lengthy uninterrupted possession may change this.

The Land Administration Project (LAP)

The trend in international law to revise the role of the nation-state (Van de Vyer, 1991: 9) and define indigenous peoples as distinct communities with specially recognised rights[56] was the background to the World Bank's LAP in Indonesia. In the 1980 the World Bank finally succumbed to international pressure and adopted a policy of 'defensive modernisation' (Ayres, 1983, 226-228). It would no longer fund projects that knowingly encroached on traditional territories being used or occupied by tribal peoples unless adequate safeguards were provided (Goodland, 1982: xi). Experience had shown that if agrarian reform is to benefit the poor, meet their needs and accommodate itself to their political, economic and environmental circumstances it must be controlled by them. Only if the local communities have a decisive role in resource use can they be expected to commit their labour to it. These were not new principles but the challenge was to reassert these values and show that, far from being backward and irrational, the values and knowledge upon which rural peoples rely may actually be relevant and efficient.

In this environment *hak ulayat* should have assumed renewed relevance. However, the Bank issued Operational Directive 4.20 on Indigenous Peoples which

---

55   Article 1(5) and 9(1) of Government Regulation No 24 of 1997.

56   In general, indigenous people retain a distinct culture, language, traditions, law and customs from the dominant group. Most importantly, they have a territorial basis. They are usually marginal groups, isolated socially, that have managed to preserve their traditions in spite of being incorporated into states dominated by other societies (Brölmann & Zieck, 1993: 187).

defined the term 'indigenous peoples' as 'social groups with a social and cultural identity distinct from the dominant society that makes them vulnerable to being disadvantaged in the development process'.[57] By this definition, indigenous peoples are described negatively, emphasising their lack of autonomy and political identity. Negative concepts have been used world-wide to represent traditional groups as pathetic or romantic, thus marginalising them. *Adat* communities' access to land resources is then reduced to a social policy issue rather than remaining a question of fundamental property rights (Chang, 1992: 849). This places the debate on a different social and legal level.

Under the LAP, priority areas are selected for systematic[58] registration, avoiding regions of uncertain jurisdiction (that is, areas with substantial areas of forest land or communal *adat* land). The project defines project areas, concentrating on Java, Sumatra and Bali, where it is believed that the LAP can have the most immediate impact in alleviating social land conflicts. Areas targeted are in units based at Local government Level II (*Kotamadya/Kabupaten*)[59] and are selected on the basis of predicted high economic and population growth. These areas are assumed to rely entirely on individual or private concepts of property and are therefore expected to be the most amenable to change.

This prioritisation is fundamentally flawed. The stated objective of LAP is to grant secure, documented title to rural landowners, thereby facilitating their access to institutional credit, securing investments in land and increasing family incomes from better productivity. The difficult issues of providing security for traditional land owners, particularly those holding communal title and those living on mineral-rich land are inexplicably deferred. Ironically, certainty of individual title also facilitates foreign investment which works to dispossess these people.

Another flaw of the registration system that will lead to continued uncertainty is the continuing validity of *adat* transactions. In *adat* land transactions, the metaphysical nature of land is highlighted. Transactions concerning this sacred entity have the ability to disturb the magical relationship between the community and the land, and hence, the cosmic balance, particularly when title is allocated or disposed. Therefore, the role of the village head (*kepala desa*) is very important. Transactions of sale (*jual*) and allocation can only take place in the presence of the chief who represents the whole community, thereby guaranteeing the validity and propriety of the transaction.[60] Through the chief, the transaction is opened to public participation and elevated to the public sector (Darmawi, 1972: 296-99).

By contrast, Government Regulation No 24 of 1997 states that the only valid form for transferring land is transfer proven by a notarial deed, drawn up by the

---

57 Personal information from a land law advisor to the World Bank, Jakarta, 26 February 1996.

58 'Systematic' registration refers to the targeting of priority areas where all land will be surveyed, measured, researched and registered at the same time. The Jabotabek Project around Jakarta is an example of such a prioritisation approach. 'Sporadic' registration refers to individuals who, of their own initiative, come and request registration (Badan Pertanahan Nasional, 1993: 25).

59 As defined under the Village Administration Law No 5 of 1979.

60 The *kepala desa* is then given a sum of money, known as *uang saksi* or witness money (a percentage of the transaction cost). He is then responsible for the transaction on behalf of his community and ensures that it does not conflict with the community's interests and laws (Soekanto, 1985: 86).

Notarial Deed Official.[61] The role of the village head is usurped by this official. The head's remaining role is to witness the notarial deed alongside the relevant local official, (that is, the central government appointee at regional level, for example, the *Camat*, or *Lurah* appointed under Law No 5 of 1979 on Village Administration)[62] and authenticating community members' *adat* rights to land for the purposes of proof for conversion of rights under the Agrarian Law.[63] The need for notarial deeds suggests that *adat* conveyance processes have been invalidated and the role of the village head as an *adat* functionary will no longer be a dominant one. This is a significant shift in power to the bureaucracy. However, due to a lack of understanding of the new concepts and the lack of enforcement the majority of transactions continue to occur in the traditional way, even if they are therefore formally invalid. This is a practical but unsatisfactory solution.

Interestingly, the *Mahkamah Agung* has supported *adat*-based cash transactions by interpreting the provisions of Government Regulation No 10 of 1961 as merely administrative and not necessary for a valid land conveyance.[64] Therefore, the conditions under Government Regulation No 10 of 1961 do not override *adat* law or the Civil Code, being only administrative directions for land officials.[65] The continued validity of these conveyances means that the value of the land register as a reflection of the true owners of the land is further impaired, despite the stated government policy of bringing certainty to land transactions (Parlindungan, 1987: 120).

Interesting examples of the practical problems this causes have arisen in the context of marriage. In one case, the husband of a childless couple intended to have his land (*barang asal*) registered in the name of his wife, to prevent his siblings claiming the property when he died. He proposed to grant (*hibah*) or sell (*jual-beli*) the property to his wife so that the certificate would be issued in her name. However, this was disallowed by the authorities, as Arts 1678 and 1467 of the Civil Code prohibit such a transaction between husband and wife, even though it is legitimate under *adat* law. The attitude of the LAP personnel is that when faced with questions from the members of the community they should decide on the basis of the written formal law rather than unwritten traditions and customs which they do not fully understand. The fact that the local people follow these customs on a daily basis is not taken into account.

As part of the LAP, an anthropological *adat* Research Project was sponsored by the Government Development Agency (*Bappenas*)[66] with the expectation that its

---

61 Article 37, Government Regulation No 24 of 1997. Under Government Regulation No 10 of 1961, a village head who authenticates a land transaction made without a notarial deed is liable to a fine or three months imprisonment. This provision was not maintained by Government Regulation No 24 of 1997 but arguably still exists.

62 For this, both the *kepala desa* and the *camat* receive a percentage of the price of the transaction. This adds to the problem of corruption and promoting the creation of multiple notarial deeds: Art 7, Government Regulation No 10 of 1961.

63 Article 25, Government Regulation No 10 of 1961: The leader's ability to authorise the opening of land has also been taken over by the regional government: Art 11, Minister of Internal Affairs Regulation No 6 of 1972.

64 *Mahkamah Agung* Decision 16 June 1976, No 1082 / K/ Sip/1976; *Mahkamah Agung* Decision 19 September 1970, No 123 / K/ Sip / 1970: For an explanation of *adat* contract law, see Himawan (1973: 3-6) and Parlindungan (1987: 100).

65 *Mahkamah Agung* Decision 12 June 1976 No 952/K/Sip/1974.

66 *Badan Perencanaan Pembangunan Nasional.*

findings would be recommendatory. The specific *adat* communities chosen for study by the Atma Jaya University Research Group engaged for the project[67] are West Sumatra, North Sumatra and Maluku. These are all areas where *hak ulayat* is clearly still practised. But they are also free of the political controversy that would be involved in any research into mineral rich Irian Jaya, or forest-covered Kalimantan, arguably locations where *hak ulayat* is under the most severe pressure.

The *Adat* Land Research Project (Badan Pertanahan Nasional, 1994: 5) has ranked the need for accuracy of data for the purpose of estimating the incidence of traditional communal land rights on non-forest land as follows:

- need for high accuracy: Java, Sumatra, Bali
- need for data of reasonable accuracy: Kalimantan, Sulawesi, Maluku
- need for approximate data: Nusa Tenggara, Irian Jaya, East Timor.

This ranking is conceptually flawed as it does not take into account the vulnerability of the more isolated groups who have no experience with, and no answer to, development and are thus most in need of the protection afforded by accurate data These people are more likely to retain their strong attachment to the land and concept of selling it is not entrenched in their way of thinking. For example, the people of the Kayan Mentarang Reserve in East Kalimantan view the compensation given to them by the forest concession holder, Sarana Trikarya Bhakti, simply as rent for the temporary use of their land. They do not understand that they have alienated their land indefinitely (Sirait, 1992: 88). The phenomenon of people inexperienced in modern commercial transactions selling their land for a pittance – for example, the price of a motorbike – is widespread in these areas.

Provision of aerial mapping has been incorporated into the second five-year phase of the LAP, but by then it will be too late. This is particularly true for areas with rapidly increasing land prices, such as Bekasi and Tangerang in Java, where sporadic registration has led to multiple certification of single parcels of land and 'land banditry' whereby false certificates are issued (Chaizi Nasucha, 1994: 3).

Implications of the Distinction
between Forest and Non-forest Land

Another difficult issue for the registration of communal land under the Indonesian land system is the arbitrary distinction made between forest and non-forest land. The exclusion of forest land from the ambit of registration has had harmful consequences for *adat* right holders living within forest boundaries. Forest land, which constitutes about 75% (or 144 million hectares) of the land area of Indonesia,[68] is administered by the Ministry of Forestry under the Forest Law[69] with non-forest parcels controlled by BPN under the Agrarian Law.

The major problem is that no consensual delineation of authority between the Department of Forestry and the Department of Agrarian Affairs has ever been

---

67   The choice of Atma Jaya University for the project was highly controversial, as at that time they did not have sufficient qualified personnel to conduct the research: personal information from a land law advisor to the World Bank, 26 February 1996.

68   Consensus Land Use Plan 1984 Indonesia.

69   Law on Forestry, No 5 of 1967.

made.[70] When forest land is developed for farming or settlement, its administration transfers to the BPN under the Agrarian Law. However, recent surveys suggest that forest cover has been reduced to 57% of the land area without any such transfers being made (Evers, 1995a: 6). The single government agency with the authority to legally recognise *adat* land rights, or grant rights over state-controlled land, is BPN but its authority is, in fact, not recognised on formally designated 'forest land', even if it is, in fact, no longer forested. This means that the Department of Forestry is, in reality, free to determine legal rights in 'forests'.[71] However, Forestry may only grant user rights. Rights of ownership will remain with the state. This has the extraordinary result that the *adat* communities occupying most of Indonesia's land area have no access to land registration services – and that includes not only indigenous groups but also villages, settlements and cultivation areas that have 'trespassed' into forest zones.

Forest zones, as they stand, were delineated on large scale maps (1:500,000) based on US Army maps produced in 1946 (Sirait, 1992: 414). Despite large scale expansion of farming and settlement into these zones over the past 50 years, people are often evicted as illegal squatters on state forest land despite having cultivated the land for many years.[72] The ill-defined extent of forest boundaries thus creates considerable uncertainty for rights to land over 15% of the land area of Indonesia.

As the Ministry of Forestry has no power to activate land titling in forests, it has sought to control the management of the land by issuing rights of use (licences or leases) to communities already inhabiting the land. This type of agreement implies that the community is relinquishing its claims to fundamental land rights for limited usufruct rights. By doing so, the community is unwittingly acknowledging the land's status as state land and admitting that they only have specified rights of use, rather than traditional tenure. Therefore, any program to recognise *adat* rights to land requires the complete renegotiation of the current forest/non-forest delineation and a clear division of power between BPN and the Ministry of Forestry.[73]

---

70 Under Art 46 of the Agrarian Law, *adat* communities are entitled to open land and to collect forest produce. The need to obtain government permission is not stated in the Article. However, in lieu of guiding regulations relating to the traditional rights of opening new land and hunting and gathering from forests, any use of forest land without permission from the Department of Forestry is considered trespassing and a criminal act: Law No 51 of 1960 on the Prohibition on Using Land without Permission (Hakim, 1976).

71 See the Law on Forestry as well as supporting regulations such as Government Regulation No 8 of 1953 regarding the Control of State Lands.

72 For example, in September of 1993, the Minister of Transmigration Siswono Yudohusodo, stated that 10,000 'forest squatter families' were to be resettled 'with the dual objective of protecting the environment and improving their welfare'. In the same breath he acknowledged the difficulty in relocating these people, as most of them had lived in the forest for many generations (Jakarta Post, 1993a).

73 In 1989 a special inter-agency Coordinating Team for National Spatial Management was established *(Tim Koordinasi Pengelolaan Tata Ruang Nasional)* chaired by *Bappenas* to draw up broad policy guidelines for institutional reform of land administration. This body encompasses senior officials from *Bappenas*, the State Ministry for Environment, BPN, the Ministry for Home Affairs and the Ministry Public Works. A noteworthy exclusion is the Ministry of Forestry.

Registration of *Hak Ulayat* as a Community Trust?

It is widely assumed in Indonesia that the real recognition of communal *adat* title in Indonesia would obstruct the government's development agenda. Officials argue that titling is directly relational to an increase in land prices. If communal lands were registrable, land consolidation, re-arrangement of land use and land acquisition for transmigration and public works projects would become prohibitively expensive. While this is debatable, it must be acknowledged that registration of communal property rights does have inherent risks. First, the legalisation of tenure leads to an increasing commodification of land which undermines the customary management systems, promoting short-term, individualistic, profit-seeking. Secondly, the formalisation of title over communal land leads to rigidity in customary systems that are no longer responsive to changes in peasant use and ownership (Colchester, 1993: 322). Finally, practical problems exist with regard to changes in community membership and the fact that the land can only be sold if *all* the community members agree, rather than a qualified majority.[74]

On the other hand, setting up legal title forms whereby land is held in a kind of trust for all members of the group would have the benefit of preventing land being offered as collateral for individual debts. It would also protect *adat* communities from intimidation or deceit by land speculators. This would require a recognition of such a trust on the registered title, with a requirement to give notice to the other beneficiaries before making a transaction. Under Brazilian law, the collective property rights of a community may not be appropriated by an individual member for personal gain. This provides a legal basis for communities to make claims against individual members profiting at the expense of the community as a whole.[75]

Assuming a policy commitment to registration of *hak ulayat* on the trust model, the problem of a legislative definition remains. No single notion of *hak ulayat* is practised nationally. Customary tenures are so diverse that principles cannot be standardised for the whole country. Similarly, *hak ulayat* is very difficult to quantify because boundaries can be natural phenomenon, for example, mountains, rivers, a specific rock or tree (Sumardjono, 1996: 14-15). Often, borders are determined by abstract phenomena, for example, 'as far as you can hear a cock crow' or on the basis of the knowledge of elders. Ghosts and spirits are present as joint guardians of the territory (Boerhan & Salim, 1972: 1-5). In Dayak communities, certain birds are regarded as messengers of the spirits or omens, and they are a part of the augury that predetermines agricultural and hunting activities. This acknowledgment continues from generation to generation, giving rise to a consciousness about the borders of traditional control of one tribe from another. These 'folk' boundaries have persisted despite contrary administrative boundaries for villages being fixed by the government.

The fact that these boundaries are recorded in human memory means that they are very difficult to ascertain and intensely subjective and contextual. The conciliatory nature of *adat* law means that it is not applied as an objective and pre-

---

74   This has been witnessed in a number of villages where the village *adat* leader who is subject to clientelistic politicking has registered the land in the name of certain community members (usually, his family and relatives), rather than in the name of the whole community: personal information from a land law advisor, World Bank, Jakarta, 26 February 1996.

75   Articles 15 and 44 of the *Estatuto das Sociedades Indigenas* 1994 (Brazil) which replaced the Indian Law 1973, No 6001 (World Bank, ndb).

existing set of rules. The nature of *adat* laws is fluid, adjusting itself to changing conditions. This is exemplified in the Minangkabau *adat* maxim:

> If the river is in spate, the washing place is shifted
> With a change of rajah comes a change of *adat* [76]

In these circumstances the likelihood of a codified form of *adat* being analogous to the living *adat* law is highly unlikely. Even in those jurisdictions where native title has long been recognised its content is largely unresolved. It appears that the answer lies in the *sui generis* nature of the rights it includes.[77] Traditional occupancy takes a number of different forms and its content is not frozen at the moment of contact with colonists and the assertion of foreign law. It is the assent of the communities themselves that validates customary law.

Guidance could be sought from the definitions used in other jurisdictions which are appropriately similar to the Indonesian context. Communal ownership under the Papua New Guinea law is:

> land which is owned, or possessed, by an automatic citizen,[78] or community of automatic citizens, by virtue of rights of a proprietary or possessory kind which belongs to that citizen or community and arises from and is regulated by custom.

The Philippines Constitution of 1987 includes provisions recognising the explicit rights of indigenous communities to their ancestral land.[79] Recent legislation includes a distinction between 'ancestral lands' and 'ancestral domains'.[80] 'Ancestral lands' cover only surface rights to land, whereas 'ancestral domains' involves the recognition and protection of the generational attachment of the community to the land, expressed as a way of life.

This applies to all areas which are habitually referred to by the traditional communities as part of their ancestral domain, including lands previously occupied but which may no longer be in their possession due to reasons beyond their control.

A further issue is the how ownership of *hak ulayat* land is to be proved. What is in question here is a community's spiritual, magico-religious relationship with its land and this is often hard to identify and express in terms acceptable to legal positivists. In the Australian native title context it has been suggested that:

> The lawyer involved in a case concerning the determination of native title may feel like an intrepid adventurer on the trail of the Yeti – quite apart from the fact that your prey is elusive, how do you recognise when you've found it? (Neal, 1995: 880).

Under various regulations, relevant proof for the conversion of *adat* rights to new rights under the Agrarian Law were limited to documentary evidence, including tax receipts dating from before 24 September 1960; an official letter of grant from the Sultan or relevant official; a verifying letter from the village head; or a letter of

---

76 *Sakali air gadang, sakali tapian baranjak, Sakali rajo baganti, sakali adat barubah* (Holleman, 1981: 24).

77 For example, in the Canadian context, see *Guerin v R* (1984) 13 DLR (4th) 321 per Dickson J.

78 An 'automatic citizen' is a person accepted as a member of the *adat* jural community by the community's members (James, 1978: 20-21).

79 Sections 5(XII), 6(XIII), 22(II).

80 Department Administrative Order No 2, series of 1993, section 3(b) and (c).

confirmation from the Assistant District Chief and proof of citizenship.[81] A much less rigid form of proof is necessary in the case of traditional communities, as in Papua New Guinea where strict rules of procedure and evidence do not apply to custom and a court may consider anything or inform itself in any way it sees fit. The problem with this approach is that customary law becomes 'lawyer-made law'. What may be fondly interpreted as custom by the courts and administrators may not accurately capture the essence of customary law as recognised by the people themselves.

In Indonesia, under Government Regulation No 24 of 1997 an Adjudication Committee was established to settle disputes between conflicting rights holders who seek to register the same piece of land (Arts 7 and 18(3)). The evidence that it can consider to determine rights to land in a first-time registration is broader than previous regulations allowed and includes written evidence, witness testimonies and statements of trustworthy parties. However, the membership of the Adjudication Committee is highly bureaucratised, with three members appointed from BPN. The local village head (another bureaucrat) or an appointed local is the fourth member. It is unclear from the regulation how this person will be appointed but it is highly likely that such a body will not be independent and will follow government policy. Other inherent problems stem from the hierarchical, clientelistic nature of inter-personal relationships in Indonesia. The members of the Committee will not necessarily be neutral; and the mediation procedure proposed by the Regulation conflicts with Indonesia's bureaucratic-authoritarian official culture and the real-politik dynamics involved in making collaborative decisions between people of differing status and rank. The creation of the Committee also presumes the con-current development of effective law enforcement mechanisms, both administrative and criminal, and the availability of quality, independent and incorruptible personnel (Sumardjono, 1995a). This is unlikely in the near future.

'Critical Pluralism' and a Workable National Land System

For the majority of Indonesians, the Agrarian Law and registration system is irrelevant. The definition of the function of land as an exploitable resource; the Western-style separation laws of mineral ownership from the surface land; and the distinction between rights *in personam* and rights *in rem* remain alien concepts to most Indonesians. Accordingly, the system of land titling under the Agrarian Law has not achieved satisfactory results because it is incompatible with the reality of legal and social practice at the local level. Likewise, the state's strong and consistent opposition to traditional land rights has not succeeded in obliterating them. In practice, traditional tenure systems remain the dominant legal vehicle in most areas of Indonesia. *Adat* rights will therefore continue to cause the state great difficulties

---

81 Government Regulation No 2 of 1962 regarding Conversion and Registration of Ex-Indonesian Rights to Land; Decision of the Internal Affairs Minister No SK 26/DDA/1970 (Art 9). It should be noted that many villagers are not registered as citizens, so this criterion provides a serious impediment to the recognition of their rights. For example, after the eruption of Mt Merapi on 22 November 1994, many thousands of farmers were forced to flee their properties. After the disaster, those who had not attended government shelters or did not have identity cards were deemed dead or non-existent and their land appropriated as state land: personal information, Yogyakarta 1994.

in asserting a centralised land administration system. They make a mockery of the clear boundaries assumed by the Indonesian land registration program under the LAP; and create a seemingly insurmountable obstacle to universal land titling. Disruption of territorial strategies by non-compliance or open resistance has rendered territorial control complicated and inefficient, and has even led to bloodshed.[82]

This means that failure to prepare viable options and procedures for dealing with land held under traditional tenure systems will simply lead to further delays in the land registration program and the government's development aims. For the registration system to be workable, state policy makers must recognise local rights deriving from local classification, modes of communication and enforcement mechanisms. How can this be done?

A new model of 'critical pluralism'[83] is needed whereby *adat* groups are given a voice. Target 'groups'[84] must be identified by a thorough study of *adat* law communities, identifying both the extent of ancestral lands and the most deserving beneficiaries of land management projects such as the LAP. It will also be necessary to create an organisational base of political support and local participation to delineate the relevant territorial bounds of their communities as well as rules regarding membership and loss of membership.

In this vision, the 'good society' does not eliminate group differences. Groups can mutually engage in dialogue which will lead to mutual correction. Cultures can then change as the result of internal challenge or interrogation by other cultures, as long as change is the result of a group's own initiative and reflective of its particularism. Otherwise, as the historical record has shown, top-down interventions, even those termed to be in the peasants' interests, can undermine peasant solvency, autonomy and initiative.

Any new land management system needs to include a strategy to address issues of the formulation of a preliminary working definition of the terms *hak ulayat* and '*adat* law community'. Only then can the incidence of *hak ulayat* and similar traditional rights in Indonesia be estimated and the extent of land covered under these rights be accurately assessed. This will require the open participation of traditional communities.

A detailed report on customary land law is also required: the precise extent of land claimed under *adat* systems and the number of people living under these systems remains a modern mystery.[85] To implement any policies, credible cartographic and anthropological data that gives satisfactory answers regarding *adat* territories, jural districts and indigenous populations across the whole archipelago is

---

82   For example, according to the traditional law of the Sou people in Irian Jaya – where the Timber company PT Yotefa Sarana Timber was recently granted a large concession without the agreement of the *adat* owners – every contravention of their territorial boundaries is punishable by death (Kompas, 1993).

83   This is the term coined by Addis (1991: 1219).

84   'Groups' also lack a precise legal meaning, but can include communities, social groups, classes, collectives and minorities. Groups are often the result of complex combinations and the issue of self-perception and perception by the surrounding community are of great importance. The presence of elements such as spontaneity, permanency, a feeling of belonging and the conviction of sharing a common past and destiny may be required (Lerner, 1993: 80).

85   Estimates of how many people are living on state forest land range from 1.5 million to as high as 65 million (Sirat, 1992: 411).

needed. Obviously this is a gigantic, complex and long-term project but before its completion, the planning of roads, development schemes etc, that may impinge on *adat* communal land should be avoided. Mapping of *adat* territories would also remedy the political invisibility of these communities and their claims. Previously, when tenurial maps were prepared local people were not consulted and local claims were largely ignored (Evers, 1995b: 1). This is now beginning to change. The current World Wildlife Fund mapping project of customary land holdings in East Kalimantan is making use of oral histories, local community sketch maps and satellite technology (Sirait, 1992: 411). These maps can form the basis of negotiations for identifying customary tenure boundaries in order to assess how the different indigenous groups organise and allocate space.

Pilot projects have been initiated to explore issues involved in the registration of communal *adat* land. However, these remain uncoordinated and overlapping and have not been incorporated into the new registration regulatory system. Measures to enhance the impact of community mapping should involve inter-sectoral coordination via the National Spatial Management Coordination Board in cooperation with the Department of Forestry.

Ultimately, the combination of proper anthropological and cartographic data with proper re-definition of key terms must lead to the incorporation of communal tenure within a national land management system. In the Indonesian context, there is no reason why a flexible system of communal title registration cannot be instigated, whereby a trustee holds the land on behalf of the community, or land is simply registered as a trust in the names of all its members.[86] Communal registered titles based on maps of *adat* territories and reports on *adat* laws would make it more difficult for land speculators to pressure individuals to sell off their land parcels. They would also put greater power in the hands of *adat* leaders who have been known to sacrifice community interests in return for personal profit.

An effective dispute resolution mechanism must also be installed. The best solution would a three-tier specialist tribunal structure (mediation, arbitration and appeal), which would largely be based on village dispute resolution methods transposed to the inter-community level. Mediators could be appointed by the local people with special knowledge of the custom of the area and flexible evidence procedures would prevail. Such a tribunal must be able to enforce its decisions.

Conclusion

> It is through the coexistence of tradition and reform in dealing with the important land tenure issues of the future that the most significant progress in rural development is likely to be made (Cleary & Eaton, 1996: 134).

In the social melange that is Indonesia, the medium through which rules are transmitted, and the social context within which they operate, are of especially varied provenance (Griffiths, 1986: 34). Each system of tenure is based on the assumptions of the community from which it springs, in which social organisation, political authority and property rights are closely interrelated. As no two societies or cultures are identical in these respects there can be no such thing as a scientifically or technically neutral management regime that is equally applicable and acceptable

---

86 In some areas which retain a high degree of *adat* tenure, it is already an unofficial policy of BPN to do so: personal information from a BPN land law official, Jakarta, 23 February 1996.

to all. Consequently, when different social systems share an interest in the same resource, there must be some accommodation unless one is to be completely obliterated by the other. One system should not be given the dominant role into which the other must be fitted as a subordinate part. A pluralistic frame is required. Therefore, attempts to formulate a generalised model of land tenure must be deliberately avoided; the historical, geographical and political context of land tenure in Indonesia is too complex for a unified model.

One of the greatest challenges for the current government will be to acknowledge *adat* land rights in a meaningful way and manage their integration into an effective land reform package. The legal complexity of a pluralist system should not deter policy-makers from the attempt to work through the problems. The social reality is that these laws exist and people continue to live by them – it is even arguable that their persistence in the face of modernity has proved their relevance to modern life. It is therefore arguable that in the face of increased dissatisfaction with modern life communal rights may in fact strengthen. Traditional communities and culture are not static. Positive value is attached to change in many aspects of social life. Resistance comes when these people are faced with dispossession without respect for their prior ownership rights and without an acknowledgment of their economic and spiritual connection with the land.

The process of adjustment toward critical pluralism will begin when *adat* communities are identified and given a voice by the legislature in the national land system. Protection of their rights by communal registration of their land would be a step towards giving them this voice.

References

Abdurrahman, H, 1984, *Hak-Hak Atas Tanah dalam Perladangan Berpindah dalam Masyarakat Suku Dayak Kalimantan*, Akademika Pressindo, Jakarta.

Abdurrahman, H, 1990, 'Konsepsi Hak Ulayat Menurut Undang-Undang Pokok Agraria', *Orientasi*, vol 4: 1.

Addis, A, 1991, 'Individualism, Communitarianism and the Rights of Ethnic Minorities', *Notre Dame Law Review*, vol 66: 1219.

Alisjahbana, ST, 1968, 'Customary Law & Modernisation in Indonesia' in Baxbaum, DC (ed), *Family Law and Customary Law in Asia: A Comparative Legal Perspective*, M Nijhoff, The Hague: 3-16.

Anas, 1972, 'Bandingan' in Boerma Boerhan and Mahjuddin Salim (eds), *Tanah Ulayat Dalam Pembangunan*, Penerbitan Fakuitas Hukum dar Pengetahuan Masjarakat Universitas Andalas, Padang: 22.

Anderson, B, 1972, 'The Idea of Power in Javanese Culture' in Holt, C (ed), *Culture and Politics in Indonesia*, Cornell University Press, Ithaca.

Ayres, R, 1983, *Banking on the Poor: The World Bank and World Poverty*, MIT Press, Cambridge.

Badan Pertanahan Nasional (Tim Persiapan Proyek), 1993, *Preparation Report for the Land Administration Project Indonesia,* Report no BPN/1/1993, May 31 (internal document prepared by the combined team of BPN officers and consultants to the LAP).

Badan Pertanahan Nasional, 1994, *Land Administration Project Report: Studies on the Registration of Traditional (Adat) Land Rights – Terms of Reference*, 12 December 1994 (internal document).

Benda-Beckmann, K von, 1984, *The Broken Stairways to Consensus: Village Justice and State Courts in Minangkabau*, Foris, Dordrecht.

Benda-Beckmann, F von & Benda-Beckmann, K von, 1991, 'Property, Politics and Conflict: Ambon and Minangkabau Compared', *Paper presented at the 8th European Colloquium on Indonesian and Malaysian Studies*, Sweden, June.

Boerhan, B, & Salim, M, 1972, *Tanah Ulayat dalam Pembangunan,* Penerbitan Fakuitas Hukum dar Pengetahuan Masjarakat Universitas Andalas, Padang.

Bowen, 1988, 'The Transformation of an Indonesian Property System: *Adat*, Islam and Social Change in the Gayo Highlands', *AE*, vol 15: 274-93.

Brölmann, C & Zieck, M, 1993, 'Indigenous Peoples' in C. Brölmann et al (ed), *People and Minorities in International Law*, M Nijhoff, Dordrecht/Boston.

Burns, P, 1989, 'The Myth of *Adat*', *Journal of Legal Pluralism*, vol 28: 1.

Chaizi Nasucha, 1994, 'Sertifikat Tanah Nasional', *Republika,* 28 February: 3.

Chang, W, 1992, 'The "Wasteland" in the Western Exploitation of 'Race' and the Environment', *University of Colorado Law Review*, vol 63: 849.

Cleary & Eaton, 1996, *Tradition and Reform: Land Tenure and Rural Development in South-East Asia*, Oxford University Press, Kuala Lumpur.

Colchester, M, 1993, 'Future Options: Pushing on a Piece of String' in Colchester and Lohmann (eds), *The Struggle for Land and the Fate of the Forests*, World Rainforest Movement, Penang; Sturminister, Newton; Ecologist, London; Zed Books, Highlands.

Cycon, D, 1991, 'When Worlds Collide: Law Development and Indigenous People', *New England Law Review*, vol 25: 761.

Darmawi, 1972, 'Land Transactions under Indonesian *Adat* Law', *Lawasia*, vol 3: 283

Departemen Sosial, 1989, *Informasi Bina Masyarakat Terasing*, Penerbitan Departemen, Jakarta.

Depdagri, 1978, *Laporan Penelitian Integrasi Hak Ulayat ke dalam Yurisdiksi UUPA*, Law Faculty, Gadjah Madah University.

Djumialdji, FX, 1995, 'Hukum *Adat* Yang Disempurnakan', *Paper given at an inter-Faculty Discussion Seminar*, UGM, Indonesia.

Dodson, P, 1983, 'Land is Sacred to Us', in Howitt & Douglas, *Aborigines and Mining Companies in Northern Australia*, Alternative Publishing Cooperative, Sydney.

Dorner, 1972, *Land Reform and Economic Development*, Penguin, Harmondsworth.

Dove, 1986, 'The Ideology of Agricultural Developments in Indonesia' in MacAndrews, C (ed), *Central Government and Local Development in Indonesia*, Oxford University Press, Singapore and New York: 121.

Durning, Thein A, 1992, *Guardians of the Land: Indigenous Peoples and the Health of the Earth*, World Watch Institute, Washington.

Eaton, 1983, 'Customary Land Disputes: Should Lawyers Be Kept Out?', *Melanesian Law Journal*, vol 11: 18-26.

Evers, P, 1995a, 'Preliminary Policy and Legal Questions about Recognising Traditional Land Rights in Indonesia', *Ekonesia*, vol 3: 1.

Evers, P, 1995b, 'Supporting Local Management Systems: Mapping and Other Strategies', *Paper from the FF Workshop*, Cisarua, Bogor, 28-29 January:

Fakih, M, 1995, 'Tanah Sebagai Sumber Krisis Sosial Di Masa Mendatang: Sebuah Pengantar' in Masruchah, U (ed), *Tanah, Rakyat dan Demokrasi*, Forum LSM-LPSM DIY, Yogyakarta: 12.

Fauzi, N, 1993, 'Politik Agraria Orde Baru: Penindasan dan Perlawanan' in, YLBHI (ed), *Demokrasi: Antara Represi dan Resistensi*, YLBHI, Jakarta.

Fauzi, N, 1996, 'Menuju Pasar Tanah Efisien: Kebijakan Pemerintah, Penguasaan Tanah dan Sengketa Tanah' (Paper in the possession of author).

Forum Keadilan, 1996, 'Akhirnya Sandera Bebas Lewat Operasi Militer', 3 June: 12

Garna, J, 1990, 'The Baduy of Java: A Case Study of Tribal Peoples' Adaptation to Development', in Ghee and Gomes (eds), *Tribal Peoples' and Development in South-East Asia*, Department of Anthropology & Sociology, University of Malaya, Kuala Lumpur.

Gautama, S and Hornick, R, 1974, *An Introduction to Indonesian Law: Unity in Diversity*, 2nd ed, Penerbit Alumni, Bandung.

Goodland, R, 1982, *Tribal People and Economic Development – The Human Ecology Considerations*, World Bank, Washington.

Gouwgioksiong, 1960, *Tafsiran Undang-Undang Pokok Agraria*, 2nd ed, PT Kinta, Jakarta.

Griffiths, J, 1986, 'What is Legal Pluralism', *Journal of Legal Pluralism*, vol 24: 34.

Hakim, SA, 1976, 'Pra-Advice Mengenai Hak Ulayat', *Paper from Hukum Pertanahan Seminar*, Jakarta, 23-27 January (copy in the possession of the author).

Harsono, B, 1971, *UUPA: Sejarah, Penyusun, Isi dan Pelaksanaanya,* 2nd ed, Djambatan, Jakarta.

Harsono, B, 1994, 'Konsepsi Yang Mendasari Hukum Agraria Nasional', *Paper given at the Universitas Trisakti*, Jakarta, 3 October, (article in the possession of the author).

Harsono, B, 1995, *Hukum Agraria Indonesia*, 6th ed, Djambatan, Jakarta.

Himawan, C, 1973, *Business Law: Contracts and Business Associations*, Lembaja Penelihan Hukum dar Criminologi, Unviersitas Padjajaran, Bandung.

Holleman, JF, 1981, *Van Vollenhoven of Indonesian Adat Law*: Selections from Het Adatrecht van Nederlandesch Indie (vol I, 1918; Vol II, 1931), M Nijhoff, The Hague.

Hooker, MB, 1978, *Adat Law in Modern Indonesia*, Oxford University Press, Kuala Lumpur and New York.

ILO, 1988, *ILO Partial Revision of the Indigenous and Tribal Populations Convention 1957 (No 107)*, Report VI(1) International Labour Conference, 75th Session.

Jakarta Post, 1993a, 8 September: 3

Jakarta Post, 1993b, 'Strange Shortage of Logs', 6 September: 5.

Jakarta Post, 1993c, 'Businessmen and Officials Implicated in Illegal Logging', 3 November: 2.

James, 1978, *Land Tenure in Papua New Guinea*, University of Papua New Guinea, Port Moresby.

Jaspan, 1965, 'In the Quest of New Law: The Perplexity of Legal Syncretism in Indonesia', *Comparative Studies in Society and History*, vol 7.

Kartodirdjo, S, 1972, 'Agrarian Radicalism in Java' in Holt, C (ed), *Culture and Politics in Indonesia*, Cornell University Press, Ithaca.

Kasim, I and Suhendar, E, 1996, 'Neglecting Justice for Economic Growth: A Critical View of the New Order Land Policies', *Paper delivered at INFID Conference X on Land and Development,* Canberra, 26-29 April.

Kato, 1979, 'Disputing and Dispute Settlement among the Minangkabau of Indonesia', *Indonesia*, vol 8: 21-67.

Katz, J and Katz, R, 1975, 'The New Indonesian Marriage Law: A Mirror of Indonesia's Political, Cultural and Legal Systems', *American Journal of Comparative Law*, vol 23: 653

Koentjaraningrat, RM (ed) 1967, *Villages in Indonesia*, Cornell University Press, Ithaca.

Koentjaraningrat, 1993, *Masyarakat Terasing di Indonesia*, Departemer Sosial dan Dewan Nasional Indonesia: PT Gramedia Pustaka Utama, Jakarta.

Kompas, 1993, 'Skephi Usulkan HPH di Tanah Adat Penduduk Asli Irja ditinjar Logi', 6 January: 7

Kompas, 1995a, 'Kodim Cimahi Undang Penduduk Cibeureum', 18 October: 10.

Kompas, 1995b, '3000 KK Merasa Diteror untuk Pembebasan Tanah', 14 November: 8.

Kompas, 1995c, 'DPR Regrets Public Transport Commissions Failure to Follow the Administrative Courts Decision', 17 November: 10.

Kompas, 1995d, 'Kasus Tanah Parabulan Minta Korban', 30 November: 15

Kroef, 1960, 'Land Tenure and Social Structure in Rural Java', *Rural Sociology*, vol 25.

Lekkerkerker, C, 1938, *Land en Volk van Java*, Wolter, Groningen.

Lerner, N, 1993, 'The Evolution of Minority Rights in International Law' in Brölmann, C et al (eds), *People and Minorities in International Law*, M Nijhoff, Dordrecht and Boston: 77

Lev, D, 1965, 'The Lady and the Banyan Tree: Civil Law Change in Indonesia', *American Journal of Comparative Law*, vol 14: 282

Lubis, TM, 1993, *In Search of Human Rights: Legal Political Dilemma of Indonesia's New Order 1966-1990*, PT Gramedia Pustaku Utama in cooperation with SPES Foundation, Jakarta.

MacAndrews, C, 1986, *Land Policy in Modern Indonesia: A Study of Land Issues in the New Order Period*, Oelgeschlager, Gunand Hain in association with the Lincoln Institute of Land Policy, Boston.

Magnis-Suseno, Franz, 1993, *Etika Jawa – Sebuah Analisa tentang Kebijaksanaan Hidup Jawa*, PT Gramedia Pustaka Utama, Jakarta.

Masruchah, UH, 1995, *Tarah, Rakyat dan Demokrasi*, Forum LSM-LPSM DIY, Yogyakarta.

Muroa, 1994, 'Recognition of Indigenous Land Rights: A Papua New Guinean Experience', *Melanesian Law Journal*, vol 22: 81

Nasution, Adnan Buyung, 1992, *The Aspiration for Constitutional Governance in Indonesia: A Socio-legal Study of the Indonesian Konstituante 1956-59*, Purtaka Sinar Harapan, Jakarta.

Neal, T, 1995, 'The Forensic Challenge of Native Title', *Law Institute Journal*, vol 69: 880-883.

Parlindungan, 1987, *Beberapa Masalah Dalam UUPA*, Alumni Press, Bandung.

Parlindungan, 1994, *Konversi Hak-hak atas Tanah*, Penerbit Mandar Maju, Bandung.

Poffenberger and McGean (eds), 1994, *Policy Dialogue on Natural Forest Regeneration and Community Mapping*, Eastwest Center, Honolulu, Hawaii.

Radcliffe-Brown, 1952, *Structure and Function in Primitive Society*, Cohne & West, London.

Roeder, 1971, 'Consolidating Party', *Far Eastern Economic Review*, 14 August: 29.

Seidman, A and Seidman, R, 1994, *State and Law in the Development Process: Problem Solving and Institutional Change in the Third-World*, St Martin's Press, New York.

Shiva, V, 1993, 'The Greening of the Global Reach' in Grecher, J, Childs, J and Cutler, J (eds), *Global Visions: Beyond the New World Order*, Southend Press, Boston : 53-60.

Singgih Praptodihardjo, 1952, *Sendi-sendi Hukum Tanah di Indonesia*, 2nd ed.

Sirait, M, 1992, 'Mapping Customary Land: A Case Study in Long Uli Village, East Kalimantan, Indonesia', Paper presented at the Borneo Research Council, Second Biennial International Conference, Kota Kinabalu, Sabah, Malaysia, July 1992.

Slaats, H and Portier, K, 1992, *Traditional Decision-Making and Law: Institutions and Processes in an Indonesian Context*, Gadjah Mada University Press, Jakarta.

Soedarso, 1976, 'Pengawasan Pemeganag Hak Ulayat Terhadap Transaksi Yang Berhubungan Dengan Tanah', *Paper from the Simposium Integrasi Hak Ulayat ke dalam Yurisdiksi UUPA di Daerah Jawa-Madura*, 26-27 April, Yogyakarta.

Soekanto, 1985, *Meninjau Hukum Adat Indonesia*, 3rd ed, Penerbit CV Rajawah, Jakarta.

Soepomo, 1962, *Bab-bab tentang Hukum Adat*, PT Penerbit Universitas, Jakarta.

Soepomo, 1963, *Hubungan Individu dan Masyarakat dalam Hukum Adat*, PT Penerbit Universitas, Jakarta.

Soerojo Wignjodipoero, R, 1982, *Kedudukan serta Perkembangan Hukum Adat setelah Kemerdekaan*, Gunung Agung, Jakarta.

Soesangobeng, H, 1975, *Pengaruh Rationalisasi Hukum Tanah Terhadap Perkembangan Masyarakat Hukum Desa*, Report on Research Conducted by Universitas Brawijaya, Malang.

Soesangobeng, H, nd, 'Understanding the Philosophy of *Adat* Land Law in Implementing the LAP: A Reflection on the Results of a Field Study at Systematic Registration Areas in Karawang and Bekasi', forthcoming in AILDF newsletter, October 1998.

Soestrisno, L, 1995, 'Tanah dan Masa Depan Rakyat Indonesia di Pedesaan' in Masruchan (ed), *Tanah, Rakyat dan Demokrasi*, Forum LSM-LPSM DIY, Yogyakarta.

Soetjipto, Adi Andojo, 1995, 'Indonesian Judges are not Free from Influence', *Kompas*, 27 November: 10.

Sumardjono, M, 1982, *Aneka Masalah Hukum Agraria*, Andi Offset, Yogyakarta.

Sumardjono, M, 1993, 'Hak Ulayat dan Pengakuannya oleh UUPA', *Kompas*, 13 May.

Sumardjono, M, 1995a, 'Pembentukan Arbitrase Pertanahan', *Kompas*, 21 June.

Sumardjono, M, 1995b, 'Pengadilan Pertanahan dan Efektivitasnya', *Kompas*, 16 October.

Sumardjono, M, 1996, 'A Study on the Land Tenure Systems and Development Cooperation in West Kalimantan (Kabupaten Sanggau)', *Report for Hukum Agraria National Seminar*, Jakarta, August.

Ter Haar, 1948, *Adat Law in Indonesia* (trans Haas and Hordyk), Institute of Pacific Relations, New York.

Ter Haar, 1950, *Beginselen en Stelsel van het Adatrecht,* 4th ed, Wolters 1939, Groningen, Netherlands: 15, translated in Soebakh Peoponoto KN 1960, *Asas-asas dan Susunan Hukum Adat,* PT Pradnya Paramita, Jakarta.

Tsuchiya, 1987, *Democracy and Leadership: The Rise of the Taman Siswa Movement in Indonesia,* University of Hawaii Press, Honolulu.

USAID (United States Agency of International Development) and Directorate General of Home Affairs 1992, *Land Titling and Mapping in Indonesia,* (1982), US Agency for International Development, Jakarta.

Vlist, L van der (ed), 1994, *Voices of the Earth: Indigenous People, New Partners and the Right to Self-Determination in Practice,* International Books NCIP, Amsterdam.

Van Vollenhoven, 1909, *Miskenningen van het Adatrecht: Vier Voordrachten aan de Nederlandsch-Indische Bestuursacademie,* EJ Brill, Leiden.

Van der Vyer, JD, 1991, 'Statehood in International Law', *Emory International Law Review,* vol 5.

Wear, P, 1995, 'Tribunal Rules Itself Out', *The Bulletin,* 12 December: 24.

World Bank, nda, *Studies on the Registration of Traditional (Adat) Land Rights – Terms of Reference* (copy in possession of author).

World Bank, 1988, *Rural Development: World Bank Experience 1965-86,* cited in Hancock, 1989, *Lords of Poverty: The Freewheeling Lifestyles, Power, Prestige and Corruption of the Multi-Billion Dollar Aid Business,* Macmillan Books, London: 35.

World Bank, 1990, *Staff Appraisal Report for Thailand – Second Land Titling Project,* August 7, Agricultural Operations Division, East Asia and Pacific Region.

World Bank, 1991, *World Development Report (2) – Poverty: The Challenge of Development,* Oxford University Press for the World Bank, Oxford.

World Bank, 1994, *Staff Appraisal Report for Indonesia – Land Titling Project,* 16 August, Agricultural Operations Division, Country Department III, East Asia and Pacific Region.

YLBHI & Jarim, 1991, *Laporan Kasus Kedung Ombo, Kasus Arso dan Kasus Cimacan,* YLBHI, Jakarta.

YBLHI, 1992, "Report on Human Rights Violations", *Indonesian Human Rights Forum,* YLBHI, Jakarta, no 3: 19.

5. Beyond Dualism: Land Acquisition and Law in Indonesia

Daniel Fitzpatrick

As with most postcolonial countries, Indonesia inherited a legal order that distinguished between formal laws of the state and customary norms of the people. The rationale for this distinction was largely economic: most colonial governments were concerned not with broad-based economic development but with export enclaves based on large-scale agricultural production and resource-extraction (Seidman & Seidman, 1994: 32). Accordingly, colonial constitutions recognised customary law in the hinterland, albeit subject to catch-all requirements such as 'natural justice, equity and good conscience' but applied European, capitalist laws to export enclaves and the commercial elite (usually European) that governed them. Many developmental economists now see this policy of economic and legal dualism as having created a clash of systems – one village-based and pre-capitalist; the other urban and capitalist – with disastrous consequences for rural areas, including indebtedness, exploitation and over-population (Greenberg, 1980: 143; Santos, 1979: 51).

Thus, the challenge of legal development in postcolonial countries is said to be to shape laws and legal institutions that overcome dualism and its consequences (Seidman & Seidman, 1994: 45-52). The orthodox Western response is 'modern' law: an autonomous system of purposive rules applied universally and uniformly by specialised state agencies (Trubek, 1972: 5). Proponents argue that this best offers the transparency, predictability and rationality necessary for a modern industrial economy (id: 5; Greenberg 1980: 130). But this orthodoxy has been much questioned. Some argue that Western-style modern law simply perpetuates the exploitation of colonial dualism (Wallerstein, 1974; Leys, 1975); others point out that legal rules and institutions transplanted from the West rarely have similar or predictable effects in developing countries (Seidman & Seidman, 1994: 44-45); others again argue that legal pluralism, not unitary state law, is the only path to broad-based sustainable development (Benda-Beckmann, 1989). Indeed, calls for a new typology to describe the relationship between law, development and dualism in postcolonial countries are a hallmark of the contemporary law and development debate (for example, Trubek, 1972: 3; Seidman & Seidman, 1994: 2-3; Greenberg 1980: 129).

Indonesian land law offers a useful case-study of aspects of this debate because it seeks to graft indigenous elements on to modernist unifying law. Indonesia's nationalists rejected colonial dualism as discriminating against autochthonous Indonesians. They were determined to have modern law and a modern nation-state. But they disagreed on the nature of this new legal order and, in particular, the role of customary law (*adat*) in it (Lev, 1962: 210). Many, largely those on the political left, saw *adat* as feudalistic and obstructive of Indonesian socio-political development. Others, however, were influenced by van Vollenhoven, who had argued that underlying the diversity of local *adat* norms there existed a pan-Indonesian pattern, an 'ur-*adat*' made up of universal *adat* principles (Burns, 1989: 3). In this notion they discerned the seeds of a uniquely Indonesian national law and spirit. The eventual resolution of this question was the syncretic sort of compromise beloved by Indonesians: the official view on legal unification is that it must be based on an *adat* law that 'does not hamper the development of a just and prosperous society' (Hooker, 1975: 27).

Indonesia's land and land acquisition laws exemplify this syncretic approach to *adat* and legal unity. The Agrarian Law of 1960 (Agrarian Law) unifies Indonesian land law by subsuming all Dutch-derived land rights, and most *adat* rights, into a series of new statutory rights. These rights are Western in nature: most are registrable (Arts 19 and 23), transferable (Arts 20(2), 24, 27, 49(3)), and mortgageable (Art 25). Yet the Agrarian Law also states that it is based on *adat* law although this *adat* law must not be inconsistent with the interests of national unity and the provisions of the Agrarian Law itself (Art 5). Additionally, it purports to incorporate a number of allegedly universal *adat* principles into formal state law. For example, it states that all rights to land have a 'social function' (a concept said to reflect *adat* principles); that the new land law of Indonesia arising out of the Agrarian Law 'will be based on *adat* principles'; and that matters involving land will be conducted in accordance with the traditional *adat* principle of mutual co-operation (*gotong royong*) (Art 13).

Indonesia's laws on land acquisition similarly purport to syncretise universal *adat* principles with Western-style law. On the one hand, their structure reflects a common assumption in land acquisition law: that a model based on written legislation and judicial review is the best means to ensure rational resource allocation whilst also minimising disputation and conflict (Kitay, 1985). A Parliamentary law grants the President exclusive power to order compulsory land acquisition; a Presidential Decision authorises regional governors to negotiate voluntary bargain and sale; and judicial review is available in respect of the assessment of compensation. On the other hand, they incorporate the same *adat* principles that are contained in the Agrarian Law, namely the concepts of social function and mutual co-operation, while also adding another: land acquisitions must be accompanied by a traditional process of deliberation (*musyarawah*).

In other words, Indonesia's laws on land acquisition are modernist in so far as they are rule-based and universalist but 'Indonesian' in that they purport to be based on *adat* law and principles. In structure, therefore, they rely on three fundamental assumptions or paradigms. First, Indonesian law consists of, or is best understood through, a dualistic division of *adat* and formal law. Secondly, unified law and uniform legal consequences may be created through universalist statutes. Thirdly, universalist statutes that syncretically incorporate *adat* principles into Western-style law best cater for legal unification in Indonesia's diverse customary environment. Through a study of Indonesia's land acquisition laws, this chapter challenges these assumptions and paradigms. It seeks to establish the following points. First, unitary law in Indonesia's pluralist environment does not have uniform legal consequences but in fact has a highly discriminatory application. Secondly, a number of normative justifications for compulsory land acquisition exist independently of, and override, the provisions of statutory law. Thirdly, incorporating universal *adat* principles into Western-style law has not succeeded in creating postcolonial national law but has been used perversely by the state to justify ad hoc bureaucratic domination of land administration. Fourthly, the relationship between formal state law and local practice is now so intertwined, and characterised to such an extent by the hegemony of state law and practice, that the traditional paradigm of dualism is no longer an accurate basis for analysis of Indonesian law.[1]

The chapter then considers possible explanations for the failure of Indonesia's land acquisition laws to achieve their syncretic and universalist objectives. Is it because of the modernist fallacy that universalist formal law of itself delivers uniformity and predictability? Is it because creating indigenous national law based on universal *adat* principles lacks the precision and institutional support necessary for formal nation-state law? Or does it bear out the dependency theorists' view that unitary Western-style law simply perpetuates exploitation of poor and traditional groups? This study agrees that the adventurism of syncretic national law has failed but asserts that this failure cannot be explained solely by modernism or dependency theory. It argues that in fact universalist law in Indonesia is curiously paradoxical: on the one hand, it illustrates modernism's flaws and partly supports dependency theory in that it is not universalist in practice and discriminates against poor and traditional groups in Indonesian society; but on the other hand, it does operate as a source of normative pressure for the state to act in a consistent and universalist way – hence the need for the state to override it on occasions through the use of state ideologies. In other words, universalist law is not intrinsically exploitative, but its subjugation to state ideology renders it very limited as an instrument of social change. Therefore, the function of formal law should not be to effect positive social change as such, but to seek to counteract, to the extent possible, the hegemony of state and bureaucratic action. This requires law that provides greater protection for those groups most subject to state hegemony and discrimination. In this anti-hegemonic pluralist endeavour there are glimpses of a proper role for formal law in postcolonial societies.

Land Acquisition Laws

The seeds of a national land acquisition law are sown in the Agrarian Law. Article 27 of the Agrarian Law provides for termination of 'a right' (*hak*) to own land, and reversion of that land to the state, where there has been 'revocation' (*pencabutan*) in accordance with Art 18. Article 18 states that rights to land may be revoked in the public interest, 'including the interests of the nation, the state and the people as a whole' on payment of 'appropriate' (*layak*) compensation. Articles 34 and 40 similarly allow for termination of business use rights and building use rights where they have been revoked in the public interest. These provisions on appropriation are confirmed by the statement in Art 6 that all rights to land have a 'social function'. This notion is said to derive from *adat* law and is interpreted in the Elucidation (Chapter II) to mean that individual rights must be balanced with the interests of the community.

---

1   The author is indebted to Milton Santos' seminal study of urban development in the Third World (*The Shared Space*) for the notion that dualism is no longer an appropriate paradigm for post-colonial development.

The 1961 Law on Revocation of Titles

The first Law on the Procedure for Revocation of Titles was passed in 1961, replacing the colonial regulation on appropriation of 1920. This colonial law was criticised as unduly restrictive of development because it required every act of appropriation to be approved by the legislature. Thus, the 1961 Law delegates exclusive power to order revocation of titles to land to the President (Gautama and Harsono, 1972: 107-109). The Elucidation to this Law states that revocation should only be ordered in matters of public importance, when all efforts to obtain the land voluntarily through a process of deliberation (*musyawarah*) have failed (Elucidation, Art 2). It gives as examples of matters of public importance the construction of highways, harbours, industrial or mining development, hospitals and health facilities and 'other enterprises that are part of the framework of realising the overall development plan' (Art 4(b)). The Elucidation also confirms that all rights to land have a social function, which is said on this occasion to mean that the interests of the individual must submit to the interests of the community (Art 3).

The President is also given exclusive power to determine the amount and form of compensation, which is to be based on the recommendations of a committee of experts (Art 3). The Elucidation states that compensation should be based on the real or actual value of the land; and explains that while, on the one hand, this will not necessarily equate to market price as that could be a 'profiteering' price (*harga catut*), on the other, it is not to be a cheap or inexpensive (*murah*) price. Compensation is also payable to those with buildings on the land or who use the land but it may take the form of money or other land or facilities, including by way of transmigration. The Presidential decision on the amount and form of compensation may be the subject of appeal to the District Court of the area in which the land is situated; but there is no right of appeal in respect of the appropriation itself (Art 8).

The state has the right to take possession of the land in question without waiting for the outcome of any appeal by the title-holder (Art 9). In addition, in an 'emergency', the Minister of Internal Affairs may order the appropriation himself, and allow the party seeking use of the land to possess it before compensation has been settled (Art 6(1)). A presidential order on appropriation and compensation is only necessary if negotiations for compensation fail to reach agreement (Art 6(2)). The Elucidation to the law gives as examples of an 'emergency' for the purposes of the law an epidemic or natural disaster which leaves its victims with an immediate need for shelter. However, the government has adopted a broader interpretation, and used the emergency power for the appropriation of land for large-scale public facilities such as sports stadia and city markets (Gautama and Harsono, 1972: 109).

The 1975 Ministerial Decree

Significantly, the non-emergency power of title revocation contained in the 1961 Law has been used only once (World Bank, 1991: 33). Since 1975, it has been eclipsed in practice by a Presidential Decree (No 55 of 1993 concerning acquisition of land). In theory, unlike the 1961 Law, these laws do not allow for compulsory acquisition of land as they require the state to achieve consensus with title-holders through traditional processes of discussion and deliberation. In practice, however, as shall be seen, they operate as de facto compulsory land acquisition statutes.

The 1975 Decree requires regional governors to establish committees to investigate and advise on matters of compensation once a request from a government agency for 'release' of title has been accepted. The appropriation committee is to consist of a large number of agrarian and district officials; a representative of the organisation that requires the land; and the village chief of the area in question. The committee must negotiate with the relevant titleholders as to the amount and form of compensation, which is to be based on the 'local public price' (*harga umum setempat*) (Art 6(1)) but may be in the form of money, land or other facilities (Art 6(2)(b)). Although the committee is not expressly required to conduct negotiations on the traditional Indonesian principle of deliberation, it must 'be guided by regulations that are based' on that principle (Art 1(3)).

The 1975 Decree on appropriation does not elaborate on the meaning of the phrase 'local public price' but does say that the factors to be taken into account in determining compensation are the location and other strategic features affecting the value of the land; and, in respect of buildings and crops, the stipulations of the Department of Public Works and/or the Department of Agriculture (Art 6(2)(a)). If the members of the committee disagree on the amount of compensation the final figure is to be obtained by averaging out the opinions of the committee members (Art 6(3)). If the titleholders do not accept the amount or form of the compensation, the committee may stick to its decision or submit the matter for resolution by the governor (Art 8(1)). The governor has the power to confirm the committee's decision or make a different decision 'shaped by finding a middle way that is acceptable to the two parties' (Art 8(2)).

The 1976 Decree

A 1976 decree of the Minister of Internal Affairs extended the operation of the 1975 decree to requests by private organisations for 'release of title' where their project is in the public interest. Unfortunately, however, this had the effect of introducing a cycle of collusion in Indonesian land development.[2] Because 'release' of land titles is usually accompanied by compensation at below market price (World Bank, 1991: 34), private developers generally eschew direct dealings with titleholders in favour of acquiring rights directly from the state through collusion with local officials. In combination with the fact that most titles in Indonesia remain unregistered, and unregistered titleholders others cannot obtain formal secured credit, the result is that ordinary occupiers of land have very little say in the processes of development in Indonesia (Fitzpatrick, 1997: 194-205).

The 1993 Presidential Decision

Apparently in response to persistent criticism of its operation, the 1975 Decree was repealed by Presidential Decision No 55 of 1993. This law follows a similar pattern to the 1975 Decree but elaborates more on the pivotal questions of assessment of compensation and the requirement of consensus based on discussion and deliberation. Thus, it continues the important role of regional authorities by stating that compensation for appropriation is to be assessed by an Appropriation Evaluation Committee, which is to be formed by regional governors in every region or sub-district (Art 6). Article 8 requires this committee to conduct deliberations

---

2   See, for example, Jakarta Post (1993a: 3).

between the holders of the land rights in question and the government agency that seeks the land in an attempt to fix the form and amount of compensation. Compensation is defined somewhat circularly as the replacement of the value of land, along with the buildings, crops, and other articles connected to it, as a result of its procurement. It is to be calculated on the basis of:

(a) the real or actual value of the land, with attention being paid to the value of the land stated in the latest Soil and Development Tax document;

(b) the market price of the buildings on the land as estimated by the regional government agency with responsibility for buildings; and

(c) the market price of the crops on the land as estimated by the regional government agency with responsibility for crops (Art 15).

Compensation may be in the form of money, substitute land, a replacement settlement, or in any other form agreed to by the parties (Art 13). However, in the case of *hak ulayat* land, which is land subject to the traditional community right of disposal, compensation may only be in the form of public development facilities or other facilities useful to the community in the area (Art 14).

The Presidential Decision repeals the 1976 Ministerial Decree and states that land acquisition under its provisions may only be carried out for government public interest projects (Art 2). It further states that land acquisitions must be carried out with a traditional process of deliberation (Arts 1, 9, 10) which is defined as a process of mutually listening, with an attitude of acceptance, to the desires and opinions volunteered by the parties holding the rights to land and the party seeking the land (Arts 1, 10). Article 19 states that, if there have been repeated deliberations but agreement as to the form or size of compensation has not been reached, the evaluation committee will issue a decision on compensation which pays as much attention as possible to the opinions, desires, suggestions, and calculations that were put forward in the deliberations. If holders of the land rights in question object to the committee's decision they may appeal to the regional Governor who will seek to settle the matter by paying attention to the calculations, opinions, and desires of all parties.

As in the 1975 Decree, the Governor is not given express power to order compulsory acquisition. Unlike the 1975 Decree, however, the 1993 Presidential decision does elaborate upon the duties of the Governor in the event of continuing disagreement by title-holders. In this event, the governor must follow the provisions of the 1961 law, and, in particular, notify the existence of a dispute to the Minister for Agriculture by way of the Minister of Internal Affairs and forward a copy of the proposed settlement to those Ministers as well as the Minister of Justice and the Minister with responsibility for the agency seeking the land. These Ministers will then forward a formal request for appropriation and compensation to the President. It is only after the President has issued an order for appropriation that the right-holders may appeal over compensation, but not acquisition, to the regional High Court (*Pengadilan Tinggi*) in accordance with the 1961 Law.

Land Acquisition in Practice

How have these laws operated in practice? The following section derives conclusions from a number of case-studies of land acquisition in practice. It is divided into three parts. The first considers the operation and interpretation of formal land acquisition law. The second describes the use of such concepts as policy, social function, *Pancasila* and development to override the provisions of formal land acquisition law. The third discusses the use of such notions as unlawful occupancy and the state's 'right of control' to allow compulsory land acquisition without reference to the land acquisition laws.

Operation and Interpretation of Land Acquisition Law

Discussion, Deliberation and Agreement

Both the 1975 Decree and 1993 Presidential Decision allow only for voluntary bargain and sale based on traditional processes of discussion and deliberation. But there are numerous examples of their use in practice to allow de facto compulsory acquisitions of rights to land. For example, the bureaucracy often asserts that the requirement of discussion, deliberation and consensus is satisfied by discussion with the village head (*lurah*) or village chief (*kepala desa*) alone. This was an argument in the Kedung Ombo case, which is discussed below, and further reports of this practice may be found in the *Jakarta Post* in April and May 1995.[3] Yet, in New Order Indonesia these officials are not traditional authority figures but civil servants who are appointed or elected pursuant to the 1979 Law on Village Government. Parlindungan (1993: 13) states that in many cases the *lurah* and *kepala desa* are younger men or women with little knowledge of local *adat* rules or particular *adat* rights. Sihombing (1980: 16) says that the application of the Law on Village Government has caused conflict in Minangkbau, particularly where village governing councils have replaced *adat* councils.

There are also consistent reports that intimidation and deceit accompany negotiations over proposed land acquisitions. For example, in one dispute, Telek Pucung village in the Bekasi Regency of central Java filed a complaint with the National Commission for Human Rights (KOMNASHAM)[4] alleging that they had been woken up in the middle of the night and made to sign blank papers (Jakarta Post, 1995a: 3). Subsequently, the Bekasi regency claimed that the land was state land; and the residents were paid compensation of Rp 150 to 250[5] per square metre. In the Kedung Ombo case, the applicants complained that the authorities had obtained thumb prints from illiterate title-holders without informing them that they were thereby agreeing to both the appropriation and the amount and form of compensation.[6] In a dispute involving land acquisition for a tourist theme park near Borobodur temple, landholders complained that large groups of men had visited individual villagers in the middle of the night; and all villagers had received letters from the National Electricity Company saying that electricity would be cut off shortly in preparation for construction of the theme park (KSBH and LBH, 1982). In a number of other cases, such as Kedung Ombo and a dispute at Plumpang in North Jakarta, security forces have accompanied officials who are outlining

---

3   See Jakarta Post (1995b: 3); Jakarta Post (1995d: 3).

4   *Komisi Nasional Hak Asasi Manusia.*

5   About AUS$00.02 − AUS$00.03 in June 1998.

6   A similar account of deceit was reported by Rancamaya village in Bogor Regency in 1994 (Jakarta Post, 1994a: 3). There are also reports of money received by villagers being far less than agreed. See, for example, Jakarta Post (1992: 7).

compensation offers to titleholders. Where there is resistance, the villagers are often labelled as 'communists' – a particularly pejorative term in New Order Indonesia.[7]

Compensation and Discrimination

The universal requirement of compensation also presents difficulties in practice. For example, the statement in the 1961 Law that the compensatable value of land is its real value, which is neither the market price nor an inexpensive price and is to take into account the social function of land, is so elusive that it allows quite different opinions to be formed on the compensatable value of land without providing predictable instruments for distinguishing between them. Similarly, the reference to 'local general price' in the 1975 Decree has little meaning in the absence both of a mature market for land in many areas, and a lack of national guidelines on heads of claims and schedules of appropriate payments.

The result is that compensation for land acquisition in Indonesia is assessed on an ad hoc, case-by-case basis without the publication of reasons. This process inevitably favours the state as all the members of the assessment committee, including the village head, are government officials, and final figures are required to be reached by averaging out the differences in their opinions. In addition, the assessment committee is also required to take into account valuations by government agencies: that is, in respect of land, the valuation of the local, government-appointed mayor, and, in respect of buildings and crops, the stipulations of the local Public Works and Agricultural offices. There is little opportunity for land-holders to obtain independent valuations because of the relative lack of private expertise in respect of valuations, and the absence of a mature market in the sale of land in rural areas. An important consequence of this is that the information available to the court in the event of an appeal is also limited. Again, this was a feature of the Kedung Ombo case.

Another significant feature of compensation assessment in Indonesia is that it discriminates in practice against owners or occupiers of land who either lack formal certificates of title to their land, or, having certificates, are socially or economically vulnerable to state coercion. These groups make up the vast majority of the Indonesian population. For example, in May 1995, 45 residents of Karet Tengsin sub-district in Central Jakarta were reported to have complained to the City Council regarding the failure of Central Jakarta mayoralty to consult with them over the appropriation of their land. The mayoralty had set unilateral offers of compensation at Rp 249,000[8] per square metre for those without certificates or other formal documents, and Rp 941,000[9] for those with such documents. The market price was said at the time to be Rp 1.5 million[10] per square metre (Jakarta Post, 1995c: 3). In another example, at Cianjar in West Java, traditional owners complained that they were yet to receive compensation as had been agreed. Many said that they had given all their original land certificates to local officials for safekeeping. The officials had asked for 10% of the value of the land to look after the certificates. Subsequently,

---

7   For example, members of Sendang Pasir village in Buleleng Regency refused to move from land that a private company had been granted a licence to develop. Subsequently, they were evicted by the military who accused them of being members of the banned 'PKI' (*Partai Komunis Indonesia*) or Indonesian Communist Party: Jakarta Post (1993b: 2).

8   AUS$33.00 in June 1998.

9   AUS$125.00 in June 1998.

10   AUS$200 in June 1998.

before the dam was completed, large numbers of new houses were constructed in the area. The new occupiers received compensation for the appropriation but not the traditional owners (Jakarta Post, 1994b: 3).

Of course, it is true that land with certificates has higher value than land without certificates and this should be reflected in compensation assessments. But it is also extremely difficult for poor or traditional groups to acquire certificates to their land in Indonesia. Certification involves travel to regional centres and incurs prohibitive official and unofficial costs. It also commonly involves converting fluid, communally-oriented customary rights to inflexible, individually-oriented statutory rights (Fitzpatrick, 1997: 180-91). Many traditional communities are reluctant to provoke the resulting disputes and loss of internal sovereignty inevitably consequent upon registration of customary titles.[11] In any event, no implementing regulations cover conversion of intermittent usufructuary rights to land into statutory titles (World Bank, 1991: 21). Finally, as shall be considered further below, certification is impossible in relation to a number of customary rights to land that were not converted into statutory rights by the Agrarian Law. In short, assessment of compensation under Indonesia's land acquisition laws purports to be uniform and universalist, save in relation to *hak ulayat* land, but in practice discriminates significantly against poor, traditional or unregistered groups in Indonesian society.

Normative Principles that override Formal Law

A related feature of land acquisition laws in practice is that, although they purport to be comprehensive codes on land acquisition, in practice they may be overridden by concepts such as policy, development, social function and *Pancasila*. This phenomenon is illustrated by the Pluit Polder and Kedung Ombo cases.

Pluit Polder

The 14 applicants in this case in the District Court of Jakarta in 1971 were the occupiers of land in Jembatan Dua in North Jakarta (Gautama, 1992, 127). This land had been appropriated pursuant to a 1969 decision letter of the Governor of Jakarta to allow for a housing development under the Pluit area development plan. It was not disputed that the applicants had been evicted from their land without agreement as to compensation. The applicants claimed that these actions contravened the 1961 law on appropriation because (1) only the President could compel appropriation; (2) appropriation was only possible after compensation had been paid; and (3) the appropriation was not in the public interest as the land was to be utilised by a private housing developer who would exploit the low prices offered to the applicants by later trading the land at market prices. The applicants accordingly sought nullification of the Governor's decision letter, a declaration that their eviction had been unlawful, and damages in the sum of Rp 50,000,000[12] for every violation of the law by the Governor.

The Governor submitted in reply that (1) the applicants had not proved that they had legal rights to the land; (2) the court lacked jurisdiction as the appropriation was a non-justiciable execution of government policy to develop Jakarta; (3) the land in question was state land pursuant to a decision dated 14 July 1960 of the Regional Wartime Administrator which sought to implement the 'Pluit

---

11   See, for example, Benda-Beckmann and Taale (1993: 19-20, 24).

12   AUS$666.00 in June 1998.

Polder' development plan; and (4) the Governor's actions were consistent with the nation's *Pancasila* ideology, the paramountcy of which had been confirmed by the Supreme Court. The High Court of Jakarta dismissed the claims of the applicants on two grounds. The first, and most significant, was that the Governor had carried out his duty as the instrument of the central government to carry out the state's development plans. The matter, therefore, involved non-justiciable execution of policy rather than any question of law. It was therefore unnecessary to consider whether there had been any violation of the 1961 Law. The second was an argument that is considered further below, namely that the land in question was land under the direct control of the state because the applicants rights were derived from the colonial *eigendom* proprietary right which had been abolished by the Agrarian Law.

Kedung Ombo

Another case illustrating the propensity of the courts not to apply formal law where it conflicts with concepts such as development and policy is the well-known Kedung Ombo case.[13] This dispute arose out the construction of a large dam at Kedung Ombo in the Genengsari sub-district of Central Java. Construction of the dam required the use of approximately 6127 hectares of land inhabited by some 60,000 families. In 1987, after an earlier offer in 1983 had been rejected, the Central Java Governor offered title-holders a combination of substitute land and monetary compensation. Shortly thereafter he declared that all title-holders had accepted this offer in accordance with the 1975 Decree. As a result, on his application, the Boyolali High Court ordered that the land and buildings in question revert to the state.

Subsequently, however, 54 titleholders brought an action in the High Court at Semarang claiming greater compensation and rescission of the order of the Boyolali High Court. At first instance in this court, and on cassation (appeal on a point of law) in the Supreme Court, the applicants adduced evidence and made submissions on the key issues in the 1975 Decree, namely discussion and deliberation; agreement by title-holders; and sufficiency of compensation.

In relation to 'discussion and deliberation', the applicants submitted that:

- The authorities obtained thumb prints from illiterate title-holders without informing them that they were thereby agreeing to both the appropriation and the amount and form of compensation.

- The inhabitants of some areas had never been included in the negotiations.

- The head of the Boyolali High Court and two local sub-district officials had said during negotiations that those who did not accept the compensation offer would be imprisoned for three months or fined Rp 10,000.[14]

- The discussion procedure was one-sided and accompanied by the intimidating presence of the police and the armed forces.

In relation to agreement with title-holders, the applicants submitted that:

- The Central Java Governor had said on a number of occasions that agreement had been reached with all the title-holders even though, for

---

13　See Dec No 2263 K/Pdt/1991 (Appeal Court of the Supreme Court); and Dec No 650 PK/Pdt/1994 (Review Court of the Supreme Court). See especially pp 102-108 and 55-58.

14　AUS$1.30 in June 1998.

example, 250 of them were protesting their case to the House of Representatives in Jakarta.

- The applicants did not wish to leave the Kedung Ombo area because they wanted to till between the high and low tide marks and use the dam water for extra income.

- The process of land acquisition contravened the Minister of Internal Affairs' Decree No 15 of 1975 as the title-holders had not accepted the compensation set by the Governor. The only way the land could be acquired compulsorily was through the use of the 1961 Law on Appropriation.

In relation to compensation, the applicants submitted that:

- Witnesses for the defendants admitted that the money was not sufficient to purchase equivalent land or buildings. Therefore, the amount of compensation offered contravened Decree No 15 of 1975 of the Minister of Internal Affairs because it was below the local public price.

- The legal status of the substitute land offered was in doubt as the correct legal procedure for transferring the rights to that land from the Ministry of Forestry (which controlled the land) to the applicants had not been followed.

- The substitute land was rugged and contained lime, making it difficult to obtain water for irrigation.

In response to the question of 'discussion and deliberation', the defendants submitted that the applicants had been invited to discussions on the question of compensation but had not attended; and that, in any event, there had been sufficient discussion and deliberation in accordance with the 1975 Decree. In relation to agreement, they submitted that compensation had been accepted in respect of most of the land necessary for the project. The people who did not accept the compensation inhabited only a small proportion of the appropriated land. In the context of the government's development drive, this was sufficient agreement for the purposes of the 1975 Decree. In respect of compensation, they submitted that the condition of the substitute land was good, near the dam water, and could be provided with certificates. The defendants also submitted that the applicants did not hold any property rights to the land or buildings in question as they lacked formal certificates of title.

The court of first instance in Semarang rejected the applicants' claim without providing reasons. This decision was confirmed at the appellate level of the Semarang district court. However, in a decision dated 28 July 1993, the cassation division of the Supreme Court overturned these decisions on the following grounds:

- The law applicable to the case was the 1975 decree, as Presidential decision No 55 of 1993 was not intended to apply retrospectively. However, even if the 1993 Presidential decision did apply, both its provisions and the provisions of the 1975 decree had been breached because there was insufficient discussion and deliberation with the title-holders and the Governor's decision had been carried out with force.

- The applicants had not accepted the amount of compensation offered by the Governor as required by Decree No 15 of 1975 of the Minister of Internal Affairs. The submerging of the land and buildings by closing the dam gates had, therefore, been illegal.

- Because the applicants were poor people the monetary compensation offered to them should have been close to the actual value of the land so as to allow them to buy equivalent land or buildings.

The court ordered that the lands and buildings that had been flooded be compensated at a rate of Rp 50,000[15] per square metre, and crops at a rate of Rp 30,000[16] per square metre. The judges did not give reasons as to how these figures were determined. The court also granted the original applicants' request for additional 'non-material' compensation of Rp 2,000,000,000.[17]

The respondents then sought a 'review' of the appeal court's decision pursuant to Law No 14 of 1970 on Judicial Powers which grants the Chief Justice discretionary powers to review Supreme Court decisions (Arts 67-72). The use, or overuse, of this review power is a matter of some controversy in Indonesia (Himawan, 1995: 1). The grounds for the review were as follows:

- Discussions and deliberations were conducted with the Kedung Ombo people and the court had erred in respect of the meaning of deliberation and discussion.
- The way in which the court had determined the amount of compensation was not expressed, and no reference was made to the calculations in the Governor's decree on compensation.
- The amount of compensation should have taken into account the equilibrium between individual and public interest, and adhered to the standard local prices stipulated periodically by the Mayor of Boyolali.
- The applicants were accepted by the court as legal owners of the land, buildings or plants in question even though they had no land certificates. The fact that most of them had letters of payment of land tax went only to prove that the tax had been paid and not proof of ownership itself.

The Review Court, consisting of Chief Justice HR Purwoto S Gandasubrata and four other judges, upheld the application for review of the earlier decision of the Supreme Court and ordered that the matter be returned to the cassation division. The court stated that two matters were of themselves sufficient to decide the case. The first was that the Boyolali District Court's orders transferring the applicants' rights to land, buildings and crops to the state were valid because (1) all rights to land have a social function, which means that individual rights succumb to the interests of the community in matters of public interest; (2) the Kedung Ombo dam was in the public interest; and (3) the law must support national development in accordance with House of Representatives Law No 111 of 1993, which was applied in similar circumstances in respect of the Mican dam in Supreme Court Decision No 135 K/Pdt/1989 of 19 July 1990. The second was that the provisions of both the 1975 Decree and the 1993 Presidential Decision had been followed by the Central Java authorities, in particular as most of the title-holders had accepted the Governor's offer of compensation. The Boyolali High Court, therefore, was entitled to transfer the applicants' rights to the state in order that the project not be delayed or neglected, in accordance with Supreme Court Decision No 578/1320/88/II/UMTU/Pdt of November 16, 1988.

---

15   AUS$6.60 in June 1998.
16   AUS$4.00 in June 1998.
17   AUS$266,000.00 in June 1998.

In this way, the *Mahkamah Agung* Review Court used the notions of social function and development to excuse apparently clear breaches of the requirements of discussion, deliberation and consensus in the 1975 Decree and the 1993 Presidential Decision. This result provides an insight into the nature and role of written law in Indonesia, namely that it is not in fact absolute and universalist but is subject to a range of ideological *grundnorms* that cluster around such concepts as *Pancasila*, policy, development and social function. In other words, written law is but one of a number of competing sources of normative references for the bureaucracy, courts and the state – and an inferior one at that.

Independent Normative Justifications for Compulsory Land Acquisition

The final relevant feature of land acquisition in practice in Indonesia is that there are a number of ways to acquire land compulsorily without reference to the laws on land acquisition. These include the notion of the state's 'right of control', the failure of formal law to convert or recognise some customary rights and the concept of unlawful occupancy.

State *Hak Ulayat*

The state's right of control *(hak menguasai negara)*, sometimes known as 'state *hak ulayat*', derives first from Art 33(3) of the 1945 Constitution and Art 3 of the Agrarian Law which both declare all land in the Republic of Indonesia to be under the 'control' of the state; and secondly from the fact that the Agrarian Law does not convert the communal right of disposal known as *hak ulayat* into a statutory right. In combination, these two matters are said to have created a 'state *hak ulayat*', in which all *hak ulayat* land is owned directly by the state and may be the subject of a grant of rights without any reference to formal law on land acquisition. In practice, this notion of state *hak ulayat* is an extremely significant aspect of compulsory land acquisition in Indonesia. Examples abound of conflict arising from its exercise (Fitzpatrick, 1997: 187)

For example, the Basic Forestry Law relies on the state's right of control to declare some 75% of Indonesia's landmass to be unencumbered state forest land; yet much of this land is either cultivated or subject to traditional hunting and gathering activities (World Bank, 1991: 22). It further states that 'community rights and community law should not hinder the fulfilment of the aims of this law' (Art 17). Similar legislative provisions overriding customary rights also apply in relation to *transmigrasi* (transmigration) projects and the granting of timber con-cessions (Colchester, 1986). As a result, and because most land rights in Indonesia are unregistered and therefore community or customary rights, in formal law many Indonesians have an extremely tenuous relationship with their land and are vulnerable to eviction without any right to compensation (World Bank, 1991: 16-25). In addition, the notion of state right of control is used to justify regional regu-lations concerning land that make no reference to the Agrarian Law: for example, a regulation in Sulawesi which states that all land is owned by the state, and a West Timor regulation that declares all sandalwood trees, wherever situated, to be owned by the state (Ruwiastuti, 1997).

In many ways, the notion of state *hak ulayat* operates more as an ideological *grundnorm*, similar to *Pancasila*, development and social function, than as a precise legal instrument. Traditionally, *hak ulayat* is an umbrella community right under which individual *adat* rights are acquired through the input of labour and commitment and lost through abandonment and neglect. Many of these individual rights were converted into statutory rights by the Agrarian Law, even though *hak ulayat* itself is not converted. But many others, as shall be seen further below, are subject to bureaucratic arguments that they either were not converted or amount to unlawful occupation of post-Agrarian Law state-owned land. In the result, while it is clear that uncultivated *hak ulayat* land falls within the state *hak ulayat*, there is no precise definition of the circumstances in which *hak ulayat* land subject to traditional individual rights similarly falls within state *hak ulayat* and may therefore be appropriated without reference to the laws on land acquisition.

Failure to Convert and/or Register

A related way in which land may be appropriated without reference to legislation arises out of the Agrarian Law conversion of *adat* rights to statutory rights. Two different arguments are commonly advanced in this context. The first is that the *adat* right of the occupiers is not included in the list of rights converted to statutory rights by the Agrarian Law, and that these occupiers may be evicted or re-settled without compensation (World Bank, 1991: 21-22). This failure to convert argument is most evident in relation to the usufructuary rights of shifting cultivators in Kalimantan, Flores and Irian Jaya where it is used to support the government's general view that shifting cultivation is an inferior form of agriculture and culture, and that shifting cultivators should be resettled in sedentary villages. But it is not restricted to these Outer Islands: for example, the Javanese *adat* right known as *yasan*, an individual right to land that accrues when forest land is cleared and cultivated, was converted expressly to *hak milik* in the Agrarian Law, yet the land office (BPN) has held that an *adat* right in Sulawesi with exactly the same characteristics was not converted and accordingly the land in question reverted to the state (Ruwiastuti, 1997). It is notable that these inconsistencies arise because the Agrarian Law only lists a small number of *adat* rights, largely from Java, and then states that these and 'rights resembling these' are converted into statutory rights. The precise definition of 'rights resembling these' has not been the subject of further regulation or judicial commentary.

The second argument advanced by the bureaucracy is that not having registered and obtained a formal certificate of title under the Agrarian Law means that whatever rights may have existed have been lost through inaction or abolition. This was a ground for decision in the Pluit Polder Case, which held that the land in question was land under the direct control of the state because the applicants rights were derived from the colonial *eigendom* proprietary right which had been abolished by the Agrarian Law. A variation, used unsuccessfully in the Kedung Ombo case, but apparently a common negotiating tactic in land acquisitions, is that occupiers of land who lack certificates of title cannot prove their title for formal purposes. Another variation, established by Regulation of the Minister for Agrarian Affairs No 2 of 1962 (Art 8), and applicable to many land transactions, is that transfers of ownership of *adat* lands without verification by the village head or village chief will lead to the transferee receiving a five year right of use only, after which time the land will revert to the state (Salindeho, 1988: 157). This affects most land transactions in Indonesia because verification by the village head or village chief incurs significant official and unofficial costs. Reliance is often placed instead on the traditional *tuan tanah* figure or its informal equivalents (Fitzpatrick, 1997:

195). In all these circumstances, *adat* rights that do not comply with the expensive and difficult requirements of formal law are left vulnerable to de facto expropriation without compensation, even though the Agrarian Law contains no direct statutory sanction, or formal time limit, relating to registration of converted rights (Gautama and Harsono, 1972: 92-97). This legal inconsistency illustrates the way in which the bureaucracy adopts a form of legal 'norm shopping', in which in any given circumstance the legal norm or ideology that best suits the interests of the state is chosen from a range of possible normative references.

Unlawful Occupancy

The third way in which land is appropriated without reference to the laws on appropriation arises out of the notion of unlawful occupancy. The 1960 Government Regulation on Unlawful Occupancy did not allow for the acquisition of rights through uninterrupted adverse possession. Yet this sort of possession is the traditional *adat* means of acquiring rights to land. It is widespread in Indonesia as a result of rapid rural-urban drift; the vacant nature of much speculative urban and peri-urban land; and large-scale occupation of former colonial plantation and private estate land (Gautama and Harsono, 1972: 12-16). Arguably, long-term possession in all these cases leads to acquisition of statutory rights as Art 56 of the Agrarian Law states that *adat* will continue to govern the acquisition of *hak milik* until (as yet undrafted) regulations are put into place and Art 27 provides for termination of a right to land in the event of abandonment. But in practice the state does not recognise that this form of possessory title may exist, at least in areas not subject to established *adat* authority, and long-term occupiers of another's land or state land may be evicted without provision of compensation, or reference in other ways to the laws on land acquisition (MacAndrews, 1986: 31-32). Examples abound in the Indonesian press of evictions in these circumstances (Fitzpatrick, 1997: 197-98). In some circumstances, occupiers have been evicted notwithstanding the fact that they have been paying land tax or have been in possession since before the passage of the Agrarian Law (Fitzpatrick, 1997: 198).[18]

Conclusions

Nature of Land Acquisition Law

What do these case-studies and conclusions say about the nature of land acquisition law in Indonesia?

First, the practice of unitary land acquisition law in Indonesia's pluralist environment does not have uniform legal consequences but in fact has a highly discriminatory application. Not only is compulsory acquisition far more likely where the occupiers lack registered interests in land, thereby leaving them vulnerable to arguments that they have no interest at all, but the assessment of compensation itself turns on whether the interests are registered or, if unregistered, whether they are in fact recognised by state law and practice. In its distinctions in treatment between occupiers with certificates and those without, its refusal to recognise a large number of customary or normative interests in land and its barriers to the certification of traditional land, the result of Indonesia's purportedly

---

18   See, for example, the case of the Rawasari traders reported in Jakarta Post (1994c: 3).

universalist land and land acquisition law is discrimination against poor and traditional groups in Indonesian society.

Secondly, a number of normative justifications for compulsory land acquisition exist independently of, and override, the provisions of statutory law. The Kedung Ombo and Pluit Polder Plan cases show that written laws may not be applied if they conflict with the malleable norms of development, *Pancasila* and the 'social function' of rights to land. The bureaucracy has also shown that the laws on land acquisition may be overridden where expropriation without compensation is justifiable on the basis of the state's ultimate right of control. In other words, a more important source of normative reference for the bureaucracy and the state is not written law but the ideologies of *Pancasila*, development and patrimonialism. Unfortunately, these ideologies are so malleable and so lacking in independent scrutiny and delineation by the courts that in effect they simply justify ad hoc bureaucratic hegemony over local community action.

Thirdly, grafting universal *adat* principles on to Western-style law has not succeeded in creating indigenous national law but has been used perversely by the state to justify ad hoc bureaucratic domination of land administration. In its traditional conception, for example, the notion of social function of rights to land represents such principles as the obligation of holders of land to increase the general wealth by making their land productive; the need to protect the poor from exploitative aspects of liberalism and capitalism; and the notion that 'rights' to land are constrained by the needs and traditional processes of local community groups. But, in its conception in New Order Indonesia, 'social function' simply represents the state's overarching right to acquire land for development without the need to refer to formal law on land acquisition. The best example of this phenomenon is the Kedung Ombo Review Court's use of the principle of social function to override otherwise applicable, unitary written law. A related example is the way in which the traditional principle of 'discussion and deliberation' has been distorted, in its application in formal law, to mean discussion and deliberation among government officials alone.

Fourthly, the relationship between formal state law and local practice is now so intertwined, and characterised to such an extent by the hegemony of state law and practice, that the traditional paradigm of dualism is no longer an accurate basis for analysis of Indonesian law. Dualism implies that there are two sectors, largely independent of each other which may validly be treated as separate subjects of study (Santos, 1979: 25). Yet this is an inappropriate description of a number of features of New Order Indonesia. In practical terms, the state and bureaucracy have far greater say over ordinary Indonesians' affairs than in colonial times. Village government has been bureaucratised; the army retains a significant internal security role; agricultural production is largely channelled through state-sponsored co-operatives; state education based on *Pancasila* and Bahasa Indonesia is widespread; and unitary laws, such the Agrarian Law and the land acquisition laws, have allowed state courts jurisdiction over matters formerly determined by *adat* authorities. In addition, and most significantly for an understanding of contemporary Indonesian law, traditional *adat* authority has eroded in almost all urban areas and most parts of Java (Fitzpatrick, 1997: 194-96). The nature of its replacement, whether legal vacuum, bureaucratic fiat or some sort of quasi-*adat*, is unclear. In other words, if dualism still exists in Indonesia, it is increasingly variegated, uncertain and subject to the overriding hegemony of state and bureaucratic action.

Modernism

Why, then, have Indonesia's land acquisition laws so clearly failed in their syncretist and universalist objectives? The answer, as in any case where law fails in its purpose, requires an assessment of basic theories of law and its relationship to socio-economic development (Trubek, 1972: 1). For example, the modernist, or legal centralist, view considers 'modern' law to be a necessary pre-condition of development and global integration in developing countries (Greenberg, 1980: 130). Modern law is said to consist of autonomous, purposive rules that are applied universally and uniformly by specialised agencies and supported by the coercive power of the state (Trubek, 1972: 5). Drawing on Weber's analysis of the role of rational law in the rise of Western capitalism, modernists argue that this type of system provides the transparency, consistency and predictability necessary for a modern industrial economy (Greenberg, 1980: 130). Some argue further that universalist autonomous rules are the only restraint on arbitrary state action, and therefore a pre-condition of participatory democracy and redistributive justice (Francke, 1972: 769). The corollary is that Western models of universalist law are appropriate to political and economic development in postcolonial countries.

Modernist assumptions are central to the leading models on land acquisition law in developing countries.[19] These prescribe universalist written law that allows for both compulsory and voluntary acquisition, and incorporates judicial review to ensure consistency, transparency and public acceptance.[20] They also require compensation in all cases to reduce conflict, guarantee protection of private property rights, and ensure efficient resource allocation (Kitay, 1985: 14). As has been seen, Indonesia's land acquisition laws largely comply with these strictures. However, this study has shown that in practice these purportedly universalist laws are subject to overriding state ideologies; that inclusion of judicial review has not created transparency, consistency and public acceptance; and that the universal requirement of compensation discriminates against poor and traditional groups in Indonesian society. In other words, Indonesia's land acquisition laws bear out the fundamental criticism of modernism, namely that it erroneously assumes that law and legal institutions transplanted from other contexts will have similar or, predictable, effects (Seidman & Seidman, 1994: 44-45).

Indigenous National Law

It is tempting to conclude from the failure of modernism that law reform in developing countries should work towards indigenous forms of national law. But this study also shows that creating indigenous national law based on a graft of universal customary principles and Western-style law can in fact encourage unrestrained ad hoc bureaucratic domination of people-state relations. This is a cautionary tale for those who see law and development as requiring either customised indigenous responses, or some sort of postmodern blending of global cultures.[21] If the relevant indigenous principles lack sufficient clarity, precision and accepted meaning to have the predictability required by formal law, and if the institutions to formulate, develop and implement those principles lack the requisite skills and governmental support, then the search for indigenous formal law is more likely to

---

19   For example, Kitay (1985); Casad & Montagne (1975).
20   For example, Kitay (1985: 14).
21   See Carty (1992: 1).

result in a legal limbo than a workable legal system. Indeed, it may be that attempting to incorporate indigenous customary principles into formal law is misconceived. One issue which requires further research is the extent to which, if at all, indigenous customary principles can be removed from their local social context and yet retain practical utility and meaning. Certainly, the development of English common law from Anglo-Saxon custom suggests that this process can lead to national law in the longer term but the Indonesian experience equally suggests that, where the customs in question are exceedingly diverse, and where the state's over-riding concern is economic development, then a fast-track process of distilling allegedly universal customary principles from local contexts and applying them to formal law can leave those principles bereft of any real value or meaning.

The *adat* principle of discussion and deliberation illustrates this point. Among the Karo Batak of North Sumatra, for example, this principle is embodied in a formal process of decision-making known as *runggun*. This entails a consensual process of deliberation before sub-clan authority figures (Slaats and Portier, 1986: 218-22). But because the determinations of the *runggun* procedure are ultimately guided by the dictates of an exogamous and patrilineal social structure, *runggun* has little meaning outside this local social structure (Fitzpatrick, 1997: 176). If, for example, it were applied to the matrilineal social structure of Minangkbau, or the shifting cultivators of Kalimantan and Irian Jaya, then very different determinations would result. When it is applied to a nation where a village for government purposes can consist of 26,000 thousand families, it loses any practical meaning or utility (Rajakgukguk, 1994: 623). In other words, because customary principles receive their colour and shape from their local social context the process of incorporating them into formal law is fraught with the risk of legal uncertainty and arbitrary state hegemony. Particularly in an era of rapid economic development, globalisation and legal harmonisation, countries such as Indonesia may not be able to afford to wait for the organic creation of indigenous national law.

Dependency Theory

If, then, the paradigms of modern law and indigenous national law both fail to fully elucidate the relationship between law and development in Indonesia, does 'dependency' theory provide a better explanation? Dependency theorists argue that modern Western-derived law simply perpetuates the exploitation of colonial dualism (Wallerstein, 1974). This exploitation has an international aspect, where world trading rules cause underdevelopment or distorted development in the third world (Greenberg, 1980). It also has a domestic counterpart in which inherited institutions of finance, government and law, in combination with Western-style laws of contract, commerce, land and labour, have created urban-based commercial elites that dominate economic activity and population movements in the countryside (Seidman & Seidman, 1994: 36; Santos, 1979).

Is this is a correct representation of land acquisition law in Indonesia? In large part, it seems so, because the major cause of discrimination and injustice in Indonesian land acquisition is that the Western nature of the Agrarian Law has resulted in a dysfunctional and disassociated system of land titles. While individualised titles in the cities, and those areas where *adat* authority has eroded, are readily converted into the inflexible, individualised categories of the Agrarian Law, *adat* titles – flexible, communal and embedded in local social structures – are not so susceptible to conversion, even if the process were made cheaper and more certain. The result, in combination with the notion of the state's right of control, is that in formal law many Indonesians have unrecognised or tenuous interests in land which leaves them highly vulnerable to eviction without compensation. In turn, this disassociation has allowed Indonesia's land acquisition laws to impact in an unfair and discriminatory way on poor and traditional groups.

Having said that, the nature and operation of Indonesia's land acquisition laws cannot solely be explained by dependency theory. If the Western nature of land acquisition law of creates exploitation, why have the bureaucracy and the courts found it necessary on occasions to override them through the use of state ideologies of *Pancasila* and development? The decision of the Appeal Court in the Kedung Ombo case suggests that universalist statutory requirements of compensation, discussion and deliberation and consensus can be a source of normative pressure on the state. In another reported case known as 'Pulo Mas', the High Court of Jakarta similarly held that acquisition without agreement by title-holders can be carried out under no other law than the 1961 Law on Appropriation (Abdurrahman, 1980: 375). In other words, universalist law can have positive effects in developing countries by putting pressure on the state to act in a consistent and universalist fashion – notwithstanding that it also can be overridden by other normative or ideological references. This conclusion suggests the need for a more discriminating criticism of modernism. Undoubtedly modernism is flawed by its assumption that law can easily be transplanted from other contexts. However, the problem is not simply the foreign nature of the transplanted law itself, but the existence of stronger normative references in the new environment. In other words, the error of modernism is not necessarily modernist law as such, but a failure to appreciate the limited role of law in developing countries. This apparent paradox is discussed further below.

Seidman & Seidmans' Theory

If, then, dependency theory also fails to fully explain the nature and operation of Indonesian land acquisition law, what alternative paradigms are available? Seidman and Seidman (1994: 122-25) have suggested that failure of law, or failure to obey law, in developing countries is best analysed through a number of questions. Are the rules inadequately formulated? Do the targets of the law have the opportunity, capacity and information to obey the law? Do relevant actors have an interest in enforcing the law? What are the inputs and processes of the law? What are the commonly held beliefs and norms of behaviour of the relevant actors?

Applying this process to Indonesian land acquisition law undoubtedly yields some useful suggestions. For example, the rules of land acquisition are inadequately formulated, and much more clarification is required on such issues as the meaning of *adat* principles of social function and deliberation; which *adat* rights were converted into statutory rights; how intermittent usufructuary rights may be converted; and the exact scope of the notion of state *hak ulayat*. Similarly, in terms of interest, there is a clear need to break the vicious cycle of collusion between officials and developers in Indonesian land acquisition. In particular, compensation must reflect market value so that there is no incentive to choose compulsory acquisition over direct bargain and sale. The definition of public interest must be more precise and enforced to exclude development for private commercial purposes. Mechanisms to alleviate the uncertainties of dealing with customary titles must be adopted. Finally, in terms of inputs and processes, more precision and enforcement regarding public consultation processes would increase public acceptance and decrease disputation and conflict.

While these proposals are practical and useful it is suggested that a flaw in Seidman & Seidman's approach is revealed by the last category: namely commonly held beliefs and norms of behaviour of relevant actors. Trubek and Gallanter have correctly noted that universalist law will only be universalist in practice if relevant officials in developing countries abandon loyalty to family, clan or tribe (1974: 1066). But what happens when, as in Indonesia, the primary loyalty of officialdom is to the state? Here lies a paradox: the state, the very body that promotes formal national law, can also subvert it. In other words, on its own, universalist law will not create universalist consequences because, for as long as the state is monolithic and hegemonic, officials will favour its overriding interests and ideologies to those of the provisions of formal law. Seidman & Seidman's response (1994: 170-95) to this is to recommend institutions that guarantee competitive electoral democracy, bureaucratic accountability, popular participation in on-going governmental decisions, and a civil society capable of acting as countervailing power to the bureaucracy. However, it is argued that this 'transforming institutionalist' approach fully fails to account for the limited role of law in developing countries, in particular the fact that law is but one of a number of competing normative and ideological references guiding state and bureaucratic action.[22] It suggests a law-based solution to a problem that law has a limited capacity to resolve. In any event, to suggest a law-based civil society, similar to that which has provided institutional restraint on the state in the West, is to participate in the erroneous assumption that postcolonial political development will mirror that of the West (Santos, 1979: 6-7). In sum, it is not enough to take a quasi-modernist approach of improving the precision of law and transforming the institutions that implement it. Because formal law in postcolonial countries is subject to overriding state ideologies, and therefore has a very limited capacity to effect positive institutional change, a less orthodox approach to its role and relationship to postcolonial development is required.

Anti-Hegemonic Pluralist Law

In all these circumstances, it is argued that law's primary role in developing countries should not be to achieve national unity or developmental objectives, but to counteract, to the limited extent possible, the current hegemony of state and bureaucracy. The starting point for this alternative approach should be a rejection of the orthodox paradigm of legal dualism in postcolonial countries. Dualism not only implies a search for unity; it also suggests that formal laws of the state exist in contradistinction to customary norms of the people. This is an inappropriate description of law and *adat* in contemporary Indonesia. If a paradigm of state and bureaucratic hegemony is substituted for dualism the paradox that formal law in developing countries is both instrument of hegemony and limited source of normative restraint becomes more apparent. In this paradox lies a more appropriate role for law in postcolonial countries. In particular, because universalist formal law in a pluralist normative environment is hegemonic, discriminatory and unfair, then those groups that are most subject to hegemony and discrimination should receive greater protection from formal law. In other words, if universalist laws (for example, the statutory requirements of discussion, deliberation and consensus) can

---

22 See for example Pozen (1976).

act as restraint on the state, then so even more could a pluralist law that required that unregistered customary interests in land either cannot be acquired, or can only be acquired, with special compensation for loss of traditional and spiritual links to the land.

This anti-hegemonic pluralist approach utilises the ability of formal law to act as a normative restraint on the state whilst also minimising its role as an instrument of hegemony. Undoubtedly, far more research and writing is required for its full elaboration. For example, a methodology needs to be created to identify those groups most subject to hegemonic discrimination, and suggest pluralist legal structures that would counter that hegemony. However, in its general outline, it suggests the need for greater understanding of social structures and ideologies in postcolonial countries (Greenberg, 1980); awareness of the differences in postcolonial political development to that of the West; recognition of the nature and rights of different groups in postcolonial societies (Rich, 1983); and research into the 'horizontal, decentralised' legal structures that could protect those groups (Paul & Dias, 1982). Specifically in relation to land acquisition, it suggests the need for prohibition or disincentives for appropriation of traditional land or land occupied by the poor; formal recognition of all traditional or normative rights to land including those of adverse possessors; and a system of title registration that is compatible with the fluidity and communal orientation of traditional rights (Fitzpatrick, 1997: 205-12).

Summary

This study is primarily a critique: it has shown that unitary law in Indonesia is neither universalist nor uniform and that indigenous national law cannot be created by adding *adat* principles to Western-style law. It suggests that the explanation for these failures lies not in modernist or dependency theory but in a view of law in postcolonial countries as, paradoxically, both source of state hegemony and as a limited normative restraint on the state. From this it is suggested that law reform should seek not to effect social change as such, but to protect those groups most subject to hegemonic pressures. This pluralist endeavour requires far greater research and elucidation, but in it there are glimpses of a more viable and accurate relationship between law and development in postcolonial countries.

References

Abdurrahman, 1980, *Himpunan Yurisprudensi Hukum Agraria* ('Collection of Jurisprudence on Land Law', Alumni, Bandung.

Basuki, S, 1992, 'The Concept of State as Landholder', *Indonesian Human Rights Forum*, no 3: 13.

Benda-Beckmann, von F, 1989, 'Scape-Goat and Magic Charm: Law in Development Theory and Practice', *Journal of Legal Pluralism*, no 28: 129.

Benda-Beckmann, von F and Taale, T, 1993, 'Land, Trees and Houses: Changing (Un)Certainties in Property Relationships on Ambon', Conference Paper: Northern Territory University Centre for South-East Asian Studies.

Burns, P, 1989, 'The Myth of Adat', *Journal of Legal Pluralism*, no 28: 1.

Carty, A, 1992, 'Introduction', *Law and Development*, The International Library of Essays in Law and Legal Theory: Legal Cultures 2, Dartmouth.

Casad, R and Montagne, R, 1975, *Expropriation in Central America and Panama: Processes and Procedures*, WS Hein, Buffalo.

Colchester, M, 1986, 'The Struggle for Land: Tribal Peoples in the Face of the Transmigration Programme', *Ecologist*, no 2/3: 99.

Fitzpatrick, DJ, 1997, 'Disputes and Pluralism in Modern Indonesian Land Law', *The Yale Journal of International Law*, vol 22.

Francke, TM, 1972, 'The New Development: Can American Law and Legal Institutions Help Developing Countries?', *Wisconsin Law Review*, vol 12: 767.

Gautama, S, 1992, *Himpunan Jurisprudensi Indonesia yang Penting Untuk Sehari-Hari (Landmark Decisions)*, ['Collection of Indonesian Jurisprudence of Daily Importance'], vol 1, Penerbit PT Citra Aditya Bakti, Jakarta.

Gautama, S and Harsono, B, 1972, *Survey of Indonesian Economic Law: Agrarian Law*, Padjadjaran University Law School, Bandung.

Gautama, S and Hornick, R, 1983, *An Introduction to Indonesian Law – Unity in Diversity* 4th ed, Alumni, Bandung.

Greenberg, DF, 1980, 'Law and Development in Light of Dependency Theory', *Research in Law and Sociology*, vol 3: 129.

Himawan, C, 1995, 'How Not to Intervene in a Judicial Process', *Jakarta Post*, 16 May: 3.

Hooker, MB, 1975, *Adat Law in Modern Indonesia*, Oxford University Press, Kuala Lumpur.

Jakarta Post, 1992, 14 April: 7

Jakarta Post, 1993a, 6 October: 3.

Jakarta Post, 1993b, 2 November: 2

Jakarta Post, 1994a, 12 August: 3

Jakarta Post, 1994b, 16 October: 3.

Jakarta Post, 1994c, 25 October: 3.

Jakarta Post, 1995a, 3 April: 3

Jakarta Post, 1995b, 13 April: 3

Jakarta Post, 1995c, 9 May: 3.

Jakarta Post, 1995d, 30 May: 3

Kitay, MG, 1985, *Land Acquisition in Developing Countries: Policies and Procedures of the Public Sector*, Gunn & Hain, Oelgeschlager.

KSBH & LBH, 1982, *Suara dari Borobudur*, Yogyakarta.

Lev, D, 1962, 'The Supreme Court and Adat Inheritance Law in Indonesia', *American Journal of Comparative Law*, vol 11: 205.

Leys, C, 1975, *Underdevelopment in West Africa: The Political Economy of Neo-Colonialism*, University of California Press.

Macandrews, C, 1986, *Land Policy in Modern Indonesia*, Boston, MA, USA, Oelgeschlager, Gunn & Hain in association with the Lincoln Institute of Land Policy

Parlindungan, AP, 1993, *Beberapa Masalah Dalam UUPA* ('Some Problems with the Agrarian Law'), Alumni, Bandung.

Paul, JCN, and Dias, CJ, 1982, 'State-Managed Development: A Legal Critique', *Third World Legal Studies*: 35.

Pozen, RC, 1976, *Legal Choices for State Enterprises in the Third World*, 1976, New York University Press, New York.

Rajakgukguk, E, 1994, 'Law, Land and the Natural Environment in the Kedung Ombo Greenbelt Area at the Central Javanese Village of Giliredjo', *Law and Society Review*, vol 28, no 3: 623.

Rich, RY, 1983, 'The Right to Development as an Emerging Human Right', *Virginia Journal of International Law*, vol 23: 87.

Ridhwan Indra HM, 1994, *The Power of the Indonesian Supreme Court*, CV Haji Masagung, Jakarta.

Salindeho, J, 1988, *Masalah Tanah Dalam Pembangunan,* Sinar Grafika, Jakarta.

Santos, M, 1979, *The Shared Space*, Methuen, London.

Seidman, R & Seidman, A, 1994, *State and Law in the Development Process*, St. Martin's Press, New York.

Sihombing, H, 1984, *Creating Indonesian National Civil Law Based on Adat Law*, University of Andalas, Padang.

Slaats, H and Portier, K, 1986, 'Legal Plurality and the transformation of normative concepts in the process of litigation in Karo Batak society' in Benda-Beckmann, von K, and Strijbosch, F (eds) *Anthropology of Law in the Netherlands*, Foris Publications, Dordrecht, Holland; Cinnaminson, USA

Soepomo, 1953, 'The Future of Adat Law in the Reconstruction of Indonesia' in Thayer (ed), *Southeast Asia in the Coming World*, Johns Hopkins University, Baltimore.

Ter Haar, B, 1946, *Beginselen en Stelsesl van het Adatrecht* (translated in Schiller, AA, and Hoebel, EA (eds), *Adat Law in Indonesia* 12-14 (1948), Djakarta: Bhratara)

Trubek, DM, 1972, 'Toward a Social Theory of Law: An Essay On the Study of Law and Development', *Yale Law Journal*, vol 82, no 1: 1.

Trubek, DM, and Galanter, M, 1974, 'Scholars in Self-Estrangement: Some Reflections on the Crisis in Law and Development Studies in the United States', *Wisconsin Law Review*: 1062.

Wallerstein, I, 1974, *The Modern World-System: Capitalist Agriculture and the Origins of the European World-Economy in the Sixteenth Century*, Academic Press.

6. The State and *Syariah* in Indonesia 1945-1995

MB Hooker

For Muslims, the authority of Islam is an alternative to the authority of the state, regardless of that state's particular ideological persuasion. This is as true now as it was for the Abbasids, the Ottomans, the former Soviet Union and the Imperial European powers of the 19th and 20th centuries. The issue has not subsided with the demise of imperialism. The successor states must still face and accommodate it. In the past 50 years, the relationship between the Indonesian state and Islam has changed constantly depending on the political circumstances of the time, ranging from oppression, conflict and control to an uneasy accommodation. It is a relationship that is difficult to characterise with any precision. It would be over-facile, for example, to describe any period of the relationship only in terms of conflict. Equally, accommodation, or attempts at accommodation, have not been overwhelmingly successful. Recently, however, the Indonesian state appears to have struck a more positive balance with Islam. The government has provided for the integration of *syariah*[1] into the rapidly developing state.

Essentially, the issue is authority. Islamic purists claim authority from Revelation; secular nationalists claim authority from the Constitution of the state. The ideal for some Muslim activists is the 'Islamic state'. However, this in itself is a contradiction. Authority can have only one locus. The issue is always who has the power to exercise authority, and how this power is to be divided, controlled and transferred. As Pakistan shows, Islamic jurisprudence provides no sufficient answer for the contemporary nation state. Indeed the arguments about the nature of the Islamic state in the contemporary Muslim world usually reduce themselves to little more than vague generalities supposedly founded in seventh century Muslim practice. On the other hand, proponents of an Islamic basis for the state can and do point to parts of Islamic law (for example, family law) where rather more specific provisions are available.

The forms and expressions of the nation-state, such as constitutions, legal codes, and the distribution and separation of powers have developed from European political history over the past two centuries. Although the nation-state and its components can encompass an Islamic element, overlay or colouring the impact of Islam can never be fundamental. An element of tension will always exist simply because the sources of authority are irreconcilable.

This is as true for Indonesia as any other state populated by Muslims. Islam has been an ideology of resistance, in both the former Netherlands East Indies (NEI) and the independent Republic. The history of *syariah* in Indonesia has been the

---

1   The whole corpus of Islamic jurisprudence.

struggle to attain a 'proper' place within a non- or even anti-Islamic polity. It was not until 1882 that *syariah* received minimal recognition in the NEI and even this was substantially reduced in 1937 (Hooker, 1984). The period from the 1880s to World War II was characterised by an intense debate within the official circles governing the NEI as to the place of Islam and its relation to law, in particular to *adat* law. The proponents of *adat* argued that the Indonesian Muslims were 'nominal' if not even 'heretical' Muslims. They came to this conclusion by emphasising the non-scriptural nature of Indonesian Islam, particularly in social custom including, especially, inheritance. The proponents of Islam, on the other hand, including especially Snouke Hurgronje, emphasised the local nature of Islamic forms and practices throughout the Muslim world. A non-scriptural expression of religion, they argued, did not make a Muslim into a 'nominal' Muslim.

On the other hand, the Japanese interregnum gave Islam a place in the wartime state for the first time (Benda, 1958) and since 1945, Islam (and hence *syariah*) has been a fundamental element of Indonesian political life. It is not as though the Japanese really promoted Islam, except possibly in the last few months of the war. What they did, however, was to give the religion a recognised space in national life. The nature and extent of this space has greatly varied in the past half century but its existence has never been called into question since.

The Colonial Religious Court System (1882-1989)

The colonial Religious Court System was the main legacy of the Dutch. In 1882, they promulgated the first regulation concerning the Colonial Religious Court system.[2] The law, revised in 1937, established Religious Courts in Java, Madura, Banjarmasin and associated areas of southern Borneo.

In 1957, the Indonesian Government promulgated regulations extending the system to the whole archipelago.[3] These regulations constituted the Religious Court system until the reforms of 1989 discussed below. Essentially, the function and content of this legislation was procedural. The majority of the provisions regulated the appointment of court officers and defined their functions. The substantive principles of *syariah* were not stated.[4] The structure of the Religious Courts was based directly on the secular model. They were collegiate; they had appeal systems; and they followed secular rules for describing, validating and filing judgments. It is not difficult to understand how this restricted the application of *syariah*. For example, the secular procedures left no room, or very little, for the application of the principles of classical (that is, Arabic) *fikh* (rules of law) and classical rules of evidence were totally excluded.

Syariah was formally limited in other ways. From 1937, the jurisdiction of the Religious Courts was quite severely restricted, mainly to matters of dowry, marriage and divorce.[5] Other claims for money or goods generally fell under the jurisdiction of the civil courts. The secular courts also had jurisdiction over property matters, as the Dutch considered them to be *adat* issues. The post-independent Indonesian

---

2   For details see Hooker (1984).

3   For details see Hooker (1984).

4   Until 1991.

5   See the revised *Priesteraad* Regulation, 1937, Art 10(3).

government has maintained the position that *syariah* should not be used to settle property disputes. This issue has and continues to cause substantial difficulties simply because family matters (as regulated in *syariah*) cannot be separated from land, the most important form of property in peasant communities.

The colonial principle that civil power had ultimate authority affected the jurisdiction of the Religious Courts. The dominance of the secular courts has been re-stated and reinforced in independent Indonesia. The Law on Judicial Authority of 1970 gives the *Mahkamah Agung* or Supreme Court overriding cassation[6] powers over all branches of the judicature, including the Religious Courts. Even at district court level, the Religious Courts were never granted exclusive jurisdiction. A dissatisfied party could apply to the district court for another adjudication on the case, based on either civil (that is, Dutch-derived) law or the *adat* of the area or district.

Although pre-war jurisprudence is scarce, Daniel Lev (1972) has illuminated two things about the post-independence workings of the Religious Courts important to the present discussion. First, the quite artificial limits on Religious Court jurisdiction are widely ignored. Religious Court judges use *fatwa* (a ruling on a point of law) as a way around the circumscribed jurisdiction. In the classical *fikh* the *fatwa* is rather formal. Indeed, its formal character has been a feature of Islamic legal history from the earliest times. Governments in Muslim history (for example, the Ottoman Empire) have used *fatawa* (plural version of *fatwa*) to validate purely secular or state interests. However, the Indonesian interpretation of *fatwa* has been quite different. *Fatawa* have provided judicial recognition to the reality of urban and peasant life, despite the restrictive (pre-1989) colonial-derived laws.

Similarly, the courts have innovatively interpreted *sjiqaq* (*shikak*), or 'serious disagreement' in divorce proceedings in the absence of any legislative provision. In the classical *fikh*, *shikak* is primarily a process of mediation with the *hakam* (arbitrator) and not a cause *for* divorce. According to the *fikh*, only the husband can initiate divorce. However, according to Lev's data, pre-1989 Religious Court practice was generally to hold that *shikak* gave women the option to initiate divorce proceedings in the Religious Courts. *Shikak*, then, appears to have been used, with court sanction, to allow wives to escape marriages when they have had no grounds for any classical *fikh* remedy. Again, this is a response to the limited jurisdiction given to the Religious Courts. The practice is not classically correct but is an attempt to overcome the restrictive colonial legacy.

Although the issue of jurisdiction has not been entirely resolved, the use of these methods eased the problem. However, the reforms of 1991 have rendered the rather sophistic use of *fatwa* and *shikak* unnecessary. These reforms will be discussed below. On a more general note it is worth recalling Hazairin's call in the early 1960s (1964) for the development of a distinctly Indonesian *Mazhab* (school of law).[7] In one sense, this is impossible but in terms of the reality of law – legal realism, itself a respectable position in jurisprudence – that position is by no means untenable. *Fatawa* and *shikak* certainly provide evidence of innovation and, I suggest, a careful analysis of *yurisprudensi* ('jurisprudence', in Indonesia, the

---

6   Review by the Supreme Court on the facts, law and reasoning of a law or court. The result might be a confirmation of the law or court decision or a direction to re-hear.

7   For the Sunni Muslim the schools of law are Hanafi, Hanbali, Maliki and Shafii. The latter is the school of adherence in Indonesia and Malaysia.

decisions of the court) from the Religious Courts from 1945 to 1990 would probably go a long way toward showing the appropriateness of Hazairin's position. To my knowledge, this has not been done.

The First Initiative on Islam:[8] The Ministry of Religion

In January 1946, the Republic of Indonesia established a Ministry of Religion with a range of functions. For the purposes of this chapter,[9] the most important were: the regulation of marriage and divorce, the organisation and staffing of the Religious Courts (*Pengadilan Agama*), and the supervision of religious foundations (*wakaf*). These functions were an advance on the pre-war position. Most importantly, they introduced a unitary scheme of *syariah* administration. This, for the first time, gave Islam a significant bureaucratic presence. However, the formal administrative jurisdiction of the Ministry and its various components remained rather restricted.

A good example is Law No 22 of 1946, which repealed the colonial Marriage Law of 1929 and replaced it with a new system of organisation. The law did not affect the substantive law of marriage. Indeed, the text does not mention Muslim marriage rules. The Law's structure and content owed much to the repealed legislation. Thus, the Law established Registrars (*pencatat*) for marriage, divorce, and reconciliation to register all such agreements, receive fees and issue copies of the registration to the parties. Persons entering into these contracts without registration could be fined and Registrars who failed to perform their functions properly could be fined or imprisoned. Although purely formal and procedural, the Law attempted to impose an Indonesia-wide and uniform administration for Muslim marriage for the first time. The Law applied only in Java and Madura until it was extended to the remaining territories of Indonesia in 1954 (Katz & Katz, 1975: 656-81).

According to the Law, Registrars are paid public servants under the control of the Ministry and the scope of their territorial competence is defined by the Ministry in terms of its own area arrangements. These revolve around the *Kantor Urusan Agama* (KUA), the Office of Religious Affairs, which is organised in a hierarchy descending from the Ministry in Jakarta down through provinces, sub-provinces and districts to village religious officials. Its function is to register marriages, divorces, and reconciliations, although in the early 1950s it did not claim competence to annul marriages. In the same period, it also undertook judicial functions on a wide range of subjects in those areas in which Religious Courts had not been established.

The KUA procedure for the registration of marriage, divorce or reconciliation is quite simple. The parties need only produce proof of identity and any previous unions. However, if the application is for a marriage certificate (*surat nikah*), a statement of prenuptial conditions must be provided. If the husband breaches these conditions, his wife may divorce him. The standard conditions are absence for six months, failure to maintain for three months, assault and neglect.

The Ministry's effect on the substantive private law of Muslims has been minimal. Its main functions are political – to promote religion generally and Islam in national politics particularly. Its lesser administrative function is to regulate

---

8   I deal with the 1945 Constitution and the *Pancasila* in the next section. For the moment, I take administrative/public law only.

9   The following summary is taken directly from Hooker (1984: 256ff).

marriage and divorce by insisting upon bureaucratic procedures. The Religious Courts have been left to effect necessary reforms.

Before 1965, the Directorate of Religious Justice within the Ministry heard appeals from decisions of the Religious Courts. The staff of the Directorate includes Muslim legal experts who provide advice to the Ministry and other government departments when requested. The Directorate also examines Religious Court decisions. This activity, combined with the importance of the Ministry as a centre of Muslim policy-making, directly brings substantive questions of Islamic principle into the arena of national politics.

The Directorate was formally given power to review decisions of the Religious Courts in respect of 'conditions and rules laid down by statute' by a Ministerial Decision in 1963 (Bambang Trawono, 1990). In an elucidation of this power the following passage occurs:

> Whether the implementation of the Ministerial Decision will be limited only to statutory [procedural] requirements or will involve the subject matter of the Religious Courts' decisions, largely based on *syariah* rules, will also be left to the discretion of the Head of the [Directorate of] Religious Justice. ... For in essence the application of religious justice cannot be separated from consideration of *syariah* rules and [the effort] to strengthen the application of *syariah* rules as an element in the positive law of the Republic of Indonesia based on the rule of law (Bambang Trawono, 1990: 493).

This statement comes close to suggesting that the Directorate had become a Court of Cassation in its own right. However, in 1965, the Supreme Court was specifically authorised to grant cassation in Muslim matters (see below). At the time of writing, the Directorate's review power seems to have been exercised infrequently, and with care. Data are sparse but, in the available cases, the Directorate has shown itself aware of the policy aspects of Islam and Muslim law.

One Supreme Court case involved the issue of jurisdiction (reported in Lev, 1972: 99-101). The suit involved the West Java Religious Court, the *Mahkamah Islam Tinggi* (Islamic Appellate Court) and the *Pengadilan Negeri* (District Court, the lowest court in the secular judicial system). There had apparently been procedural errors at all levels and in all jurisdictions. The Directorate intervened and quashed the Religious Court judgments. A later Religious Court came into issue with the secular court over the issue of the Directorate's powers. It was on the question of spheres of jurisdiction that an appeal was lodged with the Supreme Court.

The court declared that there was no legal basis for the Directorate's assumption of judicial or quasi-judicial powers. However, the court implicitly contradicted itself by finding that exercising judicial discretion (*kebijaksanaan*) might itself involve judicial elements. The court refused to interfere with any of the Islamic judicial issues in the suit.

The contradictions within this judgment merely reflect the contradictions within the Indonesian legal system. The status of 'Ministerial Decisions', the form of the law which established the Directorate's appellate function, has never been clear. The late President Soekarno introduced this form of executive law-making on 5 July 1959. On 5 July 1966, the MPRs,[10] or provisional People's Consultative Assembly, prohibited the further issuance of such Decrees and ordered a review of all such laws which contradicted the Constitution (Hooker, 1984: 260). Some were repealed,

---

10 *Majelis Permusyawaratan Rakyat* (*Sementara*), Indonesia's supreme sovereign body.

and others were upgraded to, or replaced by, statutes (*undang-undang*). Nothing has been done about this particular decision.

The Political Ideology Surrounding *Syariah*

The issue of Islam vis-à-vis the state is best approached through an investigation of past and current ideology. An obvious starting point is the Jakarta Charter (*Piagam Jakarta*) of June 1945. Although later deleted from the 1945 Constitution of which it briefly formed a part, it has been influential in the debate on the status of Islam in Indonesia. Regarding Islam, the Charter stated:

> [The state is based upon, among others] Belief in the One Supreme God with the obligation to carry out *syariah* for adherents of Islam.

The Jakarta Charter set an agenda, the simplicity or apparent simplicity of which can be misleading to positivist lawyers. It does not amount to the creation of a *Negara Islam* or Islamic state. While the Charter specifically refers to *syariah*, it is vague as to its exact scope and competence, leaving much room for debate over its jurisdiction. As discussed above, the rather restricted colonial view that *syariah* was to be restricted to certain elements of family law and *wakaf* has continued to the present day. Furthermore, the functions of the Ministry of Religion are conducted within a secular state that draws its legitimacy from a Constitution. Nevertheless, Islam as an ideology for state legitimacy can be advanced as an alternative or corrective to state practice. There are plenty of examples of past and present Muslim politicians achieving some successes in this way (Lubis, 1995).

The political dimensions of *syariah* are concerned less with its prescriptions and more with the varying ideologies which surround 'an' Islam, or a view or views of Islam. The *Qur'an* and *Sunna* (practice of the Prophet as reported in *Hadith* – tradition). are primary starting points for all Muslims. However, from thereon in, there is a wide divergence in opinion in many areas such as literature, history and philosophy. This fluidity and variation is as true for Islam in Indonesia as it is elsewhere. It has been customary to speak in terms of reformist, traditionalist and modernist Islam. These terms are of little direct importance to Indonesian law. It is more significant that the laws which reference *syariah* contain ideological references to *Pancasila*.

Pancasila is the well-known and often-asserted five fundamentals on which the Indonesian state is, or claims to be, based. The principles of *Pancasila* most important to *syariah* are its first, a Belief in One Supreme God, and fourth, which embodies a commitment to democracy. For Muslims, the reference to God embodies the *Qur'an* and *Sunna*; however, the mention of democracy refers to a political system for which these sources provide no direct authority. There is of course an Indonesian dimension to these comments. Democracy can be 'guided', and the words of God, which is how we know Him, can be interpreted variously and through the ages.

In short, there are no certainties for *syariah* in *Pancasila* – a constant theme in Indonesian Islam since independence. There are excellent current examples on the debate. For example, Bambang Pranowo (1990) poses a pertinent question: 'Which Islam and which *Pancasila*'? He notes that the New Order government seems to be moving toward an interpretation of *Pancasila*, which, while viewing it as an incorporated whole, also seems to be playing down its secularity. In his view, some degree of Islamic infusion into at least the first *sila* is now becoming government policy. He instances the use of the specifically Islamic term *taqwa* (obedience) in a wide variety of contexts, including the oath which government officials must take and the P4 (*Pancasila* education program) Guidelines. Pranowo gives other examples, and concludes that the New Order interpretation of *Pancasila* is 'more religious' and hence more acceptable to 'modernist' Islam. Evidence of this new trend may be the new regulation of *syariah*, which is the subject of the rest of this paper. Before turning to this issue, the Indonesian Constitution of 1945 must be briefly discussed.

The 1945 Constitution

The Indonesian Constitution is short and many of its provisions are vague and imprecise. There are brief references to the One Supreme God (in the Preamble and Art 29). The Constitution also provides the President with an overwhelming quantity and quality of executive power. This is most often exercised by way of 'Presidential Instruction' (*Instruksi Presiden*), which is not a statute (*undang-undang*) but has the force of law. Presidential law-making has had a long history in Indonesia since independence.

The President is also the final arbiter of *Pancasila*'s meaning and content. Taken together with his law-making powers, the implications for Islam are striking. The function and jurisdiction of *syariah* are almost exclusively under his control. Muslim views on the laws of the Indonesian Republic can and have been put successfully in the past (for example, the amendments to the Marriage Bill of 1974 before its enactment). The initiative, however, remains with the President. This is a long way from a *Negara Islam*.

Law No 7 of 1989 on Religious Justice [11]

This part highlights the significant features of Law No 7 of 1989. It is a formal law, as opposed to a Presidential Instruction, and was passed by the Peoples' Representative Council (DPR),[12] with the assent of the President in December 1989. It consists of a Preamble and seven chapters. There are three noteworthy features of the Preamble. First, religious justice is described as pertaining to the certainty of law, itself a basic function of Law No 14 of 1970 on Judicial Power. This reference to the general court structure of the Republic of Indonesia clearly indicates the full integration of religious justice within the national court system. Secondly, the pre-existing regulations on the Religious Courts (that is, the colonial and immediate post-colonial regulations) are described as 'disjointed' and thus not suited to a national system of judicial administration. Thirdly, the Preamble proposes a 'unified law ... in a national legal system ... based upon *Pancasila* and the Constitution of 1945'.

---

11   The translations of Law No 7 of 1989 and the Compilation were done by Bernard Quinn. I would like to acknowledge the excellence of his work and his generosity in allowing me to use it.

12   *Dewan Perwakilan Rakyat*, Indonesia's parliament.

General Provisions (Articles 1-5)

These provisions formally establish Religious Courts and a Religious Appeal Court. For our purposes, the most important is Art 5(1) which states that, 'the technical development of justice in the Religious Court shall be undertaken by the *Mahkamah Agung*'. However, responsibility is not totally within the ambit of the Law No 14 of 1970 on Judicial Power. Article 5(2) of the Law on Religious Justice states that the Minister for Religion is to be responsible for the organisation, administration and finance of the Religious Courts. According to the Law on Judicial Power and Law No 14 of 1985 on the *Mahkamah Agung* the Supreme Court has a general supervisory jurisdiction exercised through cassation (*kasasi*). This provision was intended to establish the Supreme Court as the final arbiter over matters arising from all branches of the Indonesian judicature. Until recently, it appears that the Director of Islamic Justice within the Ministry of Religion resolved appeals from the lower level Religious Courts.

The Composition of the Court (Articles 6-48)

These Articles establish the qualifications the religious judiciary must hold, and provide for the appointment and dismissal of judges and administrative staff. A judge must be a public servant and a 'graduate in *syariah* law or a graduate with a mastery of Islam'. Neither qualification is further defined. All officers of the court must take an oath in the name of Allah and swear to 'be faithful to and defend and apply the *Pancasila* as the basis and ideology of the state, [and] the Constitution of 1945'.

This part of the Law also regulates the perennial subject of jurisdiction. The Minister for Justice, the Minister for Religion, the Chief Justice, the Attorney General and, of course, the President generally share authority over the appointment, dismissal, suspension and arrest of judges. The President appoints and dismisses Religious Court judges on the advice of the Minister for Religion with the assent of the Chief Justice of the Supreme Court (Art 15(1)). If a judge acts criminally, negligently or culpably, the Chief Justice and the Minister of Religion must formulate appropriate investigation procedures (Art 19(3)) to ascertain whether they should be removed. The President can suspend a judge from office on the advice of the Minister for Religion with the assent of the Chief Justice (Art 21(1)). A judge can be arrested by the Attorney General (*Jaksa Agung*) with the assent of the Minister for Religion and the Chief Justice. The Minister for Religion has jurisdiction over these matters with regard to lower level administrative staff and generally supervises Religious Court judges (Art 12(1)). The new legislation has been in operation now for almost 10 years but we are little wiser as to how it actually works. The reported *yurisprudensi* is sparse and, when available, minimalist. The only constant feature is the use of *Pancasila* as a sort of basic reference point but this tells us almost nothing about legal reasoning.

The Powers of the Court (Articles 49-53)

Two points of particular interest emerge from this short chapter of the Law. First, Art 49 establishes the courts' jurisdiction over marriage, inheritance and *wakaf*. However, it goes on to provide (Art 49(2)) that marriages are to be 'based on or regulated by the operative marriage laws'. This is a reference to the Law No 1 of

1974 on Marriage, which, as will be discussed below, is also cited in the Compilation. The significance of this Article lies in its reference to *syariah* as defined in a state law – it is not a reference to *syariah* alone.

Secondly, Art 50 provides that where property or 'other civil matters' arise in cases of marriage, inheritance or *wakaf*, the general courts, that is, the civil courts, must first decide the issue. This provision retains the colonial practice of separating property matters from personal relationships. As mentioned above, it is practically almost impossible to split jurisdiction in family law this way (with the possible exception of *wakaf*). Therefore, this provision is often avoided using various devices (especially *fatwa*), or at worst, is inoperable.

Law on Procedure (Articles 54-91)

This chapter is divided into three parts: a general Article; investigation of marriage disputes; and fees. There are two interesting features in the general provisions. First, the Religious Courts must follow the laws of civil procedure operating in the civil courts (Art 54). The particular legislation is not actually specified. Secondly, Art 62 states that all decisions must 'contain the provisions of relevant regulations on the unwritten source of law which forms the basis of the decision'. This may be a reference to *adat* or local Muslim practice. Indonesian *yurisprudensi* must be examined to answer this question.

Regarding marriage disputes, the court's function is solely to regulate divorce. The Articles relevant to divorce in this chapter are clearly aimed at controlling the process of divorce by removing it from individual initiative and subjecting it to administrative procedure and, hence, delay. The same steps were taken in Singapore in the late 1950s (see Djamour, 1966) and slightly later in Malaysia.[13]

The first method of divorce regulated under the Law is *talak* (divorce by unilateral repudiation by the husband). Muslim countries throughout the world have been concerned to restrict the use of *talak*, and thus the negative societal consequences (single parent families) which follow from it. However, to destroy the right itself would be unacceptable because it is prescribed in the *Qur'an*. The Law therefore requires the husband to apply to the Religious Court to witness his declaration of *talak* (Art 66(1)). He must accompany his request with reasons for the divorce (Art 67(6)). The court is to investigate the matter within 30 days (Art 68(2)).

Article 70 sets out the restrictions on *talak* in more detail. The court may allow the husband's request if no reconciliation is possible, *and* there are reasons to justify the *talak*. Thus, the court has a measure of discretion when hearing *talak* cases. Furthermore, a wife may appeal the court's decision to allow the *talak* (Art 70(2)), an act entirely unknown in the classical *fikh*. The Religious Court is thus able to make *talak* virtually impossible to obtain.

The Law also empowers the wife to apply for divorce if her husband is imprisoned, has a physical impediment or they suffer an irreconcilable difference (*syigag*) (Art 73 ff). This is essentially a summary of *syariah fasah* divorce with the additional requirement that the husband pay alimony and maintenance (Art 78). Article 81(2) states that a divorce has formally occurred when, 'the decision of the

---

13   See the recent (post 1980s) legislation. A good summary is in Horowitz (1994), 233-94, 543-80.

court receives legal binding force'. Where does this leave *syariah*? An examination of recent *yurisprudensi* would indicate current practice.

Adultery is the final ground for divorce. Classical Islamic law requires that divorce by accusation of infidelity (*lian*) must always be supported by oath. According to the Law,[14] the husband's oath is in *fikh* form, but the wife's must be in accordance with the 'existing procedural law' which is rather more difficult to obtain.

Concerning fees, there is a familiar division of responsibility. They are regulated by the Minister for Religion with the *assent* of the Supreme Court. Finally, the Law repeals existing legislation on religious justice (Art 107(1)).

The Law can be interpreted in a number of ways and on a number of levels. The legislator clearly intended to unify administration within the Republic of Indonesia. Individual judges must subscribe to the unifying ideology of *Pancasila* and the 1945 Constitution. The Law also creates administrative diversity. Various Ministries have an interest in the administration of *syariah*. This may be bureaucratic diversity, or a representation of different bureaucratic interest groups. In the Indonesian context such formalism as the separation of powers can be quite misleading. Nevertheless, there does seem to be recognition that some functions are better kept or treated separately. For individual claimants, the real test of the Law will come in seeing whether the Religious Courts will consistently exercise the considerable administrative control they have over individual (*syariah*-based) initiatives in divorce.

The *Kompilasi* – Compilation of Islamic Law, 1991

This *Kompilasi* is certainly the most important document on *syariah* promulgated in modern Indonesia. The idea of enacting a 'Muslim Code' or 'Islamic Code' is not new. It has been discussed, to the writer's knowledge, for the past quarter century, and almost certainly in earlier years. The realities of post-independence Islamic politics are clearly the explanation for the considerable delay (Zifirdaus Adnan, 1990: 441-78).

The *Pancasila* surrounds the Compilation. Article 1 of the Elucidation states:

> For the people and nation of Indonesia which is founded upon the *Pancasila* and the Constitution of 1945 there is a right to the existence of a single national law which will guarantee the continuation of religious life based upon the principle of Belief in One Almighty God, while simultaneously representing the embodiment of the legal awareness of the Indonesian community and people.

The Compilation is not a Law (*undang-undang*), but 'a guide to applicable law for Judges within the jurisdiction of the Institutions of Religious Justice in solving the cases submitted to them' (Elucidation, Art 5). Articles 3 and 4 of the Compilation's explanatory memorandum or Elucidation – which like all the Elucidations that accompany laws in Indonesia should be read as part of the text of the law itself – appear to state what the 'applicable law' is, by setting out the following sources for *syariah*: (a) standard texts of the *Shafii mazhab*, (b) additional texts from other *mazhab*, (c) existing *yurisprudensi*, (d) the *fatwa* of *ulama*, and (e) 'the situation in other countries'. This is a formal acknowledgment of eclecticism for sources of

---

14   See the Elucidation to the Law No.1 of 1974 on Marriage for another and perhaps more complex example.

syariah. The Compilation claims to be a summary of these sources for use by Religious Court judges, but seems to overlook the *Kitab Kuning* or 'yellow books' which are the bases for instruction in the *Pesantren* (local Islamic schools) (Van Bruinessen, 1995).

The *Kompilasi* came into force by way of Presidential Instruction which, as mentioned, it is not an *Undang-undang*. The authority for Presidential Instructions is found in Art 4(1) of the 1945 Constitution, which merely states that the President 'holds the power of government in accordance with the Constitution'. The Presidential Instruction directed the Minister of Religion, 'to implement the Instruction'. The Minister then issued a 'Ministerial Decision' to implement the Instruction. The Decision declares its own legal basis to be Art 17 of the 1945 Constitution, which states that 'Ministers shall lead Government Departments' (Art 17(3)) and 'assist the President' (Art 17(1)).

The decision provides detailed instructions to various government agencies[15] to 'apply the Compilation in conjunction with other laws'. Neither the Ministry of Justice, nor the Supreme Court are mentioned. The Ministerial Decision refers to the Religious Ministry's own decisions on Organisational Structure.[16]

The Compilation itself consists of three books. The first concerns Marriage Law (Arts 1-70); Book II relates to Inheritance (Arts 171-214); and *Wakaf* is the subject of Book III. As will be recalled, the colonial legislation regulated these same three subjects. The provisions of the Compilation, however, are far more detailed. What follows is a discussion of some of the issues arising out of the Compilation.

The contents of Book I on Marriage[17] (which includes divorce) fall into three categories: (a) straight-out reproduction of *fikh*, though in a much simplified form; (b) *fikh* rules, the operation of which are contingent on the completion of bureaucratic procedures; and (c) rules of *fikh* as amended or controlled by the judicial process in the Religious Courts. These categories will be discussed in turn.

Several points flow from the straight-out reproduction of *fikh*.[18] First, the Compilation's rules are very simple statements – they are obviously drafted to be understood by judges with only a limited knowledge of *fikh*. The implication of this appears to be that these simple versions are themselves sufficient for adjudication on

---

15   'This Decision shall be delivered to the honourable:
   1.   The Minister for the Coordination of Public Prosperity
   2.   The Ministers of the Fifth Development Cabinet in the Public Prosperity sector
   3.   The Minister for Justice
   4.   The Secretary of State
   5.   The Secretary of the Fifth Development Cabinet
   6.   The Finance Supervisory Board in Jakarta
   7.   Secretary General, Inspector General, Directors General, the Head of the Religious Research and Development Bureau and the technical staff of the Minister for Religion
   8.   Heads of Bureaus, Directors, Inspectors, Head of the Religious Research and Development Centre and the Head of the Administrative Staff Education and Training Centre in the Department of Religion
   9.   The Heads of the Provincial Regional Offices of the Department of Religion throughout Indonesia.'

16   Presidential Decisions No 44 of 1974 and No 15 of 1984, Ministerial Decisions No 18 of 1975 and No 75 of 1984.

17   Chapters 1, 5-8, 12 and 18.

18   If we except the restriction on fragmentation in Art 189.

fikh. However, this view is subject to confirmation by post-1991 *yurisprudensi*. That there is no mention of any classical text tends to support this conclusion. Additionally, although it may be assumed that the rules are taken from the *mazhab Shafii* this is by no means conclusive. Again, post-1991 Religious Court *yurisprudensi* must be examined to answer these questions.

The rules of *fikh* which have been put into bureaucratic formulae are also interesting. Chapter XVI of the Compilation deals with termination of marriage. Articles 129-142 and 146-148 require a daunting quantity of paperwork to be completed before a marriage is validly terminated. Although these 'rules' do not affect the substance of *fikh*, they subject it to a secular process which actually *determines* its application. Without procedural compliance, the *fikh* will not be applied. Thus, a husband who wishes to declare *talak* must submit an oral and a written request to the Religious Court. If the judge permits the *talak*, then copies of the declaration are made and registered 'as evidence of the divorce'. The Law also contains provisions regulating the summons to attend court hearings. Various methods of delivery are specified, including the requirement that it be displayed on public notice boards and in newspapers. There are further examples of *fikh* being restricted by bureaucratic procedures in the compilation.

The purpose of these restrictions is to control personal status. The state has a vested interest in this because divorced wives and fatherless children throw a burden onto state agencies. Singapore realised this in the late 1950s and Malaysia some years later. Indonesia now grasps the point. The *ulama* still equivocate. On the one hand the much abused *talak* is divinely permitted; on the other, the social consequences are plain for all to see. To retain the divine permission but to formulate a bureaucratic obfuscation is a sensible response.

As to instances where the rules are amended and controlled by judicial processes, the policy of the Compilation is clearly stated early on in the text. According to Art 4, the validity of a marriage is determined by (a) *syariah*; and (b) the Law on Marriage. *Syariah* alone is insufficient. For example, the Law on Marriage regulates the age at which people may marry. A Muslim man's right to take more than one wife is likewise severely restricted. To enter into a polygamous marriage, the man must obtain permission from a Religious Court. Without judicial approval, the marriage 'shall have no legal force' (Art 56(3)). Referring to Art 5 of the Law on Marriage, the Compilation states that he must also obtain the permission of his existing wife or wives (Art 58(1)). However, a wife's refusal to grant permission is not absolute; the Religious Court may override it if the wife is barren, unable to fulfil her marital obligations, or has an incurable illness (Art 59 referring to Art 57).The husband must still show he is capable of behaving justly towards all his wives and children and ultimately this will be a matter of fact for the court.

Other provisions of the Compilation have a similar effect. For example, Chapter X of the Compilation aims to prevent any marriage forbidden by 'legislation or Islamic law'. The Religious Court has jurisdiction over the matter, but the Marriage Registration Office (Clerk), who must also be informed of the marriage, is forbidden 'to implement or aid in the implementation' of a marriage which contravenes the Law on Marriage (Arts 8, 68-69). Similarly, the Compilation sets out two methods for the termination of marriage (Chapter XVI): *talak*, *or*, a 'claim for divorce' (Art 114). The grounds for divorce are set out in Art 116. This part of the Compilation appears to aim to control *talak* and also to give the wife an avenue to initiate divorce. As discussed above, this option was a feature of the pre-Compilation administration of *syariah* through the use of *shikak*. *Talak* is controlled by way of judicial supervision. The Religious Court may refuse a request by a husband for *talak*, but the refusal is open to appeal and cassation (Art 130). A wife may submit a claim for divorce on specific grounds which include desertion for two years, lack of a harmonious domestic life, and imprisonment of the husband for five years. In addition, the court may order alimony payments and the protection of the wives' assets during the period of the divorce claim. The important conclusions is that *talak* is controlled, and, the wife has an initiative outside of and separate from *syariah*.

The remainder of Book I merely repeats *syariah* rules in simple form. The same is true for Book II (Inheritance) and Book III (*wakaf*). In these two areas, the Compilation is concerned with administrative procedures, and there are no substantive variations on the *fikh* rules.

From the above discussion, it is clear that 'pure' *syariah* is restricted to inheritance and *wakaf* and that in marriage and divorce it is accommodated to secular legislation and strictly controlled by the Religious Courts. Theoretically, the husband's rights in *talak* are preserved. However, a wife now has a right to divorce, though on limited grounds outside the *fikh*. The important change is that the husband's consent does not seem to be necessary: the wife's claim is by way of judicial process (*fasah*). In this respect, the Compilation has not gone so far towards secularisation as some of the Malaysian legislation where 'irretrievable breakdown' actually appears as a cause for divorce. This is, or appears to be, subsumed under *fasah* in Indonesia.

Conclusion

Several conclusions can be drawn. The first is that the recent legislation is a considerable advance over the colonial and post-colonial position. The Religious Courts are now fully a part of the national legal system with a defined and (comparatively) extensive jurisdiction. The Law on Religious Justice has certainly repaired pre-1989 internal inconsistencies. However, responsibility for various aspects of Religious Justice administration remains divided between a number of Ministries. The Supreme Court has a rather restricted function in cassation. The Ministry of Religion is the prime source of authority, and given that political power resides in the Indonesian bureaucracy – underpinned by the executive nature of the 1945 Constitution – this is not likely to change in the future. The *Negara Hukum* (state based on law) particularly where *syariah* is involved, remains problematic.

Secondly, and following from the recognition of executive control – which is ultimately located in the office of the President – one has always to consider the ideology of the executive government. For Indonesian Islam it is the *Pancasila*, in particular the first principle, 'Belief in One God'. While this is somewhat acceptable to Muslims it also carries the strong implication of secularism. The authority for *Pancasila* and its definition is in government hands. By contrast to *syariah*, its derivation is not direct from Revelation.

The practical expression of accommodation is best illustrated by the Compilation. It has been approved by the *ulama*, but ultimate approval for its implementation comes from the authority of the President in the name of *Pancasila*. Thus, we have the authority of those learned in *syariah*; the authority of the President, that is, the secular state; and the ideological authority of *Pancasila*. It is tempting to rank these authorities but I think that would be a mistake. It is probably more sensible to take them as interdependent. *Syariah* is part of the state process and, with the ebb and flow of the political process, the balance of authority will also vary.

Thirdly, we do not know how these laws are being applied. This is most likely to be found in the *yurisprudensi* of the Religious Courts. There are pre-1989 collections published; however, it appears that no detailed analysis has been done. Post-1991 *yurisprudensi* is likely to be even more interesting.

Finally, the system of religious justice in Indonesia is now, formally speaking, on a level comparable to Singapore, Malaysia and (on paper at least) the Philippines. This is worth remembering because with the increased movement of people within South-East Asia, the issue of foreign judgment recognition is likely to arise sooner rather than later. This will be a further test for the reformed religious justice system of Indonesia.

References

Benda, Harry, 1958, *The Crescent and the Rising Sun*, W van Hoeve, The Hague.

Djamour, J, 1966, *The Muslim Matrimonial Court in Singapore*, Athlone Press, London.

Hazairin, 1964, *Hukum Kewarisan...*, Tintamas, Djakarta.

Hooker, MB, 1984, *Islamic Law in South-East Asia*, OUP, Kuala Lumpur.

Horowitz, DL, 1994, 'The *Qur'an* and the Common Law', *American Journal of Comparative Law*, vol 42: 233, 545.

Katz, June and Katz, Ronald, 1975, 'The New Indonesian Marriage Law: A Mirror of Indonesia's Political, Cultural, and Legal System', *American Journal of Comparative Law*, vol 23: 653.

Lev, Daniel, 1972, *Islamic Courts in Indonesia*, University of California Press, Berkeley.

Nur Ahmad Fadhil Lubis, 1995, 'Institutionalization and the Unification of Agama courts under the New Order', *Studia Islamika*, vol 2: 1-51.

Prawono, Bambang, M, 1990, 'Which Islam and which *Pancasila*' in Budiman, Arief (ed), *State and Civil Society in Indonesia*, Monash Papers on Southeast Asia, No 22: 479-502.

Van Bruinessen, M, 1995, *Kitab Kuning*, Penerbit Mizan, Bandung.

Zifirdaus Adnan, 1990, 'Islamic Religion' in Budiman, Arief (ed), *State and Civil Society in Indonesia*, Monash Papers on Southeast Asia, No 22: 441-78.

PART III: TRADITION AND MODERNITY – SEXUALITY, MARRIAGE AND THE LAW

7. Between Crime and Custom: Extra-Marital Sex in Modern Indonesian Law [1]

Sebastiaan Pompe

In 1992 the Indonesian weekly *Tempo* (1992) reported the case of an unmarried young man who was having an affair with an unmarried girl. They saw each other regularly and, as healthy young persons are prone to do, showed each other their affection in the form of regular sexual intercourse. The parents, of course, did not know about this relationship. One fine morning, however, disaster struck as a love-bite (*cupang*) was discovered on the young lady's neck. Her parents, who evidently belonged to a different generation in both biological condition and mental outlook, were deeply shocked. They brought a charge against the young man at the Public Prosecutor's Office, which initiated legal proceedings. The young man was subsequently sentenced to three months' imprisonment.

This case is by no means unique in Indonesia. In fact, the general press and legal journals have recently begun reporting cases based on comparable facts, which often make good if somewhat tragic reading, with increasing frequency. Such cases touch upon an important legal issue in Indonesia, namely the relationship between the law of the state on the one hand, and normative systems and ideas outside state law on the other. As will become apparent, Indonesian law provides few grounds for conviction in cases like the above one, so that the question arises by what route judges reach their decisions, and what impels them to follow theses routes. This chapter will give a brief outline of the relevant issues with reference to a number of recent related cases.

Something should first be said about the general legislative background. It may be recalled that already in colonial times the Netherlands Indies Criminal Code applied to the entire territory of the Netherlands Indies and, at least in principle, to all its inhabitants, regardless of colour or creed.[2] Admittedly, Indonesian indigenous

---

1 The author was able to draw on a useful academic essay on the Balinese perspectives on this issue by Bpk E Rusdi. The author is also grateful to his female respondents for their contributions towards a more profound appreciation of some of the issues. Of course all its flaws, being partly faults of temperament, are wholly the author's responsibility.

2 The systematisation of colonial criminal law did not start with the Criminal Code, but can be traced back through the transitional penal provisions of 1848 to the Batavian Statutes of 1642. Finally, the 1872 Criminal Code for the indigenous population was a copy, with a few exceptions, of the 1866 Criminal Code for Europeans. See generally Jonkers (1946: 2).

law (*adat*) was not wholly excluded from the criminal law, but it had an essentially residual function. The plurality in the administration of justice and the distinction between directly and indirectly governed territories ensured that *adat* law remained a source for criminal law as administered by indigenous courts in the directly and indirectly governed territories (*inheemsche rechtspraak* and *zelfbestuurs-rechtspraak*). Nevertheless, the Criminal Code was declared applicable in part even in these jurisdictional systems.[3]

As we know, the colonial diversity was abandoned after Indonesian independence. The effect of this development on criminal law has been succinctly summarised elsewhere (Territoriale, 1953). The relevant colonial distinctions were abolished and criminal jurisdiction generally was transferred to a single court, the *Pengadilan Negeri*.[4] This development strengthened the position of the state vis-à-vis local communities in a much more structured and emphatic way than had been the case during colonial times. The autonomous courts had their roots in the local communities and derived their legitimacy from them rather than from the central state. The *Pengadilan Negeri*, by contrast, was a state court and served first and foremost as an instrument of state law and state policies. These organisational changes hence confirmed the superior position of the state and of state law vis-à-vis the local communities and their normative systems and values.

It is hardly surprising to see in this context that the role of state law was strengthened at the expense of local *adat*. Indeed, *adat*, which had already been residual in colonial times, was all but abolished as a source for criminal law in the independent state. The relevant legislation, Emergency Law No 1 of 1951, gives precedence to the colonial Criminal Code in an unequivocal manner, and only contains a few extra articles to cover the old *adat* laws. These articles have a transitional and residual character, and their inclusion is quite clearly meant only as a stop-gap measure pending the then generally expected inevitable decline and eventual elimination of *adat* from substantive criminal law.

The 1951 law has remained in force to the present day, and has never been supplanted or supplemented with additional legislation. Its Articles pertaining to *adat* can be briefly summarised as follows.[5] First, an act which is criminal according to both *adat* and the Criminal Code must be punished according to the Criminal Code. Secondly, an act which is criminal according to *adat* but not according to the Criminal Code must be punished according to *adat*, unless the judge considers such punishment to be incompatible with modern views. In the latter case, or in cases in which the *adat* punishment is ignored, a substitute punishment of at most three months' imprisonment (or a Rp 500 fine) may be imposed. If the *adat* punishment is more severe than a three-month prison term, a prison sentence of up to 10 years may be imposed by the judge. Evidently, although this law does give *adat* a function in the criminal law, the Criminal Code remains the prime point of reference, and as a result the application of *adat* is even more restricted.

Against this background, it is all the more remarkable that, rather than withering away, this small legislative seedling has blossomed beyond all expectations, as the judiciary is drawing *adat* more and more into the sphere of state criminal law. We shall see below how this has come about.

---

3   *Ordonnantie op de Inheemse Rechtspraak S. 1932-80; Zelfbestuursregelen* 1938.
4   Emergency Law No 1 of 1951.
5   For greater details, see Lemaire (1952: 260-02); Han Bing Siong (1961: 56).

Adat as an Extension of Criminal Liability

In March 1990 the *Mahkamah Agung*, or Supreme Court, delivered a judgment which firmly established its views on the extension of criminal liability beyond the Criminal Code.[6] The facts of this case are astonishingly commonplace: a man seduced a woman with the promise to marry her. The woman became pregnant, whereupon the man reneged on his promise.

Cases based on similar facts have surfaced a number of times in Indonesian reports. The accounts invariably mention the embarrassment which the events have caused the woman and her relatives. Whilst in this particular case a pregnancy was involved this does not appear to be an essential feature: in some of the earlier cases there was no question of pregnancy at all. In one case,[7] criminal liability was established on the mere basis of the following innocuous facts. A boy had driven through the Lombok countryside with a woman on the back of his motor cycle, whom he had dropped off at the house of a particular village head to await his return to marry her. In the event, he did not turn up at the appointed time; for the simple reason that, as it turned out, he was already married. Whilst he may have stolen a kiss or two from the girl, it was accepted by the court that sexual intercourse had not taken place with her. All the same, the boy found himself thrown in prison for two months. It should be noted that this is rather exceptional and that all the other cases support the supposition that sexual intercourse had taken place.

The Supreme Court case and its precedents indicate the Public Prosecutor's Office considers these facts to provide sufficient grounds on which to prosecute. In this case, the prosecutor based his accusation on claims of violation of both the Criminal Code and *adat*. His appeal to the Criminal Code has a history in Indonesian law. In the not too distant past, Indonesian courts have acknowledged criminal liability on the basis of the Criminal Code in comparable cases, notwithstanding the fact that the Code does not explicitly provide for these cases. The reasoning behind this was that criminal liability could be established in these cases on the basis of the theft under Art 378 of the Criminal Code. According to the interpretation of the Article in these cases, the man had 'stolen' the honour of the lady under false pretences. It is generally believed that one of the first persons to have advanced this argument was the well-known Supreme Court judge Bismar Siregar. For this reason the specific line of reasoning will hereafter be referred to as the 'Siregar argument'. It should be noted here that the theft article provides for stiff penalties. Siregar followed his line of reasoning through to the logical conclusion and made no bones about imposing the same stiff penalties as are provided for in Art 378. Thus, while still President of the Medan Court of Appeal, he applied this logic to sentence a person to three years' imprisonment.[8] The facts in the Medan case were identical to those in the 1990 Supreme Court case referred to above.

The Siregar argument has been followed in numerous lower court decisions throughout the country.[9] And, indeed, in the 1990 Supreme Court case, the Public Prosecutor based his charge on the Siregar argument.

---

6   *Mahkamah Agung* Decision No 61.K/Pid/1988, dated 15 March 1990.

7   Mataram *Pengadilan Negeri*, Decision dated 23 March 1998, cited in *Varia Peradilan* (1988).

8   Medan *Pengadilan Tinggi* Decision No 144/Pid./1983/PT Medan (no date), cited in *Varia Peradilan* (1986).

9   See, for example, Jember *Pengadilan Negeri* Decision No 198/B/1984, dated 2 March 1985; East Java *Pengadilan Negeri* Decision No 97/Pid/1985, dated 18 May 1985.

The 1990 Supreme Court case is noteworthy because it confirms a consistent line of reasoning by the court, which dismisses the Siregar argument and emphatically states that the Criminal Code does not provide for cases such as these. This is based on the argument that 'honour' is not an object (*zaak/benda*) in the sense of the relevant theft article, and that as a result one cannot speak of 'theft' here.[10]

At the same time, the 1990 Supreme Court decision confirms another line of reasoning, which as a result is becoming more and more firmly rooted in Indonesian law. It accepted the Public Prosecutor's claim that this was a case of adultery (referred to as *zina*) within the *adat* law sense; and that it was possible to convict on the basis of Emergency Law No 1 of 1951. Consequently, the man was sentenced to five months' imprisonment.

In this case, as in its precedents, the Supreme Court declared the defendant guilty because *adat* law, not the Criminal Code, had been violated, particularly where men had reneged on promises of marriage. Thus, in one of the cases referred to above,[11] the Supreme Court dismissed the Siregar argument but still found the defendant guilty of an infraction of Balinese *adat* and sentenced him to two month's imprisonment, to mention just one example.

Adat as a Limitation of Criminal Liability

In the previous cases, an extension of criminal liability beyond the limits of the Criminal Code was at issue. In this context another case should be mentioned, which to my knowledge constitutes a relative novelty insofar as the fact that the case had been tried by an *adat* tribunal was accepted as sufficient reason not to prosecute in a state court – that is, it served as a full defence.[12]

The case concerned a woman who was raped while asleep – a feat which is somehow beyond my personal comprehension but which was accepted for a fact by the court. Subsequent to the event, the man was apprehended by the local community and punished in accordance with *adat*. This punishment involved the gift of a cow and a piece of cloth by the man to the victim. Throughout the trial, the man's defence was based not upon a denial of the facts but upon the *ne bis in idem* principle. It was argued that to punish him according to the law of the state would have meant in effect punishing him a second time for the same offence, while it is a basic criminal law tenet that no one may be punished twice for the same offence.

The Public Prosecutor did not accept this argument. He took the traditional view that in criminal cases the state has a monopoly on the prosecution, trial and punishment of offenders. So he decided to take the case to court, basing his claim upon Arts 285 and 281 of the Criminal Code (rape and committing an offence against public morals), as well as on Emergency Law No 1 of 1951.

Interestingly enough, the courts at all levels decided that the claim as based on the relevant articles of the Criminal Code should be dismissed. The judges felt that

---

10   For precedents, see *Mahkamah Agung* Decision No 854.K/Pid/1983, dated 30 October 1984, cited in *Varia Peradilan* (1987).

11   *Mahkamah Agung* Decision No 854.K/Pid/1983, dated 30 October 1984, cited in *Varia Peradilan* (1987).

12   *Mahkamah Agung* Decision No 1644.K/Pid/1988, dated 15 May 1991, cited in *Varia Peradilan* (1991).

there was no question of violence being used, since the woman had been asleep; and whilst no offence could possibly have been committed against public morals as the act had taken place in private. The judges apparently decided that the term 'with the use of force' (*dengan kekerasaan/met geweld*) in Art 285 literally refers to the use of physical force. However, it should be pointed out that in colonial times the meaning of the term had been extended to include acts committed against the will of the subject.[13] Further, Art 286 appears to fully cover the case in question, since the meaning of the term 'unconsciousness' (*bewusteloosheid*) used here also applies to the state of normal sleep.[14]

The Criminal Code having been dismissed, however, the judges then turned to consider the *adat* rules. The judges of the first two lower-level courts had no difficulty in pronouncing the defendant guilty. They gave little or no consideration to the fact that he had already been punished according to *adat* law.

In this case it was the Supreme Court which did accept the defence plea. The entire case was declared inadmissible by this court and the defendant was acquitted.

A Brief Comment

The Emergency Law and the two Supreme Court cases discussed above raise a number of interesting questions about the role of *adat* within the Indonesian criminal law system. It is clear, of course, that in leaving open the possibility of criminal liability on the basis of *adat*, the Emergency Law continued a system that was already in existence in colonial times, be it in a much diluted form. Nevertheless, the conditions under which this system operates have changed dramatically over the past 50 years, as Indonesian society experienced formidable changes. The absence of comprehensive documentation and research reports on Indonesian normative systems outside the state law makes it difficult to generalise. Nevertheless, it is beyond any doubt that the significance and role of *adat* law within Indonesian society at present are much less clear than they were before independence.

In the next section I will consider these questions in general terms. I will not deal with the specifics of the Indonesian situation, which, though interesting in themselves, have limited relevance outside that country.[15] These general questions refer to how it is established what is *adat*, what the courts have done with *adat* in the context of legal reform, and to what problems the use of *adat* is giving rise in criminal justice.

---

13 *Landraad Sambas* 14 April 1913.

14 *Hoog Militair Gerechtshof*, 18 January 1935, *Indisch Tijdschrift van het Recht*, vol 141: 529.

15 One might, for example, query the substantive and geographical ambit of Emergency Law No 1 of 1951. 'Substantive ambit' relates to the question of whether exclusively only *adat* may constitute an extra-statutory basis for criminal liability, as suggested by the explicit references to '*adat*, or whether other normative systems such as religious laws are also included here. The frequent references of the courts to *zina* (adultery) make this question particularly relevant. 'Geographical ambit' refers to the geographical areas in which the law applies: are they only those areas in which the original colonial jurisdiction which this law was intended to supplant was in force, or the whole of the territory of Indonesia? It may be pointed out in this connection that the relevant articles of the Emergency Law specify that it applies to persons who until 1951 were subject to the jurisdiction of indigenous courts in indirectly governed territories (*zelfbestuursrechtspraak*) and to indigenous jurisdiction in directly governed territories (*inheemsche rechtspraak*). Quite a few categories did not come under the jurisdiction of either, however, and it is not entirely clear whether or not they have subsequently become subject to the Emergency Law.

The Determination of *Adat* by the Courts [16]

Indonesian legislation, court decisions and publications all refer to *adat* with a matter-of-factness that suggest that the meaning of the concept is beyond contention. Nothing could be further from the truth, however. Like 'custom', *adat* is marked by a number of fundamental uncertainties that preclude a facile application.

There appear to be no commonly accepted general methods and instruments by which an Indonesian court can establish the existence and precise content of a particular *adat* rule by. The reports of cases lack specific information on how court decisions as regards *adat* are arrived at. This presents considerable practical problems, of course. Very little research has been conducted on *adat* in Indonesia since independence, and the courts have no up-to-date written sources to rely on. Courts may presumably call witnesses to verify a particular *adat* rule, but this procedure is fraught with difficulties. It is seldom possible for a court to find an unprejudiced witness in a community which has been disturbed by a serious crime. Moreover, one may ask on the basis of what authority members of a particular community can claim the existence of specific *adat* rules. The members of a community are usually all too apt to assert that certain rules exist if their personal sense of justice has been injured, and such rules may be altogether different from shared normative rules.

Under these circumstances courts are having serious problems verifying the existence and content of a particular *adat* rule. These difficulties are exemplified by a series of Balinese cases decided by the Supreme Court on the basis of *adat* as laid down in an old Balinese code of law, the *Adi Agama*.[17] In these cases, the Supreme Court has invariably asserted in general terms that the Balinese code specifies that if a man induces a woman to have sexual intercourse with him by making false promises of marriage, he is liable to punishment.

It is not apparent from these cases whether the code in question still finds general acceptance within the relevant community. Surely the latter should be a relevant consideration in establishing whether a particular *adat* rule is genuine? Field reports published subsequent to the enactment of this Balinese law code suggest that it may have fallen into disuse with respect to the relevant issue. Korn (1932: 446, 478), whose authority is unquestioned, reports that it was already customary in Bali in his days for prospective marriage partners to live together as though they were married. This at least suggests that premarital sexual intercourse itself was not punishable (though leaving a woman pregnant was).

Moreover, as is pointed out by I Ketut Artadi (1980: 187-88), the relevant article of the *Adi Agama* itself is not as unequivocal as the court would have us believe. According to some sources, the article mentions sexual intercourse. Others

---

16 A number of authors have studied the way in which *adat* is applied in state courts. Among them, K von Benda-Beckmann deserves special mention, although it is impossible to do her publications justice in this chapter which is aimed primarily pointing out some recent developments in the criminal law sphere which largely fall outside the scope of her writings. Nevertheless, it can be noted that the author's findings fully support her ideas that judges do not in fact apply the *adat* as it actually exists in the field. However, whilst her critical remarks were primarily aimed at demonstrating how state law and state procedures mould *adat*, this chapter purports to demonstrate that there are underlying conceptions of state and religious morality, the reflection of which shapes the way in which *adat* is used by the judiciary.

17 See, for example, *Mahkamah Agung* Decision No 854.K/Pid/1983, dated 30 October 1984 and *Mahkamah Agung* Decision No 195.K/Kr/1978, dated 8 October 1978.

say it refers simply to the existence of a romantic relationship. Yet others assert that it only applies to partners who are already married (hence only to cases of adultery). Others again claim that it also applies to unmarried persons. Finally, there is disagreement about whether the rule applies to specific categories of individuals, such as widowers.

Another example of uncertainty about the authenticity and content of an individual *adat* rule is furnished by the Supreme Court cases in which reference is made to *zina*. In a case from Central Sulawesi, which may be taken as an illustration, the Supreme Court is found to have stated emphatically that, according to local *adat*, it is forbidden for men to entice women by means of false promises of marriage to have sexual intercourse with them.[18] This may be so, but from the published sources the existence of this rule is not so evident. Historical studies on *adat* in the 1920s reveal that in certain parts of Central Sulawesi not even extramarital pregnancy was punishable, let alone extra-marital sexual intercourse (Pandecten, 1926: 232). There is no published evidence that *adat* has changed since then, though undoubtedly it must have. Even so, it has recently been argued in Indonesia itself that the *adat* of different regions still allows at least some form of institutionalised pre- or extra-marital sexual relations.[19]

These cases raise serious questions about how Indonesian courts establish the authenticity and content of *adat* rules. It seems to be factually incorrect to assert simply that *adat* without exception or qualification disallows extra- or pre-marital sex, as the courts have steadfastly done in all the cases cited. The reason for this could be provided by the difficulties of ascertaining what is *adat*. Nevertheless, it would seem that other factors are responsible for this approach.

Adat as Judicial Projection and Instrument of Reform

The above cases support the idea that judges, rather than finding out what the relevant *adat* rule actually says, tend to project their own ideas of what it is, or even, should be, into their interpretation and application of it. In fact, in the past judges have referred explicitly to their 'own experience' and 'own research' as a reason for incorporating rules of *adat* in the civil law (Lev, 1962: 215). The outcome of this 'experience' and 'research' has sometimes deviated in spectacular ways from what the relevant *adat* rule was commonly believed to say. In fact, it is now commonly accepted that the *adat* crystallised from the 'experiences' and 'research' of the courts was totally different from the normative systems that applied in practice, and rather reflected the ideas prevailing among the state judiciary at the time. By pretending to be merely applying *adat*, the courts both obscured and legitimised legal reform. Nothing could be further removed from the normative rules applying in the field.

I would submit that this is actually the reason for the recent surge in criminal cases purportedly on the basis of *adat*: it is an outcome of a desire of judges to reform society rather than apply existing rules. Their shared objective is to make prosecution possible in cases involving extra-marital sexual relations. As is pointed

---

18   *Mahkamah Agung* Decision No 61.K/Pid/1988, dated 15 March 1990.

19   It was argued, for example, in the Indonesian legal and news journal *Forum Keadilan* (1993) that the *adat* of various regions, such as Mentawai, Minahasa and Bali, allows pre- or extra-marital sexual relations, and indeed, sometimes even encourages them, as in the case of Bakupiara in Manado.

out somewhat obliquely by Sobandi (1992: 139), Indonesian courts seem to be determined to fight the social reality of extra-marital sexual relations, and, more in particular, the practice of men inducing women by means of a false promise of marriage to have sexual intercourse with them. *Adat* is the instrument, the legitimation and the pretext in the effectuation of this category of judicial reform, in much the same way as it has been in the reform of the inheritance law in the past. It is significant in this regard that, as soon as legislation does offer a means of dealing with cases involving extra-marital sexual relations, references to *adat* are invariably omitted.[20]

In fact, imminent legislation supports and legitimises this kind of activity on the part of the judiciary in the field of criminal law. The current draft Criminal Code decrees, rather spectacularly, that the fundamental principle that no one shall be liable to criminal prosecution except by legal process shall not apply to *adat* offences (Art 1(4)). This is tending to stimulate rather than discourage continued judicial references to *adat*, genuine or projected. Moreover, this draft will make all sexual relations out of wedlock punishable with imprisonment to a maximum of five years (Forum Keadilan, 1993). This is supporting the social reform drive of the courts, which may in fact be anticipating this law rather than reflecting *adat*. Libidinous field workers, be warned.

It appears, then, that judges are not applying rules as prevailing in the field but are rather projecting their own ideas of what the rules in the field should be, and thus reforming the law. This judicial program of social reform may be partially induced by the anticipated legislative reforms but its real causes are deeper. In their campaign against extra-marital sexual relations, judges are manifesting themselves as agents of the state. Not merely enforcing state rules, they are also purveying norms of state morality – which may themselves be imbued with the rather prudish ideas of religious morality. These norms of state morality, most evident perhaps in the Marriage Regulations for Civil Servants,[21] are centred around the ideal of the harmonious family: a monogamous marriage for life – with some latitude for religious intermarriage – with a maximum of two children. Whilst these norms may in themselves be quite acceptable, they may easily evolve into instruments of intolerance. For all its references to *adat* and protestations that it is only applying the living law as generally accepted in Indonesian society, the Indonesian judiciary appears to be actually repressing *adat*. This is bound ultimately to widen the gap between the state and local communities, between the administration and the citizens.

The Defendant and the State

Of course, the fact that *adat* is being distorted by the courts does not in itself signify that the projected legal reform, whereby extra-marital sexual relations will be banned, is a bad one. This is a matter for Indonesian society to decide. Nevertheless, there are some fundamental problems attaching to criminal liability on the basis of *adat* rules, real or projected. These problems related to the lack of specificity of these rules.

---

20 See *Mahkamah Agung* Decision No 420.K/Pid/1988, dated 28 March 1988, cited in *Varia Peradilan* (1988) and *Mahkamah Agung* Decision No 1330/K/Pid/1986, dated 17 November 1986, cited in *Varia Peradilan* (1986), involving military personnel and minors.

21 Government Regulation No 45 of 1990.

The first problem is that the extension of criminal liability undermines the rights of the defendant. Contrary to the Criminal Code, *adat* rules – at least in our Western view, which may, of course, be shared by Indonesians – are generally formulated with insufficient definiteness and accuracy to give the defendant adequate opportunities to prove his innocence or provide evidence mitigating his guilt. There has been no attempt in any of the cases reported to examine and analyse the relevant *adat* rule and to establish whether the conditions specified by it have been fulfilled. This may be a typically Western approach, but judges do adopt this approach when applying the Criminal code or when examining evidence or passing judgment.

The vagueness of *adat* rules is helping prosecutors, judges, and local communities to bring particular acts under the broad umbrella of *adat* and, indeed, to tailor *adat* to their needs. Conversely, defendants are at a serious disadvantage because they do no know what precisely to defend themselves against. This may well contribute to inconsistencies in the mode of punishment. This is exemplified by all the cases discussed above. Indeed, whilst sexual intercourse seems to be the common denominator in all these cases, in one of the examples described here a boy was sentenced to prison by the court even though it had been accepted that no sexual intercourse had taken place.[22]

The vagueness of *adat* as interpreted by the courts is helping to bring very different cases within its ambit. Thus, the weekly *Tempo* (1990) reported that a married Achenese had been accused of having sexual intercourse with a woman to whom he was not married, who had become pregnant. The man had been dragged before an informal village *adat* tribunal, which condemned him to be ostracised for having violated an *adat* rule allegedly going back to the time of Iskandar Muda. The 'love-bite' case of two years later cited in the introduction to this article ended in a conviction with reference to the same Iskandar Muda *adat* rule, even though the facts were quite different. Here, both parties were unmarried and the girl did not become pregnant. This did not prevent the boy being dragged before a state court and condemned to three months' imprisonment. In neither case was the *adat* rule actually specified but it must be exceedingly broadly interpreted if such diverse facts can be brought within its ambit. It is not clear, furthermore, whether such differences in the mode of adjudication and the nature of punishments are desirable.

The second problem is that the restriction of the rules on criminal liability in its present form is limiting the rights of defendants, victims and the state. In a case mentioned above, *adat* was accepted as a full defence argument. It will be recalled that the court argued that if a case has been settled according to *adat*, the state courts no longer have jurisdiction. This means that if someone has been raped or murdered, for instance, and the injured party or his relatives have been bought off – as is the custom in certain parts of Indonesia – the Public Prosecutor may not bring the case before a court. There can be no doubt that in some instances such settlements are effected to the satisfaction of all parties involved. Indeed, some cases are solved more satisfactorily this way than the law of the state could ever do. But such settlements may also be effected under duress, with either the defendant or the victim being put under pressure.

As far as the state is concerned, there can be little doubt that its interests are negatively affected if *adat* is accepted as a full defence argument. The *ne bis in idem* principle involves that the court must declare the prosecution's case inadmissible

---

22   Mataram *Pengadilan Negeri* 23 March 1998, cited in *Varia Peradilan* (1988).

and acquit the defendant unconditionally. The court may not accept the *ne bis in idem* principle as a ground for commuting sentences (*strafverminderings* or *strafuitsluitingsgrond*). The Public Prosecutor's inability to prosecute (whether according to the Criminal Code or according to *adat*) for crimes which have already been punished under *adat* law. This undermines the state's monopoly of the enforcement of the criminal law, as it recognises the existence of a legal system beside that of the state. This assuredly is not in the interests of the state.

Finally, one may question the decision to admit *adat* as a full defence ground for technical reasons. The *ne bis in idem* rule is found in Art 76 of the Criminal Code. This article prescribes that no one can be prosecuted for an offence on which a judge has already pronounced judgment and the possibilities of appeal for which have been exhausted. Since the cases in question have not been decided by a judge, this Article strictly speaking does not apply here.

Conclusion

Indonesian society is subject to rapid change. There has been little systematic, and certainly no comprehensive, research on criminal *adat* law in the territory of Indonesia over the past decades. Neither the role nor the meaning of the concept of *adat* in modern Indonesia is exactly unequivocal. Under these circumstances, *adat* should be admitted in the criminal law system with due circumspection. On the evidence of the cases discussed here, the conclusion seems warranted that the relevant legislation requires further specification and that *adat* must be more carefully defined if the rights of the state, defendants and victims are not to be damaged by this development. It would appear, moreover, that the courts are applying *adat* not in the sense of a living law as generally accepted by society but as a construct essentially projected on the basis of state conceptions of morality. Seen in this light, references to *adat* in Indonesian criminal law may widen rather than close the gap between the state and its citizens.

References

Artadi, I Ketut, 1980, *Hukum Adat Bali dengan Aneka Masalahnya Dilengkapi Yurisprudensi*, Setia Kawan, Denpasar.

Benda-Beckmann-Drooglever Fortuijn, CE Von, 1984, *The Broken Stairways to Consensus: Village Justice and State Courts in Minangkabau*, ICG Printing, Dordrecht.

Forum Keadilan, 1993, 'Forum Utama', 21 January.

Han Bing Siong, 1961, *An Outline of the Recent History of Indonesian Criminal Law*, Nijhoff, 'Article-Gravenhage.

Jonkers, JE, 1964, *Handboek van het Nederlandsch-Indische Strafrecht*, Brill, Leiden.

Korn, VE, 1932, *Het Adatrecht van Bali*, Naeff, 'Article-Gravenhage.

Lemaire, WLG, 1952, *Het Recht in Indonesie*, Van Hoeve, 'Article-Gravenhage/Bandung

Lev, DS, 1962, 'The Supreme court and *Adat* Inheritance Law in Indonesia', *American Journal of Comparative Law*, vol 11: 205.

Magung, A, 1992, 'Pidana *Adat* pun Diakui', *Forum Keadilan* 7.

Pandecten, 1926, *Pandecten van het Adatrecht: VIII, Het Recht in zake Gezinsleven en Huwelijksontbinding*, De Bussy, Amsterdam.

Sobandi, D, 1992, 'Hukum Pidana *Adat* dalam "Yurisprudensi"', *Varia Peradilan* VIII.

Tempo, 1990, 'Berlakunya Hukum Iskandar Muda', 17 March.

Tempo, 1992, 'Titisan Zama Iskandar Muda', 10 October.

Territoriale, 1953, 'Territoriale Verscheidenheid in het Indonesisch Wetboekenstrafrecht', *Mededelingen van het Documentatiebureau voor Overzees Recht*, vol 3: 28.
Varia Peradilan, 1985, vol 25.
Varia Peradilan, 1986, vol 7.
Varia Peradilan, 1988, vol 38.
Varia Peradilan, 1989, vol 45.
Varia Peradilan, 1991, vol 72.

8. Polygamy and Mixed Marriage in Indonesia: The Application of the Marriage Law in the Courts

Simon Butt

This chapter examines the extent to which Indonesian courts have accommodated Islamic law regarding polygamy and marriages between Muslims and non-Muslims.[1] Muslims may have felt that political agitation which led to substantial amendments of a draft Marriage Law in 1973 averted radical reforms of Islamic law; and in fact strengthened and expanded both the authority of Islam and the jurisdiction of the *Pengadilan Agama* (Religious Courts). I argue, however, that, since the enactment of the Marriage Law, Islamic law has increasingly suffered at the hands of the state. Although the Marriage Law allows polygamy to exist on a formal legal level, the state attempted to make obtaining the requisite judicial consent for polygamous marriages practically impossible – with significant success. With respect to mixed marriages, in 1989 the *Mahkamah Agung* (the highest court in Indonesia) prohibited a Muslim woman from marrying a non-Muslim man without 'abandoning' her Islamic faith.[2] While prima facie the court appeared to uphold Islamic law – the *Qur'an* does not allow a Muslim woman to marry a non-Muslim man – this decision has, in fact, gone a long way towards realising Muslim fears that mixed marriage is a 'Christianising' institution.

Polygamy and mixed interreligious marriage have been controversial issues throughout Indonesia's legal history. This fact, and the political character of Indonesian Islam, are well illustrated by the debates in and outside of Parliament over the 'comprehensively and specifically secular' (Emmerson, 1976: 229) Marriage Bill, introduced in 1973.

The 1973 Marriage Bill

Muslims strongly objected to several aspects of the Bill which were contrary to Islamic law.[3] In particular (for our purposes), the Bill placed restrictions on

---

1   It will be assumed in this chapter that the government has control over the general courts and that, therefore, their decisions largely reflect state policy. See generally Butt (1997).

2   *Mahkamah Agung* Decision No 1400K/Pdt/1986, reproduced in Gautama (1992, Vol 1: 23-31).

3   Family law has been a particularly fertile ground for Muslim opposition. It is closely related to personal status from which flows legal duty. Most of the few *Qu'ranic* verses which contain legal injunctions deal with marriage, and all *fiqh* books dedicate significant space to them (Nur Ahmad Fadhil Lubis, 1994: 213-14). As Anderson (1976: 38-39) states, 'Muslims in general feel strongly that their family law must somehow remain essentially Islamic'.

polygamy and permitted interreligious mixed marriages.[4] By proposing that the civil courts adjudicate on the propriety of polygamous marriages, the Bill also significantly reduced the jurisdiction of the Religious Courts[5] – a symbol of Islamic authority and guarantor of the application of Islamic law (Hooker, 1984: 272). As Johns (1987: 218) states:

> These provisions, in effect, set civil law above the revealed law of Islam in a manner perceived as blasphemous. For a Muslim marriage to be valid, all that was necessary was a contract made in accordance with the *syariah* between the groom and the bride's father or guardian. No human authority had the right to require more.

Many Muslims believed that Islam was under threat from a 'Christianising', that is, secularising, government.[6] The Bill prompted one of the most heated debates and the largest attendance in Indonesian parliamentary history. Muslim students demonstrated against the Bill and seized control of the floor of the Indonesian parliament (DPR)[7] when the government was defending the Bill. Political stability of the country was at stake; and social and political unrest was set to break out if the draft was enacted (Katz & Katz, 1975: 663).

In the face of this intense Muslim opposition, the government enacted an amended statute which largely accommodated Muslim interests: Law No 1 of 1974 on Marriage (the Marriage Law). This Law permitted polygamous marriages and unilateral divorces, and the Religious Courts retained authority to decide on their propriety. The Article allowing interreligious mixed marriages was removed.

Why did the Government Enact the Marriage Law?

The Marriage Law was directed towards improving the social and legal status of (particularly Muslim) Indonesian women. For over 60 years many women's organisations had lobbied the government to improve the legal rights of women in marriage (Law and Society Review, 1994: 485). Islamic marriage law was largely uncodified.[8] It provided women with few rights in marriage and it left much uncertainty over how they could be protected (Katz & Katz, 1975: 656). Classical Islamic law allowed a man to take another wife without the consent of his existing

---

4   Marriage Bill, Arts 3, 49 and 11(2), cited in Weinata Sairin & Pattiasina (1994: 208-48). The Islamic prescripts dealing with mixed marriage and polygamy are discussed in more detail below.

5   This judicial branch comprises of 305 Religious Courts (*Pengadilan Agama*) and 21 Religious High Courts (*Pengadilan Agama Tinggi*) (Din Muhammad, 1995). These hear cases in which both parties are Muslims and the dispute concerns defined areas of the law, such as marriage, inheritance and trusts. See generally, Hooker (1984: 248-78) and above, Chapter 6.

6   Muslims have feared the threat of 'Christianisation' for some time. Under the Dutch, Muslims rallied to compete with Dutch-sponsored Christian missionaries. Rumours spread in 1960 that the Christians planned to convert Java in 20 years and all of Indonesia in 50 years. After the coup of 1965 and the banning of communism in 1966, Christians claimed that 2 million Indonesians had converted to Christianity. Muslims perceived the threat as real. This 'rivalry' has caused some strain and conflict in various Muslim-Christian relations (Mohammad Atho Mudzhar, 1993: 64).

7   *Dewan Perwakilan Raykat* or People's Representative Assembly.

8   Article 1 of Law No 22 of 1946 concerning registration of marriages, reconciliation and divorces required registry officials to supervise marriages but registration was not required for the marriage to be legally valid. See generally Hooker (1984: 257).

wife or wives.[9] They could be divorced on any (of their husband's) grounds and be socially humiliated in the process but could themselves initiate divorce only with extreme difficulty (Subadio, 1981: 7). Kartini (1976: 17) encapsulated the feeling as long ago as 1899:

> [C]an you imagine what hell-pain a woman must suffer when her husband comes home with another – a rival – whom she must recognise as his legal wife? He can torture her to death, mistreat her as he will; if he does not choose to give her back her freedom, then she can whistle to the moon for her rights. Everything for the man, and nothing for the woman, is our law and custom.

Before Indonesia's independence, women's organisations began to voice their concerns on a wider scale.[10] The women's emancipation movement became closely related to the independence movement (Katz & Katz, 1975: 657). After Indonesia declared its independence on 17 August 1945, women obtained more formal legal equality. The Indonesian Constitution expressly granted all Indonesian citizens equality before the law.[11] In its First Five Year Development Plan (*Repelita*)[12] 1969/70, the People's Consultative Council (MPR)[13] recognised and pledged to uphold what it termed the 'fundamental right' of equality in law, society, economics, culture and education. The state's concerns to improve the status of women were evident in a string of court decisions. The judiciary began to recognise that women had participated in the revolution against the Dutch from 1944 to 1949 and sought to redress their inferior legal status accordingly, particularly in the area of inheritance law.[14] The *Mahkamah Agung* declared invalid several Articles of the Indonesian Civil Code (*Kitab Undang-Undang Hukum Perdata*), because they were based on discriminatory grounds (Lev, 1965). In the context of this trend towards sexual equality, women's groups sought to make these legal guarantees realities and sustained their appeals for legal equality, particularly in the field of marriage law reform (Katz & Katz, 1975: 657).

Pressures also emerged from the international arena (Cammack et al, 1995: 51) and Indonesia ratified the International Convention on the Political Rights of Women in 1958.[15] By the early 1970s, most countries with large Muslim populations had instituted legal reforms to improve women's rights under Islamic law (Esposito, 1982: 49-101).

The government itself also had much to gain from unifying and codifying Indonesian marriage law, long considered particularly diverse and divisive. In fact,

---

9   However, the *Qu'ran* (4:3) forbids a man to take more than one wife if he cannot treat them equally 'in matters of food, residence, clothing and sex' (Abdur Rahman I Doi, 1989: 53).

10 In particular, *Kongres Perempuan Indonesia* (Indonesian Women's Congress), a federation of the most prominent women's organisations (established in 1928), held several congresses in pre-independent Indonesia, where the government was strongly urged to improve the marriage rights of women (Department of Information, 1975: 5).

11 Article 27.

12 *Rencana Pembangunan Lima Tahun*

13 *Majelis Permusyawaratan Rakyat*.

14 Daniel Lev (1962) has chronicled a series of *Mahkamah Agung* cases in the 1950s where the court attempted to unify the various adat laws of inheritance by recognising a widow as the heir of her husband. Before these decisions, a widow generally had only a right to property she brought into the marriage, together with a variable share in any property acquired jointly during the marriage (Hooker, 1978a: 25).

15 Law No 68 of 1958.

the desirability of unifying Indonesia's differing *adat* (traditional)[16] and religious marriage laws has been debated for over a century;[17] and the New Order often stressed the desirability of a single system of national law (Kompas Online, 1997).[18] By this is meant a unified and codified single law derived from Indonesia's diverse – and (to some extent) disintegrating – *adat*, religious and colonial laws. National law is seen as transcending local divisions, establishing and maintaining a national unity, consciousness and identity (Cammack et al, 1996: 53-54).[19]

Codification was also envisaged to inject certainty and consistency into marriage law. Much of the Islamic law relating to marriage was comprised of the prescripts contained in the assorted works of legal scholars (*fiqh*) written in Arabic centuries ago.

> The result [was] undoubtedly confusion about the bases of judgment, for one judge might use certain *fiqh* texts while other use different ones. This [was] complicated by the existence of the four Sunni schools of Islamic law, each with its own standard texts. Even within the Shafi`i *madhhab* [school of law] itself, followed by the majority of Indonesian Muslims, variations of the *fiqh* texts [were] still expected (Mohammad Atho Mudzhar, 1993: 37).

Perhaps more importantly, codification in a state-enacted statute would establish the government as the ultimate authority in the administration of marriage law and as the arbiter of its legitimacy (Johns, 1987: 217):

> The ideology of national sovereignty, which was the vehicle for independence and is now embodied in the form of the Indonesian state, is premised on the state's possession of a monopoly of law making authority within its borders. State positivism is, however, in direct conflict with Islam, which recognises ultimate law making authority in God alone. The government's marriage law was partly an attempt to establish the Indonesian state apparatus as the source of legal and social meanings (Cammack et al, 1996: 53).

Finally, the Marriage Law gained strong support from the Indonesian ruling elite, many of whom perceived (and still do) the Muslim movement as a potent political

---

16 Van Vollenhoven, the well-known Dutch *adat* scholar, divided Indonesia into 19 *adat* law circles (*adatrechtskring*), based upon cultural and language classifications (Hooker, 1978b: 192).

17 When the Civil Code was promulgated in 1848, some Indonesians advocated a single national law applicable to the entire population. Since then, there has always been pressure for unification (Gautama & Hornick, 1983: 60).

18 See Soewondo (1991-1992: 4) for a discussion of the Five Year Development Plans relating to national law.

19 The plural marriage law system inherited from colonial times had been by and large maintained in Indonesia up to 1974. It distinguished between population groups, each having its own law. To Muslims, Islamic law applied largely unamended (Marriage Law, General Elucidation, part 2(a)). For indigenous Indonesians and some Orientals, their customary law applied (Marriage Law, General Elucidation, parts 2(b) and 2(e)). The Marriage Ordinance for Indonesian Christians (S 1933, No 74) applied to Christians (Marriage Law, General Elucidation, part 2(c)). Chinese and European marriages were regulated by the Civil Code with some minor alterations (Marriage Law, General Elucidation, parts 2(d) and 2(f)). The religious basis for marriage appears to thwart the Marriage Law's goals of unifying Indonesian marriage law. Except for certain provisions on minimum age, marriage contracts and rights and duties of spouses (for which there is a common set of rules), a formal pluralism based on the distinction between Muslims and non-Muslims has been introduced into Indonesia. Indeed, the following discussion of the Marriage Law and its polygamy provisions concern Muslims only. Additionally, after the enactment of the Marriage Law, legislation has in fact started to differentiate between Muslims and non-Muslims, with separate legislation applying to each group (Pompe & Otto, 1990: 419-20).

threat (Schwarz, 1994: 163). The New Order government had suppressed the political aspirations of Islam up to this point.[20]

> It is not unreasonable to assume that the government wanted to use the marriage law to administer the coup de grace to Islamic aspirations, not the least of which was to make Indonesia an Islamic state (Katz & Katz, 1975: 660, note 41).

Polygamy

Islam allows polygamy, although it is generally regarded in Indonesia as morally reprehensible. When it occurs, it is met with 'some social embarrassment and hushed tones' (Lev, 1996b: 193). According to the *Qur'an* (4: 3), a man may marry up to four wives. The *fikh* require the marriage to be witnessed and all wives treated equally (Jawad, 1991: 185). Yet, despite the so-called 'universality' of Islam, countries with large Muslim populations have treated polygamy in different ways. In most Muslim countries, polygamy has been restricted[21] and where it is accepted, different conditions must be fulfilled before it is allowed (Pompe & Otto, 1990: 417).

Polygamy and the Marriage Law

Before the enactment of the Marriage Law, it was relatively easy for a Muslim man to practise polygamy in Indonesia. He was merely required to report his new marriage to a registrar and be fair to his wives (Katz & Katz, 1975: 672). The Marriage Law has substantially changed this position, but is nevertheless quite ambiguous. On the one hand, the principle that marriage is a monogamous institution is said to underlie the provisions of the Law;[22] and indeed, one of the main objectives of the Marriage Law was to reduce the frequency of polygamous

---

20 The suppression of Islam in Indonesia by secular forces has been a feature of Islam's more modern history. The Dutch distinguished between the religious and political aspects of Islam, allowing the former to flourish within certain bounds, and repressing the latter (Lapidus, 1988: 713). Essentially, independent Indonesian governments, whether under Soekarno or Soeharto, have maintained this standpoint, and, in some cases, strengthened state dominance over Islam. Perhaps the sharpest blow to Islamic aspirations occurred in 1945 when a provision in Indonesia's first Constitution (the *Piagam Jakarta* or Jakarta Charter) that required adherents of Islam to practise Islamic law was dropped just before the declaration of independence (Schwarz, 1994: 168). More recent examples of the suppression of Islam were the 1971 parliamentary elections, where Muslim parties suffered their worst defeat and alleged government interference. (Cammack, 1989: 57). In 1972, the government appointed the Western-educated Professor Mukti Ali as Minister of Religion who attempted to undermine the power of the Islamic organisation *Nahdlatul Ulama* and inserted secular vocational subjects into the curriculum of Islamic schools (Emmerson, 1976: 236). In 1973, the four Islamic political parties were forced to fuse into one party – the United Development Party (PPP- *Partai Persatuan Pembangunan*) – which did not even contain 'Islam' in its title. The trend of government suppression has continued since 1974 and reached its peak with Law No 8 of 1985 on Social Organisations which required that all societal organisations (including Islamic parties and groups) have the state's secular ideology – *Pancasila* – as their sole foundation (*asas tunggal*). This means that Islamic political parties must rally for support under the state-created banner of *Pancasila*, not Islam (see generally Ramage (1993)).

21 See, for example, Anderson (1976: 111-14).

22 Article 3.

marriages.[23] On the other hand, the Marriage Law allows a man to take more than one wife if he fulfils the requirements set out in the law, his religion allows it and he has obtained permission from a religious court.[24] But although the right has been maintained, cumbersome administrative procedures have quite severely limited the possibility of its arbitrary use. Banning polygamy outright would have highlighted the contest between Islamic authority (that is, divine revelation) and the state.[25]

Under the Marriage Law, the man must request permission from the Religious Court[26] before he can enter into a polygamous marriage. He must show that he:

1. has gained the approval of his wife or wives;
2. can and will guarantee to provide the necessities of life for his wives and their children; and
3. can and will act justly in regard to his wives and children.[27]

The court should then grant the husband permission to take another wife if his current wife or wives:

1. is or are unable to perform her duties as a wife;
2. suffers from physical defects or an incurable illness; or
3. is or are incapable of bearing children.[28]

Polygamous marriages carried out without judicial mandate will generally be invalid.[29] The parties can be fined Rp 7500 (approximately AUS$1.25 in early

---

23 Marriage Law, Elucidation, paragraph 4. Indeed, as shown below the state has gone a long way towards making legal polygamous marriages impossible. Signs of this approach emerged in the early 1980s when the government enacted Government Regulation 10 of 1983, which prohibits male civil servants from taking another wife from the civil service (Art 4(2)) and requires civil servants wanting to enter a polygamous marriage with a non-civil servant to obtain permission for his supervisor (Art 4). If a polygamous marriage goes ahead without permission, the public servant concerned can be dismissed (Jakarta Post, 1995a: 6). For an excellent discussion of the regulation of the sexual lives of public servants, see Suryakusuma (1996).

24 Marriage Law, Arts 3(2) and 4(1) and General Elucidation, part 4(c).

25 Many countries with large Muslim populations have adopted the same approach. 'Instead of venturing to change the substance of the divine law, the reformers could achieve their object by the purely procedural device of forbidding the courts to apply that law in specified circumstances' (Anderson, 1976: 44).

26 Marriage Law, Art 4(1); Government Regulation No 9, 1975, Art 40.

27 Marriage Law, Art 5(1); Government Regulation No 9, 1975, states that the request must be in writing (Art 40); that the wife's consent, if oral, must be pronounced before the court (Art 41(b)); that the husband must produce sufficient documentary evidence (for example an affidavit stating the husband's income or an income tax return) to show that he can guarantee the livelihood of his wives and children (Art 41(c)); and that he must prepare a written statement pledging to treat his wives and children fairly.

28 Marriage Law, Art 4(2).

29 Circular Letter of the *Mahkamah Agung* No MA/Pemb/0156/77 dated 25 February 1975 instructs that even if the man does not apply to the religious court for consent, the marriage may be valid if the court would have given its consent, that is, if the marriage fulfilled the requirements set out in the Marriage Law. *Mahkamah Agung* jurisprudence seems to indicate that the courts do not view this approach with much favour and have applied the Criminal Code (KUHP) penalty more vigorously when the court's consent has been assumed (Pompe & Otto, 1990: 425).

1998) under Government Regulation No 9, 1975[30] or can be imprisoned under the KUHP[31] (Criminal Code).[32]

The Application of the Marriage Law in the Religious Courts [33]

In what appears to be the majority of cases, the courts have followed the Marriage Law and its implementing regulation[34] quite strictly. In one well-known case, the Malang Religious Court held that a man who had based his request on his purportedly extraordinary sexual appetite, could not take another wife because 'prodigious sexual strength' was not mentioned in the law as a ground for polygamy (Sodiki, 1977: 22). In another case, the man argued that he needed another wife because he wanted more children than his existing wife could provide. The court dismissed his request after his wife testified that the couple had nine children (Sodiki, 1977: 22). The *Mahkamah Agung* itself has invalidated attempts at polygamous marriage where the man's first wife has not consented to it.[35]

However, there is also some evidence to suggest that the Religious Courts do not always refer to the Marriage Law when hearing polygamy cases, and sometimes will decide cases in 'flagrant conflict with it' (Pompe & Otto, 1990: 429). A report on the Central Jakarta District Court (Nuraja, 1985: 489-90) concluded that judges of the Religious Courts often decided polygamy cases in accordance with Islamic law rather than the Marriage Law, and therefore usually allowed polygamous marriages to go ahead. The same report revealed that, if these cases were appealed, the *Mahkamah Agung* generally overturned them, preferring to apply the state-made Marriage Law and prior *Mahkamah Agung* decisions.

Why are some Religious Court judges inclined towards the classical *syariah* and others towards the Marriage Law? Some judges appear to be wary of being overturned by the *Mahkamah Agung* on cassation (appeal) (Cammack, 1989: 67). Before 1970, the Religious Court fell under the jurisdiction of the Ministry of Religious Affairs and the *Mahkamah Agung* could not revise their decisions. The Law on Judicial Power of 1970 established that the *Mahkamah Agung* could adjudicate on decisions of the High Religious Court on cassation if requested.[36] The *Mahkamah Agung* has issued circular letters reaffirming these powers[37] and established a special Islamic panel of judges in the *Mahkamah Agung*.[38] These steps

---

30 Article 40.

31 *Kitab Undang-undang Hukum Pidana.*

32 The relevant Article of the Criminal Code is Art 279: 'Whoever marries while knowing that his existing marriage(s) constitute a prohibition to the marriage, or marries whilst knowing that that the marriage(s) of someone else constitutes an obstacle to that marriage, can be sentenced to up to five years' jail. If this is done by withholding from another party that a marriage exists, the accused can be sentenced to up to seven years' jail.' See Djoko Prakoso & I Ketut Murtika (1987: 67), for further Articles that may be relevant to illegal polygamous marriages.

33 Lev (1972a) provides the classic account of Indonesian Islamic Courts.

34 Government Regulation No 9 of 1975.

35 See, for example, *Mahkamah Agung* Decision No 435/K/Kr/1979, dated 17 April 1980 (Gautama, 1992, Vol II: 164-71) where both the man and the woman he attempted to marry were sentenced to one month in prison.

36 Law No 14 of 1970, Art 10(3).

37 *Mahkamah Agung* Regulation No 1 of 1977.

38 *Mahkamah Agung* Regulation No 3 of 1979.

seem to have influenced some Religious Court decisions regarding polygamy, although their effect is difficult to quantify.

However, other religious court judges seem to have been more influenced by their training than the threat of having their decisions overturned.[39] Pompe and Otto (1990: 430, note 64) cite government statistics on West Java to show that the religious nature of and the lack of exposure to secular law in their legal education may explain why some religious court judges are more inclined towards traditional interpretations of the *syariah* which favour polygamy. Of 104 judges, only one was educated at a state university, and six had been students of a religious institute of higher education. The others had no education beyond secondary school, though most had done additional courses in Islamic theology. Generally speaking, these judges have therefore tended to apply *fiqh* in their judgments whenever possible.

> Islamic judges emphasise Islamic doctrine as the sole source of law and regard the *syariah* rules as independently potent, whereas the *Mahkamah Agung* permits the statutory rules to stand on their own and tolerates reference to Islamic doctrine so long as the lower court's decision does not deviate from the requirements of the statute (Cammack, 1989: 67).

Although these judges may be conscious of being overturned by the *Mahkamah Agung* on cassation, they are inclined to argue that since there is no system of precedent in Indonesia, *Mahkamah Agung* jurisprudence (*yurisprudensi*) is not binding on their decisions (Cammack, 1989: 67). While this may be a good formal argument, practically speaking it is weak. The Indonesian government itself, in a report by the Institute for National Legal Development (*Badan Pembinaan Hukum Nasional* (BPHN), 1991/1992: v), has called for an increase in legal certainty through the development of jurisprudence (*yurisprudensi*), that is, the written decisions of the *Mahkamah Agung*. In fact, the report revealed that judges and lawyers use prior decisions of the *Mahkamah Agung* as a guide in making decisions or advising clients. Furthermore, in a Circular Letter, the *Mahkamah Agung* advised that published *yurisprudensi* should be followed by Indonesian courts.[40]

A Central Jakarta Religious Court decision,[41] which concerned a man who had taken a second wife without his first wife's consent, is indicative of the competing pressures, and ultimately demonstrates the increasing prominence of the state's view on polygamy. The court distinguished between the religious component (that is, a relationship between man and God) and the civil (social or legal) aspect of marriage and treated them separately. The relationship was valid with respect to religion, yet invalid in terms of the Marriage Law. The court ultimately upheld state law, but did not dismiss Islamic legal prescripts outright. The decision was upheld on appeal in the relevant Religious Court of Appeal and on cassation in the *Mahkamah Agung*.[42]

However, the days of the recalcitrant Religious Court judge appear to be numbered. In recent years, the Religious Courts have been brought under more stringent state control. Under the Religious Court Law of 1989, all Islamic court judges must hold academic degrees, pledge allegiance to *Pancasila* and the 1945

---

39   See generally Lev (1972a).

40   *Mahkamah Agung* Circular Letter No 2 of 1972.

41   Central Jakarta Religious Court Decision No 162 of 1979. This case is discussed in Cammack et al (1996: 65-66) and Cammack (1989: 72).

42   Unfortunately, whether the *Mahkamah Agung* gave any credence to the division between the religious and civil aspects of marriage has not been reported. The case is currently unavailable in Australia.

Constitution, and are appointed after an examination conducted under the auspices of the *Mahkamah Agung* (Lubis, 1994: 280).[43] Religious Court judges, like judges from other Indonesian courts,[44] must also be civil servants.[45] They are therefore required to join KORPRI (Public Servant Corps of the Republic of Indonesia),[46] the head of which is the Minister for Internal Affairs.[47] Its members are obliged to support government policy (Asia Watch, 1988: 170). In accordance with their status, judges can be reprimanded under Government Regulation No 30 of 1980 concerning the Regulations for Disciplining Civil Servants. This, it seems, will go a long way towards 'promoting' the state's legal principles in the eyes of Religious Court judges; and is beginning to compel judges to interpret the Marriage Law in line with executive policy.

The government has also attempted to limit the choices of law that can be applied in the religious courts, by codifying Islamic law regarding marriage, inheritance and charitable foundations (*wakaf*). This codification is found in the Compilation, established in 1991 by Presidential Instruction,[48] and approved by a conference of prominent Indonesian Islamic scholars (*Ulama*).[49] It purported to combine elements of classical Islamic texts, modern Islamic laws enacted by other Muslim countries, opinions and rulings of Islamic scholars and organisations, and decisions of Indonesia's Religious Courts considered most suitable for Indonesia (Cammack, 1996: 66; Mohammad Atho Mudzhar, 1993: 39-40).[50] Chapter IX of the Compilation, which deals with polygamy, is almost identical to the Marriage Law. Its implementing regulation refers to the Law in authoritative terms and is framed within the authoritative symbols of the state: the *Pancasila* and the 1945 Constitution.[51] The Compilation is not a statute: it is envisaged as a 'guide' to settle disputes in Islamic law and to 'be used by government agencies and society'.[52] However, Indonesia's strong executive system and patrimonial political culture make the Compilation as effective as a formally enacted statute (Lubis, 1995: 40). Indeed, the General Elucidation of the Compilation states that judges should use it to decide cases that come before them.[53] A *Mahkamah Agung* judge has asserted that the Islamic marriage law is now a state affair, as its principles are reflected in the Compilation, which has the force of positive law (Cammack et al, 1996: 67-68).

---

43 See generally Hooker, Chapter 6.

44 Law on the General Courts, Art 14 (1)(e).

45 Law No 7 of 1989, Art 13(1).

46 *Korps Pegawai Negeri Republik Indonesia.*

47 Presidential Decree No 82 of 1971 concerning KORPRI.

48 Presidential Instruction No 1 of 1991.

49 'This process of mobilising scholarly consensus on the content of the Compilation was clearly designed to legitimate the text, and has its source in the central role of consensus or *ijma* in classical jurisprudence. According to classical legal theory, the consensus of qualified scholars in a given generation that a particular interpretation of the revealed sources is correct ratifies that interpretation as certain. The agreement of Indonesian scholars to the text of the Compilation was intended to stamp the document as an Indonesian *fiqh*' (Cammack, 1996: 67).

50 See also Mohammad Atho Mudzhar (1993: 39-40).

51 Compilation of Islamic Law, Presidential Instruction No 1 of 1991, General Elucidation, Part 1.

52 Compilation of Islamic Law, Presidential Instruction No 1 of 1991, Introductory Consideration.

53 General Elucidation, Part 5.

This attempt to 'resolve' inconsistencies between Islamic and state law will almost certainly make Islamic judges more hesitant to challenge the state's polygamy laws in the future.

The government's efforts appear to be bearing fruit. A recent survey indicated that more Religious Court judges see themselves as part of the state bureaucracy and implementators of state law rather than as upholders of Islamic law (Lubis, 1994: 287). Some Religious Courts are beginning to uphold the Marriage Law's implicit 'monogamy' principle more stringently by restrictively interpreting the Law's polygamy procedures. They seem to be holding that equity between wives is practically impossible to quantify and implement (Law & Society Review, 1994: 483). One local official has even stated that the Surakarta Religious District Court in Central Java had ceased authorising polygamous marriages. All requests were denied if the first wife had children; and even if the man's proposed second wife was pregnant and all parties agreed to the marriage – including the first wife – the court would refuse to allow it (Cammack, 1989: 73):

> It is likely that, as the *Mahkamah Agung* consolidates its control over the Islamic judiciary, a more secularist interpretation of the marriage statute will become increasingly prevalent (Cammack, 1989: 72).

Why has polygamous marriage been rendered almost impossible? The contest between Islam and the state, together with domestic and international concern to improve the rights of women in Indonesia are relevant. However, polygamy also contradicts Indonesia's family planning policies aimed at reducing Indonesia's population (Soewondo, 1977: 287). It offends the norms of the state's ideal of 'the happy and lasting family':[54] a monogamous marriage for life with a maximum of two children (Pompe, 1994: 117).[55] Indeed, the government constantly reaffirms that a happy family is necessary for the nation's prime concern, that is, economic development (*pembangunan*).[56] Women are urged to contribute to the development climate (*iklim pembangunan*) through government-established women's organisations such as the PKK (Organisation for Family Welfare)[57] and *Dharma Wanita* (women's path or way) (the Association of Retired Civil Servants and the Wives of Civil Servants) (Gerke, 1992/1993: 46). The state constantly indoctrinates women about their role – as faithful wives, managers of the household, procreators of the nation, and mothers and educators of their children (Hull, 1976: 22) – through the ideology of State Ibuism,[58] which seeks to motivate women to assist in the *ketertiban* (order), *pembinaan* (development), and *stabilitas* (stability) goals of the state (Suryakusuma, 1987: 12; and 1996).

Polygamous marriages are quite rare in Indonesia[59] and are becoming rarer (Department of Religion, 1985/1986: 431). Polygamy, however, tends to make Muslim women anxious to the extent that some even describe it as 'disguised prostitution' (Katz & Katz, 1975: 673) and it is seen as breaking up the 'happy

---

54 Marriage Law, General Elucidation, Part 4(2).
55 The Marriage Regulations for Civil Servants provide a prime example of this state morality. See Government Regulation No 45 of 1990. Public servants are envisaged to have an 'obligation to serve as models for the rest of society' (Suryakusuma, 1996: 102).
56 See generally Ali Murtopo, (1982); Van Langenberg (1986: 19).
57 *Pembinaan Kesejahteraan Keluarga.*
58 *Ibu* literally means mother and is a term of address for an older woman or for a woman of a higher status than the addressor. The term 'state Ibuism' was coined by Suryakusuma (1987).
59 Before the Marriage Law was enacted, a series of studies indicated that only 5% of the total number of Indonesian marriages were polygamous (Gautama & Hornick, 1983: 62).

family' the New Order is attempting to promote (Jakarta Post, 1995a: 6; Jakarta Post 1995b: 7). Perhaps partly in the interests of *pembangunan*, then, the courts are refusing polygamous marriages with increasing frequency.[60]

Nevertheless, the efficacy of Indonesian polygamy law is questionable (Dirkien et al, 1989). Many commentators, especially members of women's organisations, have argued that the penalties for illegal polygamous marriage are not sufficiently severe to prevent violation of the law (Soewonto, 1976: 128). One Selong District Court judge observed that husbands found it too difficult to obtain the consent of their existing wife or wives. Many prefer to pay the Rp 7500 (approximately $AU 1.25 in early 1998) fine if they are reported rather than arduously obtaining judicial consent[61] and, indeed, many do not know the correct procedure to follow (Dirkien, 1989: 24). Unless the courts adopt the heavier penalties under the KUHP for those conducting polygamous marriages in contravention of statutory requirements, illegal polygamous marriages will probably continue.

Furthermore, some have argued that many people, especially in poorer rural areas, continue to practise polygamy because it is 'part of their culture' (Law & Society, 1994: 484; Kompas Online, 1996). Additionally, '[e]fforts to do away with polygamy have failed each time, primarily because of the symbolic importance of the *Qu'ranic* passage that allows it' (Lev, 1996: 193). One report found that men who have not been educated beyond primary school level were far more likely to engage in polygamous practices than men with higher education (Dirkien, 1989: 21-22). If the state's efforts to subsume *adat* land law prescripts within a single national land law are comparable to its attempts at reforming the law of polygamy, it will take years to change behavioural patterns in rural areas.[62]

Perhaps more importantly, most Indonesians may not be inclined to use the courts to obtain permission for a polygamous marriage as they typically hold the courts in low regard, mainly due to perceptions of judicial corruption (Fitzpatrick, 1997: 204).[63] Muslims will be reluctant to seek permission from courts they do not respect. Likewise, Indonesians also perceive litigation as expensive and time consuming (Gray, 1991: 770; Lev, 1996a: 155) and feel alienated by court processes (Lev, 1972b: 284).[64] Poerbatin (1985: 484) argues that these procedural difficulties

---

60   For an example of this trend, see *Mahkamah Agung* Decision No. 435/K/Kr/1979, 17 April 1980, cited in Gautama (1992, Vol II: 164-71).

61   The judge also said that some men would prefer to pay 50,000 rupiah than seek court approval (Abdurrahman & Riduan Syahrani, 1978: 102).

62   Even the Institute for National Legal Development (BPHN, *Badan Pembinaan Hukum Nasional*) admits that there are inadequacies in the enforcement of the Marriage Law (Hartono, 1992/1993: v). In 1960, the Indonesian government passed the Agrarian Law (Law No 5 of 1960), but it has had 'little effect in penetrating the countryside' (Hooker, 1978a: 66). *Adat* land concepts are still alive in the minds of Indonesians (Soesangobeng, 1978: 60). Indeed, although the Agrarian Law of 1960 requires that land ownership be registered only an estimated 22% of approximately 58 million plots of land have been recorded (Sumardjo, 1996: 4).

63   Society's lack of faith in the judiciary is a commonly accepted and re-occurring theme in legal circles and the press. See, for example, Jawa Pos Online (1996) and Tempo Interaktif (1996).

64   A government court, for example, is rarely aware of all the relationships at stake in a local dispute, and it may bring to bear standards alien to custom. Villages occasionally say that formal courts apply *lain hukum* (different law) '[This] refers precisely to the court's natural concern with established substantive rules, in which a village group may be much less interested than simply getting rid of a conflict with minimum social distress. In addition, settlements induced from outside may deny a community whatever benefit of social cohesion might have accrued from resolving issues internally . . . the cultural penchant for compromise of personal conflicts remains strong and it is not at all limited to villagers' (Lev, 1972b: 284-85).

seem to have limited legal polygamous marriages to the middle classes. They may be the only group aware of the need to seek the judicial permission; they can afford to do so; and they are more likely to be able to prove that they can treat their wives fairly.

Mixed Interreligious Marriages

Before 1974 the formal legal right of Indonesians to marry a partner who adhered to a different religion to their own was undisputed. According to Art 7 of the *Regeling op de Gemengde Huwelijken*s 98-158 of 1896 (GHR), a decree which first applied to Indonesians under Dutch rule, a difference in religion between prospective marriage partners could not prevent them from marrying. Mixed interreligious marriages were to be concluded according to the law of the husband (Gautama & Hornick, 1983: 59). The GHR did not require that the wife convert to her husband's religion for the purposes of the marriage; only that she cede to her husband's legal regime (Gautama, 1991: 168). This provision was problematic for both non-Muslim and Muslim women who married a Muslim man as it rendered them vulnerable to the imposition of subsequent polygamous marriage and unilateral divorce by their husbands (Katz & Katz, 1975: 680).[65]

As mentioned, Muslims generally hold mixed interreligious marriages in contempt of Islamic law. For decades they objected to the provision in the GHR which permitted such marriages. Nevertheless, the courts almost inevitably upheld this colonial regulation. In 1952, a Christian male and a Muslim female petitioned the Jakarta District Court to authorise their marriage.[66] Under the GHR, the woman was required to obtain permission from an Islamic 'priest' (*penghulu*) before she could enter into such a marriage. He had refused on the basis that Islamic law forbade it. The court granted them permission to marry, effectively holding that state law, as embodied in the GHR, held precedence over *fiqh*. The couple then married according to the Law on Christian Marriages, that is, in accordance with the husband's law. Large protests were organised by various Islamic groups[67] who saw the decision as a rejection of the Islamic belief that religion is a way of life. They protested that interreligious marriages would increase the number of Christians at the expense of Islam (Katz & Katz, 1975: 662). The girl's father, a devout Muslim, appealed to the *Mahkamah Agung*. The court upheld the GHR and decided that religious law could not bar interreligious marriages.

The Law on Interreligious Mixed Marriages after 1974

Since the enactment of the Marriage Law mixed interreligious marriage law has been in a constant state of flux. The Marriage Law and its implementing regulation do not explicitly provide either for or against marriages between Indonesian

---

65 This difficulty was overcome for Christian women by Art 75 of the Law on Christian Marriage, which states that a non-Christian man could marry a Christian women under Christian law without converting to Christianity.

66 Jakarta District Court Decision, No 342/1952, 17 June 1952, reproduced in Gautama (1992, vol 1: 2).

67 For example, over 2000 Muslims gathered at special meetings in two mosques in Jakarta alone (Gautama, 1991: 168).

nationals adhering to different religions (*perkawinan campuran* or *perkawinan antar-agama*).[68] This generated a great deal of debate over whether partners of different religions could actually marry under Indonesian law.

For example,[69] some scholars argue that the Marriage Law implicitly regulated mixed marriages. Article 2(1), which provides that the religious prescripts of the parties are to be used to conduct marriages, is seen to extend to interreligious marriages. Such marriages would be permitted only as far as these religious prescripts allowed.[70] Authors who advocate this approach[71] generally conclude that most Indonesians could not lawfully marry interreligiously unless one of them converted to the other's religion (Zubairie, 1985: 79).

Christian religious prescripts do not prohibit interreligious marriages outright. The Catholic Church does not advocate mixed marriages but adherents may intermarry if they obtain dispensation. This may be granted if the non-Catholic prospective partner agrees not to impede the Catholic party's faith; the Catholic partner promises to remain faithful to his or her Catholic conviction; and both partners are willing to give any children born out of the marriage a Catholic education (Rusli & Tama, 1984: 27). The Protestant Church does not generally prohibit its adherents from interreligious marriage (Rusli & Tama, 1984: 29).

However, it is difficult (and in most cases impossible) for Muslims, Hindus and Buddhists to marry interreligiously. Islamic law only permits marriage between a Muslim male with a non-Muslim female of a religion which adheres to the *khitab*, or sacred text – here, the Old Testament. This definition embraces Christianity or Judaism.[72] Some would also argue that this dispensation only applies where there is a lack of available Muslim women (Lubis, 1994: 232).[73] The Indonesian government does not, however, officially recognise the Jewish faith, thus restricting Muslim Indonesian men to Protestant or Catholic women.[74] This, it seems, would

---

68   Literally, mixed marriage or interreligious marriage. Interestingly, the term *perkawinan campuran* has caused confusion amongst legal scholars and registry officials. Some scholars argued that Arts 57-62 of the Marriage Law which specifically regulates marriages between foreigners and Indonesian nationals also applied to marriages between Indonesians of different religious beliefs merely because both forms of marriage are 'mixed' (Pompe, 1988: 265-66). The *Mahkamah Agung* has rejected this view. In *Mahkamah Agung* Decision No 435/K/Kr/1979, 17 April 1980, cited in Gautama (1992, Vol II: 164-71), registry officials pointed to Arts 57, 58, and 59 of the Marriage Law, stating that they were the Articles relevant to interreligious mixed marriages. The *Mahkamah Agung* decided that this view was incorrect and held that these Articles applied only to international mixed marriages.

69   Not every legal argument relating to interreligious marriage will be discussed here. See Department of Religion (1985/1986: 10; 1987/1988: 11). Pompe (1988) has provided the most clear and detailed assessment of these arguments.

70   Article 8(f); Elucidation of Art 2(1).

71   Hazairin (1974), cited in Pompe (1991: 265) and Asmin (1986: 68), is particularly well known for adopting this view.

72   Verse 5:5 of the *Qu'ran* states: '[Lawful unto you in marriage] are [not only] chaste women who are believers but also chaste women amongst the people of the Book' (Abdur Rahman I Doi, 1989: 44). The Prophet Muhammad himself is reported to have had some non-Muslim wives (Nur Ahmad Fadhil Lubis, 1994: 230-31) but some schools of Islamic legal thought still prohibit or strongly disapprove of such marriages. For a summary of these views, see Abdur Rahman I Doi (1989: 45-46).

73   Indeed, if there are many more Muslim women than Muslim men in a particular country, some *ulama* in the Muslim world are of the opinion (*ijtihad*) that it is unlawful for Muslim men to marry *kitabiyyah* women (women 'of the book') (Abdur Rahman I Doi, 1989: 45).

74   Presidential Decree No 1 of 1964 states that Indonesia recognises Islam, Protestantism, Catholicism, Hinduism and Buddhism. See also, Pompe (1992: 387).

prevent a Muslim male from legally marrying a Catholic woman if they envisaged having children, given that both their religions permit interreligious mixed marriages only if their children are brought up under their respective religions.[75] Under Islamic law, Muslim females are not allowed to marry non-Muslim males (*Qur'an* 60: 10). Hindus or Buddhists may not marry someone of another religion so non-adherents must convert before marriage.

The courts, however, did not accept that Art 2(1) extended to encompass interreligious marriages. The established view was that the Marriage Law did not explicitly provide for mixed marriages, and thus it had no effect on the existing colonial regulations which permitted interreligious mixed marriages.[76] Apparently in contravention of Art 2(1), the *Mahkamah Agung* issued a Circular letter in 1975 instructing the lower courts to apply the colonial regulations in mixed marriage cases.[77] The *Pengadilan Negeri* and *Pengadilan Tinggi* began to rule that mixed marriages could be concluded at the Civil Registry Office (which has the authority to perform marriages between non-Muslims) (Pompe, 1991: 262).[78] The *Mahkamah Agung* affirmed this approach in 1979[79] and some government officials adopted this reasoning in formal statements.[80]

Then, in 1984 the Ministry of Religion issued a guide to marriage registry officials (who conclude Muslim marriages) stating they could only register marriages between Muslims (Department of Religion, 1984: 389). By 1987 there were reports that it had become impossible to formalise interreligious mixed marriages at the Civil Registry Office (Pompe, 1991: 262). This was due to a decision made at a meeting between the Ministers of the Interior, Justice and Religious Affairs in January 1987 that civil mixed marriages could not proceed

---

75   These religious prescripts would put any children born out of the marriage in a difficult position. Their religious status would be unclear. Interestingly, Art 1 of the Marriage Law, which states that the aim of marriage is to create a happy and lasting family, prima facie seems to require that prospective marriage partners should expect to and eventually have children. On one interpretation, secular law is mirroring Christian and Islamic principles. Theoretically, this may be a way that interreligious mixed marriages will be forbidden in the future.

76   Article 66 of the Marriage Law states that the Law repeals other laws and regulations containing provisions relating to marriages to the extent that they conflict with it. Some authors emphasise that the 1973 Marriage Bill originally included both an Article stating that religious differences should not be regarded as an obstacle to marriage; and an Article regulating international interreligious marriages (Art 11). However, as mentioned above, the Article was withdrawn in the face of strong Muslim opposition to it. Some scholars argued that because the Bill distinguished between interreligious marriages and international mixed marriages and the Articles on interreligious marriage were simply withdrawn, interreligious marriage was not regulated in the Marriage Law, and thus the GHR should still apply (see generally Pompe (1988)).

77   *Mahkamah Agung* Circular Letter No MA /Pemb.0807, dated 20 August 1975.

78   There is some evidence to suggest that registry officials concluded mixed marriages not solely to comply with the Law but because they believed marriage was a better alternative to the to the couple 'living together outside of marriage' (Asmin, 1986: 67-68).

79   See, for example, *Mahkamah Agung* decision No 1650K/Sip/1974, dated 13 November 1979 (Yurisprudensi Indonesia, 1980: 111). See also Gautama (1987: 167).

80   See, for example, Decision of the Governor of East Java, 15 September 1980, concerning the Continuing Validity of The Mixed Marriage Regulations (GHR Stcb. 1898 no 158); Decision of the Head of the Jakarta Civil Registry, No 2158/-1.755.2/CS/1986 concerning Directions for the Implementation of Interreligious Marriages at the Civil Registry of the Province of Jakarta (Soewondo, 1991-1992: 19)

(Pompe & Otto, 1980: 421, note 30).[81] After 1988 there were increasingly frequent press reports of those seeking mixed marriages from the Civil Registry Office and the Board of Religious Affairs being refused (Pompe, 1991: 262).

Mahkamah Agung *Decision No 1400K/Pdt/1986*[82]

The Central Jakarta District Court strengthened this trend in 1986 when it held that a marriage between a Muslim woman and Protestant man could not be formalised.[83] Officials at the Board of Religious Affairs had refused to formalise the marriage because the prospective husband was Protestant and the marriage was thus in discord with Islam. The marriage could not be registered at the Civil Registry Office because the girl was Muslim.

The couple sued both institutions, arguing that they had acted illegally. The court denied their claims, upholding the action of the Board of Religious Affairs because the marriage was contrary to *syariah* which, the court decided, regulated mixed marriages by virtue of Art 2(1) of the Marriage Law. The court held that the Civil Registry Office had been correct in refusing their request because it was not authorised to marry a Muslim party. In the court's view, marriage between the two parties was impossible. The girl then appealed to the *Mahkamah Agung*.

The *Mahkamah Agung* panel included the President and the Vice President of the Court. Pompe (1991: 267) argues that this means the case was taken extremely seriously and the decision must have been weighed with particular care. As it had in previous rulings, the court decided that the Marriage Law did not provide for marriages between partners of different religions. However, instead of going on to hold that the GHR applied to this type of marriage by virtue of Art 66 of the Marriage Law, the court went against prior *Mahkamah Agung* jurisprudence and decided that the regulation was based on a mixed marriage system which had since been abandoned in Indonesia. Marriage was now a religious affair, not merely a civil relationship by virtue of the Marriage Law. Consequently, there was a legal vacuum (*kekosongan hukum*)[84] in the area of mixed marriage. Determined to prevent Registry Officials from obstructing mixed marriages the court found a legal basis to allow them.

The court argued that because the couple had applied to the Civil Registry Office after being refused by the Board of Religious Affairs the woman must not have wished to marry in accordance with Islam, and had in fact abandoned it. The court implied that, by lodging the request with the Civil Registry Office, the woman did not have any regard for her religious status, that is, her adherence to Islam. In short, she had apostatised. The *Mahkamah Agung* held that the couple could therefore conclude their marriage at the Civil Registry Office and ordered the institution to formalise the marriage.

---

81 As with many 'decisions' made at the ministerial level in Indonesia, it is unclear where this agreement stands in the hierarchy of Indonesian laws set out in MPRS Decree No XX/MPRS/1966. Is it a policy statement or a formal ministerial decree? Even if it were the latter, it would not appear to have legal force over the GHR which clearly allows mixed marriages.

82 Reproduced in Gautama (1992, vol I: 23-31).

83 Central Jakarta District Court decision no 382/PDT/1986/PN.JKT.PS, cited in Gautama (1992, vol 1: 20-23).

84 Literally, 'an emptiness of law'.

A Critique of the Decision[85]

Although the *Mahkamah Agung* legalised interreligious mixed marriages, its decision was relatively vague, and has injected a substantial degree of uncertainty – even inconsistency – into Indonesian law. The court did not state whether by 'abandoning her religion' the woman was left with no religion, or became an adherent to her husband's Protestant faith.

If the implication of the case is that a Muslim woman who marries a non-Muslim man effectively loses her religion, this seems to be in stark contradiction to *Pancasila*, Indonesia's state ideology, particularly its first principle, which embodies a commitment to *Ketuhanan Yang Maha Esa* (A Supreme Being).[86] All Indonesian laws (and the Marriage Law itself)[87] must be based on *Pancasila* which the MPR has decreed is the 'source of all sources of law'.[88] *Pancasila* must also underlie all judicial decisions.[89] However, one cannot claim allegiance to the Supreme Being without adhering to one of the five religions recognised in Indonesia. Thus, the *Mahkamah Agung*'s decision appears to contradict *Pancasila*, 'the *grundnorm* of Indonesian law and society as a whole' (Hartono, 1996: 23). More pragmatically, whilst one can get by without a strict observance of the rules of any faith it is a rare phenomenon for Indonesians to not at least profess a religion[90] and indeed atheism or agnosticism will lead to social ostracism in some areas of Indonesia. It is therefore ironic that, while the court attempted to bring a couple together under *Pancasila*'s third principle (the 'The Unity of Indonesia'), if the wife had no religion she would be excluded from the public service and restricted in many other areas of Indonesian life (Pompe, 1991: 269).

The *Mahkamah Agung* also seems to have detracted from Indonesia's progression towards establishing the formal legal equality of women. The court did not justify why the woman should give up her religion and not the man. There is little validity in the argument that the woman implicitly abandoned her religion because Islamic law forbade her to marry someone of a different religion (Pompe,

---

85 Pompe (1991) has written a detailed critique of the case. The following section draws significantly from his work.

86 The other four principles of *Pancasila*, a Sanskrit-derived term which literally means 'The Five Principles', are:

   2. *Kemanusiaan Yang Adil dan Beradab* (A Just and Civilised Humanity);
   3. *Persatuan Indonesia* (Indonesian Unity);
   4. *Keraykatan Yang Dipimpin Oleh Hikmat Kebijaksanaan dalam Pemusyawaratan/ Perwakilan* (Leadership of the People by Wise Policies Arrived at through a Process of Consultation and Consensus); and
   5. *Keadilan Sosial Bagi Seluruh Rakyat Indonesia* (Social Justice for all Indonesian People).

87 Elucidation, Part 3.

88 MPR Decree No XX/MPRS/1966, Memorandum, Hierarchy of Laws of the Republic of Indonesia, cited in Hartojo (1992: 10).

89 'Indonesian laws must adhere to *Pancasila* in spirit, content, and implementation' (Daman, 1993: 141). See, for example, *Mahkamah Agung* Decision No 04/K/Kr/1973, 28 August, 1974, where the *Mahkamah Agung* heard an appeal because the Demak *Pengadilan Negeri* and Semarang *Pengadilan Tinggi* had not decided the case in accordance with the first principle of *Pancasila* (Yurisprudensi Indonesia, 1974: 23).

90 Whether Indonesians actually adhere strictly to the religion they profess to have is another matter entirely. Not all Indonesian Muslims adhere strictly to Islam: the larger portion are the so-called *Muslim statistik* as opposed to the *Muslim fanatik* minority (Pompe & Otto, 1990: 415).

1991: 270). Indeed, there is as much credibility (if not more) in the argument that the man had abrogated his religion by approaching the Religious Affairs Office — which only formalises marriages conducted under Islamic law — *before* he approached the Civil Registry Office. The *Mahkamah Agung* did not consider this argument, even though some Protestant Churches are quite dogmatic about their members marrying interreligiously (Pompe, 1991: 270).[91] It is thus quite unclear whether the court discriminated against the woman because of her sex or because of her religious beliefs. Would the court have allowed a marriage between a Muslim woman and a Buddhist man, or between a Muslim man and a Hindu woman? Will a Muslim man implicitly abandon his faith if he marries a Buddhist girl? Has the court in fact consciously or subconsciously applied the colonial Mixed Marriage Regulation it purported to abrogate, which states that the woman is to cede to the religion of the man for the purposes of a mixed marriage? If so, this is a backward step for the Indonesian women's movement and indeed a breach of legal principles expounding the equality of the sexes mentioned above.

The decision can also be criticised on related constitutional grounds. In addition to the provision in Art 27 of the Constitution providing for equality of the sexes (which the court itself referred to and which, it stated, 'embraces the fundamental right ... to marry a fellow citizen, regardless of any religion'), the court cited Art 29(2) of the 1945 Constitution. This asserts that the 'state shall guarantee the freedom of the people to express and to exercise their own religion'. The provision seems to imply that the state must leave the individual to practise his or her religion, and cannot force anyone to abandon their religion (Pompe, 1991: 270). Holding that the woman had implicitly abandoned her religion or that she implicitly ceded to her husband's religion appears to contradict both these constitutional provisions. This appears to be a rare instance where both a *Mahkamah Agung* decision and the 1945 Constitution are sufficiently clear to conclude that the court's decision is unconstitutional.

Why, then, given the problems with the *Mahkamah Agung*'s decision, did the court depart from its prior decisions which appeared to be well reasoned and analytically sound? Its previous rulings, with which Muslims did not agree, were made whilst the Indonesian elite was attempting to suppress Islamic aspirations (Schwarz, 1994: 175). However, in recent years, some authors have argued that the role of religion has become so pronounced that the government has seen the need to appear to forbid marriages that do not accord with Islam (Pompe & Otto, 1990: 420). Muslims have recently indicated that they are still opposed to mixed marriages.[92] Perhaps effectively prohibiting a Muslim woman from marrying a non-Muslim man can be seen as a step towards the recognition of Islamic law.

The Soeharto elite has been courting Islamic groups for some time, possibly because the President was uncertain whether he could still rely on military support for the regime (Lindsey, 1996: 31). Although President Soeharto has not improved Islamic political representation, he has played to Islamic interests on other issues and tried to burnish his own Muslim credentials (Schwarz, 1994: 175). He injected a

---

91 Indeed, in a survey of 1000 urban Indonesians conducted by the Institute for Research, Education and Information of Social and Economic Affairs (LP3ES), only 50% of non-Muslims surveyed stated that they would accept interreligious marriages. 48% said they would reject them outright (Jakarta Post, 1997: 1).

92 In the LP3ES poll, 81% said they would not accept their relatives marrying people of different faiths. 86% of Muslims respondents (who comprised 88% of those interviewed) said they would not accept interfaith marriages (Jakarta Post, 1997: 1).

more Islamic element into the national school curriculum; gave more authority to the *agama* courts (although this is more apparent than real); helped establish Indonesia's first Islamic-style bank;[93] and made a pilgrimage to Mecca in 1991 (Schwarz, 1994: 175). The emergence of this so-called 'Islamic revival' in the late 1980s corresponds chronologically with the 1989 *Mahkamah Agung* decision.

This argument may, however, be too simplistic. From the perspective of Islamic law, the *Mahkamah Agung* has, its seems, placed the woman in a very difficult position. To abandon the Islamic religion under the Shafite School of Islamic law which applies in Indonesia is abhorrent and theoretically carries the death penalty (Pompe, 1991: 269). On this basis the *Mahkamah Agung*'s decision is impossible to reconcile with orthodox Islam.

The court has also ignored the opinion of the Indonesian Council of *Ulama* (Islamic scholars), who issued a *fatwa* (legal decision) on 1 June 1980 in response to growing concern in Muslim circles over the increasing frequency of interreligious marriages.[94] The Council, contrary to the *Qur'an* and the *fikh* texts, explicitly forbade both male and female Muslims to marry non-Muslims. This *fatwa* must have been considered particularly significant as the issue was discussed and decided at a nationwide annual conference instead of the usual limited deliberation of the *fatwa* committee (Lubis, 1994: 231).

Mohammad Atho Mudzhar (1993: 88) has argued that this *fatwa* was essentially directed towards preventing Muslim men and women from converting to Christianity. According to Nur Ahmad Fadhil Lubis (1994: 231), the fear of 'Christianisation', which is equated with secularism, has been prevalent amongst Muslims since colonial times. Converted Christian Indonesians enjoyed better treatment from the Dutch and had more chance of gaining a Western-style education. Their expertise led the New Order government to employ many Christian technocrats in key positions. Lubis interviewed several Islamic judges who perceived marriages between Muslims and Christians as 'hidden Christianisation'. They feared that such marriages would water down Islam, and increase the ranks of Christians. Some of them cited an incident where a female student of the State Institute of Islamic Studies specialising in theology had converted to Christianity to marry the son of a priest. The *ulama* seemed to decide that Christian – Muslim rivalries had 'reached such a point that, for the sake of the Muslim community's growth, the doorway to interreligious marriages had better be shut altogether' (Mudzhar, 1993: 89).

Nevertheless, it is hard to determine the practical effect of the decision. The judgment seems to have had little impact on the practices of parties who wished to marry interreligiously when many state institutions were refusing to conclude their marriages. Many Indonesians, not wishing to lose their religious status, have misrepresented their religions to marriage officials (Soewondo, 1991-1992: 35). Others have converted to their partner's religion for the purposes of the marriage, and then reverted to their original religion a short time later (Asmin, 1986: 81). Indeed, the negative social and religious implications of the decision may be pushing people into the informal and illegal sphere of *kumpul kebo* (cohabitation) (Pompe, 1988: 260). Cohabitation is on the rise in Indonesia, in particular among couples of mixed religious backgrounds (Pompe, 1988: 260; Tempo, 1984).

---

93   Government Regulation No 77 of 1992.

94   For an excellent account of the background to this *fatwa*, see Mohammad Atho Mudzhar (1993: 86-87).

Furthermore, despite the *Mahkamah Agung* decision, there have been reports that some state registration officers are still refusing interreligious marriages on an ad hoc basis (Law & Society Review, 1994: 485). In this sense, the *Mahkamah Agung* has had less of an impact in 'facilitating' mixed marriages, than feeding bureaucratic corruption. Cammack et al (1996: 65) have explained that the state does not pay Marriage Registrars for their work. They rely on a negotiated 'honorarium', paid by the couple in return for a marriage certificate. The difference between this payment and an illegal bribe is blurred, and 'social norms against bribery are comparatively weak in Indonesia'.

Conclusion

The government has not abandoned its aim of expropriating family law rules, but has found it expedient to articulate its regulatory efforts in a more Islamic idiom. In its efforts to preserve the religious grounding of Indonesian marriage rules for the Muslim majority, Islamic interests are being pressed to accept novel interpretations of Islamic law, and to recognise a larger role for the Indonesian government in interpreting the Islamic tradition (Cammack et al, 1996: 46).

The Marriage Law throws the contest between Islam and the state into stark relief. Although Muslims may have succeeded in forcing the government to cede to their interests in 1974 recent developments indicate that the state has begun to monopolise Islamic law and the *agama* courts by subjugating them to state-based authority. However, the government has instigated these changes slowly (apparently to avoid a repeat of the 1974 discontent) and, importantly, has only tampered with Islamic law and administration when it had the apparent approval of the *Ulama*. The state has not formally abolished polygamy but has made it almost impossible for Muslim men to obtain the judicial consent required to take more than one wife. The political elite therefore appears to have effectively achieved many of the goals it wished to attain when it first set out to codify Indonesian marriage law, despite the watered-down nature of the legislation it has produced. It has achieved this de facto legal transformation without inciting Muslim groups to protest at the level they did in 1974. The formal legal equality of Indonesian women has been largely established regarding polygamy. The state can claim to the international community that women's rights are protected and although some (relatively minor) concessions to Islam have been made the government has exhibited its ultimate authority over Islam with respect to polygamy.

In the area of mixed interreligious marriage, the *fiqh* has been offended, but the *Mahkamah Agung*'s prima facie adherence to *syariah* has left its decision relatively untouched by Muslim criticism. The state has, again, displayed its authority over Islam. But facilitating interreligious marriages has come at a price. The decision leaves the law of mixed marriages in Indonesia uncertain, and also tends towards contradicting one of the Marriage Law's main goals: to establish the formal legal equality of Indonesian women.

References

Abdurrahman and Riduan Syahrani, 1978, *Masalah-masalah Hukum Perkawinan di Indonesia* (Issues in Marriage Law in Indonesia), Alumni, Bandung.

Anderson, N, 1976, *Law Reform in the Muslim World*, Athlone Press, London.

Asia Watch, 1988, *Human Rights Concerns in Indonesia and East Timor*, Asia Watch Committee, USA.

Asmin, 1986, *Status Perkawinan Antar Agama ditinjau dari Undang-undang Perkawinan No 1/1974* (The Status of Interreligious Mixed Marriage Viewed from the Marriage Law No 1/1974), Dian Rakyat, Jakarta.

BPHN, 1991/1992, *Laporan Penelitian tentang Peningkatan Yurisprudensi sebagai Sumber Hukum* (Investigative Report concerning Raising Jurisprudence to a Source of Law), Badan Pembinaan Hukum Nasional, Departemen Kehakiman RI, Jakarta.

Ball, J, 1995, *Indonesian Law: Commentary and Teaching Materials*, 2nd ed, University of Sydney, Sydney.

Butt, S, 1997, *Mahkamah Agung or Makam Negara Hukum: Judicial Independence and Review in Indonesia's Negara Hukum* (unpublished Honours Thesis, Asian Studies Faculty, Australian National University).

Cammack, Mark, 1989, 'Islamic Law in Indonesia's New Order', *International and Comparative Law Quarterly*, vol 38: 53.

Cammack, M, Young, L and Heaton, T, 1996, 'Legislating Social Change in an Islamic Society – Indonesia's Marriage Law', *American Journal of Comparative Law*, vol 44: 45.

Departamen Agama RI, 1984, *Pedoman Pegawai Nikah (PNN)* (Handbook for Marriage Registry Officials), Jakarta.

Department of Religion, 1985/1986, *Perkawinan Antar Agama, Poligami dan Pelanggaran Undang-Undang Perkawinan: Laporan Akhir Penelitian* (Interreligious Marriage, Polygamy and Breaches of the Marriage Law: Final Research Report), Badan Penelitian dan Pengembangan Agama, Proyek Penelitian Keagamaan, Bagian Proyek Penelitian Kehidupan Beragama, Departemen Agama.

Department of Religion, 1987/1988, *Laporan Studi tentang Kasus Keagamaan* (Study Report concerning Cases of Religiosity), Badan Penelitian dan Pengembangan Agama, Departemen Agama, Jakarta.

Department of Information, 1975, 'Introduction', in *The Indonesian Marriage Law*, Department of Information, Republic of Indonesia, Jakarta.

Dirkien, AA Ngurah Gede, I Nyoman Mudana, AA Gede Oka Parwarta & AA Ketut Sukranatha, 1989, *Laporan Penelitian: Masalah Terjadinya Poligami tanpa Izin Pengadilan di Kecamatan Klungkung* (Research Report: The Problem of the Occurrence of Polygamy without Court Permission in the Subdistrict of Klungkung), Fakultas Hukum Universitas Udayana, Denpasar.

Doi, Abdur Rahman I, 1989, *Women in Shariah (Islamic Law)*, Ta Ha Publishers, United Kingdom.

Emmerson, D, 1976, *Indonesia's Elite Political Culture and Cultural Politics*, Cornell University Press, London.

Esposito, J, 1982, *Women in Muslim Family Law*, Syracuse University Press, New York.

Fitzpatrick, D, 1997, 'Disputes and Pluralism in Modern Indonesian Land Law', *Yale Journal of International Law*, vol 22: 171.

Gautama, S and Hornick R, 1983, *An Introduction to Indonesian Law: Unity in Diversity*, Penerbit Alumni, Bandung.

Gautama, S, 1991, 'The Marriage Laws of Indonesia with Special Reference to Mixed Marriages' in Gautama, S (ed), *Essays in Indonesian Law*, Citra Aditya Bakti, Jakarta.

Gautama, S, 1992, *Himpunan Yurisprudensi Indonesia yang Penting untuk Praktek Sehari-hari (Landmark Decisions), berikut Komentar* (Compilation of Indonesian Jurisprudence which is Important for Everyday Practice), vol 1, Citra Aditya Bakti, Bandung.

Gautama, S, 1992, *Himpunan Yurisprudensi Indonesia yang Penting untuk Praktek Sehari-hari (Landmark Decisions), berikut Komentar* (Compilation of Indonesian Jurisprudence which is Important for Everyday Practice), vol 2, Citra Aditya Bakti, Bandung.

Gautama, S, 1987, '*Mahkamah Agung* dan Keanekaragaman Hukum Perdata' (The *Mahkamah Agung* and The Variations of the Civil Law), *Hukum dan Pembangunan*, vol 17, no 2: 163.

Gerke, S, 1992/1993 'Indonesian National Development Ideology and the Role of Women', *Indonesian Circle*, vols 59 & 60: 46.

Gray, C, 1991, 'Legal Process and Economic Development: A Case Study of Indonesia', *World Development*, vol 19, no 7: 763.

Harahap, 1975, *Hukum Perkawinan Nasional* (National Marriage Law), Zahir, Medan.

Hartojo, 1992, *Himpunan Pilihan Ketetapan MPRS/MPR tahun 1966-1988 yang Masih Berlaku* (Selected Compilation of MPRS/MPR Decrees between 1966-1998 which are Still in Force), Media Wiyata, Semarang.

Hartono, S, 1996, 'An Overview of Legal Developments in Indonesia: Towards the Establishment of a National Legal System' in Creyke, R, Disney, J and McMillan, J (eds), *Aspects of Administrative Review in Australia and Indonesia*, Faculty of Law, Australian National University, Canberra.

Hartono, S, 1992/1993, 'Kata Pengantar' (Introductory Remarks), in *Laporan Akhir Pengkajian Hukum Tentang Perkawinan Campuran (Dalam Hukum Perdata Internasional)* (Final Report of the Legal Investigation concerning Mixed Marriage (in International Civil Law)), Badan Pembinaan Hukum Nasional, Departemen Kehakiman.

Hazairin, 1975, *Tinjauan mengenai UU Perkawinan Nomor 1/1974 dan Lampiran UU Nomor 1/1974*, Tinta Mas, Jakarta.

Hooker, MB, 1978, *Adat Law in Modern Indonesia*, Oxford University Press, Kuala Lumpur.

Hooker, MB, 1978, *A Concise Legal History of South-East Asia*, Clarendon, Oxford.

Hooker, MB, 1984, *Islamic law in South-East Asia*, Oxford University Press, Singapore.

Hull, VJ, 1976, *Women in Java's rural middle class: Progress or Regress?*, Gadjah Mada University.

Jakarta Post, 1995, 'Indonesia: How Women Respond to Polygamy', 29 April: 7.

Jakarta Post, 1995, 'Indonesia: Feminist Demands Polygamy be Abolished', 29 April: 6.

Jakarta Post, 1997, 'Religious Coexistence in RI Strong', 9 January: 1.

Jawa Pos Online, 1996, 'Bismar Siregar; Keributan dan Citra *Mahkamah Agung*: "Ngeri kalau Dilakukan Debat Terbuka"' (Bismar Siregar: The Disturbance and Image of the *Mahkamah Agung*: It is Scary if there is to be an Open Debate), 17 July.

Jawad, M, 1981, 'Women and the Question of Polygamy in Islam', *Islamic Quarterly*, vol 35: 181.

Johns, A, 1987, 'Indonesia: Islam and Cultural Pluralism' in Esposito, J (ed), *Islam in Asia: Religion, Politics, and Society*, Oxford University Press, USA, 1987.

Kartini, Raden Adjeng, 1976, *Letters of a Javanese Princess*, Oxford University Press, Kuala Lumpur.

Katz, J and Katz, R, 1975, 'The New Indonesian Marriage Law: A Mirror of Indonesia's Political, Cultural, and Legal System', *American Journal of Comparative Law*, vol 23: 653.

Katz, J and Katz, R, 1978, 'Legislating Social Change in a Developing Country: The New Indonesian Marriage Law Revisited', *American Journal of Comparative Law*, vol 26: 309.

Kompas Online, 1996, 'Daerah Sekilas' (A Twinkling Region), 2 October.

Kompas Online, 1997, 'Mendesak Penyempurnaan Hukum Nasional' (Perfecting National Law is Urgent), 24 May.

Lapidas, I, 1988, *A History of Islamic Societies*, Cambridge University Press, New York.

Law & Society Review, 1994, 'Comments and Discussion', vol 28: 477.

Lev, DS, 1965, 'The Lady and the Banyan Tree: Civil-Law Change in Indonesia', *American Journal of Comparative Law*, vol 14: 282.

Lev, DS, 1962, 'The Supreme Court and *Adat* Inheritance Law in Indonesia', *American Journal of Comparative Law*, vol 11: 205.

Lev, DS, 1972a, *Islamic Courts in Indonesia*, University of California Press, Berkeley, 1972.

Lev, DS, 1972b, 'Judicial Institutions and Legal Culture in Indonesia' in Holt, C (ed), *Culture and Politics in Indonesia*, Ithaca, Cornell University Press, NJ, 1972.

Lev, DS, 1996a, 'Between State and Society: Professional Lawyers and Reform in Indonesia', in Lev, D and McVey, R (eds), *Making Indonesia*, Cornell University, Ithaca, NY.

Lev, DS, 1996b, 'On the Other Hand' in Sears, LJ (ed), *Fantasizing the Feminine in Indonesia*, LJ, Duke University Press, Durham.

Lindsey, T, 1996, *The Indonesian Legal System*, Northern Territory University, Faculty of Law, Centre for Southeast Asian Law, Darwin.

Lubis, Nur Ahmad Fadhil, 1995, 'Institutionalization and the Unification of Agama courts under the New Order', *Studia Islamika*, vol 2: 7.

Lubis, Nur Ahmad Fadhil, 1994, *Islamic Justice in Transition: A Socio-Legal Study of the Agama Court Judges in Indonesia* (PhD dissertation, University of California, Los Angeles).

Murtopo, Ali, 1982, *Strategi Pembangunan Nasional* (The National Development Strategy), CSIS, Jakarta.

Mudzhar, Mohammad Atho, 1993, *Fatwas of the Council of Indonesian Ulama: A Study of Islamic Legal Thought in Indonesia 1975-1988*, bilingual edn, INIS, Jakarta.

Muhammad, Din, 1995, 'Pembinaan Hakim dalam PJP II' (The Development of Judges in the Second Long Term Development Plan) in *Seminar Akbar 50 Tahun Pembinaan Hukum sebagai Modal bagi Pembangunan Hukum Negara dalam PJP II* (Large Seminar 50 years of Legal Creation as the Base for National Legal Development in the Second Long Term Development Plan), Badan Pembinaan Hukum Nasional, Departemen Kehakiman, Jakarta.

Nuraja, 1985, 'Pelaksanaan Pasal-pasal 3 ayat (2) sampai Pasal 5 dan pasal 7 ayat (2) pada Pengadilan Agama Jakarta Utara Tahun 1980-1982' (The Implementation of Articles 3(2), 5 and 7(2) in the North Jakarta Religious Court 1980-1982), *Hukum dan Pembangunan*, vol 5: 486.

Pompe, S, 1994, 'Between Crime and Custom: Extra-Marital Sex in Modern Indonesian Law', *Bijdragen tot de Taal-, Land- en Volkenkunde*, vol 150, no 1: 110.

Pompe, S, 1992, *Indonesian Law 1949-1989: a Bibliography of Foreign-language Materials with Brief Commentaries on the Law*, M Nijhoff Publishers, Boston.

Pompe, S, 1988, 'Mixed Marriages in Indonesia: Some Comments on the Law and the Literature', *Bijdragen tot de Taal-, Land- en Volkenkunde*, vols 2e & 3e: 259.

Pompe S, 1991, 'A Short Note on Some Recent Developments With Regard to Mixed Marriages in Indonesia', *Bijdragen tot de Taal-, Land- en Volkenkunde*, vols 2e & 3e: 261.

Pompe, S and Otto J M, 1990, 'Some Comments on Recent Developments in the Indonesian Marriage Law with Particular Respect to the Rights of Women', *Verfassung und Recht in Ubersee*, vol 4: 415.

Prakoso, Djoko and I Ketut Murtika, 1987, *Azas-azas Hukum Perkawinan Di Indonesia* (Elements of Marriage Law in Indonesia), Bina Aksara, Jakarta.

Ramage, D,1993, *Ideological Discourse in the Indonesian New Order: State Ideology and the Beliefs of an Elite, 1985-1993* (Ph D Thesis, University of South Carolina), Ann Arbor.

Rozikin, Daman, 1993, *Hukum Tata Negara* (Constitutional Law), PT Raja Grafindo Persada, Jakarta.

Rusli and Tama, R, 1984, *Perkawinan Antar Agama dan Masalahnya Sebagai Pelengkap UU Perkawinan No 1, Tahun 1974* (Interreligious Marriage and its Problems, as a Supplement to the Marriage Law No 1, 1974), Shantika Dharma, Bandung.

Schwarz, Adam, 1994, *A Nation in Waiting: Indonesia in the 1990s*, Allen & Unwin, Sydney.

Sodiki, 1976, *Report on a Study of the Documentation of Fifty-Four Decisions of the Religious Court of Malang in May*: Institute of Law and Population of the Law Faculty of Brawijaya University, Malang, 1977: 22, cited in Katz, J and Katz, R, 1978, 'Legislating Social Change in a Developing Country: The New Indonesian Marriage Law Revisited', *American Journal of Comparative Law*, vol 26: 309 at 311.

Soesangobeng, H, 1988, 'Perkembangan Konsepsi Tanah Dalam Masyarakat Desa: 25 Tahun UUPA' (The Development of Conceptions of Land in Village Communities), *Kabar Seberang*, vols 19-20: 59.

Soewondo, Nani, 1977, 'The Indonesian Marriage Law and its Implementing Regulations', *Archipel*, vol 13: 283.

Soewondo, Nani, 1991-1992, *Analisa dan Evaluasi Hukum Tidak Tertulis tentang Hukum Kebiasaan dalam Perkawinan Campuran* (Analysis and Evaluation of the Unwritten Law of Custom in Mixed Marriage), Badan Pembinaan Hukum Nasional, Departemen Kehakiman, Jakarta.

Soewonto, Nani, 1976, 'Law and the Status of Women in Indonesia', *Columbia Human Rights Law Review*, vol 8: 123.

Subadio, Maria Ullfah, 1981, *Perjuangan untuk Mencapai Undang-undang Perkawinan* (The Struggle to Achieve the Marriage Law), Yayasan Idayu, Jakarta.

Sumardjo, Maria, 1996, *Real Property Ownership and Protection in Indonesia* (on file with author).

Suryakusuma, J, 1987, *State Ibuism: The Social Construction of Womanhood in the Indonesian New Order*, (unpublished MA Thesis, ISS, The Hague).

Suryakusuma, J, 1996, 'The State and Sexuality in New Order Indonesia' in Sears, LJ (ed), *Fantasizing the Feminine in Indonesia*, Duke University Press, Durham.

Tempo, 1984, 'Kumpul Kerbau Gaya Yogya' (Cohabitation Yogya Style), 16 June.

Tempo Interaktif, 1996, 'Memulihkan Muka MA Yang "Klejingan"' (Retrieving the Face of the MA which is Shaken), 29 November.

Van Langenberg, M, 1986, 'Analysing Indonesia's New Order State: A Keywords Approach', *Review of Indonesian and Malaysian Affairs*, vol 20: 1.

Wantjik, Saleh, 1980, *Hukum Perkawinan Indonesia* (National Marriage Law), 6th ed, Ghalia, Jakarta.

Weinata Sairin and Pattiasina, JM (eds), 1994, *Pelaksanaan Undang-undang Perkawinan Dalam Perspektif Kristen* (The Implementation of the Marriage Law from a Christian Perspective), BPK Gunung Mulia, Jakarta.

Yurisprudensi Indonesia, vol 1974, *Mahkamah Agung*, Jakarta, 1974.

Yurisprudensi Indonesia, vol 1980, *Mahkamah Agung*, Jakarta, 1980.

Zubairie, A, 1985, *Pelaksanaan Hukum Perkawinan Campuran Antara Islam & Kristen* (The Implementation of the Law on Mixed Marriage between Muslims and Christians), TB 'Bahagia', Pekalongan.

9. Murder, Gender and the Media: Sexualising Politics and Violence

Saraswati Sunindyo

This chapter focuses on three cases of wife or mistress murder that gained media and public attention in Indonesia in the 1980s. In contrast to other less-publicised cases of the murder of women,[1] these three seemed to entail political scandal. The perpetrators were (or were rumoured to be) functionaries of state commonly criticised for corruption and oppressiveness. It was this that drew attention to the cases and obscured the male violence against women that was involved. The media and public discourse in these cases, however, engaged representations of sexuality: the victims were 'sexualised' while the aggressors were somehow 'desexualised' by attributing their motives to a desire to protect their families.

I will argue that the representation of these three cases reconstructs gender ideology by attempting to control women's sexuality, distinguish 'good' women from 'bad' women and exclude women who do not fit into the typology of a 'good mother'. Such construction or reconstruction of gender did not take place in a political vacuum. It was linked to the substantiation of the bourgeois ideology of motherhood – that is, women as nurturer of her offspring, her husband and finally of the community and national spirit; that is, the woman's role as officially sanctioned by the Indonesian state.

The Political Context

Before 1980, Indonesian society was the site of persistent political dissatisfaction expressed in events such as the 1974 student protests known as the 'Malari Affair', a wave of student activism and the first mass protests during the New Order era. The students focused on the dependency of Indonesian economic development on

---

1   There were other cases, some solved, some not: the murder of Dewi, a career woman whose office was in the Sahid Jaya Hotel, Jakarta; the murder of Julia Jarsin, a film actress, also in Jakarta; and that of an unknown woman in Makasar, Sulawesi. These three cases gained media attention when first discovered, but inspired less public discourse and political gossip than the three cases discussed in this chapter because they lacked the political dimension of state officials as perpetrators. In 1989 there was another brutal killing in a style known as *mayat dipotong tujuh* (a corpse chopped into seven). The media sensationalised the case and the murderer was quickly arrested, put on trial and convicted. This case was a classic representation of violence against women: the victim's husband had a secret wife, and claimed that he had to kill his first wife because day-in and day-out she treated him with disrespect, that is, she never cooked breakfast and made him clean her shoes every morning before she left for work. The victim was represented as a bad wife, although the husband was convicted.

foreign aid and investment (largely from Japan). In their analyses development was closely tied to the interests of the political elite and its business collaborators. The demonstrators demanded, among other things, the dissolution of the presidential panel of personal advisors (*Aspri – assisten pribadi* or private assistant) and the eradication of corruption (ICJ, 1987: 86-88). The student demonstration was followed by violent riots in Pasar Senen, one of the major commercial districts and shopping areas of Jakarta. The Malari Affair resulted in mass arrests of student leaders and the banning of 11 newspapers and one magazine, with five of the newspapers still outlawed 20 years later.

Social dissatisfaction continued and another wave of student protests broke out in 1977-79, climaxing with the publication of a student manifesto known as *Buku Putih* (White Book). The White Book criticised the New Order Government, again focusing on its abuse of power, corruption and on economic inequities, with a very strong appeal for political changes. It was banned shortly after it appeared and student arrests and trials followed (ICJ, 1987: 90-91).

In addition to the student protests, there were many other manifestations of a generalised protest consciousness. One of the major sources of dissatisfaction with the regime was the problem of corruption and the states' incompetence in handling it despite official claims to the contrary. The police were an obvious target for the public's general resentment. One of the expressions in everyday public conversation before 1980 was the prase *prit-jigo*, a derogatory expression for the police.[2] Although a specific term, the meaning reflects a wider discontent against the whole military and the regime in general.[3]

Corruption, commonly the eliciting and acceptance of bribes, had become a well-known attribute of public officials. Another way to influence an official was to offer him sexual companions. Hotels, bars, massage parlours and other tourist facilities were sites for the 'immorality' associated with corruption and bribery.[4] Anti-corruption campaigns, however, have usually clung to the conservative position that women and sex are the main corrupting factors, rather than instruments of the main corrupting factor, the official abuse of power.

In 1979 a national newspaper, *Sinar Harapan*, published a series called *Remang-remang Jakarta*, a report on prostitution in Jakarta. The reports were published daily, and both the content and the character of the stories made the series (later published as a book) into a sensational subject of conversation (Krisna, 1979). The articles mixed sensation and sexual inquisitiveness with the exposure of decadent and corrupt bureaucrats.

Among the articles were interviews with those involved in the prostitution business, providing information about the clients and the women, including some well-known figures identified only by initials. For example, the paper ran the

---

2 *Prit* is the sound of a whistle and *jigo* is a slang term, originally from Chinese, for 'five hundred'. '*Prit-jigo*' therefore suggests that the blowing of a police whistle always leads to the extortion of Rp 500.

3 When Rene, a student from the Bandung Institute of Technology (ITB) was killed after a soccer match between the police academy and ITB, sentiment against ABRI (*Angkatan Bersenjata Republik Indonesia*, the Indonesian armed forces, which includes the police) increased. Among the banners carried by students of ITB during the funeral procession was '*Prit-jigo*' and 'ABRI *mana janjimu*' ('ABRI, what about your promise').

4 During the Malari Affair, for example, during the riot following the student demonstration, Jalan Blora, a street known for its steam-bath and massage parlour houses (covert prostitution operations), was one of the targets of mass anger.

confession of a pimp who had started out as an independent construction contractor. In order to win contracts, he had to provide women to government officials and businessmen. The story of a madam revealed that she had seven powerful men backing, or financially supporting, her (*backing* is also the term used in Indonesia) (Yuyu Krisna, 1979: 42-44). The same series revealed that a popular magazine had served as a sales catalogue for high-class prostitutes during the 1970s (Krisna, 1979: 42-44). This provocative series, however, even when published as a book, offered no in-depth analysis of prostitution.[5] As a result, the public reaction to the expose remained rooted in moral puritanism and sexism.

The Politics of Gender

The New Order Government strictly enforced an ideological approach toward the role of women and women's organisations and their voices were transformed into 'New Order fashion'. Shortly after the New Order took power in 1966, many existing women's organisations were banned, left-leaning women activists were jailed or were killed in massacres, and the national women's organisation, *Kowani* (*Kongres Wanita Indonesia*, Indonesian Women's Congress) became paralysed. This resulted from the fact that *Kowani*'s leadership had been dominated by *Gerwani* (the leftist women's movement influenced by the PKI (*Partai Komunis Indonesia*), the Indonesian Communist Party) (see Suryochondro, 1984; Wieringa, 1985). Consequently, many women's issue raised by the Old Order women's organisations and activists, such as child care and sexual harassment, were also seen as tainted and were dropped from all practical agendas.[6]

A new women's organisation was formed in 1974 called *Dharma Wanita* (Women's Duty), a national organisation headed by the First Lady of the republic, which functioned as an umbrella organisation for women's organisations in all government offices. *Dharma Wanita* membership is mandatory for every woman working in a government office and for all wives of government employees. The leadership structure parallels the hierarchy of the husbands' offices and positions. The more outspoken women's organisations were paralysed; and *Dharma Wanita* clearly did not aim to articulate women's rights issues.[7] The New Order government also launched a program for women described as Family Welfare Guidance. Described as a movement to promote 'community well-being', the program started

---

5   Instead it adhered to traditional distinctions between male and female sex drives. The book's introduction by Indonesian novelist Ashadi Siregar merely offered some views about how prostitutes, in pursuit of their own dreams, exchanged sex for money and a glamorous life. He implies that such an exchange is unacceptable to 'normal' women.

6   This was especially true during the first decades of the New Order. In the beginning of the 1980s feminist non-government organisations appeared voicing feminist issues (see Wieringa, 1985).

7   According to the New Order government, the rationale for forming *Dharma Wanita* was to strengthen national unity; to secure the loyalty of government employees; to increase political stability; to concentrate all the energy of the civil service on assisting the economic development plan; and to encourage the wives of the government employees to support their husbands' careers and responsibilities. Other goals of this organisation formulated by the New Order government included: giving guidance in promoting and strengthening women's consciousness and responsibility towards the nation; promoting the channelling of 'sisterly' sentiments under one national banner; and mobilising all wives' organisations in the direction of service to the nation (Korwani, 1978; Suryochondro, 1984)

by concentrating on women in rural areas. Today every village head's office displays a poster listing the five precepts or *Panca Dharma Wanita* (Five Responsibilities of Women). A wife is to:

- support her husband's career and duties;
- provide offspring;
- care for and rear the children;
- be a good housekeeper; and
- be a guardian of the community

(Wieringa, 1985; Notopuro, 1984; Prodjohadidjo, 1974)

Clearly this ideology of women as offspring-producers, mothers and guardians of the national interest, did not first appear when the New Order government took power, nor did it exist only because the state reinforced it through *Dharma Wanita* and its family welfare programs. The post-1965 state, however, put its weight behind these notions. While women's organisations that were concerned with women's rights issues were banned and their activities stigmatised as a result of the abortive coup of 1965, the Family Welfare Guidance program and *Dharma Wanita* were well placed, working from the top government offices to the grassroots level, promoting their creed and causes.[8]

The Supadmi Case

On 26 March 1981, the East Java Military High Court sentenced two police intelligence officers, Lieutenant Colonel Suyono and Captain Bastari, to prison, the former for six years and six months and the latter for five years.[9] Both were found guilty of attempting the premeditated murder of Mrs Supadmi (Kompas, 1981d). Suyono, who was about to be appointed as a *bupati* (regent) in an East Javanese district, botched an attempt to kill his mistress with the help of his subordinate, Bastari. The case attracted unrestrained media fascination.

Mrs Supadmi, a 'high-class' call girl, who was sitting beside her lieutenant colonel 'lover and protector' in the front seat of a police jeep, was first hit on the head by the captain from the back seat. Two shots were fired when she grabbed at the gun pointed at her head. When she realised that her 'protector' actually meant to murder her, she held her breath and pretended to be dead. The assailants took her out of the car and fired another shot at her throat. Stripped naked and thrown into a pit over 15 metres deep (the location is called *Jurang Gupit* – the Deep Pit), her

---

8   The New Order state ideology concerning women is not without contradictions. In the late 1970s the government, through its Ministry of Women's Affairs, campaigned for a 'women and development' program. It encouraged women to participate in the labour force through their *peran ganda wanita* (double roles as women). In the 1980s the New Order government promoted the sending of women to work in the Middle Eastern countries. Both married and unmarried women were eligible for this employment opportunity, leaving their families for long periods. The *Panca Dharma Wanita* precept of being a good mother and caring for children was apparently irrelevant in this case.

9   Both had been jailed from the day they surrendered to the police until the day of the sentencing. The six year, six-month period was counted from the first day they were jailed, not from the day of the verdict.

body caught on some bushes before it hit the bottom. When she heard the car leave, she crawled back to the road.

Mrs Supadmi was found by a truck driver and a forest engineer. On the way to the hospital, fearing that she was going to die, she asked her rescuers to write down the name, titles, ranks and the office addresses of her two killers. She did not die and the media craze began.

Media Construction: Contradiction

The first news concerning the matter broke four days later in *Sinar Harapan* (1980a), a major national newspaper, after a press conference held by the East Java police command. The story stated that on 23 August 1980, the forest police of Bojonegoro, East Java, found a naked woman, bloody and wounded in the neck, both thighs and palms. The Police Command of East Java had accordingly arrested Lieutenant Colonel Suyono and Captain Bastari, who confessed to shooting the victim. This news became a big and juicy issue – two police officers had attempted to murder a women in a brutal way. However, the same story also released the police finding that the motive was extortion.

> Unexpectedly, the victim, who had been a mistress of Lieutenant Colonel Suyono, had demanded a large amount of allowance, a house, and a car. If Suyono refused to give her all she asked for, she would tell his wife about their relationship. All of these demands could not be fulfilled by Suyono by any means (Berita Buana, 1980; Kompas, 1980; Sinar Harapan, 1980).

Thus four days after Mrs Supadmi was rescued and while she was still in the hospital, recovering from surgery to remove a bullet from her jaw, a statement was published attributing a very sympathetic motive to her assailant: a man in a high-ranking police department wanted to protect his family from a *wanita tuna susila* (immoral woman – the formal term for prostitute) who threatened to 'destroy' his peaceful household.

This analysis parallels Cameron and Frazer's interpretation of the hegemonic construction of sex and serial murder cases: when a man kills a woman – especially one vulnerable to being labelled loose or immoral – the act itself is unforgivable, but the motive can be understood by society at large. The murder attempted by these two policemen was clearly condemned by Indonesian society, yet the motive – to protect one's family – was upstanding and therefore comprehensible.

Two weeks after the event, an editorial 'analysis' of the 'scandal' appeared in *Berita Buana* (1980), a Jakarta newspaper. The editor drew an analogy with the British political sex scandal involving Christine Keeler and Secretary for War John Profumo, ignoring the dissimilarities – the Profumo-Keeler affair ended with Profumo losing his important political position and had nothing to do with murder, or protection of family. The editorial underscored the fact that in both cases the couple was in a relationship outside marriage; and that in the Supadmi case such behaviour presented a danger to both the police corps and the country.

> The lesson to be drawn from this is that personal relations, sexual and such, should not entangle us in extortion, and most importantly should not lead to the revelation of the country's secrets.

The editors went on:

> We hope that the incident in Bojonegoro will remain confined to those who committed the crime and will not contaminate the image of the Police Department as the protector of the society, which we laboured so long and hard to achieve. Do not let one drop of poison ruin the whole jug of milk.

Not only was sympathy denied to the victim because of her profession and her way of treating 'our' man, but also the brutal assault she experienced was submerged into 'just another sexual scandal between a state official and a prostitute'. This, according to the media, could endanger not only the persons involved, but also the country. The fact that the two assailants were members of the police department contributed, on the one hand, to the media's eagerness to cover the case. On the other hand, it obscured the violence of the crime because it was felt necessary to protect the image of the police corps and to ensure the people's continued 'trust'.

The media was eager to print any piece of information they could get on this case. Soon after Mrs Supadmi was released from the hospital, journalists crowded her house in her home town and interviewed her on what had happened (Sinar Harapan, 1980b). Stories appeared about the relationship, how she had survived the attack, how she was the flower of her village, that she had an uncle who was a retired military officer and that she had married more than once. Three weeks after the incident, the national news agency, *Antara*, reported that Mrs Suyono had hired a defence attorney for her husband and Captain Bastari. In a press conference the lawyer appealed to the media not to further publicise the case, 'to help reduce the suffering of the assailants' families'.

The trial took place in March 1981. Seven months after the incident people had not forgotten the case — testimony to the media's tenacity. The courtroom was full; people crowded the courtyard, listening to the proceedings broadcast over loudspeakers. Mrs Supadmi was cheered at her first appearance. The people came as spectators, to witness the process of 'justice', but also to see in person their 'heroine', Mrs Supadmi, who tried to hide her face during her first appearance but not thereafter. She was a heroine when people needed a symbol of their desire for justice but she seemed, at least at first, wary of the voyeurism that drew the crowd to the court building. Pictures taken of her during the trial were informally sold in the courtyard; different prices for different angles, cheaper prices for black and white than colour. But in spite of Mrs Supadmi's function as a symbol for justice, her profession (and therefore her gender and her sexuality) created contradictions. For example:

- Mrs Supadmi showed up in a dazzling outfit and looked sexy. She was wearing a light brown *kebaya*, brown high heels, and a bun hairdo. An officer in charge commented, 'Mrs Ludewijk[10] is definitely an extraordinary beauty, better than a movie star'.
- After the third day of the trial, the young and 'sexy' divorcee continued being guarded, but no longer covered her face as when she first entered the courtroom.
- Policeman's wives who attended the trial said, 'She knows how to dress herself up and be sexy' (Sinar Harapan, 1981a).

The media, however, were not the only party who sexualised the victim, the people (mostly young men) who went to the trial fell into the same contradiction. Among

---

10   'Mrs Ludewijk' was another name for Mrs Supadmi.

the remarks addressed to Mrs Supadmi were 'Sister! Come on out and let's get acquainted' and '*Salut*! You can expose the Police officer's womanising!' (Sinar Harapan, 1981b).

Mrs Supadmi was the prosecution's key witness and was the main attraction for both spectators and commentators. Her strength as a woman who had survived a brutal attack and was able to bring her attackers to court was repeatedly attributed to her 'difference' from women outside her profession. She was seen solely as a sensual and sexual being. When a case like this happens, again and again women's sexuality is constructed: the 'loose woman' category is filled with desire and sensuality; while the 'good and ordinary woman' category is totally emptied of sexuality.

As the trial progressed and the defence attorney started to challenge Mrs Supadmi's credibility as a 'responsible witness', the characterisation of the victim became clearer. She was depicted not only as a primarily sexual being, but also as a vengeful person who did not value love and devotion (see Kompas, 1981a). The two assailants, in contrast, were represented as asexual beings – men with no lust: respected, restrained and loving fathers and husbands. They became ordinary men who happened to panic and became confused under overwhelming pressure. They were also pictured as upstanding – or, at least, Captain Bastari (who was not the lover of Mrs Supadmi), was.

> The second defendant said that Mrs Ludewijk is bigger than he is, so instead of him pulling her, she was the one who successfully pulled him toward her.
> Why didn't you let yourself be pulled to her lap. Don't you think it would feel good? asked the judge
> Well, she is not my wife. If she were my wife, I would just have fallen into her lap! said the second defendant.

The judge himself fell into sexualising the courtroom by making the violent attack laughable and sexy, yet emphasising this 'asexual' nature of the attackers. Even when the sexual relationship between the lieutenant colonel and Mrs Supadmi was acknowledged, the man was not viewed as having sexual desire parallel to that of Mrs Supadmi. Either Suyono's sexuality was taken for granted as a 'natural man who needs more than one woman to have sex with' or the sexual relationship between him and the victim was just *khilaf* (at that moment he was not himself and was carried away by evil persuasion).

Unfortunately for the defence, certain facts were clear: Mrs Supadmi was still alive and had brought her case to light. The judge, the media and the public were aware that the two assailants were guilty. Despite the defence attorney's attempts to ridicule her and the media representation of her, Mrs Supadmi rejected their monopoly of the moral high ground in her testimony:

> Judge: If you felt terribly hurt, why didn't you cry?
> Mrs Supadmi: I pretended I was dead. If I cried I might have been dead by now.
> Judge: So this is a case of unsuccessful murder?
> Mrs Supadmi: It is not that it merely failed but that God protected me (Kompas, 1981a).

Her famous line, 'God protected me', represented her resistance to the normative tone inside and outside the courtroom.

The Cases of Siti Rahmini and Dietje

Six weeks after the trial of Mrs Supadmi's assailants, Jakarta was rocked by another case. A murder took place about the time of the Suyono and Bastari trial, and involved Dewanto, a high-ranking official from *Sekretariat Negara* (the state secretariat). Dewanto was secretly married to a second wife, the victim, who was his former babysitter. This case was also widely publicised, and statements about the motive were released almost immediately:

- Siti Rahmini was murdered because she demanded 'equal rights' between herself and the first wife (Suara Karya, 1981).
- According to the confession of Dewanto, Siti often undermined him by demanding this and that. She knew Dewanto's position, she knew Dewanto's weakness in marrying her without his first wife's knowledge. She used this weakness to pressure him. His evil intentions sprang from his fear that his wife would discover what he had done (Kompas, 1981e).
- According to Police Lieutenant A Tonang, Dewanto admitted that he was behind the murder of his second wife. The motive given by Dewanto was that he had always felt uneasy since he married her, that she often threatened to tell the whole affair to his first wife and the State Secretariat office. Furthermore, Siti was killed because she was too demanding. First, she asked for a house and furniture, then she asked to be formally married and finally she asked that he devote equal time to her – one night with his first wife, and one night with her (Sinar Harapan, 1981c).

Both this case and the case of Mrs Supadmi involved 'respectable' and socially powerful men. Media coverage of both cases blamed the victim for her demands and threats to unveil the identity of the key aggressor. Both claimed that the defendants acted to 'save' the family. However, there was a major difference between the courts' handling of these cases. Mrs Supadmi's case was taken to the military high court, with a strong warning from the police commander of East Java that it was the accused persons who were to be held responsible and not the police corps. During the trial, the discourse was very much characterised by the desire of the military-dominated government to both clear itself of any blame and to show that there was justice to be had in Indonesia by holding the individual defendants accountable. The judge from the military high court even admitted that Mrs Supadmi's case gained the people's attention not just because of Mrs Supadmi's profession but because of people's yearning to see justice done to those who committed crimes (Kompas, 1981b). The judge expressed concern that the two assailants were members of the police corps (and thus of the military), who were supposed to protect the people.

In contrast to Mrs Supadmi's case, the theme of sexual scandal was absent from press coverage of Siti Rahmini's murder, though it also involved violence against a mistress (notwithstanding that Siti Rahmini was married to Dewanto under Islamic law). Rahmini's case did not celebrate a protagonist or directly involve sentiments of dissatisfaction with the state, military, or police force. Although media coverage was extensive, crowds did not fill the courtroom. Whereas the judge in Mrs Supadmi's case condemned the two assailants for the immorality of stripping the victim after they thought she was dead, the judge in Siti Rahmini's case cautioned 'all second wives (*istri muda*), housemaids and especially all mothers to be cautious with their daughters and towards their maids' relations with their husbands – more so since narcotics are widely available in the underground market – [so as] not to repeat the same incident' (Kompas, 1981g). Although Dewanto was prosecuted, it was women who were warned by the judge.

Another case that was equally dramatised by the media was the murder of Dietje, a well-known model and winner of several beauty contests. She was killed in 1986. Though her death generated rumours about her involvement with some politically and economically powerful men, she was not portrayed as a voluptuous being.[11] Her status as a mother and the wife of a respected man and her fame as an image of traditional Javanese femininity in her work appeared to shield her from the media effort to demonise her.[12] Still, like Mrs Supadmi and Siti Rahmini, Dietje was constructed as a 'natural' victim of male violence because of her 'profession' and the presumption that she had sexual liaisons with very important men. Contrary to the Supadmi case, the target of sensation in the media was the possible involvement of a powerful person in the killing.

Media and public attention was higher than for the previous two cases. Daily and weekly papers printed speculation and gossip surrounding the case. In the first week of the case the media conjectured that this famous model might have had affairs with a respected Jakarta figure and pointedly mentioned that her husband was paralysed (see Jakarta Post, 1986; Kompas, 1986; Merdeka, 1986a; Tempo, 1986). The media were eager to find any crumbs of information, and rumours about the reason for the murder and the person behind it spread rapidly. Letters to the editor, an important source of media democracy in Indonesia, urged the police to find the killer (Sinar Harapan, 1986b).

Dietje's case involved questioning the police department's ability to solve the case (Depari, 1986; Merdeka, 1986b). In the Supadmi case, the wife of the assailant appealed to the media to stop the uproar humiliating her family. In Dietje's case, both her husband and the police commander demanded that the media stop publishing sensational and speculative news, claiming 'the consequences, obstructing the investigation, were too great' (Sinar Harapan, 1986a). When the police found a suspect, the media ran numerous articles about the alleged killer. In response, the president of *Dewan Kehormatan* PWI (*Persatuan Wartawan Indonesia*, the Honorary Council of the Indonesian Journalists Association) appealed to the press to keep the media attention 'objective' and respect the right to presumption of innocence of the alleged killer until a verdict was obtained.

> Journalists are particularly warned to keep in mind the journalists' ethical code on presumptions of innocence; so that it is assumed that journalists will not just compound the errors committed by the legal system (Berita Buana, 1986).

In comparison the most sympathetic analysis of Mrs Supadmi's case levelled a broader social critique and inquired whether the circumstances surrounding her attempted murder were not a sign of disappearing social responsibility in Indonesian society. 'It could be the reality of the very world of the intelligence agency which made it possible for a subordinate person to blindly follow the will of his superior' (Soenarto Sukartono, 1986).

Both cases, Supadmi's and Dietje's, involved appeals to the media to restrain publication of findings. The family of the main perpetrator in Supadmi's case did so to protect his and his family's image and the victim's family in Dietje's case

---

11 Interviews with her relatives, families and people in modelling and the fashion-design business conducted soon after her death, claimed that she really loved her husband and children and was a very soft-hearted, sweet, and hard-working woman (Kompas, 25 September 1986; Sinar Harapan, 1 October 1986; Tempo, 20 September, 1986).

12 This might not be the case in terms of the rumours circulating around her death, but the media itself did not represent her in the way it had sexualised Mrs Supadmi.

appealed for the same reason. Moreover, the Honorary Council of the Indonesian Journalists Association cautioned the media not to jump to conclusions about a particular suspect, implicitly suggesting that the police might have found the wrong person.

These three cases are not the only ones of their kind; there are other cases which the police are still unable to solve.[13] These three, however, involved public discourse and were sensationalised by the media because they highlighted issues of corruption and social dissatisfaction toward the state. The murders or attempted murders of these women gained public attention not for reasons of gender but because of the involvement of public officials.

The Discourse of Sex, Courage, and Family

The courts issued guilty verdicts in all three cases. Suyono and Bastari served prison terms. Dewanto was granted leave every Independence Day for good behaviour in prison where he taught English to the inmates. He is now a free man. Dietje's case was officially solved but gossip prevails concerning the actual killer and the 'tangible' motive. However, these three cases show over and over the construction and reconstruction of female (and male) sexuality and the family.

In the Supadmi and Rahmini cases, the assailants were involved sexually with the victims. According to his testimony, Suyono had a sexual relationship with Supadmi for two years. During the whole media craze about his wrongdoing, he was not portrayed as an 'extraordinary man' in needing more than one woman to fulfil his needs. There was no question of his male sexuality. The underlying premise was that an affair such as his was natural for a man. Suyono, and to some extent his subordinate Bastari, were simply regarded as *prajurit yang lupa akan Sapta Marga* (soldiers who happened to forget their Armed Forces' oath) (Kompas, 1981c), so they could not be considered 'courageous' soldiers. The importance of the verdict, according to the judge, was that it gave a cautionary example to the police and military corps and to the society at large (see Kompas, 1981c).

Mrs Supadmi's actions, however, were not seen as exemplary, even though her struggle to hold her breath pretending she was dead, and concealing the pain she experienced while realising that two men she trusted wanted her dead were acts of incredible courage. For Mrs Supadmi herself, and those who sympathised with her, her phrase, 'God still protected me', was a means of resistance. However, this phrase gave credit to *God* rather than to her own strength. Because of her profession her courage was not seen to be something that people could learn from. After the trial was over the Indonesian Film Artists' Association (PARFI, *Persatuan Artis Film Indonesia*) successfully protested against an attempt to have her play herself in a movie about her case. The association argued that by making Mrs Supadmi a movie star, the image of the police department would be devastated. Mrs Supadmi brought a lawsuit against PARFI through the LBH (*Lembaga Bantuan Hukum*, the Legal Aid Organisation) but to no avail (see Kompas, 1981f).

---

13   Other murder cases, such as that of Mrs Dewi, a professional woman who was killed in her office and that of Julia Jarsin, a film actress, did not provoke as much media attention or public gossip as the three cases discussed in this paper. They lacked the political dimension, as no state officials were implicated as perpetrators.

While Suyono and Bastari were being sentenced, and the news broke about the murder of Siti Rahmini by her 'respected' husband, a woman activist came to me and asked, 'Don't you think we need to give a 'family hero' medal (*medali pahlawan keluarga*) to Suyono and Dewanto for protecting their families?' In both cases – the attempted murder of Mrs Supadmi and the murder of Siti Rahmini – the perpetrators gained some sympathy for what they did to save the 'good family' from destruction. Subconsciously, violence against women and even the act of murder were in these circumstances thought to be understandable if not justified. However, 'saving the family' seems to have been solely a male motivation.

Helping, protecting and saving the family could well be the very reason why Mrs Supadmi, a village girl, became a call girl; why Siti Rahmini secretly married a man of high status and economic stability; and why Dietje was involved in modelling and planned to move into the real estate business. These women's sacrifices for their families were never mentioned nor credited. Instead, they were – to a lesser degree in Dietje's case – perceived as 'women who lusted to destroy the family'.[14]

As for Dewanto's devotion to family, there was a contradiction unexplored by both the media and the public. If he was understood to have plotted the murder of his second wife (the mother of two of his children) in order to protect his 'first' family, then there must be more than one category of family: one that is to be protected, and one 'that is not so important', regardless of the offspring.

Blaming the Victim and Beyond

The New Order government's policy on wives and women of civil employees emphasised and reformulated the role of women as mothers whose responsibility is to conserve the order of the nation and its community (see Wieringa, 1985). The media never mentioned whether Supadmi and Rahmini were good mothers. Both fell into the category of 'the other woman' and both were daughters of poor parents from remote villages. In contrast, Dietje was represented as a feminine woman and a wonderful mother and wife. Her alleged affairs with numerous powerful business and political figures did not taint the image that the media drew. In Dietje's case, her marital status and her own and her husband's class background protected her from a vicious media attack on her character.

Supadmi was identified by judges, defence attorneys and the media as 'different' from the other women. Rahmini's death was marked as a warning to wives of their husband's secret marriages with 'other' women. A new regulation barring polygamous marriage for all civil service men was enacted after this case. Though many women, among them members of *Dharma Wanita* and *Kowani*, supported the regulation, some found that it also made it harder for the wives of government employees to file for a divorce. The lesson popularly drawn form Dietje's death, in contrast, concerned the dangers of ambition in a woman.

---

14 After the trial ended, a female journalist interviewed the wife of Suyono. She was being pictured as a soft-hearted, soft-spoken and understanding wife. About Mrs Supadmi, Suyono's wife said, 'I feel sorry for her. To have to live by disturbing the peace of other people's households and looking for a husband from door to door. Certainly, there should be many ways to go to Rome'.

The three women were delineated as being outside the norm, women who have crossed the line drawn by tradition and the state's ideology of womanhood. In media representations and in public gossip concerning these three cases, women were again reminded that there are two distinct categories based on sexuality: the good and the bad. This parallels the finding of North American and European feminists who have examined themes in the cases of sex murders and serial killings. Females prostitutes are portrayed as the 'natural' victims of their killers (Caputi, 1989; Holloway, 1981; Humpreys & Carringella-McDonald, 1990; Walkowitz, 1982).[15] The acts of the killers are unforgivable but their motivations are understood by society at large and are portrayed as not having anything to do with misogyny or patriarchy (see Cameron & Frazer, 1987: 14). However, there are major differences between the construction of the killer in sex and serial murder cases and in the wife-mistresses murders examined here.

The serial and sex murders analysed in Western studies are depicted as half-beasts, half-men — sexual deviants rather than normal men. This is in sharp contrast to the way the accused in the cases discussed here were looked at. Their normality was not questioned. The claim that their motives were to protect their families assumed that they were 'normal', even upstanding, family men. In these cases, it was the *victim* who was demonised. The victim was 'abnormal' and different from respectable women. She was pictured as greedy, nagging, loose, oversexual; always demanding the impossible, she was *kurang pasrah* (not submissive enough). This was true for all the women in these cases except for Dietje who, because of her class, escaped this stigmatisation.

Even though the media made the attempted murder of Mrs Supadmi an example of how corrupt a police officer could be and demanded a conviction to discourage similar crimes of corruption, it could not refrain from also blaming the victim. Although Dietje was not overtly portrayed as a 'bad woman'[16] her death was seen as containing a lesson: 'if she had been more like any other wife, she might still be alive today'. A myth was constructed that these women were in some sense deserving victims of male violence.

Anti-government sentiment and resentment against army and bureaucratic corruption fuelled the media's frenzied interest in the Supadmi and Dietje cases and to some extent the Rahmini case. Although there were other sex murder cases during this period, only these three attracted media attention. Because the defendants were politically prominent, the cases afforded the media a rare opportunity for covert criticism of the power structure. Yet precisely this focus acted to obscure the equally important issue of male violence against women.

References

Antara, 1980, 12 September.
Berita Buana, 1980, 4 September.
Berita Buana, 1986, 30 December.
Cameron, Deborah & Frazer, Elizabeth, 1987, *The Lust to Kill*, New York University Press, New York.
Caputi, Jane, 1989, 'The Sexual Politics of Murder', *Gender and Society*, vol 3, no 4.
Depari, 1986, 'Kasus Dietje dan Citra Polri', *Kompas*, 11 October.

---

15 'Sickness' (of the murderers) and 'sin' (of the victim) are the two discursive ingredients in the construction of victim, of gender and of sexuality.

16 There were no startling revelations or sexual scandal involving important people.

Hardjito Notopuro, 1984, *Peranan Wanita dalam Masa Pembangunan di Indonesia*, Ghalia Indonesia, Jakarta.

Holloway, Wendy, 1981, 'I Just Want to Kill a Woman. Why? The Ripper and Male Sexuality', *Feminist Review*, vol 9, October.

Humpreys, Drew & Carringella-MacDonald, Susan, 1990, 'Murdered Mothers, Missing Wives: Reconsidering Female Victimisation', *Social Justice*, vol 17, no 2.

ICJ, 1987, *Indonesia and the Rule of Law: Twenty Years of 'New Order' Government*, Frances Pinter, London.

Jakarta Post, 1986, 3 October.

Kompas, 1980, 8 October.

Kompas, 1981a, 12 March.

Kompas, 1981b, 24 March.

Kompas, 1981c, 27 March.

Kompas, 1981d, 3 April.

Kompas, 1981e, 8 May.

Kompas, 1981f, 25 July.

Kompas, 1981g, 7 December.

Kompas, 1986, 25 September.

Korwani (Kongres Wanita Indonesia), 1978, *Sejarah Setengah Abad Pergerakan Wanita Indonesia*, Balai Pustaka, Jakarta.

Merdeka, 1986a, 3 October.

Merdeka, 1986b, 10 December.

Sinar Harapan, 1980a, 27 August.

Sinar Harapan, 1980b, 4 October.

Sinar Harapan, 1981a, 15 March.

Sinar Harapan, 1981b, 27 March.

Sinar Harapan, 1981c, 17 May.

Sinar Harapan, 1986a, 30 September.

Sinar Harapan, 1986b, 8 October.

Slamet Widarto Prodjohadidjo, 1974, *Pengertian Gerakan PKK dan Struktur Organisasi*, DPRD-DIY, Yogyakarta.

Soenarto Sukartono, 1986, 'Lagi tentang Kasus Mahmilti II di Surabaya', *Kompas*, 11 April.

Suryochondro, Sukanti, 1984, *Potret Pergerakan Wanita di Indonesia*, Rajawali, Jakarta.

Tempo, 1986, 4 October.

Walkowitz, Judith R, 1982, 'Jack the Ripper and the Myth of Male Violence', *Feminist Studies*, vol 8, no 3, Fall.

Wieringa, Saksia E, 1985, 'The Perfumed Nightmare – Some Notes on the Indonesian Women's Movement', Working Paper, Sub-series on Women's History and Development, no 5, Institute of Social Studies, The Hague.

Yuyu Krisna, 1979, *Menyelusuri Remang-remang Jakarta*, Sinar Harapan, Jakarta.

10. Islam & Medical Science: Evidence from Indonesian *Fatawa*: 1960-1995

MB Hooker

The purpose of this chapter is to illustrate some of the dilemmas in which Islam finds itself with respect to advances in modern medical science. This is of course a very large subject and all I do here is to take a very small sample of problems as expressed in *fatwa* [pl. *fatawa*] (or Islamic legal rulings) over the past 30 years. Coincidentally, these are also years which have seen tremendous advances in medicine and the ways in which we can now treat (or mistreat?) the human body.

For Islam, as for all religions, these new techniques raise serious and so far intractable problems in the fields of ethics and morality. Some of these are familiar to us: is an embryo 'alive'; who 'owns' it; can it be 'sold'; can it 'inherit'; and so on. These are real questions in medical ethics although they are probably fairly remote in practice for most people. But this does not, of course, detract from their difficulty. This is true for Islam as well; although the Indonesian cases have not progressed to the embryo problem yet. No doubt this will come in time.

Instead, the problems with which the Indonesian *fatawa* are concerned are at the earlier stages of scientific innovation: organ transplant, blood transfusion, contraception and family planning. Most of us have probably forgotten the ethical debate of 30 and 40 years ago on these subjects and for the younger (post-pill) generation these debates are only history. This is not true for Islam generally or for Muslims in South East Asia in particular. These issues are very much alive and continue to plague not just the conscience of the individual Muslim but also have repercussions in government health policy, in religious law and in the state criminal law. Indeed, the depth of feeling and its incidence is probably greater in Muslim countries than in the West. The reason for this is the view Islam takes of science in general and of medical science in particular.

Islam and Science

The Islamic view can be stated succinctly. It is that science is not, and cannot be, value-free. 'Value' here refers to the truths of Revelation and also to what is called the 'Islamic' or 'Muslim' context, that is, whether the science being done is ethically, morally and socially justified. The Western claim that science is pure and value free is, in the view of many Muslim scientists (or philosophers of science), just not true. Science, for them, is always value-laden and the lack of perspective from Revelation can lead to wasteful and, thus, 'illegitimate' science, to say nothing of science which is purely destructive (as in military science).

As evidence of the legitimacy of the Islamic approach Muslim philosophers of science point to the outstanding achievement of this science in the medieval period. Although achievements are undeniable in all fields of science there was also a profound decline of Islamic science in the later medieval period. This has been variously attributed to the triumph of the theologians over (the Greek-inspired) philosophy and the subsequent acceptance of a passive and authoritarian intellectualism.[1] Another reason put forward, often in conjunction with the above, is the state of political and intellectual exhaustion characteristic of the later Muslim world. This was followed by the subjection of that world to the Western powers from the 18th century, a circumstance which has only recently ceased, although perhaps not entirely. It is held by many Muslim scholars that the Western intellectual domination of Muslim thought, including scientific thought, continues simply as a consequence of the overwhelming scientific and technological dominance of the West. This is probably true and, as a consequence, the attempt to establish an 'Islamic' science is reactive, even to some degree defensive.

Consider the following. From the early 1970s, possibly earlier, we have seen a political and economic revival in the Middle East, the heartland of Islam. This was preceded, and is now accompanied, by a renewed interest in the religion of Islam. It is indeed a renewal[2] of pride and commitment to faith itself. At the same time a perceived Western dominance remains, and indeed is reinforced, as young Muslims are educated in the West or in newly-founded, but Western-style, universities at home. This melange of circumstance is conducive to a considerable debate amongst Muslim philosophers of science as to what an Islamic science can or should be.

As one might expect, there is a variety of answers which range in quality from the naive to the rather sophisticated.[3] For example, it is quite common to find the *Qur'an* 'proved' by science. This consists in reading contemporary scientific principles into passages from the *Qur'an*.[4] The results are ludicrous but, more important, the attempt betrays a serious misunderstanding both of the *Qur'an* and of science. The former does not need legitimating; it is for the believer the work of God and it stands on that alone. To suppose it needs support is to suppose, ultimately, that God needs scientific proof. This is not the Muslim position.[5] Conversely, if the *Qur'an* can be seen as justifying science then the latter has the same validity as Revelation. This cannot be, because in the Muslim view scientific facts are always relative in at least two senses. First, the facts of yesterday are often overtaken by new facts – science does not stand still. Secondly, and related, science is a product of man's mind and this, by its nature, is not capable of absolute truth.

---

1   The detailed arguments implicit here are outside the scope of this chapter. See Leaman (1985) for an introduction, especially on *taqlid* and *ijtihad*.

2   Sometimes called 'fundamentalism' – a term without meaning except to lazy newspaper editors for whom it is code for 'terrorism'.

3   A good brief summary, rather polemical, appears in Sardar (1989: 29ff) – 'anatomy of a confusion'!

4   For examples, see Sardar (1989: 29ff): 31ff.

5   Some well-intentioned Muslims do, however, come very close to this. For example, 'The Book of Signs', a popular and readily available video, illustrates the scope and depth of knowledge contained within the *Qu'ran* through the spectacular use of scientific footage and animation

Enough has now been said to indicate some of the difficulties[6] but it would be wrong to give the impression that Muslim discussion on Islam and science is wholly negative and defensive and that it is invariably naive. This is not so and there has been, and is now, vigorous discussion on the subject. I will indicate some of the main features of this but it should be clearly understood that differences of approach exist between Muslim philosophers of science. On the other hand it should also be noted that many, perhaps the majority, of Muslim scientists who are not philosophers of science are content to live in a dual world: professional scientists on the one hand and true believers on the other – and never the twain need meet.

To return to the philosophers of science, all agree that 'it is the very method of science that the Muslim scientists need tackle' (Sardar, 1989: 30ff).[7] Method here appears to mean two things. First, that it must be acknowledged that science cannot be value free.[8] There is no disagreement about this amongst the Muslim philosophers of science. The values are the Islamic values. Secondly, what are these values or, more specifically, how and by whom are they to be determined? This is the real problem.

The Muslim answer is really in two parts. First, science is held to be a matter of civilisation and each civilisation has produced its 'own' science. Greek science, for example, is not Chinese science nor is it medieval European science, though unlike Chinese science, is connected to the latter. Islam is a civilisation and therefore has its own identifiable science. It is not denied that there are Greek connections. The second part of the answer is, therefore, to identify the distinctive Islamic element or elements. It is here that Muslim philosophers of science experience difficulty. There appears to be, on the one hand, an acknowledgment that the pursuit of knowledge is always subject to a higher purpose (God's) and hence is limited by the perceived definitions of that purpose. This may of course change from time to time. Indeed, the definitions of God's purpose do change over time and they vary also from place to place. However this might be, God's purpose is taken as a fundamental datum. On the other hand, and less restrictive in practice, is the view that the material world is a reflection of spiritual value(s). Provided the obviously destructive is avoided, knowledge may be pursued as scientific method dictates. This is, in effect, the more popular view but, as is obvious from this formulation, the opportunity for disagreement is both immediate and, in fact, frequently taken.

Medicine in Islam

The evidence considered below dates from nine to seven hundred years ago. This should occasion no surprise. The main principles of Islamic theology and law were established in the 8th century of the Christian era and it is these which determine the status of medicine. The arguments and positions from that time are equally valid in 1998 and will remain as such as long as the religion of Islam exists – those who refuse to take Islam historically do so at their peril.

---

6   For other examples, see Sardar (1989: 30ff).

7   See also the contributions in al Faruqi and Nasseef (1981).

8   Indeed, due to a perceived over-emphasis on rationality Western science is not only unsuitable for Muslim societies, it has a negative value – that is, it is essentially destructive.

The first example[9] is from Ibn Hindu, an active writer and government servant in the late 10th century. As the following extract shows, he was competent in Greek philosophy and he was concerned to show that attacks on medicine, particularly from the point of view of dogma could not be justified.

> I think that (people who consider medicine worthless) are among those whom Aristotle has in mind when he declares it forbidden to enter into debates with certain people and, instead, commands (their opponents) to pray for them or to chastise them and to exercise firm control over them. In the *Kitab al-Jadl* (the Topics), he mentions that some kinds of problems, such as, for instance, the problem of the part (the atom) or the problem of eternity and createdness, must not be debated because of their obscurity and subtlety. They require the immersion of the mind in refined speculation and are not responsive to hasty thoughts and quickly applied faculties. Then, there are problems that must not be debated because of their clarity and obviousness. One should pray for the person who raise such questions and ask God to give him sound sense perceptions. He would, for instance, be the person who raises the problem of whether the fire burns or snow is cold. Then, there are problems that must not be debated because they are disruptive of the social and political situation (*siyasah*) and impugn the fundamentals of the religious law. A person who raises problems of this sort must (not be debated but) rather be chastised and prevented from advertising them. This applies, for instance, to someone who raises the problem of why it is necessary to honour one's parents or why it is not permitted to kill an innocent person. Then, there is a fourth kind of problems, which may give rise to discussion and where debate is permissible, namely, problems that are neither entirely clear nor entirely obscure, nor do they have a deleterious effect upon social and political matters. Now look, dear reader, at the person who denies the validity of medicine, and take note that he covers the eye of the sun and ignores the dawn of morn, in spite of the usefulness of physicians and the beneficial outcome of most medical treatments experienced by both the mass and the elite. Take note, further, how such a person impugn the social and political order by (attempting to) deprive people of something useful and to make them dislike some of life's conveniences. Is there anyone more in need of prayer than he be given the gift of (sound sense perceptions, and more in need of being chastised)?
>
> Thus, those who deny the validity of medicine are poor and misguided. They do not deserve to be taken seriously and to be debated. It is obvious that they are wrong (Rosenthal, 1990: 521).

As Rosenthal remarks, this passage shows a somewhat 'self righteous' attitude, but the theological argument always remains. This is to the effect that the practice of medicine, by attempting to reverse that which has occurred, that is, the illness, shows a lack of true faith. This is in fact an argument still heard today and it is a very dangerous one in a Muslim country. It essentially says that one is attempting to disrupt God's purpose or dispositions and is hence a bad Muslim – even worse, no true Muslim at all. The medical answer as expounded by Ibn Hindu and later (in the late 11th century) by 'Abd al-Wadud' is that medicine is an 'ordinary function' like eating and drinking and, as such, is necessary for life itself, which will come to an end when ordained by God in any and all cases.

We can see this well put in the following passage from Ibn al-Quff (mid-late 13th century):

---

9   This and the following two examples are taken from Rosenthal (1990 – originally published in 1969: 521).

It has been said that the will, or knowledge, or power of God, in eternity or following the (prevailing) horoscope as the astrologers say, either requires the health of Zayd and that he will not fall sick for a specified time, or it requires the change and dissolution of his temper. Now, in the first case, the science of medicine is not needed because health is going to stay in the body in question (even) without the application of the rules of medicine. In the second case, the application of medicine is of no use.

In reply we say: Just as God has destined the existence of health, He has made the proper application of medicine for the sake of health a reason for health. To a person expressing such doubts (as just mentioned), it can be said the he ought to take a respite from the task of eating and drinking. The line of argumentation suggested above either requires somehow satiety and being provided with water, or it does not require it. If it does, there is no need to employ (eating and drinking). In the second case, there is no need either for employing (food and drink) as this would be 'trifling'. All this is absurd, because it would follow from it that the existence of any food means 'trifling,' which is a denial of God's attributes (ta'til). It is an obvious error.

A further point put by the same author is that his opponents may, in their turn, also be accused of irreligion. God did not create in jest or for no purpose[10] and medicine is 'natural'. To suppose otherwise is to suppose God without purpose which is to say that one doubts His existence.

The Doctrine of Necessity

A key feature of the *fatawa* is the reference to 'necessity'. This has a wide range of meaning in English but it has no technical legal significance. In Islamic law, on the other hand, the idea in the sense of 'public interest' is a recognised principle in jurisprudence: *maslahah mursalah*. It is that which both prevents harm (*mafsadah*) and provides a benefit.

These essential parameters were established in the 13th century, particularly by al-Ghazali for whom it meant protecting religion, life, intellect, lineage and property. However, *maslahah* cannot apply in respect of specific injunctions (*muqaddarat*) of *syariah*; to allow otherwise would obviously destroy the primacy of Revelation. But given that God's purpose in the *syariah* is the welfare of man, then *maslahah* is itself a Qu'ranic objective.[11]

The public interest is classed into three: that which is essential (*daruriyyat* – religion, life, intellect, lineage and property); that which is supplementary (*hajiyyat*) to the essentials and to the negation of hardship in achieving the essentials; and that which is additional (*kamaliyyat*), that is, acts which lead to the encouragement of that which is desirable. It is only the first of these classifications – the essential – which is in discussion in Indonesian[12] *fatawa*. To be valid a rule made must be for a

---

10   *Qu'ran* XXIII

       'did ye then think

       That we had created you

       In jest, and that ye

       Would not be brought back

       To us (for account)?

11   See, for example, the *ayah* – S.21.107, S10.75

12   The last two classes raise difficult questions in their relation to *qiyas* – analogical deduction. See Mohammad Hashim Kamali (1991: 197ff) on *qiyas* and also at 276ff generally for a brilliant short account.

genuine purpose, it must be general and it must not negate or diminish any explicitly stated rule (*nass*).

There has been, and will be, considerable debate over *maslahah*[13] but surprisingly enough there appears to be little in the way of substantial disagreements between the four *Sunni* schools. This does not mean to say that there are not examples of arbitrary use or self seeking. For example, there is a *fatwa* from Indonesia prohibiting that which is clearly permitted in the *Qur'an* itself – in this case forbidding Muslim males from marrying Christian females. Such is allowed but here it was forbidden on the basis of *maslahah* for the reason that the man might not be strong enough to remain Muslim or to ensure that his children would be brought up as Muslims (Mudzhar, 1993: 90).[14]

With these introductory remarks,[15] I now turn to the Indonesian data.

The Indonesian *Fatawa*

There is a long tradition of *fatawa* in Indonesia,[16] especially in the pre-colonial period (that is before the mid-18th century). The natural development of Islam was halted by Dutch colonialism under which Islam was severely limited in its legal application and suppressed in the political sphere. Broadly speaking, the position of Islam in post-independence Indonesia is slightly better but the religion is still subject to considerable state control and restriction. This is so, despite recent reforms in 1991 and 1993.[17]

It was not until 1975 that regional councils of *ulama* (scholars) were established under the auspices of the Ministry of Internal Affairs. Representatives from these Regional Councils met later in the same year (this time under the auspices of the Ministry of Religion) and agreed to form an Indonesian Council of *Ulama* for Indonesia (*Majelis Ulama Indonesia*, MUI). The motives for the establishment of these Councils were clearly political but then everything connected with Islam is always political. A specific aim of the MUI was to control *fatawa*. For example, there are *fatawa* from the 1960s and 1970s which say that it is obligatory (*wajib*) that is, legally binding, for Muslims to vote for Islamic political parties. This is not acceptable to governments in contemporary Indonesia.[18]

The MUI therefore has as its functions the provision of *fatawa* to government (and to private individuals) on religious issues; the creation of unity between Muslims; and to represent Islam generally and in intra-religious dialogue (Mudzhar, 1993: 53ff). Indeed, if one looks at the period from 1975 to the early 1990s it is quite clear that the main function of the MUI is to support and, in some cases, to

---

13   See Mohammad Hasim Kamali (1991: 275ff) for examples. See also Muhammad Khalid Masud (1977) on al-Shatibis' theory of *Maslahah*, especially pp 173-82 for an interesting summary of 19th century and early 20th century approaches.

14   See Butt, above, Chapter 8.

15   For further references, see Rosenthal (1990) and especially Nanji (1988).

16   For literature on Islam in Indonesia see 'Indonesia', in *Encyclopedia of Islam* (2nd ed).

17   See Hooker above, Chapter 6.

18   See, for example, the papers in Budiman (1990).

justify government policy on government programs.[19] These are not our concern here but it is important to bear in mind the public policy dimension of *fatawa*.

Fatawa are not 'merely scholarly opinion' as in Malaysia but involve government and the legitimacy of government because Islam is always an alternative source of authority; that is, an authority deriving from revelation. Any government policy is, therefore, open to question or judgment deriving from the absolute value(s) that is in Revelation. Examples from Indonesia include the stunning of animals before slaughter, the use of Islamic themes in films and popular songs, attendance at Christian ceremonies and the breeding of frogs and rabbits for food (Mudzhar, 1993: 93-105). All eventually get *fatawa* to say that these things could be done on the basis of necessity and benefit.

MUI has given three *fatawa* on medical issues. These rulings are detailed, complex and fully use existing authorities.

Organ Transplants

Take first a *fatwa* on cornea transplant given in June 1979 (Mudzhar, 1993: 106-107). This was requested by the Red Cross and the MUI ruled that cornea donation was lawful provided (a) it is agreed to and witnessed by close relatives and (b) that the removal of the cornea is carried out by qualified surgeons. The actual arguments presented by the Council follow.

There is an initial reference to a *Hadith* by Abu Dawud[20] which equates the breaking of the bones of a dead person with the same action in respect of a living person. The analogy (*qiyas*) is obvious and thus the latter is also an assault. But what exactly is the interest in a corpse? The answer is found in the text books of *fikh* ('Knowledge', or rules of law).

Before looking at these sources it is important to make clear that *maslahah* is not recognised as an independent proof in the *Hanafi* and *Shafii* schools of law – the latter of course being the prevailing school in Indonesia (and Malaysia).[21] Instead, it is within *qiyas*; that is, there is no category of public interests beyond an explicit text rule and a proper analogy from it.[22] Discussion on public interest, therefore, is always conducted in terms of analogy and it is in these terms that this Indonesian *fatawa* on transplants rests.

This brings us to the text books on *fikh*. Two are cited in this *fatawa*. The first is al-Mawat's *Majmu sharh al-Muhadhdhab,* a standard work of the *Shafit* school where it is allowed that a living baby may be recovered from the body of the dead mother. The second citation is to the same text, this time to the case that where a person has swallowed another's jewels just before his death it is allowed that the corpse should undergo surgery to recover the jewels. If the person swallowed his own jewels the closest relative has the option.

---

19   See Mudzhar (1993: 61ff) for examples.

20   And also by Ibn Majah. These are two transmitters of great authority. See entries in *Encyclopedia of Islam.*

21   However, there is provision in the Indonesian legislation on *syariah* for a recourse to the *Hanbali* and *Maliki* schools of law, where *Maslahah* is directly adopted – especially in the *Maliki* where it is 'a norm by itself' (Kamali, 1991: 280).

22   This is not the case with other schools of law (Kamali, 1991: 278ff).

The MUI concluded, therefore, that these cases applied by analogy in the case of cornea transplant. Indeed it was a (classed) 'strong' analogy (*qiyas jaliyy*) since a cornea transplant has a higher purpose and good than the mere recovery of jewels. It should be noted in this case that the intention of the donor *and* the consent of the closest relatives are required. These override the *Hadith*, and it is only on the basis of consent that the technical justification through *qiyas* can be founded.

In other words, we are talking about two things; first, the morality of dealing with the human body and, secondly and dependent upon the first, the technical justification by legal process for interfering with human remains. I suggest that these two aspects of the same set of circumstances must be kept separate. This is because if we subsume the moral under the technical, justification by *maslahah* will certainly lead to 'arbitrary and self-seeking interests' (Kamali, 1991: 281), a result with which Muslim philosophers of science are always and rightly concerned. This is certainly the approach adopted in this *fatwa*.

I turn now to the second *fatwa*; in this case a request from the Head of Surgery in the Jakarta Heart Hospital in 1985 asking whether post-mortem surgery on a dead person to take his heart for transplanting was allowable (Mudzhar, 1993: 107ff). The answer was 'yes' provided that the donor had willed the donation and the nearest relatives had consented. In addition, the donation could only be made in a case of emergency where there was no other option. This last is an extra condition and not found in the earlier *fatawa*. In addition two rather general passages from the *Qur'an* are cited (*Qur'an* V: 21 and II: 195) as are two *Hadith,* both, interestingly enough, on the defence of medicine generally. This is a reminder that the state of medical science in Islam continues to be if not problematical then, at least, of concern.[23] The actual decision is based firmly, however, in analogy and the specific authorities are those cited earlier, namely that post-mortem surgery on the corpse of a woman to recover the baby and on a corpse who had swallowed jewels is allowable.

Family Planning

I turn now to family planning. In 1983 a comprehensive *fatawa* was issued by the National Conference of *Ulama* as follows:[24]

1. Islam justifies the practice of family planning exercised for the sake of the health of the mother and the child and in the interests of the education of the child. The practice must be undertaken by choice and employ contraceptives that are not prohibited in Islam.

2. Abortion practised in any form and at any stage of pregnancy is forbidden in Islam (*haram*) because it constitutes murder. This includes menstrual regulation by pills. Exception is granted only if the abortion is conducted to save the life of the mother.

---

23 See generally Rosenthal (1990).

24 This citation is taken directly from Mudzhar (1993: 109).

3.   Vasectomy and tubectomy are forbidden in Islam, except in emergency cases such as to prevent the spread of disease or to save the life of the person undergoing the operation.

4.   The use of Intra Uterine Devices (or IUDs) in family planning is justified provided that the insertion is carried out by female doctors or, in certain circumstances, male doctors in the presence of other females or the husband.

As Mudzhar (1993: 109-10) points out, no *fikh* texts are cited; instead references to Qu'ranic verses and *Hadith* are relied upon. In other words, the justification is general rather than technically legal. Contraception, for example, was known and practised at the time of the Prophet and the use of IUD is an extension of this practice. The IUD did, in fact, cause a technical problem because its use was forbidden in 1971 by a *fatawa* on the ground that its insertion involved the sight of the woman's private parts by a man not her husband. This was classed as forbidden (*haram*). However, this classification was overcome by the following reasoning.

The concept of *haram* has a number of references and the important one here is its division into two types. The first is *haram li-dhatih*, that which is forbidden as such (eg, murder, adultery). The second type is *haram li-ghayrih*, that which is forbidden because to allow it would lead to the first type of *haram* (eg, making an offer of betrothal to a woman already betrothed). The consequence of the distinction is that the first category can never be lawful while the second may become so. It is irregular (*fasid*) but not void (*batil*). Thus looking at the private parts of a woman can lead to unlawful sex which is *haram* by itself, hence the necessity for witnesses specified in the *fatwa*. Essentially then, the insertion of IUD was re-classed as *haram li-ghayrih* because the intention is not unlawful sex[25] but the prevention of undesirable consequences which therefore render it allowable.

The motive in this case is equally important. As Mudzhar (1993: 112ff) explains, the Indonesian government's national family planning policy is directed toward the stabilisation of the population and thus an improvement in the general health and welfare of society. Contraception is an essential element in this program and when one reads this *fatwa* it is quite clear that the public policy aspects play a major role.

Insemination

We may continue with the general theme of reproduction by taking three *fatawa* from the regional MUI of Jakarta (Rangkaian Fatawa/Keputusan 1980-85, Jakarta). We take first artificial insemination. There is nothing in the textbooks on this and the references to the *Qur'an* are very general.[26] The conclusion is that a direct 'injection' of the husband's sperm into his wife is allowed. However, the keeping of semen in a sperm bank, even if it is the husband's, is forbidden. The intention is to prevent sin and misuse.

---

25   There is considerable authority from the Middle East allowing this. See, for example, the authorities cited in Kamali (1991: 331).

26   For example, *Nahl* (S XVI: 27).

Furthermore, providing semen to a bank for sale or donation is forbidden. Likewise the insemination of a woman with semen from a man who is not her husband is forbidden. The term used here is *mutlaq* (absolute) which admits of no qualification. It is the strongest prohibition. The same position is adopted where a woman undergoes an artificial insemination with the semen of a man not her husband with the intention of giving up the consequent child to the donor. This is absolutely forbidden. To encourage or support such actions is also forbidden. However, the *fatwa* does conclude by saying that it may be reviewed if later pressing circumstances (unspecified) occur.

Sterilisation

The second example relates to vasectomy and tubectomy. Both are generally forbidden though the latter may be allowed to preserve the life of the woman. Obviously there are no technical rules on the matter. Instead we have a selection of verses from the *Qur'an* and some *Hadith*. None of these is particularly helpful in giving an indication of legal reasoning. For example from the *Qur'an* we have S.XXXVII: 100 which says 'O Lord!, grant me a righteous (son)' and again in S.XIX: 5-6 a plea to be granted a son. There are other examples to the same effect especially perhaps S.LXXXl: 8-9 which is cited so as to equate tubectomy with female infanticide. The point is not argued but it is suggested. In addition, there is a reference to a formal instruction from the Ministry of Health (1980) which says that sterilisation is not an option in the national family planning program. The *fatawa* explicitly approves this position, and recommends its strict enforcement.

Abortion

The third example is abortion, in this case by means of a vacuum aspirator. The technique is forbidden: it is murder and contrary to the will of God. It is recommended to the Indonesian government that criminal action be taken against those who perform it. This result does not, however, apply to accidental abortions where the intention was merely the cleaning of the womb. Again, no classical *fikh* texts are cited though we do have verses from the *Qur'an* (S.XXXVIII: 100, S ii: 205, S.LXXXI: 8-9) and *Hadiths*[27] on the sanctity of life.

Blood Transfusion

The final example is the case of blood transfusion. There are two opinions (or advice)[28] and one *fatwa* to cite. Before looking at these we should notice that in Islam blood is prohibited for human consumption. These are two verses, 'forbidden to you are the dead carcass and blood' (S.V: 3) and later also a prohibition; blood is qualified as 'blood shed forth' (S.VI: 145). This is important because the phrase

---

27   Al-Bukhari and Muslim.

28   These do not have the binding force of a *fatwa*.

'shed forth' as a qualifier will take priority. It may thus well be argued that transfusions are not 'consumption'.

In the first opinion, which is on the propriety of transfusion in general, the point was not raised. Instead, transfusion to relieve accidents or illness is an act of virtue and humane feeling. The only Qu'ranic verse cited seems to have little relevance (it is on the lawfulness of foods) (S.V: 2) and the same is true for the various *Hadith* cited. This opinion, while certainly giving effect to national or government policy is less than satisfactory.

The second opinion is similar. Here the question was whether people could give blood donations during the fasting month: would it result in an incorrect observance of the rules in fasting? The answer was that donation is permitted in this period, provided that the donor does not risk his health and so require food or drink before or after the act of donation. If the latter, then the donor has breached the fasting rules.

The final example, this time a *fatwa*, is concerned with whether the giving of blood creates a kinship between donor and donee. The term used is *nasab*, which means lineage, particularly on the patrilineal side. This is an important question because it has immediate repercussions for family law and inheritance. One may or may not marry or may or may not inherit depending upon one's position within a lineage. The primary text is S.IV: 23 which includes '[foster] mothers who gave you suck'. There is a considerable jurisprudence on this but the point for present purposes is that in the classical *fikh* the 'milk' relationship counts as a blood relationship. The obvious question in this present *fatwa*, is does a blood donor to blood donee relation give rise to the same result? The *fatwa* says no, without discussion, except that it flatly denies analogy (*qiyas*) even as a possibility. Instead, some rather unconvincing citations from *Qur'an* and *Hadith* are given (S.XVI: 116).[29]

I think it is interesting that the possibility of *qiyas* is not discussed. In a way this amounts to an avoidance of one of the considerable technical resources to be found in Islamic jurisprudence. This is a pity given the extensive and unknown future advances of medical science. I do not say that in the present instance a *qiyas* can be established to show a *nasab*-like relationship. Indeed, I think it would fail on a number of grounds particularly as to the conditions relating to the acceptance of a new ruling.[30] Additionally of course, since, as we have seen, necessity is a part of *qiyas* in Indonesian Islam, the public utility of blood transfusions would almost certainly override any purported *nasab*.[31] However, the *fatawa* form does have the advantage of allowing scope for discussion and also for testing public acceptance and national interest. It should be utilised to the full for these purposes. It is a pity it was not done in this case as the rejection of an argument can sometimes be as useful as an acceptance. On the other hand, this is not the practice of the *Ulama* any more than it is the practice of courts.

---

29 And also from Abu Daud, Bukhari and Muslim.

30 See Kamali (1991: 199ff – and especially at 200) for an example.

31 But, on the other hand, while milk is 'life', so is blood – in this case literally.

Conclusion

Although the data in this chapter are limited[32] it does show some interesting results for medical ethics.

First, it seems clear that the claims made by Muslim philosophers of science that there is an 'Islamic' value system for science is true. Abortion, for example, is forbidden and there are strict conditions on organ transplants. In other words, these are value-derived limitations and the values are the values found and justified in Revelation.

Secondly, medicine as such is a fact of life and is accepted as such. The medieval debates are, with very rare exceptions, no longer considered appropriate. Medicine is an ordinary function.

Thirdly, it is noticeable in the reported *fatawa* that the ground of necessity and public interest is one which is often defined by the state, that is by the secular authority. This has been a feature of *fatawa* throughout Islamic legal history and the persistence of this characteristic into our contemporary period should occasion no surprise. The *fatawa* is, in fact, a tool of the secular authority. Having said this, it is also true that outrageous abuse can only be short term and very limited. As the examples from Indonesia show, the technical demands of reasoning by analogy, the limitations on necessity and the definition of public interest will always restrict the possibility of abuse. I do not say that these technical aspects will entirely prevent abuse but medical science in Islam is nowhere near getting itself into the difficulties which those of us in the 'advanced' countries are now encountering. Embryo destruction, for example, can never be an issue in Islamic medical ethics.

References

Ahmad, Furqan, 1987, 'Organ Transplants in Islamic Law', *Islamic and Comparative Law Quarterly*, VII (S): 132-36.

Al-faruqim, Issmail, R and Nasseef Abdullah Omar (eds), 1981, *Social and Natural Sciences: The Islamic Perspective*, King Abdulaziz University (& Hodder & Stoughton), Jedda.

Babu Sahib, MH, 1987, 'The Islamic Point of View on Transplantation of Organs', *Islamic and Comparative Law Quarterly*, VII (Article): 128-31.

Budiman, A (ed), 1990, *State and Civil Society in Indonesia*, Monash Papers, Centre for SE Asian Studies, Clayton, Victoria.

Flon, Menachem, 1971, 'Jewish Law and Modern Medicine' in Cohn, HM (ed), *Jewish Law in Ancient and Modern Israel*, KTAV Publishing House, Jerusalem.

Hooker, MB (ed), 1983, *Islam in South-East Asia*, Brill, Leiden.

Hooker, MB, 1993, '*Fatawa* in Malaysia, 1960-1985', *Arab Law Quarterly,* vol 8: 93-105.

Kamaii, Mohd, Hashian, 1991, *Principles of Islamic Jurisprudence*, Islamic Texts Society, Cambridge.

Leaman, Oliver, 1985, *An Introduction to Medieval Islamic Philosophy*, Cambridge University Press, Cambridge.

Mudzhar, Mohd Atho, 1993, *Fatawa-Fatawa Majlis Ulama Indonesia*, Inis (XVII), Jakarta.

Masud, Muhammad Khalid, 1977, *Islamic Legal Philosophy*, Islamic Research Institute, Islamabad.

---

32 On this question of limited data I should point out that the same results, on the same reasoning, are known from India, Egypt and Syria. Exactly the same arguments are put forward: see Babu Sahib (1987) and Ahmad (1987).

Musallam, Bashir, 1983, *Sex and Society in Islam: Birth Control before the Nineteenth Century*, Cambridge University Press, Condon.

Nanji, AA, 1988, 'Medical Ethics and Islamic Tradition', *Journal of Medicine & Philosophy*, vol 13(3): 257-75.

Rosenthal, Franz, 1990, *Science and Medicine in Islam*, Vaiorum, Hampshire.

Sardar, Ziauddin, 1989, *Explorations in Islamic Science*, Mansell, London & New York.

Yaseen, MN, 1990, 'The Rulings for the Donations of Human Organs in the Light of Sharia Rules and Medical Facts', *Arab Law Quarterly*, vol 5: 49-87

11. The *Rechtsstaat* and Human Rights

Todung Mulya Lubis

This is the totalitarian idea, the integralistic idea of the Indonesian nation, as also manifested in their original statecraft ... If we want the Indonesian state to be in accordance with the nature and character of Indonesian society, then our state will be based on the integralistic staatsidee, *the state integrated with the whole people, transcending all groupings* (Yamin, 1971, vol 1: 113).

The *rechtsstaat* – the state based on law – is an ideal home for human rights as only within the *rechtsstaat* can human rights guarantees, such as the independence of the judiciary, due process of law and judicial review, survive.[1] However, the very notion of *rechtsstaat* in Indonesia has been subverted by various political, economic, cultural and legal developments that gradually weakened its foundation. As a political statement, however, a commitment to *rechtsstaat* has been made by virtually every government official in modern Indonesia.

This chapter will attempt to describe the dilemmas faced by the *rechtsstaat* under the New Order where other contrary notions exist, such as the *integralistic staatsidee*, the *beamtenstaat* (bureaucratic state) and patrimonialism. The chapter also discusses what the consequences for human rights might be. The discussion of the *rechtsstaat* will be followed by a detailed discussion of the issues of independence of the judiciary, due process of law and judicial review, three key elements of *rechtsstaat* instrumental in the protection of human rights.

The *Rechtsstaat*: Constitutionality vs Reality

Problems of Definition

Legal-political discourse over the *staatsidee* (state idea) under the New Order has been characterised by two differing and conflicting notions. One adheres to the

---

1   Synonyms to describe *rechtsstaat* include 'state based on the Rule of Law' and 'law state' or *negara hukum*, a literal Indonesian translation of the latter. Each has slightly different implications. *Rechtsstaat* implies a continental model, 'Rule of Law' implies a common law model and *negara hukum* implies a more specifically Indonesian model. The term *rechtsstaat* will be used for the reason that it is the term used in the 1945 Constitution.

literal meaning of *rechtsstaat* as stipulated in the Elucidation of the 1945 Constitution, and the other, while nominally subscribing to the *rechtsstaat* notion, also refers to the *integralistic staatsidee* of Soepomo (Suny, 1978: 10-11).[2] The official interpretation also tends to link the *rechtsstaat* to the *integralistic staatsidee* although its formal basis to said to be the *Pancasila* and the 1945 Constitution.[3]

Explanations restating the prevailing notion of *integralistic staatsidee* can commonly be found in the minutes of the DPR.[4] The 1945 Constitution, however, does not offer any definition of *rechtsstaat* aside from a statement in its Elucidation: 'Indonesia is a state based on law (*rechtsstaat*), not merely based on power (*machtsstaat*)'. The substantive meaning of *rechtsstaat* is, therefore, subject to interpretation which is frequently done subjectively by the government. The Old Order government, for example, subscribed to a *rechtsstaat* cast in terms of the romantic vision of Soekarno's notion of unfinished revolution, enabling him to interfere in the judiciary. The New Order government, by contrast, interprets the *rechtsstaat* in a sense that supports the goals of economic development, stability, security and order. Implicitly, the *rechtsstaat* is subordinated to those goals.

There are three basic ingredients of *rechtsstaat*. First, a guarantee of human rights protection in all fields irrespective of sex, race, cultural background, economic condition and political conviction. Secondly, an independent and impartial judiciary. Thirdly, strict adherence to the principle of legality (Angin Baru ..., 1966: 18; Logemann, 1954: 18). Special emphasis might be given to one element or another, depending on the circumstances. Some lawyers, for instance, stress the necessity to have an administrative court that mediates disputes between the state and its citizens, for the reason that the state must also be controlled and sentenced if it has committed a wrongdoing.[5] As is true for any other legal subject, the state is not above the law.

Abidin (1970: 47-49) argues that, in addition to these basic elements, a strong legislature is necessary to promulgate legislation that might strengthen *rechtsstaat*. Along these lines, *Persatuan Sarjana Hukum Indonesia* (*Persahi*, or Indonesian Lawyers Association) stresses that not only is a strong legislature needed but also an equally strong and functional People's Consultative Assembly (MPR).[6] They call for a 'super legislature' to guard the Constitution (Persahi, 1989: 19). For *Persahi*,

---

2   See also Simanjuntak. Suny and Simanjuntak base their interpretations of the Indonesian *rechtsstaat* solely on the 1945 Constitution. Among those who subscribe to the *integralistic staatsidee* are Padmo Wahyono (1989) and Oemar Senoaji (1989).

3   See, for example, Law No 14 of 1985 concerning the *Mahkamah Agung*; Law No 2 of 1986 concerning the General Courts; Law No 6 of 1986 concerning the Administrative Court.

4   *Dewan Perwakilan Rakyat*, People's Representative Assembly, Indonesia's parliament. See, for example, the remark made by GOLKAR on the *Mahkamah Agung* and the General Court Bills (17 September 1985). See also the reply of the Minister of Justice to remarks made by members of the DPR on the same Bills (4 October 1985): 'The government actually is applying *integralistic* principles in accordance with the spirit of *Pancasila* and the 1945 Constitution in supervising the judges by emphasising a priority on togetherness and consultation between the government and the judiciary'.

5   See the remark made by GOLKAR (*Golongan Karya*, the government party) in the DPR regarding the Draft Bill on the Administrative Court (15 June 1982): 'The *rechtsstaat* will provide adequate safeguards to prevent abuse of power by the executive. If the *rechtsstaat* is to be fully realised that means the people should have rights over the state because the state is not the Almighty ... In principle, every abuse of power which harms any individual must be monitored by the judiciary, and review can be done through the administrative court'.

6   *Majelis Permusyawaratan Rakyat*.

only a strong and functional MPR can guarantee the *rechtsstaat* because, according to the 1945 Constitution, the MPR, as the highest body in the nation, supervises the three branches of government (executive, legislature and judiciary).[7]

Suny (1978) believes that the *rechtsstaat* must always and everywhere comply with similar standards. He therefore argues that the requirements of an Indonesian *rechtsstaat* should be in accordance with international standards. He particularly stresses the importance of the rights to express opinions, the rights to organise and the rights to dissent because only the existence of these human rights is capable of securing *rechtsstaat*. The judiciary alone cannot be effective without social control and public opinion, while social control and public opinion cannot exist without the freedom to organise, to express an opinion and to dissent.

This concept of *rechtsstaat* has been enlarged over the years and credit is due to the International Commission of Jurists (ICJ) for its tireless efforts in this regard.[8] A true *rechtsstaat*, however, is a utopian idea, especially in those Third World countries obsessed with economic development where few governments regard *rechtsstaat* favourably. They fear it might gradually diminish governmental power and impose undesirable limits on certain interests. It is therefore not surprising that Indonesia's governments have held the *rechtsstaat* in disfavour, despite the encouraging rhetoric of the New Order's early years. The government continues to insist that it is in the process of fulfilling its commitment to *rechtsstaat* as it embarks on various legal development programs but top priority has always been given to economic development.[9]

Reemergence of Integralistic Staatsidee

Historically, the *integralistic staatsidee* was proposed by Soepomo for consideration by the founding fathers of the new nation that was to be proclaimed on 17 August 1945 (Yamin, 1971: 109-21). It was not clear what Soepomo meant by *integralistic staatsidee* because of its vague and general description. It seemed to represent an embodiment of the whole nation in which the leader acted as the benevolent father of the people. It also represented a strong state with an emphasis on unity, with no dualism between state and individuals since all individuals are an organic part of the state. Finally, it represented the implementation of the *asas kekeluargaan* (family principle) in accordance with the supposed communal nature of Indonesian society (Yamin, 1971: 109-21).

Soepomo offered some clues to his idea. First, he suggested that the state was the people themselves. It resulted from their embodiment as a big family, in which

---

7   See the 1945 Constitution, Arts 2, 3.

8   The standards referred to by Suny were well defined at an ICJ conference in Bangkok in 1965 as consisting of constitutional protection of human rights, an independent and impartial judiciary, fair and free general elections, recognition of the right to express an opinion, freedom to organise, freedom to dissent and civil education (Suny, 1978: 20). An earlier ICJ conference in Athens in 1955 spelled out and adopted some essential requirements to be met by the judiciary (ICJ, 1956: 5-7), and, in 1959 in New Delhi, the ICJ listed requirements to be observed by the legislature and the executive (ICJ, 1965: 11-12). Later, the ICJ linked the *rechtsstaat* to education, the legal profession and socio-economic development (ICJ, 1956: 32-51).

9   See the speech of the Minister of Justice to the DPR, when submitting the General Court and the *Mahkamah Agung* Bills (28 August 1985).

there was a total integration between *kawula-gusti* (Javanese: 'subjects-lords'). It was therefore a mistake to draw a line between the state and individual people in the state (*staat und staatsfreire gesellschaft*) (Yamin, 1971: 109-21). This logic maintained that it would be unnecessary to provide human rights guarantees to individuals within the big family as it was the duties of the individuals to the state which counted the most (Yamin, 1971: 109-21).

The second clue to Soepomo's thinking was his reference to Nazi Germany as a model *integralisticstaat* in which the leader (*Fuehrer*) appeared as a supreme leader (*kernbegriff*) in a total unity (*ein totaler Fuehrerstaat*) (Yamin, 1971: 114).[10] In Soepomo's view, a new state must be a strong state because only a strong state can bring unity and prosperity to the people. The new state must therefore be based on totalitarian ideology (*das ganze der politischen einheit volkes*). This may explain why he perceived the state as a *totaliter* idea to the extent that he even supported the idea of monarchy as a form of government (Yamin, 1971: 109-21).

The next clue was Soepomo's reference to Japan's *Dai Nippon* with its reliance on *asas kekeluargaan* as reflected in the relationship between the emperor (*Tennoo*) and the people, a notion which resembles the *kawula-gusti* relationship (Yamin, 1971: 112-14). This logic would end in rejection of the separation of power theory as incompatible with *asas kekeluargaan*, as it reflects a kind of distrust between the two groups (Yamin, 1971: 341-42). This approach may further explain why Soepomo rejected the idea of judicial review (*toetsingrecht*) when it was proposed by Yamin, as he considered it totally irrelevant in an *asas kekeluargaan* state.

Constitutionally, the *integralistic staatsidee* had been defeated when the drafters of the 1945 Constitution formally agreed to the *rechtsstaat* notion in the form of a republic, and to limited human rights guarantees (Simanjuntak, 1989: 247) Soepomo, who formulated the idea, conceded that the *integralistic staatsidee* failed to receive sufficient support and so decided not to raise the issue further (Simanjuntak, 1989: 127-30). However, under the New Order, a kind of revival of *integralistic staatsidee* has been taking place. Some ideologues of the New Order have vigorously tried to argue that the *integralistic staatsidee* was never rejected by the founding fathers in 1945, and that, constitutionally, the New Order is bound by that view (Padmo Wahyono, 1989; Abdulkadir Besar, 1972: 501-24).

The *rechtsstaat* cannot exist under the shadow of *integralistic staatsidee*, even if the government continues to reiterate that Indonesia is a *rechtsstaat* based on *Pancasila* and the 1945 Constitution.[11] In the early years of the New Order, for instance, the government attempted to restore the already weakened judiciary in order to strengthen *rechtsstaat*. A new law on judicial authority (Law No 14 of 1970) was regarded by many lawyers as a milestone in New Order legal history because it restored, or in Senoarji's terms 'recrowned', the Indonesian *rechtsstaat* (1989: 14). This law replaced Laws No 19 of 1964 and No 13 of 1965 which had empowered the President to interfere in judicial matters (Senoarji, 1989: 14; Lev, 1978).

Not everyone, however, and, in particular, not lawyers, had reason to be pleased with Law No 14 of 1970. While the law revoked the Presidential right to interfere in judicial matters, it opened the way to other forms of executive

---

10   For a stimulating debate on the totalitarian state and its relation to Nazism, see Kennedy (1987); Jay (1987); and Piconne & Ulmen (1987).

11   See, for example, the considerations of Law No 14 of 1985 and No 2 of 1986 and No 6 of 1986. See also Decrees No II/MPR/1988 and No II/MPR/1983.

interference. The Minister of Justice was given a say in judicial affairs, such as the right to control the appointment, promotion, transfer, dismissal and salary of the judges (Art 11). The lawyers were concerned that such power in the hands of the minister might inevitably weaken the judiciary and in turn threaten the existence of the *rechtsstaat* itself.

The remnants of *integralistic staatsidee* are still very influential within government circles. Laws No 2 of 1986 and No 6 of 1986, which are the current implementing statutes for Law No 14 of 1970, clearly reflect the *integralistic staatsidee*. They retain the Minister of Justice's control of the appointment, promotion, transfer, dismissal and salary of the judges.[12] Minister of Justice Ismail Saleh, in submitting the draft Bills on the General Court and the *Mahkamah Agung* to the DPR emphasised that there should be harmony between the branches of power in resolving disputes between the government and its citizens.[13]

It has been argued that the executive's control over the judiciary has been significantly strengthened and the judiciary has become an extension of the larger bureaucracy. If this is true, then the notion of the bureaucratic state or *beamtenstaat* practiced during the colonial times remains (Ong Hok Ham, 1989: 42-79).[14]

Politically, this is what happened in the New Order. The bureaucracy became very strong and succeeded in separating people from politics through its floating mass policy (McVey, 1982: 85-88). This cut the parties' relationship to their constituents. Indeed, this bureaucratic state has been significantly dominated by its top bureaucrat who is both the President and a notable individual, a fact that has led some scholars to regard the New Order as a continuation of traditional patterns of patrimonialism (Liddle, 1985: 68-90; King, 1982: 104-16). The problem for the proponents of the *rechtsstaat* is that it cannot reasonably be reconciled with reemergent patrimonialism. One can understand why Daniel Lev argues that in a state such as Indonesia, patrimonialism and legal elements are mixed, even though the former is clearly dominant. The struggle for *rechtsstaat* represents, at least in part, the struggle between the idea of a mixed form of government favouring patrimonialism and the idea favouring legal authority (Lev, 1978: 40).

The fate of *rechtsstaat* appears even more dim if considered from the perspective of economic development. Robison argues that the New Order has aspired to lead a newly-industrialising country, following in the footsteps of South Korea, Taiwan, Hong Kong and Singapore. On those grounds alone, neglect of non-economic development (in which legal development would be included) would be considered fully justified. Robison states:

> The ideologists of the New Order attempted to legitimise the regime by arguing that a period of authoritarian rule and hence, objective, scientific, and decisive policy-making was necessary, to build an industrial base for the economy and provide the precondition for future democratic government (Robison, 1988: 61).

Authoritarian rule is apparently part of the price the New Order is willing to accept for joining the club of newly industrialising countries.

---

12   Law No 2 of 1986, Arts 13 and 16.

13   Speech of the Minister of Justice to the DPR (28 August 1985).

14   See also Lev (1985: 72). In this respect, Lev might be right when he observes: '[W]ith political parties steadily weakening and the *pamong praja* (bureaucrats) securely in place, both Guided Democracy and the New Order were genetically linked to the structure of the colonial state. In this one respect, at least, the independent state was not merely similar to the colonial state. It was the same state'.

What we have seen so far represents forces not favourable to *rechtsstaat*. The hard fact is that the state has been so powerful that the *rechtsstaat* notion has had difficulty finding a toehold. Protection of human rights depends, consequently, on the mercy of the state. Unconsciously, what appears to be the prevailing notion is *integralistic staatsidee*, as perfected by legislation. Thus, while at the outset we are offered niceties about *rechtsstaat*, in essence what remains in place is the old *integralistic staatsidee*.

Independence of the Judiciary

Limited Independence

The 1945 Constitution does not explicitly state that there is to be an independent judiciary. It simply says that the *Mahkamah Agung* will run the judiciary in accordance with the law (Arts 24-25). The Elucidation to the 1945 Constitution states that 'judicial authority is an independent authority, in the sense that it is beyond the influence of the government'. What is meant by independent authority is not clear, however. As a result, it can be interpreted in accordance with whatever notion of *rechtsstaat* prevails at any given time (Lev, 1978).[15]

Before the New Order – during the *Demokrasi Terpimpin* (Guided Democracy) period – the independence of the judiciary was subverted by Laws No 13 of 1965 and No 19 of 1964. These Laws authorised the President to interfere at any time when the revolution or the national interest was at issue.[16] The judiciary was subordinated to the executive, personified by the President, who was romantically perceived as a true and genuine leader of the people. Historically, no one can deny that Soekarno was indeed the most important founding father of the nation. However, this did not give him authority to become as king in a republic (Yamin, 1971: 119, 168-73, 287-98). In formal terms, he was not above the law but his charisma allowed changes that concentrated all branches of power, including judicial power, in his hands.

As mentioned, Law No 14 of 1970 not only repealed Law No 19 of 1964, but appeared to recrown *rechtsstaat* when it acknowledged the principle of the independence of the judiciary (Senoarji, 1989: 10). At this stage, the Elucidation of Art 1 becomes very important because it defines the meaning of 'independence of the judiciary' to mean that independence is not absolute and has limitations imposed by the government. In its full text the Elucidation states:

> The independence of the judiciary should imply that there is an independent judiciary free from interference of other state institutions, free from pressures, directions or recommendations which originate from extra-judicial authorities *except in the things permitted by the law*.[17]

---

15 Compare the different interpretation of independence of the judiciary in Laws No 19 of 1964 and No 13 of 1965 with Laws No 14 of 1970, No 14 of 1985 and No 2 of 1986. In the first two, there is no independence of the judiciary, while in the last three one finds a certain degree of independence.

16 Article 19 of Law No 19 of 1964 stated: 'In the interests of revolution, the honour of the state and nation, or the urgent interests of society at large, the President can engage or intervene in court proceedings'. Article 23(1) of Law No 13 of 1965 stated 'In cases where the President interferes, the court proceedings have to be stopped and the decision of the President should be announced'.

17 Emphasis added.

Freedom in implementing judicial authority is in itself not absolute because the function of the judges is to uphold the law and to find justice based on *Pancasila* through implementation of law, and finding of its basics and principles through cases leading to decisions that reflect the sense of justice of the Indonesian people.

The words *except in the things permitted by the law* is an avenue for government incursion into the judiciary. The business of law-making has, from one point of view, always been the business of government but only as dictated by dominant political interests. From that perspective, it is unfortunate, but hardly surprising, that a policy of limiting the independence of the judiciary continues to prevail in Indonesia and in many countries throughout the world.

Expectations that the New Order would restore an independent judiciary eventually proved unrealistic, even though many people remain convinced that the independence of the judiciary can slowly evolve. Economic development would eventually require various legal safeguards which could be provided only by a strong and independent judiciary.

Political parties, especially GOLKAR, have not seemed strongly inclined to work for an independent judiciary.[18] For example, when during debates over the Draft Bill which became Law No 14 of 1970 the Minister of Justice proposed a *Majelis Pertimbangan Penelitian Hakim* (MPPH, Council for the Examination and Evaluation of Judges), a non-governmental special council, to help the government examine and evaluate the records of judges (Lev, 1978: 65),[19] the idea was rejected by most political parties. Those who did support it suggested that there should be no members from the *Persatuan Advokat Indonesia* (*Peradin*, united Indonesian Advocates) involved.[20] *Ikatan Hakim Indonesia* (*Ikahi*, Indonesian Judges Association) also voiced its displeasure with the idea (Lev, 1978: 65). The whole incident demonstrates the lack of strong support within the political system for the independence of the judiciary.

It cannot be said, however, that there has never been any support for the independence of the judiciary. Within a limited circle, particularly within *Peradin* and now *Ikadin* (the Indonesian Bar Association), the struggle to have an independent judiciary continues (Lev, 1978: 65; Tasrif, 1979: 6-29). Moreover, the rising middle class, composed of businessmen, professionals, intellectuals and religious minorities, appears to contain strong supporters (Lev, 1978: 45-49).

As Indonesian history shows, however, the cause of the independent judiciary has always been weak not just because of disagreements within the government but

---

18 Indeed, GOLKAR has been untroubled by the effects or the government's involvement in the independence of the judiciary. See, for example, remarks made by Kuntjoro Jakti during the debates over the draft Bills on Judicial Authority and the *Mahkamah Agung* (28 October 1968). Other GOLKAR members, Saljo and Malikus Suparto, made similar remarks on 11 November, 1968, continuing the debates over those two draft Bills. On 17 September 1945, Albert Hasibuan, on behalf of GOLKAR, reissued similar remarks and emphasised the importance of *integralistic staatsidee* during the debates over draft Bills on the General Court and the *Mahkamah Agung*. See also remarks made by ASS Tambuan, also from GOLKAR, at the debate over the draft Bill on the Administrative Court (12 May 1986).

19 See, for example, the remarks made by Soegyarti Wiryohardjo (*Partai Nasional Indonesia*, Indonesian National Party), Tuti Harahap (*Partai Kristen Indonesia*, Indonesian Christian Party), FX Soedjana (*Partai Katolik*, Catholic Party), Zain Bajeber (*Nahdlatul Ulama*), Kuntjoro Jakti and Saljo (GOLKAR). Interestingly, Sahat Nainggolan (*Murba*, a leftist party) and Sukarton (the military) accepted the idea of MPPH. See also ICJ (1988: 131-34).

20 *Peradin* was forced to integrate itself into a new organisation called *Ikatan Advokat Indonesia* (*Ikadin*, Indonesian Advocates Association).

also because certain remnants of the colonial period, such as the dual court system, had not totally disappeared when the new government came into being (Soepomo, 1988: 73-92). It is important to remember that the courts in the colonial period were not free from interference of administrative officers, even though at the highest level it appeared that judges enjoyed a high degree of independence (Soepomo, 1988: 73-92).

Shadrack Gutto (1988: 52-53) argues that it is unrealistic to dream about independence of the judiciary. Historically, Gutto points out the overwhelming majority of judges have tended to treat the institutional and professional independence of judges as an end rather than a means of fulfilling their primary duty of changing the society. The consequence is that most versions of the independence of the judiciary preserves the status quo and retains social inequality among the people (Gutto, 1998: 53).[21] Miliband (1973: 124-25) asks also what the judiciary is supposed to be *independent from*. He implies it would be wrong to limit the discussion on independence of the judiciary to questions involving only interference from other branches of power, because interference may come from forces other than formal powerholders (Miliband, 1973: 124).

To a certain degree, Gutto and Miliband, both 'new left' scholars, are correct. Class origin, social background and educational elitism do make their contribution to the conservative thinking of the legal professions, particularly in the case of judges who tend to be drawn from the upper strata of Indonesian society (Miliband, 1973: 124). Those from middle and lower strata who join the judiciary tend to regard themselves as the latest members of the upper stratum. Judges therefore guard their privileges and are consequently unlikely to advocate radical social transformation. Their concerns are likely to be limited to philanthropic *prodeos* and *in forma pauperises* types of charitable works which provide legal aid and advice to the needy without charge, out of feelings of professional responsibility (Gutto, 1988: 53-54).

Government Interference

A major problem faced by the judiciary under the New Order is the potential for interference by the Minister of Justice.[22] Article 5 of Law No 2 of 1986, for instance, stipulates that the organisational, administrative, and financial supervision of the court will be conducted by the Minister of Justice, even though it does imply that the Minister can only interfere in non-court proceedings, which would leave judges on the bench free and independent. In strict legal terms, therefore, the independence of the judiciary is intact.[23] But how does one draw a line between 'court' and 'non-court' proceedings. Once law has empowered the Minister to become involved in the judiciary, it is only a matter of time before he insinuates himself into the exclusive domain of the judges.

One also has to take into account the fact that judges in Indonesia are officially considered *pegawai negeri*, or civil servants, and are registered as members of the Indonesian Civil Servants Association (KORPRI), an organisation headed by the

---

21 Gutto is right when he says 'To try and demand reforms to make [the judges] independent without transforming society socially serves only to strengthen their effectiveness as agents of the minority ruling class'.

22 See Law No 14 of 1970, Art 11 and Law No 2 of 1986, Art 5. See also ICJ (1987: 61).

23 See Law No 2 of 1986, Art 5.

Minister of Home Affairs (ICJ, 1987: 61).[24] On this matter, Lev (1978: 55-56) observes:

> Indonesian judges ... conceive themselves as *pegawai negeri*, officials, and as such, members of a bureaucratic class to which high status has always attached. One implication of the role of *pegawai negeri* is that it is patrimonially associated with political leadership, to whose will it must always be responsive. It is this as much as anything else that underlies the issue of judicial independence. Whatever the daily effects of the Ministry's responsibility, it is symbolically important as a reminder of the judiciary's conceptually limited authority and the direction of its loyalties.

The concept of separation of powers gets short shrift in this case, with the executive seemingly in a domination position and leading to what Sunny described as 'executive-heavy government'.[25]

In the words of Senoaji, the government adheres to the distinction between sharing powers as opposed to separation of powers (Senoaji, 1989: 16). This means that the branches of government are seen as closely interrelated and interdependent. The government can thus justify its involvement and interference in judicial matters and relegates the judges to be shadows of the executive branch.[26] Judges' reluctance to act independently in dealing with cases that are unpopular with the government can be attributed to their circumscribed independence (ICJ, 1987: 61-62). The resulting situation is not only unhealthy but may have a devastating impact upon the *rechtsstaat* by causing citizens' loss of trust and confidence in the judiciary.

In 1981, Chief Justice Mudjono – the former Minister of Justice – questioned the constitutional validity of his former position. It was his opinion that only the *Mahkamah Agung* had been mandated by the 1945 Constitution to administer the judicial branch (Kompas, 1981b). He was referring to Art 24 of the 1945 Constitution which specifically assigns responsibility for the conduct of judicial affairs to the *Mahkamah Agung*. He then proposed that the name of the Department of Justice be changed to the Department of Law and Regulation and should concentrate on law development, the drafting of Bills and assisting the President to identify issues of importance for the politics of law.

Mudjono touched upon a basic tenet of the *rechtsstaat* and was widely applauded by professional lawyers. He was, however, ignored by government inner circles because he made the statement when he was no longer serving as Minister of Justice. Some others felt that the statement reflected Mudjono's frustration at being promoted to the highest post in the judiciary, a position that, in fact, carries no significant power.

The Place of 'Harmony'

At this juncture, the remarks made by Imam Sukarsono, a member of a military faction, during debates over the Draft Bill relating to the Administrative Courts, are worth noting. He underlined the importance of the 'spirit of harmony' in the settlement of disputes because it was the 'prevailing social value'.[27] He implied that

---

24 See also Presidential Decision No 82 of 1971.
25 Interview with Suny, 20 June 1989.
26 See the speech of the Minister of Justice to the DPR upon submitting the Administrative Court Bill (31 May 1982).
27 See the remark made by Imam Sukarsono on behalf of the military faction in the DPR concerning the Administrative Court Bill (12 May 1986).

there should be no adversarial system in court procedures because it would be contrary to the spirit of *Pancasila*. The system most suitable for the judiciary would be one based on *asas kekeluargaan*, meaning that 'togetherness' should be superior to every other value (Abdulkadir Besar, 1972: 495). Harmony must be regarded as the imperative guideline in the courtroom even though, as such, it is capable of eroding the independence of the judiciary. In this sense *asas kekeluargaan* can in fact be interpreted as an open invitation to interfere in judicial matters by anyone who is a member of the family.

Bakorstanas and Kopkamtib

There are numerous non-judicial institutions, but most notable is the *Badan Koordinasi Bantuan Pemantapan Stabilitas Nasional* (*Bakorstanas*, Coordinating Board for Assisting the Consolidation of National Stability). *Bakorstanas* is essentially part of the Defence Department, and is charged with the task of restoring, maintaining and reinforcing national stability in the broadest sense. It has offices in every region throughout the country (Asia Watch, 1986: 58-62).

The name and agency of *Bakorstanas* replaced the *Komando Operasi Pemulihan Keamanan dan Ketertiban* (*Kopkamtib*, the Operational Command for the Restoration of Security and Order) which had extraordinary powers and could interfere in any affair at any time in any place, in the name of security and order (Asia Watch, 1986: 56-62). This extraordinary extra-judicial power allowed the arrest of many alleged communists, Islamic fundamentalists and student activists with little, if any, cause (Asia Watch, 1986: 62-156).[28]

Despite the change of name, the new agency functions in a similar fashion to its predecessor and has unlimited power to do anything it chooses in the name of national stability. It has had little difficulty in interrogating activists even though doing so constitutes a violation of formal criminal procedures as stipulated in *Kitab Undang-undang Hukum Acara Pidana* (KUHAP), the code of Criminal Procedure (Law No 8 of 1981, Arts 16-31; Yap Thiam Hien, 1973: 21-29). It has been argued that the existences of agencies such as *Kopkamtib* or *Bakorstanas* indicate conditions similar to those of a state of emergency. Both *Kopkamtib* and *Bakorstanas* have denied that they function within the context of a state of emergency. Rather, each has maintained that its presence has been a need to safeguard national stability (Asia Watch, 1986: 58-62). Whatever their justification, these bodies have successfully operated beyond the ambit of judicial authority and thus in a manner inherently contrary to the *rechtsstaat*.

The tragedy of the judiciary is that it lacks support within government to be truly independent. Continued weakening of the judiciary is, therefore, inevitable. In addition, both socially and culturally, the judiciary draws minimal sustenance. Lev, for instance, argued that the weak tradition of litigation in various parts of the country also damages the judiciary (Lev, 1972: 279-80). This is not to say that legal disputes are never brought before the judiciary but rather to note that cultural hesitation, or perhaps cultural reluctance, influences the settling of disputes in court. People would rather seek mediation through local leaders, be they traditional or religious (Holleman, 1981: 301-02), or they may also try to shortcut the process by

---

28 See, for example, *eksepsi* (demurrers) read by student activists in their trials in Bandung District Court on 9, 16 and 23 December 1989.

seeking out a friend with influence in the military, among high ranking police officers or among those close to the real powerholders (Holleman, 1981: 301-302).

This preference for amicable settlements of disputes outside court is also caused by the high costs and complicated procedures involved in court cases. Furthermore, there are not enough professional lawyers available to handle cases and most professional lawyers are stationed in Jakarta and the other big cities, leaving the rural areas alienated from litigation culture (Lev, 1987: 1-47).

Economic commercialism breeds corruption (Asia Watch, 1986: 165) and this remains the worst disease of the Indonesian judiciary, although they are not alone among state agencies in this regard. Judges frequently 'trade' their decisions prompting sceptics to invent cynical jokes about the judiciary. For instance, KUHP, an abbreviation of *Kitab Undang-undang Hukum Pidana*, the Criminal Code, has been said to mean '*kasih uang habis perkara*' (literally, 'give money, case over'), implying quite directly that the settlement of the case depends on how much money was provided by the litigants to the judges (Asia Watch, 1986: 165). Everything is seen from a business perspective and it is no secret that the most prosperous judges live in the big cities where they can 'earn' substantial amounts of money to augment their relatively low salaries (ICJ, 1987: 61-62; Gutto, 1988: 52-53). The term *Mafia Pengadilan* (Court Mafia) is now commonly used to describe the activities of the Indonesian judiciary.

Not unexpectedly, the Minister of Justice denied these allegations but nonetheless prosecuted and discharged a number of senior judges in Central Jakarta District Court after obtaining sufficient evidence from a case involving one of the judges (Asia Watch, 1986: 170-71). There are other parties participating in this *Mafia Pengadilan* as well, including prosecutors, professional lawyers and those acting as legal brokers (Asia Watch 1986: 170-71), although such practices take place mostly in non-political cases, both criminal or civil. If the case is political, the judges, prosecutors or the defence lawyers will usually proceed in accordance with existing laws and regulations. What matters in political cases are political pressures, while the cost-and-benefit analysis tends to prevail in non-political cases. It can be argued that this practice is an inevitable product of the economic development taking place.

Judicial Review

Judicial review has been a subject of debate since the time of deliberations on the 1945 Constitution before independence (Yamin, 1971: 234, 336, 341, 342). The debates continue today and are still inconclusive (Tasrif, 1979: 14-20; Harun Al Raid, 1979: 37-46). There is, however, a long tradition of support for the proposition that judicial review should be vested in the *Mahkamah Agung*.

In 1945, when Yamin proposed that the *Mahkamah Agung*'s power be extended beyond being a last resort in rendering verdicts, towards reviewing possible constitutional conflicts in laws enacted by the government and the DPR, Soepomo did not absolutely reject the proposal (Yamin, 1971: 341-42). Soepomo argued that in a state based on the *integralistic staatsidee* it would be inappropriate to grant power to one branch of power to control the other because every branch of power should cooperate. For him, judicial review could only be practised in a state based on the separation of powers or, in his terms, liberal democracy (Yamin, 1971: 341).

He also declared that he could not accept judicial review because, to his knowledge, no consensus had ever been reached among constitutional scholars; and because Indonesian lawyers still lacked experience in this area (Yamin, 1971: 342).

Soepomo made no further remarks about judicial review and Yamin dropped his proposal. However, the question of judicial review was not completely forgotten, and for a very brief time in 1950 judicial review was practised by the *Mahkamah Agung* under the 1949 Federal Constitution (Arts 156-158). Neither the 1950 Provisional Constitution nor the 1945 Constitution provide for judicial review.

After the dark days of the judiciary under Soekarno, interest in judicial review reemerged in the early years of the New Order (Lev, 1978: 57-63). The New Order's promise to restore *rechtsstaat* and human rights encouraged people to begin speaking out about the imperative of judicial review. So, for example, Tasrif, a noted lawyer, referred to the famous statement of Chief Justice Marshall in *Madison v Marbury* 5 US (1 Cranch) 137, 2 L Ed 60 (1803) to propose that judicial review be granted to the *Mahkamak Agung*. The US Constitution does not say anything about judicial review either but Chief Justice Marshall argued that his oath as Chief Justice meant that it was his constitutional duty to protect the Constitution (Tasrif, 1979: 14-20; Choper, 1980: 62). Tasrif argued that the *Mahkamah Agung* was in a similar position to the Supreme Court because every Justice of the *Mahkamah Agung* took an oath similar to that taken by the American judges upon appointment to the bench. Thus, the absence of judicial review provisions in the 1945 Constitution should not prevent the *Mahkamah Agung* from acting as a guardian of the Constitution by reviewing unconstitutional laws.

Looked at from another perspective, perhaps in addition to *integralistic staatsidee* the reluctance surrounding judicial review lies in the fact that Indonesia belongs to a civil law tradition which brings with it many complexities (Cappelletti, 1971: 45-68; Rosen, 1974: 785-819; Morton, 1988: 89-110). In civil law countries, declaring legislation unconstitutional may be perceived as a political function, and therefore an unsuitable act of the judiciary. If the *Mahkamah Agung* is empowered to review such legislation after it is enacted, then it is inevitably acting as what some call a 'super-legislator' (Sri Sumantri, 1989). Also, because the civil law countries have no developed doctrine of *stare decisis*, each person affected by an unconstitutional statute might have to bring her or his own action, creating potential situations of national instability. Finally, a traditional civil law judiciary tends to be unsuited to the exercise of judicial review largely because in most cases the *Mahkamah Agung* consists of career judges who lack broad political and policy-making experience (Cappelletti, 1971: 45-68).

This is not to say that the notion of judicial review cannot be adopted. Every attempt should be undertaken to ensure that judicial review be entrusted to the *Mahkamah Agung* because while major responsibility for protecting human rights falls to the government, the role of the judiciary is also central. Judicial review is the internal procedure that restrains government from abusing its power. The question is, of course, what model of judicial review is suitable given that socio-political conditions and legal systems vary from country to country. It may be the case that the decentralised model of judicial review as practised in the United States cannot be adopted in most civil law countries because it entrusts the power to determine the constitutionality of legislation to the judiciary (Rosen, 1974: 785-819).

The centralised model in which the power rests in one special court may be more easily adopted in Indonesia. Five civil law Latin American countries – Argentina, Brazil, Colombia, El Salvador and Venezuela – practise the decentralised model. Only Guatemala subscribes to the centralised model, and entrusts its Constitutional Court with exclusive jurisdiction for determining the constitutionality of legislation (Rosen, 1974: 785-819)[29] but the court exercises its power in an anticipatory fashion (Rosen, 1974: 806-807). Any Bill passed over a presidential veto which is unconstitutional either wholly or in part is sent directly to the Supreme Court. The Supreme Court must render its decision within six days after receipt of an opinion from the Procurator General. Only if the Supreme Court sustains the Bill's constitutionality may it be promulgated as law (Rosen, 1974: 806-807).

In the framework of *asas kekeluargaan* or cooperation between branches of powers as suggested by Soepomo, anticipatory judicial review might fit into the system even though it could not affect existing laws.[30] Interestingly, such a system has legal grounds in Decree No III/MPR/1978, Art 11(3) which states, 'The *Mahkamah Agung* can render its legal advice, be it requested or not, to the other state agencies'.[31] Regrettably, anticipatory judicial review has never been practised by the *Mahkamah Agung* but it could, on its own initiative, render legal advice to both the President and the DPR concerning any draft Bill before the DPR. Of course, there is no guarantee that either the President or the DPR would listen to the advice of the *Mahkamah Agung*, but it would demonstrate the *Mahkamah Agung*'s interest in performing its constitutional role. Such a move might strengthen the position of the *Mahkamah Agung* and the judiciary as a whole. The *Mahkamah Agung*'s failure to exercise these powers points to its lack of any spirit of judicial activism or sense of independence.

Conclusion

Ultimately the human rights of citizens are defended not by the words of the Constitution, but by the institutions of due process of law and the right to association which enables citizens to insist that these institutions function as they are intended (Novak, 1985: 4). It is meaningless to have an elegant Constitution filled with human rights provisions if the rights cannot be enjoyed because of the absence of institutions upholding due process of law. In a practical sense, such rights lose their significance, and the possession paradox described by Donnelly (1985: 15-20) occurs in which human rights are constitutionally and therefore legally guaranteed but are not protected in practice.

This has been the case in Indonesia. While there appears to be no problem concerning the constitutionality of *rechtsstaat*, its implementation remains doubtful. Soeharto's government held to a narrow interpretation of *rechtsstaat* and rendered it subordinate to the larger concept of *integralistic staatsidee*, reemergent under the New Order despite its formal defeat in 1945. The notions of checks and balances, separation of powers, independence of the judiciary, due process of law and judicial review − vital foundations of *rechtsstaat* − have not been highly regarded in the

---

29 In other civil law countries, such as France and Germany, such Constitutional Courts exist to safeguard the Constitution.

30 In the case of human rights, there is an urgent need to review various existing laws and regulations such as Law No 11/PNPS/1963 on Anti-Subversion, enacted under Soekarno. No less urgent is the need to review the laws inherited from the Dutch, such as provisions in the Criminal Code. Judicial review should also touch upon existing laws.

31 See also Decree No IV/MPR/1973.

house of *integralistic staatsidee*. On the contrary, the notions of *asas kekeluargaan* and harmony prevail and the concept of *rechtsstaat* is confronted with a profoundly serious threat. Human rights guarantees are, therefore, situated in an unfavourable environment and are virtually incapable of enforcement in practice.

References

Abidin, A Zainal, 1970, 'Rule of Law dan Hak-Hak Sosial Manusia dalam Rangka Pembangunan Nasional Indonesia', *Hukum Nasional*, Vol 10: 47.

Al Raid, Harun, 1979, 'Pembahasan Terhadap Kertas Kerja Tasrif SH tentang Hak-Hak Asasi Warganegara Ditinjau dari Sudut Undang-Undang Dasar 45 dan Perundang-undangan', *Hukum dan Keadilan*, July-August: 37-46.

Angin Baru dari Simposium UI, 1966, Penerbit Angkasa, Bandung.

Asia Watch, 1986, *Human Rights in Indonesia and East Timor*, Asia Watch, New York.

Besar, Abdulkadir, 1972, 'Academic Appraisal: Tentang Tata Tertib MPR' in *Laporan Pimpinan MPRS Tahun 1966-1972*, MPRS-RI, Penerbit MPRS, Jakarta.

Baxi, Upendra, 1987, 'Law, Democracy and Human Rights', *Lokayan Bulleting*, vol 4/5: 75.

Cappellitti, Mauro, 1971, *Judicial Review in the Contemporary World*, Bobbs-Merril Company, Indianapolis.

Choper, H, 1980, *Judicial Review and the National Political Process*, University of Chicago Press, Chicago

Djaksa, Gde, IGN, 1981, 'Proses Pembahasan Penyusunan Kitab Undang-undang Hukum Acara Pidana Menuju Perlindungan Hak-Hak Asasi Manusia', paper presented at a seminar on *Hukum Rights Day*, LBH, Jakarta, 10 December.

Donnelly, 1985, 'Human Rights and Development: Complementary or Competing Concerns' in Shepard, George and Nanda, Ved P (eds), *Human Rights and Third World Development*, Greenwood Press, Westport.

Gutto, Shadrack BO, 1988, 'Judges and Lawyers in Africa Today: their Powers, Competence and Social Role with Special Reference to the Organisation and Jurisdiction of the Courts' in *The Independence of the Judiciary and the Legal Profession in English-speaking Africa*, ICJ, Geneva.

Fatwa, AM, 1985, 'Demokrasi dan Keyakinan Beragama Diadili', a defence statement read at the Central Jakarta District Court, December, LBH, Jakarta.

Feinrider, Martin, 1981, 'Judicial Review and the Protection of Human Rights Under Military Governments in Brazil and Argentina', *Suffolk Transnational Law Journal*, vol 5: 171-99.

Hadjon, Philipus M, 1989, 'Kekuasaan Kehakiman di Indonesia Sejak Kembali ke Undang-undang Dasar 1945', paper presented at the seminar on *Thirty Years of the Return to the 1945 Constitution*, Law Faculty, University of Pajajaran, Bandung, 5-6 July.

Holleman, JF, 1981, *Van Vollenhoven of Indonesian Adat Law*, Martinus Nijhoff, The Hague.

ICJ (International Commission of Jurists), 1965, *The Rule of Law and Human Rights: Principles and Definitions*, ICJ, Geneva.

ICJ, 1987, *Indonesia and the Rule of Law*, Frances Pinter, London.

ICJ, 1988, *The Independence of the Judiciary and the Legal Profession in English-speaking Africa*, ICJ, Geneva.

Jay, Martin, 1987, 'Reconciling the Irreconcilable? Re-joinder to Kennedy?', *Telos*, vol 71: 67-80.

Kennedy, Ellen, 1987, 'Carl Schmitt and the Frankfurt School', *Telos*, vol 71: 37-66.

King, Dwight Y, 'Indonesia's New Order as a Bureaucratic Authoritarian Regime: What Difference Does it Make?' in Anderson, Benedict and Kahin, Audrey (eds), *Interpreting Indonesian Politics: Thirteen Contributions to the Debate*, Cornell University, Ithaca.

Kompas, 1980, 2 February.

Kompas, 1981a, 23 July.

Kompas, 1981b, 10 August.

Kroentjaraningrat, RM, 1975, *Introduction to the Peoples and Cultures of Indonesia and Malaysia*, Cummings Publishing Company, Menlo Park.

Lev, DS, 1972, 'Judicial Institutions and Legal Culture in Indonesia' in Holt, C (ed), *Culture and Politics in Indonesia*, Ithaca, Cornell University Press, NJ, 1972.

Lev, DS, 1978, 'Judicial Authority and The Struggle for An Indonesian *Rechtsstaat*', *Law & Society Review*, vol 13: 37.

Lev DS, 1985, 'Colonial Law and the Genesis of the Indonesian State', *Indonesia*, vol 40: 72.

Lev, 1987, *Legal Aid in Indonesia* (Monash University Southeast Asian Studies, Working Paper no 44).

Liddle, R William, 1985, 'Soeharto's Indonesia: Personal Rule and Political Institutions', *Pacific Affairs*, vol 50: 68-90.

Logemann, JHA, 1954, *Het Staatsrechten van Indonesia*, NV Uitgeverij W van Hoeve, Bandung.

Lukman Hakim, 1980, *Kudengar Indonesia Memanggil*, Badan Kerjasama Pembelaan Mahasiswa Indonesia, Jakarta.

McVey, Ruth, 1982, 'The Beamtenstaat in Indonesia' in Anderson, Benedict and Kahin, Audrey (eds), *Interpreting Indonesian Politics: Thirteen Contributions to the Debate*, Cornell University, Ithaca.

Miliband, Ralph, 1973, *The State in Capitalist Society*, Quartet Books, London.

Morton, L, 1988, 'Judicial Review in France: A Comparative Analysis', *American Journal of Comparative Law*: 89-110.

Muhammad, Haji NA Noor, 1981, 'Due Process of Law for Accused of Crime' in Henkin, L (ed), *The International Bill of Rights*, Columbia University Press, New York.

Novak, Michael, 1985, 'Democracy and Human Rights' in Berger, Peter and Novak, Michael (eds), *Speaking to the Third World on Democracy and Development*, American Enterprise Institute for Public Policy Research, Washington DC.

Ong Hok Ham, 1989, *Runtuhnya Hindia Belanda*, Gramedia, Jakarta, 1989.

Padmo Wahyono, 1989, 'Hak dan Kewajiban Asasi Berdasarkan Cara Pandang Integralistik Indonesia', *Forum Keadilan*, vol 9.

Persahi, 1989, *Kerangka Landasan Pembangunan Hukum*, Pustaka Sinar Harapan, Jakarta.

Piconne, Paul & Ulmen, GL, 'Introduction to Carl Schmitt', *Telos*, vol 72: 3-14.

Robison, Richard, 1988, 'Authoritarian States, Capital Owning Classes, and the Politics of Newly Industrialised Countries: The Case of Indonesia', *World Politics*, vol 41: 73.

Rosen, Keith S., 1974, 'Judicial Review in Latin America', *Ohio State Law Journal*, vol 35: 785-819.

Senoaji, Oemar, 1989, 'Kekuasaan Kehakiman di Indonesia Sejak Kembali ke Undang-undang Dasar 1945', paper presented at *Thirty Years of the Return to the 1945 Constitution*, Law Faculty, University of Pajajaran, Bandung, 5-6 July.

Simanjuntak, Marsilam, 1989, *Unsur Hegelian dalam Pandangan Negara Integralistik* (unpublished thesis, University of Indonesia).

Soeharto, 1988, *Pikiran, Ucapan dan Tindakan Saya*, an autobiography as told to Dwipayana, G and Ramadhan, KH, PT Citra Lamtoro Gung Persada, Jakarta.

Sumantri, Sri, 1989, 'Susun Ketatanegaraan Menurut UUD 1945', a paper presented at the *Seminar on Thirty Years of the Return of the 1945 Constitution*, Law Faculty, University of Pajajaran, Bandung, 5-6 July.

Suny, Ismail, 1978, *Mekanisme Demokrasi Pancasila*, Aksara Baru, Jakarta.

Soepomo, 1988, *Sistem Hukum di Indonesia Sebelum Perang Dunia II*, Pradnya Paramita, Jakarta.

Tasrif, S, 1979, 'Hak-Hak Asasi Warga Negara Ditinjau dari Sudut UUD-45 & Perundang-undangan', *Hukum dan Keadilan*, July-August: 6-29.

United Nations, 1988, *Human Rights Status of International Instruments*, United Nations Publications.

Yamin, Muhammad, 1971, *Naskah Persiapan Undang-undang Dasar 1945*, vol 1, Penerbit Siguntang, Jakarta.

Yap Thiam Hien, 1973, 'Masalah Hukum & Penyalahgunaan Kekuasaan', *Prisma*, vol 6: 21-29.

12. Positivism and Romanticism in Indonesian Legal Thought

David Bourchier

Not long after President Soekarno revived the wartime Constitution and erected his system of 'Guided Democracy', the lawyer and novelist Sutan Takdir Alisjahbana published a short, insightful essay entitled 'Confusion in Legal Thinking'. In it he lamented the tendency for jurists of his day to regard customary law as 'the legal system most truly in harmony with the Indonesian ideal of justice'. Their efforts to build a nationalist legal order based on a romanticised vision of village life, he argued, 'had brought the development of Indonesian law and Indonesian legal thinking to a hopelessly confused and tangled impasse' (Alisjahbana, 1975: 74).

Three decades later, in the closing years of President Soeharto's long rule, official discourse on constitutional law continued to be plagued by contradictions. Soeharto's jurists routinely maintained that Indonesia was a *rechtsstaat*, a legally limited state. At the same time they rejected the doctrine of the separation of powers on the grounds that, like voting in parliament, it was not in accordance with the emphasis in traditional Indonesian culture on harmony and consensus. While Indonesia was an orderly *rechtsstaat*, it was also a '*Pancasila* Democracy', an 'Integralist State' or a 'Village Republic'. According to these supplementary doctrines, the highest priority was not law but the 'public good' as determined by a wise and benevolent father figure. The proper role of the state was not simply to regulate society but to encompass it, involving itself in all aspects of social life for the sake of the well being of the whole – the whole family as it were.

One important reason for these mixed signals is that mainstream constitutional law in Indonesia has long been informed by divergent, indeed often contradictory, traditions of legal philosophy inherited from the Dutch. These traditions have gone by many names over the centuries but for simplicity's sake I will call them 'positivism' and' romanticism'. This chapter attempts to unravel the separate histories of these two traditions and explain how they came to be superimposed in Indonesia. This will help to illuminate aspects of Indonesian constitutional development, particularly the difficulties that generations of democratic reformers have had in pressing for a separation of powers, the rule of law and executive accountability.

Positivism is used here to describe the tradition of legal philosophy that sees law as emanating from state authority rather than from God or some other source. Once laws are made by the legitimate authority, they must be obeyed by all, including those who made them. Associated historically with the Enlightenment (and more distantly with Rome), positivists favour legal systems which are rational and internally coherent, each law deriving its authority from a higher law, and ultimately from a supreme principle decided by the sovereign power. Positivist doctrines have been used to underpin absolutist, centralised, bureaucratic regimes but in their emphasis on rules they also contributed much to the growth of the *rechtsstaat*.

Romanticism, on the other hand, describes the tradition which holds that law is legitimate only if it arises organically from the history and culture of particular civilisations. Typically hostile to the rationalism and universalism of the Enlightenment, romantics emphasise the importance of the *volksgeist*, the distinctive spirit of a nation. Their tendency to look to tradition and the national past for inspiration has seen them labelled as inherently conservative, although this is not always the case.

Indonesian legal thinking derives most of its key concepts from Dutch law. During the colonial era, Dutch scholarship on constitutional law in turn took its bearings from Germany, especially the enormous German literature on the philosophy of law. This is why so many German terms appear in Indonesian texts on constitutional law – even in the official Elucidation of the 1945 Constitution. It is therefore to Germany that we need to look to examine the origins of some of the key ideas that are still being played out in Indonesia.

The story begins, for our purposes, in the early 19th century, when the German fascination with the French Revolution turned to dread. Humiliated by the defeat of the German speaking-principalities at the hands of Napoleon's armies and horrified by Robespierre's terror in France, figures associated with the Romantic movement turned their backs on what they described as the 'mechanistic' Enlightenment concept of humanity and the universe, including natural law, social contract theory and the idea of popular sovereignty. They also opposed the trend in Germany, accelerated by the Napoleonic conquest, towards the establishment of a modern, liberal, bureaucratic regime. They saw this trend as undermining the traditional pattern of social relations based on obligation in favour of an artificial, impersonal relationship between the atomistic individual and the centralised state.

The juridical movement associated with German romanticism was the Historical School of Law (*Historische Rechtsschule*). Founded by Friedrich Karl von Savigny and his student Georg Puchta around 1815, this school flourished for several decades and influenced legal and political philosophy well into the 20th century. Accepting the romantic view of the nation state as an entity possessing an organic unity above and beyond the concerns of individuals, the members of this school argued that law, like language and custom, was a product of slow, unconscious distillation of the living traditions of particular people. Law, they held, could not be created by legislators, nor transplanted from one context to another. It had to be *discovered*. On this basis Savigny argued against efforts to introduce a Napoleonic codification of law in Prussia. Renewal and unification of German civil law could only be achieved, he argued, through an exhaustive scholarly investigation of its historical development. The task for jurists, then, was to dig into the national culture and discern what was part of national consciousness and what was not. The Historical School spawned a series of encyclopaedic studies from about 1810 onwards into the customs, languages and folk law of the people of Germany in an attempt to extract a set of principles on which a national legal system could be built.

By 1840, a dispute over the reception of Roman law into Germany had split the Historical School into two hostile camps. The 'Germanists', who included the brothers Grimm, argued in favour of preserving the uniqueness of indigenous German culture and rejected any attempt to incorporate 'corrupt' law derived from non-German, and particularly Roman sources (Eikema Hommes, 1979: 198). The

'Romanists', on the other hand, led by Savigny and Puchta, had by this time come to believe that Roman law had penetrated so deeply into the German national culture that much of it could be regarded as in tune with the *volksgeist*.

The split was exacerbated by Savigny's penchant for abstract logic and system building which drew him ever closer to the methods of the rationalistic Natural Law philosophies which the Historical School had been founded to oppose. Confronted by the increasingly apparent impracticality of deriving all law from custom, the Romanists, and in particular Puchta, stressed the central role of state jurists in formulating law (Whitman, 1990: 124). They were to do this not by digging into the national past but by developing legal maxims on the basis of reason from a closed system of axioms without reference to external factors such as religious, social or economic values (Gale, 1982: 144).

Savigny's Historical School thus set in train two sharply different approaches to jurisprudence. The first, stemming from the Germanists, emphasised the importance of historical specificity and saw law as an essential feature of social solidarity: the glue that held society together. The Romanists, meanwhile, helped to lay the foundations of legal positivism, developed further by Rudolf von Jhering and Georg Jellinek, which regarded law as an instrument of state authority and domination (Turner, 1993: 495). Due to its practicality and its attractions to the managers of the emerging bureaucratic states of central Europe, positivism eventually won the day.

The romance with the *volksgeist* lived on, however, finding favour with conservative politicians and jurists not only in Germany but also in Holland. Both rejected the 'anarchic' doctrines of liberal individualism and socialism, preferring a more old fashioned and cosy provincialism. Jacques Oppenheim, for example, the head of the prestigious School of Law at Leiden University at the turn of the century, was a strong proponent of the notion that viable political orders could not be constructed from artificial rules but rather had to evolve out of custom (Oppenheim, 1893).

Oppenheim's student, Cornelis van Vollenhoven, was the most influential advocate of the ideas of the romantics in Dutch debates about colonial policy. Like the folklorist Jakob Grimm, van Vollenhoven was a powerful supporter of what he called *volksrecht* (law emerging from the people) as opposed to *juristenrecht* ('lawyer's law'). The latter, he argued, had derived from alien (Roman) traditions that had corrupted and suppressed the indigenous customs and law of the non-Roman European peoples (van den Bergh, 1986: 80). The battle against the encroachment of positivism in Europe, however, was all but lost; a comprehensive Napoleonic-style civil code having been adopted in the German Empire in 1896.

Van Vollenhoven instead took the fight to the Indies, where liberals and business interests were successfully lobbying the colonial government to abolish the old racially stratified legal order and bring the whole population of the Indies under a unified European-style private property-oriented legal system. Just as the Germanists attacked the Romanists for their 'sin against the historical spirit' (Eikema Hommes, 1981: 198), van Vollenhoven attacked the colonial authorities and their advisers for trampling on time-honoured *adat* traditions by attempting to impose alien notions of ownership, punishment and compensation on Indonesian communities. To deny indigenous communities their law and a degree of sovereignty over their land, he maintained, would not only betray the spirit of the government's so-called Ethical Policy, but would consign *adat* to the same destiny as Dutch common law which jurists had 'squeezed ... into the matrix of Roman law' (Holleman, 1981: 22).[1]

Between 1904 and the late 1920s, debates raged between van Vollenhoven's 'Leiden school' and the proponents of a unified legal system associated with Utrecht University.[2] Thanks in part to the eloquence of his appeals, and the way in which his lyrical and magisterial writings on *adat*[3] caught the imagination of the Dutch public, van Vollenhoven and his supporters succeeded in convincing the colonial government to preserve a pluralistic legal system in which Europeans were covered by European law and local indigenous communities were serviced by local courts dispensing local justice. Such were the successes of van Vollenhoven and his disciples, Savigny's Historical School is said to have had a more enduring impact in Indonesia than anywhere else in the world (van den Bergh, 1986: 78).

But what was good for the romantic *volksrecht* movement was not necessarily good for Indonesia. The *adat* lobby's victory simply crystallised the existing situation in which the 'native' side of the racially segregated justice system obeyed Historical School principles, while the European side, and the machinery of the centralised bureaucratic state, operated according to the logic of positivism. The entrenchment of a two-tiered legal system reinforced the power of often reactionary local elites and rendered local communities in many cases even more vulnerable to outside intrusion than they had previously been (Lev, 1985: 64, 66). More important in the longer term, many Indonesian lawyers were won over by the arguments of the *adat* lobby that 'Western' models of law and government, with their emphasis on individual rights and impersonal rules, were inappropriate for Indonesia. This was partly because the *adat* lobby was seen as siding with the Indonesians against the excesses of colonial capitalism. It was also because van Vollenhoven's glorification of *adat*, particularly the communalistic values he claimed made Indonesian *adat* unique, was taken genuinely to heart by many young lawyers 'thirsty for praise' as Alisjahbana (1975: 73) put it, 'of the values of their society and culture which had suffered so many humiliations in the twentieth century'. This persuaded not only lawyers but also parts of the broader nationalist movement to take on board two of the assumptions of the *adat* law lobby. First, that Indonesia's system of governance must reflect its *volksgeist*; and, secondly, that the *volksgeist* was embodied in the country's system of customary law, with its accent on harmony, balance and reciprocity.[4]

Evidence of the way in which European romantic ideas were incorporated into Indonesian legal thought can be found in the writings of the Leiden-educated *adat* scholar, Dr Raden Soepomo. As the primary author of the 1945 Constitution, Soepomo had a considerable influence on subsequent discourse about the legal

---

1   Van Vollenhoven was equally disparaging of Islam's universal pretensions, both as a threat to the survival of *adat* and to the colonial order in general, but on this score he found fewer causes for disagreement with the authorities.

2   A good account of the debates can be found in Burns (1989).

3   Van Vollenhoven's major work is the three volume, *Het Adatrecht van Nederlandsch-Indië* (*The Adat-Law of the Netherlands Indies*, 1918, 1931, 1933). This work is in the same vein, and driven by a similar impulse, as the large and extremely detailed studies of local cultures in Europe written by Germanists.

4   An important exception was lawyers in private practice, who tended to be in favour of doing away with the patchwork of *adat* realms and institutions and building up a modern, rational, unified system of law (Lev, 1985: 67). Most communist and Muslim nationalists were likewise unpersuaded by *volksgeist* arguments.

foundations of the state. In his inaugural lecture as professor in the Law Faculty of the University of Indonesia in 1941, Soepomo drew heavily on van Vollenhoven and other Dutch authorities to argue that Indonesian society – in sharp contrast to the West – was communally-oriented and gave precedence to the interests of the whole over those of the individual (Soepomo, 1970). Soepomo's acceptance of the theoretical underpinnings of the Leiden approach to the study of law was not exceptional. Indeed, thanks largely to the close institutional links between Leiden and the Jakarta law school, the premises and assumptions of the Historical School found an important place in the legal education system alongside the 'standard' positivist canon of legal theory.

Indonesia's first foreign minister Ahmad Subardjo, who was educated at Leiden but did not study *adat*, was also deeply impressed by the romantics of the Historical School. Recalling his years in Europe in the 1920s he wrote admiringly of von Savigny and how he had been struck by the parallel between his account of the imposition of alien Roman law on Germany and the situation in Indonesia. Subardjo (1978: 135) wrote that he had been

> impressed by von Savigny's concept that unless law was rooted in the culture and history of a people, it would undermine the state. This was a clear sign for me that the system of Dutch law in my country had obstructed the natural growth of Indonesian *adat* law. Von Savigny's famous phrase '*Das Recht ist und wird mit dem Volke*' ('the law is in and of the people')[5] reinforced my view that our struggle for independence must look for its strength in our nation's identity to oppose the powerful alien influences.

Subardjo was confirmed in his ideas by his experience living in 1930s Japan, where he was witness to the nationalist reaction against doctrines seen as flowing from the European Enlightenment: socialism, communism, liberalism and legal positivism. One of Subardjo's closest friends in Japan was Professor Toyo Ohgushi, a prominent nationalist ideologue. Subardjo recounted enthusiastically how Toyo and many of his colleagues condemned the way in which Western theories, and in particular the legal thought of positivists such as Jellinek, had dominated in Japan at the expense of historically evolved indigenous conceptions of power (1978: 199).

There was a surprising congruence between the theoretical perspectives of the Leiden-educated lawyers and the Japanese cultural nationalists. Both sympathised with the conservative, communalistic and anti-liberal stream of thinking that arose in Europe in reaction first to the French Revolution and later to the social dislocation and alienation wrought by industrialisation. Both advocated casting off western legal frameworks in favour of a 'return' to indigenous Asian values although for different political reasons. This is why Subardjo found himself on the same wavelength as one of Japan's most militant right wing nationalists. This is also why, during the Japanese occupation of Indonesia, Soepomo found a receptive environment for his ideas about state and society.

Like the Dutch, the Japanese brought their disagreements about law with them to Indonesia. In some ways they were less tolerant of legal pluralism than the Dutch, taking important steps to unify and rationalise the complex colonial legal system (Lev, 1973). At the level of ideology, however, they supported the idea that Indonesia should look to its own cultural traditions as a source not only of pride but also of law. Japanese-sponsored journals such as *Keboedajaan Timoer* (Eastern

---

5   Savigny's original sentence was *Das Recht wird nicht gemacht, es ist und wird mit dem Volke*.

Culture) and *Asia Raya* (Greater Asia) extolled traditional culture and virtues, promoting such concepts as *gotong royong* (the spirit of cooperation). One of the first advisory bodies the Japanese set up was the Research Council on Adat and Past State Organisation (*Panitia Pemeriksa Adat dan Tatanegara Dahoeloe*), bringing together nationalist politicians Soekarno and Hatta with several Leiden-educated lawyers, including Soepomo.

On the eve of independence, Soepomo was one of sixty-two prominent Indonesians appointed by the Japanese to an assembly whose task it was to draft a Constitution. As a prominent scholar and the most senior Indonesian legal functionary to serve the occupation regime, Soepomo was put in charge of a drafting subcommittee. In a speech to the assembly on 31 May 1945, Soepomo recalled the advice of a senior Japanese official urging the delegates to be careful not simply to imitate other government systems but rather adapt any future system of government to the specific character of the nation (Yamin, 1959: 111). This was, Soepomo said, very germane advice, which he translated into an axiom of the Historical School: 'A state's internal organisation is intimately related to its legal genealogy (*rechtsgeschichte*) and its social structure' (Yamin, 1959: 111).

Transcripts of the constitutional debates of 1945 reveal the ways in which both positivist and romantic legacies informed the thinking of the delegates to the assembly. They were in no doubt, for instance, that their first task was to decide on a *staatsidee*, a cardinal principle from which all 'lower' laws, including the constitution itself, would be derived. The image of the state as a hierarchy of laws crowned by a *staatsidee* is pure positivism. There was also a broad consensus that the internal structures of the colonial state and the mass of positive law it generated should be retained more or less intact.[6] At the same time several delegates insisted that the Constitution reflect Indonesia's folk tradition of deliberative and consensual decision-making. Soepomo made an impassioned plea for the rejection of western philosophies of liberalism and communism on the grounds that they were out of tune with the communalistic principles underlying *adat*. Arguing that the traditional relationship between leaders and their people was characterised by familial trust and mutual obligation, Soepomo maintained that there was no place for divisive concepts such as political rights in the constitution. He proposed instead a totalistic state philosophy he called 'integralism' (*teori integralistik*) (Yamin, 1959: 110-11).

Democratic-minded members of the Assembly such as Mohammad Hatta successfully resisted some of Soepomo's proposals. In other respects the Constitution accommodated Soepomo's desire to frame the state as a village writ large, leading to real inconsistencies. While Art 2 (3), for instance, specifies that all decisions of the MPR (*Majelis Permusyawaratan Rakyat* or People's Consultative Assembly) be made on the basis of voting, there is a concurrent emphasis on the need for *musyawarah* (deliberation), with its clear reference to 'village style' consensual decision-making.

This points to a more general contradiction in the Constitution between its stated commitment to *rechtsstaat* principles (ie binding rules) and its extreme flexibility. The loose phrasing of the Constitution was in part a product of Soepomo's wish to keep the text adaptable. But Soepomo's opposition to proposals

---

6   This was to find legal expression not long afterwards in Art II of the Transitional Provisions of the 1945 Constitution; and in Paragraph 1 of Government Decree No 2 of 1945, stating that 'All state institutions and regulations existing prior to the formation of the Indonesian Republic on 17 August 1945 shall be regarded as authoritative unless they are superseded or in conflict with the Constitution'.

that the powers of the government be balanced by the provision of political rights to the population suggests that he supported giving maximum discretion to those in power. This impression is reinforced in this passage of the Elucidation of the Constitution, written by Soepomo in 1946:

> The most important aspect of government and state life is spirit (*semangat*) – the spirit of state officials, the spirit of government leaders. While the wording of this Constitution is intentionally familistic, if state officials and the leaders of government are individualistically inclined, the Constitution will of course be meaningless in practice (Art IV, Elucidation of the 1945 Constitution).

Full independence in 1949 saw a flight from romanticism. The Allied victory and four years of revolution helped bring to power a group of leaders bitterly opposed to the Japanese and what Sutan Sjahrir, Indonesia's first Prime Minister, called 'feudalistic solidarism' (Sjahrir, 1968: 28). The adoption of a resolutely democratic Constitution in 1950 ushered in a period of remarkably free political life that lasted for almost a decade.

But the legacy of Romanticism was not extinguished so easily. Elements of the gentry associated with conservative political parties hankered after a system of rule that would restore the 'natural' social hierarchy. And a substantial number of Dutch-trained lawyers committed to extending *adat* philosophies to national life continued to teach in civilian and military law schools, disseminating their ideas to Indonesia's future elite.

In the mid 1950s, when President Soekarno and the army leadership sought alternatives to the multi-party democracy which had marginalised them from positions of formal power, it was to lawyers such as Professor Djokosutono, Dean of the University of Indonesia's Law Faculty, that they turned, to help them steer a course towards a more authentically 'Indonesian' – and less democratic – system of government. Drawing on a range of continental legal thinkers from Carl Schmitt to Jakob Grimm, Djokosutono argued that Indonesia had been too quick to adopt 'abstract' European conventions such as parliamentarism after 1945 (Djokosutono, 1982). Constitutional structures, he argued, should reflect the prevailing 'natural and cultural' conditions of society rather than abstract ideals (see, for example, Djokosutono, 1982: 11). In the years between 1956 and 1959 Djokosutono played an important role as a supplier of political, legal and doctrinal formulas which helped legitimise the increasingly prominent political profile of both General Nasution's army and the President.

As Soekarno stepped up his calls for a return to Indonesia's 'national personality', indigenist rhetoric – especially the idea of *gotong royong* – came to stand for opposition to parliamentary democracy. For both his radical and conservative allies, the image of the communalistic village provided a counterpoint to what they saw as the divisiveness and foreign-inspired individualism of the existing political system. But each group used indigenist rhetoric in its own way. For many radicals, calling for a return to a *gotong royong* society was a way of declaring their opposition to the whole system of Western derived law in Indonesia, which many saw as bourgeois and overly positivistic: preoccupied with statutes and precedents rather than revolutionary justice. For conservatives a return to a more 'Indonesian' political system promised strong, decisive government at the centre, military participation in government and a reduction of party influence in the towns and villages.[7]

Soekarno's 1959 decree resurrecting the 1945 Constitution marked the beginning of the end for the *rechtsstaat*. His Guided Democracy explicitly rejected all forms of 'textbook thinking' and was contemptuous of any attempt by lawyers or the courts to stand in the way of his drive to 'return Indonesia to the rails of the Revolution'. In 1964 he underscored his disdain for legal processes by issuing Law No 19 of 1964 on Judicial Powers, formally authorising himself to intervene in matters of jurisdiction and thereby abolishing the principle of the separation of powers.

Soeharto's military-backed New Order regime, in contrast, placed an enormous rhetorical emphasis on legality and constitutionalism. Among its first legislative priorities, realised in Resolution No 20 of the Interim MPR of 1966, was to establish a clear hierarchy of 'legal products' from the Constitution down to Presidential Decisions, Ministerial Instructions and so on. This was intended to reimpose a strict positivist logic onto the chaotic administrative legacy of the Soekarno years, reinforcing bureaucratic lines of command. At the same time it formally elevated the *Pancasila* as the supreme legal principle, 'the source of all sources of law', which could not be altered by any government authority without 'destroying the state itself' (Ketetapan ..., c.1967: 53, 56).

Government spokespeople frequently drew attention to Resolution No 20 as proof that the New Order was firmly committed to upholding the rule of law (see, for example, Ali Moertopo 1975: 125). But designating the *Pancasila* as 'the source of all sources of law' might just as well be seen as having cancelled out any guarantee that the rule of law would prevail. Just as Soekarno used the symbol of Revolution to justify sweeping legalism aside so Resolution No 20 paved the way for the Soeharto government to do precisely the same. Formally ensconcing a principle as malleable as the *Pancasila* at the very pinnacle of the hierarchy of positive law made it possible to declare anything legal and to interpret the Constitution in any way that was held to be 'in accordance with the *Pancasila*'. Long-time security chief Yoga Soegomo (1986: 16) was candid about the utility of the arrangement: '*Pancasila* is the legal basis of authority. Hence, any political action based on the norms of *Pancasila* ideology is in accordance with the law and legitimate'.

On the face of it, New Order ideology was all about modernisation and economic development. Yet, as I have argued elsewhere (Bourchier, 1996: Chapter 6), Soeharto's ascendancy also marked the return to influence of conservative lawyer-ideologies steeped in the romantic thought world of *adat*. Under their guidance, the *Pancasila* was drained of revolutionary, leftist resonances and made to stand for the 'organic', 'harmonious' essence of the Indonesian nation. Resolution No 20, then, might be seen as representing a conjunction of the two traditions of legal thought that have been discussed in this chapter. In specifying a strict hierarchy of laws, the New Order's jurists were following the positivist legal principles upon which their colonial forebears had originally built the administrative

---

7   Many conservatives appear to have shared the hopes of *adat* lawyer, Mohammad Nasroen, who, like Soepomo in 1945, argued for a political order based on 'traditional' village values and institutions in his 1957 book *Asal Mula Negara* (The Origins of the State). Sarwono Djaksonagoro's paper entitled 'The Village as a Model' provides an excellent statement of the 'feudal' ideals prevailing among the Javanese *pamong praja* (bureaucratic) elite in the late 1950s. See the translated extracts in Feith and Castles (1970: 198-200).

bureaucracy. Enshrining the *Pancasila* as the highest legal principle, however, imposed a different, and in some ways contradictory logic onto the system. The view of law and authority in the *adat* tradition of scholarship, on which New Order explications of the *Pancasila* drew, had little time for the impersonal, rational principles characteristic of legal positivism. Romantic constructions favour a fluid and totalistic concept of authority, in which relations between the rulers and their people are governed not by fixed rules consistently applied but by a diffuse paternalism resting on the concept of the 'public good'. Resolution No 20, then, might be seen as having formally subordinated the entire 'positive' legal and constitutional apparatus of the state to a logic in which written law counted for little.

Running positivism and romanticism together in this way presented New Order ideologues with some complicated problems. One of the most systematic expositions of constitutional theory under the New Order is to be found in a 1990 Doctoral dissertation by the constitutional lawyer Hamid S Attamimi, Deputy Cabinet Secretary from 1983 until 1993. Attamimi brought to his study a good knowledge of the philosophy of law in general and German positivist theory in particular. His thesis attempted to remind legislators and legislative drafters of the positivist logic underlying the system of public law in Indonesia; and stressed the importance of abiding by its dictates – that is, orderliness, internal consistency and respect for a structured hierarchy of legal norms. But he was also keen to defend an interpretation of the Constitution that provided for an expanded concentration of power in the office of the President, where he worked. That argument required him to draw on Soepomo's 'village republic' concept to depict the President's position as analogous to that of a traditional village head, with a wide range of responsibilities, many of them unwritten (Attamimi, 1990: 106-109, 126, 144-88). This led him into serious conceptual difficulties, however, partly because of his stylised vision of what constituted a 'traditional village' but mainly because he was unable to show how the positivist principles he espoused could be upheld when combined with 'village' style organicist logic. The lack of fit between the two constitutional models is perhaps most obvious in the contrast between the intricately stratified pyramid he used to represent the positivist concept of the legal order, and the circular diagram complete with feedback loops he used to illustrate a traditional village (Attamimi, 1990: 110a, 290a).

There are few signs, however, that Soeharto ever worried himself with these kinds of theoretical problems. For him, any doctrine that could justify and prolong his power was good, regardless of how incoherent it may have been. Declaring his support for the rule of law and making a show of legality was useful in some circumstances. In other circumstances he ignored the law completely, presenting himself as the champion of development or the protector of his people. An example of the latter was his decision in the early 1980s to order the abduction and execution of around 5000 suspected criminals throughout the country. Although questions surrounded the exact identity of the assassins (they were dubbed the 'mysterious shooters') little serious effort was made to construe these killings as legal or to disguise the fact that they were being carried out with the active backing of the security apparatus.[8] Soeharto went as far as to claim personal credit for the campaign of 'shock therapy' in his autobiography. 'This was done', he wrote, 'so

---

8   On the killings and their political context see Bourchier 1990. Burns (1984: 7) suggested that there was a precedent for the killings in the 'misplaced sympathy of Dutch adat scholars for extra-legal sanctions'.

that the general public would understand that there was still someone capable of taking action to tackle the problem of criminality' (Soeharto, 1988: 364).

In terms of the conceptual framework discussed in this chapter, Soeharto combined the positivist and romantic traditions in a way that was useful to him and destructive of both. He exploited the absolutist potential of positivism, effectively crippling all constitutional curbs on his power. And from the romantic tradition he assumed all the prerogatives of a traditional leader minus the accountability that he would have had to exercise if he had not been so insulated from the population by the armour of the state.

Soeharto's rule has left deep scars on the body politic. His institutionalisation of an absolutist presidency made it impossible for regulatory authorities and institutions such as the courts to function in any way other than as tools of power. Open and constructive debate was quashed on the grounds that Indonesian culture did not recognise the concept of opposition. Those who spoke about the separation of powers or tensions between workers, and employers, civilians and the military, state and society were liable to be condemned as un-Indonesian. Such dichotomies, it was said, belonged to liberal, individualistic cultures. In Indonesia, there was 'unity and oneness between the state and the people' (Darji, 1995: 35).

This kind of language was not always easy for critics to respond to, because in some respects they shared with government officials assumptions about the nature of Indonesian culture and the need for law to reflect society's ideals. Student leader Heri Akhmadi (1981: 23), for instance, at his trial for insulting the head of state, accused the judges and the public prosecutor of 'embracing legal positivism' and ignoring 'the spirit of the 1945 Constitution, *Pancasila* and ... our spirit of freedom as a nation'.

It is not difficult to sympathise with Heri Akhmadi. On balance, however, it is governments, not the ordinary people, that stand to gain more from such 'romantic' appeals. Considering the history of legal romanticism in Indonesia and elsewhere, reformers in post-Soeharto Indonesia would be well served by resisting the allure of romanticism and insisting on clear rules that apply to all.

References

Alisjahbana, S Takdir, 1975, *Indonesia: Social and Cultural Revolution*, Oxford University Press, Kuala Lumpur (first published 1961; translated from Indonesian by Benedict Anderson).

Attamimi, A. Hamid S, 1990, *Peranan Keputusan Presiden Republik Indonesia dalam Penyelenggaraan Pemerintahan Negara*, dissertation for the degree of Doctor of Laws, Postgraduate Faculty, University of Indonesia, Jakarta.

Bergh, GCJJ van den, 1986, 'The Concept of Folk Law in Historical Context: a Brief Outline' in Benda-Beckman, K von and Strijbosch, F (eds), *Anthropology of Law in the Netherlands; Essays on Legal Pluralism*, Verhandelingen van het Koninlijk Instituut voor Taal-, Land- en Volkenkunde No 116, Foris Publications, Dortrecht-Holland/ Cinnaminson-USA.

Bourchier, David, 1990, 'Law, Crime and State Authority in Indonesia' in Budiman, Arief (ed), *State and Civil Society in Indonesia*, Centre of Southeast Asian Studies, Monash University, Melbourne.

Bourchier, David, 1996, *Lineages of Organicist Political Thought in Indonesia*, unpublished PhD Dissertation, Politics Department, Monash University, Clayton, Melbourne.

Burns, Peter, 1984, 'Crime Wave in Indonesia: Negara Hukum Tidak Jadi', paper presented at the 5th Asian Studies Association of Australia Conference, Adelaide, 1984.

Burns, Peter, 1989, 'The Myth of Adat', *Journal of Legal Pluralism and Unofficial Law*, No 28: 1.

Darji Darmodihardjo, 1995, 'Proses Penuangan Pandangan Integralistik Indonesia dalam Undang-undang Dasar 1945', *Mimbar*, 71/XII 1994/95.

Djokosutono, 1982, *Kuliah Hukum Tata Negara*, Ghalia Indonesia, Jakarta (compiled by Harun Al Rasid in 1959).

Eikema Hommes, Hendrik Jan van, 1979, *Major Trends in the History of Legal Philosophy*, North-Holland Pub Co, New York, Amsterdam, Oxford.

Feith, Herbert and Castles, Lance (eds), 1970, *Indonesian Political Thinking 1945-1965*, Cornell University Press, Ithaca.

Gale, Susan Gaylord, 1982, 'A very German legal science: Savigny and the Historical School', *Stanford Journal of International Law*, vol 18, No 1, Spring.

Heri Akhmadi, 1981, *Breaking the Chains of the Oppression of the Indonesian People: Defence Statement at His Trial on Charges of Insulting the Head of State*, Translation Series (Publication No 9), Cornell Modern Indonesia Project, Cornell University, Ithaca.

Holleman, JF (ed), 1981, *Van Vollenhoven on Indonesian Adat Law*, M Nijhoff, The Hague.

Ketetapan-Ketetapan MPRS; Hasil-hasil Sidang Umum ke-IV Tahun 1966, Hasil-hasil Sidang Istimewa Tahun 1967 dengan Undang-undang Dasar 1945 (c 1967), CV Pantjuran Tudjuh, Jakarta.

Lev, Daniel, 1973, 'Judicial Unification in Post Colonial Indonesia', *Indonesia*, No 16, October.

Lev, Daniel, 1985, 'Colonial Law and the Genesis of the Indonesian State', *Indonesia*, No 40.

Moertopo, Ali, 1975, 'Pembinaan Hukum dalam Masa Pembangunan', *Seminar Pendidikan Hukum: Reorientasi Pendidikan Hukum Pada Fak. Hukum Universitas Gadjah Mada Dalam Akselerasi Pembangunan Negara Republik Indonesia*, Fakultas Hukum Universitas Gadjah Mada, Yogyakarta.

Nasroen, Mohamad, 1957, *Asal-Mula Negara*, Beringin, Jakarta.

Oppenheim, Jacques, 1983, *De Theorie van den Organischen Staat en hare waarde voor onzen tijd*, JB Wolters, Groningen.

Sjahrir, Sutan, 1968, *Our Struggle*, Modern Indonesia Project, Cornell University, Ithaca, New York (translated from Dutch by Benedict Anderson).

Soeharto, 1988, *Soeharto: Pikiran, Ucapan dan Tindakan Saya* (Otobiografi seperti dipaparkan kepada G Dwipayana and Ramandan KH), PT Citra Lantoro Gung Persada, Jakarta.

Subardjo Djoyoadisuryo, Ahmad, 1978, *Kesadaran Nasional*, Gunung Agung, Jakarta.

Soepomo, 1970, *Hubungan Individu dan Masjarakat dalam Hukum Adat*, Pradnya Paramita, Jakarta (first published 1941).

Turner, Bryan, 1993, 'Outline of a Theory of Human Rights', *Sociology*, vol 27 No 2, May.

Van Vollenhoven, Cornelis, 1918, 1931, 1933, *Het Adatrecht van Nederlandsch-Indië*, EJ Brill, Leiden.

Whitman, James Q, 1990, *The Legacy of Roman Law in the German Romantic Era; Historical Vision and Legal Change*, Princeton University Press, Princeton, New Jersey.

Yamin, Mohammad, 1959, *Naskah Persiapan Undang-undang Dasar 1945*, vol 1, Jajasan Prapantja, Jakarta.

Yoga Soegomo, 1986, *Perbandingan antara Demokrasi Eropa dan Demokrasi Pancasila di Indonesia sebagai Subyek Penelitian Demokrasi*, Pustaka Kartini/ PT Sarana Bakti Semesta, Jakarta.

13. Not your Local Member

Sugeng Permana[1]

Teacher: Children, children. Get out your notebooks. Carefully take down what I have to say. Today is 1 October, the Day of the Supernatural Power of *Pancasila*. The Chief Justice of the *Mahkamah Agung* is installing the members of the People's Consultative Assembly (MPR)[2] as well as the new Parliament (DPR)[3] of our Republic of Indonesia. The MPR will meet in March for its once-in-five-years gathering.

Our country is not a kingdom, a military junta or a communist state, whose sovereignty lies in the hands of a king or a leader from the military or the working class ruling arbitrarily. No, Art 1(2) of the 1945 Constitution states that 'sovereignty is in the hands of the people, and is fully enacted by the MPR'.

The MPR consists of members of the DPR, along with delegates from the provinces and from functional groups. The Constitution stipulates that the MPR chooses the President and regulates the direction of the state. The President then makes laws together with the DPR.

In our beloved Indonesia today the DPR has 500 members, and the MPR 1000. It is constituted like this: each member of the DPR represents 400,000 people and each member of the MPR represents 200,000 of our people. Are there any questions?

Student: Yes, sir. In the newspapers and on television they say there are elected and appointed representatives. Can you explain how that is the case, sir?

Teacher: In the last election the representatives that were elected to the DPR were only those members belonging to the parliamentary factions of GOLKAR,[4] the United Development Party (PPP)[5] and the Indonesian Democratic Party (PDI).[6] There are 325 from GOLKAR, 89 from the PPP and 11 from the PDI. On the other hand, 75 members were appointed as the ABRI[7] faction. As a result, out of 500 DPR representatives, 425 were elected and 75 were appointed by the President.

Student: Excuse me, sir. I have a question. Each member of the DPR is supposed to represent 400,000 people, aren't they, sir?

---

1 Translation by David Williams.
2 *Majelis Permusyawaratan Rakyat.*
3 *Dewan Perwakilan Rakyat*, People's Representative Assembly.
4 *Golongan Karya.*
5 *Partai Persatuan Pembangunan.*
6 *Partai Demokrasi Indonesia.*
7 Armed Forces of the Republic of Indonesia, *Angkatan Bersenjata Republik Indonesia.*

Teacher: Yes. Work it out yourself. 200 million Indonesians divided by 500 means each member of the DPR represents 400,000 people, correct?

Student: In that case, the 75 ABRI members times 400,000 makes 30 million people. Is that right, sir? In that case our country must have the largest military force in the world.

Teacher: No, our country's armed forces don't even reach a million. But ABRI membership in the MPR/DPR is a special right not possessed by the other civil political parties. Furthermore, that privilege is needed for these changing times in order to protect *Pancasila* and the 1945 Constitution. You children have to understand this well. For the moment we will not consider it to be in conflict with Art 27 of the Constitution about the equality of all citizens. Try and read thoroughly about this topic by yourselves.

Student: But tell us how the ABRI representatives get chosen, sir. Are they chosen by the ABRI leadership, or by the President, or like our election of student representatives, by a meeting of ABRI members conducting an open election?

Teacher: Enough, enough! Don't ask about such matters. Later on you will understand when you are at university. Then you will study about democracy in theory and practice. For the present, just accept the fact that Indonesia is a *Pancasila* Democracy.

Now I will explain about the membership of the MPR. The 500 DPR members automatically become members of the MPR. The other 500 members are appointed by the President. It works like this. Each provincial parliament selects its provincial delegates. They can be military area commanders, governors, chairmen of the provincial parliament, or just anybody considered to have enough authority to represent a region. So in practice the President just has to appoint the delegates suggested from below, a total of 149 people.

Then there are the functional group delegates consisting of 100 people. They are appointed by the President. The process of candidature and election is never clear. Nor are the groups which get represented ever announced. Amongst the 100 are people like Mr Yogi Memet (Interior Minister) and Mrs Hartini Hartarto (wife of another cabinet minister).

Student: Sir, does Mr Yogi represent the functional group of Ministers of State, while Mrs Hartini Hartarto represents the functional group of Wives of Ministers?

Teacher: Now, I don't know how it works. In the school text book it is not at all clear what the functional groups are and how their delegates are chosen.

Aside from that, the President also appoints members to the MPR from the three political parties, depending on the balance of power in the DPR. Thus, GOLKAR gets another 163, the PPP 45, the PDI 5 and ABRI gets 38 more.

Student: During the general election one campaigner said that all members of the MPR ought to be directly elected. How many are elected that way right now, sir?

Teacher: Those elected directly are only the 325 from GOLKAR, the 89 from PPP and the 11 from PDI, 425 in total. So out of 1000 people in the MPR, only 42.5% were elected and 57.5% were appointed.

Student: Sir, if 57.5% of the MPR was appointed by President Soeharto and later the MPR chooses Mr Soeharto as President again, won't fractious foreign journalists make the headline: 'The Soeharto People's Assembly elects Soeharto as President'?

Teacher: That's enough, try not to think about whatever outsiders might feel like writing. What is clear is that the composition of the MPR and the DPR is the best that we have for the present. What is the evidence? No one dares to oppose the system, and that includes the intellectuals and the respected religious leaders. The only ones who do not like it are small groups who have been shoved aside or are on state pensions, or students and young people who are always demanding that the laws on politics be rescinded. But they only ever indulge in empty chatter. They have no idea how to rescind the laws or what to replace them with. That is enough of this lesson for today.

Student: Excuse me please, sir. One final question. According to Art 2(1) of the Constitution there should only be delegations of regional and functional groups in the MPR. But we have also put them in the DPR. What do you think, sir? I also once read in the newspaper that GOLKAR is actually not a political party. But then what are they doing occupying the DPR? Surely it is enough for them to just be in the MPR. What do you think?

Teacher: That is enough, my boy. Don't go trying to count the number of clauses in the Constitution you consider to have been broken. They have not been broken, it is just that they have yet to be fulfilled exactly as originally intended. It takes time. Maybe in the future when *Pancasila* has become more truly supernaturally powerful. Possibly at that time the Constitution will be enacted consistently and as purely as the driven snow. That is all for now. See you tomorrow. Good afternoon.

14. Regional Government and Central Authority in Indonesia

Peter Holland

Introduction

Since independence Indonesia has sought to strike an appropriate balance between central government and the regions. Complete decentralisation has been regarded as a threat to national unity and the country's historical ideals. However, Indonesia has a plurality of cultures, regional divisions and ethnic groupings. It consists of over 13,000 islands stretching 5119 kilometres from east to west and 1880 kilometres from north to south. There are over 300 ethnic groups each with its own traditions and culture such as the Javanese, the Minangkabau, the Batak and the Balinese. This diversity militates against a complete centralisation of power.

There have been two trends in the evolution of the relationship between the central government and the provincial authorities in the five decades since the declaration of independence in 1945. One is the process of nation building – the establishment of the authority of the central government throughout the country. The second is the delegation of authority from the centre to the provinces to satisfy regional aspirations and to implement development programs.

Indonesia today is still in a state of transition with a tension between central authority and regional autonomy. The Law on Regional Government of 1974, which establishes the basic framework of regional and local government, reflects this tension. Kahin (1994: 204) has said that 'neither under the Dutch nor in the subsequent nearly half century of independence has anything more than lip service been paid to ... a government structure allowing for considerable devolution of power from the centre'. Recently, however, there have been significant developments in the powers and authority of regional governments, including a pilot program of regional autonomy in 1995 and a new system of local taxation beginning in 1998. The resignation of President Soeharto in May 1998 has released further pressures for decentralisation. A study of regional government can therefore provide an insight into the functioning of the Soeharto regime and some of the issues confronting his successors.

Local Government and the Constitution

Indonesia has operated under three Constitutions. In 1945 the Republic of Indonesia was established as a unitary state. Then followed a period of conflict against the Dutch who attempted to reimpose colonial rule. In 1949 Indonesia acquired a new but short-lived Constitution as the Netherlands formally transferred sovereignty to the Republic of the United States of Indonesia in which the Republic of Indonesia would be one of the member states. However, the federal states established by the Dutch had no legitimacy and the federal structure collapsed. A new Constitution in 1950 therefore provided for a unitary state. On one view this history has meant significant local autonomy is perceived as an unacceptable remnant of the Dutch-imposed federal idea of the 1949 Constitution. Maryanov (1958), however, has argued that in incorporating the federal states into the new unitary state in 1950 the Republic promised to implement considerable decentralisation.

The 1945 Constitution was reintroduced by Presidential Decree in 1959. The 1945 Constitution provides for a system of local government within a unitary state. Article 18 says:

> The division of the area of Indonesia into large and small regional territories together with the structures of their administration, shall be prescribed by statute, with regard for, and in observance of the principles of deliberation in the governmental system of the state, and the traditional rights in the regional territories which have a special character.

The Elucidation of the Constitution provides that because Indonesia is a unitary state, it 'will not have within its jurisdiction areas which have the character of "states"'.

The local government system established pursuant to Art 18 of the Constitution is a pyramid with the Ministry of Home Affairs at the apex. Regional government is divided into four main levels. The first tier is the province (*propinsi*) headed by a governor appointed by the central government. The second tier of government is the regency (*kabupaten*) headed by a regent (*bupati*) or the municipality (*kotamadya*) headed by a mayor.[1] The 27 provinces in Indonesia are subdivided into 241 regencies and 56 municipalities. The third tier is the subdistrict under the leadership of a subdistrict head (*camat*) and the fourth is the village (*desa*).

The fundamental issue in the history of local government in Indonesia has been the degree of control to be retained by the central government and how it is to be exercised. Specific questions include the process of appointment of regional heads and representative bodies; methods of supervision; powers; the role of the civil service and political parties; and financial relations between the centre and the regions.

Regional Government: The 1948 System

The Republic of Indonesia inherited from the Dutch a state based on strong centralised administration with a shell of largely powerless regional representative bodies. Thus Indonesia did not take over a functioning decentralised system of

---

1   The province is formally known as *Daerah Tingkat* I (Level 1 Region) and the *kabupaten* as *Daerah Tingkat* II (Level II Region).

government. The Dutch had begun experimenting with a system of administrative and political decentralisation from 1903. Some key features of the system in Java, which gradually developed after reforms in 1922, continue today. In particular the governor or regent was an appointed official and the local bodies had a double function – execution of central government policies as well as decision-making in their own area of responsibility.

In 1948 the Republic of Indonesia enacted a law on the regions which in theory involved significant decentralisation of power. Law No 22 of 1948 provided for a system of regional government in Java, Sumatra and Borneo. Subsequently Law No 44 of 1950 extended this to Eastern Indonesia consisting of the areas of Sulawesi, Maluku and Nusa Tengara. The 1948 Law provided that the autonomous regions

> must, as an absolute condition, have a democratic organisation in which power must be in the hands of the people of the region … The highest instruments of authority must be held by a Regional Representative Council the organisation of which must be determined by election.

Power was divided into two types. Article 24 provided for 'co-operating administration' which involved regions participating in the administration of central government in tasks delegated to them. Further Art 23 provided that regions were to exercise autonomous powers in their household affairs (*rumah tangga*). Subsequent legislation provided for 15 such powers including irrigation, maintenance of roads and public buildings, agricultural programs, fisheries, health services, veterinary services, social welfare and supervision of marketing and distribution.

The Law provided for a system of government at the provincial, district and village levels. There were to be representative institutions at each level. Each region was to have an elected Regional Representative Council (DPRD, *Dewan Perwalikan Rakyat Daerah*) which was a legislative body.[2] Each region was also to have a Regional Executive Council (DPD, *Dewan Pemerintah Daerah*) elected by the members of the DPRD.[3]

The key position was the head of the region (*kepala daerah*) – the governor of the province or the regent (*bupati*) heading the regency. The primary responsibility of the *kepala daerah* could be seen either as representing the people of the region or as implementing the policies of the central government. The Law provided for the appointment of the *kepala daerah* by the central government from a list of candidates submitted by the representative council. Article 18(1) provided that 'the Regional Head of a province is appointed by the President from at least two, and at the most four, candidates nominated by the provincial Representative Council'.[4]

The Law also enabled the central government to supervise local government. These provisions included veto powers of the *kepala daerah* over decisions taken by bodies lower in the hierarchy,[5] controls over financial matters[6] and the right of central government to direct the local government to act in a certain manner.[7] For example, Art 36(1) provided that:

---

2 Article 3(4).

3 Article 13(1).

4 The President appointed heads of provinces, the Minister for Home Affairs appointed heads of *kabupaten* and the head of the province appointed village heads.

5 Articles 36 and 42.

6 Articles 33 (loans) and 36 (annual budget).

7 Article 25.

The Regional Head supervises the work of the Regional Representative Council and the Regional Executive Council and has the right to delay the operation of decisions of the Regional Representative Council and the Regional Executive Council when, in his opinion, such decisions conflict with the general interest or with laws or Government Regulations or regulations of higher regional governments, when those decisions are taken by a Regional Representative Council below the province.

In practice there was a significant difference between the reality and the theoretical position under the 1948 Law (Legge, 1961). There was no attempt to implement the Law at the lowest level. Villages therefore continued to operate on customary lines with elected heads and significant autonomy. Instead of elected bodies, provisional regional councils were appointed by the central government. The central government appointed regional heads, ignoring the names proposed by the regional representative bodies, and thus stripped these bodies of some of their most significant powers. The central government appointed members of its own administrative service, the *pamong praja*,[8] thus reverting to the colonial practice of appointing an official to head local government. The 1948 legislation therefore failed to establish an effective, decentralised local government system.

Regional Rebellions in the 1950s

The position of regional government today is significantly shaped by the historical legacy of the regional rebellions of the 1950s. These included a pro-federalist revolt in the South Moluccas until 1950; the *Darul Islam* insurgency in West Java from 1948; a revolt in Aceh from 1953; a revolt in South Sulawesi from 1951; and the PRRI-Permesta rebellions of 1957-58.[9]

There were a variety of factors which influenced these challenges to central authority. In the 1950s there was a fundamental conflict of economic interest between the export producing Outer Islands and Java, a net importer (Feith, 1962: 26-7). When the national elections in 1955 resulted in three of the four main parties being Java-dominated,[10] this conflict escalated into rebellion in exporting regions such as Sumatra and Sulawesi. There was also a religious factor in the regional challenges, beginning with the *Darul Islam* movement in West Java and later in other areas where Islam had a strong hold such as Aceh and South Sulawesi. A third factor behind the regional rebellions in the 1950s was the pattern of civilian-military relations. The factionalism in the army and the army's disdain for civilian politicians had continued for years after an unsuccessful attempt by the army central leadership on 17 October 1952 to force President Soekarno to dissolve Parliament. This

---

8   In the New Order referred to as *pegawai negeri*.

9   *Pemerintah Revolusioner Republik Indonesia* – Revolutionary Government of the Republic of Indonesia (PRRI). In 1960 this developed into the RPI which was formed from the 'Islamic States' of Aceh and South Sulawesi and the 'States' of Tapanuli, East Sumatra, West Sumatra, Riau, Jambi, South Sumatra, North Sulawesi, Moluccas and South Moluccas. See Ichlasul Amal (1992).

10   The three Java based parties were PNI, *Partai Nasional Indonesia* or Indonesian Nationalist Party (22.3% votes, 57 seats), NU, *Nahdlatul Ulama*, the traditionalist Muslim party (18.4% votes, 45 seats) and PKI, *Partai Komunis Indonesia*, the Indonesian Community Party (16.4% votes, 39 seats). *Masyumi*, another Muslim party, was strong in the Outer Islands with 20.9% of the votes and 57 seats (Feith, 1962: 434).

factionalism culminated in local army commanders and their forces joining regional rebellions.

A further factor behind the regional challenge to central authority in the 1950s was the geo-political position of Indonesia. In the 1950s the Americans grew afraid that Indonesia could be 'lost' to communism as had China. American policy was therefore to prevent a unified Indonesia falling to the communists by supporting the regional dissident movements (Kahin, 1994; Kahin & Kahin, 1995). Ethnic rivalry was a fifth factor in the rebellions of the 1950s. Some groups such as the Minangkabau and South Sulawesians perceived the assertion of central authority as Javanese colonialism. They frequently called for the appointment of *anak daerah* (native sons) to regional positions of authority. For example, the appointment of Ruslan Muljoharjo, a Javanese, as Governor of Central Sumatra led to the proclamation of the PRRI rebellion in 1958.

The final factor behind the regional rebellions in the 1950s was the failure of post-independence governments to establish a decentralised local government system and grant significant regional autonomy. For example, the 1957 Permesta rebellion in South Sulawesi demanded that the central government increase regional autonomy, pay more attention to the economic development of the region and allocate 70% of the seats in the proposed *Dewan Nasional* (National Council) to provincial level representatives, with a view to that body ultimately attaining the status of a Senate (Feith, 1962: 545).

Thus, despite the rejection of the concept of a federal system in 1950, after independence there was a feeling that the diversity of Indonesia justified significant autonomy for the regions. The government responded to the regional challenges, which by 1957 had culminated in full-scale rebellions, in two ways. One way was to provide for a new system which promised to allay regional concerns with significantly increased regional autonomy. It seemed therefore that the pressure from the regions for significant autonomy was successful. Indonesia began an experiment with a strongly decentralised system of local government under Law No 1 of 1957. The experiment however was short lived. The second response to the regional rebellions in 1957 was to view the problem as a military one. In March 1957 President Soekarno proclaimed the 'State of War and Siege'. The imposition of martial law lasted until 1963 and effectively transferred authority from the provincial civilian leaders to the army. The 1957 Law was therefore not only short-lived, it was also never properly implemented.

Law No 1 of 1957 – The Decentralised System

The 1957 Law set out general principles but required further legislation and ministerial regulations to actually establish the system of government for which it provided. Some aspects of the 1957 system continued and built upon the 1948 system. There was a hierarchy of local administration. At each level there was also to be a Regional Representative Council (DPRD).[11] The DRPD was to be chaired by the regional head[12] and had the power to make regulations.[13] There was also to be a Regional Executive Council chosen from the DPRD with responsibility for

---

11   *Dewan Pemakilan Rakyat Daerah*: Article 7.
12   Article 6.
13   Article 36.

executing the decisions of the DPRD and the day-to day running of the regional government.[14] However, there were important differences between the 1957 law and its predecessors, particularly regarding the powers of local government; the role of the regional assemblies; the role of the regional heads; and the method of central government supervision.

The 1957 Law envisaged the election of regional heads at the provincial and district levels rather than their appointment by the central government. Article 23 provided for future legislation establishing direct popular elections. In the interim, Art 24(1) provided that 'until the legislation referred to in 23(1) is passed, the Regional Head for the time being is to be chosen by the Regional Representative Council, having regard to the qualities of knowledge and ability necessary for the office'.

Consequentially the responsibility and the powers of the *kepala daerah* to supervise regional assemblies were reduced since he or she was no longer a central government functionary. In particular the ability to veto regulations was removed. Instead Arts 64 and 65 provided a veto power for the Minister for Home Affairs. As Legge (1961) has explained, the central government's supervisory powers were thus dramatically weakened as the Minister, unlike the governor or regent under the 1948 system, did not sit in the regional representative bodies. The Minister was thus not able to dominate the assemblies through informal and traditional powers. The removal of the appointed official at the head of local government meant that the DPRD was to be the basic instrument of the local government system.[15] The Law, for the first time, thus gave power to the regions to control their own local government activities.

A feature of the 1957 Law was that considerable powers were delegated to regional government. A major change from previous laws was the method of division of powers between the central government and the provinces. Article 31 gave the DPRD authority over all local matters which were not legislated for at the central government level such as foreign affairs, defence and currency. In contrast, the earlier laws had enumerated the powers of the provinces leaving all residual power to the centre. Genuine autonomy requires an independent financial base and Law No 32 of 1956 therefore provided that regional governments were to receive eight specific state taxes;[16] a proportion of other taxes;[17] and direct financial assistance for poorer regions.

The 1957 Law reflected the temporary political weakness of the central government in the face of the regional revolts. The Law was thus short-lived because when the rebellions were defeated the powerful forces of Guided Democracy, the President and the army, had a common interest in strong central power. Furthermore genuine decentralisation would have caused major problems as the regions lacked the competent staff and financial ability to fulfil their expanded role. The central government was able to ignore the provisions of the 1957 Law when it deemed it advisable. For example, in Sulawesi the central government acted to secure the

---

14   Article 19, Art 44.

15   Article 7. So, for example, first level regions should have one representative for every 200,000 inhabitants, with a minimum of 30 representatives and a maximum of 75.

16   Urban land tax, household tax, motor vehicle tax, road tax, poll tax, a slaughter tax, copra tax and a restaurant tax.

17   Income tax, wages tax, stamp duties, property tax, company tax, and the proceeds from extra duties levied on products produced within their boundaries.

support of traditional rulers and to diffuse the rebellion by appointing noble *anak daerah* (locals) to important posts such as the regencies of Luwu and Bone without election by regional councils. The 1957 Law was moreover never fully operative since in March 1957 a state of emergency was declared which meant that the military commander in each region was more powerful than the regional head. The experiment with significant devolution of power to the regions came to a formal end in 1959.

Presidential Decree No 6 of 1959

By 1959 there had been a change in the constellation of Indonesian politics. The claims of regional leaders to political autonomy had been lost through military defeat. Also parties and parliament had lost their legitimacy with the President and the army emerging as the two dominant forces.[18] At the national level the 1950 liberal Constitution was replaced by the presidential Constitution of 1945 by Presidential Decree. President Soekarno's concept of Guided Democracy was adopted to replace the system of Western liberal democracy. In accordance with this political philosophy the regional autonomy and democratisation which had been promised in the 1957 Law was withdrawn.

In 1959 central control over regional government was formally re-instituted. Important aspects of Law No 1 of 1957 were suspended by Presidential Decree No 6 of 1959.[19] The fundamental structure of central control in the 1959 system was similar to that under the 1948 system. The central government appointed governors and regents following nomination of a list of candidates by the regional representative councils 'having regard to conditions of education, ability, and governmental experience which will be determined in a Presidential Regulation'.[20] The position of the regional head as both chief executive of the region and representative of the centre was restored.[21] In practice the central government ignored local nominations in a number of cases, especially for the position of governor.

The 1959 Presidential Decree withdrew the delegation of powers to the local government.[22] The existing DPRD continued but, stripped of their powers and independence, their role was only a pale shadow of their position under the 1957 system.[23] The Decree restored the supervisory powers of the regional heads as an instrument of central government. Thus a governor had a preventative veto over decisions of the DPRD when in his opinion they conflicted with 'the main lines of state policy, the general interest or legislation of a higher level'.[24] Further each

---

18 Alternatively, the situation could be viewed dominated by as a triangle of forces, the President, the army and the PKI.

19 The constitutional position of this action is controversial. It can be argued that a Presidential Decree without the approval of Parliament cannot suspend an Act of Parliament. On the other hand the government argued that no approval of Parliament was required since the measure was designed to implement the earlier Presidential Decree which had re-instituted the 1945 Constitution.

20 Article 4(4).

21 Article 14.

22 Article 14(2) and (3).

23 Article 18.

24 Article 15.

DPRD was no longer to elect an executive from its own members, to be responsible to it. The Regional Executive Councils were replaced by Daily Government Boards (*Badan Pemerintah Harian*) appointed by the Minister for Home Affairs for provinces and the provincial governor for regencies.[25]

In 1959 therefore the experiment with significant local autonomy initiated by the 1957 Law was ended. The central government machinery in the provinces was strengthened. There were two other developments which restricted regional autonomy. All major decisions were subject to the approval of the army territorial organisation and in the rebellious regions a large number of Javanese officials came in with the invading troops and stayed (Amal, 1992: 95). The 1959 system continued until 1974 when it was radically revised.

The Guided Democracy period (1957-65) saw the emergence of a stronger central government able to impose its control over the regions. The army replaced political parties as the main force behind the government. However, central government control was still uncertain in 1965 due to the weakness of the economy. The inability of the central government adequately to support the regions financially led to illegal revenue raising to support local needs including smuggling and unofficial levies on trade. Regional discontent did not disappear but overt defiance of Jakarta was no longer possible. The economic weakness of the central government under Guided Democracy created a de facto federalism where the central government had to bargain with the regions to have its policies implemented (Mackie, 1980: 674-5).

Regional Government in the New Order

The New Order period has seen dramatic changes in central-provincial government relations. Under the Soeharto government, Laws in 1974 and 1979 established a comprehensive system of regional government. This system remained, however, deeply rooted in Indonesia's historical experience. Vatikiotis (1993: 63) has said that the hallmark of Soeharto's Indonesia was 'the totally successful extension of state power to all corners of society'. The state has controlled political parties, universities, students and intellectuals, unions, the media, trade associations, religion, the judiciary, mass organisations and other groups. Naturally this projection of power has included central government dominance of regional and local government.

There are three reasons why the issue of local government emerged as an important political phenomenon in the New Order period (Magenda, 1987). One was the perceived need for a strong central government to provide stability. The second was the emphasis on economic development implemented at the local level through a well-planned and well-financed process. This saw an expansion of the role of local government into a multiplicity of functions including planning, economic development and social welfare. The third feature was the 'depoliticisation' of Indonesia under the New Order. To achieve its primary objectives of political stability and economic development the New Order government adopted a policy which has consciously and successfully attempted to limit political activity in the villages.

---

25   Article 19.

The establishment of the New Order in 1965 did not immediately change the centralised framework of central-provincial government relations created by the 1959 system. However, by the 1970s the central government had vastly greater financial, administrative and logistical resources than ever before. This included control over the army, the abolition of regional warlords and control over Parliament and the political parties – especially after the first elections in the New Order period in 1971.[26] There were other factors which enabled Indonesia to become much more integrated in the 1970s. These included effective promulgation of a common national language; economic development; and improved transport and communications technology. Reflecting this mix of influences, a new law on regional government was enacted in 1974. The Law in theory required a decentralisation of power but it had the immediate impact of virtually abolishing any real regional autonomy.

The 1974 Law on Regional Government repealed the 1957 Law which had been suspended by the 1959 Presidential Edict. The legislation spelt out in detail the division of power between the central government and the provinces and laid out for the first time a clear conceptual framework for central-provincial relations. The 1974 Law maintained the system of local government with each province being divided into three levels.[27] Three important aspects of this Law are the provisions for village government, the powers vested in the governors and regents, and the division of power between the central and regional governments.

Village Government in the New Order

Article 88 of the 1974 Law provided that legislation on village governance would later be enacted. Under the Old Order Indonesia had been one of the most 'political' nations in the world. It was characterised by a multiplicity of parties, popular mobilisation and political conflict in the villages. The fragmentation of Indonesian society was taken to its extreme in the slaughter following the attempted 'coup' in 1965. An important element of the New Order policy of political stability and economic development was therefore to de-politicise the villages and to implement central bureaucratic controls over them.

Law No 3 of 1975 on Political Organisations introduced the 'floating mass' concept. Party branches below the regency level were to be closed down. Villagers' political preferences were to be expressed only through elections every five years. However, the floating mass concept did not adversely affect the government political organisation, GOLKAR, since the government was able to use the formal channels of the village heads, the bureaucracy and the military to continue to mobilise votes. An example of the power of these forces was raised by a minority party representative concerning the 1992 elections who claimed that a number of government officials had proclaimed their regions to be 'political party free' meaning that every resident was expected to vote for GOLKAR. The officials would declare anyone a 'communist' if they dared to say that they would vote otherwise (Jakarta Post, 1992a).

---

26 An interesting contrast to the period of the 1950s is that GOLKAR, the government political organisation, generally attracts greater support from the outer regions than in Java.

27 Article 3.

Law No 5 of 1979 on Village Government was a key instrument in the extension of central control down to the village level. It established a detailed administrative structure for Indonesia's 63,000 villages. The 1979 Law stood in contrast to a short-lived predecessor from the Old Order period. In Law 19 of 1965 President Soekarno had attempted to establish a 'third level' of regional government below the province and the regency. As a populist president, Soekarno expected the Law to raise mass support for his regime to counter the growing power of the army and Muslim groups. The Law was passed in September 1965 only one month before the attempted coup. It provided for the transfer of significant power to village councils and yet for significant central government control of the villages. However, the 1965 Law was repealed early in 1966. In contrast to the centralisation of the 1965 Law, the 1979 Law was claimed to be a movement towards greater decentralisation and regional autonomy. In reality, however, the 1979 Law has increased central control over local government.

The Elucidation to the 1979 Law states that the then existing situation with each region having its own system of local administration impeded the 'guidance and necessary direction' required for improved living standards and effective government. A feature of the 1979 Law on Village Government is therefore an attempt to model village administration throughout the archipelago on the Javanese village or *desa*. The *desa* is a self-contained unit with a powerful headman, reflecting the high population densities and hierarchically ordered society of Java.[28] However, conditions elsewhere in Indonesia are different. For example, in North Sumatra clans are more influential than village ties. In Aceh, villages are subject to a supra-authority grouping several villages under one local leader.[29] This policy may therefore be counterproductive because village administration may become less able to fulfil central government policies if its formal structure has been divorced from its traditional cultural and popular base.[30]

The 1979 Law incorporated village administration into the central government apparatus. Village heads had previously been elected and had immense traditional power, as was demonstrated in the villagers' voting patterns in the 1955 elections (Feith, 1962: 430-4). Pursuant to the Law, villages were divided into *kelurahan* and *desa*. Villages which were centrally located or administratively strategic were designated *kelurahan*. They had no right to conduct their own affairs.[31] The *lurah* (head of the *kelurahan*) is a civil servant appointed by the governor for an unlimited term with, therefore, responsibility only to the central government hierarchy.[32] *Desa* are the remaining villages which have not been 'upgraded' into *kelurahan*. The *kepala desa* remains an elective office but subject to significant new prerequisites and supervision by the central government hierarchy.[33] All other positions in the *desa* are appointed. The Law also replaced the existing village councils with two bodies; the elected LKMD (Village Public Security Council) and the appointed

---

28   For an analysis of the village system in Java, see Sullivan (1992). Sullivan emphasises the importance of the sub-village units (the *rukun warga* and the *rukun tetangga*); their historical precedents particularly from the period of Japanese occupation during World War Two; and their important role in the New Order political and economic structures.

29   For a study of the implementation of the law in Riau, see Kato (1989).

30   For a case study on Bali, see Warren (1993) and Warren (1990).

31   Article 1.

32   Articles 24 and 31.

33   Articles 4-10.

LMD (Village Consultative Council).[34] Neither body however, in contrast with the earlier village councils, is capable of exercising effective supervision of the *kepala desa* or *lurah*. The result of the 1979 Village Law therefore is the growth in central bureaucratic power at the expense of local political forces which had once dominated village government.

The 1979 Law reveals conflicting attitudes of the central government towards decentralisation and public participation. Although the government has a proclaimed policy of participation and decentralisation, the effect of the Law is to ensure more efficient control of local government by the centre. To the extent that power has been decentralised, this has not focused on a genuine devolution of authority to elected officials and representative bodies at the village level. Instead, as discussed below, power has been devolved to the regencies and *kecamatan* which are within direct central government influence and supervision.

The *Kepala Daerah* and the DPRD

The 1974 Law on Regional Government established a centralised hierarchical system of regional government. Article 13 provides that the district government consists of the regional head (*kepala daerah*) and the regional representative council (DPRD). However, in contrast to the 1957 decentralised system, power is vested in the *kepala daerah* rather than the DPRD. Article 22(1) provides that the *kepala daerah* 'exercises the rights, authority and obligations of the leadership of the district governance'.

The *kepala daerah* is explicitly made a functionary of the central government rather than an independent leader of the district, again in contrast to the 1957 system. Article 22(2) provides that 'in exercising the rights, authority and obligations of governance of the district, the *kepala daerah* is part of the hierarchy answerable to the President through the Minister for Home Affairs'.

The controls over the *kepala daerah* vested in the DPRD are limited. The main formal mechanism is under Art 22(3). It requires that the *kepala daerah* make an account of his or her responsibilities to the DPRD at least once a year or when requested. The governor is given full authority within the province over all other officials for coordinating government offices and keeping law and order. All civil servants within the province report to him or her. In turn the governor, as *kepala daerah* of the province, is responsible to the central government for all activities within his or her area. At the lower levels the regents and *camats* have similar authority within their areas.

Article 38 provides that the *kepala daerah* with the agreement of the DPRD may enact regulations for the district. The Law further provides in Art 39(1) that 'district regulations or decisions of the *kepala daerah* must not conflict with the public interest, statutes or regulations of higher level district authority' and in Art 39(2) that 'district regulations may not control a matter which is already regulated by statute or regulations of a higher level district authority'. Another limit on legislative power to ensure a balance of power in the three levels of local government is Art 39(3) which provides that 'district regulations may not regulate a matter which is vested in the household business of a lower level district authority'.

---

34   *Lembaga Ketahanan Masyarakat Desa* (LKMD) and *Lembaga Musyawarah Desa* (LMD): Art 17.

To administer the province the governor has a secretariat (*Sekretariat Daerah*) consisting of offices such as finance, personnel and audit.[35] The governor is also advised by a range of bodies including the Provincial Development Planning Body (*Bappeda*) which co-ordinates planning, the Bureau of Finance (*Biro Keuangan*) and the Development Bureau (*Biro Pembangunan*) which has responsibility for the implementation of development plans. There are also offices of central government departments (*Kantor Wilayah* or *Kanwil*) in each province with responsibility for centrally administered programs but which also report to the governor. In addition each province and regency has offices (*dinas*) providing services in areas such as public works, agriculture, health and education.

Finally the Law provides the central government with various supervisory powers. An example is Art 35 which states that, if the DPRD cannot perform its functions and duties, such that it may damage the district or the nation, after consulting with the governor, the Minister of Home Affairs may exercise the rights of the DPRD.

The Indonesian system therefore provides for regional parliaments but they possess few powers.[36] The DPRD works with the governor or regent in preparing legislation and the budget but does not have overriding powers, acting mainly as an advisory body.[37] As at the national level the provincial and regency bodies are controlled by the government through a combination of reservation of seats and domination of the elections by the government political organisation, GOLKAR. The future of the DPRD is unclear. On the one hand the Home Affairs Minister in the 1988-93 cabinet, Rudini, made the controversial suggestion that the DPRD be abolished because the supreme rulers were the governors and regents who are answerable to the central government not to the local council members (Jakarta Post, 1994a). On the other hand his successor as Minister of Home Affairs, Yogie S Memet, said that the regional councils have a crucial role as 'mediator and facilitator' between the administration and the people (Jakarta Post, 1995b). The composition and powers of the DPRD are therefore important issues for the post-Soeharto Indonesian government.

The Appointment of Governors and Regents

The most powerful positions in regional government are clearly the *kepala daerah* – the governors or regents, unlike the 1957 system where the focus of power was the elected DPRD. Article 17 provides that the term of office for the *kepala daerah* is five years, which coincides with the central government election and cabinet appointment process.

Article 14 provides conditions and requirements for *kepala daerah*. Some of these are objective such as age, academic qualifications and government experience. Others reflect the nature of the Indonesian state such as belief in god, not being involved in the 1965 coup and faithfulness to the 1945 Constitution and the President. Other requirements such as 'fairness' and 'honesty' may be essential but appear unusual as formal requirements to an outside observer. In 1997 the Director

---

35 Articles 47-48.

36 There is also provision for regional representation in the central parliament, both the DPR and the MPR. However, the system is structured to prevent regional-based parties or blocs.

37 Articles 27-30.

General for Public Administration and Regional Autonomy, Oman Sachroni, claimed that civilians were ineligible to become governors because only people from the civil service or the military had the experience required under Art 14 (Jakarta Post, 1997a).

The Law provides for input by the local community but ultimately, as a representative of the central government, the *kepala daerah* is appointed by the centre. For provincial governorships, for example, Art 15(1) requires the DPRD to elect a short list of as few as two candidates. This is not, however, a completely free choice, for in addition to the requirements of eligibility discussed above, the Article first requires consultations between the governor, the head of the DPRD and the leader of factions in the DPRD. There is thus an opportunity for the central government, through the incumbent governor, GOLKAR fraction leaders in the DPRD or other sources to exert significant influence behind the scenes in the determination of the short list by the DPRD. Ultimately the President, through the Minister for Home Affairs, decides who will be appointed. If he or she is not prepared to make the appointment from the short list he or she will remit the matter to the DPRD for reconsideration.[38]

A key issue in an examination of regional government in Indonesia therefore is who is appointed and how. There are two important groups to examine in the appointments of *kepala daerah*: the armed forces (ABRI) and the local political forces. In recent years there has been a significant move to demilitarise regional government and to give greater weight to the aspirations of local political groups.

In the early years of the New Order it was widely accepted that the military dominated positions in local government. The Indonesian armed forces have both a civilian and military role under the 'dual function' (*dwi fungsi*) doctrine. The territorial role of the armed forces developed early in the life of the republic when it was facing regional insurrections and a communist-led revolt. The army today is represented in every settlement down to the smallest hamlet.[39] This military penetration of the bureaucracy has been formalised through the *Dewan Kekaryaan* which assigns military personnel to civilian tasks.[40] Its central board is responsible for placements as provincial governors. Its provincial boards recommend officers for positions such as regents and its boards at the residency level propose officers for civilian positions at the subdistrict or village level. This system has permitted tight government control over the regions, easier implementation of government policies and domination of positions of power by the military.

In recent years, however, there was some demilitarisation of the Soeharto New Order which has included positions in regional government. This is a reflection of economic development, political stability and tensions between ABRI and President Soeharto. In the late 1970s half the cabinet and over two-thirds of the regional governorships were military officers and at the district level 56% of offices were held by ABRI (Jenkins, 1984: 3). In the late 1980s the period of demilitarisation began. Former Home Affairs Minister General Rudini stated that at the start of his term in 1988 58% of governorships and regencies were in the hands of ABRI officers but by its end in 1993 this had fallen to 40% (Jakarta Post, 1993c).

However, ABRI has recently appeared to be reluctant to relinquish its active role in local government. One prominent commentator, Amir Santoso (1994), has

---

38   There is a similar process for regency appointments.
39   For an analysis of the parallel roles of military and civilian officers, see Jenkins (1984: 46).
40   Functional Service Board.

identified two factors behind this reluctance. The first factor is that ABRI has doubts about the capacity of civilians to run local government bureaucracies. In particular Santoso believes ABRI is still feeling the trauma of the regional rebellions of the 1950s and does not want to take the risk of regional disintegration by giving too much power to civilians. It has been argued that multi-ethnic Indonesia would disintegrate, like Yugoslavia and the Soviet Union, if it adopted fully fledged democracy and devolution of power.[41] The second factor behind ABRI's desire to continue to dominate the top administrative positions of local government relates to the Presidency. The appointment of the President is made by the MPR which includes representatives of the regions. ABRI wants to ensure that the presidency (and vice-presidency) remains in its hands or at least in the hands of a civilian who will co-operate with ABRI. Control of positions of power in the regions may therefore be a significant factor in determining the political development of post-Soeharto Indonesia.

In the appointment of civilian governors and regents, recent years have seen significant conflict between the centre and local political forces, especially following the 1992 parliamentary elections and the re-election of President Soeharto by the MPR in 1993. In a number of cases the wishes of the local GOLKAR faction did not tally with those of the government and GOLKAR's central executive board in Jakarta. The threat to the government was that there might be mass defections to other parties if the central organisation imposed its preferred candidate. This is an interesting echo of the conflict between local interests and central authorities in the 1950s.

The appointment of governor in Central Kalimantan in 1994 is an instructive example of the tension between the centre and the regions. The governorship had been held for more than 10 years by non-locals. The outgoing governor Soeparmanto, a Javanese, and the local GOLKAR chapter promised that GOLKAR would vote in the DPRD for a prominent local leader, Nihin, the regent of North Barito. The executive board of the GOLKAR provincial chapter ordered all 31 councillors of the faction to vote for Nihin in the 45 member local legislative council. However, the central government preferred Karna Suwanda, a Sundanese, who was also a member of GOLKAR. Karna, the central government's choice, won the DPRD election with 24 votes while Nihin came second with 21. Ten GOLKAR DPRD members had disobeyed the provincial authorities and voted for Karna. Protests and demonstrations broke out when Nihin's supporters in the GOLKAR faction charged that the election was rigged. Nihin's GOLKAR supporters threatened to resign and there were allegations that the GOLKAR members who had voted for Karna had accepted bribes from 'outside elements' (Jakarta Post, 1993d). The threat to defect was not withdrawn until the Minister for Home Affairs capitulated and made both candidates withdraw from the contest with another election to be held in six months time to break the impasse.

The government and the central GOLKAR Board have used a variety of methods to assist their favoured candidates in gubernatorial elections. For example, when a new governor was about to be elected in Aceh in May 1993, the GOLKAR board in Jakarta sent a senior official to try to persuade the local DPRD councillors

---

41   For example, State Secretary Moerdiono told the DPR Commission I which oversees Home Affairs that 'openness without a clear conceptual basis such as *glasnost, perestroika* and the democratisation implemented in the Soviet Union ended with the break up of the country. Is that what we want?' (Jakarta Post, 1992b).

to vote for a Jakarta-based candidate, a GOLKAR activist, instead of Dr Syamsuddin Mahmud, the head of the provincial planning board. The Acehenese, however, elected the latter who had been involved in the development programs for a long time. Similarly in 1992 the governor of West Sumatra won re-election against the wishes of the central government.

There were similar disputes in the appointment of regents in Sintang (West Kalimantan), Viqueque (East Timor), Deli Serdang (North Sumatra), East Sumba (East Nusa Tenggara) and Kutai (East Kalimantan). In some cases such as Kutai (East Kalimantan) the Minister of Home Affairs annulled the DPRD elections and ordered new elections to resolve the conflict. In other cases, however, the Minister has forced the governor to appoint the central government's choice as regent. For example, in East Timor in 1994 the Governor, Abilio Jose Osorio Soares, succumbed to pressure to appoint the central government's candidate to head a regency in the province.

In the regency election held in Viqueque in January 1994 a local-born figure Afonso Hendriques da Costa obtained seven votes, the same number as that of Lt Col I Ketut Lunca, with a third candidate obtaining one vote. All three names were sent to the Minister for Home Affairs who appointed Lunca because his opponent had at one time deserted GOLKAR for the PDI (Indonesian Democratic Party).[42] Governor Abilio had opposed Lunca's appointment because the local people insisted that a local person be appointed. The governor at first refused to inaugurate the regent but ultimately said he had no choice because the decision had been made by the Minister. As a representative of the central government the governor was obliged to support whatever decision his superiors made. Many organisations in Dili issued statements of rejection when the decision of the government was made known. For example, the chairman of the East Timor Council, Parada, said: 'I'm ashamed to talk about integration if the aspirations of the East Timorese are neglected' (Jakarta Post, 1994b).

What is the cause of the recent conflicts in appointment of *kepala daerah* and the success of local political forces in this struggle? It is suggested that there are at least three separate sources of this conflict, the struggle between the technocracy and the politicians; the conflict between central and regional politicians; and the central government's need to take local political aspirations into account in order to achieve its policies.

One source of the conflict between the centre and the regions is the hostility of government officials to the political parties. There is a belief that party conflict within the bureaucracy in the Old Order was destructive. Party loyalties were detrimental to the solidarity of the ministry and each change of government in the 1950s meant that dismissals and replacements of officials occurred on a large scale, making impossible the achievement of continuity and efficiency. An important element in the New Order restructuring was therefore to depoliticise the bureaucracy (Ward, 1974: 33). In Government Regulation No 6 of 1970 certain categories of civil servants were forbidden membership of political parties. Subsequently Government Regulation No 20 of 1976 required government employees in key positions to have the permission of their superiors before joining a political organisation while other government employees had to inform their superiors.[43]

---

42 *Partai Demokrasi Indonesia*

43 Article 2. All government employees are required to join the Civil Service Corps (KORPRI) which supports GOLKAR at each election and expects all its members to vote accordingly.

Thus a significant source of the recent conflict between the centre and the regions may be the opposition of local politicians to the continued dominance of power in the regions by the central technocracy.

A second source of empowerment of the regions is the conflict amongst the elite which has many aspects with the key one being the presidential succession. Control over the levers of power at the regional level permits influence in the appointment of the regional representatives for the MPR and also boosts power within GOLKAR for inclusion in the list of candidates for elections. Local political forces had some success in challenging the control of regional appointments by the central technocracy and the government in the period after the 1992 elections and the 1993 MPR. Perhaps this increase in regional power only reflected a conflict within the elite in the relatively open era of *keterbukaan* (openness) beginning in late 1980s. However, the closure of *Tempo* magazine in 1994 and the authoritarian controls over the 1997 general elections showed that *keterbukaan* had ended.

It is suggested, though, that there is a third source underlying the increased local influence in regional appointments which is not as transient as *keterbukaan*. The central government needs to secure the willing participation of the regions to achieve its policies in economic growth and community development. This suggests that the future is unlikely to see a return to the overwhelming central dominance of the past. A 1970s government structure will not be able to cope with the vastly more complex public policy demands of a rapidly industrialising economy in the 21st century. The future therefore is likely to involve a local government system which vests a degree of autonomy in local bodies, particularly as the new government of President Habibie is less secure than that of President Soeharto and will need to broker support from the outer regions. An important step towards this future was made with a 1995 pilot program which conferred significant powers on selected regional governments.

The Powers of Regional Government

The 1974 Law on Regional Government states its objective is 'real and responsible (local) autonomy' (*otonomi yang nyata dan bertanggung jawab*) whose purpose is to secure development. However, the system established under the 1974 Law has involved a massive centralisation of power. There are two concepts of decentralisation: administrative decentralisation and political decentralisation. The former involves delegation of authority for program implementation to lower levels. However, the programs and budgets are determined by the central authorities. Political decentralisation involves delegation to lower levels of decision-making authority and control of revenue sources (Amal, 1994). Until 1995, the system established under the 1974 Law involved decentralisation only in the former sense as the Department of Home Affairs has been able to determine what could be done by the regional governments.

The two major forces of the New Order, the military and the technocrats, have emphasised economic development. However, the development projects have still concentrated power in the centre. There has been little power sharing – either between the central and regional governments or between the bureaucrats and the community. Development planning is controlled by the central government through *Bappenas* (the National Planning Agency). Hill (1991: 5-44) has shown how optimal development would involve strengthening the planning and implementation apparatus at the local level. An example is the statement of the Governor of East Timor, Abilio Soares, that 'it is high time for the central government to give wider autonomy to all provinces to manage their own respective affairs. If it continues its centralist policies, the poverty in the eastern region of Indonesia will never be eliminated' (Jakarta Post, 1993c).

In recent years there have been significant increases in the powers and responsibilities of regional governments to implement central government policies in areas such as economic development and environment protection. For example, in October 1993 the government announced a new package of deregulation under which investment licensing procedures were reduced and restrictions eased. Part of the package was to decentralise some of the investment licensing jurisdiction to the regency level. The then Minister of Industry, Tunky Ariwibowo, said that the complicated licensing process at the provincial level had been among the major hindrances to the establishment of new industrial plants in the country (Jakarta Post, 1993b). Two of the multiple layers of bureaucratic administration of land permits were abolished and there was significant decentralisation and increased autonomy for regency administrations.

The 1995 Autonomy Project

The system established under the 1974 Law has involved a very limited decentralisation of power. This can be seen from the provisions concerning the appointment of the head of government; the budget system; the relationship between the DPRD and the government bureaucracy; and the limits on the DPRD authority in general. However, in April 1995 the government announced a pilot project to devolve greater autonomy on the regions.[44] The project was based on 26 selected regencies located on all the major Indonesian islands.[45] The project was to run for two years and if successful was to be implemented nationwide.

There are clearly a number of forces underlying the pilot program. The movement to greater regional autonomy accords with the trend throughout the world. Decentralisation is seen as a key to stronger economic performance. Countries such as the Philippines, South Korea, Thailand and India have successfully developed more decentralised systems of government. In introducing the program, President Soeharto stated that Indonesia should reassess the respective roles of the central government and the regions. He said that there is no more room for a centralised administration in a world that is rapidly changing and that too great a centralisation could stunt the growth of creativity and initiatives in society (Jakarta Post, 1995a).

---

44   Government Regulation No 8 of 1995.

45   The regencies included Aceh Utara (Aceh), Simalungun (North Sumatra), Tanah Datar (West Sumatra), Kampar (Riau), Batanghari (Jambi), Muara Enim (South Sumatra), Bengkulu Selatan (Bengkulu), Lampung Tengah (Lampung), Bandung (West Java), Banyumas (Central Java), Slemen (Yogyakarta), Sidoarjo (East Java), Badung (Bali), Lombok Tengah (West Nusa Tenggara), Timor Tengah Selatan (East Nusa Tenggara), Kutai (East Kalimantan), Sambas (West Kalimantan), Kotawaringin Timur (Central Kalimantan), Tanah Laut (South Kalimantan), Gowa (South Sulawesi), Minahasa (North Sulawesi), Donggala (Central Sulawesi), Kendari (Southeast Sulawesi), Maluku Tengah (Malaku), Sorong (Irian Jaya), Alleu (East Timor).

The essence of the pilot program was the empowerment of regional administration in its relationship with the central bureaucracy. Under the program each of the 24 agencies representing a government ministry in the regencies was put directly under the command of the regent. The central branch offices would be abolished and most of their tasks transferred to new agencies created by the regencies. The agencies therefore were no longer subject to direct control from the central government.

The areas of responsibility handed over to the regencies included health, fisheries, education and culture, public works, animal husbandry, home industries, public housing, social services, manpower, land transport and tourism. Under the program therefore virtually all affairs were decided and administered at the regency level. The principal exceptions were security, justice, international relations, monetary affairs and some general administration. One limit on regency independence was that the provinces were required to formulate strategic policies to be implemented by the regencies.

The project is the first clear effort to implement the decentralisation aspirations of the 1974 Law. Such a decentralisation has been long delayed by the national trauma caused by the regional revolts of the 1950s. There was thus still significant opposition in 1995 to greater regional autonomy with sections of the central bureaucracy fearing the impact on national unity and development. The ministries of education and culture, information and religious affairs in particular objected to delegating aspects of their authority to the regencies.

As a result of this opposition from central government ministries the pilot program experienced a slow implementation. In April 1996 the director general for regional autonomy, Sumitro Masik, admitted that only six of the 50 steps to full autonomy in the 26 districts had been completed. Nevertheless at the end of the two-year pilot program the government concluded that it had been successful.

In July 1997 President Soeharto said that the program to delegate authority to the regency administrations would continue and dismissed fears of national disintegration. He emphasised that local authorities had to have more say in their development affairs because they deal directly with the people, which would leave the central government to concentrate on strategic affairs (Jakarta Post, 1997b). A few days later State Secretary Moediono explained that the move towards regional autonomy was necessary because authoritarian regimes are doomed to fail. He said that their excessive controls create passive, uncreative people and that authoritarian regimes become inefficient over time because they have to carry too many responsibilities (Jakarta Post, 1997c).

Some serious issues remain to be addressed in the assessment of the pilot program and its application throughout Indonesia. A major concern is that the regional head is still a functionary of the central government. The regional head is not subject to significant responsibility towards the regional legislative council. A more significant political reform may therefore be to strengthen the position and authority of the legislative councils. Another concern is the problem of differing levels of income or economic development between regions. The pilot program was based on more affluent regencies. Even if it has been successful, what implications does it have for less advanced regencies? A third concern with the pilot project is that officials in Jakarta may still perceive autonomy only as a process of the central government turning over limited affairs and resources to local authorities. In particular there has been a reluctance to provide local administrations with sufficient financial powers, quality personnel and adequate infrastructure. However, in July

1997 a new system of local taxation was enacted which appears to provide a sound financial base for significant regional autonomy.

Reform of Local Taxation

The 1974 Law makes provision for the financial affairs of local government.[46] The governor has power to levy taxes, set up local enterprises and, with the approval from the Department of Home Affairs, to borrow money.[47] However, in reality the regions have in the past been held in financial thrall by the central government. Central government grants became a significant source of provincial revenue, particularly the *Inpres* program. Local governments received about 80% of their revenue from the central government. Local governments therefore had little fiscal autonomy and central priorities largely determined expenditures. In the mid 1980s, however, the decrease in oil revenues began to force attention on raising local revenues, improving the tax base and considering the economic impact of local taxation (Hill, 1991: 47-8; Ranis & Stewart, 1994; Booth, 1986; Booth, 1995: 68-73).

The most significant development to implement the proclaimed decentralisation policy of the central government was the reform of local taxes and fees which came into effect on 1 January 1998. The pressures on local administrations to raise revenue had led to a proliferation of local taxes and levies. Many were uneconomic to collect, were used to extort bribes or were clearly detrimental to business. In July 1997 a new reform package slashed the number of local taxes from 42 to 9 and local fees and levies from 192 to 30. Provincial administrations are permitted to collect only three taxes, on motor vehicles, on motor vehicle transfers of ownership and on petrol. Regency administrations are permitted only six taxes, on hotels and restaurants, entertainment services, advertisements, street lighting, quarried minerals and ground water. The central government will set maximum rates for the nine taxes and local authorities have five years to phase out other existing taxes and levies. The revenue from the new taxes will rise as the local economies grow. Therefore, in contrast with the past, the new tax regime provides an incentive for local administrations to take initiatives to boost economic activity. The new tax regime also provides a stronger financial base for decentralised decision-making on economic and social development.

Conclusion

The 1974 Law on Regional Government provided the first comprehensive system of regional government in Indonesia. The Law was built upon an historical heritage including experiments in decentralised government in both the colonial and independence periods. The 1974 Law was designed to give the provinces a reasonable amount of formal decision-making and autonomy while retaining the central government's control. Until recently, however, the dominant feature of the local government system has been the dominance of the centre. Only in recent years

---

46   Article 28.
47   Article 61.

have there been significant moves towards greater regional autonomy. These include increasing the influence of the local constituency in determining regional leaders and the empowerment of regional governments, especially through the 1995 pilot program on regional autonomy and the 1997 reform of local taxation.

Improvements in regional powers and independence have been driven partly by transient factors and partly by deep-rooted factors. The latter include the need to secure regional involvement to achieve the policy objectives of the New Order government, especially for economic and social development. It is possible that the political and historical forces opposed to full regional autonomy will continue to prevail. These include the fear of national disintegration and the strength of economic and political nationalism. The economic situation of 1998 poses perhaps the greatest crisis since 1966 for Indonesia and the future for the nation is unclear, despite the resignation of Soeharto and the installation of his Deputy, Dr BJ Habibie as President.

One reaction to the resignation of President Soeharto has been openly expressed aspirations for Indonesia to become a federation. For a long time this has been a taboo topic in Indonesia. It can at least be predicted that the regional authorities in post-Soeharto Indonesia will continue to carry increased responsibilities. However, it is too early to predict whether this will involve the regions being given independent decision-making authority or only additional responsibilities for the implementation of central government programs. The recent experiments in regional government constitute significant steps in the direction of real regional autonomy. Whether this continues may depend on the make-up and policies of the Habibie government and its successors and the extent to which they are prepared to accept regional demands in order to establish their own legitimacy.

References

Amal, Ichlasul, 1992, *Regional and Central Government in Indonesian Politics: West Sumatra and South Sulawesi 1949-1979,* Gadjah Mada University Press, Yogyakarta.

Amal, Ichasul, 1994, 'The Dilemmas of Decentralisation and Democratisation' in Bourchier, D and Legge, J (eds), *Democracy in Indonesia: 1950s and 1960s*, Centre of Southeast Asian Studies, Clayton, Melbourne.

Booth, A, 1986, 'Efforts to Decentralise Fiscal Policy' in MacAndrews, C (ed), *Central Government and Local Development in Indonesia*, Oxford University Press, Oxford.

Booth, A, 1995, *The Oil Boom and After*, Oxford University Press, Oxford.

Feith, H, 1962, *The Decline of Constitutional Democracy in Indonesia*, Cornell University Press, Ithaca.

Hill, H, 1991, *Unity and Diversity: Regional Economic Development in Indonesia since 1970,* Oxford University Press, Oxford.

Jakarta Post, 1992a, 10 April.

Jakarta Post, 1992b, 13 November.

Jakarta Post, 1993a, 7 September.

Jakarta Post, 1993b, 25 October.

Jakarta Post, 1993c, 22 November.

Jakarta Post, 1993d, 23 December.

Jakarta Post, 1994a, 4 January.

Jakarta Post, 1994b, 24 February.

Jakarta Post, 1995a, 14 July.

Jakarta Post, 1995b, 12 October.

Jakarta Post, 1997a, 9 July.

Jakarta Post, 1997b, 10 July.

Jakarta Post, 1997c, 14 July.

Jenkins, D, 1984, *Soeharto and His Generals,* Cornell Modern Indonesia Project, Ithaca.

Kahin, AR, 1994, 'Regionalism and Decentralisation' in Bourchier, D and Legge, J (eds), *Democracy in Indonesia: 1950s and 1960s,* Centre of Southeast Asian Studies, Clayton, Melbourne.

Kahin, AR and Kahin, G McT, 1995, *Subversion as Foreign Policy: The Secret Eisenhower and Dulles Debacle in Indonesia,* Washington University Press, Seattle.

Kahin, G McT, 1970, *Nationalism and Revolution in Indonesia,* Cornell University Press, Ithaca.

Kato, Tsuyoshi, 1989, 'Different Fields, Similar Locusts: *Adat* communities and the Village Law of 1979 in Indonesia', *Indonesia*, vol 47: 89.

Legge, JD, 1961, *Central Authority and Regional Autonomy in Indonesia: A Study in Local Administration, 1950-1960,* Cornell University Press, Ithaca.

MacAndrews, C, 1986, *Central Government and Local Development in Indonesia,* Oxford University Press, Oxford.

Mackie, JA, 1980, 'Integrating and Centrifugal Forces In Indonesian Politics Since 1945' in Fox, J (ed), *Indonesia: Australian Perspectives*, Research School of Pacific Studies, Australian National University, Canberra.

Magenda, BD, 1987, 'Indonesia' in Ahn, Chung-si (ed), *The Local Political System in Asia: A Comparative Perspective*, Seoul National University Press, Seoul.

Maryanov, 1958, *Decentralisation in Indonesia as a Political Problem,* Cornell Modern Indonesia Project, Ithaca.

Ranis, G and Stewart, F, 1994, 'Decentralisation in Indonesia', *Bulletin of Indonesian Economic Studies*, vol 30, no 3: 41.

Santoso, Amir, 'Local administrations deserve greater autonomy', *Jakarta Post*, 4 January 1994.

Sullivan, J, 1992, *Local Government and Community in Java: An Urban Case Study,* Oxford University Press, Oxford,

Vatikiotis, MR, 1993, *Indonesian Politics Under Soeharto,* Routledge, London.

Ward, K, 1974, *The 1971 Election in Indonesia: An East Java Case Study*, Monash University, Melbourne.

Papers on Southeast Asia no 2, Centre for Southeast Asian Studies,, Melbourne.

Warren, C, 1990, *The Bureaucratisation of Local Government in Indonesia: The Impact of the Village Government Law* Centre of Southeast Asian Studies, Working Paper no 66, Melbourne.

Warren, C, 1993, *Adat and Dinas: Balinese Communities in the Indonesian State,* Oxford University Press, Oxford.

15. Decentralisation Versus Administrative Courts: Which Path Holds Greater Promise?

David Linnan

Which holds greater promise for increasing popular participation in Indonesian government: decentralisation and devolution of authority to the local level or judicial review of high-level executive acts in an administrative court setting? Placing such choices in opposition would seem undesirable but, speaking as of 1995, Indonesian legal scholars and reformers in general eagerly embrace administrative courts, while barely acknowledging administrative devolution or government reform itself as worthy of attention.

The purpose of this chapter is to examine whether this perception is accurate, where it comes from and whether it is a mistake in the longer term. The problem is that, upon close examination from the legal perspective, administrative courts in the *negara hukum* (rule of law) setting may be less effective than devolution in popularising government in a constitutional sense. I take the view that decentralisation is more likely to bear fruit in the near to medium term. Therefore articulating the legal basis and structure of relations within the executive branch deserves closer legal scrutiny as an approach to increasing popular participation in Indonesian government (or, employing Indonesian terminology, within development).

The Dutch Law Legacy within the *Negara Hukum*

To stress devolution over judicial review should not be mistaken as revisiting the discredited argument that 'Western-style' democratic government or laws are somehow inappropriate for Indonesian culture and society, a view expressed in connection with the claimed 1950s failure of parliamentary government and the *Konstituante* (Consitituent Assembly).[1] Similarly, it is not based in the common observation that the Indonesian judicial system suffers from insufficient independence, occasional irregularities and problematic formal issues such as whether the senior levels of the judiciary can instruct judges and revise judgments in the lower courts outside the appeals process. Instead, it is based on a sophisticated appreciation of legal limitations in employing judicial review to harness the executive anywhere. There is both a general problem, which has not gone unnoticed

---

1 The *Konstituante* was established under the 1950 Provisional Constitution to draft a new Constitution. It was dissolved by Soekarno in 1959 before it could reach agreement on a draft. See Nasution (1992: 1-5).

among thoughtful Indonesian legal scholars,[2] and special problems involving Indonesia's Dutch law legacy.

Part of Dutch law's problematic legacy involves seemingly indirect influences on governmental structures in the aftermath of the colonial period (adopting the view that institutional approaches to law and government outlast a sovereign). From a comparativist's standpoint, several historical oddities of Dutch legal development give it a distinct profile comparing Dutch constitutional and administrative law to classic Continental administrative law states such as France and Germany.

One historical oddity is that in the Netherlands a republican form of government preceded the 19th century monarchy, which started as a limited constitutional monarchy, rather than developing into one.[3] During the republican period itself the Netherlands was a confederation of states, with decisive power maintained in the sovereign provinces. The confederation became a unified state, but, as a result of its historical development, was a decentralised state without ever having been a federal one. While eroded over time in connection with central government control of finances, Dutch institutions incorporated a tradition of local and regional government. This included advisory councils alongside corporate authorities with regulatory power over trade, industry and the professions. While no single reason exists, democratic elements in this historical tradition may account for Dutch administrative law's emphasis on procedural due process under legality review more than the abstract civil law doctrine of separation of powers.

Dutch administrative law developed relatively late and in a different historical context to Germany or France where administrative law was articulated in opposition to a powerful central executive in the form of absolutist monarchy in Germany and a powerful centralised revolutionary government in France. This in turn may be the best explanation why it seems traditionally less inclined to restrain untrammelled executive power. Dutch administrative law is a relatively weak, procedurally-oriented corpus compared to classic Continental administrative law systems as they exist in France or Germany, which may account for why some recent Indonesian administrative law scholarship arguing for restraints on executive power seems to borrow more from German than Dutch administrative law concepts.

Traditional Dutch constitutional law only consistently implemented separation of powers in relation to the judiciary. Executive and legislative competencies were mixed. The traditional problematic aspect of this approach was Dutch law's dualism. The monarch appointed the Netherlands government directly (that is, the executive), which was then not formally responsible to the elected legislative branch. In parallel, under traditional Dutch approaches law-making by executive decree may predominate. These constitutional borderlands spill over into administrative law.

Against this background, institutional structures under the 1945 Constitution and the related concept of the *Negara Hukum berdasarkan Pancasila* (rule of law

---

2   See, for example, Lotulung (1993: 121-22). This is separate and apart from traditional civil law interpretations of separation of powers doctrines precluding judicial review of the 'constitutionality' of executive acts in favour of a 'legality' review.

3   The 1579 Union of Utrecht, a treaty of confederation concluded among sovereign provinces, is generally considered the first Dutch constitutional document. The resulting Republic of the United Netherlands lasted until creation of Batavian Republic in 1795 in changes wrought during the Napoleonic Wars. The French-influenced era of revolutionary republics lasted 1795-1814, with the modern Dutch monarchy being introduced under the 1815 Constitution of the Kingdom of the Netherlands.

based on the *Pancasila*) may be nationalistic icons in a political sense but they have some reasonably close legal analogies, if not parallels, to Dutch constitutional and administrative law. Here we recall Indonesian problems in the formal, legal relationship between the President, his Ministers, the *Dewan Perwakilan Rakyat* (DPR or People's Representative Council, Indonesia's legislative body) and the *Majelis Perwakilan Rakyat* (MPR or People's Consultative Assembly, Indonesia's supreme sovereign body). Under the 1945 Constitution in legal theory Ministers are responsible to the President rather than the DPR. The President himself is responsible theoretically only to the MPR. The parallel lies in Dutch law's traditional problem with limited ministerial responsibility (now mitigated through custom) resulting technically from the location of popular sovereignty outside legislative institutions. This is not to argue that the 1945 Constitution was patterned on Dutch law but rather only that its drafters' exposure to the peculiarities of Dutch law and institutions are visible.

Beyond permissible scope of delegation issues, legality review in any administrative law setting will be problematic if the executive controls law-making in detail through general grants of authority under legislation. The dimensions of 'executive law-making' through regulation should resonate with those familiar with Indonesian practice where presidential and ministerial decrees predominate over legislation in most areas. If ministerial policy assumes the character of law through delegated regulation, traditional administrative law constraints separating legality review from policy review vanish. This may be viewed as positive by some but in theory it magnifies separation of powers problems. In practice it risks disappointment given that the judiciary is not realistically in a position to articulate coherent policy under circumstances of rapid, ongoing social change.

The Dutch legacy is more directly present in Indonesian administrative law, both through Indonesian law's incorporation of Dutch law before Independence and because Indonesia's Law on Administrative Justice of 1986 drew heavily on Dutch models.[4] Here I am less concerned with administrative review within the executive in place prior to the Law on Administrative Justice (*administratief beroep*), the *Badan Peradilan Semu* (quasi-judicial body), or specialised review by the *Majelis Pertimbangan Pajak* (Tax Review Council). Instead, I focus on Arts 1365 and 1401 of the Dutch Indies Civil Code. These include general provisions on torts, applicable under Art 2 of the Dutch Law on Judicial Organisation, which gave ordinary courts jurisdiction over suits involving infringement of private rights, irrespective whether the infringement was by a private citizen or the state.

The traditional protection of individual rights through the ordinary courts is itself a Dutch historical development reflecting the idea that, despite French law's influence, the Netherlands itself only developed a separate system of general administrative court review of executive actions following World War II, that is, after Indonesian independence. Following *Hoge Raad* (High Court) jurisprudence, pre-independence judicial review of executive acts was possible in ordinary courts. The older Dutch law originally permitted government liability only on the basis of 'private rights' ideas, following civil law distinctions between public and private law.[5]

---

4   The most 'modern' general administrative law text was co-authored by Dutch and Indonesian scholars under the auspices of the Dutch-Indonesia legal cooperation program which also supported drafting of Indonesia's Law on Administrative Justice of 1986. See Hadjon, ten Berge et al (1993).

5   For a more complete presentation of Dutch Civil Code Art 1401 jurisprudence, see Ybema & Wessel (1978: 442-47).

Beginning in 1919, however, the *Hoge Raad's* substantial expansion of the concept of what constituted 'unlawful' *(onrechtmatig)* acts, coupled with its 1924 abandonment of distinctions between private and public law as a criterion of government liability, enabled substantial 'legality review' in the administrative law sense under the Civil Code. The ebb and flow of subsequent *Hoge Raad* jurisprudence through the 1930s changed and narrowed government liability. Doctrines articulated provided special limitations on the kind of public law norms which would support tort claims and, in parallel to privilege doctrine in conjunction with sovereign immunity ideas in the common law sense, concluded that the executive acting within its discretion would not be liable for damages in tort. To an extent not statutorily defined, the breadth of discretion conceded would be determined by the nature of the administration's task and the circumstances of its execution (conceding broad discretion in areas such as defence, maintenance of public order and foreign affairs). Under Indonesia's 1986 Law on Administrative Justice, many of the same exclusions are achieved in the technical definition of what is an 'administrative act' for review purposes.[6]

Limits on discretionary exercises of power as avoiding liability were articulated by the *Hoge Raad* in 1949 – again, this occurred after Indonesian Independence, with the result these limits were not incorporated formally into Indonesian law as part of the general reception of Dutch law in 1945. Beyond unlawfulness as the traditional test, government liability for acts that might otherwise be deemed discretionary was extended to arbitrary or capricious acts, the test being that the government in weighing the interests at stake could not reasonably have reached its decision at issue, hence no such weighing of interests took place.[7] It also included acts by which the government exercises a power for a purpose other than envisioned by the statute creating the power *(detournement de pouvoir)*.[8]

The final development in connection with limitations on discretion comes through the application of 'general principles of proper administration', failure to adhere to which the *Hoge Raad* indicated in 1963 was not an independent illegality ground but rather only provided inferential evidence of arbitrary or capricious behaviour.[9]

Dutch lawmakers, however, subsequently inserted 'general principles of proper administration' into the Dutch Administrative Justice Code alongside the three other grounds for challenging administrative acts.[10] These served as the model for Art 53(2) of the Indonesian statute which specifies grounds for review of administrative acts. Its function is to substantially widen grounds for review of administrative acts given that 'general principles of proper administration' is now a term of art under Dutch law encompassing both procedural and 'substantive' due process grounds.

The problem under Indonesian circumstances is that the 1986 Law on Administrative Justice omitted 'general principles of proper administration' as a ground for judicial review of administrative acts (limiting permissible grounds to challenge decisions to illegality, *detournement de pouvoir* and arbitrary or

---

6   Thus, importantly for Indonesian purposes, acts of the military are essentially excluded from the definition of reviewable acts.

7   Decision of 25 February 1949, [1949] *Nederlandse Jurisprudentie* 558 (Hoge Raad).

8   Decision of 14 January 1949, [1949] *Nederlandse Jurisprudentie* 557 (Hoge Raad).

9   Decision of 4 January 1963, [1964] *Nederlandse Jurisprudentie* 204 (Hoge Raad).

10   Section 8(1) of the *Wet Administratieve Rechtspraak Overheidsbeslissingen*.

capricious acts). Ever since, Indonesian judges have tried to reinsert 'general principles of proper interpretation' in a broad interpretation of illegality by arguing in effect that the principles are now part of Indonesian legal consciousness (because executive acts will be subject to much narrower review if these broad principles are unavailable).[11]

The problem with such a strategy is that it does not answer the obvious question of what the Indonesian law-makers thought they were doing in omitting the provision the judiciary is now trying to read back into the statute. Beyond the simple legislative history question, however, the Dutch Civil Code doctrinal roots discussed above (shared formally through Independence) point to the underlying problem now buried in the statutory grounds for challenging executive acts in the administrative court setting. The real issue is how much discretion exists in the executive, whether phrased in terms of privilege-type doctrine under tort law or in administrative law. Here we recall the initial institutional legacy of Dutch law. It will be doubly difficult for the judiciary effectively to control an executive in situations where the executive customarily articulates law under extremely broad delegation from the legislature.

Current Decentralisation Initiatives

Initial remarks on decentralisation's cool reception addressed a general lack of interest in Government Regulation No 8 of 1995. This regulation was experimental and provided for significant reordering of personnel and authority in 26 districts to move central government functions into local government. In an institutional sense, central ministries are called upon to transfer responsible personnel and authority out of their regional offices and into the local offices of general government, thus reordering the traditional *kanwil-dinas* system.

The significance of this regulation can only be appreciated in light of the fact that it revives legal encouragement of local involvement in government dating back to the Old Order, effectively frozen at the beginning of the New Order period. In fact, it represents a tentative step towards decentralisation within the current government framework. If localism succeeds, enhancement of popular participation in local government will become necessary.

Given articulated problems with judicial review of executive acts, devolved competences and increased local involvement may be a more realistic approach to increase popular participation in government.

However, the new decentralisation measures do face a variety of legal and practical obstacles. Much as Dutch concepts heavily influenced the 1986 Law on Administrative Justice, so Government Regulation 8 of 1995 draws upon German law ideas of decentralised government within a Continental administrative law state. A variety of administrative law issues within the executive must therefore be addressed once substantive competences are devolved. Further, the issue of finance for decentralised government remains open. In practice, local government during the New Order has been financed by grants from the central government. Reordering of state-federal or local-central responsibilities for governmental activity in any country requires the means to pay for newly acquired responsibilities. Otherwise, if the old arm of government retains the power of the purse, despite a nominally novel

---

11 See generally, Indroharto (1994: 164-84) (commentary on Art 53).

distribution of formal competences the old arm of the government can exercise veto power by refusing to fund. Government Regulation 8 of 1995 addresses this problem on a temporary basis by providing in the near term that already budgeted funding will follow reordered personnel and competences as they are transferred within government.

Such a temporary solution does not address the longer term local finance problem. Competing suggestions appear to include guaranteeing local government a share in national government revenue (a *Finanzverfassung* approach following German practice) or allowing local government to levy significant taxes or similar charges directly to finance local activity (representing a significant change from current practice). These are the kind of significant public law issues yet to be addressed under the concept of decentralisation.

This discussion of decentralisation leaves aside the issue of ABRI influence in local governance via *muspida* (*musyawarah pimpinan daerah*, literally consultation of area leadership, under which local military commanders sit in council with local civilian leaders). *Dwi fungsi*, or ABRI's dual function doctrine, presents broader challenges to the idea of better governance through administrative courts to the extent acts of the military are excluded from review under the 1986 Law on Administrative Justice.

References

Hadjon, Philpus M, JBJM ten Berge et al, *Pengantar Hukum Administrasi Indonesia* (*Introduction to the Indonesian Administrative Law*), Gadjah Mada University Press, Yogyakarta.

Indroharto (1994) *Usaha memahami undang-undang tentang peradilan tata usaha negara*, Vol II, Sinar Harapan, Jakarta.

Lotulung, Paulus Effendi, 1993, *Beberapa Sistem tentang Kontrol Segi Hukum terhadap Pemerintah*, 2nd ed, PI Citra Aditya Bakti, Bandung.

Nasution, Adnan Buyung, 1992, *The Aspiration for Constitutional Government in Indonesia: A Socio-Legal Study of the Indonesian Konstituente 1956-1959*, CIP-Gegevens Koninklijke Bibliotheek, The Hague.

Ybema, SB and Wessel, J, 1978, 'Redress of Grievances Against Administrative Action' in *Introduction to Dutch Law for Foreign Lawyers*, Kluwer BV, Deventer: 435-59.

16. Between State and Society: Professional Lawyers and Reform in Indonesia

Daniel S Lev

In few discussions of fundamental change in Indonesia are lawyers likely to get much attention as agents of it. The neglect is understandable as until recently lawyers have had relatively little influence on anything, let alone fundamental change. Moreover, their peculiar ideological vision – the 'law state', *rechtsstaat*, rule of law or *negara hukum* in the Indonesian variant of the idea – is no match for the glamour of such more obvious revolutionary claims as those of communism or Islam or even 'development' Yet, in the Indonesian setting, the idea is at least equally ambitious and nearly as radical.

Gradually, during the past 30 years of New Order change, private lawyers have grown more conspicuous as the interests they represent have become more salient, the audience for *negara hukum* appeals has expanded and the government has found it more and more difficult to ignore demands for reform. To explain why a relatively small group of reform lawyers has exerted quite so much influence is the purpose of this chapter. I will trace the recent history of the professional advocacy, the tension between reform lawyers and the state over *negara hukum* issues, and the response of officialdom to the challenge of the advocacy.

Lawyers in Indonesian Society

In Indonesia's legal system there are five types of assistance on which individuals or groups rely in dealing with one another or the state bureaucracy: informal intermediaries, bush lawyers (*pokrol bambu*), notaries, advocates and legal aid. The most pervasive form of representation is informal mediation, useful everywhere more or less in proportion to the legitimacy, accessibility and reliability of formal institutional procedures. In Indonesia informal patterns of transaction, involving kin, ethnic, religious, friendship or associational ties generally supersede formal ones. Only a few points need to be made here about the process. First, it reinforces existing patterns of informal authority and influence. Secondly, those without much influence to begin with have limited resources of informal assistance. The higher one's standing the more influential relationships one has. For those with influence, informal connections offer special advantage, which helps to explain why reformers often emphasise the need for formal procedures and controls. Thirdly, informal mediation is the primary competition of formal representational roles.

These latter – notaries, bush lawyers (*pokrol bambu*), advocates and legal aid – differ in function and stratificatory location. The notariat is only tangentially relevant to our concerns, for it has never been politically salient. In Indonesia (like other civil law countries) notaries make up a quiet centre of lawyerly gravity. Responsible for the essential documentary work of private law, their work is usually secure and steady, for 'authentic documents' are always necessary. The size of the notariat is restricted by regulation of the Ministry of Justice, with quotas for each major city. Because of their number, which they campaign constantly to restrict, and the inescapability of their services, notaries occupy a comfortable and prosperous economic-legal space. Concentrated in major cities, their services drop off precipitately at the edge of urban commercial activity. Since the New Order economic boom, from the late 1960s on, when notarial activity and income rose dramatically, the notariat has come under pressure for reform – its governing legislation dates from 1860 – but little has yet been done about it.

Unlike notaries, who have nothing directly to do with courts, *pokrol bambu* and advocates are basically litigators, fundamentally alike but also quite different. *Pokrol bambu*, bush-lawyers, are more closely related to advocates than barefoot doctors are to trained physicians.[1] Few advocates ever admit it, but *pokrol bambu* are simply low status advocates. What distinguishes the two roles are formal education and, generally, the kinds of clients whom they represent. Formal procedural rules do not require trained counsel; anyone at all may appear in court. It is difficult to estimate just how many *pokrol bambu* there are, however, as they come in many shapes, from the legally incompetent influential who merely accompanies friends in court, often as a show of force, to the experienced attorney, perhaps a former court clerk, who knows his way through procedure as well as most trained counsel.

Pokrol bambu survive in part because their genetic kin, advocates, have never been influential enough to eradicate them. There have never been enough advocates to go around but in any case *pokrol bambu* represent clients whom advocates do not serve. Advocates and *pokrol bambu* share an overlapping market for legal services primarily in the cities and to some extent among well-off farmers. Beneath a vague stratificatory boundary, however, advocates seldom drift and clients do not seek them out. Here *pokrol bambu* have consistently represented poorer, but not destitute, clients. For villagers who singly or collectively can afford some payment, or an attractive contingency fee, up through better off landholders, traders, and the urban commercial and bureaucratic petite bourgeoisie, *pokrol bambu* offer the advantages of lower charges and accessibility.

Yet there are distinct limits to what *pokrol bambu* can do in and beyond litigation. Lacking training and degrees, status, social legitimacy, confidence, contacts in the government or the press and an ideological conception of their professional role, *pokrol bambu* do not speak, or are not heard, on the social conditions and interests of their clients, who are clients rather than a clientele. They have no say on institutional issues within the legal system and do not count in questions of legal reform.

---

1   On *pokrol bambu*, see Lev (1973a). *Pokrol bambu* is a pejorative term but more commonly used and recognised than others that have appeared.

By contrast with the steady existence in this century of informal mediation, the notariat and *pokrol bambu*, none of which has evolved all that much, the advocacy is a study in disequilibrium. Unlike the others, which enjoy a constant market for their services, the demand for advocates has always been elastic. Economic factors count for a great deal in the history of the advocacy since the revolution but, while the profession has always been responsive to economic change, many advocates have been equally sensitive to the political and institutional settings of their work.

From their beginning in the colony during the 1920s, Indonesian advocates made up a small new group of accomplished, independent professionals. Politically nationalist by and large, they were also committed to the idea of a modern state rid of colonial administration but built around the Dutch legal institutions and codes in which they made their ways (Lev, 1976).[2] With independence, as Dutch lawyers left during the early 1950s the reach of local advocates extended upwards into the corporate economy but not much lower into the rest. The profession then was neither substantial nor exceedingly well-off, but reasonably secure, prestigious and confident. After 1959, however, under Guided Democracy, the advocacy's sources of economic and political support dried up. Growing emaciated as the economy sank underground, the advocacy was also disengaged politically and ideologically from the Soekarno regime.

These conditions changed dramatically in the years following the coup of 1965, when economic growth in the New Order startled the advocacy awake. Foreign investors especially required legal assistance and advice, and increased foreign and domestic commerce meant increased commercial negotiation, conflict and litigation. Having nearly starved, the profession now saw a huge feast spread before it. It fattened, multiplied and mutated. Until the mid-1960s the number of advocates in Indonesia had probably never risen above 250 or so, about the same as in the last years of the colony. Between 1966 and 1970 the size of the advocacy at least doubled. From 1971 through late 1984, according to the Ministry of Justice rolls, a total of 1075 new advocates registered. Twice that number, perhaps, did not bother to register, which saved them trouble and did not prevent them from practising. By the early 1990s uncertain estimates of the number of legally educated private practitioners, both registered and unregistered, ranged from 3000-10,000 or more nationwide.[3] Sometime during this period of expansion the ratio of advocates to population surpassed that in the colony, about one per 350,000 at best, and now may be in the vicinity of one per 20,000 or better.

At the same time, other dimensions of the profession began to change radically. Once the advocacy began to grow during the late 1960s, its average age declined as

---

2 By 1941, the last year of the colony, of a total of 206 advocates in the colony 81 were Indonesian, divided almost evenly between ethnic Indonesian and ethnic Chinese lawyers (*Regeerings Almanac*, 1941/II: 156-59). Although ethnic Indonesian lawyers have been politically more active and outspoken than ethnic Chinese lawyers (with striking exceptions) ideologically there is relatively little difference between them.

3 That many practising lawyers did not bother to register as advocates reflects the disarray into which the profession fell during the Guided Democracy years. Until the 1980s the government was not interested in regulating the advocacy. Voluntary registration, often an expensive inconvenience, bestowed no obvious advantages. Consequently, it is hard to ascertain precisely how many lawyers are actually in private practice at any time. The figures given here are approximated from information in the Ministry of Justice and the membership lists of *Peradin*, the advocates' association, for 1977. See Peradin (1978: 131-48). *Peradin*'s membership was restricted to registered advocates but not all registered advocates joined *Peradin*.

experienced seniors retired and younger lawyers took up private practice. Moreover, for the first time in its history the profession attracted lateral recruits from the ranks of retired judges, prosecutors and other civil servants, who introduced new elements and consequent tension over style, ethics and ideology. Economic change also triggered a structural metamorphosis in the profession. For most of its history the advocacy had been a relatively homogeneous order of specialists in litigation, as in the European model. But in the New Order private lawyers diversified, specialised and stratified along lines of new economic opportunity. The features of private lawyering were redefined by the emergence of a stratum of non-litigators, 'consulting lawyers', specialising in commercial legal counselling and negotiation. These are a new breed of solicitors or office lawyers who are not notaries but do not fit the traditional mould of advocates. The most successful of them inhabit new multi-member law firms established in Jakarta since the late 1960s. Many consulting lawyers did not register with the Ministry of Justice until they were compelled to do so in the 1980s. Nor did they join the most prominent professional association, *Peradin*, some of whose members did not, in any case, recognise them as advocates. But their income and status have promoted them to the elite of the private legal profession.

These changes naturally affected the social and political outlook of the profession. The most prosperous private lawyers generally have disengaged from common issues of Indonesian state and society. Financially successful attorneys prefer to attend exclusively to their professional work. Consulting lawyers (and a few advocates) exist in a busy, lucrative and comfortable commercial stratosphere – often suitably located in new tower offices – well insulated from the everyday miseries of the courts and of clients who have to deal with them. While they may sympathise with reformers, they also tend to detached or cynical views that excuse uninvolvement and justify political quiescence. Many feel indebted to the New Order for their prosperity, moreover, and see no reason to raise extraneous non-professional issues. And some, particularly former judges and prosecutors who rely on government contacts, are disinclined to imperil these advantages through critical activism of any sort, whatever their views otherwise. In 1978, when *Peradin* (*Persatuan Advokat Indonesia*, Indonesian Advocates Association) proclaimed itself to be a 'struggle organisation' dedicated to reform, a few members were uneasy enough to help establish a counter-organisation, HPHI (Peradin, 1978: 98).[4]

Yet the new prosperity and public recognition of the advocacy also supported the reform efforts of legal activists for whom the *negara hukum* amalgamated professional necessity, political ideology and social program. Their most important creation was the legal aid movement, which began with the Legal Aid Institute (*Lembaga Bantuan Hukum*, LBH) of Jakarta. Founded with *Peradin* sponsorship in 1970, the LBH institutionalised the political vision of reform advocates. It will not be dealt with at length in this essay, whose focus is the advocacy proper.[5] In brief, however, the LBH provides legal assistance to the poor but also has become Indonesia's most prominent center of social-legal and political-legal reform activity.

---

4   On the new organisation of attorneys, the *Himpuan Penasehat Hukum Indonesia* (Indonesian Legal Counselors Association, HPHI), see Tempo (1979: 17). Other associations of private lawyers that emerged during the next several years recruited both certified advocates and unregistered practitioners. See Abdurrahman (1980: 265ff).

5   On LBH see Lev (1987) and the sources cited there.

Advocates and the *Negara Hukum*

Like the modern Indonesian state itself, the *negara hukum* (a literal translation of the Dutch *rechtsstaat*) is an imported concept but (also like the state) its significance can only be understood in an Indonesian context. Although various groups have supported an Indonesian rule of law, professional advocates have been its most articulate and generally most liberal spokesmen (Lev, 1978). Their commitment to the *negara hukum* is best understood in related terms of professional interest and ideological orientation, which can be traced most clearly against the background of their professional evolution.

Earlier than most nationalists in the colony, advocates knew what kind of independent state they wanted. The colonial legal system distinguished unequivocally between European and colonial-Indonesian conceptions of political and social order, creating a striking contrast for attentive lawyers.[6]

On the European side the symbolic focus of the legal system was the judiciary, staffed by well-trained, respected public and private lawyers, including Indonesian advocates themselves. The written codes were rigorous, precise and enforceable. Governmental authority was limited by written rules, which also accorded individuals well-defined and actionable rights. All this was predicated on normative values of legal equality, certainty, and predictability; and it applied only to those with European legal status.

On the Indonesian side, symbolic (and real) political-legal authority vested not in courts but in the administrative bureaucracy, particularly the *pangreh praja* (now the *pamong praja*), the local arm of the Ministry of Interior (Sutherland, 1979). Unlike the European codes of civil and criminal procedure, the Revised Indonesian Regulation (HIR)[7] for Indonesians was relatively loose, with less stringent controls over the exercise of official authority and fewer protections for individuals. Substantively, Indonesians were subject to the diverse rules of local customary (*adat*) law, applied in several areas outside of Java by customary courts governed by their own procedural norms. What was certain and predictable in this, from the advocate's point of view, were the prerogatives of patrimonial authority, refined and shored up for the purposes of colonial administration but resting still on a 'traditional' social order for which the lawyers had little sympathy. Its primary attributes had to do not with legal equality but social and political hierarchy, not individual rights of citizens but the discretionary privileges of officials. Here there was room for informal intermediaries and supplicants but not for lawyers, for whom clear rules and justiciable rights were minimal requirements of their role.

That advocates leaned to the 'European' concept is not surprising. They made that choice in part by joining the advocacy instead of the public bureaucracy, the preferred calling of the Javanese aristocracy which supplied the first Indonesian lawyers. Their professional advantage lay in retaining the structure of the European, not the Indonesian, side of the legal system, but this also implied an ideological

---

6   In the complex legal system of the Netherlands East Indies, the Indonesian side was no less a Dutch creation than the European side, but worked by different principles. Not only were there distinct courts and procedural codes, but equally distinct substantive law regimes, with catchment areas of uniformity or connection where it suited various interests. Under indirect rule, Indonesian elites were allowed considerable local authority enforced by colonial administrative power. On colonial legal structure, see, inter alia, Alting (1926) and ter Harr (1948). The discussion that follows draws on Lev (1985).

7   *Herziene Indonesich Reglement.*

interest in refashioning Indonesian social and political values to suit a state basically liberal in design. Advocates joined, or helped found, those parties that promised such change. They applauded the Japanese decision during the wartime occupation to eliminate the plural colonial judiciary in favour of unified courts but regretted the retention of the weaker courts for Indonesians rather than the stronger courts for Europeans.

During and after the revolution, they consistently pressed for institutional reforms that favoured limited government, procedural uniformity and legal equality. Early in the revolution, however, the government adopted the colonial procedural code for Indonesians instead of the more elaborate codes for Europeans. It was an omen of things to come. In positions of authority, advocates fairly consistently undertook to abolish traditional local privileges, to eliminate *adat* courts, to create a nationally unified judiciary and to strengthen the courts against executive aggression, but the political odds were heavily against them (Lev, 1976; 1973b).

Although advocates were disproportionately influential as part of a small educated elite, they were still hopelessly outnumbered and lacked the middle class support their vision required. Even among the minuscule group of legally trained Indonesians – about 400 when the Japanese army arrived – advocates were a minority. Most indigenous lawyers had joined the colonial government as judges in the *Landraad* (superior court for Indonesians), administrators, and scholars; and their experience on the Indonesian side of the colonial legal system promoted an ideological perspective that favoured a powerful state in control of a submissive society.

The spread between the two political-legal orientations was made acutely clear in July 1945, when Indonesia's first Constitution was drafted, in a debate between Mohammad Yamin and Raden Soepomo. The West Sumatran Yamin made the most elaborate case for the kind of state professional advocates generally preferred. He proposed a constitutional bill of rights; a *Mahkamah Agung* (Supreme Court) with powers of judicial review; and clearly-separated legislative, judicial and executive functions. Drawn from the United States model, his ideas departed radically from the institutional experience of the colony. The premises on which his ideas rested – a sharp distinction between state and society, recognition of individual interests and rights, limited government, and institutional controls over political authority – challenged all the constructs of political authority that underlay the administration of Indonesian society as it was most fully developed in colonial Java (Yamin, 1959: 330-37).[8]

The Javanese Soepomo was the colony's most prominent Indonesian legal scholar. Closely associated with the conservative *adatrechtpolitiek (adat* law policy) conceived in Leiden, he worked in the Department of Justice during the 1930s, taught in the law faculty and then served as legal adviser to the Japanese occupation administration. The most influential legal technician in the independence preparatory commissions of 1945, Soepomo was chiefly responsible for drafting the document that became the Constitution of 1945. If some nationalist leaders accepted the institutional heritage of the colony simply because it was easier, requiring no political imagination, Soepomo understood it intimately and consciously preferred it.

---

8   While Yamin, who practised as an advocate for only a short time in the 1930s, represented well the political ideas of the profession, his proposals probably went further than most advocates at the time were willing to go. It may be that he also spoke for Sumatran worries about the inevitable domination of independent Indonesia by the Javanese heartland. One can read his ideas as promoting control either over the Indonesian state or over a Javanese-dominated Indonesian state.

He dismissed Yamin's proposals out of hand, arguing that Indonesian jurists had no experience with the system Yamin wanted. The alternative model of Continental civil law, equally prestigious in the world outside, was already in place, already adapted to Indonesian conditions and already known by the political leaders and officials who would have to staff the independent state.

Soepomo's political agenda was more interesting than mere administrative conservatism. Committed to preserving not only the existing legal order but the authority of the *priyayi* aristocracy on which colonial administration in Java had depended, his line of argument flowed smoothly from the ideology of colonial-Javanese patrimonialism (Soemarsaid Moertono, 1968; Sutherland, 1979). Liberal individualism was out of the question, he insisted, for the state is conceived as a family and the good of the family must supersede that of the individual member. The constitutional rights Yamin wanted were unnecessary, for such rights were against the state. On this point Soepomo was right, but he assumed state and society to be indivisible, led by an ascriptive elite responsible for ascertaining and defending the interests of state-society. The evident superiority of this elite, and the totality of its responsibility, rendered external control not only superfluous but obtrusive and even subversive.[9]

Yamin's proposals were voted down in 1945, but Soepomo's were not fully endorsed either. Following the revolution, the parliamentary regime of independent Indonesia rather vindicated the views of the advocates, though not entirely to their satisfaction. The elegant Dutch procedural codes were supplanted by the simpler HIR; and new national courts descended from the colonial *Landraden* for Indo-nesians rather than the European *Raden van Justitie*. But it was not a bad time for the profession and advocates remember it as a period of great promise (Jamaluddin Dt Singo Mangkuto, 1973: 37-38). The ideological symbols were right: consti-tutionalism, parliamentarism and the *negara hukum*. During the 1950s many advocates were in the government and active in political parties, depleting the profession, especially of ethnic Indonesian lawyers. Those who still practised were complacent. Despite the turmoil of the parliamentary years, they had reason to suppose that their professional livings were secure, that the legal system would continue to honour them, that public legal institutions would eventually catch up to the advocates' own high standards and that Indonesian society would become progressively more 'law-minded'. Shaky as the parliamentary *rechtsstaat* seems in hindsight, private lawyers thought it natural and inevitable. The *negara hukum*, though beset by evolutionary problems, was to their minds an accomplished fact, secured by the provisional parliamentary Constitution of 1950.

But the *negara hukum* proved to be even more provisional than the 1950 Constitution. As Guided Democracy took form from 1957, all the supports advocates had taken for granted – a legitimate private economy, autonomous and effective legal process and constitutionalism – collapsed. Beneath the new regime's surface radicalism lay essentially reactionary administrative premises drawn self-consciously from the myths of the classical Javanese state; and less openly but more profoundly from the memory of colonial practice. Soekarno's emphasis on revolutionary movement (including *hukum revolusi*, 'revolutionary law') and a

---

9   Unlike the Federal Constitution of 1949 and the Provisional Constitution of 1950, the 1945 Constitution provides few institutional controls over executive authority and no constitutionally stipulated political rights. For Soepomo's arguments, see Yamin (1959: 337ff) and, for an English translation, Feith & Castles (1970: 188-92). See also Bourchier, Chapter 12; and Lubis, Chapter 11.

patrimonially conceived populism ('the message of the people's suffering') endowed political and bureaucratic leadership with maximum discretionary authority, much as Soepomo had originally intended. Legal process was rendered ritually peripheral to political and administrative prerogative freed of institutional controls.

Soekarno treated the liberal *negara hukum* as a weak challenge to his own vision of a self-realised Indonesian nation-state, the instrument of conservative elements bent on surrendering Indonesian creativity to European political fashion. He dealt with the lawyers mercilessly, making their prized constitutionalist ideas a special target of his contempt. In two crowning legislative gestures, politically pointless by that time but symbolically cutting, Soekarno tossed out the principles of separation of powers and judicial independence.[10]

The Guided Democracy years edified few lawyers of any sort, but advocates suffered most professionally and ideologically. Public lawyers – particularly judges but prosecutors too – felt the loss of institutional autonomy, yet retained the advantages of official status at a time of rising bureaucratic authority. As compensation for their loss of independence, courts and prosecution, like the rest of the bureaucracy, were relieved of controls and became increasingly corrupt, self-serving and unaccountable. As judges, prosecutors and police were drawn into explicit cooperation with local administrative and security officials (the *Caturtunggal*), advocates, nakedly unofficial, lost procedural leverage and their clients suffered for it. Professional satisfaction evaporated even faster than professional work. During the Guided Democracy period the advocacy was, on the whole, stunned and stagnant, with few new recruits. As if to demonstrate that the profession still hung on, despite everything, a dozen or so senior advocates finally organised a national association, *Peradin*, in March 1963.

When Guided Democracy capsized in a sea of blood following the coup of October 1965, advocates were prominent among the enthusiastic crowd who cheered and tried optimistically to shape a successor regime. At no previous time were private lawyers as a group so politically engaged and in public view as they became during the early New Order. *Peradin* seniors and a few new recruits involved themselves ardently in the political and ideological issues. They were active in reform efforts in and out of the legal system, in public meetings and seminars, in parliamentary hearings and in the press.[11] As fierce holdouts against Soekarno's bandwagon, most advocates had unassailable political credentials but in addition many of the key issues of New Order politics were their issues – restoring legal process, institutional reform, constitutionalism and human rights. Because of the experience of Guided Democracy, but also because fundamental features of Guided Democracy survived into the New Order, the perspective of advocates on the state acquired support among a wider and more critically interested audience than ever before. Not in any formal sense and not exclusively, yet quite clearly, advocates spoke to and for this audience.

Soekarno's explicit rejection of *rechtsstaat* symbols had paved the way for their revival. Demands for reform after 1965 were framed partly by the reaction against

---

10   Law No 19 of 1964 on Judicial Authority and Law No 13 of 1965 on the Organisation of the Civil Judiciary.

11   See, for example, Tasrif (1971), long-time chairman of *Peradin*. In 1968 the famous Yap affair, in which police and prosecution officials tried to intimidate the civil rights attorney Yap Thiam Hien by detaining him in jail, helped to raise important symbolic legal issues around the advocacy.

Guided Democracy's abuses, conveniently though simplistically represented as failures of legal principle. Rhetorically, at least, all the major forces behind the New Order favoured the *negara hukum*, but there were profound differences over what it meant. At odds were two antithetical images of the proper relationship between law and public authority rooted in quite different conceptions of the relationship between state and society.

The principal protagonists were the army and state bureaucracy on the one hand and a growing universe of self-consciously private, non-governmental groups on the other. To the extent that the government conception did not simply mask the actuality of military force and political privilege, its impulse was fundamentally bureaucratic and took for granted the priority of state interests. The other *negara hukum* was parliamentary and judicial in institutional conception and favoured a better balance between state and private interests. While advocates and like-minded groups sought legal predictability, protection of private social interests, and constitutional limits on state power, army leaders sought stability, fuller control over a diverse society, expansion of state power and consolidation of the army's special claim to leadership.

It was hardly a match. Once General Soeharto had succeeded Soekarno as President in 1967-1968, army leadership was not likely to concede institutionalised controls over political and bureaucratic authority. Who could possibly man such controls? Not military officers, obviously, for this would threaten armed forces unity; and not civilian political interests, which, in Soeharto's contemptuous assessment, had had their chance and failed. By this view, legal process could not serve as an autonomous instrument of social and political management, for any measure of institutional independence must proportionately diminish the responsibilities (and prerogatives) of political leadership.[12] Despite occasional public assurances to the contrary, the legal system was conceived to be subordinate to the prior claims of political and bureaucratic authority.

This line of reasoning, never made explicit but commonly understood, traces back through Guided Democracy and Soepomo's exposition in 1945 to the principles of colonial administration on the Indonesian side.[13] In effect, the regime trumpetted constitutionalism and legal process but had the resources necessary to behave as it wished. Confidence in this reality justified the creation of an elaborate security apparatus, staffed and run by the military, whose extra-legal procedures paralleled and, at will, either superseded or subordinated conventional legal process. Legal officials generally accepted their submerged role as a matter of course. Even judges took it for granted that they were bound, like the rest of the bureaucracy, to the purposes of executive leadership. Any other view endangered their careers and

---

12   To put the argument differently, at its best, the government's monopoly of responsibility for political and social order could not be realistically subjected to limits imposed by law, for 'law' is fundamentally an instrument of the regime, within which, it followed, no effective institutional recourse could exist without fragmenting public authority. Anderson (1972) traces the Javanese sources of this worry about dispersing authority. A compelling but worrisome analysis, it has the disadvantage of distracting us from a straightforward understanding of the interests of the regime in rejecting controls.

13   As New Order tensions grew, the lines of debate established in 1945 between Soepomo and Yamin re-emerged. The government revived the authoritarian 'integralist' position of Soepomo in service to a corporatist ideology, while critics dug deeply into the constitutional debates of 1945 in search both of a constitutionalist foundation and a fuller understanding of the ideological sources of the government's case. See Simanjuntak (1989); Buyung Nasution (1992); Lubis (1993).

violated the bureaucratic ethos of the New Order administration. Acceptance was rewarded with bureaucratic privilege and insulation.

Consequently, while concessions were made to demands for administrative and judicial probity, they could not be enforced for lack of effective institutional machinery or useful political recourse. Assurances of improvements in judicial procedure – the Cibogo agreements of the late 1960s and early 1970s – did not hold for long (Peradin, 1978: 101).[14] The government deflected an effort, led by judges and advocates but with wider support, to allow the *Mahkamah Agung* powers of judicial review over legislative and executive acts (Lev, 1978: 56ff).[15] Complaints against judicial corruption and prosecutorial abuses, as routine in the New Order as under Guided Democracy, went essentially unanswered. Sporadic promises by the government to control corruption also consistently came to nothing. A new statute on judicial organisation (Law 14 of 1970) provided for legal representation of accused persons from the time of arrest but the implementing legislation it required was not forthcoming.[16] Each of these reforms was intended to impose restrictions on bureaucratic privilege, discretion and prerogative, diminutions of public authority conceded on paper but rejected as long as possible in practice.

The same reform issues illuminate the other *negara hukum*, which increasingly emphasised the legitimacy of private interests, assuming the separation of state and society and the necessity of an autonomous legal order that transcended both. The interests at stake in this evolving ideology belonged predominantly to a growing intellectual, professional, and commercial middle-class and to religious and ethnic minorities: whoever lacked consistently dependable influence in the administration. The lesson of Guided Democracy, confirmed in the New Order, was that if you could not share in the power of the state, you needed protection against it. On this view, state and society had parted ways and now confronted one another.

Unlike the parliamentary period, when *negara hukum* principles and issues were rarely discussed seriously, they now became common fare in the press and in professional, academic and intellectual circles. Key questions revolved persistently around the related problems of confining executive authority and protecting private citizens and interests. Without inside influence or organised power, groups outside the government sought routine institutional access and redress within it. The judiciary, for lack of anything better, became the symbolic focus of this ambition. Advocates had a special interest in the courts, but for nearly all groups with weak links to power an independent judiciary had some appeal. From early 1966 onwards there were widespread demands to restore the separation of powers, assure judicial independence, erect institutional (that is, judicial) controls over executive-

---

14   Cibogo was the site of three meetings, in 1967, 1970, and 1973, among officials of the Ministry of Justice, judiciary, prosecution and police to bring some order, efficiency and fairness to criminal trial process especially. Advocates were particularly concerned with the difficulties of obtaining case records from the courts, seeing their clients in good time, speeding up trials, reducing their costs and other problems that obstructed adequate legal representation. See also Abdurrahman (1980: 89ff, 174ff).

15   In this quest advocates supported the demands of the judicial corps, but their purposes were different. While most judges wanted to enhance their institutional stature in bureaucratic terms, advocates sought a stronger and more effective judiciary that would distance itself from the bureaucracy and impose legal controls over executive authority. The brief and shaky alliance did not alleviate the considerable hostility between judges and advocates.

16   The same law provided for administrative courts, which finally came into being only 20 years later, in 1991.

bureaucratic authority and surround the entire political system with a fence of legal process. A new literature on private rights developed around the problem of protecting citizens from official abuse.

These ideas became mainstays of protest against the New Order regime from the late 1960s through the 1990s. Professional advocates embraced them most enthusiastically and consistently. Stimulated by their own activism and public visibility but also frustrated by the absence of change and no longer optimistic, *Peradin* seniors adopted them as a program. In late 1977, at a *Peradin* congress dedicated to 'The Role of Advocates in the development of a *Negara Hukum*', Chairman Suardi Tasrif and his colleagues pushed through this resolution:

- that the corps of advocates as one element of the *penegak hukum* (maintainers of the law) shares responsibility with lawyers in other fields and with society generally for developing an Indonesian *negara hukum*, as affirmed in the elucidation of the 1945 Constitution.

- that the Indonesian *negara hukum* is responsible for guaranteeing and respecting fundamental human rights for all citizens both in their political and in their social life, so that a just and prosperous society based on the *Pancasila* is achieved for all the Indonesian people.

- that to attain these goals *Peradin* is obliged to intensify its role so as to become a struggle-organisation (*organisasi perjuangan*) in its essential commitment to establish Truth, Justice and Law.

Later a new charter-oath (*Ikrar Peradin*) pledged advocates to defend human rights; to pursue the struggle to establish truth, justice and law; to promote democracy, clean government and an independent judiciary based on the *Pancasila*; to fight for representative bodies that truly serve the people's interests; to obey the advocates' code of ethics; to defend the weak and the poor; to oppose all arbitrariness and oppression; and to be open to criticism and correction from any quarter.[17] The two documents, unabashedly idealist, are also unashamedly disregarded by most private lawyers. Yet they represent authentically the professional and political values to which advocates lay claim.

For most advocates professional interests and experience defined issues of reform. Litigating lawyers especially perceived the failings of the regime most acutely in the conditions under which they represented their clients. It is largely for this reason that litigating attorneys, not consulting lawyers, have always been in the forefront of reform efforts. In court their troubles multiplied if they insisted on legal correctness. It was not simply a matter of judicial corruption, in which some advocates came to participate more or less equitably in the so-called 'judicial mafia' of collusive prosecutors, judges and private lawyers. Rather the problem was (and remains) that these were just about the only terms on which advocates could claim something more than pro-forma membership in the judicial system. For the most part they were kept at a distance, as outsiders, for which they and their clients suffered. Most (not all) judges resented advocates as well-off, self-serving, unofficial, private intruders upon public authority. Not only were the courts inefficient and expensive, because of extraordinary fees, and execution of judgments highly uncertain but advocates were often treated contemptuously, ignored by judges, obstructed and occasionally even forbidden to enter courtrooms.

---

17   See Peradin (1978: 97-98) for the resolution and the oath.

Although civil litigation was difficult enough, so that some advocates avoided it if at all possible, and others gave it up altogether in favour of office practice, criminal process incurred the most serious adversities. Criminal defence was treacherous, filled with abusive police, corrupt and extortionate prosecutors, bureaucratically-minded judges who favoured prosecutors as colleagues and regarded defence attorneys as interlopers.[18] Advocates raised a perpetual din over these problems on behalf of their clients and themselves, leading now and then to open conflict with judges.[19] Relatively little has ever come of their protests, for the judiciary is protected by the mantle of bureaucratic privilege. Prosecutors and judges have been transferred or even dismissed – occasionally as the result of extraordinary efforts by private lawyers – but their institutions have gone relatively untouched for to do more would challenge essential features of the regime itself.

Reform-minded advocates were (and still are) frustrated at every turn: politically because their *negara hukum* was not in the foreseeable future, and professionally, as barristers, because the one institution that meant most to them, the judiciary, was impervious to their wishes for fundamental reorientation and acceptance. Responding to this push factor, as well as to the pull of more lucrative and comfortable work, advocates who could do so turned to commercial legal counselling, where, at a distance from judicial wretchedness, their interest in reform either faded or decayed into cynicism.

Yet the efforts of advocates and allied reformers did not go entirely unrequited. *Peradin* and its offspring, the *Lembaga Bantuan Hukum* or Legal Aid Institute (LBH), had good press and the government's own purveyance of *negara hukum* rhetoric, regarded cynically by some officials but seriously by others, also lent credibility to its critics. At parliamentary hearings *Peradin* spokesmen were heard, often sympathetically, and their positions showed up fragmentarily in significant new legislation.

There have been statutory reforms, although no one committed to change regards them as unequivocal victories. Politically the most important of them has to do with criminal procedure, ideologically (as well as practically) important because it defines critical relationships between state and citizenry. Of all the laws promulgated since 1966, the two most heralded – largely as a result of debates set off by professional advocates and legal aid lawyers – were Law No 14 of 1970 on Judicial Organisation and the new code of criminal procedure of 1981 (*Kitab Undang-undang Hukum Acara Pidana*, KUHAP). The first was a disappointment to reformers, in part because it failed to give the *Mahkamah Agung* review powers but also because concessions of principle favourable to accused persons were not implemented by the ancillary legislation required. A little over a decade later, KUHAP went further to meet demands for reform. A milestone in post-

---

18 In a society in which advantage inheres in official status many advocates have long been troubled by their lack of it. Their solution to the problems of advocacy is official recognition, through a law and at least semi-official status. See, for example, Sastrayuddha (1971). Others, conscious and proud of the private tradition of professional advocacy and resentful of the state, have opposed any law at all governing private practice; but they are a small minority. See Wirjanto (1971: 27-33); Abdurrahman (1980: 189ff).

19 See Peradin (1978: 34-41), the opening address by Suardi Tasrif; Tasrif (1971: especially 22-42, 77ff); Yap Thiam Hien, (1973: 8-16). *Hukum dan Keadilan, Peradin*'s late journal, frequently ran articles and commentaries by advocates on the difficulties of criminal and civil process. *Ikadin*'s *ERA Hukum* (which lasted briefly), the independent *Forum Keadilan* (Justice Forum) and the daily press continue to do so.

revolutionary legal history, it is Indonesia's first new major code, replacing at last the procedural regime of the HIR rules of criminal procedure define. The attention paid to criminal process in Indonesia indicates how much political issues, or state/society issues, have dominated public debate about legal change.

Even the subdued satisfaction legal reformers drew from these statutory developments did not last, however, for they were accompanied by none of the political and institutional changes that might have made sense of them.[20] The government itself felt no obligation to abide by the spirit or even letter of the new procedural code on any issue of political concern. Not only did political dissidence remain subject to the extra-legal powers of the security apparatus, but even common criminality was treated without a blink of recognition of legal proprieties. During the early 1980s, with President Soeharto's blessing, military death squads killed thousands of the petty criminals and racketeers living on the periphery of the New Order's prosperity.[21] The existence of a criminal code and the KUHAP, just promulgated, were rendered utterly trivial, but the murderous project won loud and widespread public applause before some in its audience had second thoughts. Legal reformers, prominent advocates above all, shouted their dismay into the wind.[22]

Legislative reform unaccompanied by institutional reform – and unreinforced by apposite political reform – is likely to prove a bit airy but not entirely meaningless. For all its failings in practice, the new code of criminal procedure nevertheless confirmed the growing importance of fundamental legal issues, and of legality itself, in political discourse; and it constituted a recognition, at least, of legitimate private (or citizen) interests in the organisation of the legal system and of private rights as defenses against official abuse of power. The code established ideological footholds and commitments that are useful to reformers in continuing debates over political and legal change. It may be little, but it is not irrelevant in a long and complex political evolution.

The Advocacy and the State

Neither is the professional advocacy irrelevant to this evolution but its influence necessarily depends on a receptive audience. The salience of the reform advocacy from the late 1960s has been precisely the result of an interested audience, a new

---

20 Among other innovations, for example, the KUHAP disentangled the functions of police and prosecution, making the police solely responsible for preliminary investigation – the result of criticism of the prosecution as well as police eagerness to extend their authority – and subject to suits for wrongful damages. In addition, it provided a wholly new procedure of pre-trial judicial review of arrest and detention, potentially a means of control over repressive organs. Finally, the code implemented (within limits) the principle of legal representation of accused persons from the time of arrest. Not one of these innovations has worked according to promise, largely because of the resistance of the institutions responsible for them. See Fitzpatrick (Chapter 24).

21 President Soeharto takes credit for these *Petrus* (*penembak misterius* or mysterious gunmen) killings in his memoirs (Dwipayana, & Ramadhan, 1988: 364-67), in the first, withdrawn, edition. A persuasive analysis of the *Petrus* affair is available in Bourchier (1988).

22 The *Petrus* affair was hardly the only deviation, however. The reforms intended by the new code of criminal procedure are daily undercut by institutional resistance. For critical discussions of the KUHAP in practice, see 't Hart & Nusantara (1986); Nusantara et al (1986). See also ICJ (1987), especially the chapter by J 't Hart, 'Aspects of Criminal Justice' (at 166ff).

middle class generated by the New Order's own economic policies.[23] As in Korea and Thailand, for example, economic and social change unmatched by political change – an expanding private economy, a diversifying middle class and an authoritarian monopoly for a governing class – was bound to create tension. The tension results, in part, from the incompatibility of two quite distinctive constructions of state/society relations, formulated earlier as divergent versions of an Indonesian *negara hukum*. As support for a more liberal construction has grown among private groups, often organised self-consciously in new NGOs, the government has had a harder time riding herd over a slightly unruly and recalcitrant crowd. The regime has had no difficulty in asserting its prerogatives but its claims to legitimacy for them are wearing thin. The recent history of the professional advocacy itself illustrates the stakes involved in conflicts between public and private claims to authority and the institutional consequences once the battle is joined.

In the politics of the legal system after 1965, as in the politics of nearly everything else in Indonesia, the motor of state ran on military fuel. From the start administrative institutions – the central bureaucracy and *pamong praja* – were subject to control by military appointees. The formal legal system followed suit more slowly. Early symptoms of independence among legal officials were simply suppressed. Then, one by one, public legal institutions were dealt to military officials, a policy which served the twin interests of political security and patronage.

The national police had been incorporated into the armed forces since the late Guided Democracy period. After 1971, when the independently inclined police commandant Hugeng Imam Santoso was dismissed, his successors toed the line. In the case of the prosecution there was never any question of genuine autonomy. In 1966 General Soegih Arto was appointed Chief Public Prosecutor (*Jaksa Agung*) and his successors were drawn from the military. The Ministry of Justice and *Mahkamah Agung* were left in compliant civilian hands for a few years. In the late 1970s, however, the Ministry was turned over to retired Lt Gen Mudjono, succeeded by retired Lt Gens Ali Said and Ismail Saleh. Finally, the *Mahkamah Agung*, packed with several retired officers appointed after 1974, was given over to Mudjono in 1981 and on his death in 1984 to Ali Said. By 1981 retired army officers were in command of the entire core of the legal system. Only in the early 1990s, particularly in the new cabinet of 1993, were amenable civilians back in the chief chairs of the *Mahkamah Agung* (Purwoto Gandasubrata) and Ministry of Justice (Oetojo Oesman).

The silent notariat and peripheral Islamic judiciary aside, the one significant legal institution which the military did not dominate was the advocacy, a prime source of noisy and irritating criticism. Gradually the profession moved into focus on the regime's crosshairs.

Though still a moving target, the advocacy was weaker than its public voice implied. The stimulating effect of economic expansion on private legal practice also set off difficult issues of professional evolution and regulation. So quickly did the profession change, becoming vastly more heterogeneous and less intimate, that it

---

23   Until the New Order period very little at all was written about the advocacy. Only a few standard law texts even mentioned private lawyers. During the late 1960s, however, *Peradin* began to publish its own journal, *Hukum dan Keadilan* (Law and Justice), under the able direction of Suardi Tasrif, a former newspaper editor (*Abadi*) who took a law degree and began practice only in the early 1960s. The first book on the advocacy, Soemarno P Wirjanto's *Profesi Advokat* appeared only in 1979. See also Abdurrahman (1980); Prodjohamidjojo (1982); Silaban et al (1992).

lost organisational capacity to deal with its problems. Apart from consulting lawyers, who shared little of the tradition, many new litigating attorneys had joined the profession out of backgrounds in the civil service and military that did not fit well either. *Peradin*, with about 800 members at peak, represented only a fifth or so of the graduated private lawyers actually practising throughout the country. Other organisations were much smaller. None of the associations, including *Peradin*, offered members substantial professional advantages. In *Peradin*'s case the inclination of senior advocates to enforce its ethical code discouraged some lawyers from joining and drove a few out.

The advocacy's inability to organise effectively and to discipline its members was due in part to lack of government interest in regulating the profession. The Ministry of Justice did little more than register advocates, from whom unofficial fees were extracted in the process but, as the procedural code did not preclude anybody else from practising, it hardly mattered whether lawyers registered or not.

Most advocates hoped for limited government intervention on their terms: a law governing practice, for example, that would lend the advocacy legitimacy, define its professional rights and responsibilities and eliminate or restrict non-degreed bush-lawyers. *Peradin* leaders also dreamed of a national bar association, whose establishment required government assistance. The danger, however, given the antagonism to advocates among the courts, prosecution, police and Ministry of Justice, was that any government attention might take a bad turn. This is exactly what happened in the early 1980s, as public law officials set about bringing the advocacy under control.

No one doubted the need for professional regulation but there was good reason to suspect the motives behind sudden official interest in it. Available evidence indicates much less concern in the administration for protecting the public from disorderly legal practice than in extending bureaucratic authority, whose fullness was seriously challenged – not only in the legal system – by expanding private groups. Since the 1970s the NGO movement had aggressively taken hold, spawning independent reform organisations with little respect for either public policy or officialdom. The original model was *Peradin*'s Legal Aid Institute, which had grown into a national foundation with a dozen active branches around the country.

No less in the legal system than in other sectors of the public bureaucracy, the effect of these non-governmental rumblings was to reinforce corporatist urges to assert official predominance. The antagonism between public and private lawyers added intense animus. Judges and prosecutors resented professional advocates their independence, and all the more their constant accusations of official corruption, incompetence and abuse of authority. They were eager to silence their critics and to run a test of prerogatives in which their parent institutions, including the Ministry of Justice and the *Mahkamah Agung*, would have to back them. But there were other political reasons for reining in the advocacy. In political trials since 1966 defence attorneys from *Peradin* and the LBH had embarrassed the government at home and abroad by challenging the staged affairs and turning them into platforms of political criticism. Private lawyers were prominent among the human rights activists whom administration spokesmen regarded as a threat to the regime, along with hidden communists and assorted other evils.

During the early 1980s legal officials initiated a strategy designed first to absorb *Peradin* and other lawyers' organisations into a single national association and then to impose official disciplinary control over the entire profession. In 1981 at *Peradin*'s congress in Bandung, *Mahkamah Agung* chairman Mudjono, Minister of

Justice Ali Said and Chief Public Prosecutor Ismail Saleh each proposed that the advocacy required a unified organisation (*wadah tunggal*).[24] It was left to Ali Said, first as Minister of Justice and later as *Mahkamah Agung* chairman, to achieve the new *Ikadin* (*Ikatan Advokat Indonesia*, Indonesian Advocates League).

Many advocates responded favourably in the hope that a national association sponsored by the government would improve professional opportunities and ease intercourse with the bureaucracy. Senior *Peradin* leaders were sceptical, to put it mildly. The appeal of a national bar association was dampened by worry that Ali Said was mainly intent upon eliminating *Peradin*'s influence. The agents meant to accomplish this end, they feared, were military law graduates who, acting as a group with official support, would amass enough support to dominate the new association.[25]

Peradin's misgivings delayed but could not avoid the inevitable. *Ikadin* was formally established in November 1985 with Harjono Tjitrosubeno of *Peradin*, by prior agreement, as its first chairman.[26] Many lawyers nevertheless held *Ikadin* at arm's length. Despite pressure from Ali Said and Minister of Justice Ismail Saleh, *Peradin* and other associations refused to disband and submerge themselves completely, as individual members, in *Ikadin*. Instead, they engaged in a slow battle with the government for control of the organisation. On every crucial issue *Ikadin* leaders fought for organisational autonomy and self-governance to which the Ministry of Justice responded by tightening control over registration requirements, imposing quotas of advocates, like the notariat, for major cities and dividing the profession organisationally.[27] Even so, the advocates held out. In *Ikadin*'s first balloted elections in 1988 the military law graduates did not come through as Ali Said had assumed and tried to assure they would. The winners were Harjono Tjitrosubeno and a slate of candidates in which *Peradin* figured prominently.

---

24   The idea of a *wadah tunggal* – a single receptacle – was not new. In 1967, when *Peradin* was riding high along with other aggressive critics of the old order of Guided Democracy, acting president Soeharto had issued a statement recognising *Peradin* as the sole organisation of professional advocates. A decade later, when *Peradin* had lost favour in the regime, the approval was tacitly withdrawn as new associations were allowed and probably encouraged. At about the same time the notion of a *wadah tunggal* for advocates was resuscitated as an anti-*Peradin* instrument. For a brief discussion of the history of the new association IKADIN, see the first edition of Era Hukum (1987: 212ff).

25   Since the 1950s the Academy of Military Law (AHM) and College of Military Law (PTHM) had graduated a steady flow of military lawyers, as many as 1200 or more by the 1980s. On the political-administrative side of the army they have represented a large bloc of useful personnel, usually linked to such key regime figures as former vice-president Sudharmono and Ali Said, now both retired.

26   For a slightly ironic review of *Ikadin*'s history, see Era Hukum (1987: 212-14).

27   Not all practising advocates were quick to join IKADIN. As of late 1986, of 1125 advocates registered in the Ministry of Justice and practising in the jurisdiction of appellate courts (*Pengadilan Tinggi*) across the country, only 645 were enrolled as members of IKADIN (Era Hukum, 1987: 240). The Ministry of Justice brought compelling pressure to bear, however, both by requiring registration of all practising lawyers and refusing it before registrants joined IKADIN. At about the same time, it imposed quotas, like those for the notariat, on the number of advocates for each major city. Jakarta lawyers especially had to search for cities nearby with vacancies. Still, the Ministry failed to squeeze all practising lawyers into IKADIN. Although the initial plan was to incorporate both advocates and *pengacara praktek* – 'practical lawyers', including *pokrol bambu* – advocates predictably objected and won on the issue. In early 1988 the Ministry approved a separate organisation established for *pengacara praktek*, the *Ikatan Penasehat Hukum Indonesia* (Indonesian Legal Advisors Association, IPHI). See Indonesia Reports (1988: 27). Consulting lawyers, distancing themselves from advocates, also were allowed to create their own organisation.

In the meantime Ismail Saleh and Ali Said undertook to surround the profession with a fence of disciplinary requirements, which advocates contested fiercely. By any reasonable legal standard, the official actions were egregiously messy. The criteria applied, however, were not legal but political, in which case the administration had all the advantages.

An ad hoc opportunity to move against the advocacy, and a particularly bothersome advocate, arose in 1986, when Adnan Buyung Nasution, founder of the LBH, committed a breach of etiquette in the trial of Lt Gen Dharsono (ret) for subversive complicity in the Tanjung Priok riots of September 1984. What followed was unprecedented, and clumsy, as the Minister and judicial officials, eager to make an example of Nasution, made up the rules as they went, oblivious to the least subtle legal questions.[28] A provision from a new law (No 2 of 1986 on the Lower Courts) was applied ex post facto. Ismail Saleh accused Nasution of contempt of court, a concept quite absent from Indonesian (and civil law) procedure.[29] A first instance judge, without hearing Nasution, handed down an awkward 'administrative decision' – which he later called a 'report' although he had granted Nasution a right to appeal from it (to whom was never made clear) – recommending that the Minister of Justice revoke the advocate's certification. *Ikadin* leaders, denying the government's sole authority to punish its members, insisted that the association would handle the matter itself. The ethics board of the Jakarta branch of *Ikadin* heard the case and recommended a reprimand for Nasution. But Ismail Saleh refused to be preempted. Setting aside even the limited (and in principle inapplicable) requirements of the law, and ignoring protests from *Ikadin* and abroad, he revoked Nasution's registration for a period of one year.[30]

A coup de grace aimed at the advocacy followed. In July 1987 the Minister of Justice and Chairman of the *Mahkamah Agung* issued a 'joint decision' on procedures for supervising and regulating legal counsel.[31] The two officials construed Art 54(4) of Law No 2 of 1986 to allow the judiciary far reaching supervisory authority over private practitioners for the sake of 'guiding and developing' the profession. A fundamental purpose of this supervision appears in Art 3(c) of the document, which provides that measures can be taken against legal counsel who 'act, behave, bear themselves, speak or issue statements that indicate

---

28 Nasution's case is dealt with briefly in Lev (1986: 4-5). Nasution, the founder of the Legal Aid Institute and a fiery, outspoken and occasionally grandstanding critic of the government, was an ideal target, for damaging someone of his reputation might give all other activist advocates pause.

29 Contempt of court is mentioned in passing, in English, in the general considerations of the elucidation to Law No 14 of 1985 (on the *Mahkamah Agung*) at p 4 where it is recommended that a law be drafted to provide for measures to be taken against acts undermining the authority or dignity of the courts. Ismail Saleh had no legal grounds at all to level the charge against Nasution. There is irony in the issue, however, for in earlier years advocates were the first to wonder whether the common law concept might help to strengthen the courts and assure efficient execution of judgments. But in the hands of the judicial bureaucracy the notion of contempt took a nasty turn, appealing to judges as a weapon to be used against critics, advocates above all.

30 Nasution later sued the Minister of Justice, on grounds, inter alia, that the law (No 2 of 1986) had been applied *ex post facto*. Predictably, the case was thrown out by the South Jakarta *Pengadilan Negeri* (State Court, the court of first instance), in part on the significant reasoning that the ex post facto rule did not apply to administrative law in which public interest is the governing consideration (Kompas, 1988).

31 KMA/005/SKB/VII/1987- M.03-PR.08.05 of 1987. On 25 November 1987 the *Mahkamah Agung* issued a circular (No 8 of 1987) with an elucidation of the joint decision and instructions for implementing it.

lack of respect for the law, statutes, public authority, the courts, or their officials'. For the rest, the joint decision essentially removed disciplinary authority from the advocates' association to the judiciary and the Ministry of Justice, vitiating the profession's claim to autonomy.

Advocates sent up an outraged howl of protest, attacking the joint decision as an unlawful attempt to destroy their independence, to reverse the entire history of the profession and silence them forever. Despite support for the profession from other groups including, of course, legal aid circles and the press, legal officials stood their ground. At hearings of Parliamentary Commission III on a new Bill governing legal assistance, 40 advocates, led by Harjono Tjitrosubeno, showed up to protest quietly with T-shirt messages. Members of the Parliamentary Commission were sympathetic and challenged the government position represented by Ismail Saleh who eventually conceded that the joint decision might give way to a new law but otherwise, like Ali Said, stonewalled criticism. Insisting that the joint decision would be administered impartially, he nevertheless made clear that the government intended to have its way against the advocacy. Later in the year advocates were denied police permission to hold a retreat to discuss the issue.

On 12 July, in reaction to the joint decision, *Ikadin* issued a hurried defence that made the case for professional independence:

> The special character of the advocate and the profession of advocacy, recognised universally in various international conferences and declarations, lies in autonomy ...
>
> [I]n this joint decision no freedom is left to legal counsel, for every act, attitude, and expression is under the control and authority of the chairmen of the first instance courts, the chairmen of the appellate courts, the chairman of the *Mahkamah Agung*, and the Minister of Justice. ...
>
> [T]he wide authority vested by this joint decision [in the courts and Ministry] will cause legal counsel to lose moral courage to carry out their functions in and out of court in accord with the free and autonomous character of their profession. In turn legal counsel will always posture and proceed only according to the taste and whim of the judge, which will greatly damage those who seek justice in particular and legal development in general (Dewan Pimpinan Pusat Ikatan Advokat Indonesia,1987).

Thereafter the administration was unrelenting in its effort to tame the lawyers, whose main advantage by then lay in latent resources of unruliness, disorder and disunity. The details are unnecessary here but in short the Ministry of Justice, hoping to eliminate the influence of the *Peradin* group, later supported its own candidate for the chairmanship of *Ikadin*, setting off a conflict in the organisation that led in early 1991 to an embarrassing incident in which members of the rival factions came to unlawyerly (and largely incompetent) blows (Tempo, 1990). To the astonishment and dismay of the Minister whose purpose all along had been to unite and control the advocacy, *Ikadin* promptly split into two organisations, one more or less amenable to official bidding, the other, the old *Peradin* group, still defiant. When last heard from on the issue of advocates, not long before he retired, the Minister was said to be disgusted with the lot.

Lawyers and Change

It is not the end of the matter. If the battle of the lawyers were merely a sideshow in Indonesian politics, it might be, but the conflict is at the centre of a struggle over the political and ethical dimensions of the Indonesian state.

Private lawyers, more consistently than most, have long challenged the terms of Indonesian political organisation. They are among those most often accused of having lost touch with Indonesian culture, of being too 'Westernised', the imprecation generally levelled against those who question the habits of authority. There is some truth in the charge. By education, training and function, advocates trace their role back through the European middle ages, not to an Indonesian historical prototype – *Ikadin*'s motto, like *Peradin*'s, is *Fiat Justitia Ruat Coelum*, Let Justice be Done though the Heavens Fall. But is any national political structure, including the state itself, the bureaucracy, party or army without the historical stamp of European intervention? What is more to the point is that the uses of advocacy, the support for the ideas of private lawyers and the impact of the legal aid movement set off by *Peradin* are the result not of European influence but of distinctly Indonesian claims. Economic and social change in Indonesia has by now produced enough social power and ideological equipment to sustain a long argument over the limits of state authority.

In the debate thus far, state leaders have had the power to ward off challenges, but their ideological defences are crumbling. Even officials, both military and civilian, have to admit (and do, increasingly) that corruption and abuse of authority are at levels that cannot be dismissed as trivial and that it is getting harder – not impossible by any means, or even all that difficult yet, just harder – to buy the support of a middle class that is growing doubtful about the existing state.

None of this means that the lawyers are close to success, or even, for that matter, that they are key players in the political drama. But the reformers among them provide the ideological rationalisations for political change, as indeed lawyers have elsewhere through much of modern history. Legal systems, as they actually work, record essential codes of political relationship and authority. Indonesia's political codes, no less outmoded than legal ones from the colony, cannot be maintained without too high a price for both regime and state. A small pride of professional advocates has had remarkable influence in framing the debates over legal and political change, and is likely to pursue them long into the future.

References

Abdurrahman, 1980, *Aspek-Aspek Bantuan Hukum di Indonesia* (Aspects of Legal Assistance in Indonesia), Cendana Press, Jakarta.

Anderson, BRO'G, 1972, 'The Idea of Power in Javanese Culture' in Holt, C (ed), *Culture and Politics in Indonesia*, Cornell Press, Ithaca: 1-71.

Alting, JH Carpentier, 1926, *Grondslagen der Rechtsbedeeling in Nederlandsch-Indie*, Martinus Nijhoff, Hague.

Bourchier, D, 1988, 'Crime, Law and State Control in Indonesia' in Budiman, Arief (ed), *State and Civil Society in New Order Indonesia*, Centre for Southeast Asian Studies, Melbourne: 177-214.

Dewan Pimpinan Pusat Ikatan Advokat Indonesia, 1987, *Pernyataan Pendirian Ikadin atas Keputusan Bersama Ketua Mahkamah Agung dan Menteri Kehakiman Republik Indonesia tentang Tata Cara Pengawasan, Penindakan dan Pembelaan Diri Penasihat Hukum*, 12 July.

Dwipayana, G and Ramadhan, KH, 1988, *Otobiografi*, Citra Lamtoro Gung Persada, Jakarta, 1988.

Era Hukum, 1987, *Laporan Satu Tahun Berdirinya Ikadin 10 Nopember 1985-10 Nopember 1986* (First year report on the establishment of *Ikadin*, 10 Nov 1985-10 Nov 1986), November: 212ff.

Feith, H and Castles, L, 1970, *Indonesian Political Thinking 1945-1965*, Ithaca, Cornell University Press.

ICJ, 1987, *Indonesia and the Rule of Law: Twenty Years of 'New Order' Government*, Frances Pinter, London.

Indonesia Reports, 1988, November: 27, citing *Editor*, 1988, 23 July.

Kompas, 1988, 22 July, from *Indonesia Reports*, 1988, vol 36, November: 26-27.

Lev, DS, 1973a, *Bush-lawyers in Indonesia: Stratification, Representation, and Brokerage* (Berkeley: Center for the Study of Law and Society, working paper no 1).

Lev, DS, 1973b, 'Judicial Unification in Post-Colonial Indonesia', *Indonesia*, October: 1-39.

Lev, DS, 1976, 'Origins of the Indonesian Advocacy', *Indonesia*, vol 21, April: 135-69.

Lev, DS, 1978, 'Judicial Authority and the Struggle for an Indonesian Rechtsstaat', *Law and Society* Review, vol 13: 37.

Lev, DS, 1985, 'Colonial Law and the Genesis of the Indonesian State', *Indonesia*, vol 40, October: 57-75.

Lev, DS, 1986, 'Adnan Buyung Nasution, Indonesian Civil Rights Lawyer Under Attack', *Human Rights Internet Reporter*, vol 11, no 2, June: 4-5.

Lev, DS, 1987, *Legal Aid in Indonesia* (Monash University Southeast Asian Studies, Working Paper no 44).

Lubis, Todung Mulya Lubis, 1993, *In Search of Human Rights: Legal-Political Dilemmas of Indonesia's New Order, 1966-1990*, Gramedia, Jakarta, SPES.

Peradin, 1978, *Album Kongres V Peradin* (privately published).

Mangkuto, Jamaluddin Dt Singo, 1973, 'Masa Depan Professi Advokat di Indonesi' (The Future of the Profession of Advocacy in Indonesia) in *Penataran Pengacara Muda se-Indonesia*, April: 34-48.

Moertono, Soemarsaid, 1968, *State and Statecraft in Old Java*, Ithaca, CMIP.

Nasution, Adnan Buyung, 1992, *The Aspiration for Constitutional Government in Indonesia: A Socio-legal Study of the Indonesian Konstituante 1956-1959*, CIP-Gegevens Koninklijke Bibliotheek, The Hague.

Nusantara, Abdul Hakim G, Pangaribuan, Luhut MP and Mas Achmad Santosa, 1986, *Studi Kasus Hukum Acara Pidana* (Case Studies in Criminal Procedure), Djambatan, Jakarta.

Prodjohamidjojo, Martiman, 1982, *Penasihat dan Bantuan Hukum Indonesia: Latar Belakang dan Sejarahnya* (Indonesian legal Counsel and Assistance: Its Background and History), Ghalia Indonesia, Jakarta.

Regeerings Almanac, 1941/II: 156-59.

Sastrayuddha, 1971, 'Hambatan-hambatan bagi Advokat dalam melaksanakan tugasnja' (Difficulties for advocates in performing their functions), *Hukum dan Keadilan*, vol 2, no 5, July/August: 17-27.

Silaban, Sintong; Aldentua Siringoringo, & Susy Mahyudiarni Devianty, 1992, *Advokat Muda Indonesia: Dialog tentang Hukum, Politik, Keadilan, Hak Asasi Manusia, Profesionalisme Advokat dan Liku-liku Keadvokatan* (Young Advocates in Indonesia: Dialogues on Law, Politics, Justice, Human Rights, Professionalism, and Intricacies of the Advocacy) Pustaka Sinar Harapan, Jakarta.

Simanjuntak, Marsillam, 1989, *Unsur Hegelian dalam Pandangan Negara Integralistik* (Hegelian Elements in the Integralistic View of the State) (Thesis submitted to the University of Indonesia Faculty of Law)

Sutherland, Heather, 1979, *The Making of a Bureaucratic Elite*, Heinemann, Singapore.

Tasrif, Suardi, 1971, *Menegakkan Rule of Law dibawah Orde Baru* (Consolidating the rule of law under the New Order), *Peradin*, Jakarta.

Tempo, 1979, 21 April: 17

Tempo, 1990, 4 August.

Ter Harr, B, 1948, *Adat Law in Indonesia*, IPR, New York.

't Hart, AC and Nusantara, Abdul Hakim G., 1986, *Hukum Acara Pidana dalam Perspektif Hak Asasi Manusia* (Criminal Procedure in the Perspective of Human Rights) YLBHI and LBH-Jakarta, Jakarta.

Wirjanto, Soemarno P, 1971, 'Fungsi dan organisasi Advokat', *Hukum dan Keadilan*, vol 2, no 5, July/August: 27-33.

Wirjanto, Soemarno P, 1979, *Profesi Advokat*, Alumni, Bandung.

Yamin, Muhammad,1959, *Naskah-Persiapan Undang-Undang Dasar 1945* (Preparatory Documents of the 1945 Constitution) Prapantja, Jakarta.

Yap Thiam Hien, 1973, 'Hukum Acara Pidana' (Criminal Procedure) in *Penataran Pengacara Muda se-Indonesia*, April: 8-16

17. The *Eksekusi* of the *Negara Hukum*: Implementing Judicial Decisions in Indonesia

Simon Butt

In its first Five-Year Development Plan (*Repelita*)[1] of 1969/70, the Indonesian People's Consultative Council (MPR)[2] set out how it envisaged the operation of law in Indonesia would change under the New Order government. The constitutionally enshrined[3] *negara hukum* (literally, 'law state') was described as consisting of three basic principles: formal and substantial legality; an independent judiciary; and recognition and protection of fundamental human rights.

This chapter will focus on the principle of judicial independence. It will examine how, apparently under the weight of government pressure, the *Mahkamah Agung*[4] has manipulated a lacuna into the law by which judicial decisions are implemented or executed (*pelaksanaan eksekusi putusan*).[5] In several recent cases, the court has been prepared to thwart the effect of its own decisions by 'recommending' that they not be implemented. This, combined with allegations that corruption,[6] collusion[7] and government interference[8] are prevalent during the judicial decision-making process, has prompted much of Indonesian society to lose any remaining faith[9] in courts they have been reluctant to use for many years.

To be truly independent, the judiciary must not only hand down impartial decisions. It must also be able to enforce its decisions. If judicial decisions are treated with contempt, the *negara hukum* cannot exist. The principle of legality will

---

1   *Rencana Pembangunan Lima Tahun*
2   *Majelis Permusyawaratan Rakyat*.
3   See the General Elucidation to the 1945 Constitution.
4   Supreme Court, Indonesia's highest court.
5   Literally, 'the implementation of the execution of a decision'. As we shall see, whilst there may be no express legal provisions directing that *Mahkamah Agung* decisions to be implemented, it is strongly arguable that Art 2(1) of the Law on Judicial Power implicitly requires it.
6   Such allegations are commonplace in the Indonesian media. See, for example, Forum Keadilan (1991), Forum Keadilan (1992), Inside Indonesia (1997).
7   See, for example, Yasonna H Laoly (1996), Republika Online (1996a), Indonesia-L (1996b).
8   See, for example, Suara Pembaruan Online (1996a), Suara Pembaruan Online (1997a), Forum Keadilan (1996), Jakarta Post (1995).
9   Society's lack of faith in the judiciary is a commonly accepted and re-occurring theme in legal circles and the press. See, for example, Republika Online (1996b); Republika Online (1996c); Jawa Pos Online (1996a), Java Post Online (1996b), Kompas Online (1996a), Kompas Online (1996b), Kompas Online (1996c), Kompas Online (1997a), Tempo Interaktif (1996), Jakarta Post (1994).

be compromised if the government can ignore judicial determinations on the exercise of state law-making authority and activity.[10] Laws that protect human rights will have no effect if the judiciary cannot enforce them.

The State of the Law and Ideal Implementation of Judicial Decisions [11]

Decisions in civil cases are enforced on the directive of the Chief Justice of the *Pengadilan Negeri* (State Court, the court of first instance) in which the dispute arose.[12] Before a decision can be implemented it must have 'certainty status' (*mempunyai kekuatan hukum yang tetap*), that is, it must be unreviewable by a higher court. Certainty status is attributed to decisions of the *Pengadilan Negeri* which have stood for 14 days without a request for an appeal to the *Pengadilan Tinggi* (High Court) being lodged. *Pengadilan Tinggi* decisions are said to have 'certainty status' if they are not appealed within three weeks in Java or Madura, or six weeks in the rest of Indonesia. Decisions of the *Mahkamah Agung*, the final court of appeal, also have 'certainty status' (Dermawan, 1986: 10).

After a decision of the court has achieved 'certainty status', the unsuccessful party can comply with the decision on its own initiative (*secara sukarela*). However, this rarely happens. The court is therefore often required to compel implementation of the decision (*dengan paksa*). This leaves it to the successful party to take the initiative to approach the court to have the decision implemented (Syahrani, 1988). The recalcitrant party is called before the Chief Justice of the *Pengadilan Negeri*, who should then direct that the decision be carried out within eight days.[13] The implementation of the decision is then supervised and enforced by the court clerk (*panitera*) or bailiff (*juru sita*) in accordance with the Chief Justice's directive.[14]

If the decision concerns the payment of money and is not implemented within eight days the court can take any chattels owned by the unsuccessful party. If the value of that property is insufficient to cover the amount owed, then land or fixtures can be taken as security for payment[15] and may be sold by auction if the debt is not repaid.[16] If the decision instructs the unsuccessful party to do something and that party refuses to act, the original decision will be altered to put a monetary value on the act.[17] That amount is then extracted in the same way as a debt.

10　See Lotulung (1997); Lev (1978); Indra (1987); Lubis (1991). For discussions on the operation of Indonesia's new administrative courts, see Quinn, Chapter 18; and Millie, Chapter 19; Bedner (1997a); Quinn (1994). For a colourful and lively discussion of the practical workings of these courts, see Bedner (1997b).

11　For summaries of the law of implementation of judicial decisions, see generally Subekti (1989: 130-38) and Muhamman (1990).

12　Article 195(1) *Reglemen Acara Perdata* (HIR); and Art 206(1) *Rechtsreglement Buiten gewesten* (RBg).

13　Article 192(2) HIR and Art 207(1) RBg.

14　Law on Judicial Power of 1970, Art 33(3).

15　Article 197(1) HIR and Art 208 RBg.

16　Article 200(1) HIR and Art 215(1) RBg.

17　Article 225(1) HIR and Art 259(1) RBg.

These provisions do not appear to work well in practice. A substantial number of *Mahkamah Agung* civil law decisions have been treated with contempt by unsuccessful parties (including the government), who have either refused to adhere to orders of the court, or have not responded until many years after the decision has been handed down (Indonesia-P, 1996; Kompas, 1993a).[18] Several factors contribute to this state of affairs. According to many recent reports, Indonesians generally hold judicial decisions in low regard. Unsuccessful parties may therefore be reluctant to comply with a court decision that they do not respect.

Additionally, the law on execution in civil matters is largely undeveloped.[19] First, no law establishes how long the court should take to call on the reluctant party to adhere to a decision after the successful party has requested that the decision be implemented. This often causes substantial delays in the execution of a decision (Dermawan, 1986: 60). Secondly, it appears that the Chief Justice of the *Pengadilan Negeri* can delay the execution of a decision for any reason (Dermawan, 1986: 61). Thirdly, it also appears that the *Mahkamah Agung* must direct the *Pengadilan Negeri* to implement its decisions. Without this directive, the *Pengadilan Negeri* will not implement the *Mahkamah Agung*'s decision. The *Mahkamah Agung* has on several occasions relied on this loophole to prevent cases being implemented when its decisions have gone against government interests. Specifically, the Chief Justice of the *Mahkamah Agung* has employed the power his court holds to supervise and advise all lower courts[20] to instruct the *Pengadilan Negeri* to either delay the implementation of, or effectively invalidate, its own decisions.

For example, in the *Kedung Ombo* case[21] the *Mahkamah Agung* ordered the government to pay a substantial amount of compensation to villagers whose land it had compulsorily acquired in order to build the Kedung Ombo dam. After waiting a substantial period for the government to comply with the decision, the villagers requested the court to compel the government to pay them the compensation. The government, however, requested that the implementation of the decision be delayed (Suara Pembaruan, 1994). On 8 October 1994 Chief Justice Purwoto granted a stay of implementation pending a review of the *Mahkamah Agung* decision by a

---

18 Gray (1985: 115) has described several cases which were not, or could not be, implemented. In one case, a man tried to have a squatter removed from his land and was successful in the *Mahkamah Agung* but the *Pengadilan Negeri* avoided ordering action on the decision. In another case, two Japanese businessmen were convicted of tax evasion and sentenced to two years' jail. However, apparently neither was imprisoned and at least one returned to work with the same company.

19 There is very little Indonesian legal academic work on the civil law dimension of contempt of court. Most scholarly writing on contempt of court appears to discuss its criminal elements (see, for example, Hamzah & Waluyo (1989)). This seems to reflect the undeveloped nature of the law of civil contempt.

20 According to Art 32 of the Law No 14, 1985 on the *Mahkamah Agung*, the *Mahkamah Agung*:
1. in implementing judicial power is to carry out the highest form of supervision over all types of courts;
2. is to supervise the behaviour and the actions of judges in all courts in carrying out their tasks; and
3. has the authority to give direction, reprimand, or warning to all courts when deemed necessary.

Subarticle (4) states that the supervision and authority referred to in subarticles (1) to (3) cannot reduce judicial independence in investigating and deciding a case.

21 Much has been written on the *Kedung Ombo* case. See eg Fitzpatrick (1997: 199-202); In the Name of Development (1995); and Forum Keadilan (1994b: 102 and 1994c: 102).

different panel of judges.[22] He took this action even though the Law on Judicial Power[23] and the Law on the *Mahkamah Agung*[24] stipulate that a review can only be heard regarding a decision which has 'certainty status'. As mentioned above, these decisions – of which a decision of the *Mahkamah Agung* is one – are the *only* decisions that, under Indonesian civil law, *can* be executed (Forum Keadilan, 1994a: 11). Therefore, the review should not have impeded execution.

The Execution of Administrative Court Decisions

Indonesia's newly-established administrative courts[25] have also found it difficult to 'persuade' the government to comply with some of their decisions in which government action has been declared invalid. The administrative courts require the executive's cooperation to enforce their orders (Quinn, 1994: 74-75). While the executive has often acted upon decisions of the administrative courts, it has not always complied with them and there has been conflict between the courts and the government over enforcement. In an illuminating article on the problems facing the administrative courts, Bedner (1997a: 200-203) points to dozens of press articles highlighting the problems these courts have had in enforcing their decisions against the government. He reports that the house of one judge was pelted with stones and rotten meat when he requested compliance from a government agency. In 1991 and 1992 alone, the Minister of Administrative Reform sent 19 letters to government departments which had refused to obey the orders of the court.[26]

---

22 The *Mahkamah Agung* review is set out in Varia Peradilan (1995b). The review, which took one month, was the fastest in the *Mahkamah Agung*'s history. The court usually takes at least 2-3 years to conduct such reviews (Republika, 1994). It is legal for the *Mahkamah Agung* to review its own decisions in the sphere of civil law (Law on the *Mahkamah Agung*, Art 34). This option, first available under *Mahkamah Agung* Regulation No 1 of 1969, was intended to provide an avenue for the review of court decisions made under the Old Order which conflicted with law or were influenced by extra-judicial forces (Tasrif, 1971). This review process has, however, become an 'invariably' requested channel by which aggrieved parties (including the government) have challenged *Mahkamah Agung* decisions made after 1966 (Jakarta Post, 1995: 1). Indeed, the process seems to have extended to the review of criminal law decisions. Muchtar Pakpahan, an outspoken critic of the government was acquitted by the *Mahkamah Agung*. Dissatisfied, the government requested the court to review the acquittal. The *Mahkamah Agung* sentenced the accused to four years' jail (Mahkamah Agung Review No 55/K/Pid/1996). However, to the credit of the court, the review process has not always been used exclusively to further government interests. See the *Ohee* case, below.

23 Article 21.

24 Article 34.

25 The administrative courts were established by Law No 5 of 1986 and implemented with Government Regulation No 7 of 1991

26 Cf Quinn, Chapter 18. According to Bedner (1997a: 203), the established procedure to attempt to obtain compliance is for the applicant to approach the court which heard the case at first instance and request it to contact the superior of the defendant. If this does not result in compliance, the judge will appeal to the President. Bedner states that this has happened twice, but unfortunately does not report on the outcome of these requests.

The Hanoch Hebe Ohee Land Case

The most controversial recent instance of the *Mahkamah Agung* delaying the execution of its own decision is the *Ohee* Case. The Chief Justice of the *Mahkamah Agung* 'permanently delayed' the execution of the court's order by sending a letter to the Head of the Jayapura *Pengadilan Negeri* 'recommending' that the decision not be implemented.

The 62 hectares of land in dispute in Sentani, Jayapura, was communally owned by the Ongge and Ohee clans according to local *adat* (traditional) law. It was taken over by Allied troops in 1945-47. When the Dutch returned, they made a verbal agreement to lease it for 10 years, but never paid the amount agreed upon. In 1969, the territory was reintegrated into the administration of the Republic of Indonesia and the ownership of all Dutch assets in Irian Jaya was transferred to the Indonesian government's representatives in Irian Jaya. No mention was made in the Dutch-Indonesian agreement (the New York Agreement of 1962) of this land as traditional land occupied by the government. This meant that it was still regarded as land owned by the clan.

When in 1984 the Irian Jayan government expropriated this land, Hanoch Hebe Ohee successfully appealed to the Jayapura *Pengadilan Negeri* for more compensation than was initially offered. He argued that the compensation had been calculated under the assumption that the land was state-owned. The court agreed that the oral agreement for the lease of the land was valid, thus proving the clan's ownership of the land. The Irian Jayan *Pengadilan Tinggi* upheld this decision on appeal.[27]

In 1985, the *Mahkamah Agung* heard the case on cassation and overturned the *Pengadilan Tinggi* decision. In stark contrast to the lower courts, it held that under the New York Agreement, where the Indonesian Government agreed to pay 600 million guilders to Holland as compensation for Dutch land 'acquired' in Indonesia, the 62 hectare property in dispute was transferred to the state (Varia Peradilan, 1995a: 23). However, in 1988 the *Mahkamah Agung* reviewed its own decision and upheld Hanoch's claim. The court ordered the Governor of Irian Jaya to pay Rp 18.6 billion (approximately AUD\$2,480,000 in June 1998) in compensation for the loss of the use of the land (Forum Keadilan, 1995d: 99).

The Irian Jayan provincial government refused to pay this sum, stating that it was not a matter of having the funds to pay the compensation, but a matter of rights (Forum Keadilan, 1995a: 92). It maintained that the reasoning of the 1985 *Mahkamah Agung* decision was correct, that is, that the land had been transferred to the state by the Dutch. After waiting three years for the government to act on the judgment, the plaintiff requested the *Mahkamah Agung* to order the Jayapura *Pengadilan Negeri* to implement the decision. In response, the Irian Jayan Governor requested that the execution of the decision be delayed on the grounds that he had to consult with his superior, the Minister of Internal Affairs. The Governor met with the Minister, arguing that the compensation should be the responsibility of the central government. The Governor then applied to *Mahkamah Agung* Chief Justice, Soerjono, for a stay of execution so that the matter could be taken over by the Minister. The Interior Ministry studied the case, and said it was 'consulting' with the *Mahkamah Agung* (Forum Keadilan, 1995a: 92).

---

27   Decision No 21/Pdt/1985/*Pengadilan Tinggi*.Jpr, 27 November 1985.

Perhaps as a result of this consultation, in early April 1995 the Chief Justice of the *Mahkamah Agung*, Soerjono, issued a letter (*surat sakti*) addressed to the Chief Justice of the Jayapura *Pengadilan Negeri*. The letter essentially overturned the previous decision of the *Mahkamah Agung*, stating that:

> because the party required to pay compensation to the plaintiffs is the Governor of Irian Jaya … who is not a public legal entity (not having his own funds), *Mahkamah Agung* Decision No 381 PK/Pdt/1989 cannot be executed.[28]

The relevant defendant should have been the Irian Jayan government, which was the legal entity (*badan hukum*) holding the land in question. The Chief Justice stated later that his letter to the Jayapura Court was only 'advice' and not legally binding and that the decision of *Mahkamah Agung* in question still stood. The Governor remained liable to pay compensation, and the decision was final because it could not be appealed. The letter, he said, only expressed his opinion that the decision could not be implemented (Forum Keadilan, 1995b: 97). However, in the hierarchical structure of the civil service the letter was just as effective as a judicial decision (Indonesia-L, 1996a). The Jayapura Chief Justice said he would 'reluctantly obey' the Chief Justice of the *Mahkamah Agung* (Forum Keadilan, 1995d: 100).

The letter (or, more accurately, decision) can be criticised on several grounds. First, Chief Justice Soerjono later attempted to justify his decision by stressing that the defendant was an administrative official and not a public legal entity (which, in this case, should have been the provincial government). Thus, he could not be the defendant in a civil case such as this. However, many observers have condemned this approach on legal grounds. Governments are public legal bodies and governors are the representatives of provincial governments. According to the Law on Regional Government, '[t]he head of the region represents his or her region in and out of court'.[29] Regional governors are not simply individuals but heads of provinces empowered to represent the local people. Thus, the Governor was an appropriate defendant.

Secondly, even if we assume that the letter was sound on legal grounds, Art 32 of the Law on the *Mahkamah Agung* quoted above does not seem broad enough to allow the court to re-evaluate and re-interpret its own 'final' decisions and to 'fill in the gaps' on the law of execution by correspondence. The Law implies that the *Mahkamah Agung* is to play a supervisory role and to notify a local court if it believes it has acted improperly but not effectively to overturn the decision. Furthermore, the *Mahkamah Agung* is the highest court in the land. It is, therefore, doubtful that this law could be construed to permit the Chief Justice to supervise the *Mahkamah Agung* in this manner. Assuming that the Chief Justice has the legal authority to do this, a more appropriate action in Indonesian legal culture would have been for him to have sent a written reprimand to the responsible *Mahkamah Agung* judges for their 'errors'.

Thirdly, according to the Law on Judicial Power of 1970 the main role of the judge is to accept, investigate, adjudicate and settle or complete (*menyelesaikan*) cases that come before the court.[30] Arguably the judicial role is therefore not fulfilled merely when the decision is handed down but requires that the decision be enforced. Conversely, interfering with the implementation of a court decision could be seen as a breach of the law.

---

28   Letter of the Chief Justice of the *Mahkamah Agung* No KMA/126/IV/1995.

29   Law No 5 of 1974 on the Principles of Regional Government, Art 23(1).

30   Article 2(1).

Fourthly, it has been mentioned that before composing the letter, the Chief Justice met with the government to discuss the decision. The independence of the judiciary was thereby compromised – in appearance, at the very least.

It is likely the government interfered to avoid the flood of cases that could have resulted if the decision had been successfully implemented. According to Irian Jayan Land Office Chief, JS Serpara, there are over 80 cases similar to Hanoch's. He fears all the land passed to the Indonesian Government by the Dutch Government in 1962 may be lost to private hands (Forum Keadilan, 1995d: 99).

Indeed, the *Mahkamah Agung* has heard an almost identical case and resolved it in the same way.[31] Soccer coach Fistus C Yom took a dispute between himself and the Governor and the Head of the Regional Land Affairs Office to the Jayapura District Court. At issue was the appropriation of his land for an Air Force base. Again the land was formerly leased by the Dutch. He demanded compensation. He was unsuccessful at first instance and on appeal but the *Mahkamah Agung* held that he was entitled to compensation. Dissatisfied with the decision, the government lodged an appeal for a review of the decision. The *Mahkamah Agung* accepted this appeal but upheld its previous decision, requiring the government to pay Fistus compensation.

Still dissatisfied, the Head of the Jayapura Land Affairs Office, Soni Harsono, wrote a letter to the Chief Justice of the *Mahkamah Agung*, asking that the execution of the decision be delayed. He argued that the land was communal, and thus could be transferred to the state.[32] He also argued that the land should be governed under the Law on Land Reform (Law No 56 Perpu 1960), which restricts individual land ownership. The letter also expressed Harsono's fears that a flood of similar cases would inundate the courts if the decision was implemented. Chief Justice Gandasubrata agreed to delay execution, and, as occurred in Hanoch's case, sent a letter to the Jayapura District Court, stating that the decision could not be executed because the defendant was not a legal entity with its own funds.

Surat Sakti

It appears *surat sakti* letters are a commonplace. In May 1995, after retiring from the *Mahkamah Agung* bench, Gandasubrata stated:

> We [the *Mahkamah Agung*] often receive requests from the government to cancel or delay the execution of a *Mahkamah Agung* ruling in the name of development (The Australian, 1995).

According to the daily newspaper *Kompas* (1993b),[33] the validity of these *surat sakti* has been subject to legal challenge. RJ Kaptin Adisumarta was aggrieved by a *surat sakti* issued by the then Chief Justice, Gandusbrata, again, delaying the implementation of a land dispute decision. He instigated legal proceedings against the Chief Justice in the Jakarta Administrative Court.

In a preliminary hearing, Administrative Court Chief Justice Benyamin Mangkoedilaga dismissed the claim because, he argued, *surat sakti* were judicial decisions, not administrative ones, and therefore administrative courts lacked

---

31 See Forum Keadilan (1995c: 102-103).

32 See Haverfield, Chapter 4; and Fitzpatrick (1997: 180-82; 186-87)

33 The author is indebted to Julian Millie for this reference.

jurisdiction to hear disputes arising from them. The decision is disappointing (especially from Mangkoedilaga, the judge now well known for his courageous decision in the *Tempo* case). Although the judiciary is said to be independent from government and other non-judicial influence (Law on Judicial Power, Art 4(3); MPR Decree No II/MPR/1978, Art 11) judges are required to be civil servants (*pegawai negeri*) (Law Concerning the General Courts, Art 14(i)(e)). They must be members of KORPRI (Public Servant Corps of the Republic of Indonesia),[34] and, as such, must support government policy (Asia Watch, 1988: 170).[35] In essence, then, judges are part of the wider bureaucracy. Ironically, *surat sakti* which uphold government interests are probably better seen as administrative (or executive), not judicial, decisions.

Because *surat sakti* are the only type of unreviewable judicial decisions in Indonesia, they are therefore the only judicially proclaimed decisions with real 'certainty status'.[36] *Surat sakti* appear to have become institutionalised to form the final stage of an impractical five-tier judicial system. A case may begin at the *Pengadilan Negeri*, be appealed to the *Pengadilan Tinggi*, heard on cassation in the *Mahkamah Agung*, reviewed by the *Mahkamah Agung* and then be subject to the Chief Justice's self-instigated mandate to veto the decision (most likely in response to pressure from non-judicial forces). In these circumstances it is hardly surprising that Indonesians are losing faith in the judiciary: obtaining final resolution in the courts is now more costly and time-consuming[37] than ever before.

Conclusion

The Indonesian press has perhaps been the most often-used forum for the *negara hukum* debate. The government has been openly and rightly criticised for its interference in judicial processes. Yet one gets the impression that the judiciary has, generally speaking and probably unfairly, shouldered more of the blame for ceding to government interests. The press seems to concentrate more on the dwindling confidence Indonesian society has in the courts rather than the pressure the government puts on judges. Perhaps by encouraging the media to portray the judiciary as untrustworthy, the government (at least partially) seeks to legitimise its interference with and subordination of the *Mahkamah Agung*.

The existence of cases which are impossible, or at least very difficult, to enforce serves to undermine greatly the claim that Indonesia is a *negara hukum*. The implementing stage of judicial processes provides another means for government interference in court decisions, thus contradicting the independence of the judiciary, an important element in the *negara hukum*. These cases also serve to undermine the

---

34 See Presidential Decree No 82, 1971 concerning KORPRI.

35 Recalcitrant judges can be reprimanded under Government Regulation No 30, 1980 on the Regulations for Disciplining Civil Servants.

36 A telephone call from the Chief Justice of the *Mahkamah Agung* to the Chief Justice of the *Pengadilan Negeri* in which the case arose is often an effective substitute for a *surat sakti* (Kompas, 1993a).

37 The *Mahkamah Agung*'s case backlog was estimated at 17,599 cases in 1997 (Jakarta Post, 1997) and increases by approximately 50-100 cases per month (Suara Pembaruan Online, 1996b).

principle of legality. The law has no effect if its final arbiter, the courts, cannot or do not have their will imposed and the law upheld.

References

Adji, Oemar Seno 1979, 'An Indonesian Perspective on the American Constitutional Influence' in Beer, L (ed), *Constitutionalism in Asia: Asian Views of the American Influence*, University of California Press, Berkeley.

The Australian, 1995, 'Ex-Chief Justice talks of Pressure on Courts', May 30.

Bedner, A, 1997, 'Administrative Courts in an Executive-Dominated State: The Case of Indonesia' in Zhang, Y (ed), *Comparative Studies on the Judicial Review System in East and Southeast Asia*, Kluwer Law International, The Hague.

Dermawan, I Gede, 1986, *Laporan Penelitian: Eksekusi Perkara Perdata Dalam Praktek* (Research Report: The Execution of Civil Cases in Practice), Fakultas Hukum Universitas Udayana.

Fitzpatrick, D, 1997, 'Disputes and Pluralism in Modern Indonesian Land Law', *Yale Journal of International Law*, vol 22: 171.

Forum Keadilan, 1991, 'Dagang Hukum tanpa Malu-malu (Legal "Trading", without Shame)', 17 September.

Forum Keadilan, 1992, 'Menyiasati Musabab Dagang Hukum' (Investigating the 'Trade' of the Law), 17 September.

Forum Keadilan, 1994a, 'Keadilan' (Justice), 15 November: 11.

Forum Keadilan, 1994b, 'Harapan Tenggelam di Kedung Ombo' (Hopes Drown in Kedung Ombo), 24 November: 26.

Forum Keadilan, 1994c, 'Kedung Ombo, Balik ke Titik Nol' (Kedung Ombo, Back to Square One), 8 December.

Forum Keadilan, 1995a, 'MA: Surat Pembatalannya' (The *Mahkamah Agung*: Its 'Overturning' Letter), 27 April: 92.

Forum Keadilan, 1995b, 'Dampak Surat Sakti Ketua?' (The Impact of the Chief Justice's Letter?), 11 May: 97.

Forum Keadilan, 1995c, 'Wibawa Mahkamah Setelah "Sukma" Soerjono' (The Authority of the *Mahkamah Agung* after Soerjono's Letter), 11 May: 99.

Forum Keadilan, 1995d, 'Fistus "Disalib" Sebelum Hanoch' (Fistus 'Crucified' before Hanoch), 11 May: 102-103.

Forum Keadilan, 1996, 'Tempo dan Mahkamah' (Tempo and the *Mahkamah Agung*), 1 July.

Gautama, Sudargo and Hornick, R, 1983, *An Introduction to Indonesian Law: Unity in Diversity*, 3rd ed, Penerbit Alumni, Bandung.

Gray, CW, 1985, *Indonesian Public Administration: Policy Reform and the Legal Process,* Ann Arbor, Michigan.

Hamzah, Andi and Bambang Waluyo, 1989, *Delik-delik Terhadap Penyelenggaraan Peradilan (Contempt of Court)* (The Crimes of Contempt of Court), Sinar Grafika, Jakarta.

In the Name of Development: Human Rights and the World Bank in Indonesia, 1995, Lawyers Committee for Human Rights and the Institute for Policy Research and Advocacy, USA.

Indonesia-L, 1996a, 'High Court disappoints again', 14 June.

Indonesia-L, 1996b, 'Mereka Bicara: Prof Dr H Busthanul Arifin, SH: Di *Mahkamah Agung*, Malaikat Pun Akan Berkolusi' (They Speak: Professor Dr H Busthanul Arifin, LLB: In the *Mahkamah Agung*, Even an Angel would be involved in Collusion), 2 August.

Indonesia- P, 1996, 'Muladi: Banyak Eksekusi *Mahkamah Agung* Diabaikan Pihak yang Kalah' (Muladi: Many *Mahkamah Agung* Executions Ignored by the Defeated Party), 5 February.

Indra, Muhammad Ridhuran, 1987, *Kedudukan Lembaga-lembaga Negara dan Hak Menguji menurut Undang-undang Dasar 1945* (The Position of State Institutions and the Right to Review according to the 1945 Constitution), Sinar Grafika, Jakarta.

Inside Indonesia, 1997, 'Courting Corruption', January-March.

Jakarta Post, 1994, 'Oetojo admits legal abuse in judicial system', 12 December.

Jakarta Post, 1995, 'How Not to Interfere in a Judicial Process', 16 May.

Jakarta Post, 1997, 'Court can't Review Law says Oetojo', 4 June: 1

Jawa Pos Online, 1996a, 'Bismar Siregar; Keributan dan Citra *Mahkamah Agung*: "Ngeri kalau Dilakukan Debat Terbuka"' (Bismar Siregar, The Upheaval and the Image of the *Mahkamah Agung*: 'It is Frightening if there is to be an Open Debate'), 17 July.

Jawa Post Online, 1996b, 'Mendongkrak Kembali Wibawa *Mahkamah Agung*' (Revamping the Authority of the *Mahkamah Agung*), 5 November.

Kompas, 1996a, 'Putusan Bermasalah, Peradilan Disorot' (Problematic Decision, the Court is spotlighted), 4 June.

Kompas, 1996b, 'Aksi Mengontrol "Surat Sakti"' (Action to control 'surat sakh'), 4 June.

Kompas Online, 1996a, 'MA Dinilai Tidak Taati Asas Kedaulatan Rakyat' (*Mahkamah Agung* Evaluated to not Adhere to the Principle of Democracy), 27 May.

Kompas Online, 1996b, 'Di Antara Putusan Kontroversial' (Between Controversial Decisions), 13 July.

Kompas Online, 1996c, 'Majelis Kehormatan *Mahkamah Agung* yang Terlupakan' (The Forgotten Respect for the *Mahkamah Agung*), 16 August.

Kompas Online, 1997a, 'Ketua MA: Perbaikan Citra MA Melalui Pengurangan Tunggakan Perkara' (Chief Justice of the *Mahkamah Agung*: Improve the Image of the *Mahkamah Agung* by Reducing the Case Backlog), 3 February.

Kompas Online, 1997b, 'Pernyataan Kemandirian MA Masih Perlukan Pembuktian' (The Statement of the Independence of the MA needs to be Proven), 5 February.

Lev, DS, 1972, 'Judicial Institutions and Legal Culture in Indonesia' in Holt, C (ed), *Culture and Politics in Indonesia*, Cornell University Press, Ithaca, 1972.

Lev, D, 1978, 'Judicial Authority and The Struggle for An Indonesian Rechsstaat', *Law & Society Review*, vol 13: 37.

Lotulung, P, 'Judicial Review in Indonesia' in Zhang, Y (ed), *Comparative Studies on the Judicial Review System in East and Southeast As*, Kluwer Law International, The Hague, 1997.

Laoly, Yasonna H, 1996, 'Kolusi: Fenomena atau Penyakit Kronis' (Collusion: A Phenomenon or Chronic Disease) in Aldentua Siringoringo Tumpal Sihite (ed), *Menyingkap Kabut Peradilan Kita: Menyoal Kolusi di Mahkamah Agung* (Exposing the Haze of our Courts: Problemising Collusion in the *Mahkamah Agung*), Pustaka Forum Adil Sejahtera, Jakarta.

Lubis, Todung Mulya, 1993, *In Search of Human Rights: Legal-Political Dilemmas of Indonesia's New Order, 1966-1990*, PT Gramedia Pustaka Utama, Jakarta.

Lubis, Todung Mulya, 1991, 'Judicial Review Dalam Perspektif Hukum Tata Negara' (Judicial Review in the Perspective of Constitutional Law) in Benny K Harman Hendarti (ed), *Konstitusionalisme, Peranan DPR dan Judicial Review* (Constitutionalism, the Role of the DPR and Judicial Review), YLBHI, Jakarta.

Muhamman, Abdulkadir, 1990, *Hukum Acara Perdata Indonesia* (The Indonesian Law of Civil Procedure), PT Citra Aditya Bakti, Bandung.

Quinn, B, 1994, *The Administrative Review Act of 1986: Implications for Legal and Bureaucratic Culture* (Honours thesis, Faculty of Asian Studies, Australian National University, Canberra.

Republika, 1994, 'Batalnya Kasasi Kasus Kedung Ombo Apalagi harus Diperbuat Warga Kedungpring?' (The Overturning of the Kedung Ombo Cassation Hearing. What More Must the People of Kedungpring do?), 9 November.

Republika Online, 1996a, 'Hakim: Antara Independensi dan Kolusi' (Judges: Between Independence and Collusion), 15 April.

Republika Online, 1996b, 'Wawancara Trimoelja: *Mahkamah Agung* Memang sudah Bobrok' (Interview with Trimoelja: The *Mahkamah Agung* has indeed Degenerated), 21 April.

Republika Online, 1996c, 'Siapa yang Tepat Menggantikan Soerjono' (Who is Appropriate to Replace Soerjono), 26 July.

Suara Pembaruan, 1994, 'Tanpa Harus Tunggu PK Tergugat Eksekusi Putusan Kemenangan Rakyat Kedung Ombo Bisa Dilaksanakan' (Without Waiting for the Review the Successful Kedung Ombo People's Decision can be Implemented), 18 September.

Suara Pembaruan Online, 1996a, 'Mulya Lubis: Putusan PK MA Itu Tragedi Hukum' (Mulya Lubis: The Decision of the *Mahkamah Agung* Review is a Legal Tragedy), 22 November.

Suara Pembaruan Online, 1996b, 'Tajuk Rencana: Negara Hukum Bukan "Negara Undang-undang"', 14 November.

Suara Pembaruan Online, 1997a, 'Luhut: Peradilan Bukanlah Proses Musyawarah Mufakat' (Luhut: Court is not a Process of Deliberation and Consensus), 5 July.

Subekti, 1989, *Hukum Acara Perdata* (The Law of Civil Procedure), Binacipta, Bandung.

Syahrani, Riduan, 1988, *Hukum Acara Perdata di Lingkungan Peradilan Umum* (The Law of Civil Procedure in the General Courts), Pustaka Kartini, Jakarta.

Tasrif, S, 1971, *Menegakkan Rule of Law Dibawah Orde Baru* (Upholding the Rule of Law under the New Order), vol 1, Persatuan Advokat Indonesia (*Peradin*), Jakarta.

Tempo Interaktif, 1996, 'Memulihkan Muka MA Yang "Klejingan"' (Retrieving the Face of the *Mahkamah Agung* which is 'Shaken'), 29 November.

Varia Peradilan, 1995a, 'Kasus Tanah *Adat* Irian Jaya Surat Ketua MA' (The Irian Jayan Land Case: The Letter of the *Mahkamah Agung*), vol 112: 23.

Varia Peradilan, 1995b, 'Putusan Peninjauan Kembali Kasus Waduk Kedung Ombo' (The Review of the Kedung Ombo Dam Case), *Varia Peradilan*, vol 112: 24.

18. Indonesia: Patrimonial or Legal State?

The Law on Administrative Justice of 1986 in Socio-Political Context

Bernard Quinn

On 29 December 1986, Indonesia's then President Soeharto ratified Law No 5 of 1986 on Administrative Justice. For the first time, Indonesians were to have the right to challenge bureaucratic decision-making practices which were in breach of the principles of administrative law through the courts.

The appearance of administrative law in the Indonesian context was an enigma. The Soeharto government had consistently attempted to ensure that the constitutional checks on the exercise of the executive powers of government were disabled. The legislative processes are kept under tight government control through the careful engineering of an electoral system which minimises political awareness and participation. The judiciary is effectively part of the bureaucracy and possesses no powers of constitutional review. Its power to test the legality of subordinate legislation has never been used.

In this context, the Law on Administrative Justice raised two questions. First, could administrative law operate as an effective tool by which to introduce an ethos of legality into bureaucratic decision-making practices? Secondly, did the development of administrative law imply a shift in the balance of power within the Indonesian state from the executive to the judiciary; and through this from state to civil society?

The Enigma of Administrative Law in a Patrimonial State

Unlike the Soekarno regime before it, Soeharto's New Order demonstrated a marked concern for the formal legal legitimacy of its actions through an emphasis on the rhetoric and symbolism of constitutionalism and the rule of law. Under Soeharto, Indonesian public law theory focused upon the attempt to create a *negara hukum* (nation based on law). The concept of the *negara hukum* is analogous to the concept of the rule of law; however, the Indonesian government's version of the concept stresses that the *negara hukum* is to be maintained by reference not to

Western constitutional theories such as separation of powers but to Indonesian theories of state.[1]

Indonesian constitutional theory is founded upon the concept of the 'integralistic' state developed by *adat* law scholar Professor Raden Soepomo.[2] This model, which views the Indonesian republic as an organic unity modelled upon the traditional village unit, underpins the Constitution of 1945 of which he was the key drafter. The theory of the village republic holds that the interests of the individual are not merely subordinate to, but inherently consistent with, the interests of society as a whole. It is inconceivable that there could be conflict between the interests of state and the individual. This fundamental assumption is expressed by the Javanese phrase *manunggaling kawula lan gusti* – the unity of authority and people. The basal values of the social and political system are harmony, order, unity and totality, and the imperatives of maintaining these absolute values require strong government.

A principle fundamental to comprehending the integralistic state and the values underpinning it is that of *kekeluargaan*, the family principle, stressed by the nationalist and educator Ki Hadjar Dewantara. *Kekeluargaan* conceptualises the state as a family, with the government as father figure acting in the interests of the people and having unquestionable authority and unlimited discretion, in so doing. These principles are referred to in the preamble to most Indonesian legislation. It is therefore unsurprising that the Constitution of 1945 contains no specific indication of a doctrine of separation of powers. Nevertheless, a 'division' of the functions of government has been embodied in a resolution of the MPR or Peoples Consultative Assembly[3] which locates the source of the division as an implication from the structure of the Constitution (Wahyono, 1992). Yet in this version of the division of powers the executive remains supreme.

After coming to power in 1965, the Soeharto government implemented a corporatist strategy for channelling political participation away from less controllable political institutions such as political parties into various state-endorsed representative bodies (MacIntyre, 1991: 23). This process, supported ultimately by military power, resulted in government control over the political and electoral process and thus the legislature. Executive control over the legislative process has had a profound impact upon legislative style. Laws lack detail, often resembling vague policy statements. This apparent legal vacuum disguises the reality that laws passed by the legislature serve as guidelines for formulating and implementing regulations and decrees (Hartono, 1995: 8). The vast bulk of Indonesian law takes the form of constantly changing, interconnected and often conflicting governmental decrees and decisions, presidential decrees, directives and instructions, ministerial decisions and other forms of subordinate law made by the executive (Hartono, 1995: 8). This creates obvious difficulty and uncertainty in identifying the formal instrument under authority of which bureaucratic decisions are made.

Nor is the judiciary independent of the executive. The formal status of a judge is that of a civil servant appointed by the President. The Constitution of 1945 provides for a Supreme Court (the *Mahkamah Agung*) independent of the other arms of government. However, the review powers granted to the Supreme Court by the Law on Judicial Powers of 1970 are severely limited. Pursuant to Art 26(1) of that

---

1   Much of the scholarly work on *negara hukum* and its political implications has been done by Daniel Lev. This section draws heavily upon his contributions.

2   See Reeve (1990: 157); and Bourchier, Chapter 12.

3   *Majelis Permusyawaratan Rakyat.*

Law the Supreme Court (*Mahkamah Agung*) has no power of constitutional review and can only determine whether regulations, decrees, directives, instructions and other subordinate forms of law conflict with statute. Even then, if the court finds a subordinate law invalid, it has no power to quash it. Only the administrative agency which made the invalid law can rescind it. In any case, the Supreme Court has displayed a marked reluctance to exercise even those limited powers of review which it does possess,[4] a fact which should not be surprising given the status of judges as members of the bureaucracy.

As a result of the supremacy of the executive within the constitutional framework, the Indonesian administration has remained unaccountable to the legislature or the judiciary. This has resulted in what Weber described as patrimonial administrative practices. Bureaucrats struggle for the patronage of their superiors and for more clients for themselves. Consequently, administrative decisions often reflect, or are influenced by, the personal interests of more powerful bureaucrats rather than the application of formal legal rules and procedures. This contrasts to Weber's rational-legal model of administration, characterised by a separation of official and private interests in the mind of the bureaucrat; and a respect for formal rules and regulations in the administrative decision-making process. The development of the Indonesian bureaucracy has involved a gradual replacement of patrimonial characteristics by rational-legal traits. However, this process of change has not eradicated many of the patrimonial aspects of administration, leading Lev (1978: 40) to characterise it as an essentially patrimonial bureaucracy with gradually strengthening rational-legal influences.

While the enactment of the Law on Administrative Justice prima facie represents a fresh attempt by the Indonesian government to develop a more rational-legal approach to administrative decision-making, it is by no means the first attempt to do so. Reacting to public protest about the patrimonial tendencies and corruption within the bureaucracy, the Indonesian government has, over the years, attempted to impose a number of other controls upon modes of bureaucratic decision-making. These include judicial control through application of the anti-corruption laws by the general courts (Crouch, 1978: 294); top-down controls via special 'good conduct operations' carried out by the state security apparatus (formerly *Kopkamtib*, now *Bakorstanas*); and internal controls via Presidential and ministerial directives setting out decision-making codes of conduct. Each of these measures has met with only limited success. Their application has been marked by an inability to affect decision-making practices above the very lowest levels of the administration. The lowest level administrators have effectively acted as a buffer, absorbing the sanctions which the public demand while protecting the real power-holders. In the absence of a strong legal culture these challenges to patrimonialism in the past have been largely symbolic. This raises the question of whether the Law on Administrative Justice is a measure more likely to encourage genuine administrative reform.

The preamble to the Law on Administrative Justice describes the general position of administrative law within the context of the theory of Indonesian law and state developed by the Soeharto government. While emphasising the shared interests of government and society, the need for harmonious relations between the two and the way in which government policy necessarily represents the public interest, the Law inherently acknowledges – by introducing the very concept of

---

4   An example is the *Prioritas* case. See Tempo (1993).

administrative law – that public and individual interests may diverge. This was probably the first time that the New Order government recognised in law that there are individual, protectable interests which may conflict with the interests of the community as a whole as expressed by government policy.

The Preamble to the Law on Administrative Justice identifies two specific objectives of the administrative law courts. First, the courts must protect individual interests from injury by government decisions. Secondly, through doing this, the courts must facilitate the development of 'efficient, effective, clean and authoritative' administrative organs. Essentially, this second broad objective implies the elimination of corrupt and patrimonial administrative decision-making.

Prima facie, therefore, the Law offers some potential for the protection of private interests and the resulting development of a culture of legality and rationality in administrative decision-making. Whether this potential is realised depends upon three related factors. The first is the extent to which the Administrative Courts are willing to enforce the provisions of the Law on Administrative Justice and allow the challenge of government decisions. The second is the ability of the courts to capture public confidence, and present the court system as a viable avenue for the protection of individual interests against the improper or illegitimate exercise of the power of the state. Finally, much depends upon the willingness of the bureaucracy to obey court orders in the absence of any compelling enforcement mechanisms.

The Role of the Administrative Court Judges

The way in which the judiciary interpreted the grounds of review in the Law on Administrative Justice was the first indication of their determination to ensure that the Administrative Courts operated as an effective check on bureaucratic decision-making. The grounds established by the Law for review of an administrative decision are derived from the Dutch Administrative Justice Code.[5] These grounds, contained with Art 53(2) of the Law on Administrative Justice are as follows:

(a) the decision under challenge conflicts with operative law;

(b) the administrative body or official, in making the decision under challenge, used their authority for a purpose other than that for which it was granted; and

(c) the administrative body or official, after taking into account all the interests affected by the decision, should not have made, or failed to make, that decision.

However, the Dutch Code contains an extra ground of review which translates as the principle that the decision-making process must conform with general principles of proper administration, entrenched in the general legal consciousness (Schwarze, 1992: 189). These may be viewed as analogous to the principles of natural justice or procedural fairness. The deliberate omission of this ground of review by the drafters of the Law on Administrative Justice had the potential to render the available grounds of administrative review extremely narrow. However, even before the administrative courts were established the future judges remedied this deficiency by implying the principles of proper administration into the first ground of review. (Indroharto, 1991: 297). This inference was based upon the statutory duty of judges

---

5 *Wet Administratieve Rechtspraak Overheidsbeslissingen* (Wet AROB).

to 'discover and apply' the legal values alive within the Indonesian community.[6] The principle of proper administration was said to be one such accepted legal value. When the Administrative Courts commenced operation, judges showed no hesitation in moving outside the express statutory grounds of review and relying upon the inferred grounds of proper administration.

An analysis of the cases passing through the Administrative Courts since they were established in 1991 suggests that they are in fact protecting a range of interests, which were previously beyond legal protection, against arbitrary administrative decision-making filling what were critical gaps in the legal system. The most important of these interests relate to private property rights, public sector employment, the provision of public services, taxation and general human rights issues.

In many of the cases heard by the Administrative Courts, the judges have shown remarkably strong resolve in the face of government pressure. For example, publicity surrounded Justice Amarullah Salim, the Chair of the Jakarta Administrative Court, when he publicly demanded, and forced, the attendance of Jakarta Deputy Mayor Basofi at a hearing . Enormous public support was given to the Chair of the Medan Administrative Court, Justice Lintong Oloan Siahaan, when he was terrorised by security personnel after handing down a decision against them (Forum Keadilan, 1993a). Perhaps more significantly, there was widespread media coverage of the decision of the Semarang Administrative Court which held a decision by the Civil Director of the Department of Justice void (Forum Keadilan, 1993d). Here, the court proved willing to overturn a decision by one of the most powerful bureaucrats in its own department. The display by judges in the Administrative Courts of a reasonable degree of impartiality, by contrast to the reputation of other members of the Indonesian judiciary, resulted in the public placing great hope and faith in the new court system.

The Administrative Courts have also been relatively free of the regular reports of judicial corruption which have plagued other courts. When these reports have arisen in relation to the Administrative Courts they have been promptly and harshly dealt with. The only serious allegations of corruption have been against two judges in Jakarta, who were accused of accepting bribes. The Minister for Justice, Ismail Saleh, and Chairperson of the Supreme Court, Purwoto Gandasubrata, publicly condemned the actions of the judges (Forum Keadilan, 1992). After an Administrative Appeals Court investigation and a Supreme Court evaluation the judges were dismissed.

The integrity and impartiality of Administrative Court judges in hearing claims against the administration of which they are a part is not merely due to the good character of the particular judges. The Administrative Court judges also have a personal, professional and political interest in establishing a more independent judiciary. While they are acting, and perceived as, bureaucrats, Indonesian judges continue to lack the recognition, salary, prestige and aura of 'legal mysticism' associated with the judiciary elsewhere. What we may be witnessing in the 'courageous' decisions of Administrative Court judges is an attempt to assert the demands of the judiciary to be independent from the other branches of government. By standing between the individual and the state, the judges may be able to develop a source of prestige and recognition derived from public support upon which may be constructed an accepted doctrine of judicial independence.

---

6   Law on Judicial Powers, Art 26.

The Attitude of the Executive Towards the Courts

The effectiveness of the Administrative Courts has been enhanced by the fact that the bureaucracy has, on the whole, demonstrated a willingness to respect court decisions. One of the main concerns about with the court system before it commenced operation was whether it would command the respect of the administration. This was seen as crucial to the development of public confidence in the court. At the 1993 National Judicial Conference, it was noted that the authority of the Administrative Courts had been challenged several times.[7] The cases indicate, however, that government agencies have generally complied with Administrative Court decisions.

There are several reasons for this. First, the insistence of the Administrative Courts that their orders be implemented coupled with the publicity they have received has made violations relatively rare. Secondly, Justice Olden Bidara, the Deputy Chair of the Administrative Law division of the Supreme Court has noted that the Administrative Courts have a policy of only making an order if they are confident that it will be enforceable (Forum Keadilan, 1993b: 17). Hence, an official will never be summonsed to the court personally if his or her legal representative can provide an adequate explanation of the bureaucrat's actions. This reduces the risk of the court being embarrassed through a breach of its orders. It also reduces the risk of the court embarrassing the government by handing down a decision with which the government is unwilling to comply. This ensures that the administration does not feel overly threatened or disempowered by the judiciary. As a result of this pragmatic strategy most ministers have issued departmental circulars ordering their departments to comply with, or implement, any decision of the Administrative Courts (Forum Keadilan, 1993c).

Public Perceptions of Administrative Law –
The Role of the Media

The media has also played a crucial role in raising expectations about the potential of the courts to protect the public from arbitrary government decision-making. From 1986 when the Law on Administrative Justice was passed, the media actively promoted the Administrative Courts as a potential source of individual justice and legal reform. This created an environment of expectation in which the government was encouraged to ensure that the courts were formed by 1991, performed their duties as promised and were obeyed by government agencies. Without the media, public expectations would not have been raised, and the Administrative Courts may well have been the paper tigers that many expected.

Indeed, the media has an interest in encouraging the development of the Administrative Courts. One of the characteristics of the Soeharto government was the strict control it maintained over the media through decisions to grant and revoke press licences. The arbitrariness with which such decisions were often made was

---

7　These are listed in Forum Keadilan (1993b: 17-19). On at least three occasions, authorities had breached interim orders to postpone the demolition of buildings while the court evaluated the validity of the demolition orders. At Plumpang this left some 3000 families homeless. In another case, the North Jakarta Fisheries Office had initially disregarded an order to reopen a dock which they had shut down. It only complied after the breach was widely reported in the press

illustrated in July of 1993 by the revocation of the press licences of three of Indonesia's most popular news magazines – *Tempo, Editor* and *Detik.*[8] In 1991, Minister for Justice, Ismail Saleh, had foreshadowed that such decisions would not usually be justiciable because they were essentially policy decisions and rarely in the written form as required by the Law on Administrative Justice to attract the court's jurisdiction (Editor, 1991: 36). Justice Benyamin Mangkoedilaga's decision in the *Tempo* case held otherwise. The Indonesian media were, for the first time, presented with a forum within which they could challenge detrimental administrative decisions which threatened their ability to freely determine the content of publications.

Implications of Administrative Law for Indonesian Public Law Theory

In answer to the first of the questions posed at the outset of this chapter, the foregoing discussion suggests that the Administrative Courts are introducing concepts of due process and procedural regularity into bureaucratic decision-making processes where none previously existed. While it is probably going too far, in the absence of clear evidence, to say that this has altered administrative and bureaucratic culture in Indonesia, the introduction of concepts which form the basis of any rational legal administration is a start. Ultimately, the effect of administrative law on bureaucratic culture will depend upon the determined efforts of the executive government, at the highest levels, to reform itself through other measures which support the efforts of the Administrative Courts. Whether this is likely to occur as a result of domestic or international economic and political pressures is beyond the scope of this chapter.

The willingness of the administrative courts to hold the executive accountable for administrative decisions, contrary to the expectations of many, raises the second question posed at the outset. Does the development of administrative law signify a deeper shift in power away from the executive towards the judiciary; or away from the state towards civil society?

One political theory of Indonesian state provides an adequate framework within which to explain the appearance of courts apparently providing significant opportunities for citizens to challenge bureaucratic decisions. The bureaucratic-authoritarian model of state analyses the process of change from patrimonial to rational-legal administration in terms of the nature of the institutions and mechanisms constructed by the state to legitimise its rule. Bureaucratic-authoritarian regimes cultivate a multiple-legitimacy base of tradition, charisma, efficiency and rational and legal principles, with particular reliance upon legal legitimacy derived from formal legal structures (King, 1982: 110). Patrimonialism is not the only force at work in such regimes. Ultimate authority resides in the military who adopt a technocratic, bureaucratic approach to policy-making with a consensual decision-making process amongst a ruling group. Policies are then implemented by a large bureaucracy rather than directly by the military.

Another characteristic of such a regime is the attempt to create a conformist mentality by invoking vague, inclusivist values and national symbols. To aid this process, radicals, critics and media freedom are often repressed. Such regimes also operate within a context of rather apathetic acceptance of the regime by the bulk of

---

8   For more information on the *Tempo* case, see Millie, Chapter 19.

the population and an active discouragement of the mobilisation of mass support by the ruling elite (King, 1982: 111). Popular support is to be mobilised only at election time, when it is carefully controlled and employed as a source of legitimacy.

However, most importantly from the legal perspective, bureaucratic-authoritarian regimes construct a series of corporatist organisations through which they channel opposition to the regime into a controllable form. These can be categorised into inclusionary or exclusionary poles (Stephan, 1978). While both utilise state-designated representative organisations, at the inclusionary pole these organisations facilitate the orderly communication of demands up to policy-makers, rather than suppressing them. Exclusionary corporatism excludes social groups from policy-making while creating the appearance of participation.

There is ample evidence for a process of exclusionary corporatism in Indonesia; however, there are indications that some of the more powerful corporate structures have now begun to influence government policy, gradually becoming effective channels linking social groups to the government, for example business groups through KADIN[9] and Environmental groups through WALHI[10] (MacIntyre, 1991: 247). This indicates that the style of corporatism employed by the Indonesian government may be moving towards a more inclusionary type. My argument is that the Law on Administrative Justice can be seen as part of this shift in corporatist strategy applied in the legal sphere – what I call 'legal corporatism'. The administrative court system can be viewed as a means of channelling public discontent through the officially-sanctioned mechanism of the curial process where it can be controlled. At the same time it gives the impression of legal legitimacy to administrative decision-making by virtue of its mere existence and its stated purpose of ensuring bureaucratic accountability.

This raises the question of whose discontent the Administrative Courts seek to control. The cases suggest that the courts primarily represent a concession to the interests of the Indonesian middle class which has grown out of the economic prosperity of the New Order period and its consequences – increased urbanisation; the spread of secondary and tertiary education; the expansion of manufacturing and tertiary industries; increased real-estate ownership; the increased income from industrial, commercial and investment activities; and the expansion of a better paid bureaucracy (Mackie, 1990: 111).

The essential feature of these private sector middle groups is that their conception of the *negara hukum* is fundamentally different from that of the other proponents of the concept. The middle classes generally are the holders of values which conflict with many of the patrimonial values of Indonesian administrators. The most important of these for our purposes is the notion of the separation of society from state, a notion predicated upon the existence of a civil society with interests independent of public authority. This growing awareness of distinct private rights is really a prerequisite to the development of any administrative law system.

Patrimonialism threatens the private rights of the middle classes in three ways. First, it creates an environment which lacks the predictability and certainty which is required to nurture investment opportunities. In particular, patrimonialism prevents the protection of private property rights. Secondly, patrimonialism runs counter to middle class ideals which demand administrative accountability, open administrative process and popular participation in the political and administrative

---

9   *Kamar Dagang dan Industri*, the Indonesian Chamber of Commerce and Industry.
10   Indonesia's umbrella environmental protection organisation.

processes. Finally, the inefficiencies created by patrimonialism within a huge bureaucracy are perceived as a threat to the economic development process which gave rise to the rapid growth of the middle classes, and upon which they rely for their continued existence.

The Indonesian middle classes have now reached a size and political significance sufficient to compel the government to offer administrative law as a concession to their demands for the protection of their interests against patrimonial decision-making practices. The most important of these interests relate to private property rights, public sector employment, the provision of government services, human rights issues and taxation – precisely those issues that now dominate the work of the Administrative Courts.

While the Administrative Courts represented a concession to middle class demands, Indonesia's poor have been, unsurprisingly, largely unable to protect themselves from patrimonial decision-making practices through the Administrative Courts. The urban and rural poor rarely have a significant property right which the law will recognise, even where they have lived on a piece of land for 20 years or more. They do not work in the public sector, rely upon government services or pay tax. The issues which effect the working classes most, such as labour relations, are not raised frequently in the Administrative Courts. While the elucidation of the Law on Administrative Justice cites industrial relations arbitration decisions as an example of those which can be challenged in the courts, at the time of writing, I could find no evidence that any such case had been decided. This is despite the fact that the past few years has seen an astonishing increase in working class industrial action in urban industries.

Conclusion

The Law on Administrative Justice of 1986 may prove to be a landmark in Indonesia's legal history as a *negara hukum*, or nation of law.

In Weberian terms, the Indonesian administration tends towards patrimonial decision-making practices. According to Weber, such bureaucracies may be expected to undergo a transition towards more rational-legal modes of decision-making. Theories of bureaucratic power within the Indonesian state differ on the issue of how far the process of transformation described by Weber has taken place. The bureaucratic-authoritarian model of state analyses the process of change from patrimonial to rational-legal administration in terms of the nature of the institutions and mechanisms constructed by the state to legitimise its rule. The model describes the construction of such institutions and mechanisms by the state as state corporatism. Exclusionary state corporatism involves the construction of mechanisms which satisfy public demands for accountability without actually providing that accountability. It is a kind of symbolic legitimation. Inclusionary state corporatism, on the other hand, employs institutions which control dissent by providing some minimum measure of genuine bureaucratic accountability through state-sanctioned mechanisms.

The Law on Administrative Justice appeared to represent a move away from an exclusionary strategy towards more genuine attempts to provide some level of bureaucratic accountability. The creation of a system of Administrative Courts empowered those adversely affected by bureaucratic decisions to challenge such decisions directly, without having to rely upon the government to act on their behalf. It is too early to determine whether patrimonial bureaucratic culture is being transformed by the existence of the Administrative Courts. However, the impact of individual court decisions may be felt throughout the bureaucracy, encouraging at least an awareness among decision-makers that rational-legal decision-making is expected of them.

There are three main contributions made by administrative law. First, an analysis of the cases passing through the Administrative Courts since their formation in 1991 suggests that they are protecting a range of interests against arbitrary decision-making which were previously beyond legal protection – essentially interests of the growing Indonesian middle classes. Secondly, the Administrative Courts may well have initiated a process of increasing public confidence in the ability of legal institutions to provide justice. Finally, the courts have provided at least some judges with a platform of public support from which they may eventually be able to demand a more independent and meaningful role for the judiciary in the development of Indonesian law.

The use of the court system to challenge government action successfully suggests some shift in the balance of the powers of government away from the executive and towards the judiciary. Ultimately this may imply a movement of some of the power of the state to civil society. However, while the middle classes have been the beneficiaries of this shift, Indonesia's poor have been largely unable to protect themselves from patrimonial decision-making practices through the Administrative Courts.

In short, the Administrative Courts appear to represent a hybrid form of corporatist strategy. While the courts represent a move towards inclusionary state corporatism for the middle classes, they function as exclusionary legal institutions for lower socio-economic groups. There is no guarantee that when repression and exclusivist corporate strategies are no longer effective means of controlling the working classes, inclusionary corporate and legal mechanisms will be any more effective in containing their demands for political change.

For the moment however, social forces are compelling the Indonesian government to move away from empty rhetoric about the rule of law. In the Administrative Courts, at least some of the Indonesian people may be seeing their first glimpse of a future *Negara Hukum*.

References

Crouch, H, 1978, *The Army and Politics in Indonesia,* Cornell University Press, Ithaca.

Editor, 1991, 'Intern tapi Ekstern', 2 March: 31.

Forum Keadilan, 1992, 'Katabelece ke PTUN', 1 October: 35.

Forum Keadilan, 1993a, 'Menggugat Bakorstanasda, Menangkap Pendeta', 4 February: 25-26.

Forum Keadilan, 1993b, 'Mahkota Hakim akan Kembali?', 18 February: 17.

Forum Keadilan, 1993c, 10 June: 56-57.

Forum Keadilan, 1993d, 24 June: 24.

Indroharto, 1991 *Usaha Memahami Undang-Undang Peradilan Tata Usaha Negara*, Pustaka Sinar Harapan, Jakarta.

King, 1982 'Indonesia's New Order as a Bureaucratic Polity, a Neopatrimonial Regime, or a Bureaucratic-Authoritarian Regime: What difference does it make?' in *Interpreting Indonesian Politics: Thirteen Contributions to the Debate*, Cornell Modern Indonesian Project, Ithaca.

Lev, D, 1978, 'Judicial Authority and The Struggle for An Indonesian Rechsstaat', *Law & Society Review*, vol 13: 37.

McIntyre, Andrew, 1991, *Business and Politics in Indonesia*, Allen and Unwin, Sydney.

Mackie J, 1990 'Money and the Middle Class' in Tanter, Richard and Young, Kenneth (eds), *The Politics of Middle Class Indonesia*, Centre of Southeast Asian Studies, Monash University, Melbourne.

Reeve, David, 1990, 'The Corporatist State: The Case of Golkar' in Budiman, Arief (ed), *State and Civil Society in Indonesia*, Monash Papers on Southeast Asia no 22, Melbourne: 151-77.

Schwarze, J, 1992, *European Administrative Law*, Sweet and Maxwell, London.

Stepan, A, 1978, *The State and Society: Peru in Comparative Perspective*, Princeton University Press, Princeton.

Tanter, Richard and Young, Kenneth (eds), 1990, *The Politics of Middle Class Indonesia,* Centre of Southeast Asian Studies, Monash University, Melbourne.

Tempo, 1993, 26 June.

Wahyono, Padmo, 1992, 'Democracy in Indonesia: *Pancasila* Democracy' in Beer, L (ed), *Constitutional Systems in Late Twentieth Century Asia*, Asian Law series no 12, School of Law, University of Washington, Uni of Washington Press.

19. The *Tempo* Case:

Indonesia's Press Laws, the *Pengadilan Tata Usaha Negara* and the *Negara Hukum*

Julian Millie

In June of 1994, publication of Indonesia's most prominent current affairs magazine was made illegal by the issue of notices of decision from the Department of Information. This prohibition sparked an effort by the magazine to regain its legal status by means of legal proceedings. This effort captured widespread attention. It was less the legal issues at stake than the novelty of the attempt to restrain government action by using the legal system which created interest and, in some quarters, optimism. This was especially the case after the orders sought were granted in Indonesia's newly established administrative law court, the *Pengadilan Tata Usaha Negara* (PTUN).

In the first part of this chapter an attempt is made to provide a background to the *Tempo* case by outlining the legislative framework which was at issue in the case. The chapter then follows the progress of the case from the first decision in the PTUN, through an unsuccessful appeal by the minister in the *Pengadilan Tinggi Tata Usaha Negara* (administrative court of appeal) and finally to the granting of the minister's *kasasi* (cassation, appeal) application in the *Mahkamah Agung* (the highest court in Indonesia). The third part examines aspects of the *Tempo* case using the rubric of constitutionalism.

The justification for adopting the lexicon of constitutionalism when discussing the *Tempo* case stems from Indonesian constitutional theory, which defines the Republic as a state in which power is to be exercised within institutional limits.[1] First, the elucidation to the Constitution states that Indonesia is a *negara hukum*, a state based on law. Secondly, the 1945 Constitution establishes the structure of the state and is the express source of power of the state's organs and it confines them to specific roles in government. Thirdly, a hierarchy of legislation is established in Decree No XX/MPRS/1966 of the MPR (the Peoples' Consultative Assembly and Indonesia's sovereign body).[2] According to that Resolution, the 1945 Constitution is the supreme written law in the hierarchy of legislation and 'in accordance with the principles of *negara hukum*, each legislative product must be explicitly based upon and have as its source the legislation in force at the higher levels' (Para (3) of Part II (A)). It may be concluded, then, that principles of constitutionalism were intended to play a role in the Republic's state structure.

---

1   See Lev (1978), Mackie (1963) and Soemantri & Saragih (1993).
2   *Majelis Permusyawaratan Rakyat.*

Part 1: Legislative Background of the SIUPP

An examination of the legal background to the *Tempo* case reveals the perilous existence of media organisations in Indonesia. The term *pembreidelan* (banning) used to describe the removal of *Tempo's* publishing licence originated from the regulatory framework of the colonial *Persbreidel Ordonnantie* of 1931, which empowered the Governor General of the Netherlands Indies to prohibit publications which threatened public security (Atmakusuma et al 1980: 146). In the late 1950s it was made mandatory for publishers to possess a licence, known as a *surat izin terbit* (SIT), the continued possession of which was explicitly linked to the content of the publication concerned (Atmakusuma et al 1980: 153-56). In 1966, the New Order government with one hand abolished the concept of the SIT through the Law on the Press No 11 of 1966, while with the other – and in the same statute – it created transitional provisions which required publishers to hold a SIT for the duration of the transitional period (Art 20(1)(a)).[3]

Article 4 of the Law on the Press[4] – which reads 'Censorship and *pembreidelan* are not to be imposed on the Indonesian national press' – was to become one of the central issues in the *Tempo* case. Despite this provision, the government withdrew or 'froze' the SITs of many publishers throughout the 1970s and early 1980s, including, briefly, that of *Tempo* in 1982 (Siregar 1995: 79).[5] The withdrawals varied in stringency, from temporary to permanent. They also varied in the manner of notification, with some publishers simply being told by telephone that their SIT had been cancelled. Criminal penalties could be imposed on publishers who published without possessing a SIT.

This transitional period came to an end with the enactment of the Law on the Press No 21 of 1982. The era of the SIT was over. A new licence, however, was brought into existence by Art 13(5), which reads:

> Every press publication produced by a press corporation requires a *surat izin usaha penerbitan pers* (permit for press publishers), abbreviated to SIUPP, which is issued by the government. Provisions concerning the SIUPP shall be put into effect by the government after hearing the opinion of the *Dewan Pers* (Press Council).

What was the difference between the SIT and the SIUPP? Circumstances surrounding the enactment of Law No 21 of 1982 lead to the conclusion that the SIUPP is directed at the regulation and administrative aspects of enterprises involved in the press industry. The Minister of Information's explanation of the Law when it was under consideration by the DPR (People's Representative Assembly or parliament)[6] was that 'these licensing provisions (SIUPP) are based on a desire to create a more stable process of growth in the press industry' and that 'SIUPP will be useful as a mechanism for the development of publishers particularly in regard to the business aspects' (Simorangkir, 1986: 73). This demarcation between the use of licensing provisions as a regulation of management and business aspects of publishing on the one hand and as a means to regulate the content of publications on the other was prominent in the submissions made to the DPR. Needless to say, the result of the

---

3   Indonesian legislation concerning the media is gathered in Simorangkir (1986).
4   Press Laws No 11 of 1966 and No 21 of 1982 contain Art 4 in identical terms.
5   Atmakusumah et al (1980: 181) contains a detailed history of the *pembreidelan* of Indonesia Raya.
6   *Dewan Perwakilan Rakyat.*

withdrawal of the SIUPP and the SIT was the same; further unlicensed publication was again punishable by criminal penalties.

In addition to the statutes, ministerial regulations also played a role in the *Tempo* case, namely Minister of Information Regulation No 1 of 1984 concerning SIUPP. This regulation addressed issues such as levels of ownership in media enterprises, employment issues and the corporate form publishers should take. Article 33 of the Regulation sets out the circumstances in which the Minister of Information may cancel a SIUPP. Again, it is a general requirement that the Minister must first 'hear the Press Council (*Dewan Pers*)'.[7] Eight specific circumstances are prescribed. Two relate to compliance with provisions concerning ownership levels and administrative procedure. Five impose minimum productivity levels. Clause (h), however, enables the Minister to cancel a SIUPP when:

> In the estimation of the *Dewan Pers* ... the relevant publisher and the publication no longer reflects, in the management of its publication, the existence of a press which is healthy, free and responsible.

It is from this Clause, seemingly at odds with the provisions of the Law creating the SIUPP framework and prohibiting *pembreidelan*, that the Minister of Information derives the power to withdraw a SIUPP and thus prevent publication on the grounds of content. To the knowledge of the author there has never been a cancellation of a SIUPP on the basis of the other grounds although failures to comply with the administrative procedures seem to be common, even in well-established publishers.[8]

The apparent conflict between the Law and the Regulation had encouraged one attempt to contest the withdrawal of a SIUPP before the *Tempo* case. Surya Paloh's 1992 application to the *Mahkamah Agung* to contest the legality of the withdrawal in 1987 of the SIUPP of his newspaper *Prioritas* was the first application for judicial review of a regulation in Indonesia. It failed due to the lack of formal procedure for such an application. By the time the procedure had been established, the application had been discontinued (Bujono et al 1995: 10).

Part 2: The Tempo Case

Tempo magazine was established in 1971 and by the time of its final edition had achieved a readership of approximately one million (Hadad 1995: 17).[9] In the spirit of its motto *enak dibaca dan perlu* (pleasant to read and essential), the magazine combined concise reporting with a glossy, attractive format.

In its 11 June 1994 edition *Tempo* ran a story describing the concerns of the Indonesian Finance Minister Mar'ie Muhammad in relation to the price of German

---

7   The *Dewan Pers* was established in Chapter 3 of the 1966 Press Law. Its duty is to 'assist the Government in nurturing the growth and development of the National Media'. The head of the *Dewan Pers* is the Minister of Information (Art 7).

8   According to Siregar (1995: 89), 'There has not yet been a cancellation of a SIUPP based on the other provisions. Moreover, *Kompas*, for example, has still not yet transferred 20% of its shares to its employees (in accordance with Art 16(1) of *Permenpen* No 1 of 1984)'. A recent report, however, indicates the Department of Information intends to withdraw the SIUPP of a number of inactive publications (Forum Keadilan, 1997: 93).

9   This estimation is based on five readers per copy sold.

naval vessels ships purchased at the instigation of the Minister for Research and Technology, Dr BJ Habibie.[10]

In a speech given in Lampung on 9 June 1994 President Soeharto had hinted that action would be taken against elements of the Indonesian media as a result of the reporting of this issue (Sulistyadi 1995: 101). The editorial chief of *Tempo* was sufficiently concerned by the prevailing atmosphere to contact a member of the Press Council who assured him there would be no *pembreidelen* (Kesaksian 1995: 256). Later on, a member of the Press Council testified in the Jakarta PTUN that the Council had not recommended to the Ministry of Information that *Tempo*'s SIUPP be withdrawn and indeed had never been consulted on the issue (Kesaksian 1995: 280).

Nonetheless, on 21 June 1994, a notice of decision effecting the cancellation of the grant of SIUPP was issued to the weekly magazines *Tempo* and *Editor*, and the weekly tabloid *Detik*.[11] From that point on, PT Grafiti Pers (the owner of *Tempo* and holder of its SIUPP) and the employees involved in the production of *Tempo* faced criminal penalties if they continued to publish the magazine.

Two applications were issued in the newly established PTUN, one being the application of editorial chief Goenawan Mohamad, the other the application of 43 employees of PT Grafiti Pers. The respondent in both applications was the Minister of Information, Harmoko. On 3 May 1995, the Jakarta PTUN, headed by Judge Benyamin Mangkoedilaga, found in favour of the applicants.[12] In this unexpected decision, the court found that the act of withdrawing the SIUPP had the same effect as *pembreidelan*. Accordingly Art 33(h) of the Regulation of Minister of Information Regulation No 1 of 1984 was in conflict with the prohibition on *pembreidelan* contained in Art 4 of the Law on the Press No 21 of 1982. For this reason, the court set aside (*menyingkirkan*) the Regulation. Furthermore, the court decided the Minister had not acted within the power granted to him and had failed to follow the 'principles of good government'. The court judged that the Minister's decision was void and ordered that a new SIUPP be issued. The decision was confirmed by the five judges who announced their judgment of the Minister's appeal in the Administrative Court of Appeal on 21 November 1995.

Three judges of the *Mahkamah Agung* handed down their judgment on a further appeal (*kasasi*) of the Minister of Information on 13 May 1996.[13] The crucial finding of the *Mahkamah Agung* was that the withdrawal of *Tempo*'s SIUPP could be distinguished from *pembreidelan*; and that there was therefore no conflict between the Regulation and the superior Law. In the context of the then crisis of confidence in the Indonesian *Mahkamah Agung* the eventual failure of the two *Tempo* applications was not a surprise to the participants. After the decision had been handed down, editorial chief Goenawan Mohamad commented:

> in the current political constellation, it should not be hoped that the MA would produce an independent or virtuous decision (Kompas, 1996: 13).

---

10 The connection between this particular story and the withdrawal of the SIUPP is widely accepted, as is revealed in the testimony of Jacob Oetama in the PTUN of 9 May 1995 (Kesaksian 1995: 279). The Ministry for Information has never acknowledged the connection.

11 The notices of decision are reproduced in Hasibuan et al (1994: 98-110).

12 See generally Forum Keadilan (1995b).

13 See Kompas (1996: 1, 13), Gatra (1996: 68-69), Forum Keadilan (1996: 21-22).

Part 3: The Tempo Case and Indonesian Constitutionalism

Clear guarantees of individual rights are omitted from the 1945 Constitution. Since the return to this Constitution in 1959 this feature has been entrenched in policy by successive governments. In contrast to this emphasis on the priority of *kepentingan umum* (the interest of the general public) at the cost of *kepentingan perorangan* (interest of the individual), the PTUN has accorded greater priority to *kepentingan perorangan* in both its legislative foundation and some of its decisions.

Although Law No 5 of 1986 emphasises that 'the aim of the PTUN is in fact not to give protection to individual rights only, but at the same time to protect the rights of society',[14] Art 53(1) of the Law stipulates who may apply to the court, namely 'a person or legal entity who or which believes its interests have been damaged by an administrative decision'. The meaning of 'interest' is not defined in the Law or its Elucidation and, as there is no constitutional precedent or guideline concerning the nature of individual rights, it may be concluded that the ambit of the term is to be determined at the court's discretion.

The *Tempo* case brought before the court an important question concerning the nature of the loss which must be suffered for an applicant to possess the standing to apply to the PTUN. The opposing sides of the question were summarised in the appeal memoranda of the parties. One of the grounds of the Department's appeal was that the damage claimed by Goenawan Mohamad's appeal was not to an interest (*kepentingan*) which was able to satisfy the requirements of Art 53 (1). The Department's appeal memorandum stated:

> *Tempo*'s SIUPP was issued to Grafiti Pers Pty Ltd (the owner of *Tempo*) ... the person with the right to represent the company is Eric Samola (President and Director of the Company).

Goenawan's memorandum in reply stated:

> Article 53(1) of (Law) No 5 of 1986 does not limit the (class of) person having the right to apply. ... Goenawan Mohamad has suffered a loss of prestige and status as the editorial chief, and his livelihood as editorial chief has disappeared ... (Kompas, 1995e).[15]

The court was in a position to choose between a narrow or broad interpretation of Art 53(1). A decision that Goenawan's *kepentingan* could not sustain an application would have suggested that access to relief from the PTUN would be difficult for applicants who have suffered loss as a result of a government decision but cannot show a formal legal nexus with the parties affected by the original decision. The Jakarta PTUN rejected the Minister's objections and thereby opted for a broad interpretation of Art 53(1). The *Mahmakamah Agung* approved this interpretation, and conceded that Goenawan Mohamad had suffered loss in his capacity as editorial chief and that he therefore had standing to make an application to the PTUN (Soerjadi 1995: 57-60).

---

14   Paragraph 1 of the General Elucidation of Law No 5 of 1986.

15   Goenawan Mohamad had been advised by his counsel that a shareholders' meeting should be convened in order to resolve that the action be brought by the directors of PT Grafiti Pers. This was not undertaken. The majority shareholders in the company were ethnic Chinese business people and Goenawan Mohamad felt that they wished to avoid a confrontation with the government (personal conversation with Goenawan Mohamad's representative, Jakarta, June 1995).

Review of Legislation

The absence of checks and balances on the executive by the judicial branch has its origin in the debates of the Committee for the Preparation of Independence in 1945. Soepomo, the ultimate drafter of the Constitution produced by that committee, did not believe the concept of judicial review should be applied in the *kekeluargaan* (family-like) state. Soepomo said it was not proper for one organ of government to review the results of the labours of the other organs of government because they are all equal in level and for this reason should cooperate. Judicial review, he argued, could only exist in a liberal state which ascribed to the theory of the separation of powers (Lubis 1992: 25). For this reason, the Constitution made no mention of a judicial power of review.

The debate over judicial review has continued since 1945 and was at its most intense in the period leading up to the passage of the Law on Judicial Power No 14 of 1970 which made it clear that the courts had no power to review Laws passed by the DPR (Seno Adji 1993: 224-26; Lev 1978: 57-62). Opponents of the Soepomo view continue to argue for a constitutional court but without success.[16] Historically Soepomo's argument has prevailed to the extent that the *Mahkamah Agung* has to date not even exercised the lesser power to review regulations and other subordinate legislation granted to it in Art 26 of Law No 14 of 1970 *(Forum Keadilan,* 1995b).[17]

The decision in the *Tempo* case, however, signalled a departure from the stagnant state of judicial review in Indonesia. If the three judges hearing the case had regarded Law No 5 of 1986 (the empowering statute of the PTUN) as the exhaustive source of the administrative court's power they would clearly have considered themselves to be bound by Regulation of the Minister of Information No 1 of 1984 regardless of whether it contradicted the Law on the Press. This is because No 5 of 1986 does not include a *hak uji* (power of review of written law) amongst the court's powers. To the surprise of many, the judges led by the Chief Judge Benyamin Mangkoedilaga stated in their decision 'that ministerial regulation has been put aside *(singkirkan)* by us in this case'. Although the term *menyingkirkan*[18] is not mentioned in the Law No 5 of 1986, it appears the judges considered that because the regulation conflicted with superior law the court was not bound to apply it; and that any decisions of the executive based upon the Regulation would be legally void. Implicitly then the judges considered that the PTUN's jurisdiction included this limited form of legislative review or *hak uji*.

The *hak uji* aspect of the court's decision came under scrutiny at appeal level. The Department's legal representatives indicated that one of their grounds of appeal was that the court had exceeded its jurisdiction. They argue that the *penyingkiran* (putting aside of the regulation) was in reality a *perbuatan uji material* − an act of

---

16 Recent manifestations include the statement of Justice Din Muhammad, the head of the *Makamah Agung's* Centre for Research, Development, Education and Training, in Kompas (1995b: 10); and Albert Hasibuan's comments in Kompas (1995c: 10).

17 See also the interview with former Chief Justice Ali Said in Tempo (1995). Anecdotal evidence links the paucity of applications under Art 26 to the extreme delays in proceedings before the *Makamah Agung* and the reluctance of litigants in commercial matters to undertake such a prolonged endeavour.

18 The decision in no way requires the law to be amended, nor, it is presumed, is the Department obliged to refrain from issuing further decisions based on the *Permenpen*. The writer of this thesis asked Judge Mangkoedilaga what the effect of his decision was upon the *Permenpen*. He replied that the law was still valid but that in the matter before him it had been put aside.

reviewing the substance of a law – and that only the *Makamah Agung* is empowered to conduct such a review (Kompas, 1995e: 10).

In the first appeal of the decision, the Appeal Court of the PTUN approved the *penyingkiran* as a legitimate use of judicial power. Importantly, the *Mahmakah Agung* at *kasasi* level did not seem to disapprove of the *penyinkgiran* of the Regulation by the PTUN (*Kompas*, 1996: 1,13,15). A tentative conclusion may then be made that the PTUN's jurisdiction does include the power to put aside a regulation where the court judges it to be in conflict with a superior provision.

Despite appearing not to dispute the power of the PTUN to set aside regulations, the *Mahkamah Agung* did make two objections to the manner of exercise of the *penyingkiran*. First – and here is the most disappointing aspect of this decision – the *Mahkamah Agung* did not agree with the conclusions of the lower courts concerning the compatibility of the legislation in issue. The court found no conflict between Art 4 of Law No 11 of 1966 nor Law No 21 of 1982 and Art 33(h) of Regulation of the Minister of Information No 1 of 1984. In short, the court created a facile distinction between the withdrawal (*pencabutan*) of a SIUPP and *pembreidelan*. In support of this distinction, the *Mahkamah Agung* drew on the evidence of a former director of the Press and Graphics Development Body (Kesaksian 1995: 293-303). His torturous evidence was that the withdrawal (*pencabutan*) of a *SIUPP* was different from *pembreidelan* in that the *pembreidelan* was permanent, whereas the *SIUPP* could be returned to the holder after it had been withdrawn (*dicabut*) (Kesaksian 1995: 293-95). Historical evidence does not seem to completely support his testimony.[19] Furthermore, in his evidence he conceded that a withdrawn SIUPP had *never* been returned to the same SIUPP-holder to enable recommencement of publication under the same journal title as before the withdrawal (Kesaksian 1995: 300). The second objection of the *Mahkamah Agung* to the PTUN's decision was that it had first put aside Art 33(h) of Regulation of the Minister of Information No 1 of 1984 but had then relied on the very same regulations to order the Minister to reissue the SIUPP (Kompas, 1994: 13).

Whatever the outcome in the *Mahkamah Agung*, the PTUN judge's assumption of the power to set aside the regulation was a significant event for the Indonesian judiciary. It was a rare occasion on which a court has adjudicated on the validity of written law. The executive of the Republic of Indonesia has traditionally produced regulations in conflict with superior law without any institutional restraint. The *Tempo* decisions provided a stark demonstration of the potential of the PTUN to impose legal constraints on executive action.

Separation of Powers and the Judiciary

Recent years have seen a dramatic decline in the image of the Indonesian judiciary. At least two constitutional phenomena have contributed to this situation. The first is the structural conflict whereby the *Mahkamah Agung* is responsible for the day-to-day management of the judiciary, yet the Department of Justice is responsible for the appointment, promotion and termination of judges (Lev 1978: 65-66). The second is the contentious issue of the constitutional supremacy of the MPR pursuant to Art 1(2) of the 1945 Constitution.

---

19   Concerning the duration of *pembreidelan*, see Atmakusuma et al (1980: 146-47).

By contrast, the very establishment of a court such as the PTUN could be regarded as a formal hallmark of a state in which there is a more pronounced separation of the organs of state. It is too early to conclude, however, that the PTUN will in substance function as an effective and independent check upon the executive. First, the enforcement provisions of Law No 5 of 1986 put the final decision to order Ministerial compliance in the hands of the President, who is, of course, the head of the executive (Muchsan 1992: 88-89). The executive therefore retains an ultimate discretion to resist any PTUN order. Secondly, the general low regard in which the judiciary is held may adversely affect the reception of orders of the PTUN by the bureaucracy (Meliala 1996: 70).

Despite this, aspects of the *Tempo* case showed the potential of the PTUN to function independently and energetically. The creativity of the Jakarta PTUN in carrying out a de facto judicial review of Regulation of the Minister of Information No 1 of 1984 has been discussed above. In the context of the long-simmering public discontent regarding the use of the SIUPP regulations by the Minister of Information to prevent publication on the grounds of content, and the routine interference in the judiciary by the executive, the decision to set aside the Regulation was extremely courageous.

Like their counterparts in the general courts, the judges of the PTUN are appointed by the executive upon the recommendation of the Minister for Justice.[20] They are therefore subject to 'general supervision, as civil servants, carried out by the Minister of Justice'.[21] It is difficult to identify the reason why the same forces which hamper the independence of the *Mahkamah Agung* did not have a similar effect on the PTUN in the first two *Tempo* cases. A plausible explanation is a combination of the 'snowball' effect of the phenomenon of the PTUN's gaining great public support in high-profile cases and the desire of judges to properly fulfil their independent role. Lev has written that Indonesia's judges supported moves toward a liberal constitutionalist state in the late 1960s more out of preoccupation with their own status rather than conviction as to the beneficial role of the judiciary in such a state (Lev 1978: 55-65). Following this line of reasoning, judicial independence reflects well upon the status of Indonesian judges, as it would in the judiciary of any state. In Judge Benyamin Mangkoedilaga's words:

> whether we wish to or not, the efforts to start (strengthening the judicial power) must come from us ourselves (the judges). We must make ourselves worthy of the task. A judge must be professional, especially a PTUN judge, so that our decisions can be accepted. If we make decisions which people will laugh at, how then can we wish to be respected? (Kompas, 1995d: 10)

Epilogue

Having identified the PTUN as tending towards a system in which the exercise of power by the government is restrained by law – a key element of *negara hukum* – the question arises as to how the jurisdiction will develop. Current circumstances lead to the conclusion that there is no certain trend in Indonesia. The unconvincing decision of the *Makamah Agung* in the *Tempo* case has to some extent dulled enthusiasm for the PTUN with the same gloom which envelopes the public image of

---

20   Article 16(1) of Law No 5 of 1986.
21   Article 13(1) of Law No 5 of 1986.

the *Makamah Agung* despite the fall of Soeharto in May 1998. The passage of time will allow evaluations to be made concerning the rate of execution of orders of the PTUN by the executive. One interesting issue is the spate of PTUN applications in which the plaintiffs have suffered loss in their professional lives as a result of government action traceable to their non-professional lives as political figures.[22] These cases have established the PTUN as a forum for overt political confrontation between citizen and state. In the current climate of reform in Indonesia it seems likely that these cases may be decided in such a way as to eradicate the disparities described in this chapter and make the PTUN a genuine check on the executive. This would be an important step towards the realisation of a *negara hukum* which in substance reflects the ideals reflected in its formal structures.

References

Abdullah, Rozali, 1992, *Hukum Acara Peradilan Tata Usaha Negara*, Rajawali Pers, Jakarta.

Atmakusumah and Swantoro, P, 1980, 'Pembreidelan Pers Dalam Sejarah Indonesia' in Surjomihardjo, A (ed), *Beberapa Segi Perkembangan Sejarah Pers di Indonesia*, Proyek Penelitian Pengembangan Penerangan Departemen Penerangan RI, Jakarta: 141-254.

Beer, Lawrence W, 1979, *Constitutional in Asia: Asian Views of the American Influence*, University of California Press, Berkeley.

Beer, Lawrence W, 1992, *Constitutional Systems in Late Twentieth Century Asia*, University of Washington Press, Seattle and London.

Bujono and Hadad, 1995, 'Tonggak Sejarah Dari Ponggak Halim' in Bujono, Hadad and Setia (eds), *Mengapa Kami Menggugat*, Yayasan Alumni Tempo, Jakarta: 9-18.

Djiwandono, J Soedjati, 1990, *SIUPP dan Cita-cita Negara Hukum*, Paper M48/90, Centre for Strategic and International Studies, Jakarta.

Forum Keadilan, 1995a, 19 January: 98.

Forum Keadilan, 1995b, 25 May.

Forum Keadilan, 1996, 1 July: 21-22.

Forum Keadilan, 1997, 29 December: 93.

Gatra, 1996, 22 June: 68-69.

Hasibuan, Santoso, Siregar, Utami, 1994, *Bredel 1994*, Aliansi Jurnalis Independen, Jakarta.

Kanyeihamba, GW, 1984, 'Constitutional Obligation in Developing Countries' in Marasinghe ML and Conklin WE (eds), *Essays on Third World Perspectives on Jurisprudence*, Malayan Law Journal, Singapore.

Kesaksian-kesaksian, 1995, in, *Mengapa Kami Menggugat*, eds Bujono, Setia and Hadad, Yayasan Alumni Tempo, Jakarta: 243-303.

Kompas, 1994,14 June: 13.

Kompas, 1995a, 4 June: 9.

Kompas, 1995b, 17 June: 10.

Kompas, 1995c, 1 July: 10.

Kompas, 1995d, 26 July: 10.

Kompas, 1995e, 14 August.

Kompas, 1996, 14 June: 13.

Lev, DS, 1978, 'Judicial Authority and the Struggle for an Indonesian Rechtsstaat'. *Law Society Review,* vol 13, Fall: 37-71.

Lembaga Penelitian, Pendidikan dan Penerangan Ekonomi dan Sosial, 1990, *Hukum dan Politik di Indonesia, Kesinambungan dan Perubahan,* Lembaga Penelitian, Pendidikan dan Penerangan Ekonomi dan Sosial, Jakarta.

---

22 Two such applications were those of Arief Budiman in relation to his removal from his academic post at Universitas Kristen Satya Wacana; and Sri Bintang Pamungkas in relation to his removal by the President from his position in the DPR. See Millie (1995: 32).

Loqman, L, 1996, 'Tempo', *Gatra*, 22 June: 67.

Mackie, Jamie, 1963, 'Aspects of Political Power and the Demise of Parliamentary Democracy in Indonesia' in Spann, R (ed), *Constitutionalism in Asia*, Asia Publishing House, Bombay: 90.

Mangkoedilaga, Benyamin, 1983, *Lembaga Peradilan Tata Usaha Negara, Suata Orientasi Pengenalan*, Ghalia Indonesia, Jakarta.

Manus, et al,1993, *Tokoh-tokoh Badan Penyelidik Usaha-usaha Persiapan Kemerdekaan Indonesia*, Departemen Pendidikan dan Kebudayaan, Direktorat Sejarah dan Nilai Tradisional, Proyek Investarisasi dan Dokumen Sejarah, Jakarta.

Meliala, A, 1996, 'Humanisme PTUN', *Forum Keadilan*, 1 January: 70.

Millie, J, 1995, *The Indonesian Negara Hukum and the Pengadilan Tata Usaha Negara; Contrasts in Constitutionalism*, Unpublished Honours Thesis, Monash University, Melbourne.

Muchsan, 1992, *Sistem Pengawasan Terhadap Perbuatan Aparat Pemerintah Dan Peradilan Tata Usaha Negara Di Indonesia*, Liberty, Yogyakarta.

Nasution, Adnan Buyung, 1992, *The Aspiration for Constitutional Government in Indonesia: A Socio-legal Study of the Indonesian Konstituante 1956-1959*, Pustaka Sinar Harapan, Jakarta.

Pranarka, AMW, 1985, *Sejarah Pemikiran Tentang Pancasila*, Yayasan Proklamasi, Centre for Strategic and International Studies, Jakarta.

Quinn, Bernard, 1995, 'Indonesia: Patrimonial or Legal State? The Administrative Justice Act of 1986 in Socio-Political Context', paper presented at the conference *Indonesian Law: The First 50 Years*, University of Melbourne, September.

Seno Adji, 1980, *Peradilan Bebas — Negara Hukum*, Erlangga, Jakarta.

Seno, Adji, 1993, 'Kekuasaan Kehakiman di Indonesia Sejak Kembali ke UUD 1945' in Soemantri and Saragih (eds), *Ketatanegaraan Indonesian Dalam Kehidupan Politik Indonesia – 30 Tahun Kembali ke Undang-Undang Dasar 1945*, Pustaka Sinar Harapan, Jakarta.

Simorangkir, JCT, 1986, '*Pers, SIUPP dan Wartawan: Ketentuan-ketentuan Mengenai Pers, SIUPP dan Wartawan dan Beberapa Komentar*', Gunung Agung, Jakarta.

Siregar, Liston P, 1995, 'SIUPP, Cucu Persbreidel' in Bujono, Hadad and Setia (eds), *Mengapa Kami Menggugat*, Yayasan Alumni Tempo, Jakarta: 75-90.

Soemantri, Sri, 1993, 'Susunan Ketatanegaraan Menurut UUD 1945' in Soemantri and Saragih (eds), *Ketatanegaraan Indonesia Dalam Kehidupan Politik Indonesia – 30 Tahun Kembali Ke Undang-Undang Dasar 1945*, Pustaka Sinar Harapan, Jakarta.

Soerjadi, T, 1995, 'Legal Standing' in Bujono, Hadad and Setia (eds), *Mengapa Kami Menggugat*, Yayasan Alumni Tempo, Jakarta: 57-60.

Soetomo, 1983, *Peradilan Tata Usaha Negara di Indonesia*, Usaha Nasional, Surabaya.

Tempo, 1995, 25 May.

20. The Transformation of Indonesian Commercial Contracts and Legal Advisers[1]

Veronica Taylor

In the 50 years since it gained independence, Indonesia achieved striking economic growth. Post-colonial oil-dependency was replaced with diversified economic activity and steady, impressive growth in Indonesia's GNP (MacIntyre, 1994: 244). Until recently, its status within regional trade groupings had similarly increased. When the APEC Heads of government met in 1994, the Bogor Declaration on trade liberalisation emphasised both Indonesia's status as host nation and the extent to which it has transformed its own economy (Australia-Japan Research Centre, 1994). However, as the global economic integration proceeds, the rules have changed. Major creditors such as the World Bank demand not only evidence of industrialisation, structural adjustment and a healthy balance of payments but also transformation of a state's political, social and legal infrastructure (World Bank, 1992; World Bank, 1993). The collapse of the rupiah in late 1997 has led to a wholesale re-evaluation of Indonesia's development and a consequent flight of capital to other economies.

Linking law with economic development is not a new idea. Development theorists have traditionally seen a 'modern' legal system as integral to a state's economic growth. The legal yardsticks of 'rational' modernity are relatively clear – a 20th century state should guarantee transparency and certainty in the allocation of contract and property rights (Weber, 1954). In particular, the state should be concerned with the form and content of consumer and commercial transactions; the venues and procedures for resolving commercial disputes; and regulation of areas of public interest such as competition, intellectual property rights, occupational health and safety and the environment. Adherence to the 'rule of law' is another litmus test. In theory, law should be universal and uniformly applied and the state should be willing to establish and submit itself to an independent judiciary. An independent private legal profession is usually considered essential for the actual enforcement of individuals' rights and for mounting challenges to improper acts by the state. In

---

1   This research was financed by the ARC between 1992 and 1994 as part of a study by the Asian Law Centre at the University of Melbourne of the Internationalisation of Contracts within Asia.

each of these areas Indonesia now increasingly (although incompletely) conforms to the paradigm of the modern legal system.

Contracts continue to be an important vehicle for economic development, foreign investment and the transmission of legal culture. New types of commercial contracts cross national boundaries in the briefcases of multinational executives and their legal advisers. Indonesia, like many developing economies, recognises that foreign investment and trade inevitably results in legal change. In areas such as franchising, distribution, banking and finance, Indonesia has no specific legislation regulating the new forms of contract on which such businesses are based. De facto legal rules are drawn from the standard-form contracts prepared in countries such as the United States and Australia, and European and Anglo-American law and practice. As KFC fast food restaurants compete with local *ayam goreng* vendors, so do foreign contract forms and legal services challenge Indonesia's legal infrastructure.

In this chapter I look at how globalisation is affecting Indonesian law and practice in commercial contracts. I analyse some of the 'problem' areas that foreign businesspeople and their lawyers identify as making contracts uncertain and difficult to enforce in Indonesia: the role of the patrimonial state, the colonial contract legacy and the lack of legal infrastructure for dispute resolution. Pressure is now mounting internationally and domestically for contract law reform in Indonesia but the direction of change is not yet clear.

Whether states such as Indonesia do, in fact, naturally evolve along a common 'modern' legal trajectory continues to provoke intense debate.[2] In the past decade the 'legal evolution' debate seems to have been overtaken by other intellectual currents. The first 'of these alternative agendas' is international trade theory, within which 'free trade' perspectives predominate. These demand that participant states have the attributes of a 'modern' legal system and more. A new emphasis on 'fair' free trade calls for not only the removal of tariff and non-tariff barriers to trade but also transparency of legal regulation, the removal of overly onerous or discriminatory regulations and the harmonisation of commercial law in form, substance and application (Trebilcock & Howse, 1995: 25-48). Not too far below the 'fair trade' agenda is the assumption that the legal rules and institutions that facilitate free trade are those that the West (more usually the United States) already has in place. The calls for change to national laws that do not fit the Western model can also be understood as an application of globalisation theory to law.

'Globalisation' is the second legal buzzword of the decade. It is usually understood as external and internal pressures on domestic legal systems that flow from the integration of global capital and labour markets. In one sense, globalisation is not a new phenomenon: colonising states and world powers have frequently provided compelling models of law or procedure that could be chosen by developing states, or imposed by persuasion or force. What seems to distinguish globalisation from movements such as colonisation (and in the case of Indonesia, Islamicisation)[3] is the rapidity of developments in technology and information exchange, and the multiplication of the actors who are dictating or influencing legal change. Some of the actors, or 'change agents', are well established – United Nations affiliates and similar bodies developing multinational model rules and

---

2   See, for example, Trubeck (1972).
3   See, for example, Cammack (1989).

treaties, such as UNCITRAL and UNIDROIT come to mind immediately.[4] These bodies have pursued the unification and harmonisation of private commercial law for much of this century but globalisation and the proliferation of change agents have accelerated and complicated the process.

Some individual states are enormously influential in legal change – the United States, for example, is a magnetic legal model because of its economic and political power. The US has increasingly wielded this power bilaterally against trading partners. In the area of intellectual property rights, for example, it has vigorously pressed most Asian countries to adopt (fairly uniform) laws to protect foreign and local patents, trademarks and copyright (Nimmer & Krauthaus, 1992; Antons, Chapter 22). In the post-WWII period, multinational corporations have also emerged as de facto legal drafters and regulators. Their contributions to a new *lex mercatoria* include a dramatic increase in contract standardisation; industry-wide choices of commercial arbitration in preference to litigation; and the development of commercial rules which are not articulated in legislation but are nevertheless regarded as binding.[5]

Taken together, these pressures are making national jurisdictional boundaries permeable (Nimmer & Krauthaus, 1992). A key consequence of globalisation is that the individual nation-state no longer has exclusive control over the nature and content of its legal system. It is buffeted by extra-national influences. Trends and pressures across developed countries and between developed and developing countries increasingly drive developments in local law. Lawrence Friedman (1994) has suggested that the end result may be the emergence of a 'global' modern legal culture. But complete convergence of commerce and law across the globe is not inevitable. As this glimpse of commercial contracting in Indonesia suggests, globalisation will inevitably alter formal contracting and local legal infrastructure but powerful local political and cultural factors will also shape the extent and form that such change may take.

Most descriptions of the business environment in Indonesia down play the role of law as a social institution. In private exchange transactions, legal rules are depicted as absent, irrelevant or incompatible with the relationships and social norms that govern agreements.[6] The received wisdom is that relationships dominate legal rules in Indonesia, to the extent that 'lack of regulatory consistency, the unenforceability of contracts and the uncertain proprietorial security of investments and specialised technologies' have become major concerns for foreign investors (MacIntyre, 1994: 258). Economists working on Indonesia have been vocal in asserting that, 'the legal system has become a drag on both growth and fairness and autonomous rules are now necessary' (McKendrick, 1992: 106).

4　United Nations International Trade Law Commission (UNCITRAL) and the International Institute for the Unification of Private Law (UNIDROIT).

5　For example, Rosett (1992). Rosett cites the 'Banker's Rules dealing with documentary letters of credit: Uniform Customs and Practice for Documentary Credits', the International Chamber of Commerce Commission on Banking Technique and Practice (5th ed, 1983). Another example is the International Chamber of Commerce INCOTERMS defining commonly-used terms in the international carriage of goods.

6　For example, Kawashima (1974).

The Asian Law Centre at the University of Melbourne is currently testing this assertion in a project on the internationalisation of contracts in Asia.[7] By interviewing Australian and local lawyers, law reformers and bureaucrats in Asia, the Centre is building up a selection of contract case studies of international contract law and practice within each system. This chapter represents one of the contract 'snapshots' that highlights tensions between Indonesia's colonial contract legacy, the practice of patrimonial business relationships and pressures to reform local legal infrastructure.

An International Joint Venture in Indonesia

One of the transactions in the Centre's study was a foreign and domestic joint venture to create and operate a commercial bank in Indonesia. The parties included the foreign bank, the Indonesian counterpart and Indonesian financial regulators. Major local and international law firms provided the transaction advice.

The documentation underpinning the transaction was a Joint Venture Agreement (JVA); the Articles of Association of the Joint Venture Company; and a Technical Assistance Agreement. The latter was negotiated between the parties but also required intensive lobbying and education of government bureaucrats to familiarise them with how a foreign company runs a banking business.

Indonesia has special regulations on banking joint ventures. As a result, the transaction required major coordination – documents had to be checked by the Ministry of Finance and then ultimately approved by the Ministry of Justice. Inter-departmental liaison was particularly time consuming. A number of new bureaucrats were responsible for this transaction and it took time to build the necessary relationships. From the lawyer's point of view, a transaction moves much more quickly through regulatory channels if the lawyer knows bureaucrats 'on the inside'. Typically the basis for these professional relationships is graduation from the same university or high school. It is maintained through lunches, tennis, or – for men in their 40s or 50s – games of golf. Family connections are also important. Lawyers usually open discussions with bureaucrats by making small talk and mentioning family and acquaintances in common.

The Ministry of Finance provides standard form documentation for banking joint ventures and requires the JVA, particularly the Articles of Association, to be translated accurately into *Bahasa Indonesia* (although the English language version is usually the governing version). In this transaction the JVA was prepared in English. Some of the precedents (models) for the documentation were drawn from the participating law firms' files; others were customised for this transaction. Much redrafting was done at the request of the Ministry of Justice. In particular, clauses proposed by the foreign partner were frequently rejected. The foreign partner's law firm in their home jurisdiction tended to draft first and ask questions later. Consequently, the response to the question 'Do you have an equivalent for our local stipulation x?' tended to be 'No'. In trying to adopt stimulations common in banking transactions in their home jurisdiction, the lawyers were attempting to graft a sophisticated model of an international banking joint venture onto a legal system

---

7   A project undertaken by Malcolm Smith, Veronica Taylor and Kumar Menon, with Sarah Biddulph, Sean Cooney and Peter Neustupny. At the time of writing, 50 interviews had been conducted in Japan, Korea, Indonesia, Malaysia and Australia.

that had very few equivalent legislative provisions and practices. The Ministry of Justice accepted some of the suggestions but rejected many others.

The dispute resolution procedure in the JVA was suggested by the Ministry of Justice. It provides for arbitration under the Indonesian arbitration body BANI,[8] recommended as the most common and reliable form of dispute resolution available in Indonesia. The arbitration clauses stipulate Indonesian law as the governing law and adopt the UNCITRAL rules of arbitration.

One of the lawyers acting for the foreign bank regarded this as a 'fairly typical' joint venture but it was, at the time, the only one of its kind in Indonesia. Not surprisingly, it experienced problems in the early stages. One example concerned the start-up date. The foreign partner wanted to start operations on a Monday and to advertise the joint venture in Monday's newspapers. The Ministry of Finance had promised approval for the proceeding Saturday but this had not transpired. The law firm tried to lobby the Ministry to allow the bank to commence operations but the Ministry was firm. The foreign partner, though anxious to start trading, was told that they would print the advertisements at their peril.

The incident illustrated a more general problem that the bank's legal advisers identified − trying to explain to a foreign client why government officials might renege on assurances without blinking or give undertakings that simply fail to materialise. The incident also symbolised some of the friction between the joint venture partners and the foreign partner's perceptions about how to conduct business in Indonesia.

The Indonesian party was concerned that the foreigners were being too aggressive in their dealings with the Ministry of Finance. The Indonesian partner appeared to want to 'have the upper hand' in dealing with the Ministry, probably because of close friendships between senior Indonesian bank officers and people in the Ministry. As a result, the Indonesian joint venture partner tended to side with the Ministry of Finance stance, even in situations that seemed unreasonable to their foreign partner. The Indonesian partner had a much stronger sense of the importance of ongoing relationships with the Ministry. By contrast, the foreign partner focused exclusively on overcoming hurdles ahead of the start-up date, only later coming to appreciate the importance of ongoing relationships with Ministry officials.

How should we characterise the transaction at this point? I suggest that we can identify a number of themes, the first being the importance of the relationships underpinning the transaction.

Relational Contracting in a Patrimonial State

Historically, the development of private business interests in Indonesia has been based on personal or familial connections to those in power. The call for a consistent and predictable legal framework for contracting in Indonesia is a direct response to this pattern of patrimonial business relationships within an authoritarian, interventionist state (MacIntyre, 1994: 245). The post-independence Constitution legitimated an active role for the state in fostering commercial development by expressly including the principle that economic activity should be organised on the basis of joint endeavour; and that the state should control key sectors of the economy for the benefit of the people (MacIntyre, 1994: 246, citing Art 33). This it

---

8   *Badan Arbitrase Nasional Indonesia,* the Indonesian National Arbitration Body.

did through a nationalisation program and preferential funding of state-owned enterprises. Such a move was accepted in part because of scepticism about free-market capitalism and because of the paucity of private business activity outside the immigrant Chinese trading communities.

Private actors had to rely on preferential treatment by powerful patrons. As parliamentary democracy declined after 1957, patronage was more likely to be found among senior civilian and military officials:

> Commercial success was closely correlated with the position of a business person's patrons in government. Firms grew largely on the basis of preferential government treatment: those which had access to subsidies and various rent-taking opportunities were about to accumulate the capital necessary for further expansion (MacIntyre, 1994: 248).

Economic policy under the Soeharto regime remained interventionist and continued to extend preferential support for state-owned enterprises, buoyed by revenues from the 1970s oil boom. State ownership predominated in the banking sector, which provided subsidised credit to priority sectors of the economy and indigenous borrowers. During the 1970s, trade and foreign investment were both heavily regulated through restrictions on access to business sectors and the imposition of onerous requirements for transferring control to local interests (MacIntyre, 1994: 250).

A slump in both oil and commodity prices in the 1980s demanded a change of policy direction. Indonesia responded by adopting a neo-liberal solution: structural adjustment; deregulation of the banking industry; the reform of local and foreign investment laws; and the lowering of tariff and non-tariff barriers to trade (MacIntyre, 1994: 254). This 'strategic retreat' by the state has meant that the private sector is now dominant within the economy but as MacIntyre argues (1994), the effects of long-term state domination of business linger in the patterns of business-government interaction.

The dominant form of interaction between government and business remains the patrimonial or clientelistic relationships between individual business people and senior government figures. Under Soeharto, these included a number of Chinese Indonesian figures and members of the President's immediate family, who in turn functioned as proxy political patrons for other investors.

These patrimonial relationships, however, create a number of dissatisfied outsiders: local business people who do not enjoy the special privileges of those linked to government patrons; foreign investors who find the price of buying into and sustaining a patronage relationship too high; and external agencies such as the World Bank. In the past, business disquiet with the status quo has either been stifled, or not expressed publicly (especially in the case of Chinese entrepreneurs). Collective action by business communities was largely unknown – government-sponsored organisations such as the national Chamber of Commerce and Industry (KADIN)[9] remained compliant toward government policy, with the leadership rewarded with preferential access to government contracts. But those outside the patrimonial networks have a vested interest in arguing for a more level commercial playing field, 'which is likely to have the effect of promoting a less uneven political playing field for business' (MacIntyre, 1994: 258).

In the past, law did not threaten the scheme of presidential family or privileged patron contracting that developed in Indonesia. From the parties' point of view, the

---

9   *Kamar Dagang dan Industri.*

legal system simply furnished formalities that may contain standards of performance and rights of enforcement, but which were subordinate to the power dynamics of the more complex long-term relationship. Commercial outsiders are impatient with this approach. They argue that better laws and more transparent regulation would operate to discipline both the state and business – to wean them away from clientelistic favouritism and promote more open, efficient competition and further economic development.

This 'legislative lag' is evident in a range of areas, including the banking joint venture described above. In part it is the product of Indonesia's colonial contract legacy.

The Colonial Contract Legacy

The colonial legal legacy in Indonesia was Dutch civil law. Recent and projected legislative reform in commercial law preserves Dutch concepts, as well as elements of Islamic law and *adat* (traditional customary law), while incorporating aspects of Anglo-American commercial law. As with other systems embodying 'legal pluralism', the national legal system dominates indigenous law but *adat* remains relevant for domestic and international commercial transactions, particularly in relation to ownership of land (Hooker, 1975).[10]

The legal rules that govern contracts in Indonesia are found primarily in the Dutch-style Civil Code and partially revised Commercial Code, although many of the Code provisions are now regarded as obsolete or inappropriate for current commercial transactions. Commercial parties routinely seek to 'contract out' or exclude the operation of archaic parts of the Code from their own contracts. The fact that there is no authorised or standardised translation of the Civil Code into English also symbolises its lack of pungency. A number of projects in Indonesia have aimed for changes to commercial and consumer contracting.[11] The reality, however, is that these are not necessarily the areas of priority law reform and can only proceed as far as the human resources allocated to them allow.

At the same time, Indonesian Code provisions are now overlaid with domestic legislation dealing with specific forms of transactions and with international conventions and principles dealing with contract.[12] The most important of these in the transaction discussed above are the foreign investment regulations and the rules applying to banking as a newly-liberalised sector. As in many legal systems seeking to attract foreign investment and new technology, the Indonesian government supervises foreign-invested joint ventures. Joint ventures involving a foreign partner

---

10 Singapore, Hong Kong, the Philippines and Korea arguably also fall into this category but there are other ways in which indigenous law is supplanted or ignored. In Hooker's typology, Australia is an example of colonial laws which marginalised indigenous laws. Thailand, Japan and Taiwan illustrate the voluntary adoption of Western law and the PRC is an example of the abolition of a traditional indigenous legal system in favour of revolutionary ideology.

11 Two of the most important were the contract law study and reform project conducted by a team under Prof Sunaryati Hartono; and the US-funded ELIPS project in the Ministry of Finance, headed by Normin Pakpahan.

12 Examples include the Convention on the International Sale of Goods (Vienna Convention) and the International Principles for International Commercial Contracts (completed by UNIDROIT in 1994 and available for voluntary adoption). See, for example, Bonnell (1992).

must be approved by the Capital Investment Coordinating Board (BKPM)[13] and the Ministry of Justice.[14] Further approvals may be needed from other relevant agencies, including the Ministry of Finance, depending on the nature of the joint venture. One practical effect of this is that a joint venture agreement must be in writing, so it can be approved. Adoption of a standard form agreement is not compulsory, but agreements tend to be drafted in a form known to be acceptable to the government agencies (Tumbuan, 1992). More flexibility is shown for other kinds of contracts, for example, licensing agreements.

The Indonesian regulatory agencies also monitor the agreement. In this case BKPM requires six-monthly and annual reports to be filed.[15] Amendments to the JVA require prior approval; additional finance requires approval from the Bank of Indonesia; and amendment to the articles of association of the joint venture company and certain other matters must be referred to the Ministry of Justice.[16] Importation of goods in connection with the JVA requires an import licence from the Ministry of Trade and approval is required from the tax authority. In addition to this local legal supervision, the transaction may also be subject to international regulation, one example being double taxation treaties in force between the investor's country and the host country.

In common with most civil law systems, Indonesia's Civil Code prescribes relatively few requirements for contract formation. Transactions between local parties continue to be oral or only partially evidenced in writing – for example, the necessary documentation for transfer of real property. This opens the way for the introduction of foreign or 'globalised' contract forms and practice. Demand in Indonesia for written commercial contracts with detailed provisions (or as one practitioner puts it, 'the documents from Hell') is usually imposed by the investor,[17] by government regulation, by multinational practice[18] or by international agencies such as the World Bank (Upham, 1994). In the banking joint venture discussed above, the precedents being used by the Indonesian and foreign lawyers involved were not Indonesian but a distillation of English and United States banking law and practice. Although the transaction marked the absorption or acceptance of some of the foreign banking joint venture model into Indonesia, it was a negotiated process –

---

13 *Badan Koordinasi Penanaman Modal.*

14 Presidential Decree No 21 of 1991, Art 3, Paragraph 1.

15 A joint venture company is obliged to establish a Board of Management which, under Art 44 of the Indonesian Commercial Code, is charged with the management of the affairs of the company including any joint venture agreements entered into by it and is accountable to the General Meeting of Shareholders.

16 The articles of association of the joint venture company may be amended only by an extraordinary resolution of a general meeting of shareholders. The amended articles must, in turn, be approved by the Ministry of Justice (Tumbuan, 1992: 106-107).

17 Such demands frequently originate in the 'West'. However, note the statement made by Japanese Prime Minister on his August 1994 visit to Vietnam, where he indicated that the development of legal infrastructure would be necessary for attracting private investment from Japan. Such pronouncements are significant, given Japan's prominent position within the World Bank and the pattern of inward investment in developing Asian countries originating in other regional economies.

18 An example would be the leverage of a foreign franchisor in Indonesia, which, until 1997, had no positive law or industry code of conduct dealing specifically with franchises. However, this area is now regulated by Government Regulation No 16 of 1997, dated 18 June 1997; and Decree of the Minister of Industry and Trade No 259/MPP/Kep 7/1997, dated 30 July 1997. For an overview of these regulations, see Ibrahim and Weiss (1997/1998: 43).

the Ministry of Finance rejected or directed changes to as many provisions as it accepted.

The demand for rule-based certainty and state-of-the art contract drafting and regulation is a familiar one. Foreign investors the world over want a clear and comprehensive framework of contract and company laws, competition law and policy, taxation, intellectual property protection and competent, timely legal adjudication in courts, tribunals and arbitration centres. The governments of developing economies have a stake in providing the legal framework. Developing 'modern' commercial law contracts; attracting foreign investment by providing a sympathetic legal environment; and adjudicating commercial disputes are all ways of enhancing political legitimacy.

However, it would be wrong to characterise comprehensive legal rules and improved legal services as the 'modern' replacement for relational contracting. Law is embedded in the same cultures from which commercial transactions are formed. In areas where states allow private parties autonomy over their own transactions, relational, economic and social aspects of the business deal are usually more important to the participants than the legal requirements. When trouble hits, the legal 'rules' governing contracts in most societies may be invoked but are seldom tested in formal dispute proceedings. Even in the United States, business people have been found to rely on 'reciprocal trust' as the binding element in their transactions, fostered by trade customs, 'unwritten laws', repeat trading and potential damage to reputation as a method of enforcing performance.[19] Studies of relational contracting in Taiwan and the PRC, where Chinese business communities prefer to rely upon informal networks of relationships rather than law to protect their interests, have drawn similar conclusions (Jones, 1994; Winn, 1994).

In cross-cultural, off-shore investment in Indonesia, the parties are usually compelled to acknowledge the importance of the social and political relationships underlying the deal. For foreign investors, contract law and legal advice provide an additional, 'residual form of security' (Deakin et al, 1994: 337). They provide a basis for negotiations with a new partner in an unfamiliar environment and for planning and executing the rules of performance for the project. Should problems arise, contract law acts as a 'fall-back' position and a basis for predicting when a court or arbitral tribunal's adjudication may be sought and what results are likely. This is the value of the commercial certainty claimed for contract rules. The real 'certainty' of the rules, however, is usually somewhat less – the transaction problem scenario will be strongly influenced by a matrix of factors, including the identity of the parties; their relative leverage in the transaction; the quality of the legal advice available; the cost of submitting to formal adjudication; the availability of a 'rules that fit the transaction' type and the capacity and competence of the tribunal.

Cracks in the Legal Infrastructure

The choice of commercial arbitration as the dispute resolution mechanism in the joint venture discussed is typical of such transactions in Indonesia. It represents a conscious decision by the investor (and here, the Ministry of Finance) to insulate the transaction from the Indonesian court system.

---

19 Campbell and Harris (1992: 184) suggest that 'the adequate form of self-interest in long-term contracts is co-operation'. See also Deakin et al (1994).

Disquiet about the capacity, competence and neutrality of Indonesian courts dealing with international commercial matters is fairly widespread. In other interviews in this study lawyers described four perceived problems with the courts:

(1) judges are not trained to a level where they can comprehend foreign invest-
    ment documentation in English and are not comfortable with international
    transactions;

(2) to foreign clients, it appears that the courts are biased in favour of the
    Indonesian party;

(3) both lawyers and their foreign clients believe that judges may be corrupted
    through bribery; and

(4) decisions made by courts in commercial cases are not consistent.

Arbitration under Indonesian law in Jakarta represents the best of a limited range of choices. Unlike Australia, Indonesia draws a distinction between international arbitration conducted locally, and domestic arbitration. By locating possible future arbitration in this transaction in Jakarta, the lawyers hope to have it treated as local, and therefore enforceable arbitration. In theory, the enforcement of an 'inter-national' arbitral award in Indonesia should also be possible: Indonesia ratified the New York Convention on the Recognition and Enforcement of Foreign Arbitral Awards in 1981,[20] which requires enforcement to the extent that the foreign award is not contrary to public policy.[21] However, in practice, enforcement is still difficult and there have been few cases in which this has been done successfully through Indonesian courts.[22]

Although a preference for informal dispute resolution and avoidance of socially destabilising litigation is often represented as being 'Asian' in origin, this transaction suggests that the choice is one of compromise rather than culture. Despite the apparent care in drafting and the attempt to insulate the transaction as far as practicable from local law and the court system, the lawyers had little illusion about the outcome if the transaction began to unravel.

Changing Roles for Transaction Advisers

The lawyers in this transaction were conscious of their role being wider than that of legal strategists; they became comprehensive transaction advisers. Lawyers in many Asian countries have traditionally been few in number and concentrated in litigation roles. The globalisation of trade and business, however, has meant that legal services have changed dramatically for both lawyers and their clients in Asia. Lawyers in our study were very conscious of acting as cultural 'buffers', softening or diverting potential sources of friction between their client and the other party. They regarded themselves not only as legal experts but as cultural informants and advisers on local government and business practice. Foreign lawyers working in Indonesia are restricted by local law from giving legal advice. Not surprisingly, their

---

20 Presidential Decree No 34 of 1981.

21 In disputes between an investor and the Indonesian government, the Convention on the
    Settlement of Investment Disputes between States and Nationals of Other States (ICSID)
    applies and was ratified by Indonesia in 1968.

22 On arbitration in Indonesia, see generally, Green, Chapter 21.

focus was on promoting a workable transaction rather than preparing for possible litigation.

In this transaction one of the major difficulties was a clash of personalities among the clients. The foreign managers appointed to oversee the joint venture had no previous experience in Indonesia and, initially, little understanding of Indonesian business culture. Their tendency, in the eyes of some of their legal advisers, was to 'go full bore' and not to pull back when the situation demanded it or the Indonesian parties expected it. One example occurred in negotiation regarding whether Indonesian technicians would be paid at the same rate as foreign technicians performing the same work. For the Indonesian partners this was a sensitive issue which would colour perceptions of the competence of their Indonesian personnel and of the quality of technical transfer. When the foreign partners became irate during discussions their lawyers would try to persuade them not to show aggravation because it would result in significant loss of good will.

The gender dimension of the transaction was also interesting. In a country like Indonesia where class tends to trump gender in the professions, the participation of women in transactions as businesspeople, lawyers or bureaucrats is not remarkable. Where, as here, women lawyers are among those on both sides of the transaction, foreign clients often assume that they are secretaries waiting to take coffee orders. The comfort zone for European and American clients is a grey-headed senior male Western lawyer heading the transaction. Female lawyers are conscious of the time it takes to earn respect from such foreign clients.

The Trajectory of Transformation

This brief discussion of a banking joint venture is not intended as a template for the direction of legal change in Indonesia. It merely samples some of the dynamics in an international contract transaction in the 1990s. Ultimately, the preliminary data from the study as a whole is intended to challenge undifferentiated views of Indonesian contracts. The case studies suggest that international influences and industrialisation are inducing change in the form and content of contracts in Indonesia, as in most Asian legal systems. However, these international 'models' are in turn moulded to some degree by local legal characteristics and culture. Although it is possible to draft a contract that appears 'international' and standardised on its face, local people, culture and law become vitally important when contracts are interpreted or enforced. While it is important to trace the contours of contract 'globalisation', we should be aware that the convergence of contract laws and practices through the Asia-Pacific region to 'known' or imagined benchmarks may be a mirage.

References

Australia-Japan Research Centre, 1994, *Implementing the Bogor Declaration: Report*, Australia-Japan Research Centre, Australian National University.

Bonnell, MJ, 1992, 'Unification of Law by Non-Legislative Means: The UNIDROIT Draft Principles for International Commercial Contracts', *American Journal of Comparative Law*, vol 40: 617-33.

Cammack, M, 1989, 'Islamic Law in Indonesia's New Order', *International and Comparative Law Quarterly*, vol 38: 53-73.

Campbell, D and Harris, D, 1992, 'Flexibility in Long-Term Contractual Relationships: the Role of Co-Operation', *Journal of Law and Society*, vol 20: 166

Deakin, S, Lane, C and Wilkinson, F, 1994, '"Trust" or "Law"? Towards an Integrated Theory of Contractual Relations between Firms', *Journal of Law and Society*, vol 21: 329-49.

Friedman, LM, 1994, 'Is There a Modern Legal Culture?', *Ratio Juris*, vol 7: 117-31.

Hooker, MB, 1975, *Legal Pluralism: an Introduction to Colonial and Neo-Colonial Law*, Clarendon Press, Oxford.

Ibrahim, R and Weiss, R 1997/1998, 'New Franchise Regulations Enter Indonesian Investment Scene', *Asia Law*, vol 9: 43.

Kawashima, T, 1974, 'The Legal Consciousness of Contract in Japan' (translated by C Stevens), *Law in Japan*, vol 7: 1-22.

McKendrick, D, 1992, 'Indonesia in 1991: Growth, Privilege and Rules', *Asian Survey*, vol 32, no 2: 106, cited in MacIntyre (1994: 258).

MacIntyre, A, 1994, 'Power, Prosperity and Patrimonialism: Business and Government in Indonesia' in MacIntyre, A (ed), *Business and Government in Industrialising Asia*, Allen and Unwin, Sydney.

Nimmer, RT and Krauthaus, PA, 1992, 'Globalisation of Law in Intellectual Property and Related Commercial Contexts', *Law in Context*, vol 10: 80-103.

Rosett, A, 1992, 'Unification, Harmonisation, Restatement, Codification, and Reform in International Commercial Law', *American Journal of Comparative Law*, vol 40: 683-97.

Taylor, V, 1998, '"Asian" Contracts: An Indonesian Case Study' in Milner, A and Quilty, M (eds), 1998, *Australia in Asia: Episodes*, Oxford University Press, Melbourne.

Trebilcock, M and Howse, R, 1995, *The Regulation of International Trade*, Routledge, London and New York.

Trubek, D, 1972, 'Toward a Social Theory of Law: An Essay on the Study of Law and Development', *Yale Law Journal*, vol 82: 1-50.

Tumbuan, FBG, 1992, 'Indonesia' in Buhart, J (ed), *Joint Ventures in East Asia: Legal Issues*, Graham and Trotman and the International Bar Association, London: 106-34.

Upham, FK, 1994, 'Comment: Speculations on Legal Informality: On Winn's "Relational Practices and the Marginalisation of Law"', *Law and Society Review*, vol 28: 233-41.

Weber, M, 1954, *Max Weber on Law in Economy and Society,* Simon & Schuster, New York, cited in Fitzpatrick, P, 1992, *The Mythology of Modern Law*, Routledge, London: 88.

Winn, JK, 1994, 'Rational Practices and the Marginalization of Law: Informal Financial Practices of Small Businesses in Taiwan', *Law and Society Review*, vol 28: 193-241.

World Bank, 1992, *World Bank Support for Industrialisation in Korea, India and Indonesia*, World Bank Operations Evaluation Department, Washington DC.

World Bank, 1993, *The East Asian Economic Miracle: Economic Growth and Public Policy*, Oxford University Press, New York, cited in MacIntyre (1994: 261).

21. Arbitration:

A Viable Alternative for Resolving Commercial Disputes in Indonesia?

Stephen B Green

The strong economic growth experienced by Indonesia over the decade up to 1997 saw commercial opportunities open up throughout the Indonesian economy.[1] In addition to the large Australian companies doing business in Indonesia, 'thousands of small and medium-sized Australian businesses' became involved in bilateral commerce (Davis, 1995: 102; Featherstone, 1995). Most, if not all, of these firms lack the first-hand experience and knowledge that the larger companies have developed over many years of doing business in Indonesia. In addition, smaller businesses may not have the resources to engage large accounting or law firms before venturing into the Indonesian market. While Indonesia still presents opportunities for Australian firms despite the recent crisis, doing business there is clearly not the same as doing business at home. Australian business investors, in particular small and medium-sized firms, therefore need to be aware of the situation they may face if problems arise between them and an Indonesian partner.

Although business relations between an Australian and an Indonesian party are neither more nor less immune to problems than those conducted solely between Australian parties, a difference is thought to exist in the manner in which Indonesian parties tend to handle disputes. The generic information on doing business in Indonesia includes the advice that Indonesians avoid confrontation and adversarial systems of dispute resolution, 'prefer[ing] to settle conflicts by consultation and consensus' (Hudson, 1994: 29). The same has been said of other Asian countries, notably Japan.[2]

One observer's view of the long-standing myth that Japanese corporations do not litigate is that each party involved in the dispute will make a rational assessment of the options available and adopt the dispute resolution strategy that best suits them in the circumstances (Taylor, 1995: 28). If, for instance, an adversarial method of dispute resolution is considered by one party to be the best option in the circumstances, this assessment may well overshadow any cultural predisposition toward non-adversarial means of resolving disputes. There are indications that Indonesians also employ such calculated behaviour. For example, use of litigation

---

1   The Indonesian economy grew at a rate of 7.1% between 1985 and 1995, and attained real Gross Domestic Product (GDP) growth of 7.8% in 1996 (Source: World Bank).

2   The discourse that addresses this issue includes: Kawashima (1963); Haley (1978, 1991) and Ramsayer (1988).

for tactical purposes in Indonesia has been noted in the environmental field (Trubek et al, 1994: 491-92) and also in civil cases (Imanuddin & Haryoso, 1995), where appealing against lower court decisions has been widely used as a means to delay payments or execution of the ruling.

There is a general perception among foreigners that they will experience substantial difficulties in enforcing their legal rights in Indonesia, this being described as '*the* most notable' problem facing foreign businesses in Indonesia (Davis, 1995: 102 – emphasis added). It is therefore desirable to consider the procedures available for resolution of commercial disputes involving foreign and Indonesian private parties.

Dispute resolution can be divided into two classes: formal and informal methods of resolution. Parties may seek recourse to the formal mechanisms of dispute resolution, the courts and arbitration, immediately when a dispute arises or after all other attempts to settle the dispute using informal mechanisms have failed. It is more often the case than not that lawyers become involved in the dispute resolution process only when the parties are considering or engaged in litigation or arbitration. These formal mechanisms of dispute resolution are the focus of this chapter.

The situation envisaged is one in which a foreign and an Indonesian party enter into a private commercial agreement. For whatever reason the relationship between the parties breaks down, with the foreign party seeking to enforce its legal rights against the Indonesian party, whose main assets are in Indonesia. The foreign party's prime concern, given that it expects a favourable outcome, will be the implementation of the decision or award against the Indonesian party. Having made the decision to pursue formal, or non-consensual, dispute resolution it has two options: litigate or arbitrate.

The foreign party must choose first whether to litigate in or outside Indonesia. As Indonesian law currently stands, for all practical purposes only the first option exists.

Enforcement of Foreign Judgments in Indonesia

As a rule, a decision of a condemnatory nature (principally money judgments) of a foreign judge or court is not enforceable in Indonesia. An express prohibition against the enforcement of foreign judgments is embodied in Art 436 of the Civil Procedure Code for Europeans (BRv),[3] but the status of the BRv in Indonesian law is unclear given that it has been superseded by the Revised Indonesian Regulation (RIB).[4] The BRv probably remains operative under Art II of the 1945 Constitution which states that all Dutch colonial laws continue in force until replaced by the laws of the Republic of Indonesia.[5] Thus, the BRv is referred to where the RIB is silent, there is no other relevant legislation and the relevant provision is not

---

3   Regulation of 8 November 1847, S 1847: 52 & S 1849: 63 (*Reglement op de Burgerlijke Rechtsvordering* – BRv). This was enacted during the Dutch colonial period when a dual court system existed in Indonesia. In this chapter, 'S' refers to Staatsblad van Nederlandsch-Indie (Government Gazette of the Netherlands Indies).

4   S 1941: 44 (Dutch text), 1 Husin 366 (Indonesian text) (*Herziene Indonesische Reglement* – HIR; *Reglement Indonesia jang Dibaharui* – RIB).

5   In 1959 President Soekarno unilaterally decreed a return to the 1945 Constitution (Presidential Decree No 150 of 1959), which has applied since then.

unconstitutional (Hornick, 1977: 98). The alternative argument is that the BRv as a whole is unconstitutional: having been enacted by a colonial ruler and being based on the racial categories of colonial law it is fundamentally repugnant to the basic principles of the Indonesian Constitution. Article 436, therefore, survives only as a guideline.

Although this debate has not been tested in a reported decision it is generally assumed that the BRv is still valid (Hornick, 1977: 98-99). Article 436 provides, inter alia, that:

(1) except as provided in Art 724 of the Commercial Code[6] and in other legislation,[7] judgments rendered in foreign courts may not be executed in Indonesia.

(2) such cases may be commenced, retried and decided in an Indonesian court (Hornick, 1977: 98).

The situation, then, is that a foreign party who has obtained a foreign judgment requiring execution against property in Indonesia will have to bring a new action in an Indonesian court.[8] In the new action, the Indonesian court is not bound by any of the findings of the foreign court. If the parties agree to submit to a foreign jurisdiction Indonesia will consider it a contractual obligation of the parties to comply with the foreign judgment, provided it is not contrary to Indonesian public policy (Hornick, 1977: 101). Whether there was such an agreement, or whether the defendant submitted to the foreign jurisdiction, are questions for the Indonesian court to decide.[9] Thus, even if the parties expressly stipulate a foreign jurisdiction in their contract as the forum in which any disputes between them are to be heard, an Indonesian court has considerable discretion to decide not to force the Indonesian party to comply with the foreign judgment and would not assist with the important aspect of enforcement.

Using Indonesian Courts

A foreign party is likely to face considerable difficulties in pursuing litigation in Indonesia, regardless of whether the action was originally commenced there, or was commenced after being pursued abroad because it could not get its judgment enforced. Mistrust of the Indonesian court system seems fairly common among foreign investors and their legal advisers (Taylor, 1998: 175; Taylor, Chapter 20). Observers have described the Indonesian judicial system as being: 'ill-equipped to

---

6   Article 724 of the Commercial Code refers to decisions on 'general average' under Indonesian maritime law.

7   No other legislation in respect of foreign judgments has been enacted (Hornick, 1977: 99; Huda unpub).

8   BRv, Art 436(2).

9   These conditions are not dissimilar to those imposed by the Foreign Judgments Act 1991 (Cth). See s 7(2)(a)(xi): registration must be set aside if enforcement would be contrary to public policy; s 7(2)(a)(iv): registration must be set aside if the foreign court did not have jurisdiction, with jurisdiction being determined by whether, amongst other things, there was any agreement between the parties to submit any dispute to the courts of the foreign country, and s 7(5) sets out the circumstances in which a defendant is taken not to have voluntarily submitted to the jurisdiction of the foreign court. The Foreign Judgments Act does not extend to judgments made by Indonesian courts.

deal with commercial matters particularly those with international dimensions' (Trubek et al, 1994: 486-87), 'inefficient and slow' (Della-Giacoma, 1995), 'capricious and unreliable' (Coudert Brothers, 1998: 8), and as being 'subject to intimidation from the executive branch of government' (Sreenivasan, 1995). In a country report on Indonesia, the World Bank stated:

> [T]he courts are overburdened and understaffed; there is little specialisation, with all types of cases going to general courts and judges; ... and there is a lack of confidence in the fairness of the trial process (Della-Giacoma, 1995).

These problems are not unique to Indonesia's legal system, and some, such as the cost and time involved in litigation, are faced by litigants throughout the world, including those in Australia (see Pheasant, 1998). It must also be recognised that both the judiciary and the Indonesian government, aware of the negative impact these perceptions create amongst foreign investors, have been willing to address these issues. For example, in response to concerns about judicial corruption, the Indonesian government is reported to have doubled judges' salaries (Ford, 1995; Gray, 1995: 18; Jakarta Post, 1996).[10] The *Mahkamah Agung* (Indonesia's Supreme Court) has also discussed various ways of improving efficiency, including tightening the criteria for appeal against lower court verdicts (Imanuddin & Haryoso, 1995) and implementing an alternative dispute resolution system (Kompas, 1995a; Kompas, 1995b; Suara Pembaruan, 1995; Jakarta Post, 1995).

The poor perception that many foreigners have of Indonesia's judicial system will not, however, change overnight. Indeed, a report prepared from a poll of 400 expatriate managers working in Asian countries stated, in relation to Indonesia:

> [P]rudent foreign businesses usually insist on a contract clause specifying that disputes will be resolved by an arbitration panel in a third country (Sreenivasan, 1995).[11]

Nevertheless, it would be more prudent to select Indonesia as the forum for litigation, and Indonesian law as that governing a contract. This is because, as already discussed, if a matter relating to a contractual agreement involving an Indonesian party has to be litigated, it will only be possible to enforce the judgment through an Indonesian court.

Arbitration

Arbitration is the resolution of a dispute in a binding manner by an independent tribunal, which may be composed of one or more people. It is usually formal and adversarial in nature. The tribunal's decision, called an award, is final and legally binding, subject to any right of appeal to the courts.[12] The parties to a transaction may agree to arbitration after a dispute has arisen; or they may require its use in

---

10   In 1995, a middle-ranking executive in a private company earned around six times more than a senior Indonesian judge would each month (Della-Giacoma, 1995). It is uncertain whether all judges received salary increases. It is known that District Court judges did (personal communication, Judge Mangkoedilaga, Jakarta Administrative Court).

11   The 1995 poll covered the countries of Singapore, Hong Kong, Japan, Malaysia, Thailand, Taiwan, South Korea, China, Indonesia and the Philippines and was conducted by the Hong Kong-based research agency Political and Economic Risk Consultancy.

12   The extent to which an award is legally binding, should a party refuse to abide by its terms, will depend on whether the jurisdiction in which enforcement is sought will recognise and enforce the award.

resolving future disputes by including a mandatory arbitration clause in their contract.

One of the advantages claimed for arbitration as a means of dispute resolution is that it does not possess the potential hazards of a national court (Craig, 1985: 57), such as a perceived bias against foreign parties. Other advantages are typically summarised as being relative informality, familiarity by arbitrators with technical subjects, privacy, and savings in time, money and effort. However, these advantages may not exist in reality (Redfern, 1976).

Arbitration is generally divided into two categories. One is ad hoc arbitration, where the rules and procedures used in the arbitration are uniquely fashioned, to a greater or lesser extent, to resolve a particular dispute, and have no life beyond that dispute. The other category is institutional arbitration, conducted under the auspices of one of the many arbitral institutions around the world. It is this second category that is the main focus of this chapter.

Indonesian law recognises dispute settlement through arbitration,[13] with the BRv containing provisions on arbitration and the execution of arbitral awards.[14] Foreigners involved in a dispute with an Indonesian party must usually decide whether they want a domestic or foreign arbitration, that is an arbitration within or without Indonesia. As discussed below, domestic arbitrations are usually enforceable in Indonesia but this is not always the case, as the distinction between domestic and foreign awards is not always clear cut. In one arbitrator's experience of trying to register a final award in Indonesia, a combination of factors (the arbitrator was Australian, the award was written in English, and one of the parties was a Swiss corporation) apparently led the District Court Registrar to conclude that the award was 'foreign' and therefore unregistrable. This was despite the arbitration having been conducted in Indonesia, and the award having been made according to Indonesian law (Pryles, 1993).[15]

In theory, the enforcement of a foreign arbitral award in Indonesia should be possible: in 1981 Indonesia acceded to the New York Convention on the Recognition and Enforcement of Foreign Arbitral Awards of 1958.[16] In addition, the *Mahkamah Agung* has held it does not have authority to adjudicate a contractual dispute where the parties provided for arbitration in the contract.[17] However, in practice enforcement is still difficult, and as yet there is no clear evidence that this has been done successfully through Indonesian courts (Himawan, 1998).

Recognition and Enforcement of Foreign Awards in Indonesia

Indonesia's accession to the New York Convention by Presidential Decree 34 of 1981 was subject to two reservations. First, it would apply the New York Convention only to the recognition and enforcement of awards made in the territory of another contracting state. Second, it would apply it only to disputes arising out of

---

13 Elucidation to Art 3(1) of Law No 14 of 1970.

14 BRv, Arts 615-651.

15 The issue of whether the award was foreign or domestic ended up before the *Mahkamah Agung* (Pryles, 1995: 76).

16 Presidential Decree No 34 of 1981, Lembaran Negara 1981 No 4.

17 Reg No 2924 K/sip/1981.

legal relationships, whether contractual or not, which were considered commercial under Indonesian law.

In case No 2944 K/Pdt/1983,[18] the *Mahkamah Agung* found that Decree No 34 of 1981 required a set of implementing regulations to enable the enforcement of a foreign award and that these implementing regulations had not been issued (Gunanto, 1991: 153). Some legal sources, however, maintain that the decree does not require implementing regulations and that the *Mahkamah Agung* acted too rigidly in interpreting the decree (Gunanto, 1991: 153-54). Another case was also decided in an unfavourable light, the court holding that the meaning of the New York Convention was vague.[19]

To end this uncertainty, the *Mahkamah Agung* passed its Regulation No 1 of 1990. This set out the criteria and procedures for the enforcement of foreign arbitral awards. The following conditions have to be met:

(a) the award must be rendered by a tribunal in a country which is a party to a bilateral or multilateral convention with Indonesia concerning the reciprocal recognition and enforcement of foreign arbitral awards;[20]

(b) the award must relate to a cause of action that would fall within the scope of commercial law as the term is understood in Indonesian law;[21] and

(c) the award must not contravene Indonesian law and public order or public policy.[22]

The procedure for enforcement is that an applicant must obtain a writ of execution from the *Mahkamah Agung* by registering an application with the office of the Registrar of the Central Jakarta District Court. The application must be accompanied by:

(a) an original or authenticated copy of the arbitral award, with an official translation in *Bahasa Indonesia*;

(b) an original or authenticated copy of the underlying contract on which the award was based, with an official translation; and

(c) a statement from the Indonesian diplomatic representative in the country where the award was made, stating that the country is bound by a bilateral or multilateral treaty with Indonesia concerning recognition and enforcement of foreign arbitral awards.[23]

The application must be submitted by the Central Jakarta District Court to the *Mahkamah Agung* within 14 days of the lower court receiving it. The *Mahkamah Agung* will then issue a writ that must be enforced by the Central Jakarta District Court or transferred to an appropriate court having jurisdiction over the matter.

The introduction of these regulations did not, however, entirely resolve the question of enforceability. One vital test remains: whether a foreign arbitral award is contrary to public policy. Article 4(2) of Regulation No 1 of 1990 defines public

---

18 Decision of the *Mahkamah Agung* dated 29 November 1984 (*Navigation Maritime Bulgars, Varna v PT Nizwar*).

19 *Trading Corp of Pakistan v PT Bakrie Brothers*. Full details of this case were not available at the time of writing.

20 Regulation No 1 of 1990, Art 3(1).

21 Regulation No 1 of 1990, Art 3(2).

22 Regulation No 1 of 1990, Art 3(3); Art 4(2).

23 Regulation No 1 of 1990, Art 5.

policy as the fundamental principles of the legal and social system in Indonesia (Gautama, 1998).

The first writ of execution, based on Regulation No 1 of 1990, was issued by the *Mahkamah Agung* in 1991. The writ was to enforce an award of US$146 million made by an arbitral tribunal in London under terms and conditions laid down by the Council of the Refined Sugar Association. A settlement was agreed under which Yani Haryanto was to pay ED & F Man (Sugar) Ltd US$27 million over three years. Haryanto paid a first instalment of US$9 million before suspending further payments, questioning the validity and status of the underlying contracts in the Central Jakarta District Court.[24] Haryanto contended that under Presidential Decree 43 of 1971 and Decree 39 of 1978 only the Indonesian government procurement agency (BULOG)[25] – and not private individuals such as himself – could import sugar. The Central Jakarta District Court held that the underlying contracts were contrary to public policy and thus invalid. This decision was confirmed by the Jakarta Appellate Court and the *Mahkamah Agung*.[26] Ultimately, the *Mahkamah Agung* rendered the writ of execution unenforceable holding that enforcement had become irrelevant (Gautama, 1998: 32). This decision generated controversy among Indonesia's legal scholars and lawyers, who questioned the court's interpretation of public policy.

Domestic Arbitration:
The Indonesian National Board of Arbitration

The limitations associated with litigation focus attention on arbitration as the preferred formal method of dispute resolution. However, enforcement of a foreign arbitral award in Indonesia is, despite the implementation of regulations, not automatic as reciprocity and public policy requirements must be met. The alternative is domestic arbitration, that is, arbitration conducted in Indonesia and governed by Indonesian law. As already mentioned, locating arbitration in Indonesia and making it subject to Indonesian law does not of itself guarantee that an award will be treated as domestic and therefore registrable and enforceable (Pryles, 1993). If a stronger nexus is required between the arbitration and Indonesia, having an arbitration conducted under the auspices of Indonesia's national arbitration body should fulfil this requirement.

BANI,[27] the Indonesian National Board of Arbitration, was established in 1977 at the initiative of KADIN,[28] the Indonesian Chamber of Commerce and Industry. Pursuant to Art 1(2) of its Constitution, BANI is an independent and autonomous body. Its functions include administering arbitration, both national and international, and giving binding advice regarding questions arising from a contract. It is composed of a chairman, a vice-chairman, three members and a Secretary, and has its headquarters in Jakarta. It maintains a list of arbitrators consisting of retired justices of the *Mahkamah Agung*, law professors, experts in finance and other

---

24   Case No 499/Pdt/G/VI/1988 [*ED & F Man (Sugar) Ltd v Yani Haryanto*].

25   *Badan Urusan Logistik.*

26   Case No 1250K/Pdt/1990 decision of the *Mahkamah Agung* dated 14 December 1991.

27   *Badan Arbitrase Nasional Indonesia*

28   *Kamar Dagang dan Industri*

prominent persons (Subekti, 1980: 60-61; Widinugraheni, 1996). After two decades BANI is only now starting to build up an international panel of arbitrators (Lawyer, 1998).

BANI prides itself on the fact that its fees (Rp 250,000 for registration; between Rp 150,000 and Rp 1.25 million (depending on the amount of the claim) for administration; and between 0.5% and 10% of the amount of the claim as the arbitration fee) are far less than those charged by other international arbitration bodies, such as the International Chamber of Commerce (ICC) and the International Centre for the Settlement of Investment Disputes (ICSID). This raises a question about BANI's financial viability, especially given the low number of cases it hears on an annual basis, an average of three cases decided per year for the period 1983-1992; and because KADIN − an organisation for Indonesian businesses − has provided substantial financial assistance to BANI.[29] There is, however, no plan to commercialise BANI (Widinugraheni, 1996).

Between 1979 and 1992 BANI handled 53 cases: 31 decided, 16 discontinued and six pending. In 1990 it handled five cases, in 1991 two cases, and in 1992 five cases (Abdurrasyid, 1993). In 1994, BANI dealt with 15 business disputes, over 90% of which were international (Suditomo, 1994). One explanation for the low volume of work BANI receives is that Indonesian businesses prefer mediation to arbitration.

Foreign Perceptions of BANI

To obtain information on the use by foreign lawyers of BANI, including their awareness and perceptions of this body, I prepared a questionnaire that was forwarded to:

(a) 29 lawyers in Australia with relevant experience in the area;

(b) lawyers from seven Australian law firms working at their firms' Indonesian affiliates' offices;

(c) a business consulting firm which advises on doing business in Indonesia; and

(d) the Australian Centre for International Commercial Arbitration (ACICA).

Twenty-one responses were received, of which information from 18 is summarised below.[30]

(a) Most lawyers recommend that their clients include an arbitration clause when contracting with an Indonesian party. They also recommend that arbitration take place outside Indonesia, usually under either United Nations Commission on International Trade Law (UNCITRAL), or the ICC rules. They do *not* recommend arbitration in Indonesia using BANI facilities.

(b) Reasons for recommending that arbitration take place outside Indonesia include: familiarity with, and the convenience and neutrality of, such a

---

29   An average of Rp 7,700,000 (AUD$1283.33 in June 1998) a year for the period 1988-1992.

30   Three respondents indicated that they were unable to make any useful contribution to the study.

forum; lack of confidence in the Indonesian legal system; and a lack of information on the procedural rules for arbitration in Indonesia.

(c) Reasons for not recommending BANI include: unfamiliarity with, and concerns as to the adequacy of, its facilities; a general uncertainty about BANI; and a perception that it is unreliable.

(d) The reasons for choosing a dispute resolution process not connected with Indonesia are as outlined at (b) and (c). Additional reasons include preference for a recognised arbitration centre, and client familiarity with other rules and fora.

(e) All respondents listed informal methods of dealing with disputes that they had been involved with.

(f) Of the formal mechanisms for dispute resolution, litigation was mentioned as a potential method of resolving a dispute. One respondent referred to an occasion where litigation was employed by the other side, and another did not discount its use if other means did not achieve the desired result.

(g) Australian lawyers had negligible direct or indirect experience of arbitration by BANI.

(h) No clear consensus emerged from the survey as to why BANI is under-utilised as a dispute resolution centre. Some of the possible reasons put forward included BANI's low profile; the lack of readily available information about BANI; and a general lack of confidence in, and a negative perception of, the Indonesian legal system.

(i) Most respondents felt unable to comment on BANI's neutrality and efficiency, or on the commercial acumen of its decisions and staff.

(j) Most respondents, again because of lack of direct experience, were not prepared to comment on whether Indonesian courts enforced BANI awards, or intervened in BANI proceedings.

(k) There appears to be no widespread awareness of the relationship between KADIN and BANI. The few comments that were made on this subject indicate that the effect of any relationship between BANI and KADIN would diminish the perception of BANI's independence.

(l) The consensus among respondents was that there is insufficient information available on BANI's services. There was a strong call for information on BANI's rules, its panel of arbitrators, and its success in resolving disputes.

The Procedural Rules of BANI

BANI's rules have been described by one of its former chairmen as being 'very simple' (Subekti, 1979: 11). Others have commented on their simplicity, stating that they may need 'to be supplemented in the parties' arbitration agreement' (Hudson, 1994: 29). If both parties agree, the tribunal will hear and decide a dispute according to other rules of procedure, such as ICC or UNCITRAL rules. However, an agreement not to be governed by the BANI rules must be explicit and in writing (Art 4(2)).

Formation of the arbitral tribunal is said to follow a system commonly used in most rules of arbitration, particularly the UNCITRAL rules (Subekti, 1979: 11).

However, the BANI rules (Art 5) are far less detailed than the UNCITRAL provisions (Arts 10-15). Unless the parties have agreed otherwise, each party is allowed to appoint one arbitrator, which they must do in the initial pleading (the request for arbitration in the case of the claimant, and the answer in the case of the respondent). There is nothing in the rules to prevent a party from appointing an arbitrator of foreign (non-Indonesian) nationality, and the Chairman of the Board can permit the arbitrators of both parties, upon their mutual agreement, to choose the third arbitrator from outside the list of BANI arbitrators (Art 5(3)). It is unclear, however, whether this would remove the original requirement that the Chairman of the Tribunal be of Indonesian nationality. Although parties are not obliged to choose BANI members as arbitrators in all but one instance BANI members have been appointed. Notably, no foreign national has ever been appointed (Hornick, 1991: 595).

Although the BANI rules do not stipulate the language of arbitration, a distinguished commentator has said that the arbitration will be conducted in *Bahasa Indonesia* unless the parties have specified another language (Hornick, 1991: 596).

Once a party has executed an arbitration agreement or a contract containing an arbitration clause, refusal to appear before an arbitration tribunal without an acceptable reason (it is not clear to whom the reason must be acceptable) is considered a breach of contract (Arts 11 and 12 deal with this situation) (Subekti, 1979: 11). If the respondent chooses to ignore the proceedings of the tribunal the hearing will continue in the respondent's absence and an award will be made in the claimant's favour, save where in the opinion of the tribunal the claim is 'not based on the law or justice' (Art 12(1)).

Articles 12(2) and (5) give respondents a de novo hearing in circumstances where they oppose an award made in their absence. Respondents are given three opportunities to appear and state their case before a final and binding award is made against them. An award made by BANI has the same legal force as a district court decision. While there is no right of appeal to the *Mahkamah Agung* (Abdurrasyid, 1994: 7; Widinugraheni, 1996)[31] a party can seek to have an award nullified by a district court for breach of Art 643 of the BRv which provides that:

> In case the arbitral award is not appellable, it can be challenged as being null and void when:
>
> (1)   the decision is rendered beyond the limits of the agreement;
> (2)   the decision is given by virtue of an agreement which is void or which has expired;
> (3)   the decision is given by a number of arbitrators who were not competent to decide in the absence of the others;
> (4)   subjects have been decided upon which were not claimed or the award had allowed more than what was claimed;
> (5)   the award contains controversial dispositions;
> (6)   arbitrators have omitted to decide upon one or more subjects which according to the agreement were submitted to their decision;
> (7)   the arbitrators have infringed procedural formalities which have to be followed on penalty of nullity (but this will be only the case when according

---

31   This statement is in conflict with, '[t]he BANI Rules are silent as to whether an award can be appealed' (Hornick, 1991: 597); 'the Law of the Supreme Court of 1950 (re-enacted as the Law of the Supreme Court of 1985) contains provisions for appeal against such awards' (Subekti, 1980: 60); and 'appeal from arbitral awards to the Supreme Court is allowed' (Gautama, 1998: 25).

to explicit stipulations in the agreement the arbitrators had to follow the normal court procedure);

(8)   documents have been decided upon which after the decision had been rendered, are acknowledged to be false or have been declared false;

(9)   after the decision has been rendered, decisive documents which had been retained by one of the parties are recovered;

(10) when the decision was based upon fraud or guile, committed during the hearings is later on discovered (Indonesian National Board of Arbitration, 1979: 39-40).

These provisions are 'imperative, absolute and may not be disregarded by the parties in an arbitration clause or an arbitration agreement' (Abdurrasyid, 1994: 9).

Pursuant to Art 17 of BANI's rules, the award can stipulate the time in which the losing party must abide by the decision. If at the end of this period the losing party has not abided by the terms of the award it is submitted to the District Court for execution (Art 18). An award shall be executed according to the provisions in the BRv (Art 19).

Given that the procedure for execution of an award made by BANI is the same as for a domestic arbitral award enforceability does not appear to present the same difficulties as those met by the successful party trying to register a domestic award not conducted under the auspices of BANI. However, as there are no reported instances of any recent attempts to enforce a domestic award, and as it is believed that all BANI awards have been complied with voluntarily (Suditomo, 1994; Hornick, 1991: 573), it cannot be stated with absolute certainty that enforcement of BANI awards will always be problem-free.

Conclusion

Of the two formal mechanisms for resolving a dispute between foreign and Indonesian parties to a private agreement, domestic arbitration in Indonesia appears to be the least problematic when it comes to the critical issue of enforcement.

It may be necessary to demonstrate a clear nexus between the arbitration and Indonesia in order to get the award recognised as domestic and thus registrable by a district court in Indonesia.

There is a very strong, though untested, basis for assuming that by using BANI the award will be treated as domestic and therefore enforceable in Indonesia. However, using BANI is not without potential problems, stemming in particular from the simplicity of its rules. This could be overcome by supplementation of its rules in the contractual arbitration provision; or by expressly providing that other specified rules (for example, those of UNCITRAL) are to be used.

Foreign lawyers lack awareness of BANI's rules and services, and the potential benefit it offers to clients because its awards are enforceable in Indonesia. Their limited knowledge of BANI appears to be derived from 'talk' within the profession rather than from direct experience. Respondents to the author's survey indicated that there was not enough information available on what BANI offers. They wanted more information on its rules and profiles of its arbitrators. BANI would not find it too difficult to meet such a request, though it could require a change in its way of thinking.

An issue raised by the survey results is that, while an arbitration clause is usually included in private contracts between Australian and Indonesian parties, arbitration is not in practice widely used as a method of commercial dispute resolution. The preference expressed in the survey results for informal dispute resolution mechanisms may simply reflect pragmatic commercial concerns. To avoid, or at least minimise, problems associated with resolving commercial disputes in Indonesia it is imperative that foreign parties understand how the system works. Unless they do it is unlikely to work for them.

References

Abdurrasyid, P, 1993, *Memorandum Badan Arbitrase Nasional Indonesia*, Jakarta, in possession of SB Green, Canberra.

Abdurrasyid, P, 1994, *Arbitration: An Indonesian Perspective*, Jakarta, in possession of SB Green, Canberra.

Coudert Brothers, 1998, *Survey of Asia Pacific Insolvency and Restructuring Regimes*, Coudert Brothers, Hong Kong.

Craig, L, 1985, 'International Ambition and National Restraints in ICC Arbitration', *Arbitration International*, vol 1: 49-81.

Davis, B, 1995, 'Indonesia Seeks Funds for Infrastructure', *ABM*, vol 15, June: 100-104.

Della-Giacoma, J, 1995, 'Indonesian Legal System Seen Hampering Investment', *Reuters News Service*, Reuter Business Briefing, 25 June.

Featherstone, 1995, 'Medium Companies Focus on Asia Links', *Australian Financial Review*, 21 March: 5.

Ford, M, 1995, 'Getting Law in Order', *Business Times* (Singapore), Reuter Business Briefing, 15 June.

Gautama, S, 1998, 'Indonesia' in Van den Berg, A (Gen ed), *International Handbook on Commercial Arbitration*, Kluwer Taxation Publishers, Deventer.

Gray, J, 1995, 'Indonesia braces for change', *Asia Law*, vol 7, September: 16-20.

Gunanto, H, 1991, 'Implementing Regulations for the 1958 New York Convention on the Recognition and Enforcement of Foreign Arbitral Awards in Indonesia' in Ko Swan Sik, Pinto, MCW and Syatauw, JJG (eds), *Asian Yearbook of International Law*, vol 1, Martinus Nijhoff Publishers, Dordrecht.

Haley, JO, 1978, 'The Myth of the Reluctant Litigant', *Journal of Japanese Studies*, vol 4: 359-90.

Haley, JO, 1991, *Authority Without Power: Law and the Japanese Paradox*, Oxford University Press, New York.

Himawan, C, 1998, 'Indonesia: Law – Missing Link in Stabilizing the Rupiah', *Jakarta Post*, Reuter Business Briefing, 6 April: 1.

Hornick, RN 1977, 'The Recognition and Enforcement of Foreign Judgments in Indonesia', *Harvard International Law Journal*, vol 18: 97-108.

Hornick, RN, 1991, 'Indonesian Arbitration in Theory and Practice', *The American Journal of Comparative Law*, vol 39: 559-97.

Huda, M (unpublished), 'International Commercial Dispute Resolution in Indonesia'.

Hudson, T, 1994, 'Indonesia Lapses on Company Law', *Asian Business Review*, June: 29-30.

Imanuddin & Haryoso, 1995, 'Indonesia: Court Plan to Limit Appeals Criticised', *Jakarta Post*, Reuter Business Briefing, 24 January.

Indonesian National Board of Arbitration (ed), 1979, *Arbitration in Indonesia and International Conventions on Arbitration*, Penerbit Alumni, Bandung.

Jakarta Post, 1995, 'Indonesia: Chief Justice Endorses Plan for Mediation System', Reuter Business Briefing, 23 August.

Jakarta Post, 1996, 'Indonesia: Corrupt Judges Must Be Punished – Bismar', Reuter Business Briefing, 12 February: 2.

Kawashima, T, 1963, 'Dispute Resolution in Contemporary Japan' in von Mehren, AT (ed), *Law in Japan: The Legal Order in a Changing Society*, Harvard University Press, Cambridge Massachusetts.

Kompas, 1995a, 'It's about Time to be Formed, Alternative Dispute Resolution', 13 February.

Kompas, 1995b, 'Priority, the Establishment of an Alternative Dispute Resolution Centre', 14 February.

Lawyer, 1998, 'Indonesia: International-Jakarta Crisis Halts Arbitration Plans', Reuter Business Briefing, 19 May: 5.

Pheasant, B, 1998, 'Companies Shun Courts in Disputes', *Australian Financial Review*, 25 September: 21.

Pryles, M, 1995, 'The International Arbitration Regime in the Asia-Pacific Region', *The Arbitrator*, vol 14: 69-83.

Pryles, M, 1993, 'Foreign Awards and the New York Convention', paper presented to the *Annual Conference of the Institute of Arbitrators, Australia* in Queensland, Australia, May.

Ramsayer, JM, 1988, 'Reluctant Litigant Revisited: Rationality and Disputes in Japan', *Journal of Japanese Studies*, vol 14: 111-23.

Redfern, A, 1976, 'Arbitration: Myth and Reality', *International Business Lawyer*, vol 4: 450-53.

Sreenivasan, V, 1995, 'Singapore: S'pore has the Best Legal System in Asia – Perc poll', *Business Times* (Singapore), Reuter Business Briefing, 20 July.

Suara Pembaruan, 1995, 'Alternative Dispute Resolution', 15 February.

Subekti, R, 1979, 'Introducing the Indonesian National Board of Arbitration' in *Arbitration in Indonesia and International Conventions on Arbitration*, ed The Indonesian National Board of Arbitration, Penerbit Alumni, Bandung.

Subekti, R, 1980, 'The Judicial System of Indonesia', *The Indonesian Quarterly*, vol 8: 52-61.

Suditomo, AS, 1994, 'Arbitration Body is Slowly Coming of Age', *Jakarta Post*, Reuter Business Briefing, 24 October.

Taylor, VL, 1995, 'Adding Another Side to the Iron Triangle – Lawyers', *Asian Business Review*, April: 28-29.

Taylor, VL, 1998, '"Asian" Contracts: an Indonesian Case Study' in Milner, A and Quilty, M (eds), *Australia in Asia: Episodes*, Oxford University Press, Melbourne.

Trubek DM, Dezalay Y, Buchanan R and Davis JR, 1994, 'Symposium: The Future of the Legal Profession: Global restructuring and the law studies of the internationalization of legal fields and the creation of transnational arenas', *Case Western Reserve Law Review*, 44: 407-98.

Widinugraheni, P, 1996, 'Indonesia: Benefits of Arbitration Are Not Widely Known', *Jakarta Post*, Reuter Business Briefing, 10 July: 10.

22. Intellectual Property Law Reform in Indonesia

Christoph Antons

When the current wave of reforms in Indonesian intellectual property law began towards the middle of the 1980s, it ended a period of several decades during which intellectual property law had been a neglected area of Indonesian law. While most of the relevant statutes and international agreements from the colonial period had been left in force after the independence of Indonesia on the basis of transitional provisions of the respective Constitutions,[1] their practical relevance was limited and little had been done to replace them with a national legislation. Only trade mark law was somewhat an exception to this generally bleak picture and was comparatively well established. Trade mark law had been quite extensively used during the colonial period[2] and decisions based on the colonial legislation continued to be reported during the 1950s. In 1961, the Colonial Trade Marks Law had been replaced by a new Trade Marks Law[3] which was still basically a translation of the former law.

The 1980s brought a sudden revival of interest in intellectual property protection. A new Copyright Law was introduced in 1982[4] and again revised in 1987.[5] A Patent Law[6] followed in 1989 and a new Trade Marks Law replaced the 1961 Law in 1992.[7] This development was accompanied by a large number of administrative decrees[8] providing, for instance, for the formation of a Copyright

---

1   The Colonial Trade Marks Law and Copyright Law, both of 1912, remained in force at first on the basis of Art II of the Transitional Provisions of the 1945 Constitution and then based on similar provisions of the 1949 Constitution of the United States of Indonesia and the 1950 Provisional Constitution of the Republic of Indonesia. After the return to the 1945 Constitution the validity of the legislation depended again on Art II of the Transitional Provisions of that Constitution. The validity of the Colonial Patent Law, however, ceased with independence as its substantial examination of patents in the Netherlands was regarded as conflicting with Indonesia's sovereignty, see Antons (1991b: 366).

2   See the list of cases in Antons (1995: Annex I).

3   Law No 21 of 1961 on Factory Marks and Trade Marks, in, *Lembaran Negara Republik Indonesia* 1961 No 290. As for an English translation, see Kaehlig (1993).

4   Law No 6 of 1982 on Copyright.

5   Law No 7 of 1987 on Amendment of Law No 6 of 1982 on Copyright. Texts incorporating the revised parts can be found in Simorangkir & Panggabean (1988) and Hutauruk (1988). For an English translation see Kaehlig (1993).

6   Law No 6 of 1989 on Patents, in *Lembaran-Negara Republik Indonesia* 1989 No 39.

7   Law No 19 of 1992 on Marks. An Indonesian version of this text can be found in Saleh (1994: 485-517). English translations of the Laws can be found in Kaehlig (1993).

8   The collection of Saleh (1994), contains 8 Government Regulations, 2 Presidential Decrees, 11 Decrees of the Minister of Justice and 3 circular letters of the Minister of Justice.

Council,[9] the appointment of special investigators for copyright violations,[10] the translation and reproduction of copyright protected works for educational and scientific purposes,[11] the importation of raw materials or certain patented products for domestic pharmaceutical products,[12] the registration of patent attorneys[13] and outlining details of the registration of patents, trade marks or copyright protected works.[14] There were also many important international activities beginning with Indonesia's ratification of the WIPO Convention in 1979 (Intellectual Property, 1979: 219), followed by a confirmation of Indonesia's membership in the Paris Convention for the Protection of Industrial Property in 1983[15] and by a number of bi-lateral treaties for the protection of copyright with the United States, Australia and the European Community between 1988 and 1992.[16]

These international activities culminated in the ratification of the GATT Agreement on Trade-Related Aspects of Intellectual Property Rights, Including Trade in Counterfeited Goods, concluded in 1993 (the TRIPs Agreement).[17] As a result of the TRIPs Agreement, reservations against some aspects of the other international agreements were dropped and in 1997 Indonesia ratified the Berne Convention for the Protection of Literary and Artistic Works, the Patent Cooperation Treaty, the WIPO Copyright Treaty and the WIPO Trademark Treaty (IP Asia, 1997b: 4). Reservations against Arts 1-12 and 28(1) of the Paris Convention were also removed by Presidential Decree No 15 of 1997 (IP Asia, 1997a: 4).

To understand that these remarkable changes in Indonesian intellectual property law were achieved within little more than a decade and to gain an impression of likely future developments in this field, one needs to know the political and economic reasons behind these reforms. There were several coinciding factors. Most importantly, improvements in transport and communication technology had led from the 1970s on to an increasing fragmentation of industrial production and had allowed the partial or complete transfer of production facilities to countries where production was most cost-efficient.[18] With their low level of wages, a few developing countries, in particular in Asia, offered the most attractive conditions for such a transfer. Their apparent success in accelerating industrial development subsequently led to a paradigm change in development theory from import substitution

---

9   Government Regulation No 14 of 1986 on the Copyright Council.

10 Decision of the Minister of Justice No M.04-PW.07.03 of 1988 on Copyright Investigators; Circular Letter of the Minister of Justice No M.01-PW.07.03 of 1990 on Responsibility for Investigation of Criminal Copyright Infringements.

11 Government Regulation No 1 of 1989 on Translation and/or Reproduction of Copyright Protected works for Education, Science, Research and Development.

12 Government Regulation No 32 of 1991 on the Importation of Raw Materials or Certain Patented Products for Domestic Pharmaceutical Products.

13 Government Regulation No 33 of 1991on the Registration of Patent Attorneys.

14 Regulation of the Minister of Justice No M.01-HC.03.01 of 1987 on the Registration of Copyright; Government Regulation No 34 of 1991 on Procedures for Application for Patent Registration; and Government Regulation No 23 of 1993 on Procedures for Application for Trade Mark Registration.

15 See the declaration of President Soeharto in Industrial Property (1983: 366).

16 As to the texts of these agreements, see Kaehlig (1993).

17 See the text of this agreement in the International Review ... (1994: 209-37). See also Djaman (1994: 135); Harjowidigdo (1994, 129); Priapantja (1995: 2).

18 See Robison et al (1987); Ruggie (1993: 32-33).

models to approaches favouring export-led development. International financial institutions like the World Bank and the IMF endorsed this approach and tied the granting of their credits to the creation of conditions favourable to export-led development (Robison et al, 1987).[19] In this context, the World Bank demanded a complete reform of the Indonesian legal system as 'an important prerequisite if the shift towards a less government-regulated environment for the private sector is to be successful' (Vatikiotis, 1989).

Due to its massive earnings from oil and gas as an OPEC country, Indonesia was able to resist these changes for quite some time and pursued a fairly protectionist economic policy until the middle of the 1980s (Simandjuntak, 1994: 211-12; Bresnan, 1993: 246-60). With the decline of the price of oil that accounted for roughly two-thirds of Indonesia's budget and export earnings between 1974 and 1984, this policy was no longer sustainable (Simandjuntak, 1994: 218; Bresnan, 1993: 260, 283). It became increasingly necessary for Indonesia to attract foreign investment and to create a legal infrastructure conducive to this aim. These fundamental changes in the Indonesian economy coincided with the growing importance of trade in services and new technologies for the industrialised nations which resulted in an increasing interest in intellectual property protection. In particular the United States government detected a correlation between the US trade deficit and losses of American companies abroad due to weak intellectual property protection (Ullrich, 1988: 131).

Indonesia became one of the main targets of a US crusade for improvements in intellectual property protection. In 1987, the country was threatened with the withdrawal of import privileges under the GATT 'Generalized System of Preferences' if there were no rapid improvements in this area of law (Gielen, 1988: 102; Gingerich & Hadiputranto, 1987: 7-8; Antons, 1991a: 81; Antons, 1991b: 371-72). Since the late 1980s, Indonesia along with many other East and Southeast Asian countries was also repeatedly placed on the 'priority watch list' for possible sanctions under s 301 of the US Omnibus Trade and Competitiveness Law (Antons, 1991a: 78).

The new Indonesian intellectual property legislation that was put into place under these coinciding pressures has again been revised in 1997 to bring the different laws into accordance with the recently concluded GATT-TRIPs Agreement. The following parts of this chapter examine some of the controversial issues under the current legislation in the areas of copyright, patent and trade mark law and finally assess the future of intellectual property protection in Indonesia in particular with regards to the TRIPs Agreement.

Copyright Law Reform in Indonesia

In 1982, a new Copyright Law (UUHC, *Undang-Undang Hak Cipta*) replaced the colonial *Auteurswet* 1912, but was criticised from the outset because of its insufficient scope of protection. The period of protection granted amounted to only 25 years after the death of the author. Foreign works were only protected if first publication of the work occurred in Indonesia and Art 10 went so far to allow an appropriation of the copyright by the State in the 'national interest' (Simorangkir,

---

19   See also the summary of the World Bank Report on Indonesia of 1981 in Robison (1986: 379-80).

1988: 64-65; Gielen, 1988: 101-102; Antons, 1991b: 371). The revision of 1987 increased the period of protection for original works to lifetime of the author plus 50 years, for derivative works and for works made by a legal entity to 50 years after first publication and for photographs, computer programs and compilations to 25 years after first publication. The scope of copyright protection was extended to cover also video recordings, sound recordings, computer programs and batik. Foreign works first published abroad were now also protected provided such a protection was guaranteed under a bi- or multilateral agreement.[20]

A further revision of 1997 was intended to bring the Indonesian Copyright Law into line with the TRIPs Agreement.[21] Among the more important changes in the new legislation is the introduction of rental rights for cinematographic works and computer programs and the introduction of a new Part IIIA dealing with licences and of a new Part VA covering neighbouring rights to copyright (*hak-hak yang berkaitan dengan hak cipta*). The term 'neighbouring rights' refers to a diverse group of rights of performing artists, producers of sound recordings and of broadcasts which are protected under the International Convention of Rome of 26 October 1961.[22] In common law countries, copyright extends to these rights, although it is in general regarded as a somewhat lesser form of an 'entrepreneurial copyright'.[23] Before the 1997 revision, performers' rights, sound recordings and broadcasts were included in the list of copyright protected works in Art 11 and the concept was little discussed in the Indonesian literature, which was still struggling to develop a terminology for these rights.[24]

While the revision of the Copyright Law has now addressed the matter, the approach chosen has created many new ambivalences. The reason for the distinction between copyright protected works and subject matter protected by neighbouring rights is that neighbouring rights are supposed to protect useful but not necessarily particularly creative material. Therefore, it is argued that this material does not deserve the same length of protection as 'classical works'. Moral rights, the different rights of an author to prohibit distortions of a work, do also not usually extend to 'subject matter other than works', as this material is called in the Australian Copyright Act. To achieve the rationale of this two tier protection, it is therefore essential to make a clear decision whether material should be subjected to copyright proper or to neighbouring rights.

Unfortunately, the new Indonesian legislation avoids such a decision and as a result creates much confusion with regards to the extent of the protection granted. The reason is that the rights of performers, producers of sound recordings and broadcasting organisations are now specifically regulated in the new Part VA, but have not been deleted from Art 11 which lists examples of copyright protected original works. The producer of Part VA material receives, thereby, a choice to seek protection under neighbouring rights or copyright principles. In view of the reduced

---

20 For a summary of these changes, see Gielen (1988, 101-107); Gingerich & Hadiputranto (1987: 7-10) and Kaehlig (1988: 18-19).

21 See Law No 12 of 1997 on Amendment to Law No 6 of 1982 on Copyright as Amended by Law No 7 of 1987 in: *Lembaran Negara Republik Indonesia Tahun 1997 No 29*.

22 As to the history of neighbouring rights, see Cohen Jehoram (1990: 75-91); Cohen Jehoram (1991: 266-70).

23 See Goldstein (1994: 191-94); Ricketson (1984: 136); McKeough & Stewart (1997: 155).

24 Simorangkir (1982: 66) translated the term literally from English as *hak-hak tetangga* and suggested as alternatives *hak berdekatan* (associated right) or *hak saluran* (channelled right), whereas Rosidi (1984: 86), preferred *hak cipta sampingan* (secondary right).

length of the protection for neighbouring rights, this decision will hardly ever be made in favour of neighbouring rights. However, even within the copyright part of the Law, there is confusion with regards to the length of the protection. Under Art 26(1) most of the material of Art 11 receives a protection period of lifetime of the author plus 50 years. This protection period is reduced in Art 27(1) for a selected group of works to 50 years after first publication. Performances, sound recordings and broadcasts are mentioned in both Art 26(1) and Art 27(1).

What constitutes a copyright protected work in Indonesia can be derived from the definition of the 'creation' in Art 1(2) and from the definition of the 'author' in Art 1(1). According to Art 1(2), a work is 'the product of any labour of an author in a special form and showing originality in the fields of science, art and literature'. An author is defined in Art 1(1) as 'an individual person or several persons together creating a work following their inspiration on the basis of intellectual capacity, imagination, skilfulness, competence or expertise which is manifested in a special form and is bearing personal character'. The earlier mentioned Art 11 contains also a list of copyright protected works. As Art 12 lists those works for which copyright protection is expressly excluded, the list in Art 11 is obviously only of an exemplary nature.[25] This conclusion is occasionally still disputed.[26] It is confirmed, however, by a declaration of Deputy Secretary of State Bambang Kesowo during the 1990 'Indonesia Copyright Enforcement Workshop' that the Indonesian Copyright Law protects works in the fields of science, art and literature and specifies in Art 11 'all sorts of works' covered by the Law (Kesowo, 1990: 26).

Another feature of the work that deserves some discussion is 'originality' as a condition for copyright protection. The 1997 revision has added the requirement of originality (*keasliannya*) to the definition of 'creation' in Art 1(2). It is also mentioned in the definition of the 'author' in Art 1(1), which demands that the work created must have 'personal character' (*bersifat pribadi*). The question, how much 'personal character' a work must possess or how 'original' it must be to be eligible for copyright protection, is still one of the most remarkable distinctions between the Anglo-American copyright tradition and Continental European perceptions of copyright.

For the Anglo-American concept of originality it was traditionally sufficient if the work originated from the author independently of the degree of creativity,[27] whereas Copyright Acts of Continental European countries usually demand a 'mark of personality of the creator of the work' or 'an imprint of personality'.[28] The consequence is that many works which are copyright protected in common law countries would only receive protection under neighbouring rights or competition law in Continental Europe. Indonesian copyright law is based on a Dutch tradition but shows also influences from common law countries. The question is, therefore, which concept of originality applies.

---

25 See Rosidi (1984: 57); Simorangkir (1990); Prawiroe (1989); Antons (1995: 68-73).

26 See Sinaga (1990) and the officials cited in Kaehlig (1993: 13).

27 See *University of London Press Ltd v University Tutorial Press Ltd* [1916] 2 Ch 607, cited in: Ricketson (1994: 110-11); See also Ricketson (1991: 183-99). As to the current position in the US, see the *Feist* decision of the US Supreme Court of 27 March 1991, in *Ars Aequi, Jurisprudentie en annotaties: Intellectuele eigendom* 1954-1992, Ars Aequi Libri, 1992, 348-52 and the note by Cohen Jehoram, 352-53.

28 See Dreier & Karnell (1991: 155).

On the one hand, the definition contained in the official Elucidation to Art 1(1)[29] points to an Anglo-American concept of originality. The term 'personal character' itself, on the other hand, seems to be a translation of the *eigen persoonlijk karakter* of the Dutch Copyright Law. Furthermore, Art 11(1)(a) protects besides books and brochures also 'all other written works'. This could possibly be interpreted as an adaptation of Art 10(1) of the Dutch Copyright Law which grants a 'pseudo copyright' to non-original writings,[30] thereby indicating stronger requirements for 'original writings'. A further indication for a Continental European concept of originality is the above mentioned creation of a separate neighbouring rights protection in the new Chapter VA, although the amendment lacks clarity and leaves the former copyright protection of the same material as an option.

The question of who is regarded as the author of a work is dealt with in Arts 1(1) and Arts 5-9. To facilitate the proof of authorship, the copyright may be registered in the copyright register of the Directorate for Patents, Trademarks and Copyright, situated in Tanggerang near Jakarta. If the registration violates a pre-existing but unregistered copyright, the owner of that right can file a cancellation claim with the District Court (*Pengadilan Negeri*) of Central Jakarta (Art 36(1)). This claim must be filed within nine months after the publication of the copyright registration in the State Gazette (Art 36(2)). This period of limitation is exactly the same as the one for trade marks under the former Trade Marks Law of 1961. It created enormous problems with that legislation, because the State Gazette appeared at times with a backlog of up to six years.[31] In addition, the Supreme Court developed during the 1980s the rather strange interpretation that the claim had to be filed exactly within the nine-month period. Therefore, claims were not only rejected if filed after the expiry of this deadline but also if filed too early when the State Gazette was not yet published.[32] The practical consequence of this approach and the backlog in the publication was that applicants had to wait for up to six years for the publication of infringing registrations.[33] The Trade Marks Law of 1992, therefore, introduced a new Trade Mark Bulletin specifically for the publication of trade mark registrations. Such a special gazette is not yet available in the field of copyright, however, and one can only hope that the Supreme Court will not extend its approach to the limitation period under the former Trade Marks Law to that under the Copyright Law and that the State Gazette will in future appear on time.

The Copyright Office has so far mostly decided the above mentioned question as to where to pitch the level of originality in favour of a low level approach and it has been willing to register trade marks, wrappers, packaging designs and industrial designs as 'works'. This has allowed trade mark pirates to abuse the copyright

---

29 'The author has to create something which is original in the sense that it is not a copy'.

30 As to this provision see Cohen Jehoram (1993: 20-22) and Cohen Jehoram (1992a: 340-42). As to the question whether this interpretation could be adopted in Indonesia, see Antons (1995: 78-80).

31 See Decision of the *Mahkamah Agung* No 226PK/PDT81 dated 30 September 1983, 'Jim Willie/ Swallow Globe Brand': 20; Decision of the *Mahkamah Agung* No 36PK/Pdt/1984 dated 16 February 1985 'Bagus/Lily Ball': 8; Decision of the *Mahkamah Agung* No 1026K/Sip/1982 dated 17 November 1982, 'Levi's': 2.

32 See Decision of the *Mahkamah Agung* No 36PK/Pdt/1984 dated 16 February 1985 'Bagus/Lily Ball': 8, 13; Decision of the *Mahkamah Agung* No 2674K/Pdt/1983 dated 30 March 1985, 'Lanvin': 12-13

33 See Kaehlig (1993: Trademarks under the 1961 Trademark Law 50-58); Antons (1995: 332-33).

registration as an obstacle to the enforcement of trade mark rights. The reason is that Art 6(2)(d) of the Trade Mark Law prohibits the registration of trade marks which use a copyright protected work of someone else. Trade mark pirates who achieve entry into the copyright register are thereby enabled to counterclaim for copyright infringement in trade mark infringement proceedings brought against them. This is a particularly difficult obstacle for the trade mark owner as a registered copyright can only be cancelled by a court decision, but not by the Copyright Office.[34] There are as yet no published court decisions dealing with this sort of registrations, which is perhaps not surprising given the fact that they are meant to delay trade mark enforcement and there is rarely an intention to defend them in court.

The state maintains a fairly strong role in the current Indonesian Copyright Law. Article 8, for instance, distinguishes for works created in the course of employment between government officials and other employees. If there is no different agreement between the parties, the copyright in works created by government officials in the course of their employment and used for purposes of this employment belongs according to Art 8(1) to the state as their employer, whereas the copyright in works created by employees in the private sector remains with the employee. The revision of 1997 has extended this Copyright ownership of the state to private parties who create a work on government order (Art 8(1a)). Part Four of the Copyright Law was originally named 'Copyright to objects of national culture' and allowed the President in a particular controversial provision to expropriate authors in the national interest with the approval of the Copyright Council. The revision of 1987 has abolished the controversial Art 10(3) and (4) and changed the title of this part to 'Copyright to works of unknown authors'. The government conceded in the Elucidation accompanying the revision that an expropriation of authors was not appropriate and that the compulsory licensing provisions of the Copyright Law would be sufficient to safeguard the interests of the state. The explanation concluded that the publication of works that are considered important for defence and security politics can still be prohibited.[35]

Article 10 in its current form contains areas in which the state exercises the copyright. These areas are pre-historical and historical works and other objects of national culture (Art 10(1)) as well as 'products of popular culture' which have become collective property (Art 10(2)). The article mentions as examples for such products stories, tales, fairy tales, legends, chronicles, songs, handicrafts, choreographies, dances, calligraphies and other 'works of art'. Calligraphies, batik and choreographies are also eligible for individual copyright protection under Art 11(1)(e), (h) and (k). In such cases the judge would have to decide whether, for example, a batik would be a non-traditional batik or a batik painting protected under Art 11(1)(k) or whether it would constitute a traditional design in which case Art 10(2) would apply.[36] In the same way, calligraphy or choreography would receive individual copyright protection rather than protection under Art 10 if sufficiently original.

Article 10 implements folklore protection as envisaged by the Tunis Model Copyright Law for Developing Countries drafted by the World Intellectual Property Organisation (WIPO) and UNESCO in 1976.[37] This approach ignores, however,

---

34 Cf Rouse & Co (1997: 22-23); Roosseno et al (1995: 13); Roosseno (1997: 11).
35 See the text of the Elucidation in Hutauruk (1988: 33).
36 Elucidation to Art 11 in Hutauruk (1988: 34-35).
37 Cf Weiner (1987: 86).

more recent criticisms that copyright is not the appropriate means for such a protection, because most of the protected works would hardly be 'original'; the time bar for copyright protection would be inappropriate; and the individual rights granted by a Copyright Law would be hard to reconcile with the collective rights to folklore that are often granted by traditional law. The latter argument has been raised in the Indonesian literature as well. This literature has interpreted Art 10(2)(b) which says that the Indonesian state exercises the copyright in 'products of popular culture' with regards to foreign countries as a limitation to the copyright of the state in the sense that the domestic use of such material in Indonesia by Indonesians would be free.[38]

Article 15 allows the government to secure the translation and reproduction of copyrighted works that have not been translated into Indonesian or reproduced in Indonesia within three years 'in the interest of education, science and research and development activities'. This aim is achieved in three steps: the first step is a certified letter by the government to the copyright owner ordering her or him to provide for a translation or a reproduction of the work within 18 months.[39] If the copyright owner refuses or does not reply within eight months, the government can order the copyright owner to grant a licence to an Indonesian publisher to translate or reproduce the work in Indonesia.[40] The government can itself take on the translation or reproduction of the work under Art 15(1)(c) and Arts 7, 17 and 18 of Government Decree No 1 of 1989 if the copyright owner does not grant the licence within 10 months or the Indonesian licensee does not implement the licence.

The revision of 1987 introduced a new Art 16 allowing the government to prohibit the publication of works that are in conflict with government politics in the fields of defence and state security, morality and public order after hearing the advice of the Copyright Council. The government mentions as reasons for this fairly problematic censorship provision the belittling of 'religious values' and of 'questions of ethnic groups and races'. The provision seems to target mainly certain separatist, anti-Chinese and Islamic tendencies but also publications regarded as communist, to mention only a few areas where the government could use its very wide discretion on this basis. While Art 16 prevents the publication of certain works, Art 17 allows the publication of a work in the government owned radio or television 'in the national interest' even without prior consent of the copyright owner.

Patent Law Reform in Indonesia

As mentioned above, the Patent Law was the only piece of the intellectual property legislation of the Netherlands East Indies not to survive independence. During the first few decades after independence, the only protection available was a provisional registration of an invention in order to safeguard priority under a future patent legislation. This provisional protection was based on a Decree of the Ministry of Justice of 1953.[41] The system of provisional registrations was abolished with the

---

38   See Rosidi (1984: 79-80); Simorangkir (1982: 136).
39   Article 15(a) of the Law on Copyright; and Art 3 of Government Regulation No 1 of 1989.
40   Article 15(1)(b) of the Law on Copyright; and Art 6 of the Government Decree No 1 of 1989.
41   See Announcement of the Ministry of Justice of 12 August 1953, No JS 5/41/4, in: *Berita Negara* No 69 (1953).

introduction of the new Patent Law in 1989. At that time, about 13,000 patent applications had been provisionally registered. Article 131 provided, however, that only the approximately 4500 applications registered during the last 10 years before the coming into force of the Patent Law could apply for re-registration under the new provisions.[42] Finally, only 1663 provisional applications were in fact refiled (Priapantja, 1997: 34). The Patent Law has been substantially revised in 1997 to fulfil the requirements of the GATT TRIPs Agreement.[43]

To receive patent protection in Indonesia, an invention must be novel, contain an inventive step and be applicable in industry (Art 2(1)). As to prior art information harmful to novelty, the Patent Law distinguishes between prior publication in writing which will be taken into account regardless of whether it has occurred in Indonesia or abroad and a prior publication through oral explanations, demonstrations and the like which will be harmful to the novelty of the invention only if the publication has occurred in Indonesia (Art 3).[44] Neither the Law nor the Elucidation specifies how many documents might be used to assess what constitutes the prior art base.[45] Problematic is further the wording of Art 5 which describes the requirements for 'industrial applicability'. An invention is there described as 'industrially applicable', if it can be produced or used 'in different branches of industry' This would be quite different from the requirement in s 116 of the WIPO Model Law for Developing Countries on Inventions which served as a model for the Indonesian legislation (Gautama, 1990; Patents: 63) and only requires the possibility of production or use in 'any kind of industry'. In view of the clear wording of Art 5 it is difficult to simply conclude that the provision is incorrectly worded (Kaehlig, 1993: 5) and it will be left to the courts to decide the exact requirements in this area.

Article 7 contains a list of inventions that cannot be patented. The revision of 1997 has deleted products and processes related to food and beverages and to animal and plant varieties from this list. Still not patentable are inventions concerning processes or products which are in conflict with current legislation, the public order or morality, inventions concerning methods for medical examination, therapy, treatment and operation and inventions concerning theories and methods in the areas of science and mathematics. The exclusion of inventions that are in conflict with current legislation is a rather conservative provision that precludes a flexible adaptation to technological changes if these changes happen to be ahead of legislative developments.[46]

The paramount importance of Indonesia's economic development is repeatedly mentioned in the preamble of the Patent Law as the motive for its introduction and it is expressed in a number of different provisions throughout the Law. An example is

---

42 See Gingerich (1989: 18-19). Cf also Priapantja (1997: 34), who uses slightly higher figures here.

43 See Law No 13 of 1997 on Amendment to Law No 6 of 1989 on Patents, in: Lembaran Negara Republik Indonesia, 1997, No 30. Printed also in: *Perubahan Undang-Undang tentang Hak Cipta, Paten dan Merek Tahun 1997* (1997: 39-103).

44 This distinction is in line with Art 114(2)(a) of the WIPO Model Law for Developing Countries on Inventions, see Gautama (1990: 60-61).

45 Cf, for example, s 7(1)(b) of the Australian Patent Act, which allows taking into account information made publicly available in two or more related documents, or through doing two or more related acts, if the relationship between the documents or acts is such that a person skilled in the relevant art in the patent area would treat them as a single source of information.

46 Cf the different approach in Art 5 of the WIPO Model Law for Developing Countries on Inventions.

Art 8 which allows the President to postpone the granting of a patent by Presidential Decree. According to the official Elucidation to the provision, the President can use this discretion, if an invention is 'considered important for the population or for the acceleration of the implementation of development programs in certain fields'.[47] The discretion does not extend to inventions for which a patent has already been granted or which can be the subject of an application claiming a priority right.

According to Art 11(1) of the Law, the right to the patent belongs to the inventor or to the legal successor of the inventor. The definition of the inventor in Art 1(1) has been revised in 1997 and is now restricted to a natural person or several persons together. It no longer includes a legal entity. Employees' inventions are regulated in Art 13 which contains a general transfer of the rights to the invention to the employer, if there are no different contractual arrangements. Article 13 does not distinguish between inventors in private employment and those in public service and it applies, therefore, also to inventions of academics in public and private universities.[48]

One of the most confusing parts of the Patent Law before the 1997 amendment was the recognition and partial protection of two different forms of prior use. Most Continental European Patent Acts grant such a limited protection to a prior user, for example to someone who independently from the patentee made the same invention and had not applied for a patent but had begun to use the invention at the time of the patent application.[49] Articles 14-16 of the Indonesian Patent Law allow a so-called 'prior inventor' (*penemu terdahulu*) to continue the use of the invention in spite of the granting of the patent to someone else. The term 'prior inventor' is rather misleading in the Indonesian context. It is used in American patent law which employs a 'first-to-invent' system where the right to an invention is based on the inventive act and not on registration. Indonesia, however, has established a 'first-to-file' system and the right to an invention follows from the patent registration. What the provisions of Arts 14-16 intend, therefore, is clearly a prior user protection as in most of the European Patent Acts. As in these Acts, the Indonesian legislation allows the 'prior user' to continue the use of the invention and a certificate confirming this right can be obtained from the Patent Office (Art 16 Patent Law). Before 1997, the Indonesian Patent Law contained in Art 22 a similar but more general provision which was more restricted in its implications and did not use the term 'prior inventor' (Antons, 1995: 215-17). The conflict between these provisions has now been resolved by the revision of 1997, which abolished Art 22.

With the consent of the Minister of Justice, the patent office may refrain from the publication of an invention which under normal circumstances precedes the substantive examination if such a publication would be in conflict with the 'defence of the security of the State'. The Elucidation to this provision allows the interpretation that the 'security of the State' refers to traditional security interests vis-à-vis threats from abroad but might also include domestic security threats.[50] The provision gives, therefore, a potentially wide discretion to the Patent Office and the Minister of Justice to withdraw an invention from the public.

---

47   Cf the text of the Elucidation in Saleh (1994: 292).

48   See Antons (1995: 184-85).

49   Cf for the examples of Germany, the Netherlands and Switzerland: Hubmann (1988: 102-103); Wichers Hoeth (1993: 53-55); Troller (1983: 81-82).

50   See Antons (1995: 203-204).

If a patent application is rejected, Art 68 allows the applicant to appeal to a special Patent Appeal Commission (*Komisi Banding Paten*) which is an independent body within the Ministry of Justice.[51] The decision of the Patent Appeal Commission is final (Art 71(2)). This is justified in the Elucidation to the 1992 version of the provision with the technical nature of the decision. For the same reason, the Elucidation to the provision also excludes an administrative appeal. This means in practice that a large percentage of the patent litigation in Indonesia will take place in a tribunal. It presumably also means that the interpretation of important parts of the legislation by this Commission will never be published, since the Official Patent News (*Berita Resmi Paten*) will only report the outcome of the appeal (Art 65(3) of the Patent Law) whereas the reasons for the rejection will be reported only to the applicant (Art 62(2) and (3) of the Patent Law). The revision of 1997 has shortened the period between the appeal and the beginning of the hearing of the appeal by the Commission from 12 to three months (Art 71(1)).

Important limitations on the rights of a patentee are to be found in Arts 20 and 21. According to Art 20, the import of patented products or of products that are produced by using patented processes is not regarded as an implementation of the patent. The former version of Art 21 allowed the import of a patented product or of a product produced by using a patented process by someone other than the owner of the patent. This provision was supplemented in the interest of the Indonesian pharmaceutical industry by Government Regulation No 32 of 1991. The Annex to this Government Regulation listed 50 pharmaceuticals which could be freely imported.[52] Article 21 has now been amended and a new para (2) has been added to Art 17, which deals with the rights of the patentee. Article 21 in conjunction with Art 17(2) now gives the patentee a right to prohibit such imports, provided that the patentee has begun with the production and the implementation of the process patent in Indonesia. This provision, therefore, still leaves the patentee unprotected against unauthorised imports, if he/she does not immediately implement the patent.

The granting of compulsory licenses is regulated in Arts 81-93. Such a compulsory licence can be obtained if a patent has not been worked in Indonesia for three years after it has been granted in spite of the opportunity for commercial exploitation (Art 82). Alternatively, a compulsory licence can also be obtained at any time by another patentee if the implementation of his/her patent is not possible without infringement of the patent in question (Art 88(1)). In this case, it is necessary, however, that the second patent clearly contains elements that represent a technological progress in comparison to the earlier granted patent (Art 88(2)). Following the TRIPs Agreement, provisions have been added to ensure that the patentee is first given a possibility to grant a licence voluntarily (Arts 83(1)(a)(3); 88 (2a)(a)).

A problematic provision is Art 89(1)(a) which allows the patentee to claim cancellation of the compulsory licence if 'the reason for the granting of the compulsory licence no longer exists'. The Elucidation to Art 89(1) points out that this refers to the non-use of the patent for three years. The question remains, then, whether a change in other conditions for the granting of a compulsory licence, for example in the public need for the products in question, is irrelevant. More importantly, however, the provision would allow the patentee to file a cancellation

51   The Elucidation to Art 68(3) stresses the independence of the Commission from orders of the Ministry of Justice or the Patent Office.
52   See Antons (1997: 334).

claim shortly after the compulsory licence has been granted if she/he finally decided to implement the patent. This could be disastrous for the licensee who has possibly made large investments to take up the production of the patented product.[53] Article 89(1) in its current form, therefore, reduces the attractiveness of compulsory licences and this can hardly be in the interest of the Indonesian government. It will be interesting to see whether the courts will interpret the provision in a restrictive manner or whether the government will finally decide to revise it.

Articles 104-108 of the Patent Law allow the government to undertake the implementation of a patent that is regarded as 'very important for the defence of the security of the State' (Art 104(1)). The decision whether this is the case is made by the President after consultation with the Ministers of Justice and Defence and is implemented by Presidential Decree. As mentioned above, the term 'defence of the security of the State' can potentially be interpreted fairly widely and could also include internal security and order. The patentee is released from the payment of annual fees and receives a compensation but no licence fees.[54] The decision of the government to undertake the implementation of the patent is final and cannot be appealed (Art 107).

The revision of 1997 has raised the period of protection for a patent from 14 to 20 years after the filing of the application (Art 9(1) Patent Law). However, Art 42 which allowed an extension for a further two years has been cancelled. Articles 6, 10 and 109-113 contain regulations about petty patents which are now protected for 10 years after the granting of the petty patent. As the petty patent system applies a domestic novelty standard, a petty patent will easily and quickly be granted. Domestic companies in Indonesia have occasionally used these advantages to file specifications of overseas standard patents as petty patents. Four cases dealing with such practices are currently pending in the Indonesian courts.[55]

Trade Mark Law Reform in Indonesia

In 1961, the Trade Marks Law No 21 of 1961 replaced the Colonial *Reglement Industrieele Eigendom*. Both statutes were based on the principle of first use granting the right to a trade mark to the first user of the mark in Indonesia. A registration of the trade mark was possible but created only a rebuttable presumption that the registered owner of the trade mark was also the first user in Indonesia.[56] The system not only made it possible to establish a trade mark right through token sales, but also allowed 'trade mark entrepreneurs' to register internationally well-known trade marks years in advance only to sell the rights to these registrations back to the original owner, once the product was introduced to Indonesia. Much publicised were the law suits of an Indonesian company, which allegedly owned hundreds of registrations of well-known trade marks (Lumenta, 1994: 14) in 1993 and 1994 against such famous foreign companies as Pierre Cardin, Levi Strauss and Alfred Dunhill. The aim of these law suits was to prohibit those companies to use their own

---

53   Cf s 133(6) of the Australian Patent Act, which achieves a balance of these interests by requiring that 'the legitimate interests of the licensee are not likely to be adversely affected by the revocation'.

54   Cf Art 105(3) and Art 106(2) as well as the Elucidation to Art 106(2).

55   See Kusoy (1996c: 31).

56   See Antons (1991b: 369).

trade marks in Indonesia because such use would infringe upon the registration of the Indonesian company. Most trade mark owners in such cases prefer buy-back arrangements to prolonged court battles with uncertain outcome (Antons, 1995: 345-46).[57] Two decrees of 1987 and 1991 for the protection of well-known trade marks[58] were early attempts of the Minister of Justice to restrict this practice.

A new Trade Marks Law was enacted in 1992 and came into force on 1 April 1993. As the other parts of the Indonesian intellectual property system, the Law was amended in 1997 to achieve compliance with the GATT-TRIPs Agreement. The amendment added a Chapter IXA with a protection for geographical indications and indications of origin. Under the current Trade Marks Law, the right to a trade mark follows no longer from first use but from first registration in Indonesia. The scope of the Law has been expanded to cover also service marks and collective marks. Whereas a colour combination can now be registered as a trade mark, make-up and packaging are still excluded from trade mark protection. These features may only be considered as elements of the trade mark for the question of deceptive similarity. Article 1(1) defines a trade mark as 'a sign in the form of a picture, a name, word, letters, figures, a combination of colours or a combination of these elements, which has the capacity to distinguish and is used for activities of trade in goods or services'. The last part of this definition is different from, for example, Australian trade mark law where it is only required that a trade mark is 'used, *or intended to be used*, to distinguish goods or services'.[59] There are indications, however, that Art 1 of the Indonesian legislation has the same meaning and that a clarification was regarded as unnecessary.[60]

Articles 5 and 6 provide which trade marks cannot be registered. Article 5(a) prohibits the registration of trade marks which are in conflict with moral or public order. According to the explanatory memorandum, the concern of this provision is in particular the protection of religious symbols. In the past, Chinese trade marks were occasionally refused registration based on this provision (Gautama, 1986: 28; Kaehlig, 1993; Trademarks under the 1961 Trademark Law: 4)[61] but this policy has been abolished after the restoration of diplomatic ties between Indonesia and the People's Republic of China. Article 5 was at times also used to refuse registration of trade marks that deceive about the geographical origin of a product (Gautama, 1986: 28; Gautama, 1992: 16-17).[62]

Signs that have become public property are not registrable (Art 5(c)), for example, a skull on top of two crossed bones as a sign for 'danger' (Kaehlig, 1993; Trademarks under the 1992 Law on Marks: 3). Also not registrable are marks that are not sufficiently distinctive (Art 5(b)). The latter case concerns especially marks that are only descriptive and contain for example merely the generic name of a

---

57   The *Mahkamah Agung* criticised this practice in the 'Seven Up' decision (*Mahkamah Agung* Decision No 3027K/Sip/1981 of 29 December 1982, in: Gautama & Winata (1987: 240)).

58   Decree of the Minister of Justice No M.02-HC.01.01.1987 and M.03-HC.02.01 of 2 May 1991.

59   See s 17 of the Australian Trade Marks Act and McKeough & Stewart (1997: 424), emphasis added.

60   The substantive examination of Art 25(2) focuses only on the conditions of Art 5 and 6. It is, therefore, not clear whether the use demanded by Art 1(1) is a condition for the registration of the mark.

61   See also the 'Flying Wheel' case, decision of the District Court of Central Jakarta No 33/1972 G dated 3 October 1973.

62   As to a similar approach in the Netherlands, cf Gielen & Wichers Hoeth (1992: 197).

product or a statement about the product's quality. Very often used as an example for a descriptive mark is the decision of the District Court of Central Jakarta in the 'Supermi' ('Supernoodle') case.[63] This actually merely descriptive mark was in the end accepted because it was written in a distinctive manner and had acquired distinctiveness through continued use as a trade mark. While a descriptive word can thus acquire distinctiveness through continued use as a trade mark, a trade mark can also loose its distinctive character if continually used as a generic name.[64] In the case of the trade mark 'Aqua' for mineral water, a claim based on deceptive similarity of the owner of that trade mark against the registration of the concurring marks 'Club Aqua' and 'Asian Aqua' was rejected at first instance because the court regarded the Latin word 'Aqua' as descriptive. In revising this decision, the Supreme Court unfortunately did not comment upon the interesting argument of the plaintiff that the meaning of a Latin word would hardly be understood by the vast majority of the Indonesian population. The Supreme Court decided, however, in favour of the plaintiff and concluded that 'Aqua' had acquired distinctiveness through continued use as a trade mark.[65]

Article 6(1) of the Trade Marks Law prohibits the registration of trade marks which conflict with earlier registered trade marks. The courts have distinguished between trade marks consisting of words, trade marks consisting of pictures and combinations of pictures and words. The courts consider meaning but also sound of the words in word marks, whereas the overall impression of the mark becomes important in the case of combined word/picture marks. Furthermore, the registrations must concern the same kind of products or services. This is the case, if the products or services are from a technical and economic viewpoint so closely related that they give the impression to originate from the same company or the same manufacturer.[66] Also prohibited is the registration of names, photos and names of legal entities of well-known persons (Art 6(2)(a));[67] of national symbols, flags and the like (Art 6(2)(b)); of official signs, seals or stamps (Art 6(2)(c)); and of trade marks that make use of a copyright protected work of someone else (Art 6(2)(d)).

The registration of well-known trade marks was for a while prohibited by the above mentioned Decrees of the Ministry of Justice. The first of these decrees of 1987 prohibited the registration of well-known trade marks only for goods of the same kind. This decree was replaced by a second Decree in 1991, which covered also goods which were not of the same kind, but restricted the protection to trade marks well-known 'in Indonesia as well as abroad'.[68] This Decree was abolished in 1993 (Kusoy, 1994: 25-26) and it was explained that well-known marks were now exclusively regulated under the new Trade Marks Law. However, until the revision

---

63   Decision No 904/1970 dated 30 January 1971, in Gautama & Winata (1987: 57-62).

64   See the 'Lysol' decision of the District Court of Batavia of 12 October 1938, *Indisch Tijdschrift van het Recht*, Vol 149, 1939, 385.

65   Decision of the District Court of Central Jakarta No 706/Pdt.G/D/1987/PN.JKT.PST. dated 14 September 1988 and *Mahkamah Agung* No 757K/Pdt/1989 dated 30 March 1992, in Gautama (1993, 1-32). See also Tempo (1988a); Tempo (1988b).

66   See Soemodiredjo (1963: 19) and the 'Imam Mekah' case, decision of the District Court of Jakarta No 2407/1953 G. dated 2 March 1955, 'Seven Up', decision of the District Court of Jakarta No 122/1974 G. dated 30 July 1974, 'Teijin', decision of the District Court of Jakarta No 590/1973 G. dated 7 January 1975.

67   As to problems with this provision, see Antons (1995: 305-307).

68   Cf Antons (1992: 309-11).

of 1997, the former Art 56(3) was the only provision in the Trade Marks Law of 1992 clearly covering well-known trade marks. It made a cancellation claim by the owner of a well-known trade mark subject to a prior registration of the mark. While this clearly showed the intention of the legislators to protect such marks, trade mark lawyers still had to search the Law to find a more detailed basis for their claim. A rather peculiar wording in the former Art 6(2)(a) was supposed to provide this basis (Maulana, 1995: 386). However, the provision protected 'trade marks and names of legal entities belonging to another well-known person'. The emphasis was, therefore, clearly on the well-known owner of the trade mark and not on the reputation of the mark as such. Strictly applied, the provision protected well-known trade marks only in cases where the owner happened to be well-known.

The revision of 1997 has now removed these remaining doubts and provided an unambiguous protection for well-known trade marks in Art 6(3), at least as long as they are used for goods of the same kind. Unfortunately, however, owners of well-known trade marks which are used for goods not of the same kind are referred to a future government Regulation for further conditions their trade marks need to fulfil (Art 6(4)). Under these circumstances, cancellation claims will remain difficult for the time being. During the last few years, a substantial number of unauthorised registrations of well-known trade marks were in fact renewed. Since an application for renewal is not published by the Trade Mark Office, it is difficult for the real owners of such well-known marks to object (Kusoy, 1997a: 58; Kusoy, 1995: 57).

The new Trade Marks Law has abolished the principle of 'first use' in favour of a 'first-to-file' system, but first use is occasionally still important under the current legislation. The reason for this is Art 4 which makes the registration of a trade mark dependent on good faith of the applicant. This good faith relates to an earlier use by someone who has chosen not to register the mark. As the established interest of such a prior user is, therefore, protected, the large number of cases on the question of 'first use' decided under the former legislation may still be consulted.[69]

The Trade Mark Office examines the application as to formal requirements and publishes the application in a Trade Mark bulletin (*Berita Resmi Merek*) that has replaced the State Gazette as medium for publication. The subsequent substantive examination focuses on obstacles to registration from Arts 5 and 6. In the case of a rejection of the application, the applicant can appeal to a Trade Mark Appeal Commission, a similar body to the Patent Appeal Commission mentioned above. As with decisions of that Commission, a decision of the Trade Mark Appeal Commission is also final (Art 34(2)). Consequently, the appeal procedure under the Trade Marks Law raises the same concerns as that for patent applications. However, in contrast to the procedure under the Patent Law, the Elucidation to Art 34(2) of the Trade Marks Law allows an appeal to an administrative court in case of procedural mistakes by the Trade Mark Appeal Commission.

This alternative venue for an appeal has become important, because of the difficulties in forming the Trade Mark Appeal Commission. These difficulties were at first due to the lack of an implementing Government Regulation referred to in the Law. After the Government Regulation was finally issued in August 1995,[70] it required a further Decree of the Minister of Justice to appoint the members of the Commission. As of May 1997, these appointments had not been made. By this time,

---

69   See Antons (1995: 313-23); Kaehlig (1993; Trademarks under the 1961 Trademark Law: 9-15).

70   See Kusoy (1996b: 67); Roosseno (1996: 13).

approximately 500 appeals were awaiting a decision (Kusoy, 1997a: 58). As the District Court declared itself no longer responsible to decide cases of rejections of applications under the Trade Marks Law of 1992, frustrated applicants began to turn to the administrative courts. However, apart from the lack of competence of the administrative judges in intellectual property matters, such administrative judgments cannot immediately order the Trade Mark Office to reverse a decision in favour of the applicant (see Quinn, Chapter 18). Furthermore, the administrative court would only consider questions of law, but could not examine a trade mark as to substantial similarity with an earlier registered mark.[71]

The granting of licences is now explicitly regulated in Chapter 5 of the Trade Marks Law. Article 48 gives considerable discretionary power to the Trade Mark Office to restrict the granting of licences if it holds the opinion that a licence can, either directly or indirectly, have negative effects on the Indonesian economy or on the capability of Indonesians to handle technology.[72] The registration of licences has also been made difficult by the absence of necessary implementing regulations (Maulana, 1995: 380; Roosseno, 1997: 10-11).

The Future of Intellectual Property Law in Indonesia after the GATT Agreement

The outcome of the Uruguay Round of GATT and the new TRIPs Agreement obliges Indonesia to bring her legislation into accordance with the Agreement until 1999.[73] The amendments of 1997 are a significant step towards achieving this goal. Nevertheless, officials occasionally give the impression that the government wanted to reach this compliance in steps through several amendments.[74] Remaining problem areas in the field of copyright are in particular the confusing regulation of neighbouring rights and the contradictions in the protection periods for some of the material. In the field of patent law, a judicial review must be allowed for the cases of Arts 104-108, where the government takes on the implementation of a patent.[75] The TRIPs Agreement also requires the regulation of a few other areas such as industrial designs, confidential information and integrated circuits. Legislation covering these areas is currently being prepared.[76] Already enacted is a new Customs Law of 1995 covering the border control of infringing material;[77] and a new Government Regulation of June 1997 outlining requirements for franchising agreements (Kusoy, 1997b).

The most serious difficulties remain, however, in the enforcement and administration of intellectual property rights in Indonesia. Mechanisms for judicial review still need much improvement and there is an unnecessarily large number of implementing regulations, which take often years to be issued by the government or the

---

71　Cf Media Indonesia (1997).

72　See Gautama & Winata (1993: 26). The Patent Law contains a similar provision in Art 78.

73　See Art 65(2) of the Agreement and Harjowidigdo (1994: 129).

74　Cf the report on the trade mark legislation in Media Indonesia (1997), that the General Directorate for Copyright, Patents and Trade Marks wishes to amend the trade mark legislation further until it is in line with the Agreement.

75　Cf Art 31 of the TRIPs Agreement.

76　See Roosseno (1997: 11).

77　See Kusoy (1996a).

Ministry of Justice. A substantial backlog has already developed in parts of the intellectual property system with about 500 undecided appeal cases on file with the Trademark Appeal Commission and approximately 29,000 pending trade mark applications in the Trade Mark Office (Kusoy, 1997a; Managing Intellectual Property, 1997: 15-17). There is also a need for a better understanding of overlaps between different areas of intellectual property protection to avoid the registration of infringing trade marks as copyrights or of petty patents which infringe upon foreign standard patents. As the recent economic turmoil in Indonesia has increased the economic pressures for reforms, we will presumably see further amendments and new legislation in the near future. In view of the time pressure under which these revisions take place, one can only hope that the Indonesian intellectual property system will nevertheless be developed in a sufficiently consistent manner and will not become 'patch up' legislation which is difficult to interpret and only results in new opportunities for infringers.

References

Antons, C, 1991a, 'Intellectual Property Law in ASEAN Countries: A Survey', *European Intellectual Property Review*, No 3: 78-84.

Antons, C, 1991b, 'The Development of Intellectual Property Law in Indonesia: From Colonial to National Law', *International Review of Industrial Property and Copyright Law*, vol 22, No 3: 359-76.

Antons, C, 1992, 'Note on the Decision of the District Court of Central Jakarta in the "Davidoff" Case', *Gewerblicher Rechtsschutz und Urheberrecht – Internationaler Teil*, No 4: 309-11.

Antons, C, 1995, *Urheberrecht und gewerblicher Rechtsschutz in Indonesien*, PhD thesis, University of Amsterdam.

Antons, C, 1997, 'The Indonesian Patent Act of 1989', *International Review of Industrial Property and Copyright Law*, vol 28, No 3: 320-47.

Berita Negara, 1953, No 69.

Bresnan, J, 1993, *Managing Indonesia: The Modern Political Economy*, Columbia University Press, New York.

Cohen Jehoram, H, 1990, 'The Nature of Neighbouring Rights of Performing Artists, Phonogram Producers and Broadcasting Organizations', *Columbia – VLA Journal of Law & the Arts*, vol 15, No 1: 75-91.

Cohen Jehoram, H, 1991, 'Hybrids on the borderline between Copyright and Industrial Property' in Association Littéraire et Artistique Internationale, *Copyright and Industrial Property – Congress of the Aegean Sea II*: 263-80.

Cohen Jehoram, H, 1992a, 'Note on the decision of the Hoge Raad of 4 January 1991, "Grote Van Dale"', *Ars Aequi – Jurisprudentie en Annotaties: Intellectuele Eigendom 1954-1992*, 4th ed, Ars Aequi Libri, Nijmegen: 340-42.

Cohen Jehoram, H, 1992b, 'Note on the Feist Decision of the Supreme Court of the United States', *Ars Aequi – Jursiprudentie en annotaties: Intellectuele eigendom 1954-1992*, 4th ed, Ars Aequi Libri, Nijmegen: 352-53.

Cohen Jehoram, H, 1993, 'Netherlands' in Geller, P (ed), *International Copyright Law and Practice*, vol 2, Matthew Bender, New York.

Djaman, FS, 1994, 'Beberapa Aturan dan Kebijakan Penting di bidang Hak Milik Intelektual', *Varia Peradilan*, No 106: 135-46.

Dreier, T & Karnell, GWG, 1991, 'Originality of the Copyrighted Work' in Association Littéraire et Artistique Internationale, *Copyright and Industrial Property – Congress of the Aegean Sea II*: 153-66.

Gautama, S, 1986, *Hukum Merek Indonesia*, 2nd ed, Penerbit Alumni, Bandung.

Gautama, S and Winata, R, 1987, *Himpunan Keputusan Merek Dagang*, Penerbit Alumni, Bandung.

Gautama, S, 1990, *Segi-Segi Hukum Hak Milik Intelektual*, Penerbit PT Eresco, Bandung.

Gautama, S, 1992, *Undang-Undang Merek Baru*, Penerbit Alumni, Bandung.

Gautama, S, 1993, *Himpunan Jurisprudensi Indonesia yang penting untuk praktek sehari-hari (landmark decisions) berikut komentar*, vol 5, PT Citra Aditya Bakti, Bandung.

Gautama, S and Winata, R, 1993, *The New Indonesian Trademark Law*, Penerbit Alumni, Bandung.

Gielen, C, 1988, 'New Copyright Law of Indonesia: Implications for Foreign Investment', *European Intellectual Property Review*, No 4: 101-107.

Gielen, C and Wichers Hoeth, L, 1992, *Merkenrecht*, WEJ Tjeenk Willink, Zwolle.

Gingerich, DJ and Hadiputranto, SI, 1987, 'Indonesia amends its Copyright Law', *East Asian Executive Reports*, vol 9, No 11: 7-10.

Gingerich, DJ, 1989, 'Indonesia: New Patent Law', *IP Asia*, vol 10, November: 18-23.

Goldstein, P, 1994. *Copyright's Highway: From Gutenberg to the Celestial Jukebox*, Hill and Wang, New York.

Harjowidigdo, R, 1994, 'Mengenal Hak Milik Intelektual yang Diatur di dalam TRIPs', *Varia Peradilan*, No 111: 129-43.

Hubmann, H, 1988, *Gewerblicher Rechtsschutz*, 5th ed, CH Beck, Munich.

Hutauruk, M, 1988, *Hak Cipta Terbaru*, Penerbit Erlangga, Jakarta.

Intellectual Property, 1979, vol 18.

Industrial Property 1983.

International Review of Industrial Property and Copyright Law, 1994, vol 25.

IP Asia, 1997a, 'Effective Ratification of Paris Convention', September.

IP Asia, 1997b, 'Patent, Trademark, WIPO Copyrights Treaty and Bern Convention Ratified', September.

Kaehlig, CB, 1988, 'Copyright Law Amendments', *IP Asia*, January: 18-19.

Kaehlig, CB, 1993, *Indonesian Intellectual Property Law*, PT Tatanusa, Jakarta.

Kesowo, B, 1990, *Implementasi Undang-Undang Hak Cipta – Konsepsi, Problema dan Peningkatan Efektifitas Pelaksanaannya*, paper delivered at the Indonesia Copyright Enforcement Workshop, Jakarta, 19-20 March.

Kusoy, EL, 1994, 'Improvements in the protection for well-known trademarks', *IP Asia*, June: 25-26.

Kusoy, EL, 1995, 'Indonesia', *APAA News*, No 22: 56-58.

Kusoy, EL, 1996a, 'Customs law ratified', *IP Asia*, March: 4-5.

Kusoy, EL, 1996b, 'Indonesia', *APAA News*, No 23: 64-69.

Kusoy, EL, 1996c, 'Indonesia', in 'Patent Law Developments', *IP Asia*, September: 31-33.

Kusoy, EL, 1997a, 'Current Status of the Trademark Law and Its Enforcement in Indonesia in 1996', *APAA News*, No 24: 57-60.

Kusoy, EL, 1997b, 'Franchise Agreements Now Subject to Regulation', *IP Asia*, September: 30-32.

Lumenta, JB, 1994, 'Intellectual Property Enforcement: Recent Developments', *APAA News*, No 21: 13-14.

Managing Intellectual Property, 1997, 'Emerging Markets Survey: Indonesia', March.

Maulana, IB, 1995, 'Indonesian Trademark Law', *International Review of Industrial Property and Copyright Law*, vol 26, No 3: 376-87.

McKeough, J and Stewart, A, 1997, *Intellectual Property in Australia*, Butterworths, Sydney.

Media Indonesia, 1997, 'Komisi Banding Merek: Suatu Keharusan?', 14 May.

Perubahan Undang-Undang tentang Hak Cipta, Paten dan Merek Tahun 1997, 1997, Pustaka Salendro, Jakarta.

Prawiroe, NR, 1989, *Potret Undang-Undang Hak Cipta*, Berita Yudha, 18 February.

Priapantja, CC, 1995, *The Current Status of Intellectual Property Rights and Enforcement in Indonesia*, paper delivered at the AIPLA Annual Meeting, 27 October.

Priapantja, CC, 1997, 'TRIPs encourages revision of Patent laws', *IP Asia*, April: 34-36.

Ricketson, S, 1984, *The Law of Intellectual Property*, Law Book Co, Sydney.

Ricketson, S, 1991, 'The Concept of Originality in Anglo-Australian Law' in Association Littéraire et Artistique Internationale, *Copyright and Industrial Property – Congress of the Aegean Sea II*: 183-201.

Ricketson, S, 1994, *Intellectual Property: Cases, Materials and Commentary*, Butterworths, Sydney.

Robison, R, 1986, *Indonesia: The Rise of Capital*, Allen & Unwin, Sydney, etc.

Robison, R, Higgott, R and Hewison, K, 1987, 'Crisis in economic strategy in the 1980s: the factors at work' in Robison, R, Hewison, K and Higgott, R (eds), *Southeast Asia in the 1980s: The Politics of Economic Crisis*, Allen & Unwin, Sydney.

Roosseno, THN, Kusoy, EL, & Priapantja, CC, 1995, 'Intellectual Property in Indonesia', *APAA News*, No 22: 12-14.

Roosseno, THN, 1996, 'Developments in Intellectual Property in Indonesia', *APAA* News, No 23: 12-13.

Roosseno, THN, 1997 'Indonesia', *APAA News*, No 24: 9-11.

Rosidi, A, 1984, *Undang-Undang Hak Cipta: Pandangan Seorang Awam*, Penerbit Djambatan, Jakarta.

Rouse & Co Intl, 1997, 'Getting it Right in Indonesia', *Managing Intellectual Property*, September: 18-23.

Ruggie, JG, 1993, 'Unravelling Trade: Global Institutional Change and the Pacific Economy' in Higgott, R, Leaver, R and Ravenhill, J (eds), *Pacific Economic Relations in the 1990s: Cooperation or Conflict?*, Allen & Unwin, Sydney: 15-38.

Saleh, KW, 1994, *Undang-Undang Hak Cipta, Paten dan Merek Serta Peraturan Pelaksanaannya*, Ghalia Indonesia, Jakarta.

Simandjuntak, DS 1994, 'The Role of the State in a Gradual Marketization: Recent Experience of Indonesia' in Vu Tuan Anh (ed), *The Role of the State in Economic Development: Experiences of the Asian Countries*, Social Science Publishing House, Hanoi.

Simorangkir, JCT, 1982, *Undang-Undang Hak Cipta 1982* (UHC 1982), Penerbit Djambatan, Jakarta.

Simorangkir, JCT, 1988, 'Catatan-Catatan mengenai: Sejarah UU Hak Cipta di Indonesia', *Persahi*, September 1988: 58-66.

Simorangkir, JCT and Panggabean, MU, 1988, *Undang-Undang Hak Cipta 1987: Undang-Undang Nomor 6 tahun 1982 tentang Hak Cipta sebagaimana telah diubah dengan Undang-Undang Nomor 7 tahun 1987 tentang perubahan atas Undang-Undang Nomor 6 tahun 1982 tentang Hak Cipta dengan komentar*, Penerbit Djambatan, Jakarta.

Simorangkir, JCT, 1990, 'Pendaftaran Karya Cipta tidak Wajib Tapi Perlu', *Suara Pembaruan*, 9 March.

Sinaga, VH, 1990, 'Sanksi Pelanggaran Hak Cipta', *Pelita*, 6 June.

Soemodiredjo, S, 1963, *Merek Perusahaan dan Merek Perniagaan*, Lembaga Administrasi Negara, Jakarta.

Tempo, 1988a, 'Aqua, Merk Siapa?', 20 August.

Tempo, 1988b, 'Aqua, Siapa yang Punya?', 1 October.

Troller, 1983, *Immaterial guterrecht: Patentrecht, Markenrecht, Muster- und Modellrecht, Urheberrecht, Wettbewerbsrecht*, vol I, 3rd ed, Helbing & Lichtenhahn, Basel-Frankfurt am Main.

Ullrich, H, 1988, 'GATT: Industrial Property Protection, Fair Trade and Development' in Beier, FK and Schricker, G (eds), *GATT or WIPO? New Ways in the International Protection of Intellectual Property*, Symposium at the Ringberg Castle, 13 to 16 July 1988, VCH Publishers, Weinheim.

Vatikiotis, 1989, 'Order in Court', *Far Eastern Economic Review*, 15 June.

Weiner, JG, 1987, 'Protection of Folklore: A Political and Legal Challenge', *International Review of Industrial Property and Copyright Law*, vol 18, No 1: 56-92.

Wichers Hoeth, L, 1993, *Kort begrip van het intellectuele eigendomsrecht*, 7th ed, WEJ Tjeenk Willink, Zwolle.

23. Indonesian Islamic Banking in Historical and Legal Context

Abdullah Saeed

In 1992, Bank Muamalat Indonesia (BMI), Indonesia's first major Islamic bank, was established with the backing of President Soeharto and his then-Minister Dr BJ Habibie, now Indonesia's third President. Soeharto himself contributed to the bank's initial capital and he leaned on the elite to join him. In 1994, the bank had launched Indonesia's first Islamic insurance company, Syarikat Takaful. By 1995, the bank had assets of US$112,000,000 and returns to depositors were comparable with Western-style banks. By 1997 BMI had established 52 rural Islamic banks and 800 credit cooperatives and its activities were continuing to expand, not least because of a growing Islamic consciousness encouraged by the Soeharto government as part of the strategy to expand its political support.

There can be little doubt that BMI has now established Islamic banking as a player in Indonesia's commercial sector. This will inevitably force changes to the practices of secular banks in Indonesia, particularly in light of the role bank failures have played in the current economic crisis in that country. This chapter seeks to explain the rise of Muamalat and Islamic banking in Indonesia in the broader historical and legal context of Islamic thinking and the rise of modern theories of Islamic banking.[1]

Modernism and Neo-Revivalism

Although 'Islamic banking' is a term commonly used in the late 20th century, it is a phenomenon that needs to be understood in the context of Islamic revivalism *(tajdid)* which began in the Islamic world in the 19th century. This revivalism emerged against the so-called 'corruption' of religion and the moral laxity and degeneration seen as prevalent in Muslim society at the time. It was essentially a call to a 'going back' to the 'original' Islam and to a shedding of both the super-stitions inculcated by popular forms of sufism, and the idea that the traditional schools of law were not infallible (Rahman, 1979: 317). The revivalism of the 19th century led to two distinct trends within Islam: 'modernism' and 'neo-revivalism' (Saeed, 1996: 5-8).

The Islamic modernist movement emerged in the latter part of the 19th century. It called for fresh attempts to revive *ijtihad*[2] to derive relevant principles from the

---

1   A significant part of the historical and legal aspects dealt with in this chapter is based on the author's earlier work, Saeed (1996).

2   Legal reasoning and interpretation of *syariah* (Islamic law).

Qur'an and authentic *Sunna*, and to formulate necessary laws based on those principles. Modernists criticised what they called the 'atomistic' approach to deriving rules from the *Qur'an* and also the early jurists' failure to understand its underlying unity. According to the modernists, to insist on a literal implementation of the rules of the *Qur'an*, shutting one's eyes to the social change that had occurred, and was so palpably occurring, was tantamount to deliberately defeating its socio-moral purposes and objectives (Rahman, 1982: 2-19).

The modernists also called for selective use of the *Sunna*; the exercise of systematic original thinking with no claim to finality; a distinction to be made between the *shari'a* and *fiqh* (Islamic jurisprudence); the avoidance of sectarianism, and a reversion to the characteristic methodology (but not necessarily to the law) and solutions of the classical schools, extinct and extant (Mahmassani, 1961: 92-8; Iqbal, 1960: 129, 151, 171-73; Husaini, 1980: 23; Saeed, 199).

Neo-revivalism, which became an influential movement in the first half of the 20th century, was in part a continuation of the revivalism of the 19th and early 20th centuries, and a reaction to the excesses of secularism in the Muslim world (Muzaffar, 1986: 10-12). Neo-revivalism focused, inter alia, on the following important issues: resistance to the 'Westernisation' of the Muslim community (*umma*), advocation of the self-sufficiency of Islam and of Islam as a way of life, and the rejection of any reinterpretation of the *Qur'an* or *sunna* (Muzaffar, 1986: 9-12). The most important neo-revivalist movements appeared in Egypt and the Indian subcontinent: the Muslim Brotherhood founded by the Egyptian reformer Hasan al-Banna (d 1949), and the *Jama'at Islami* (Islamic Party) founded by the Pakistani scholar Abu al-'A'ala Mawdudi (d 1979).

The neo-revivalists argued that Islam, as a God-given religion and founder of a brilliant civilisation, had answers for all the modern day ills of both the East and the West (Qutb, 1965; Mawdudi, 1970). By a return to Islamic beliefs, values and law, they argued, Muslims could begin to re-establish themselves as they had been in the past; and once again could become a contributor to world civilisation, reversing the course of humiliation they had undergone under the colonialism and imperialism of the West. According to Chandra Muzaffar (1986: 10):

> [F]undamental to this belief is an explicit recognition that the *Qur'an* and *sunna* lay out a complete way of life whose sanctity and purity should not be tarnished by new interpretations influenced by time and circumstances.

Based on this view, the function of *ijtihad* according to the neo-revivalists would be to arrive at solutions to problems not explicitly covered by the *Qur'an* and the *sunna*. In line with this, the neo-revivalists emphasised areas such as *Qur'an*ic punishments (*hudud*); and family laws based on the *Qur'an* and *Sunna*. They also identified interest on loans as *riba* (forbidden usury) (Rahman, 1979). They argued that Muslims should implement these principles without reinterpretation.

Even though both modernism and neo-revivalism have been significant in shaping Islamic thought in modern history, it is the neo-revivalist movement that has been the more influential in the development of Islamic banking theory. This theory was developed mainly in order to put into practice the traditional interpretation of *riba* embraced by the neo-revivalists in the area of banking and finance.

The Emergence of Islamic Banks

In the 19th century, Western interest-based banks began to be established in the Muslim world. While some leading figures like Muhammad Rashid Rida (d 1935), the famous disciple of Muhammad 'Abduh (d 1905), attempted to accommodate some forms of interest (Homoud, 1986: 115ff), the progress of Islamic revivalism in the 19th and 20th centuries led many *ulama* (scholars of religion) and reformers to resist the interest-based banks and their services. It was mainly the neo-revivalists represented by Muslim Brotherhood of Egypt and *Jama'at Islami* of Pakistan, that, with their considerable following throughout the Islamic world, kept alive the issue of the prohibition of interest as well as the necessity for the development of alternative Islamic financial institutions. The founder of the Muslim Brotherhood, Hasan al-Banna (d 1949, in a letter sent to Arab and Muslim heads of state in 1947, urged them to reform their banking systems according to the teachings of Islam. Among the reforms, he requested the re-organisation of the banks on an interest-free basis:

> Let the government provide a good example in this domain by relinquishing all interest due on its own particular undertakings, for instance in the loan-granting banks, industrial loans etc (Banna, 1978: 130)

Sayyid Qutb, the ideologue of the Muslim Brotherhood, in his interpretation of *riba*-related verses in the *Qur'an*, also condemned bank interest and accused modern banks of 'eating the bones and flesh' of the poor borrowers and 'drinking their sweat and blood' under the umbrella of the interest-based system (Qutb nd: 12). In the Indian subcontinent, the *Jama'at Islami,* led by Abu al-A'la Mawdudi, continued to condemn interest and the interest-based banking system. Mawdudi himself wrote several works on the issue (1984, 1986).

Condemnation of the institution of interest and efforts to develop a model of an interest-free Islamic bank continued simultaneously in the 1950s and 1960s. (Qureshi, 1967; Mawdudi, *al-Riba*; Sadr, 1973; Najjar, 1985). Islamic banking theory developed under the influence of neo-revivalist thinking until Islamic banks began to be established on a large scale in the 1970s, largely due to the huge increase in the revenues of some conservative Islamic countries as a result of the oil price rise during that decade. The oil revenue which began to flow into Saudi Arabia, Kuwait, the United Arab Emirates (UAE), Qatar and Bahrain was an important determinant in the development of Islamic banks.

Although the earliest Islamic banking experiments like that of Malaysia in the mid-1940s; the Indian Jama'at Islami in 1969 (Khan, 1987: 52-54); Egypt's Mit Ghamr Savings Banks (1963-67); and the Nasser Social Bank (1971), cannot be linked to Arab oil wealth, the accelerated growth of Islamic banks at national and international levels occurred after the oil price rises of 1973 and 1974. Almost all Islamic banks established in the 1970s in the Middle East were partly, and in some cases totally, funded by oil-linked wealth. The Islamic Development Bank, whose initial capital was approximately US$2 billion, had a majority shareholding of more than 60% held by the oil-producing Saudi Arabia, Kuwait, United Arab Emirates and Libya. The Dubai Islamic Bank, the Kuwait Finance House, the Bahrain Islamic Bank, the Qatar Islamic Bank, the Faisal Islamic Banks of Bahrain, Niger and Senegal, banks of the Al-Baraka group of Shaykh Saleh Kamil and Dar al-Mal al-Islami (DMI) of the Saudi Prince Muhammad al-Faisal were almost totally funded by oil wealth, while the Faisal Islamic Banks of Egypt and of Sudan – and many other Islamic banks in non oil-exporting countries – were partly funded in this way, at least initially. The most active countries in contributing the necessary capital for Islamic banks, at private or public sector levels, have been Saudi Arabia, Kuwait and the UAE, the leading oil exporters of the Gulf.

The most important momentum to develop an international Islamic bank at inter-governmental level, was given by the Organisation of Islamic States Conference with the active support of the late King Faisal of Saudi Arabia. The purpose of this bank, the Islamic Development Bank (1975) was to foster economic development and social progress in member countries and Muslim communities, individually as well as jointly in accordance with the principles of the *shari'a* (IDB, 1990: 1). Not only did Muslim nations become members of the newly created Islamic Development Bank but some of them (for instance, Kuwait, UAE, Sudan, Egypt) also began to promote Islamic banks in their countries by promulgating special laws and decrees for their establishment, or by becoming shareholders. A number of other Islamic countries like Bangladesh, Tunisia, Bahrain and Malaysia, for instance, followed suit and became shareholders in the Islamic banks in their countries. Today, there is perhaps no Muslim government that has not dealt in some way with the Islamic banks. Three countries in particular, Pakistan, Iran and Sudan, have attempted to transform their economies from interest-based ones to Islamic ones. Growing confidence in Islamic banking led to more accommodation of Islamic banks, even by so-called secular governments of Muslim countries. By 1998, in addition to the Islamic banking systems of Iran, Pakistan and Sudan, the number of private sector Islamic banks, in fact, stood at more than 50 with assets of several billion dollars. As Islamic revivalism continues to gain ground in almost all Muslim societies, many governments are likely to face pressure from their populations to abolish interest which is perceived to be *riba*, and to establish Islamic banks.

The Interpretation of *Riba* as Interest: the Raison d'etre of Islamic Banking

Contemporary Muslim scholars have differed as to whether the *riba* prohibited in the *Qur'an* applies to modern bank interest. These differences appear to stem from one basic issue: should the emphasis be on the rationale for the prohibition of *riba*, that is, injustice, or should it be on the legal form in which *riba* came to be formally conceptualised in Islamic law? The modernist trend is towards the former, while the neo-revivalists support the latter view.

Modernists such as Fazlur Rahman (1964), Muhammad Asad (1984), Sa'id al-Najjar (1989) and 'Abd al-Mun'im al-Namir (1989) tend to emphasise the moral aspect of the prohibition of *riba*, and relegate the 'legal form' of *riba*, as interpreted in Islamic law to a secondary position. They argue that the *raison d'être* for the prohibition is injustice, as formulated in the *Qur'an*ic statement (2: 279), *la tazlimuna wa-la tuzlamun* (Do not commit injustice and no injustice will be committed against you). It is this reason, according to the modernists, which makes the prohibition morally sustainable in a changing socio-economic environment. According to Muhammad Asad (1984: 633):

> Roughly speaking, the opprobrium of *riba* (in the sense in which this term is used in the *Qur'an* and in many sayings of the Prophet) attaches to profits obtained through interest-bearing loans involving an *exploitation of the economically weak by the strong and resourceful* ... With this definition in mind, we realise that the question as to what

kinds of financial transactions fall within the category of *riba* is, in the last resort, a moral one, closely connected with the socio-economic motivation underlying the mutual relationship of borrower and lender.

The Pakistani scholar, Fazlur Rahman, remarked on the attitude of many Muslims towards interest (1979: 326):

> Many well-meaning Muslims with very virtuous consciences sincerely believe that the *Qur'an* has banned all bank interest for all times, in woeful disregard of what *riba* was historically, why the *Qur'an* denounced it as a gross and cruel form of exploitation and banned it, and what the function of bank interest [is] today.

For these scholars, it appears that what is prohibited is the exploitation of the needy, rather than the concept of the interest rate itself. It is the type of lending that attempts to profit from the misery of others. Many writers of this trend attempt to differentiate between various forms of interest practised under the traditional banking system, advocating the lawfulness of some, while rejecting others (Saleh, 1986: 29; Saeed, 1995, 1996). The rejection is generally based on a perceived injustice in a particular form of interest.

The modernists, however, have failed so far to carry the day in the debate on *riba*. Their views, and the 'exceptions' to the *riba* prohibition they have advocated, have been met by neo-revivalist critics with both economic and scriptural counter arguments, and their position has been weakened (Saeed, 1996: 41-50). One of the leading Islamic banking theorists, Siddiqi (1983b: 9-10), says:

> Efforts of some pseudo-jurists to distinguish between *riba* and bank interest and to legitimise the latter [have] met with almost universal rejection and contempt. Despite the fact that circumstances force many people to deal with interest-based financial institutions, the notion of its essential illegitimacy has always remained.

The position of the modernists is further undermined by two factors: their inability to present a consistent theory of *riba* on the basis of the rationale of prohibition which is specified in the *Qur'an*, and the rise of Islamic banking institutions inspired by neo-revivalist thinking on the issue of *riba*, which declare that 'any interest is *riba*, and as such is prohibited'.

The now dominant neo-revivalist view emphasises the legal form of *riba* as expressed in Islamic law, and insists that the words specified in the *Qur'an* should be taken at their literal meaning, regardless of what was practised in the pre-Islamic period. According to this view, since the *Qur'an* has stated that only the principal should be taken (in repayment of a loan), there is no alternative but to interpret *riba* according to that wording. Therefore, the existence or otherwise of injustice in a loan transaction is irrelevant. Whatever the circumstances, the lender has no right to receive any increase over and above the principal (Abu Zahra, 1970).

Although several leading neo-revivalists like Mawdudi and Sayyid Qutb have discussed to some extent the issue of injustice in *riba*, they have generally refrained from stating that it is injustice which is the raison d'être of the prohibition. According to Mawdudi (1986: 7):

> [T]he contention that *zulm* (injustice) is the reason why interest on loans has been disallowed and hence all such interest transactions as do not entail cruelty are permissible, remains yet to be substantiated.

Following this line of thinking, neo-revivalist writers have interpreted *riba* in a way which would not allow any increase in a loan. Mawdudi defines *riba* as 'the amount that a lender receives from a borrower at a fixed rate of interest' (1988 I: 213).

Perhaps one of the most important documents on Islamic banking, the Council of Islamic Ideology Report is more explicit (CII, 1983: 7):

> There is complete unanimity among all schools of thought in Islam that the term *riba* stands for interest in all its types and forms.

Chapra (1985: 57) states that '*riba* has the same meaning and import as interest'. For these, the prohibition of *riba*, interpreted as interest, is axiomatic. Mohammad Uzair (1984: 40), an Islamic banking theorist, asserts that interest in all its forms is synonymous with *riba*, and claims the existence of consensus on the issue.

> By this time, there is a complete consensus of all five schools of *Fiqh* ... and among Islamic economists, that interest in all forms, of all kinds, and for all purposes is completely prohibited in Islam. Gone are the days when people were apologetic about Islam, and contended that the interest for commercial and business purposes, as presently charged by banks, was not prohibited by Islam.

Profit and Loss Sharing (PLS) as the basis of Islamic banking

Islamic banking theorists envisioned that the investment and financing activities of the Islamic bank would be based on the two legal concepts of *mudaraba* and *musharaka*, alternatively known as profit and loss sharing (PLS). These theorists contended that the Islamic bank would provide its extensive financial resources to the borrowers on a risk sharing basis, unlike the interest-based financing in which the borrower assumes all risks.

In Islamic law, *mudaraba* is a contract between two parties whereby one party, *rabb al-mal* (investor), entrusts money to a second party, *mudarib* (user of the funds), for the purpose of conducting trade or a business venture. The *mudarib* does not invest any funds but contributes his labour and time and manages the venture according to the terms of the contract. The profit, if any, will be shared between the two on a pre-agreed proportional basis. The loss, if any, will be borne by the investor alone unless the *mudarib* is negligent or has breached the terms of the contract, in which case, the *mudarib* should bear the loss (Saleh, 1986: 103; Abu Saud, 1980: 66; El-Ashker, 1987: 75). In the early literature on Islamic banking, it can be seen that the theorists took this contract from Islamic law and adopted its key features. The theorists believed that *mudaraba* financing could be the ideal form of Islamic finance since the capital assumed the risk, a form of finance which was needed to provide loans to those who did not have access to funds under the traditional interest-based system. However, the experience of Islamic banks with *mudaraba* was not a pleasant one: the contract was too risky since the bank, as provider of finance, assumed all risks but had to rely on the *mudarib* to manage the venture. Many Islamic banks which attempted to utilise *mudaraba* had to scale down its use due to the losses and inherent risks. The use of *mudaraba* thus declined sharply, its importance remaining in theory rather than in practice. Where *mudaraba* is used, it is mainly in short-term commercial ventures where the bank can reduce the risk to a negligible level and the return is virtually certain. Hence, *mudaraba* loses one of its key features, that is, risk (Saeed, 1996: 55-59).

The second key concept of PLS is *musharaka* (partnership). It is described by the International Islamic Bank for Investment and Development as one of 'the best financing methods of Islamic banks' (IIBID *Tamwil*: 6) and is based on the participation of the bank and the seeker of finance (the potential partner) in a given project, and ultimately, in the profit or loss arising. The profit sharing ratio is agreed upon in advance. That ratio does not have to correspond to the capital contribution ratio but the loss, if any, will have to be strictly in line with the capital contribution ratio. The terms and conditions should be in accordance with the principles pertaining to *musharaka*, and are agreed upon beforehand, between the bank and the partner. The bank would usually contribute to the capital of the venture and leave the management to the partner (IIBID *Tamwil*).

Musharaka has been conceived in Islamic banking as a mechanism for bringing together labour and capital for the socially beneficial production of goods and services. It can be used in all occupations which are run according to profit. Although several writers on Islamic banking appear to use the term *musharaka* in the sense of participation in investment projects (Mukhtar, 1987: 300-302), the term is used by Islamic banks in a much broader sense. For these banks, *musharaka* can be utilised for purely commercial purposes which are usually of a short term nature, or for participation in the equity of short to long- term projects (Saeed, 1996).

Like *mudaraba, musharaka* is for Islamic banks a risky method of financing and this risk has led them to use *musharaka* either on a restricted scale or in very short-term commercial *musharakas* where the outcome is almost certain. In fact, it is this latter form of *musharaka* which is more commonly utilised in Islamic banking. The bank protects its interest by means of the terms of the contract, guarantees and risk-minimising strategies – to the extent that *musharaka* as developed in Islamic law often appears to have only a distant relationship to that adopted by Islamic banks. In fact, the PLS forms of finance to be provided by the Islamic banks and as envisioned in the literature, that is, *mudaraba* and *musharaka,* have become the least significant due to the inherent risk and uncertainty associated with the outcome. This appears to be true for most Islamic commercial banks. Thus it could be said that the Islamic banks established so far are not, generally speaking, pure PLS banks, but also make extensive use of other methods of financing, such as mark-up trading or leasing of capital goods (Nienhaus, 1983: 37). The extent of PLS financing is described by Homoud (1988: 43), a theoretician on Islamic banking, as follows:

> The Islamic banks practise *mudaraba* with utmost caution. The banks can only rarely find trustworthy people. There is no law in Islamic countries which regulates the relationship between the investor and the *mudarib*, and there is nothing to prevent the *mudarib* from misusing the funds by thousands of unlawful means. ... The grim result is that the Islamic banks' utilisation of this method of financing has contracted sharply, and is being replaced by other methods of financing which do not help to realise the objectives of the *shari'a.*

From 'Profit and Loss Sharing' to 'Profit Sharing'

Though Islamic banking theorists argued that Islamic banking should be based on Profit and Loss Sharing (PLS) rather than interest or pre-determined return based financing, Islamic banks, in practice, have found from the very beginning that PLS-based banking is difficult to implement as it is risk-laden and often the outcome uncertain. The practical problems associated with this financing have led to its gradual decline and to a steady increase in the utilisation of what some would refer to as financing mechanisms with pre-determined returns, and which are thus somewhat akin to interest (Saeed, 1996).

One of the most important and commonly used such financing mechanisms is *murabaha*, a contract developed in Islamic law. In *murabaha* there are three parties, A, B and C. A requests B to buy some goods for A. B does not have the goods but promises to buy them from a third party, C. In this, B is a middleman and the *murabaha* contract is between A and B. This *murabaha* contract is defined as a 'sale of a commodity at the price which the seller (B) paid for it originally, plus a profit margin known to the seller (B) and the buyer (A)' (Jaziri 2: 278-80). Since its inception in Islamic law, the contract of *murabaha* appears to have been utilised purely for commercial purposes. Udovitch suggests that *murabaha* is a form of commission sale, where a buyer who is usually unable to obtain the commodity he requires except through a middleman, or is not interested in the difficulties of obtaining it by himself, seeks the services of that middleman (Udovitch, 1970: 221).

Islamic banks have adopted *murabaha* to provide mainly short-term finance to clients essentially as a deferred payment sale under several labels. The clients use *murabaha* extensively to purchase consumer or capital goods or for working capital purposes where payment is deferred. *Murabaha*, as utilised under Islamic banking, is founded on two elements: (a) the purchase price and related costs; and (b) an agreed upon mark-up (profit) (Saleh, 1986: 94). The basic features of a *murabaha* contract (as a deferred payment sale) are the following:

(i) the buyer should have knowledge of all related costs and the original price of the commodity, and the profit margin (mark-up) should be defined as a percentage of the total price plus costs;

(ii) the subject of the sale should be goods or commodities against money;

(iii) the subject of the sale should be in the possession of the seller and owned by him and he should be capable of delivering it to the buyer; and

(iv) payment is deferred (Mohammed, 1989: 3-4; Saeed, 1993).

Murabaha, as conceived here, is utilised in any financing where there is an identifiable commodity to be sold (Khan, 1984: 39-40; CII, 1983: 15).

Islamic banks in general have been using *murabaha* as their major method of financing, constituting approximately 75% of their assets (al-Tamimi, 1986: 33; Saeed, 1996). Even for the Islamic Development Bank (IDB), more than 70% of its total financing, over a 10-year period (1977-88), was on a *murabaha* basis, that is in its foreign trade financing (IDB, *Annual Reports*).

Several reasons can be given for the popularity of *murabaha* in Islamic banking investment operations. First, *murabaha* is a short-term investment mechanism and is convenient compared with profit and loss sharing (PLS). Secondly, mark-up in *murabaha* can be fixed in a manner which ensures that the banks are able to earn a return comparable to that of interest-based banks with which the Islamic banks are in competition. Thirdly, *murabaha* avoids the uncertainty attached to earnings of businesses under a system of PLS (Ahmad, 1985: 24). Finally, it does not allow the Islamic bank to interfere with the management of the business since the bank is not a partner with the client but their relationship is that of creditor and debtor (Saeed, 1993, 1996).

A number of other investment mechanisms which are similar to *murabaha* in terms of the pre-determinability of return are used in addition to *murabaha* and one such example is leasing *(ijara)*.

Criticism of Predetermined Return-based Financing

It has often been argued by several critics of Islamic banking practices that the mark-up and profit-margin techniques in trade and leasing are nothing other than interest by a different name. From an economic point of view, they argue, there is indeed no substantial difference between mark-up and interest. The main difference between the two is a legal one: the bases for interest are loan contracts, while mark-up or rent is founded on sale or lease contracts (Saeed, 1996). These legal differences do not seem to make the profit margin in *murabaha* much different from the fixed interest on a loan. In economic terms, it is argued, financing on the basis of mark-up in price (*murabaha*) has no merit over the interest-based system, except that genuine financing cannot be provided under mark-up agreements if there are no goods to be transacted (Zaidi, 1988: 29). Zaidi says (1988: 29):

> In my opinion the cost of credit in bank financing on the basis of *murabaha* or mark-up in price, is the same as in the case of financing on the basis of simple interest, except that in *murabaha* financing, the price agreed remains the same even if the payment is not made on the due date.

Ziauddin Ahmad (1985: 23-4), one of the theoreticians of the Islamic banking movement, was highly critical of the replacement of interest by 'mark-up':

> [That] replacement of interest by a technique like 'mark-up' does not represent any substantive change becomes apparent if one ponders over [sic] the philosophy behind the prohibition of interest. It is easy to see therefore, that the mark-up system, and for that matter all other devices which involve a fixed pre-determined return on capital, are no real substitutes for interest. It has also been pointed out that *bay' mu'ajjal* [*murabaha*] are trade-specific practices rather than financing techniques. Their use may therefore be alright for those engaged in trade as a profession but it is stretching the permission in *shari'a* too far to use them as general financing devices.

The theorists of Islamic banking from the 1950s to the late 1970s did not envisage Islamic banking operating on a 'mark-up' basis. They saw it as being based on profit and loss sharing (PLS) within the concepts of *mudaraba* and *musharaka*. The Council of Islamic Ideology report (Pakistan), perhaps the most important document on Islamic banking, allowed the use of *murabaha* type products only hesitantly and even then limited them to unavoidable cases in the process of change to the interest-free system. It also warned that 'it would not be advisable to use it widely or indiscriminately in view of the danger attached to it of opening a back door for dealing on the basis of interest' (CII, 1983: 124).

Even though *murabaha* is allowed by many early jurists, its relevance has remained to trade, which involve goods. The problem arises when this instrument is utilised extensively in financing. Banks, by nature, are not traders in goods but financiers. According to the Council of Islamic Ideology (CII, 1983: 124):

> The fact of the matter is that 'mark-up' is a crude trading practice which has been permitted by certain religious scholars under specified conditions. Its permissibility is questioned by other scholars. In any case, it is a device which is relevant in the contract of transactions between a seller and buyer of goods. Banks are not trading organisations. They are essentially financial institutions which mobilise funds from the general public and make them available to productive undertakings. It should, therefore, be abundantly clear that if the banking system is to be Islamised, mark-up is no solution and some way has to be found which preserves the financial character of the banking institutions and steers clear of interest which is prohibited by Islam.

Therefore, one could argue that a change from an interest-based system to a mark-up based system is probably a change of name, leaving the substance intact. Considering the implications of the mark-up system, Siddiqi (1983b: 139). succinctly summarises the whole issue in one sentence: 'For all practical purposes this [the mark-up system] will be as good for the bank as lending on a fixed rate of interest'. Recognising the same implication of the mark-up system, the Council of Islamic Ideology is highly critical of it:

> There is a genuine fear among Islamic circles that if interest is largely substituted by 'mark up' under the PLS operations, it would represent a change just in name rather than in substance. PLS under the mark-up system was in fact the perpetuation of the old system of interest under a new name (CII, 1983: 97, 121).

Because of its inherent dangers, Siddiqi argues in favour of excluding *murabaha* type products from Islamic banking altogether. He says (1983b: 139):

> I would prefer that *bay' mu'ajjal* [*murabaha*] is removed from the list of permissible methods altogether. Even if we concede its permissibility in legal form, we have the overriding legal maxim that anything leading to something prohibited stands prohibited. It will be advisable to apply this maxim to *bay' mu'ajjal* in order to save interest-free banking from being sabotaged from within.

However, in their defence, Islamic banks argue that the *Qur'an* allows trade, that is buying and selling at a profit, and *murabaha* is also buying and selling at a profit. Since there are no legal restrictions on the amount of profit one can make from a particular sale, Islamic banks are theoretically free to charge whatever mark-up they can in a *murabaha* contract. These banks also tend to interpret *riba* as occurring mainly in the context of financial transactions, that is, contractual obligations to pay an increase by the borrower in a loan. They argue that since products like *murabaha,* leasing and hire-purchase are not, strictly speaking financial transactions (or exchange of money for money), an increase as profit in these transactions should not be considered *riba* whatever similarities they have to fixed interest (Saeed, 1993, 1996). A Western observer of the progress of Islamic banking remarks (Nienhaus, 1986: 44):

> For the Islamic banks, especially their advisers in Islamic law, the prohibition of interest is not mainly an economic problem, as it is for Muslim economists, who claim the allocative and distributive superiority of an interest-free system, but it is first and foremost a legal prescription. Prohibited is any predetermined positive return to the provider of capital in a purely financial transaction, that is, where an entrepreneur receives from a bank liquidity or money for utilisation at his own discretion. *Murabaha*, mark-up or *ijara*, leasing, are not such purely financial transactions, because the entrepreneur does not receive liquidity or money but real assets, that is, merchandise or machinery.

Banking Services Offered by Islamic banks

The banking services provided by the Islamic bank are also justified according to *shari'a* while various contracts developed in Islamic law, such as *wadi'ah* (trust), *wakalah* (agency) and *sarf* (currency exchange) are used as bases for provision of these services. Where possible, these services are provided on the basis of a fee or commission. PLS based deposits, that is, investment deposits, are on the basis of *mudaraba*.

Islamic banks accept several types of deposit: current account, savings, special investment and general investment. Current account deposits are accepted on the basis of *wadi'ah* (trust) in which the depositor is not interested in a return but merely safekeeping of the funds by the bank. The bank generally seeks from the depositor permission to use the funds but any profit on the use will belong to the bank. Since the depositor is not taking any risk, this is deemed at *shari'a* to be acceptable. The bank provides the depositor with cheque books and the depositor may withdraw the funds at any time.

Like current accounts, savings account deposits are strictly for safekeeping purposes. This means that the bank holds the funds on the principle of *wadi'ah* and is not obliged to give any return to the depositor. However, the bank may, at its own discretion, allocate a share of any profit to these deposits.

Investment deposits are by far the most common form of deposit with an Islamic bank. Investment deposits are made by clients who are interested in a return on their funds which the bank accepts on the basis of *mudaraba*. The depositor in this case is the *rabb al-mal* (investor) and the bank the *mudarib*. The bank would accept these funds for specified periods of time and use them in its investment operations. Since the funds are placed on a PLS basis, the bank and the client share in the profit, and the profit-sharing ratio is agreed upon in advance. If a loss results, the depositors (investors) will bear such loss.

Investment deposits can be general or specific. General investment deposits are those deposits placed with the bank without specifying how and where they are to be invested. The bank has total freedom to invest these funds and the depositors cannot dictate to the bank how this should be done. In the case of specific investment deposits, the investor specifies how and where the deposits are to invested, and the bank is obliged to invest the funds in line with those instructions. Such deposits are usually large and come from wealthy individuals or corporate clients.

Other banking services include foreign exchange services; travellers cheques; money transfers (both local and international); correspondent banking services; trustee services; and safe-deposit services.

The Emergence of Islamic Banking in Indonesia

Indonesia, though the most populous Muslim country, has been relatively slow to introduce Islamic banking. It was some 20 years after the emergence of the modern Islamic banking that the government decided that support for an Islamic bank project would be a prudent gesture towards the Muslim community. As mentioned, this should perhaps be understood in the context of former President Soeharto's support for such projects as a means of legitimising and strengthening his Islamic credentials.

Islamic banking in Indonesia is not isolated from the Islamic banking context in other parts of the Muslim world. In fact, it closely follows the practices of Islamic banks elsewhere. Much of the above discussion applies to Islamic banking in Indonesia. The tension between the neo-revivalists and modernists regarding the interpretation of the foundation texts as well as how Islamic law is to be developed and applied also exists among Indonesian Islamic scholars *(ulama)* although the terminology used to refer to the trends noticeably differ.

In Indonesia, as in some other Islamic countries, it was the government which was the key to establishing an effective Islamic bank. A first attempt, led by the traditionalist Islamic organisation, Nahdlatul Ulama, led in 1990 to a surprising partnership with Christian ethnic Chinese financiers in Bank Summa. At best a quasi-Islamic institution, this bank also conducted Western-style banking operations. It did not accept the neo-revivalist reading of *riba* and charged interest on its loans. It had, however, established a network of rural community credit banks before it collapsed in 1992 by reason of mismanagement. The *Majelis Ulama Indonesia* (MUI – Indonesian Council of *Ulama*) had also explored the idea of an Islamic bank in a workshop held in August in 1990 in Cisarua. The idea was later confirmed by the MUI's 4th National Congress. A working group[3] was then entrusted to develop a concrete plan for establishing an interest-free bank and Soeharto, then President of Indonesia, provided much-needed government backing for the project. In particular, he pushed a number of prominent figures, including several ex-ministers and Muslim businessmen to take part.[4] The involvement of ICMI (*Ikatan Cendikiawan Muslim se-Indonesia* – the Association of Indonesian Moslem Intellectuals) and in particular BJ Habibie, then its head and now President, was also important for the realisation of the project. An organisation largely controlled the by state, ICMI has been a key instrument for implementing government policy towards Islam in Indonesia.

Backed by the top level of government and the government's key Islamic organisation, Bank Muamalat was established in a relatively short time and enjoyed the broad official and religious support that Bank Summa was never able to obtain. An important boost was the willingness of the Soeharto-headed foundation, *Yayasan Amal Bhakti Muslim Pancasila,* to lend funds for the initial deposit on an unconditional basis. This deposit was a prerequisite for the Bank's application for a Preliminary Licence, a requirement in the establishment of banking institutions. A further political move was Soeharto's personal invitation to several leading figures to the Bogor Palace in November 1991 to subscribe to shares in BMI, with the result that Rp500 billion was subscribed and BMI opened with Rp106 billion as paid-up capital. On 1 May 1992, Bank Muamalat Indonesia began its operations and a grand ceremony on 15 May at the Sahid Jaya Hotel again confirmed the full support of the President and cabinet.

BMI's Operations

In line with Islamic banks in other parts of the Muslim world, BMI, is managed by a Board of Directors under the supervision of a *Shari'ah* Supervisory Board. It also has a Board of Commissioners. The *Syariah* Supervisory Board is established in consultation with the Central Indonesia Council of *Ulama*, with its key function being to ensure that the products marketed by the bank are in line with Islamic principles.

---

3   Consisting of M Amin Aziz (chair), Syahrul Ralie Siregar, A Malik and Zainulbahar Noor.

4   These included: Ginanjar Kartasasmita, Alamsyah Ratu Perwiranegara, Hartarto, Arifin M Siregar and Azwar Anas, Sukamdani Sahid Gitosardjono, Probosutedjo, Mohamad Hasan, Abdul Latief Agus, Sudwikatmono, E Kowar, Hutomo Mandala Putra and Abu Rizal Bakrie.

The basic products offered by the bank are as follows.

- Gathering of public funds: (a) *wa'diah* giro accounts; (b) *mudharabah* deposits; (c) *mudharabah* savings; and(d) *mudharabah* and *takaful* deposits
- Funds channelling products: (a) *mudharabah/qiradh* profit sharing-based financing; (b) *murabahah* working capital financing; (c) *al-bai' bithaman ajil* investment financing; and (d) *al-qardh al-hasan* service financing
- Other services: (a) foreign currency transactions; (b) provisions of guarantees; (c) issue of letters of credit; (d) transfers; and (e) other banking service

Islamic banking in Indonesia, although still in its early stage, and not yet playing a major role in the economy, has been very well received. In spite of there being among Indonesian *ulama* a degree of openness regarding the interpretation of Islamic legal texts regarding commerce in particular, there remain, as in other parts of the Islamic world, a substantial number of Muslims who believe that interest is *riba* and is prohibited. They are therefore reluctant to deal with the interest-based banks. Moreover, because a significant proportion of the population remains poor, savings are limited. Considering the perceived bias of traditional banks against lending to low income earners it is not surprising that these groups have difficulty in dealing with the banks. The banks for their part see low income earners as poor risks, unable to provide adequate security or guarantees. This combination of factors virtually guarantees a market for an Islamic banking institution that will service the poor.

From its beginning in the 1960s, Islamic banking literature stressed that one function of an Islamic bank would be to reach low income groups. In this sense, Islamic banks had a mission as the Islamic world was at the time comprised largely of low income people, who had no access to bank funds. In practice this emphasis survived at varying degrees in different countries depending on the level of poverty or affluence in the country and the disposition of the banks concerned. A number of Islamic banks continue to attempt to serve low income clients via interest free loans *(qard hasan)* or small grants from the *zakat* funds.

There being sound economic reasons as well as theoretical ones, Bank Muamalat has a similar disposition. It has been working to reach low income groups in major cities as well as in villages by opening branches in cities and playing a leading role in establishing rural branches and village credit cooperatives.

Though Bank Muamalat is an Islamic bank, its business and products are open to people of any faith. As for the shares, although the BMI's articles of association do not limit its shareholders to Muslims, share purchases by non-Muslims are not likely to be approved for the time being to protect the bank's Islamic identity. In terms of performance, the bank's pre-tax profit of Rp 7 billion in 1995 was up 15.33% on 1994. To date, profits have grown at an average annual rate of 31.7%. As a percentage of total credit, year-end 1995 problem loans stood at 3.34%, with bad loans at 0.34%. In these respects, BMI's performance has been similar to that of the average commercial bank over the same period. Of course, the impact the economic difficulties of 1997-98 will have on the performance of Bank Muamalat Indonesia and on its future development remains to be seen but it is possible that the failure of 'mainstream' Western banks may lead to new deposits for Islamic banks that place a priority on serving low-income clients – now the growing majority of Muslim Indonesians.

Conclusion

Islamic banking emerged in the 1960s as a result of a number of interrelated factors, the most notable being the perception that modern bank interest is *riba*, which is prohibited in the *Qur'an*. Other factors were the emergence of a powerful neo-revivalist movement in the 20th century and the availability of vast resources in petro-dollars, a result of the 1973 oil embargo by the oil producing and exporting countries of the Arab Middle East.

Islamic banking theorists of that time accepted the view that interest is *riba* and rejected the modernists' arguments that it should be interpreted in the light of modern social and economic realities. They also believed that Islamic banking should be based on profit and loss sharing, both in deposit mobilisation and investment/financing. Islamic banking was to correct those practices of traditional banks which placed too much emphasis on security and guarantees in financing. It was argued that Islamic banks could play a significant part in the social and economic advancement of the less developed Islamic communities by providing funds to those who had skills but lacked the capital. As it turned out, however, most Islamic banks were commercial banks with profit maximisation as a key objective. They could not rely too much on pure PLS based financing as the risks in PLS were great and the shareholders as well as the depositors would not countenance losses or comparably lower returns. From the very beginning therefore, Islamic banks relied more on pre-determined return based financing such as *murabaha* and *ijara* (leasing) and other similar financing mechanisms and much less on pure PLS based financing.

Despite the criticisms of many Islamic banking theorists, Islamic banks have apparently earned the respect of their Muslim clientele and have grown rapidly throughout the Muslim world, including Indonesia. The history of Islamic banking shows that it has the ability to provide most of the services traditional banks provide to their customers in both deposit mobilisation and financing, and that it can provide a comparable return to its depositors.

Indonesia's Islamic bank, Bank Muamalat Indonesia, a relative newcomer in international terms, has generally followed the practices of Islamic banks in other parts of the Muslim world. Islamic banking is still, however, in its early stages in Indonesia and it remains to be seen whether it can play a significant role in the faltering Indonesian economy.

References

Abu Saud, Mahmud, 1980, 'Money, Interest and Qirad' in Khurshid Ahmad (ed), *Studies in Islamic Economics*, Islamic Foundation, Leicester.

Abu Zahra, Muhammad, 1970, *Buhuth fi al-Riba*, Dar al-Buhuth al-'Ilmiyya, Kuwait.

Ahmad, Ziauddin., 1985, 'The Present State of Islamic Finance Movement', *Journal of Islamic Banking and Finance*, Autumn: 7-48.

al-Tamimi, Youne, 1986, 'Experience of Islamic Banks in the Middle East', *Journal of Islamic Banking and Finance*, Spring: 55-62.

Asad, Muhammad, 1984, *The Message of the Qur'an*, Dar al-Andalus, Gibraltar.

Banna, Hasan al-, 1978, *Five Tracts of Hasan al-Banna (1906-1949)*, trans Charles Wendell, University of California Press, Berkeley.

Chapra, M Umer, 1985, *Towards a Just Monetary System*, Islamic Foundation, Leicester.

CII (Council of Islamic Ideology), 1983, *Consolidated Recommendations on the Islamic Economic System*, Council of Islamic Ideology, Islamabad.

El-Ashker, Ahmed Abdel-Fattah., 1987, *The Islamic Business Enterprise*, Croom Helm, Kent.

Homoud, Sami, 1986, *Islamic Banking*, Arabian Information Ltd, London.

Homoud, Sami, 1988, 'Siyagh al-Tamwil al-Islami: Mazaya wa 'Aqabat Kulli Sigha'. *Majallat al-Bunuk al-Islamiyya*. (63).

IDB (Islamic Development Bank), 1990, *Technical Cooperation Programme among IDB Member Countries*, Jeddah.

IDB (Islamic Development Bank), 1980-1993, *Annual Reports*.

IIBID. *al-Tamwil bi al-Mudaraba*, IIBID, Cairo.

Iqbal, Sir Muhammad, 1960, *The Reconstruction of Religious Thought in Islam*, Sh Muhammad Ashraf, Lahore.

Ismail, Abdul Halim, 1992, 'Bank Islam Malaysia Berhad: Principles and Operations' in Abod, Sheikh Ghazali Sheikh, Syed Omar Syed Agil and Aidit Hj Ghazali, *An Introduction to Islamic Finance*, Quill Publishers, Kuala Lumpur.

Jaziri, 'Abd al-Rahman al-, *Kitab al-Fiqh 'ala al-Madhahib al-Arba'a*, 6th ed, al-Maktabat al-Tijariyya al-Kubra, Cairo, nd.

Khan, Abdul Jabbar, 1984, 'Divine Banking System', *Journal of Islamic Banking and Finance*, Winter: 29-50.

Khan, Shahrukh Rafi, 1987, *Profit and Loss Sharing: An Islamic Experiment in Finance and Banking*, Oxford University Press, Karachi.

Mawdudi, Abu al-A'la, 1970, *al-Hadarat al-Islamiyya*, Dar al-'Arabiyya, Beirut.

Mawdudi, Abu al-A'la, 1986, 'Prohibition of Interest in Islam', *Al-Islam*. June: 6-8.

Mawdudi, Abu al-A'la, *al-Riba*, trans Muhammad 'Asim al-Haddad, Dar al-Fikr, Beirut. nd.

Mawdudi, Abu al-A'la, 1984, *Economic System of Islam*, Islamic Publications, Lahore.

Mawdudi, Abu al-A'la, 1986, *Towards Understanding Islam*, IIFSO, Kuwait.

Mawdudi, Abu al-A'la, 1988, *Towards Understanding the Qur'an*. trans Zafar Ishaq Ansari, Islamic Foundation, Leicester.

Mohammed, Ismail Hassan, 1989, 'Islamic Banks' Practices in *Murabaha*'. paper presented at the 5th Expert Level Meeting on Islamic Banking Studies, held in Abu Dhabi, 18-20 March.

Mukhtar, Ibrahim, 1987, *Bunuk al-Istithmar*, Maktabat al-Injlo al-Misriyya, Cairo.

Muzaffar, Chandra, 1986, 'Islamic Resurgence: A Global View' in Taufik Abdullah and Sharon Siddique (ed), *Islam and Society in Southeast Asia*, Institute of Southeast Asian Studies, Singapore: 5-39

Najjar, Ahmad A al-, 1985, *Bunuk bila Fawa'id*, IAIB, Cairo.

Najjar, Sa'id al, 1989, 'Si'r al-Fa'ida Yu'addi Wazifa Hayawiyya fi al-Nizam al-Iqtisadi al-Mu'asir' in Salah Muntasir (ed), *Arbah al-Bunuk*, Dar al- Ma'arif, Cairo: 35-42

Namir, 'Abd al-Mun'im al, 1989, '"Ala Ayyi Asas Jara al-Hukm bi Hurmati Ribh" fi al-Bunuk?' in Salah Muntasir (ed), *Arbah al-Bunuk*, Dar al- Ma'arif, Cairo: 53-60.

Nienhaus, Volker, 1986, 'Islamic Economics, Finance and Banking: Theory and Practice', *Journal of Islamic Banking and Finance*, Spring: 36-54.

Nienhaus, Volker, 1983, 'Profitability of Islamic PLS Banks Competing with Interest Banks: Problems and Prospects', *Journal of Research in Islamic Economics*, Vol 1, no 1.

Qutb, Muhammad, 1965, *al-Insan bayna al-Maddiyya wa al-Islam*, Dar Ihya' al-Kutub al-'Arabiyya, Cairo.

Qutb, Sayyid, *Tafsir Ayat al-Riba*. Dar al-Buhuth al-'Ilmiyya, nd.

Qureshi, Anwar Iqbal, 1974, *Islam and the Theory of Interest*, Sh Muhammad Ashraf, Lahore.

Rahman, Fazlur, 1979, 'Riba and Interest', *Islamic Studies*, March 1964: 1-43.

Rahman, Fazlur, 1980, 'Islam: Challenges and Opportunities'. in Welch, Alford T and Cachia, Pierre (eds), *Islam: Past Influence and Present Challenge*, Edinburgh University Press, Edinburgh.

Rahman, Fazlur, 1982, *Islam and Modernity: Transformation of an Intellectual Tradition*, University of Chicago Press, Chicago.

Saeed, Abdullah, 1993, 'Islamic Banking in Practice: A Critical Look at the *Murabaha* Financing Mechanism', *Journal of Arabic, Islamic & Middle Eastern Studies*, Vol 1, no 1: 59-79

Saeed, Abdullah, 1995, 'The Moral Context of the Prohibition of Riba in Islam Revisited' *American Journal of Islamic Social Sciences*, vol 12, no 4, Winter: 496-51.

Saeed, Abdullah, 1995b, 'Islamic Banking in Practice: the Case of Faisal Islamic Bank of Egypt', *Journal of Arabic, Islamic & Middle Eastern Studies*, vol 1, no 3: 28-46.

Saeed, Abdullah, 1996, *Islamic Banking and Interest: A Study of the Prohibition of Riba and its Contemporary Interpretation*, EJ Brill, Leiden: 169.

Saeed, Abdullah, 1997, 'Ijtihad and Innovation in Neo-Modernist Islamic Thought in Indonesia', *Journal of Christian-Muslim Relations* (October).

Saleh, Nabil A, 1986, *Unlawful Gain and Legitimate Profit in Islamic Law*, Cambridge University Press, Cambridge.

Siddiqi, Muhammad Nejatullah, 1989, 'Impact of Islamic Modes of Finance on Monetary Expansion', paper presented at the 5th Expert Level Meeting on Islamic Banking Studies. March.

Siddiqi, Muhammad Nejatullah, 1980, 'Muslim Economic Thinking: A survey of Contemporary Literature' in Khurshid Ahmad (ed), *Studies in Islamic Economics*, Islamic Foundation, Leicester.

Siddiqi, Muhammad Nejatullah, 1983a, *Banking without Interest*, Islamic Foundation Leicester.

Siddiqi, Muhammad Nejatullah, 1983b, *Issues in Islamic Banking: Selected Papers*, Islamic Foundation, Leicester.

Siddiqi, Muhammad Nejatullah, 1985, *Partnership and Profit-Sharing in Islamic Law*, Islamic Foundation, Leicester.

Sadr, Muhammad Baqir al-, 1973, *al-Bank al-Laribawi fi al-Islam*, Dar al-Kitab al-Lubnani, Beirut.

Udovitch, A., 1970, *Partnership and Profit in Medieval Islam*, Princeton University Press, Princeton.

Uzair, Mohammad, 1978, *Interest-Free Banking*, Royal Book Co, Karachi.

Uzair, Mohammad, 1983, 'Impact of Interest Free Banking', *Journal of Islamic Banking and Finance*. Autumn: 39-50.

Zaidi, Nawazish Ali, 1988, 'Islamic Banking in Pakistan', *Journal of Islamic Banking and Finance*. Summer: 21-30.

24. Culture, Ideology and Human Rights:

The Case of Indonesia's Code of Criminal Procedure

Daniel Fitzpatrick

The question of culture is prominent in current human rights literature largely because of the challenges and contradictions of cultural relativism. Extreme cultural relativists argue that 'rights' only exist when particular societies perceive them as such. As cultural constructs, they lack any autonomous existence and therefore cannot be said to be universal (Pollis & Schwab, 1979). This view, uncomfortably suggestive of an absolute inability to explain or understand other cultures lacks many proponents (Schirmer, 1988: 93), although it does give succour to the 'Asian values' argument that restriction of civil and political liberties in Asia is justified by a distinct regional view of human rights. Yet, few also would argue the opposite view: that Western human rights law and legal institutions may be applied, *mutatis mutandis*, to Asian societies. After all, the history of postcolonial law reveals clearly that transplanted law and institutions rarely operate with similar effects in their new environment (Seidman & Seidman, 1994: 44-45). Thus, the orthodox formulation is that international human rights norms must be infused with contextual and cultural specificity (Pritchard, 1996: 153-54, 166-68). But how is this to be done? What is the middle way between universalism and cultural relativism?

Western lawyers tend now to accept that cultural factors may validly produce different human rights outcomes, but argue that culture cannot be a 'metanorm': cultural practices that conflict with international standards must be condemned (Alston, 1994: 20; Falk, 1992: 46-52). Alston (1994: 19-20) argues further that international human rights standards are best seen as concentric circles: central norms that relate to the physical and mental integrity of the person are less responsive or susceptible to cultural influences than more peripheral norms such as treatment of detainees and freedom of thought. In contrast, a prominent Muslim writer, An-Na'im, asserts that culture must play a more dynamic role than mere subordinate normative influence. He argues that a major cause of human rights violations in the Third World is the lack of local cultural legitimacy of international human rights standards and institutions (1992: 1-5). If human rights instruments are to be truly universal, they must be based on genuine cross-cultural normative consensus rather than the views and values of a dominant culture. This quest for consensus requires intense intra- and inter-cultural dialogue, which may ultimately result in a need to modify international human rights standards (1994: 62-69).

An-Na'im further argues that international human rights efforts can only gain cultural legitimacy if they relate directly to, and work as much as possible through, local 'folk models' (id: 1994: 70-71). This approach has resonances of the 'dependency' argument that, in the context of postcolonial oligarchic governments, formal Western-style law has operated as an instrument of hegemony rather than an autonomous restraint on the state (Greenberg, 1980). Thus, for example, it is sometimes said that Western criminal law and institutions in postcolonial countries actually suppress human rights because they establish a centralised and hierarchical system based on the coercive powers of a hegemonic state (Greenburg: 133-36). In support of this view dependency theorists note that colonially derived laws and institutions, such as legislation, courts, prosecutors and lawyers, have assisted in perpetrating systematic human rights violations; yet human rights guarantees in many postcolonial constitutions – separation of powers, independence of the judiciary and free elections – rarely worked to prevent them (Seidman & Seidman, 1994: 20, 27-36). The corollary is that a more appropriate system for postcolonial countries would be culturally sympathetic, horizontal and decentralised law and legal institutions. In relation to criminal law, this entails traditional folk models of adjudication and punishment.

At first glance, the folk model approach is an intellectually satisfying answer to the human rights and culture debate. It satisfies demands for cultural specificity and is consistent with the increasing focus on 'group' rights and the plight of indigenous peoples. But, quite apart from the fact that traditional folk models have eroded significantly in the Third World as a result of urbanisation and development, the focus on folk models has a major flaw, namely that many of the abuses that human rights instruments are aimed at – summary executions, arbitrary detention and torture – are the result of activities of modern nation-states rather than intra-cultural phenomena. Indeed, Doughty (1988: 43) argues that 'all that transpires under the rubric of human rights is related directly to the creation and internal operation of nation-states and the relationship of one state to another'. Similarly, in a study of Latin America, Fruhling (1992: 254-55) concludes that human rights violations are essentially the conduct of social and ethnic divisions created by the modernising process in new nation-states which lack institutional mechanisms for dealing with those divisions. In other words, because postcolonial nation-states have an undeveloped institutional superstructure, they cannot assert their authority over their citizens by non-violent means. Notably, this approach is a direct challenge to many aspects of the human rights and culture debate. It suggests that human rights should be viewed more in the context of nation-state ideologies and institutions than through a prism of cultural difference (Howard, 1992).

These issues, then, raise a number of fundamental questions concerning the relationship between law, culture, ideology and institutions. Why have human rights laws and institutions so often failed in practice in postcolonial countries? To what extent have technical flaws in those laws contributed to their failure? Should the proper approach be to reform institutions, and if so which institutions and how? What role does cultural illegitimacy play in human rights violations? Do Western-style law and institutions actually suppress human rights in a postcolonial environment? Would decentralising criminal punishment to traditional groups provide greater protection of human rights? Is the problem not so much cultural as intrinsic to the creation and spread of nation-states? Are ideologies, and in particular the overriding loyalty of bureaucratic oligarchies to postcolonial nation-states, more important factors than culture?

This chapter considers these issues through a study of Indonesia's Code of Criminal Procedure (KUHAP).[1] It begins with an analysis of cultural patterns in Indonesia. It then considers the provisions and operation of the KUHAP and analyses the institutions that implement it. It concludes, in essence, that cultural relativities in Indonesia have a far less important role in human rights violations than national institutions and ideology.

Cultural Patterns in Indonesia

Does Indonesia's Western-style Code of Criminal Procedure lack cultural legitimacy? Is there an 'Indonesian' culture through which international human rights standards may be implemented? These questions require analysis of cultural patterns in Indonesia. The starting point is the difficulties of discerning one 'Indonesian' culture.

Regional Diversity

Before the arrival of the Dutch, the Indonesian archipelago consisted of a large number of sultanates, kingdoms, clan-groups and city-states. The Dutch took control of the archipelago over a number of centuries but did not seek 'national' law or institutions. Their system was profoundly pluralist: European law was used to rearrange agriculture, particularly in Java, into large export-oriented plantations whilst the balance of the colony was left largely to its diverse customary practices (Gautama and Harsono, 1972: VII-X). Independent Indonesia's rulers have sought to overcome this pluralism. They have promoted a national mythology largely based on anti-colonial unity and historical figures such as Gadjah Madah, prime minister of a Java-based archipelagic empire. They have also overseen the spread of a national language, *Bahasa Indonesia*, formerly a lingua franca derived from Malay.

Nevertheless, in reality Indonesia remains extraordinarily diverse in religious, social, ethnic and linguistic terms. In Sumatra, the Acehnese are strongly Islamic and rebellious; the Minangkbau are Islamic but matrilineal; some Bataks are patrilineal Christians and others are Muslim; and the Niasians are (or were until recently) stone-age animists. In Java, the Sundanese are strongly Islamic, *santri* Muslims, while East and Central Javanese tend towards *abangan* Islam, a syncretic combination of pantheistic animism with Hindu and Islamic beliefs. A related group in Java is adherents of *kebathinan*, a system of Javanese mystical belief in natural and ancestral spirits. The Balinese are Hindu and strongly communalistic. Sulawesi consists of both Christians and Muslims. The Eastern islands of Nusa Tenggara are Christian or animist and largely consist of subsistence or shifting cultivators. The East Timorese are Catholic, secessionist and, in company with Irian Jaya and certain remote islands of indigenous peoples, are not from the proto-Malay stock of the rest of Indonesia. In Kalimantan and Irian Jaya, various tribal groups of animist, shifting cultivators or hunter-gatherers vie with transmigrants from Java, Madura and,

---

1 *Kitab Undang-Undang Hukum Acara Pidana.*

increasingly, Nusa Tenggara. All of these groups largely retain their own languages and customs, save in Java and urban areas where customary authority has been eroded and the effects of industrialisation are more apparent.

Common Features of Indonesian Cultures

Anthropologists generally agree that there are certain common features of Indonesian societies. One is the insistence on maintaining an appropriate equilibrium between individuals, the community and the cosmos (Warren, 1993: 38). This equilibrium is embedded in the intense interaction between living and spirit worlds in all traditional Indonesian societies. Thus, failure to fulfil ritual and ceremonial obligations to appease the spirit world, particularly in relation to agricultural fertility and forest produce, is seen almost universally to lead to social disaster. In turn, this focus on ritual and cosmology fosters communal solidarity, which creates another common principle, namely that collective interests outweigh those of the individual (Hooker, 1978: 55). But it is important to recognise that this collectivist principle is not static. Another common belief in Indonesia is the centrality of dualist forces – birth/death, planting/harvest, rights/obligations, egalitarian/hierarchical tendencies, locality/kinship loyalties – and the rich role that *adat* plays in balancing them (Warren, 1993: 33-48). In addition, traditional life in Indonesia is not circumscribed by autonomous village or kinship communities but involves a complex interaction of kinship, territorial tea, hierarchical, religious, agricultural and external influences (Geertz, 1980: 47-48; Warren, 1993: 1).

However, for the purposes of the human rights and culture debate, and in particular questions of cultural context and legitimacy, it is difficult to see how these highly generalised principles create an 'Indonesian' culture. They may be sufficient to lead to the conclusion that the centralised, inflexible, hierarchical and secular nature of Western-style criminal law and institutions is culturally inappropriate to Indonesia. But apart perhaps from their support for regional folk models of criminal law, they provide little guidance on the question of culturally specific implementation of international human rights standards, both inter-culturally and in people-state relations, in the nation of Indonesia. Indeed, such common principles as may be discerned among Indonesian cultures – equilibrium, dualism and spirituality – are so lacking in specificity and autonomous existence that their ability to found pan-Indonesian institutions of adjudication and punishment must be doubted.

In these circumstances, is it possible to discern more specific and useful pan-Indonesian beliefs through a process of distilling universal *adat* principles from careful study of diverse regional customs in Indonesia? This process has a cherished tradition in Indonesia. The Leiden School of *adat* research primarily devoted itself to proving, from common features of regional *adat*, the ultimate existence of a pan-Indonesian 'ur-*adat*' (Burns, 1989: 1-29). The Indonesian government then adopted this notion of universal *adat* principles as a potent national myth. It has thus applied the traditional principle of discussion and deliberation to parliamentary procedure, and incorporated the notion of the 'social function' of rights to land into Indonesian land law. Yet, this process of distilling and applying universal *adat* principles must now be questioned. Burns (1989) has shown that the Leiden school's belief in universal *adat* principles primarily arose in response to colonial proposals to impose Western codified law throughout the archipelago. Thus, their efforts were flawed by political motivations: if it could be shown that *adat* had sufficiently uniform and predictable characteristics to be regarded as 'law', then a more ethical alternative to Western codification could be pursued.

Further, it is now apparent that, in the transformation of universal *adat* principles from colonial argument to national myth and aspect of formal law, these principles have lost much of their original meaning and value. In relation to parliament, for example, discussion and deliberation essentially means rubber-stamping government proposals. In relation to land law, 'social function' simply means the right of the state and bureaucracy to exercise ad hoc control over the rights of individual or customary landholders (Fitzpatrick, 1997: 202-204).

A Cultural Cause of Human Rights Violations?

If, then, the question of common Indonesian cultural beliefs is highly indeterminate, and therefore culturally specific implementation of international human rights standards is problematic, can the inquiry be reversed? Is it possible to say that cultural factors actually contribute to human rights violations in Indonesia? Mulya Lubis (1993: 297-98), a prominent Indonesian human rights lawyer, argues that, although the national ideology of *Pancasila* is highly significant, three cultural factors have hampered the protection of human rights in Indonesia: first, the strong belief in social hierarchy which, in the Javanese context in particular, includes an 'unshakeable' belief in the pre-determination of one's place in society, either as *kawula* (subject) or *gusti* (lord); secondly, the 'cultural obsession for harmony'; and, thirdly, the fact that 'in most parts of the country, Indonesian society is not rights-based but duties-based'. A number of other commentators have also identified cultural lack of emphasis on individualism and individual rights as undermining Indonesia's support for human rights.[2]

Although Lubis's view must be respected, as with much writing on Indonesia notions such as one's pre-determined status as 'lord' or 'subject' are Java-centric rather than pan-Indonesian. Indeed, egalitarian tendencies are quite strong in Bali and the 'outer islands' (Warren, 1993); in Aceh (under the influence of Islam); and in matrilineal Minangkbau (West Sumatra). In any event, to the extent that notions of hierarchy and communism are pan-Indonesian, they must be considered in their proper context. They are not absolute or autonomous cultural principles but part of an interplay of oppositional forces (egalitarian/hierarchical, individualist/ communalist) that is regulated by *adat* and ultimately influenced by the world of natural and ancestral spirits. Thus, hierarchical figures and communal obligation are not laws unto themselves, but subject to *adat* principles of equilibrium and ritual obligations to the spirit world.

In these circumstances, to transpose a general cultural tendency to hierarchy and communalism into autonomous principles governing and explaining the actions of state officials is entirely misconceived. As with most postcolonial countries, Indonesia faces a new situation and new challenges as the structure and ideology of a nation-state impacts on traditional loyalties to region, race and religion. In this new context, vague formulations of pan-Indonesian cultural beliefs are little guide to the actions of state officials.

---

2   See, for example, Lev (1972: 301-302); Djodjodigoeno (1952: 42).

KUHAP

The following section considers specific provisions of KUHAP, identifies their technical flaws and analyses the institutions and ideologies involved in implementing them. Ultimately, it is concerned not so much with listing transgressions of KUHAP but analysing the respective roles of culture, technical flaws, institutional weaknesses and nation-state ideologies in their occurrence.

KUHAP was promulgated in 1981, replacing the Dutch colonial code of 1848 known as the HIR.[3] It establishes a number of fundamental rights for criminal defendants that were not provided for in the HIR. These include a presumption of innocence; a right to legal assistance; a right to be free of duress during interrogation and trial; and a right to compensation for illegal arrest, detention and/or seizure of property. Yet there are repeated, credible reports of consistent violations of KUHAP.[4] These violations are particularly apparent in cases of political or regional unrest that threatens national unity. Indeed, in areas of rebellion or secessionist movements such as Aceh and East Timor, KUHAP clearly has little meaning or application. Transgressions of KUHAP are also widespread in ordinary criminal cases. Torture, mistreatment, anti-terrorist and fabrication of evidence appears commonplace (US State Department, 1992). The military is also regularly involved in ordinary criminal matters arising out of civil disputes such as land acquisition and labour conflicts.

Investigations

KUHAP gives police exclusive powers of investigation and interrogation. The former powers of prosecutors to undertake investigations themselves are abolished: they are simply limited to prosecution itself (Art 137) and the implementation of court decisions (Art 270). This lack of supervision over the initial stages of police investigation and suspect detention has been identified as a significant formal defect in KUHAP (UN Special Rapporteur, 1991: 18). In addition, although the police must have a reasonable presumption that a criminal act has been committed before they can begin an investigation (Arts 102(1), 106), judicial review of this requirement is not available (Lubis, 1993: 119) and there is no other sanction for its violation.

Arrests

Unless the offender is 'caught in the act', a warrant is required in order to make an arrest where a 'criminal act', as defined in the Criminal Code, has been committed (Art 18). A warrant is not required in respect of lesser crimes, known as 'offences' in the criminal code. In these cases, an arrest may be made pursuant to a failure on two consecutive occasions to comply with a summons (Art 19(2)). Warrants must identify the suspect, give reasons for his arrest, briefly outline the nature of the case against him, and state the place of interrogation (Art 18(1)). A copy of the warrant must be delivered to the suspect's family (Art 18(3)). To be 'caught in the act' is to be caught whilst committing a criminal act, or 'some time after', a vague phrase

---

3 *Herziene Indonesish Reglement.*

4 See, for example, Asia Watch (1989, 1990); LBH (1991); Indonesian Human Rights Forum (1991); ICJ (1991); Lawyer's Committee (1993); and US State Department (1992).

which grants police considerable leeway in deciding whether or not to obtain a warrant.

An arrest in cases of a 'criminal act' requires a strong presumption on the basis of sufficient initial proof that such an act has been committed (Art 17). A suspect must be released one day after arrest unless pre-trial detention has been ordered (Art 19). There is a right of compensation for unlawful arrest (Art 82), although there is no provision which states that an unlawful arrest 'taints' subsequent proceedings in any way. In addition, although there is no lawful authority to do so, 'arrests' are often made by the military. Perversely, this then makes it difficult to complain of non-compliance with KUHAP as it is not an 'arrest' under it (Lawyer's Committee, 1993). In addition, it appears that in practice arrests without warrants are common: if pre-trial detention procedures are instituted, arrest warrants are simply backdated (Lawyer's Committee, 1993: 20).

Detention

A significant reform introduced by KUHAP is its regulation of pre-trial detentions. Under the old Dutch HIR, indefinite detentions could be ordered on 30-day renewable periods. Under KUHAP, pre-trial detention is limited to offences carrying a sentence of greater than five years imprisonment as well as a large number of other crimes enumerated in KUHAP (Art 21(4)). In all other cases the suspect must be released, with or without bail or personal guarantees, within one day of arrest. Depending on the stage of the investigation or proceedings, police, prosecutors and judges all have the power to order pre-trial detention. In every case, however, a detention order identifying the suspect, outlining the reasons for the detention, briefly explaining the nature of the suspected criminal act, and stating the place of detention must be presented to the suspect and a copy given to his or her family (Arts 21(2) and (3)). The threshold requirement for a detention order is a strong suspicion on the basis of sufficient evidence that the suspect will disappear, damage or destroy evidence, and/or repeat the criminal act (Art 21(1)). A detention order may be suspended or withdrawn by either police, prosecutors or a judge with or without bail or personal guarantees (Art 31).

There are two formal deficiencies in the pre-trial detention provisions. The first is that detention may be ordered by the police themselves thus allowing suspects to be pressured into making admissions by threats of detention. This is compounded by the second deficiency, namely, that KUHAP contains no requirement for a detainee to be brought promptly before a court. KUHAP contemplates three types of detention order. In the first, the police may detain a person on their own authority for a maximum of 20 days (Art 24(1)). This is extendable for a further 40 days by a prosecutor (Art 24(2)). The court cannot further extend this type of detention and the suspect must be released at the end of the 60-day period (Art 24(4)). In the second, the prosecutor may order an initial detention of up to 20 days. This detention is extendable for a further 30 days by the chairman of a competent district court (Art 25(2)). In the third, a judge of a district court may order an initial detention of up to 30 days which is extendable for a further 60 days by the chairman of the court (Art 26(1) and (2)). In this way a suspect may be detained for up to 60 days without judicial involvement and for up to 90 days with judicial consent.

Pre-Trial Procedure

Another important reform established by KUHAP, and one which commenced with high hopes for its success, is the establishment of a pre-trial procedure to determine whether the arrest and/or detention of a suspect is lawful (Arts 77-83). A request for a pre-trial hearing may be made by the suspect, his family or counsel (Arts 79, 124). If the arrest or detention is determined to be unlawful by a judge then the detainee is to be released immediately and the amount of any compensation determined (Arts 82 (3)). There is no appeal from pre-trial determinations in respect of arrests, detentions and compensation (Art 83). KUHAP does not provide any criteria by which the amount of any such compensation may be established, although an implementing regulation states that the amount of compensation may range from Rp 5000 to 3,000,000 (approximately A\$3.20 to A\$2000).[5] This would appear to be too restrictive, even for a country with low average per capita income.

While the establishment of the pre-trial procedure is laudable, a number of matters undermine its effectiveness in practice. First, the court's jurisdiction is limited to the lawfulness of arrest or detention: any complaints about mistreatment are to be filed with the police, the very body that will be the subject of the complaint. Further, these complaints are heard before military courts. Secondly, there are simply not enough lawyers, particularly in rural areas, to allow legal assistance to most suspects before the trial itself (ICJ, 1991: 174-78). The irony is that challenges to the validity of arrests or detentions may only be made at the pre-trial hearing, and not at the trial itself. Thirdly, there are no regulations governing non-appearance by government officials at pre-trial detention hearings. It appears to be common for this to happen, thereby leading to postponement of the hearing to the point where the pre-trial procedure is no longer available because the trial itself has begun. Fourthly, there are a number of reports of intimidation of applicants for pre-trial detention or their families (ICJ, 1991: 174-78).

Fifthly, because there is no right of appeal from pre-trial detention determinations, those decisions are said to lack predictability and uniformity. Sixthly, whilst the Indonesian Government has formally affirmed the independence of the judiciary, the operation of that independence in practice is questionable. Many Indonesian judges see themselves as part of the apparatus of the state: an attitude reinforced by their express categorisation as public servants.[6] They are also subject to subtle administrative influences. All courts save for the *Mahkamah Agung* (Indonesia's highest court) are under the direct administrative control of the Ministry of Justice which determines postings, transfers and promotions of individual judges.[7] Sometimes the pressure on judges is not so subtle. There are a number of reports of intimidation in politically sensitive cases.[8] Sometimes judicial orders are simply flouted.[9] The result of all these factors is that approximately only 5-10% of pre-trial detention applications are successful, and most defence lawyers prefer now to adopt informal means of resolving human rights violations during detention (Lawyers Committee, 1993: 31).

---

5   Government Regulation No 27 of 1983, Art 12.
6   Government Regulation No 27 of 1983, Art 12.
7   Law No 2 of 1989, Art 5. See also Lubis, 1993: 103; and Lev, 1987: 37-71.
8   See, for example, Indonesian Human Rights Forum (1993: 26).
9   See, for example, Indonesian Human Rights Forum (1992: 25).

Interrogation

A suspect must be interrogated 'immediately' after arrest by the relevant police officer (Art 50). There is a right to be informed of what is presumed against him at the beginning of an interrogation (Art 51). Statements of suspects and witnesses must be recorded in their own words (Art 117(2)) and signed by them, and the police, after they have approved their contents (Art 118(1)). A refusal to sign must be recorded in the police report along with the reasons for such refusal (Art 118(2)). Information by a suspect is to be given without pressure of any kind (Arts 117, 52). There appears to be, in theory at least, an express right to silence during interrogation as Art 66 states that a suspect shall not be burdened with the duty of providing evidence.[10]

These are comprehensive safeguards. Nevertheless, they are undermined, first, by the lack of penalty for their violation; and, secondly, by the fact that KUHAP gives judges no discretion to exclude illegally obtained evidence. Individual judges may, of course, give little weight to admissions obtained by duress, but one consequence of the lack of judicial independence discussed above is that this is rarely done. This problem is compounded by the fact that neither a prosecutor nor a judge can order an independent investigation into allegations that statements were obtained by duress (UN Special Rapporteur, 1991: 7).

Legal Assistance

KUHAP improves significantly on the HIR in that it establishes a right to legal assistance from the beginning of the police investigation itself and not simply at the time of trial. It also does not limit the right to legal assistance to offences carrying the death penalty – as was the case under the HIR. Nevertheless, the right does remain quite restricted in practice because free legal aid is only available to crimes carrying sentences of five years' imprisonment or more (Art 56). The right to legal assistance, other than in cases of free legal aid, includes the right to counsel of one's own choosing (Art 55). Legally aided suspects must accept the legal adviser who is assigned to them. Counsel has a right of access to his client at all stages of the investigation (Arts 69 and 70). This expressly includes the right to be present at, and listen to, interrogations (Art 115(1)).

Clearly enough, the presence of counsel during interrogation serves to prevent the possibility of unfair interrogating techniques. Nevertheless, the extension of the right to legal assistance to include investigations has not been as effective as might be thought (UN Special Rapporteur, 1991: 10). In practice, detainees often do not receive legal assistance because they are unaware of that right and there is no obligation on the part of police to inform them that it exists (UN Special Rapporteur, 1991: 1). In any event, particularly in rural areas, there is often no lawyer available. When they are available, there is a monetary disincentive for them to represent poorer clients. If they are lawyers assigned to clients who cannot afford

---

10 Professor I Made Widayana, Dean of the Faculty of Law, University of Bali, believes that KUHAP does contain a formal right to silence (interview July 1993); Professor Marjono Reksodiputro, then Dean of the Faculty of Law of the University of Indonesia also believes that the right of a defendant to remain silent is implicit in KUHAP (cited in Asia Watch, 1989, *Human Rights in Indonesia and East Timor*: 150). However, Professor J t'Hart of the Netherlands does not believe that KUHAP contains a right to silence (see International Commission of Jurists, 1992: 188).

assistance, the amount payable by the state in respect of trial, appeal and cassation procedures is limited by a 1980 regulation to a maximum of Rp 100,000 (approximately AUD$13.30 in June 1998).[11] In practice, legal aid lawyers say they often receive less.

The right to legal assistance has also been weakened by ministerial regulations or the lack thereof. For example, KUHAP allows counsel the right to communicate with his or her client 'at every moment'. But a Kafkaesque 1983 Ministry of Justice regulation interprets this to mean 'at every moment during office hours'.[12] The result is said to be either that many interrogations are conducted at night or police stations are mysteriously closed whenever a lawyer comes to visit in ordinary hours (Lawyer's Committee, 1993: 38-39). In addition, KUHAP does not specify when police must notify suspects of their right to legal assistance: nor is there any sanction for failure to allow such access. It appears that, in political cases, the right to legal assistance or access is routinely denied until after investigation and detention periods are complete (Lawyer's Committee, 1993). Where lawyers complain to the court, judges are said usually to be unwilling to write a formal order for access to be granted. There are also reports of violence and intimidation against detainees or their families who request legal assistance (Lawyer's Committee, 1993).

Client/Counsel Confidentiality

KUHAP impliedly recognises the confidentiality of client/counsel communication. However, it establishes a number of significant exceptions to that confidentiality. These include:

- Article 70 allows for a client/counsel relationship to be 'closely watched' if counsel fails to heed police warnings about abuse of his right to communicate with his client. Repeated abuse of this right may in fact lead to counsel's being banned from representing the client in question.

- Article 71(2) states that the police can listen to discussions between counsel and client where the charges include crimes against the security of the state.

- Article 62 states that written communications between counsel and client may be censored or examined where there is 'enough reason to presume that the correspondence is being abused'.

The Trial

The KUHAP establishes a number of important procedural safeguards for the conduct of Indonesian trials. These include a presumption of innocence: a suspect shall not be burdened with the duty of providing evidence (Art 66); a right to be present in person at the trial (Arts 152 and 154); and a right to be tried 'immediately' (Art 50). The judge is also obliged to ensure that nothing will be done and that no questions will be asked that will cause a defendant or witness not to be free in answering. This obligation is one of the few that is subject to sanction: failure to ensure the unpressured giving of evidence will annul the decision (Art 153). Certain fundamental principles are also laid down by the criminal code:

---

11 Regulation of the Minister of Justice No M.02-UM.09.08 of 1980.
12 Regulation of the Minister of Justice No M.14-PW.07.03 of 1983, Art 17.

charges are to be based on specific legal provisions (Art 1); criminal laws are to have no retrospective operation (Art 2).

The court must be convinced on the basis of two pieces of 'legal evidence materials' that the accused committed the crime in question (Art 183). A suspect may not, therefore, be convicted on the basis of a confession alone. However, 'legal evidence materials' are defined broadly. They not only include the testimony of a witness, information by an expert, a letter, and a statement of a defendant, but also 'an indication' (Art 184), that is, 'an act, event or situation which because of its concurrence whether between one or the other, with the criminal itself, indicates the occurrence of a criminal act and the person committing it' (Art 188(1)). Such an 'indication' can only be obtained from the testimony of a witness, a letter or a statement by a defendant (Art 188(2)).

One of the more problematic aspects of the safeguards established by KUHAP relates to the right to remain silent at trial. This right probably does exist in KUHAP: Art 66 says that an accused shall not be burdened with the duty of giving evidence. However, Art 175 states that if a defendant refuses to answer a question, the Chairman of the Court 'shall suggest' that he or she answer it, 'after which the examination shall be continued' (Art 175). In a society such as Indonesia which is highly respectful of authority, this 'suggestion' is likely to persuade many suspects to answer. In any event, it has been said that in practice any continuing refusal to answer questions will be treated as an aggravating circumstance in the penalty or as pointing by implication to the guilt of the accused (ICJ, 1991: 188).

Any theoretical right to remain silent is also undermined significantly by the practice of 'splitting' trials. Because there is no obligation in Indonesian law to prosecute matters involving more than one offender in the one trial (see Arts 141, 142), a practice has arisen whereby defendants in one case, particularly 'political' trials, are summoned as witnesses in a related case and compelled to give evidence which is subsequently used against them in their own trial (Asia Watch, 1989: 150). The problem is compounded by the further practice of refusing to allow the defence to have access to the evidence given in the related trial (Asia Watch, 1989: 150).

Indonesia's Special Criminal Laws

In practice, the procedural safeguards contained in KUHAP are sidelined to a significant extent by special criminal laws which provide exceptions to those safeguards. These include the Anti-Subversion Law: the Anti-Corruption Law; the Narcotics Law and the Economic Crimes Law. This article will only consider the Anti-Subversion Law as it is the most widely used of these special laws.

The Anti-Subversion Law was promulgated as a Presidential Decree in 1963 and became a statute in 1969.[13] The scope of its application is potentially very broad. It defines 'subversion' to include 'any action' that could 'distort, undermine or deviate from the ideology of *Pancasila* ... or otherwise destroy or undermine the power of the state or the authority of the lawful government', or that could 'arouse feelings of hostility ... or anxiety among the population'.

The *Pancasila* is Indonesia's official state ideology. It has five very broad elements:

---

13 Law No 11/PNPS/1963; Law No 5 of 1969.

(1) Belief in one God;

(2) A just and civilised humanitarianism;

(3) A united Indonesia;

(4) Democracy guided by wisdom through consultation and representation;

(5) Social justice for all Indonesian people.

Actions that distort, undermine or deviate from any one of these elements is subversion as defined and is punishable by death, life imprisonment or a prison sentence of a maximum of 20 years. 'Subversion' is, therefore, an extraordinarily broad and vague concept. This theoretical breadth of application is reflected to some extent at least in practice: the Minister of Justice in July 1988 estimated that the number of convictions under the anti-subversion law (that is, excluding those detained without trial) 'probably reaches the thousands' (Asia Watch 1989: 138).

KUHAP allows for its provisions to be suspended in respect of charges or detentions under the Anti-Subversion Law (Art 284(2)) and the Anti-Subversion Law contains a number of exceptions to KUHAP's procedural rights. The most significant of these is the Attorney-General's right to detain suspects for a maximum period of one year (Art 7). KUHAP's pre-trial procedure to determine the lawfulness of an arrest or detention and consequent compensation does not apply. Periods of pre-trial detention under the anti-subversion law are also not deducted from any final sentence.

Even where the procedural rights established by KUHAP do apply, they are often ignored in practice. Asia Watch (1989, 1990) and the International Commission of Jurists (1991) have catalogued a number of examples of non-compliance with KUHAP in 'political' trials, including the refusal of the right to counsel of one's own choosing and the refusal to call witnesses on behalf of the defence. There is such a widespread fear of *Bakorstanas*,[14] the military body charged with investigation of subversive activity that the courts are very reluctant to make rulings against them. In fact, the courts have cited the *Bakorstanas* operating 'Instructions', which grant very broad arrest and detention powers, to excuse illegal actions by *Bakorstanas* personnel (Lubis, 1993: 106-107). This judicial reluctance to make rulings against *Bakorstanas* is reflected in the fact that, in 1989, only one subversion conviction had ever been overturned on appeal (Asia Watch, 1989: 6-7). In addition, in areas of secessionist unrest, such as Aceh or East Timor, *Bakorstanas* conducts virtually all arrests and detentions, and in practice operates without reference to any law or court (Lawyer's Committee, 1993: 20).

Conclusion

Law, Ideology and Institutions

Clearly there are a number of technical flaws in KUHAP, particularly relating to the lack of implementing regulations and absence of sanction for its violation. Identifying these flaws generates a number of proposals for reform: for example, clearer guidelines for arrest and detention; reduction of detention periods; removal of the right of police to order detention; removal of actions against police and

---

14　*Badan Koordinasi Bantuan Pemantapan Stabilitas National*, Co-ordinating Agency for National Stability and Security.

military from military courts to civil courts; judicial review of all arrest or detention decisions; and empowering prosecutors and the courts to order independent investigations of mistreatment in detention. However, it is important to recognise that these technical flaws are not explanations for the consistent failure of KUHAP in practice, but convenient loopholes for the authorities to avoid compliance with KUHAP. In fact, the real cause of consistent violation of KUHAP is not technical but ideological and institutional. That is why in political cases, particularly in Aceh and East Timor, there is no pretence of following KUHAP.

The ideology in question is the notion of an 'integralist' state: that people-state relations are familial rather than libertarian (Schwartz, 1994: 8). This conception, said to be more consistent with an Indonesian cultural propensity to avoid criticism and dissent, arose first in post-Independence constitutional discussions (id.). In New Order Indonesia, it has been transmuted into the ideology of *Pancasila*. Although the precise boundaries of *Pancasila* are unclear, in its core conception it encompasses the primacy of national unity, social stability and a patrimonial state. All social organisations, including religious and legal entities, must adopt *Pancasila* as their governing ideology (Law No 8 of 1985). It is a compulsory subject in schools and universities. Indeed, in all fields of activity in contemporary Indonesia, notions such as *Pancasila* state, *Pancasila* democracy and *Pancasila* law are the malleable metanorms by which law, civil activities and people-state relations are judged.

Buyung Nasution has astutely commented that advocates of integralist ideology did not envisage that 'state power welded by the state's functionaries might also be used to serve the particularistic interests of the rulers, that it might be used against the interests of the people and that it might take the form of repression'.[15] In other words, integralist ideology assisted the natural tendency in all postcolonial countries for state officials, including the military and police, to become part of a new oligarchic ruling class (Seidman & Seidman, 1994: 145-70). This class adopted colonial institutions for control and exploitation to amass great wealth and patrilineal prestige. Because the bureaucracy, for reasons of expertise and broad discretion, controlled these institutions, their participation in postcolonial commercial endeavours and political controls became essential. This then fostered collusive arrangements with business and politicians, thereby creating what Seidman & Seidman call the 'bureaucratic bourgeoisie'. The primary feature of the bureaucratic bourgeoisie is that it operates in its own ruling class interests rather than for the benefit of the people (Seidman & Seidman, 1994: 145-70).

Thus, in Indonesia integralist ideology has combined with the postcolonial institutional propensity to oligarchy to create a patrimonial state which commands the loyalty of its officials in a way that transcends region, race or religion. This is the problem of the '*pegawai negeri*'. State officials, particularly in rural areas, are the new ruling class: arbitrary, capricious, laws unto themselves. There are few institutional restraints because they are the institutions. The people are subordinate, 'spectators to development', instinctively frightened of authority figures (Schwarz, 1994: 246). And at the apex of this new ruling class is the military. Although in its 'dual function' role, it is an anti-communist, anti-Islamic force for national unity and stability, it is not simply a neutral arbiter of political, religious and ethnic tensions. It is embedded in the oligarchic patrimonialism of Indonesia: both profiting from economic development and ensuring that the profits of development are retained within the oligarchy – hence its involvement in land and labour disputes.

---

15   This statement is quoted in Schwarz (1994: 8).

Culture

In Indonesia, institutions and ideology, not culture, are the context in which implementation of international human rights standards must be assessed. The concept of an 'Indonesian' culture is highly uncertain. To the extent that there are common principles such as hierarchy and communalism, they are embedded in regional cultures – circumscribed and defined by an interplay of *adat*, dualism and spirituality. They are not autonomous principles explaining official action in a new nation-state. In turn, this conclusion suggests that, for the purposes of the human rights and culture debate, questions of cultural legitimacy and cultural context in implementing human rights standards must be carefully defined. For example, if, in a multi-cultural country such as Indonesia, questions of pan-cultural legitimacy and context are highly indeterminate, how is it possible to talk of an 'Indonesian' cultural context for implementing the international prohibition of torture or cruel and unusual punishment? Or to say that this prohibition is culturally illegitimate? The true context for human rights violations in Indonesia, at least, is the impact of a new nation-state across many cultures not a chimerical search for pan-Indonesian cultural values.

This conclusion also affects An-Na'im's quest for cross-cultural consensus on fundamental human values on which to base international human rights standards. The Indonesian experiment – distilling pan-Indonesian principles from a multi-cultural archipelago and applying them to national law – shows, first, that a quest for cross-cultural consensus can reveal few principles of sufficient autonomy or precision to enable formulation of cross-cultural 'legal' standards; and, secondly, that the transformation of culture-specific notions into autonomous 'universal' principles can fundamentally change their character. Undoubtedly, of course, cross-cultural analysis is a worthwhile pursuit, but a more viable alternative to An-Na'im's quest for cross-cultural normative consensus would be to seek greater international insight into the institutions and ideologies of nation-states, particularly in relation to their application and creation in multi-cultural, racial and religious societies.

In these circumstances, An-Na'im's emphasis on traditional folk models as culturally legitimate implementers of human rights standards must also be carefully circumscribed and defined. For intra-cultural 'crimes' (leaving aside the question of subjecting traditional punishment to global standards of justice and equity) there is little doubt that folk models of adjudication and punishment are far better means of maintaining social equilibrium and cultural cohesion than hierarchical, centralised, Western-style systems of criminal law. Indeed, the Indonesian government is considering incorporating some traditional crimes and punishment into a proposed new Code of Criminal Procedure (Widayana, 1993). But in Indonesia, most human rights violations occur in people-state relations or in an inter-cultural context. In any event, customary forms of authority have been significantly eroded by urbanisation, transmigration and government-sponsored development. Accordingly, although folk models are appropriate in theory, their role in culturally legitimate application of international human rights standards can in practice only be limited.

Law Reform

Ultimately, theoretical questions of the relationship between human rights and culture, law, institutions and ideologies are concerned with explaining why human rights violations occur and generating practical proposals to minimise their repetition. Thus, in relation to human rights violations in Indonesia, it has been concluded that culture is of marginal relevance; law has some normative influence but far less than ideology; institutions are oligarchic; and ideology commands the loyalty of officials in a way that transcends region, race or religion. Therefore, in the first instance, reform of criminal law in Indonesia is recommended. Particular suggestions are to remedy technical flaws in KUHAP and de-centralise intra-cultural crimes to traditional societies with demonstrated cultural cohesion. But equally, it is recognised that these reforms can at best be of limited effect: they will be ineffective without accompanying institutional and ideological change. The difficult questions are: how is this change to occur and what is the proper role for law in it?

Seidman and Seidman (1994: 170-95) argue that institutional change in a postcolonial environment is best effected through law-based institutions that guarantee competitive electoral democracy; bureaucratic accountability; popular participation in ongoing governmental decisions; and a civil society capable of acting as countervailing power to the bureaucracy. Their view is that, because law helped create postcolonial oligarchy it can be used to remedy it. The author questions whether this approach in Indonesia would be too much of a Western, law-based solution to a society in which formal law has a very limited role. For example, as has been seen, the Indonesian military largely operates without reference to law: its justifications and loyalties are ideological and political rather than legal. There-fore, it is difficult to see how law-based reform, including competitive elections and bureaucratic accountability, could succeed in reforming it – even if reform of this kind were allowed at all.

In other words, precisely because law and legal institutions are of little effect in Indonesia at present, they cannot be used instrumentally to effect institutional change. Rather they must evolve first in substance and effectiveness from political, social and ideological change. It is in change of this kind, not questions of culture or application of Western-style law, that the greatest prospects of improving human rights in Indonesia may be found.

References

An-Na'im, A, 1992, 'Towards A Cross-Cultural Approach to Defining Standards of Human Rights: The Meaning of Cruel, Inhuman or Degrading Treatment or Punishment' in An Na'im, A (ed), *Human Rights in Cross-Cultural Perspectives*, University of Pennsylvania Press, Pennsylvania: 19.

An-Na'im, A, 1994, 'Cultural Transformation and Normative Consensus on the Best Interests of the Child' in Alston, P (ed). *The Best Interests of the Child: Reconciling Culture and Human Rights*, Clarendon Press, Oxford and Oxford University Press, New York.

Alston, P, 1994, 'The Best Interests Principle: Towards a Reconciliation of Culture and Human Rights' in Alston, P (ed), *The Best Interests of the Child: Reconciling Culture and Human Rights*, Oxford University Press: 1.

Asia Watch, 1989 *Human Rights in Indonesia and East Timor: an Asia Watch report,* New York (available from Human Rights Watch).

Asia Watch, 1990 *Injustice Persecution Eviction: A Human Rights Update on Indonesia and East Timor*, Asia Watch, New York.

Burns, P, 1989, 'The Myth of *Adat*', *Journal of Legal Pluralism*, No 28: 1.

Carty, A, (ed.), 1992, *Law and Development*, The International Library of Essays in Law and Legal Theory: Legal Cultures 2, Cambridge, Dartmouth.

Djojodigoeno, M, 1952 *Adat Law in Indonesia,* Jajasan Pembangunan, Jakarta

Doughty, PL, 1988, 'Crossroads for Anthropology: Human Rights in Latin America' in Downing, TE, and Kushner, G (eds), *Human Rights and Anthropology*, Cambridge, Mass., Cultural Survival Inc: 43.

Falk, R, 1992, 'Cultural Foundations for the Protection of Human Rights' in An Na'im, A (ed), *Human Rights in Cross-Cultural Perspectives*, University of Pennsylvania Press, Pennsylvania: 44.

Fitzpatrick, D, 1997, 'Disputes and Pluralism in Modern Indonesian Land Law', *Yale Journal of International Law*, vol 22: 171.

Fruhling, H, 1992, 'Political Culture and Gross Human Rights Violations in Latin America', in An Na'im, A (ed), *Human Rights in Cross-Cultural Perspectives*, University of Pennsylvania Press, Pennsylvania: 253.

Gautama, S and Harsono, B, 1972, *Survey of Indonesian Economic Law: Agrarian Law*, Padjadjaran University Law School, Bandung.

Geertz, C, 1980, *Negara: The Theatre State in Nineteenth-Century Bali*, Princeton University Press, Princeton.

Greenberg, DF, 1980, 'Law and Development in Light of Dependency Theory', *Research in Law and Sociology*, 3: 129.

Hooker, MB, 1975, *Adat Law in Modern Indonesia*, Oxford University Press, Kuala Lumpur.

Howard, RE, 1992, 'Dignity, Community and Human Rights' in An Na'im, A (ed), *Human Rights in Cross-Cultural Perspectives*, University of Pennsylvania Press, Pennsylvania: 81.

Indonesian Human Rights Forum, 1992, *Newsletter on Development and Human Rights in Indonesia*, July-September, No 5, Indonesian Human Rights Forum, Melbourne.

Indonesian Human Rights Forum, 1993, *Newsletter on Development and Human Rights in Indonesia*, January-March, No 6, Indonesian Human Rights Forum, Melbourne.

ICJ (International Commission of Jurists), 1991, *Indonesia and the Rule of Law: twenty years of 'New Order' government*, Pinter, London.

Lawyer's Committee for Human Rights, 1993, *Broken Law Broken Bodies: Torture and the Right to Redress in Indonesia*, Lawyer's Committee for Human Rights, New York.

LBH (Yayasan Lembaga Bantuan Hukum Indonesia), 1991, *Summary of the Observations of Legal Process in the Cases in Aceh*, LBH, Jakarta.

Lev, D, 1972, 'Judicial Institution and Legal Culture in Indonesia' in Holt, C (ed), *Culture and Politics in Indonesia*, Cornell University Press, Ithaca.

Lev, D, 1987, 'Judicial Authority and the Struggle for an Indonesian Rechstaat', *Law and Society*, vol 13: 37-71.

Lubis, TM, 1993, *In Search of Human Rights*, PT Gramedia Pustaka Utama, Jakarta.

Pollis, A and Schwab, P, 1979, 'Human Rights: A Western Construct of Limited Applicability' in Pollis, A and Schwab, P (eds), *Human Rights: Cultural and Ideological Perspectives*, Praeger Publishers, New York: 1.

Pritchard, S, 1996, 'Asian Values and Human Rights', in *Proceedings of the Fourth Annual Meeting*, Australian and New Zealand Society of International Law: 153.

Schirmer, J, 1988, 'The Dilemma of Cultural Diversity and Equivalency in Universal Human Rights Standards' in Downing, TE and Kushner, G (eds), *Human Rights and Anthropology*, Mass, Cultural Survival Inc, Cambridge: 91.

Schwarz, A, 1994, *A Nation in Waiting: Indonesia in the 1990s*, Allen & Unwin, Sydney.

Seidman, A and Seidman, R, 1994, *State and Law in the Development Process: Problem-Solving and Institutional Change in the Third World*, St Martin's Press, New York.

Singarimbun, M, 1975, *Kinship. Descent and Alliance among the Karo Batak*, University of California Press, Berkeley.

United Nations Special Rapporteur, 1991, *Report of the Special Rapporteur, Mr P Kooijmans, pursuant to Commission on Human Rights Resolution 1991/38*, United Nations, Geneva.

US State Department, 1992, *1992 Country Reports*, US State Department, Washington.

Warren, C, 1993, *Adat and Dinas: Balinese Communities in the Indonesian State*, Oxford University Press, Kuala Lumpur

Widayana, I Made, *Interview July 1993*, Dean of the Faculty of Law, Udayana University, Bali.

25. 'But a Shadow of Justice': Political Trials in Indonesia

Spencer Zifcak

Ratna Sarumpaet is one of Indonesia's best known actresses. In 1997 she wrote a play called 'Marsinah'. Marsinah worked in a factory in Eastern Java. In 1994, fed up with her poor working conditions and angry about the meagre remuneration she and her colleagues received, Marsinah, just 23, led an unauthorised strike. A few days afterwards she was raped brutally and murdered. The identity of her killer remains uncertain. Marsinah became a martyr to the trade union cause.[1]

Ratna Sarumpaet's one-woman play dealt with key aspects of Marsinah's short life. At times, however, she would step out of role, step forward on stage and address her audience on the parallels that could be drawn between the conditions oppressing her subject and those which still prevail in the country at large. About 600 people attended the first performance in Jakarta and were held in thrall. The success was short-lived, however. The Indonesian authorities prohibited any further performances in the capital and the play itself drifted into oblivion.

The prohibition marked Sarumpaet. It sharpened her appreciation of political repression and provoked her engagement in oppositional political activity. Around her she gathered a small but dedicated group of activists – artists, lawyers, journalists and students. In March 1998, she convened a 'People's Summit', timed to coincide with the re-election of General Soeharto as President of Indonesia by the People's Consultative Assembly (MPR).[2] It was hardly an imposing affair. Some 50 people turned out to attend the meeting which took place in a small hotel in central Jakarta. Moments before the meeting was scheduled to begin Sarumpaet was approached by the hotel management and told that the hotel could no longer house the event as the police had forbidden it. She took to the podium and announced that the summit could no longer continue. She apologised and expressed regret that freedom of speech and expression no longer appeared to exist in Indonesia. The meeting, she said, would have to be abandoned but before it was she asked that all present join her in singing the national anthem and in saying a prayer for Indonesian democracy. The participants complied and then left the premises.

Outside they were met by the constabulary. The police converged upon Sarumpaet who clung to the arm of a foreign diplomat. She was encircled by several supporters including her young daughter who begged that her mother should not be taken. Sarumpaet cried out in English and Indonesian for an arrest warrant. 'I am the arrest warrant' the supervising officer replied. Subsequently, she and nine others – including her daughter – were detained and transported to prison. They remained

---

1   For Marsinah, see Fehring, Chapter 26.
2   *Majelis Permusyawaratan Rakyat.*

there pending trial until their sudden release by the newly-appointed President Habibie in May.

I was present at the legal proceedings in which Sarumpaet challenged the validity of her arrest. A statuesque and striking woman said to have the 'highest cheek bones in all of Java', Sarumpaet made her entrance to the North Jakarta District Court (*Pengadilan Negeri*) accompanied by a bevy of defence lawyers and security guards. It was the day on which the judge would deliver his decision. There was little optimism among the 250 or so Sarumpaet supporters who crammed the courtroom.

The judge began by summarising the evidence provided by defence witnesses — the prosecution had called none — but that was as far as his commitment to procedural fairness would take him. Having noted the circumstances of the meeting and the arrest as Sarumpaet had described them he proceeded to cite the provisions of the relevant law. Noting that the law required that any person holding a meeting that might undermine the stability of the state must have an official permit, he said simply that the defendant had been caught 'red-handed' without one. Pre-judging the substantive issue, he concluded that Ratna's arrest had proceeded on reasonable grounds as she had self-evidently broken the law and that, therefore, such defects as there were with the arrest procedure and warrant must be considered as a mere administrative triviality. The case, he said, should proceed to trial. There followed a remarkable series of events.

Ratna's defence lawyer jumped to his feet and screamed at the judge at the top of his voice. He demanded that the judge examine his conscience and accused him of political complicity. Procedural protections under Indonesia's Code of Criminal Procedure (KUHAP)[3] were valueless, he declared. 'From now, even to sing the National Anthem and to call for prayer is a criminal offence in this country'.

At this point heavily-armed security guards entered the courtroom and ushered the judge out the back door. As he left, Sarumpaet herself leapt onto the bar table and delivered a political speech ex tempore to cheering supporters. The security guards returned and ushered her through the throng into a waiting police wagon but not before she had stepped onto its stair, turned and issued a further denunciation of the court and its 'political justice'. She was returned to prison to await her next appearance on the politico-legal stage.

Political Law

The law under which Ratna was charged is sweeping in scope and of intensely political origin. Together with the Anti-Subversion law, the Law on Political Activity was first issued as a Presidential Decree by former President Soekarno when Indonesia appeared on the brink of confrontation with Malaysia in the early 1960s.[4] After the bloody massacres of 1965-66 and Soekarno's subsequent replacement, the 'New Order' government of President Soeharto promised that all decrees conferring emergency powers would be reviewed. The first provisional Parliament established under the New Order government was given two years during which to

---

3   *Kitab Undang-Undang Hukum Acara Pidana*. See Fitzpatrick, Chapter 24 for a detailed discussion of KUHAP.

4   The Law on Political Activity, Presidential Decree No 5 of 1963 was reincorporated by statute into Indonesian law as Law No 5 of 1969.

determine whether these and other decrees issued by Soekarno were in the interests of the people and whether they were constitutional. It had been widely assumed that the Law on Political Activity and the Anti-Subversion Law would be repealed. Instead, in 1969, the decrees were incorporated into Indonesian law by statute with references to threats to Soekarno's 'Guided Democracy' replaced with threats to *Pancasila* the theoretical linchpin of General Soeharto's New Order regime.[5]

In summary the Law on Political Activity provides that no political meeting, gathering or other similar activity shall take place without an official permit. There are a number of features of this Law which merit particular attention. First, it requires that the organisers of any and every political meeting having more than five participants must obtain a permit from the police before it can be held. This gives the police carte blanche to determine whether and when people may gather to discuss matters of contemporary political concern. Secondly, the meetings in relation to which a permit must be obtained are those which might have the effect of 'undermining the state'. Such a definition makes it exceptionally difficult for organisers to determine whether a permit is required and, correspondingly, affords the authorities a virtually unlimited discretion to determine whether any particular meeting falls within that definition. Thirdly, the Law does not require that a meeting should be reasonably likely to undermine the state. Rather it makes it sufficient that such an effect may possibly occur. Fourthly, the Law does not set down any criteria in relation to which a judgment about whether a meeting might undermine the state should be made. This renders the judgment subjective and arbitrary.

Ratna Sarumpaet was also charged under a second law which, as with the first, had been used with increasing frequency during 1998. This law, which is contained in Indonesia's Criminal Code, forbids a person from expressing 'hate or insult to the government of the Republic of Indonesia'[6] The law is taken directly from a Dutch statute designed originally to suppress the pre-war nationalist movement and carries with it a maximum gaol term of seven years. Again there appear to be no clear legal criteria in relation to which a judgment about whether a person has expressed 'hate' or 'insult' might properly be made.

The companion Anti-Subversion Law suffers from all these defects and more.[7] The Law describes a wide range of activities that might be considered subversive. These include, for example, actions which could distort, undermine or deviate from the official State ideology of *Pancasila*; otherwise destroy or undermine the power of the State; or disseminate feelings of hostility or arouse disturbances or anxiety among the population or broad sections of society or between the Republic of Indonesia and a friendly state.[8]

It is not necessary that any of the acts described should actually have endangered the Republic. It is sufficient to demonstrate merely that such an effect

---

5   *Pancasila* consists of five components: 1. A Belief in Almighty God 2. A commitment to just and civilised humanity 3. A commitment to the unity of Indonesia 4. A commitment to democracy, led by the inner wisdom of consensus arising out of deliberation of the people's representatives 5. Social Justice for the whole of the Indonesian people. These are set out in the Preamble to the Indonesian Constitution of 1945.

6   The Criminal Code (KUHP or *Kitab Undang-Undang Hukum Pidana*) Arts 154, 155. The Criminal Code also makes it an offence punishable by a maximum of six years gaol to engage in 'Deliberate disrespect for the President or Vice-President': Art 134.

7   The Law on Subversion, Presidential Decree No 11/1963 incorporated as a statute by Law No 5 of 1969.

8   Article 1(1)(a), (b) and (c).

were possible. Further, a person charged may be convicted even though he or she did not intend the consequence concerned and was not responsible for it.[9] It is sufficient that the person might have been 'expected' to know that the relevant consequence might eventuate. Quite whose expectation this might be is legally unclear although in practice it has become that of the government.

The Anti-Subversion Law sweeps aside a host of procedural protections normally guaranteed to detainees by Indonesia's Code of Criminal Procedure. Among other things it accords wide power to the military and to prosecutors to search premises and seize material; to investigate cases; and to imprison suspects for up to one year without trial. This latter period of detention is renewable indefinitely. Any person may be called as a witness in the proceedings including any professional person whose duties of confidentiality would normally prevent their evidence from being tendered. A refusal to give evidence is punishable by gaol. The sweeping nature of these procedural exemptions has resulted in the substantial abuse of the rights of political detainees (Amnesty International, 1997a).

Following the arrest and detention of many political activists involved in the peaceful occupation of the premises of the Democracy Party of Indonesia (PDI)[10] in July 1996, the Indonesian Human Rights Commission (KOMNASHAM)[11] called upon the government to repeal the subversion law. It argued that the law contradicted existing criminal statutes; encouraged the abuse of human rights because of that contradiction; and that its general nature permitted the government to apply its provisions arbitrarily. In so doing, the Commission added its voice to those of the United Nations (UN) High Commissioner for Human Rights, the UN Special Rapporteur on Torture and the International Commission of Jurists (ICJ) among many others (ICJ, 1987, 1998).

Until July 1996, it seemed that the Indonesian government had responded to the sustained international criticism of these repressive laws by moderating their use. Since then, however, they had been invoked with renewed vigour. More than 200 people had been imprisoned under the laws just described in Jakarta alone.

The Anti-Subversion Law in Action

On my first working afternoon in Jakarta I met Dr Sri Bintang Pamungkas. We encountered each other in a small holding room at the back of the South Jakarta District Court where Bintang was awaiting the recommencement of his trial on charges of subversion. Small, animated, bespectacled, expressive and rueful he reminded me a little of Woody Allen as he held court among his family and friends. I asked him how he felt. 'Well, you know, one has to be brave – and always optimistic' he responded.

Bintang, 53, had been a Professor of Technology at one of Jakarta's major technical universities. Subsequently, he became a member of parliament representing the Islamic PPP party (United Development Party).[12] In 1994 he travelled to Europe and while there delivered two speeches, one in the Hague the other in Berlin, critical of the undemocratic nature of the Soeharto regime. In the

---

9   *Mahkamah Agung* Decision No 20/Kr/1969, dated 17 July 1971.
10   *Partai Demokrasi Indonesia.*
11   *Komisi Nasional Hak Asasi Manusia.*
12   *Partai Persatuan Pembangunan.*

speeches he described Soeharto as a dictator, a term regarded by the authorities as particularly offensive.

It was Bintang's misfortune to precede Soeharto in Berlin by only two weeks. Upon his arrival, Soeharto was met and publicly embarrassed by a small but vocal band of protesters. In an interview soon after he was visibly angry and upset. Not long after Soeharto's return to Jakarta, Sri Bintang was arrested and charged with sowing hatred against the President. He was found guilty and imprisoned for a term of two years and 11 months. The University stripped him of his teaching position. No connection between Bintang and the demonstration was ever established. The conviction rested solely on the content of Bintang's addresses abroad.

Soon after his release from prison, Bintang resigned from the PPP and established his own political party, the PUDI (Indonesian United Democracy Party).[13] Under a package of political laws enacted in 1985, however, only three parties were officially to be recognised – GOLKAR, the government 'non-party' political organisation, the PPP and the PDI, the party led by Megawati Soekarnoputri, the daughter of former President Soekarno, before her engineered removal. Bintang travelled the country seeking support for his plans for a more democratic and radically decentralised Indonesian republic. Then he had the temerity to declare his candidacy for the Presidency in the elections to be held in March 1998. Everyone knew that only one nomination for President would go forward, that of Soeharto. With Bintang's declaration, however, official patience ran out. He was arrested and charged once more with subversion.

The indictment made interesting reading. Five events were recounted as evidence of subversive activity. Bintang, it is said, organised a meeting to announce the formation of his new political party; another to develop its constitution; another to declare the party's formation and adopt its constitution; and another to declare his candidacy for President. Finally, it says, he sent out greeting cards to his supporters announcing the imminent dissolution of the New Order government and the introduction of his own.

In court that afternoon, Bintang delivered his demurrer. He spoke eloquently, energetically and without pause for two and half hours. He agreed that the events set down in the indictment had occurred but argued that they did not and could not constitute subversion. The prosecution, he said, had simply taken it for granted that the meetings he had organised were subversive. But it had never demonstrated how or why this might be the case. All the meetings described had been publicly announced and conducted. Without conspiratorial, secretive or agitational components it was difficult to understand how any subversive intent could be proven. The simple formation of a political party did not in and of itself demonstrate an intention to overthrow the state ideology and neither did a declaration of one's candidacy for President. His party's manifesto, he said, had explicitly embraced *Pancasila* ideology.

As he moved from the particulars of the indictment to more general observations upon political freedom and suppression, Bintang's presentation became ever more passionate. The Anti-Subversion Law, he argued was cast so widely that any intellectual writing on government could be outlawed at the government's behest. He acknowledged that he had criticised the operation of Indonesian democracy but in doing so he had sought only to expose the strength of executive power, corruption wherever it existed and gross inequalities of wealth and

---

13 *Partai Uni Demokrasi Indonesia.*

power. Everyone, he said, acknowledged the existence of these social characteristics privately. He had sought simply to draw them into the public domain. Such fair comment, he pleaded, could not be regarded by any reasonable person as either subversive or dangerous to the continuation of the Indonesian State.

He looked directly at his judges and concluded:

[T]he activities in which I have been engaged represent entirely legitimate political action. I have sought only to exercise freedom of speech and freedom of assembly. Every one of my activities has been consistent with the United Nations framework for human rights, with the rule of law, with the Indonesian constitution and with the fundamental tenets of democracy. Who are you to convict me for this?

A Partial Judiciary

Throughout his presentation, Bintang's eyes darted between the three judges, assessing and accusing but theirs rarely rested upon him. One of the most disconcerting elements of this trial and the others was the self-evident unwillingness of members of the judiciary to engage with the accused and their representatives except when absolutely necessary.

In delivering his decision in Ratna Sarumpaet's proceeding the judge never once looked at her. In Bintang's case, the presiding judge with whom I had spoken before the afternoon session at least made eye-contact from time to time and recorded the odd note. His two colleagues, however, stared distractedly at the ceiling, out the high windows, into their hands, at movement in the gallery, at the heavily armed security police in the doors of the court – focusing it seemed, every-where, except upon the lively and intense defendant claiming their attention. Their expressions betrayed no trace of concern or attentiveness but rather boredom, listlessness and the occasion flash of irritation as Bintang turned his argument to corruption not only in government but also in the judiciary. A less inspiring reception to legal argument would be hard to imagine.

Without a genuinely independent judiciary, trials like this become an elaborate charade. In the ordinary courts of Indonesia, in the recent political cases, no trace of independence could be discerned. There are a number of reasons for this. The Indonesian judiciary is directly responsible to the Minister for Justice. It is not administered as a separate and distinct judicial hierarchy but forms part of the executive arm of government. Judges' appointment, remuneration, promotion and reward therefore are in the gift of the Minister and the government. In political cases, it can reasonably be expected that a decision favourable to the government will be rewarded, a decision adverse to it, penalised.

While the significance of judicial independence is acknowledged in the higher levels of the administration, its practical application and import is not. So, for example, in a speech in April 1998, Muladi, the recently appointed Minister for Justice, urged his judges to be more courageous and less conformist in their decision-making. To encourage them, he cited the example of one judge in Yogyakarta who had made a decision to free an accused after having found that there was insufficient evidence to link him to the murder of a well-known journalist. That judge, he said, had been promoted soon after to head a Jakarta District Court (Jakarta Post, 1998). That it might be inconsistent with judicial independence for a judge to be promoted following an approved decision and that the promotion should have been effected directly by the executive seemingly went unappreciated.

Appointments to the country's highest court, the *Mahkamah Agung* are made routinely from the ranks of the military, the government and the civil service. No appointment from the private legal profession has ever been made.

In political cases, proceedings are routinely prejudiced by statements from senior military and governmental officials implying the guilt of the parties being tried. For instance, in Sri Bintang's case a senior General was quoted as saying that the accused's mailing of greeting cards deriding Soeharto's prospects for re-election was clear evidence of subversive activity. During the course of earlier trials of PRD (People's Party for Democracy)[14] activists in 1997, Soeharto himself had said that the PRD 'had conducted activities which had the characteristics of insurgency' (Amnesty International, 1997b).

In subversion trials, the court's setting can also be intimidating. In all the proceedings I witnessed, heavily armed guards stood at the hearing room doors and patrolled the corridors. Plain clothes intelligence officers were ever present.

Judges are very poorly remunerated leaving them open to monetary and political inducement. To supplement their meagre incomes, many judges engage in commercial activities beyond their profession so producing undesirable conflicts of interest. In the private legal profession disillusionment with the calibre and partiality of the judiciary has become so great that, in civil cases, every effort is made to reach a settlement before a matter reaches court. In commercial cases, private arbitration or mediation has become the preferred method of dispute resolution. Acknowledging some of these problems, in 1998 Justice Minister Muladi announced a 'war' on judicial corruption. It has been met with reservation amongst the judges and considerable scepticism in the legal profession. Nevertheless, there are hopes that some inroads will be made.

Procedural Bias

In such an environment, it is unsurprising that partial, political decisions should be made in party political proceedings. But bias extends considerably further into trial procedure. To take only the most recent example, on 11 February 1998, 122 people were arrested for having taken part in a demonstration. The demonstration, which took place in the main shopping street of Jakarta, had been in favour of lower food prices. The demonstrators, some of whom were loosely associated with the PDI, were rounded up and incarcerated at the central metropolitan police station. 65 of them were subsequently removed to another police detention centre.

The demonstrators challenged the validity of their arrest and detention, invoking the pre-trial procedures in KUHAP (the Code of Criminal Procedure).[15] On the day of their hearing, their families, friends and supporters gathered at South Jakarta District Court to catch sight of their colleagues and loved ones. They were destined to be disappointed. Six separate court rooms had been set aside to process the demonstrator's appeals but the defendants did not arrive. Their lawyers made inquiries and late in the afternoon it emerged that the police had refused to permit them to leave their cells to attend. The defence took their complaints about this refusal to the bench and all the cases were stood down until the following day.

---

14 *Partai Rakyat untuk Demokrasi.*
15 See Fitzpatrick, Chapter 24.

That next day exactly the same thing occurred. The defendants were not released. Their lawyers again protested to the judges who asked that the defence proceed without the clients. There followed a heated interchange the result of which was another adjournment with the judges indicating that they would decide overnight whether they could and would proceed in the defendants' absence. On the third day, the defendants failed to emerge yet again. The judges did not order their attendance but indicated that they were willing to proceed to a determination. All the defence lawyers walked out of court, leaving the judges and the prosecutors to themselves. There followed a troubling scene in which the name of each defendant was read out followed by a one sentence statement from the judges in each court that the arrests had been made in accordance with the law.

This is but one of many startling instances of legal irregularity in the conduct of criminal proceedings (ICJ, 1998). During my visit I observed many other deficits in trial procedure principal among which were:

- the ready acceptance by the court of the validity of arrests in spite of the fact that the prosecution failed to call either the arresting officers or any other witnesses to demonstrate that reasonable grounds for an arrest existed.

- the refusal by the court to inquire into claims by defence witnesses that their earlier contradictory evidence had been obtained under duress.

- the refusal by the court to require the prosecution to specify clearly how certain events could constitute subversion within the meaning of the term in the Anti-Subversion Law.

- the refusal by the court to step in and prevent defence lawyers being called as witnesses against their own clients.

- the intervention by the court to prevent difficult and pertinent questions being put to prosecution witnesses, such intervention being justified on the grounds that the questions were irrelevant.

One of the most alarming failures of the courts has been their refusal to countenance the release of detainees held on remand when the initial case against them has collapsed. Instead, the judges have connived in continuing their detention after having been given notice by the prosecution that entirely new and different charges would be laid. Defendants thus found themselves confronted by a moving feast of allegations, charges and indictments that cohered only on the first day of their trial. The proceedings against Dr Muchtar Pakpahan, the leader of SBSI (Indonesian Prosperous Workers' Union)[16] – the independent trade union that until recently was not recognised by the Indonesian government – is the most celebrated case in point.

Dr Muchtar Pakpahan

I met Dr Muchtar Pakpahan in his hospital room in central Jakarta, before his surprising release from prison soon after President Habibie's appointment in May 1998. He had been ill for more than a year, having been diagnosed with a large tumour on his lung. His requests to obtain treatment overseas had been denied repeatedly by Soeharto's government although a Canadian medical team was

---

16   *Serikat Buruh Sejahtera Indonesia.*

eventually permitted to assess him. His transfer from prison to hospital appears to have been beneficial. He told me on the first day we met that he was feeling considerably better than he had done. For a 44-year-old man, however, his movements were measured and slow.

Despite his poor health, his close relationship with his wife and four children and constant harassment by the authorities for almost two decades, Pakpahan's commitment to his cause seemed undiminished. He retained his position as head of the SBSI, the union he helped to establish in the late 1970s to organise and agitate for minimum wages and conditions for workers whose labour has too often been abused. He speaks passionately about his social responsibility and the plight of Indonesia's people following the recent collapse of the Indonesian economy.

In April 1994, Pakpahan and 10 of his colleagues were arrested in Medan in Northern Sumatra and charged with inciting workers to demonstrate and to strike. He had been elsewhere at the time of the demonstration but was nevertheless held responsible. To these charges a later one of sowing hatred against the President was added and Pakpahan was convicted of the latter in November 1994. He was sentenced to three years and upon appeal the sentence was increased to four. Pakpahan requested judicial review of the conviction and sentence before the Supreme Court of Indonesia. In October 1995, his application for review was successful and he was acquitted.

Then, on 29 July 1996, two days after the government-backed break up of the occupation of the headquarters of the PDI by supporters of its toppled leader, Megawati Soekarnoputri, Pakpahan was re-arrested, interrogated and charged with subversion. Although the foundation for this charge and others was unclear, the implication appeared to be that Pakpahan had masterminded the occupation and had been responsible for the subsequent violence. In fact, at the time of the violence, he had been in another part of Java, three hours away, addressing a regional meeting of his union. He says he had no prior knowledge whatever of the 27 July occurrences.

In the event, these initial charges were dropped, the authorities realising apparently that there was no evidence which could plausibly link Pakpahan with the 27 July events. A raft of new subversion charges, however, were brought in their stead. Among other things these related to the publication of Pakpahan's book 'Portrait of the Indonesian Nation' (1996), a critical analysis of the operation of Indonesian democracy; to speeches and interviews that he had given in Europe; and to his composition of a song 'Love Letter for Marsinah'.

To further secure their quarry, the government, through the *Kejaksaan Agung* (Chief Prosecutor's office), initiated a review of Pakpahan's earlier acquittal by the Supreme Court. The court re-convened with surprising speed and overturned its own previous decision. It proceeded to re-impose the four-year sentence that had initially been handed down.

Muchtar Pakpahan retained his sense of humour in the face of this adversity. I told him that I was somewhat mystified by the fact that he had been arrested on one set of charges relating to the 27 July 1996 riots but that he was now defending himself in court on a completely different set. He paused for a moment and his face broke into the broadest grin as he observed wryly 'it is a complete mystery to me too'. Later we spoke about elections in Northern Sumatra in which the local authorities are alleged to have manipulated the electoral rolls to ensure the success of their favoured candidate. 'That member of parliament', he said, 'represents the computer'.

No one, however, can doubt the sincerity and earnestness of his cause. In response to a question about the content of his book he gave me a 45-minute lecture on the deficits of Indonesian democracy which are its subject. In the book, Pakpahan argues that in every facet of Indonesian political life power has been centralised in the hands of the President. A portfolio of political laws introduced in 1985 restricted the number and nature of officially recognised political parties. Presidential appointments to the Parliament ensured that the New Order government retained legislative control and that Soeharto would be unchallenged in elections for President. Even where opposition political parties are permitted, parliamentary candidates have been screened for their suitability. In the regions too, the local mayors could be elected only if they met with official approval. Newspapers must be licensed by the government and some which, like *Tempo*, had been too critical of government policy have had their licences revoked. The police have no genuinely autonomous prosecutorial discretion, acting where required on governmental orders. The judiciary, while notionally independent, is subject to the overarching control of the Ministry of Justice. The constitution, the book concludes, is therefore of only symbolic importance.

In Jakarta's legal and diplomatic circles it is widely accepted that such a description of Indonesian rule is accurate. I asked Pakpahan, therefore, why he thought he had been targeted by the authorities while many others have not.

> It is because the government knows that it is only organised labor that can bring about change. It has learnt the lessons of Eastern Europe and South Africa. It does not want those events to be repeated in Indonesia. That is why I am being kept here ... It is why the Cabinet has decided that I should serve another five years in gaol.

Counterpoints

In Indonesia, there are of course competing perspectives on the delicate subject of political justice. Government officials, prosecutors and judges with whom I spoke were at pains to emphasise that Indonesia's legal norms and legal system differed from the Western models with which I was familiar. It is unhelpful, they argued, to apply Western concepts and standards to a country and to a system in which Eastern cultural and legal traditions prevail.

The key to understanding these traditions is the concept of *adat* law (see ICJ, 1987, Ch 2). At one level, *adat* can be understood simply as the traditional, uncodified law of the Indonesian people which preceded and now complements the codified law introduced by the Dutch colonial rulers and their successor nationalist governments. At another level, however, *adat* can be appreciated as a system of rules and practices devoted to the attainment and maintenance of a community consensus arrived at by mutual consultation. On this view, justice consists not primarily in the application of explicit rules but rather in decisions which uphold and promote the general well-being. This is an understanding of the law that is more collective than individual in character.

Among the Javanese in particular, the underlying cultural value attached to consensus is pervasive. Traditionally, outward expressions of dissatisfaction and hostility are frowned upon. Disagreements are finessed rather than arbitrated. Mutual assistance and compromise are preferred to argument and enforcement. Balance, equilibrium, co-existence and harmony are valued over conflict, contract, dissent and diversity.

It is such values that are called in aid by governmental officials when criticism of Indonesia's human rights record are made. So, for example, the Indonesian government has cautioned Western observers with respect to their defence of individual rights. These, it is said, should be balanced by 'the rights of the community, in other words, balanced by the obligation equally to respect the rights of others, the rights of the society and the rights of the nation' (Republic of Indonesia, 1995). Such an orientation is said to be more consistent with the cultural traditions and customs prevalent in developing countries where the interests of the community must of necessity prevail over those of the individual if economic growth and prosperity is to be achieved – if hunger, ignorance, backwardness and disease are to be defeated.

So much might well be conceded in a state which fostered plural discussion and deliberation regarding national purposes albeit within a wider civic and cultural framework. The problem in Indonesia, however, is that values, principles and traditions having distinctive and significant merit have been dragooned into the service of the state and now serve to mask the deeper reality of authoritarian rule.

Thus, the rights of the nation metamorphose into the rights of the ruler. The principles of *Pancasila*, the state ideology, become personified in the President. Alternative political perspectives are swept aside in the name of consensus. Critics are crushed to preserve a governmentally defined harmony. Those not with the government are designated as its enemies and as the enemies of the *Pancasila* state. The idea of community is transmogrified through ideology into tyranny.

On the broader political plain, the government is often heard to argue that Indonesian society is inherently unstable. The fragile unity which has been achieved and which has brought to its people a degree of prosperity until recently unknown can only be endangered by permitting too much diversity, difference and dissent. To fracture the republic would be to invite chaos and confusion.

So much may again be admitted. Indonesia's political history has from time to time been bloody and the memories of the political carnage of 1965 still exert a powerful influence on the Indonesian political psyche. Yet it is hard not to feel that the dangers of disintegration are exaggerated in order cement the government's pre-eminence. There is no guerilla warfare here as, for example, there has been in the Philippines. Except in East Timor separatist tendencies appear sporadic and muted. Despite the fall of Soeharto, the political opposition is divided and the union movement remains in its fledgling stages. Non-governmental organisations promote legal and democratic reform and act for individuals in trouble but their collective strength remains limited.

To contain these movements, however, the government, in partnership with the military, has amassed a repressive state organisation of truly formidable dimensions. As one senior diplomat remarked to me 'the mechanisms of political suppression are as pervasive as they were in the former USSR. The problem is that they are less sophisticated and therefore are worse'.

Conclusion

In his holding room at North Jakarta District Court, I asked Muchtar Pakpahan whether he saw any prospects of success in defeating his prosecution for subversion. 'My success', he responded, 'will not be here'.

My success lies in the fact that more people now dare to say the truth. When I began in 1978 I was the only labour leader in Indonesia. Now there are many and many more will follow.

I then asked whether he had a message for the international community.

Tell your people in Australia that I am in gaol because I stand for worker's rights, for the rule of law, for human rights and for democracy. Tell them that it is better to die in justice than live in fear.

It is sincerely to be hoped that neither Pakpahan nor his fellow prisoners of conscience will ever be required to exercise such a choice.

References

Amnesty International, 1997a, *Indonesia/East Timor, The Anti-Subversion Law: A Briefing*, AI Index: ASA 21/3/97, February 1997.

Amnesty International, 1997b, *Indonesia: The Trial of Thought*, AI Index: ASA 21/19/1997, April 1997.

Jakarta Post, 1998, 23 March.

ICJ (International Commission of Jurists), 1987, *Indonesia and the Rule of Law: Twenty Years of New Order Government*, H Thoolen (ed), Frances Pinter, London.

ICJ, 1998, *Report on Anti-Subversion Trials in Indonesia*, ICJ, Sydney.

Pakpahan, Muchtar, 1996, *Portret Negara Indonesia*, Pustaka Forum Adil Sejahtera, Jakarta

Republic of Indonesia, 1995, *Indonesia's Position on Human Rights*, Position Paper, Embassy of Indonesia for Canada.

26. Unionism and Workers' Rights in Indonesia – The Future

Ian Fehring

The current state of trade unionism within Indonesia is characterised by limited effectiveness, government and military control and an uncertain future. The prospects for change have dramatically changed with the unexpected appointment of Dr BJ Habibie as the third President of Indonesia on 21 May 1998. This chapter briefly outlines the history and structure of trade unions in the New Order period and the current difficulties experienced by the Indonesian trade union movement.

Trade Unions in the New Order Period

Following the imposition of martial law after the 1965 coup trade unions were effectively banned. Their activities and existence were unacceptable to the military, especially those of the *Sentral Organisasi Buruh Seluruh Indonesia* (SOBSI)[1] which was affiliated to the PKI, the Indonesian Communist Party.[2] By 1973, President Soeharto and the Indonesian Armed Forces (ABRI)[3] felt that the situation was secure enough to allow the formation of trade union organisations. The Indonesian government was at that time reorienting investment and industrial policies due to a decline in oil revenues. Export-oriented industries were to be encouraged especially within the labour intensive sectors such as textiles. In that year the *Federasi Buruh Seluruh Indonesia* (FBSI)[4] was brought into existence. It was an extremely limited and ineffectual organisation and was restructured in November of 1985 when its name was changed to the *Serikat Pekerja Seluruh Indonesia* (SPSI).[5]

From the very beginning of the SPSI, ABRI was centrally involved in its creation, structure and operation. It was Admiral Sudomo, the then-Minister of Labour, who orchestrated the changes which brought the SPSI into existence in November of 1985 at the second congress of the FBSI (Witjes, 1987: 12-13). Sudomo addressed that congress and advocated structural changes which in fact occurred.

The FBSI had been a federation of 21 unions which were industrially based and vertically integrated structures. They had local and regional officials who reported to a central executive. It was the individual unions which had representation in the federal structure which made up the FBSI (Witjes, 1987: 12). This vertically

---

1   Central Organisation of All-Indonesian Workers.
2   *Partai Komunis Indonesia.*
3   *Angkatan Bersenjata Republik Indonesia.*
4   All-Indonesian Workers' Federation.
5   All-Indonesian Employees' Union.

integrated federal structure was unacceptable to Sudomo who openly criticised FBSI's effectiveness and capacity to perform its role as seen by the government. The SPSI by comparison was a centralised organisation of nine departments, having appointed officials and a centralised bureaucratic structure. It was a far more centrally-controlled organisation and one which was in effect under the direct control of the Minister of Labour and other state agencies.

This need to centralise and corporatise the Indonesian trade union movement arose within an environment where ABRI was exercising its political influence throughout the government in the face of economic crisis. In particular the decline of world oil prices was placing the Indonesian government under immense financial strain. Within this context the need for ABRI to remain in control and to exercise greater influence over possible sources of opposition was heightened.

It is also important to note that the SPSI does not include any employees of government departments or government owned industries. These are covered by *Korp Pegawai Republik Indonesia* (KORPRI, the Indonesian Civil Service Corps). The Indonesian government has never claimed that KORPRI is a trade union. By ensuring that all state employees are covered by this body the capacity of the broader trade union movement to organise and exert pressure is weakened.

One of the new challenges which face the Indonesian government and the trade union movement in the late 1990s is the transfer of government employees to the private sector as the program of privatisation embarked upon by the government gathers pace. The privatisation program will take employees out of the jurisdiction of KORPRI. Whether they will be covered by a new union or be admitted to the SPSI is unclear and probably unresolved in the government's thinking.

Pancasila Industrial Relations

During the 1980s Sudomo also promoted the concept of *Pancasila* Industrial Relations (*Hubungan Industrial Pancasila* or HIP). This involved a re-working of the traditional notion of *Pancasila* as embodied in the 1945 Constitution. It was General Ali Murtopo who first discussed HIP in 1974 (Katjasungkana & Masduki, nd: 2) at the time the FBSI was emerging, but it was Admiral Sudomo who developed the concept, gave it a more precise formulation and set up the structures which made HIP work in reality (Lambet, 1996: 3). The concept which Sudomo developed had as its central thrust that industrial relations should be conducted, rhetorically at least, in the following context.

1. Partnership and production;
2. Partnership and profit;
3. Partnership and responsibility towards
   (a) God the almighty;
   (b) nation and state;
   (c) the community;
   (d) fellow employees and family;
   (e) the employee.

The HIP thus provided a bland and easily manipulated framework of ideological justification for industrial stability and the involvement of ABRI to ensure industrial stability and national security. In effect, *Pancasila* industrial relations became a part of the ideological and political dominance exerted by ABRI and the forces it represents over Indonesian society.

It was also during this time that Law No 8 of 1985 on Social Organisations was strenuously debated within the Indonesian parliament[6] and generated considerable tension. The Law required that all organisations adopt *Pancasila* as their respective ideology. This concept of a state ideology which is must be adopted by all social organisations has a considerable Orwellian dimension. The Law and *Pancasila* industrial relations together represented a tightening of control by ABRI over the social institutions of the Indonesian State.

The HIP operates at all levels of industrial relations within Indonesia and it is not just an overriding ideological formulation. It reaches down to the day-to-day operations of employer and employee relationships. At the national level there is the Department of Labour;[7] the SPSI; the *Panitia Penyelesaian Perselisahan Perburuhan Pusat* (the Central Labour Dispute Arbitration Committee, 'P4P'); and various national employer bodies.

This structure is re-produced at the regional levels. However *Kodim*,[8] *Polres*[9] are also involved and the *Walikota*[10] and *Bakorstanas*[11] have co-ordinating roles particularly when there is industrial unrest or strikes.

At a local level there are SPSI units and officers from the Ministry of Labour and members of *Koramil*[12] and *Polsek*[13] will be involved if there are industrial disputes or disturbances. Regional and national bodies can reinforce any of these local units if the matter requires greater attention.[14]

Trade Union Recognition

As part of the strengthening of government control, and the promotion of the SPSI, the Soeharto government carefully regulated trade union recognition. Labour Decree No 5 of 1987 required that for a union to obtain recognition it must have representation in:

1. 20 provinces;
2. 100 district level organisations; and
3. 1000 workplaces.

This regulation in effect maintained and buttressed the existence of the SPSI against any competition; and, in fact, the New Order government repeatedly made it clear that it did not want, and would not accept, the development of rival unions.

---

6   The DPR, *Dewan Perwakilan Rakyat* or People's Representative Council.

7   *Departemen Tenaga Kerja*, literally, the Department of the Workforce. The term 'Labour' is used instead of 'Workforce' throughout this chapter for convenience.

8   *Komando Distrik Militer*, District Military Command.

9   *Polisi Resort*, District Police.

10   Mayor.

11   *Badan Koordinasi Bantuan Pemantapan Stabilitas National*, Co-ordinating Agency for National Stability and Security.

12   *Komando Rayon Militer*, Sub-district Military.

13   *Polisi Sektor*, Sub-district Police.

14   For a description of how the various agencies work, see YLBHI (1994: 2-4).

However, in Labour Regulation No 3 of 1993 some relaxation of the registration requirements were allowed and Labour Decree No 5 of 1987 was declared void. In the new regulation, Art 2(a) provided that:

1. Trade unions shall be registered with the Ministry of Labour; and
2(a). A trade union must have representation in at least:
    (a) 100 workplaces;
    (b) 25 regions;
    (c) five provinces.

Alternatively if the nature of the industry in which the union is operating is of a 'special kind' it must have at least 10,000 members. There was no definition or assistance in determining what an industry of a 'special kind' was to be. This left the Ministry of Labour with considerable flexibility in deciding whether to accept registration of a union.[15]

Article 2(c) of the regulation goes on to require that a trade union which seeks to register should first obtain a recommendation from an existing trade union federation. This in effect gave the SPSI a veto over the registration of new unions as it was hard to see why the SPSI would of its own volition allow other unions to gain registration. Recognition would, however, draw new unions into the system and would minimise the accusations which are made against the Indonesian government that it does not allow democratic and independent unions to exist. As discussed below, such criticism has been particularly strong from the United States which is an important supplier both of aid and trade preferences to Indonesia.

Despite the legislative protections it has received, SPSI has, however, consistently failed to fulfil the role cast for it by government. The SPSI at best has only claimed membership slightly in excess of 1 million workers – only approximately 6% of the total workforce (Jakarta Post, 1993a). To give another example of this inability to attract worker support, Ministry of Labour Decree No 1 of 1994 required any company of more than 25 employees to form a 'company union'[16] and provided that such a union must be a part of the SPSI. Fauzi Ibrahim, the Jakarta Region head of the SPSI, has stated that of the more than 8000 companies in his area covered by the decree only 781 had SPSI branches (Jakarta Post, 1996). The SPSI's failure to recruit and represent workers given the strong institutional support it received under Soeharto amounted to a major failure. General Feisal Tanjung, then the commander of ABRI commented on this in 1991:

> There is a prevalence of labour problems which occur within company or industrial circles which results in demonstrations in the form of strikes, and even cause considerable damage as a result of an emotional attitude which has tended to be destructive. In my opinion, these problems occur due, among other things, to the weakness or unclearness of the rules which govern the rights and obligations of workers and employers, worsened by the rather ineffective role of the local SPSI, or in some cases, by the continued non-establishment of the SPSI. Under such conditions, it is almost impossible to develop at the spirit of partnership between employer and workers in a fairer manner, as indicated by the values of *Pancasila* labour relations in every company.[17]

---

15 Article 2(b) also requires that a trade union federation have at least 10 trade union members who fall within the above criteria.

16 Article 4.

17 The speech was given to the National Working meeting of the SPSI in Bogor on the 7 December 1991 and was titled 'The Role of ABRI in Enhancing the Implementation of Pancasila Industrial Relations'.

Two comments should be made about Tanjung's comments. First, he was openly critical of the inability of the SPSI to manage and control industrial relations. Secondly, he made his comments as the leader of ABRI and he made them directly to the SPSI at its national level.

On 14 and 15 April 1994, rioting broke out in the Sumatran city of Medan. The rioting degenerated into anti-Chinese violence which resulted in one death and many injuries. The rioting followed months of industrial disputes in the region and an upsurge in organising in the area by an alternative and unrecognised trade union, *Serikat Buruh Sejahtera Indonesia* (SBSI).[18] These events were used by ABRI and other conservative forces to resist the move to more democratic and independent unions. They were also used to justify increased military involvement in industrial disputation and to a general tightening of the political environment within Indonesia.

General Hartono who was then head of SOSPOL – the Socio Political Department of *Bakorstanas* – commented on industrial disputation in the wake of the Medan riots:

> If they are not co-ordinated in the early stages labour issues will develop and spread. And if they are left unattended they may even turn into violence that would necessitate more difficult actions. *Bakorstanas* involvement in industrial relations should be seen in the context of guarding national stability (The Australian, 1994b).

Like General Tanjung before him, General Hartono again criticised the SPSI saying that it had largely failed to organise and protect the interests of its membership. He said that its ineffectiveness had helped foster the growth in recent years of unofficial independent unions such as the SBSI.

At the SPSI congress of November 1995, held in a climate of rising industrial activism, the organisation formally adopted a new structure. That structure had been under debate since the early 1990s and was to provide for 13 sector-based unions linked to a separate federation. Each union was to be entitled to control membership contributions and to develop independent policies. With these changes the SPSI had its last chance to operate as an effective trade union movement or be relegated to obscurity. Official strikes had increased from 114 in 1991 to 1130 in 1994 (Tjajo, 1996) and, although it is hard to locate reliable up-to-date figures, anecdotal evidence suggests that this wave of unrest has continued to escalate since then, demonstrating that the SPSI's 1995 restructuring did nothing to reverse its decline as an effective tool for government control of the workforce.

The Emergence of New Unions

Law No 18 of 1956 specifies the rights of workers to organise and engage in collective bargaining and Law No 14 of 1969 includes the right to establish and become a member of a democratically formed trade union and to conclude collective labour agreements. Article 11(1) states that '[e]very worker has a right to establish and become a member of a worker's association'.

These laws are said to be consistent with Art 28 of the 1945 Constitution which relates to freedom of association and of assembly. However, the vague rights they

---

18 Indonesian Prosperous Workers Union.

confer must be seen in the context of the Department of Labour regulations referred to above and to the political realities which operate on the ground.[19]

Yet, even in the face of these weak formal protections and formidable legal and political obstacles new labour formations did emerge. The *Serikat Buruh Merdeka* (SBM)[20] or 'Solidarity' as it was known was founded in December of 1990. In response to what was clearly seen as dissident behaviour Admiral Sudomo (who by then held the position of Minister for Political and Security Affairs) asserted that the SPSI was the only labour union recognised by the government and warned workers not to set up a rival union as it was obvious that the government would not recognise it (Jakarta Post, 1990). Solidarity soon collapsed as a result of this government opposition and consequent employer hostility.

The second independent union, SBSI, emerged in April 1993. Shortly after it held its first national congress, the Minister for Labour, Abdul Latief, continued to assert the government's opposition to independent unions. He said:

> There is no place in the Indonesian labour movement for SBSI or SBM. The government will not recognise these two labour unions because they were established by individuals with political interests (Jakarta Post, 1993b).

SBSI has emerged as the strongest advocate of worker rights within Indonesia. Muchtar Pakpahan, its leader, was jailed for three years in November 1994 for his alleged involvement in the Medan riots of March that year. He was subsequently released in May 1995 due to a failure by the government to process his appeal but in October 1996 the *Mahkamah Agung* (Indonesia's highest court) convicted him again and increased the sentence to four years. Pakpahan was arrested in August 1996 following rioting in Jakarta after the 26 July takeover of the PDI[21] offices. He was charged with various criminal offences and subversion for the publication of his book, 'Portrait of an Indonesian State'. His trial was delayed due to his ill-health yet in mid-1998 he remained in prison awaiting his frequently-postponed trial.

A third union which has caused considerable embarrassment to the Indonesian government is the Alliance of Independent Journalists (AJI), established in 1994. The government has refused to recognise this union. Given the sensitivity of the Indonesian government to media criticism it is hardly surprising that an independent trade union for journalists is not encouraged or recognised. This was particularly so following the banning of the news magazines *Tempo*, *Editor* and *DeTik* in May 1994. The openness which had emerged in the early years of the 1990s was by then clearly in decline. The jailing of AJI members Ahmad Taufik and Eko Maryadi for 34 months each for breach of Art 154 of the Indonesian Criminal Code put the case of Indonesian unionists back on the international stage. They had both been active in the formation and activities of the AJI and their charges related to their activities in that organisation.

It is important to consider the context in which these three unions have emerged and the response of the Indonesian government both as to their emergence and to the continuing problems within the SPSI itself. In many disputes that occur in

---

19 For example, on 1 July 1990 General Try Sutrisno, then Vice President of Indonesia, warned of growing anti-*Pancasila* activity among workers. He warned that certain groups would try to utilise the gaps between groups in the society to create disturbances and threaten security and order. He further warned that the ABRI would be vigilant against the anti-*Pancasila* activity (Indonesian Times, 1990).

20 Independent Workers Union.

21 *Partai Demokrasi Indonesia*, Indonesian Democratic Party.

Indonesia the issue of representation is an important factor. In a study of 87 strikes during 1994, 22 involved, amongst other demands, that workers not be represented by the SPSI (Abdullah, 1994). The restructuring of the SPSI is a partial attempt to deal with these problems. The SBSI, however, has developed a prominent role in criticising the government and in advocating for worker's rights. It is seen by many workers as the legitimate voice of their interests.

The strength of SBSI and the dramatic failure of SPSI undoubtedly contributed to two of President Habibie's first decisions on assuming office: he released Pakpahan and announced that trade union regulation would be relaxed. Accordingly, on 27 May 1998 Labour Minister Fahmi Idris confirmed the new government's decision to recognise the opposition union, SBSI, and to permit other unions to operate legally. He stated that unions could exist if their main aim was to improve the well-being of workers and the quality of work (South China ... 1998). He also stated that new rules would be announced with respect to union recognition. As at the date of writing, however, new regulations have not been made public and the extent of the reforms remains to be seen.

The Right to Strike

As mentioned, *Pancasila* industrial relations has been used as an ideological framework to restrict and control the right to strike. Strike action by workers has been discouraged and minimised. The procedures which unions and workers are required to adopt before they can legally take strike action are complex and designed to curtail worker action. Ministry of Labour Decree No 1108 of 1986, for example, requires that if a dispute is not resolved at the bipartite or tripartite level then it must be taken to the regional office of the department of Labour for further conciliation. It is only if a dispute is not resolved at this stage that legitimate strike action can be taken.

This requirement, which obviously restricts and significantly curtails industrial action, was until recently buttressed by Ministry of Labour Regulation No 62 of 1993. This regulation enabled a company and the Ministry of Labour to require workers to sign a written agreement that they would resume their employment within a specified time. A failure to provide such written agreement would result in the employees' being deemed to have resigned their employment.

Further Ministry of Labour Decree No 4 of 1986 expressly states that workers cannot be absent from their employment for more than six consecutive days without proper justification or they are considered to have resigned.

The effect of these restrictive regulations on the right to strike has been controversial within Indonesia. They were criticised by a number of non-government organisations (NGOs) and become the subject of industrial campaigns. Partly because of criticism and industrial unrest Decree No 62 of 1993 was withdrawn late in 1993 (Katjasungkana & Masduki, nd: 3).

The Minimum Wage

The minimum wage of workers within Indonesia is controlled by government regulations. The rate of the minimum wage is based upon the *Kebutuhan Fisik*

Minimum (Minimum Physical Needs or KFM). The actual rate at which the government sets the minimum wage varies from one region to another and is determined by the *Dewan Penelitian Pengupahan Daerah* (the Local Wage Research Council or DPPD). This body, using the KFM as a basic formulation, determines what the wage rate should be for any particular region. The DPPD recommends to the Ministry of Labour the appropriate rate which is then regulated by government decree.

The DPPD is composed of 10 public servants, three trade union members and three company representatives. This is in accordance with Ministry of Labour Regulations No 131 of 1970. The trade union representatives are from the SPSI and the public servants representatives come from a range of government agencies. The deliberation of the DPPD which obviously have important ramifications for workers and their families are conducted in secret. Ministry of Labour Regulation No 20 of 1971 specifies that the minutes of DPPD meetings can only be made available to its members and the deliberations it engages in before formulating a rate for the minimum wage can only be attended by members of the council. This leads to the most extraordinary situation where perhaps the most important condition for workers is decided without public scrutiny or public knowledge of the factors which have led to the decision or how such decisions are reached.

The minimum wage rate has been the subject of industrial disputes in the recent past. The minimum wage rate per day for Jakarta has been Rp 5750[22] since 1 April 1997 (Herald Tribune, 1997). There was no increase in April 1998 due to the severe economic problems of the country (The Age, 1998).

The inability of workers or their representatives to participate in any meaningful way in the setting of minimum wage rates is simply another example of the control that has been exercised by the Indonesian government as part of its consistent policy to minimise wage increases so that economic development can proceed. With the effect of the recent economic problems still sweeping through the Indonesian economy and inflation running out of control, official intervention in industrial disputes will, if anything, be exacerbated. The Minister of Labour has estimated 8.7 million workers were unemployed by April 1998 and that this figure will increase to 13.4 million by 1999.

The Labour Law of 1997

After many months of debate, the DPR,[23] the Indonesian parliament, passed a new Labour Law on 11 September 1997. The Law does not come into operation until 1 October 1998 and is subject to Presidential approval. The Law aims to repeal many of the existing labour and industrial relation laws but it is unlikely to significantly change the industrial realities of Indonesia – for example, it still only recognises the SPSI. as the legitimate trade union for workers. Likewise strikes will only be legal if they have been notified to relevant authorities seven days before they take place and do not involve street demonstrations (Jakarta Post, 1997).

Parliament has indicated, however, that eight regulations will have to be drafted and issued before the bill can be proclaimed. Whether these new regulations are completed and the new law is proclaimed in the current economic climate must be

---

22   About AUS$0.70 in June 1998.
23   *Dewan Perwakilan Rakyat*, the People's Representative Council.

very uncertain. It is now clear that, in any case, the new Law has been superseded by political events in Jakarta and the reforms promised by both Habibie and his Minister for Labour. It is now probable that the 1997 Law will be abandoned or replaced by a new statute even before its commencement date.

Foreign Pressure in the Reform of Indonesian Industrial Relations

Pressure has been mounting on Indonesia for some years with respect to workers' rights and the existence of independent trade unions. With the election of the Clinton administration in the United States this pressure was significantly increased. In June of 1992 Asia Watch and the International Labour Rights Education and Research Fund petitioned the United States government with respect to Indonesian labour rights and practices.[24] The Office of the Trade Representative (Carla Hills) agreed to review the Indonesian case. Material was presented by the petitioning organisations in October of 1992 and the Indonesian government submitted an official response in November of that year. The United States initially gave Indonesia until February of 1994 to conform with minimum requirements with respect to worker and trade union rights or suffer the withdrawal of trade preferences granted under the Trade and Tariff Law of 1984 ('GSP').

The GSP requires that countries which receive trade preferences from the United States comply with a number of minimum standards, including the right for workers to organise, to collectively bargain and to form trade unions. The loss of trade preferences would undermine Indonesia's strategy of providing low cost labour to manufacturing export industries and would also no doubt generate political dissension within the Indonesian business elite, exacerbating the political tensions resulting from the current monetary crisis.

Although President Clinton has extended trade preferences to Indonesia, subject to continuing review, US Secretary of State Madelaine Albright criticised the Indonesian government and its response to the calls for a more democratic society as recently as April 1998 (Financial Review, 1998). It is an interesting development that as the globalisation of the world economy continues and countries like Indonesia expand their economies to participate they also open up an arena for political debate as to the structure of their trade unions. Indonesia's economic collapse makes it especially vulnerable to foreign pressure for industrial reform.

The Marsinah Case

It is suggested that the killing of Marsinah, a young labour activist, and the events surrounding the subsequent trial, conviction and ultimate freeing of those accused of her murder, highlight the practical realities of *Pancasila* industrial relations in Indonesia. In particular, it illustrates the length to which ABRI is prepared to go to control unionism. Although there is no final or hard evidence that ABRI was directly involved in Marsinah's death, it was certainly extensively involved in the dispute which led to her murder. In any case, whether or not Marsinah's killers were

---

24   See Asia Watch (1993).

ABRI officials does not detract from the extensive involvement of ABRI in the dispute and other disputes of a similar nature.

Marsinah was a found dead on 8 May 1993.[25] She had been employed by PT CPS which was a watchmaking factory located in Porong, East Java. There had been an industrial dispute at the factory for some months before the death and a strike occurred at the factory on 3 and 4 May 1993. The strike arose from negotiations which had been occurring at the factory which involved the local work unit of the SPSI. Discussions had been occurring over the issue of wage increases and the proposed 20% increase in the minimum wage for the East Java region. At that time, East Java's minimum wage was set at Rp 2250.[26] Workers at PT CPS were only being paid Rp 1700,[27] which was below the official minimum daily wage rates.

Marsinah and other workers came to the view that the company was not complying with its legal obligations and that the SPSI was not adequately representing them in their negotiations with the company. On 3 May 1993 a number of workers did not enter the factory at the required time of 6.00 am and encouraged other workers not to go into work. Officials from the *Koramil*, *Polres*, the Department of Labour and the regional office of the SPSI arrived at the factory later in the morning. During the course of that day a number of workers were taken to the *Koramil* offices and were questioned. It is important to note that the workers were being held at the local military headquarters and interrogated by military officers. It was suggested that they were accused of being involved with the PKI, an extremely intimidating threat to make in Indonesia where the Communist Party is an illegal organisation and hundreds of thousands of leftists were executed in the mid-1960s. The workers were therefore placed under enormous pressure to abandon their claims.

A typed list of demands which the workers had formulated previously were provided to the military officers in charge:

1. an increase in wages in accordance with Ministry of Labour Decree No 50 of 1992 from Rp 1700 to Rp 2250 per day which should have been current since 1 May 1992;

2. the calculation of overtime payment in accordance with Ministry of Labour Decree No 72 of 1984;

3. an agreement for menstrual leave with minimum pay;

4. health guarantees in accordance with Regulation No 3 of 1992, *jaminan sosial tenaga kerja* (Workers Social Security Law);

5. inclusion of *Astek* (workers insurance);

6. provision of bonus for *Hari Raya* celebrations at the end of the Islamic fasting month of Ramadan;

7. a rise in food and transport allowances;

8. dissolution of the PT CPS SPSI work unit because it did not conform with the basic constitutional SPSI organisational guidelines;

9. on time payment of pregnancy leave;

---

25   The details of the death and background are taken from YLBHI (1994).

26.   About AU$0.30 in June 1998.

27   About AUS$0.22 in June 1998.

10. raising the training wage level to the wage received by workers who had been employed for one year;

11. existing workers' rights could not be withdrawn;

12. after the strike ends the company is prohibited from transferring, intimidating and dismissing workers involved in the strike (YLBHI, 1994: 11).

On 4 May the strike continued and more workers were involved. *Koramil*, *Polsek* and *Kodim* officials were all in attendance and involved in attempts to get the workers to resume their employment duties. In the course of the day negotiations occurred between management and worker representatives. Officials were also present from the regional office of the SPSI, the Department of Labour and the local Commander of *Koramil*. After considerable negotiations substantial agreement was reached on the workers' demands although not all matters were agreed to and some modification to the demands were made. The only worker demand which was expressly rejected was the dissolution of the SPSI unit at the factory. This is hardly surprising given the involvement of government officials in the negotiations and the importance for them of having the SPSI in existence in an obviously troubled industrial environment. It would be inconceivable for government officials to agree to such a demand given both the strong pressure exerted by central government officials and the military for the existence of the SPSI and the role SPSI plays in government attempts to co-ordinate and discipline the industrial workforce.

Perhaps surprisingly, the workers' demands were, in general, met or compromises reached. By the end of the 4 May, the dispute had been resolved by negotiation. A letter had been signed by all parties setting out the mutually agreed results.

There is nothing to suggest that the demands at the PT CPS were unusual or in any way radical. Their quick resolution through negotiations on the second day indicates that the company was prepared to concede nearly all of the demands and certainly those demands which were within the company's power to accede to.

That same afternoon, however, 13 workers who had been involved in the negotiations were summonsed to attend at *Kodim* the following morning. *Kodim* is the district military command and requiring the workers to attend there was a significant escalation of the dispute. Again, after substantial interrogation and threats that they were involved in the PKI the 13 summonsed workers were required to sign letters of resignation from PT CPS. These letters of resignation were sought by the *Kodim* officers and, it would appear, not by management directly. No doubt the *Kodim* officials saw this intervention as part of their role to ensure industrial peace and stability at the factory after the dispute and to ensure that there were no further re-occurrences of strike action. One can imagine that they would be embarrassed even to report to higher officials that there had been industrial disputation on 3 and 4 May.

In any case, whether or not the company officials sought the resignations, the close involvement of the military highlights the working relationship which exists between management and ABRI forces. It also highlights the ideological basis on which ABRI officers operate when they deal with what are day-to-day industrial matters.

Marsinah subsequently became aware of the forced resignations of her 13 fellow workers and decided to take further action to prevent the dismissals taking effect. She was last seen attempting to deliver a letter to company management protesting that the resignations were not genuine and had been forced by the military. Her body was found three days later on the 8 May some 200 km from the factory. After medical examination her death was found to arise from torture after she had been raped.

Subsequently, national and international publicity was given to the case and charges were eventually laid against a number of individuals for her murder (YLBHI, 1994: 20-21). Following her death, Marsinah's case was first investigated by the local police with involvement of regional and national police as the publicity around the case gathered. The investigation appears to have been inadequate and proper procedures were not carried out. On 30 September military intelligence therefore became involved in these investigations. On that day military intelligence (*Intel*, a component of *Bakorstanas*) arrested a number of suspects without warrant and interrogated those suspects for 19 days before obtaining admissions to the crime of murder. The interviews were conducted at military offices and the arrests and the interrogations were carried out by *Intel*. Again this highlights the involvement of ABRI and its various agencies in what had become by this time a major public affair with respect to industrial relations within in Indonesia. The involvement of *Bakorstanas*, to the exclusion of the local and regional police, indicates the seriousness with which ABRI viewed the Marsinah case. The growing public attention to Marsinah's death and the underlying industrial relations difficulties that it symbolised were issues which ABRI wished to contain by disposing of them as quickly as possible.

In December 1993, the trial of the first of accused came before the Surabaya District Court (*Pengadilan Negeri*). At that trial one of the witnesses, an official of the Ministry of Labour, indicated that the department operated a secret organisation known as the *System Inteligine Sidoarajo*. The official testified that the organisation was designed to exchange information and maintain links between company security staff and *Kodim*. The official testified that similar organisations existed in almost all companies across Indonesia.

While the court was continuing with the proceedings the first defendant retracted her admissions. Shortly afterwards all of the remaining defendants retracted their admissions which they all alleged had been obtained from them under torture. Convictions were nonetheless recorded at the end of the trial. All nine defendants appealed to the *Mahkamah Agung* and were acquitted in May of 1995. Following the acquittals the investigation was reopened. No new charges have been laid but Indonesian newspapers have repeatedly speculated as to the identities of the ABRI personnel who are widely believed to have been responsible for the murder.

The Indonesian Legal Aid Foundation (LBH)[28] and the National Human Rights Commission (KOMNASHAM)[29] both investigated the Marsinah case and the surrounding circumstances; and their reports were instrumental in persuading the *Mahkamah Agung* that the convictions could not stand. The KOMNASHAM released findings on 4 April 1994 which drew on LBH's investigations. The Commission, which was then headed by Ali Said, a former Chief Justice, came to the conclusion that there had been a number of irregularities in the arrest, detention and interrogation of the suspects. It was also suggested that there were other people possibly involved in the murder who had not been brought to trial. The Commission urged the government to act upon its findings and to further investigate the surrounding circumstances of Marsinah's death.

---

28 *Yayasan Lembaga Bantuan Hukum Indonesia.*

29 *Komisi Nasional Hak Asasi Manusia.*

The findings and recommendations of the KOMNASHAM put the Indonesian government in a more difficult position and placed pressure on President Soeharto to find both a political solution to the case and to moderate ABRI's role in industrial relations. The Supreme Court acquittals relieved some of this pressure and officially the case was closed in September 1997 for lack of evidence. Marsinah nonetheless remains a potent symbol of opposition to government and military repression of workers (see Zifcak, Chapter 25). If it is ever demonstrated that ABRI were implicated directly in the murder of Marsinah then this will dramatically increase pressure on the Indonesian government to exclude ABRI from industrial relations matters. We will have to await future developments to see whether or not this case is ever solved but the political dilemma at the heart of the Marsinah case remains.

Conclusion

The current situation is one characterised by an ineffectual and numerically weak official trade union and the emergence under difficult conditions of independent trade unions and various NGOs committed to improving the rights of Indonesian workers. These trends are occurring within a context of the increasing instability within the Indonesian regime following the fall of President Soeharto. The recent decision to permit new and independent trade unions to operate will have profound consequences for industrial relations in Indonesia. There will probably be sudden and unexpected policy changes and dramatic repositioning within the government by various competing factions.

The explosive circumstances which led to the rioting in Medan in 1994 and in Jakarta in 1998 may again emerge with more dramatic consequences. The International Monetary Fund rescue package, initially settled in 1997, has been repeatedly re-negotiated because of the concerns that price rises are fuelling extensive unrest. The failure to deliver speedy economic recovery has already led to a massive fall in real wages and a rapid increase in unemployment. This, combined with the release of Pakpahan and the recognition of alternative unions, is a recipe for industrial turmoil unless real reform is delivered quickly. The government may be forced to review not just the status of trade unions but the basic philosophy beneath its whole industrial relations policy.

Whether President Habibie can hold office and establish an effective government remains to be seen. The winds of change are blowing with considerable force but their direction is by no means clear.

References

Abdulah, F, 1994, 'Price hikes motivate labor strikes', *Jakarta Post*, 15 February.
Indonesian Times, 4 July 1990.
Asia Watch, 23 January 1993, *Indonesia: Charges and Rebuttals over Labor Rights Practices*.
Financial Review, 30 April 1998.
Herald Tribune, 23 January 1997.
Indonesian Times, 4 July 1990.
Jakarta Post, 1990, 19 December.
Jakarta Post, 1993a, 7 July.
Jakarta Post, 1993b, 8 September.

Jakarta Post, 1996, 16 January.

Jakarta Post, 1997, 12 September.

Katjasungkana, N and Masduki, T, *Labour, State and Democracy Workers Solidarity*, Jakarta, copy in possession of author.

Lambet, R, *Authoritarian State Unionism In New Order Indonesia*, October 1993 Asia Research Centre, Murdoch University.

Roehadi, K, 1982, *Achieving Good Labour Relations in Indonesia*, copy in possession of author.

South China Morning Post 27 May 1998

The Age, 15 April 1998.

The Australian, 1994b, 14 May.

Tjajo R, 1996, *Workplace Health and Safety*, paper given at the Comparative Labour Law and Employment Relations in Asia Conference, Melbourne, February.

Witjes, Ben, 1987, *The Indonesian Law on Social Organisation*, Nijmegen.

Workers Solidarity Forum, *Statement on the GSP*, Jakarta, 3 February 1994.

YLBHI, March 1994, *A Preliminary Report On The Murder Of Marsinah*, Indonesian Legal Aid Foundation Jakarta.

27. Overlapping Sovereigns:

Some Reflections on the Case Concerning East Timor

Gerry J Simpson[1]

The independence of every country is the right of every nation,
with no exception for the people of East Timor
Indonesian Foreign Minister Adam Malik,
17 June 1974

Timor is an island 600 kilometres off the north-west tip of Australia and approximately 2200 kilometres from Jakarta. It lies at the Eastern end of the Sunda Archipelago.[2] In 1893 the island was divided between the Netherlands and Portugal with Holland incorporating West Timor as part of the Dutch East Indies. West Timor became part of the independent state of Indonesia when Indonesia gained its independence from the Dutch in 1949. East Timor remained a colony of Portugal until 1975 when the Portuguese withdrew from the island. In 1975 Indonesia invaded East Timor[3] and began an occupation marked by systematic degradation of East Timorese cultural life.[4] The United Nations Security Council passed two resolutions condemning the invasion in 1976[5] and the General Assembly passed a

---

1   Many thanks to Pedro Pinto Leite and Roger Clark for formative early work, both activist and academic, on the subject of East Timorese self-determination.

2   East Timor consists of the eastern portion of the island as well as the enclave of Oe-cussi, Atauro Island and Jaco Islet. It totals some 19,000 square kilometres.

3   Since 1960, East Timor has been a non-self-governing territory according to the United Nations. Portugal was declared East Timor's Administering Power in 1960 under GA Res 1542 (15 UN GAOR, Supp (No 16) 30, UN Doc A/4684 (1960), a role it rejected until 1974, just before it relinquished physical control over the island. Portugal remains East Timor's official Administering Power under Chapter 11 of the UN Charter even though de facto authority is now exercised by the Indonesians. The political events leading up to the invasion are described in Elliot (1978: 238-40).

4   Figures vary but it is thought that between 100,000 and 200,000 East Timorese have lost their lives as a consequence of the Indonesian occupation. See generally Human Rights ... (1977). Clark (1981: 321); and Testimony of Shepard (1977). 'It is clear that the people of East Timor have been denied the exercise of the most fundamental of human rights under Indonesian rule' (Australian Senate Standing Committee, 1983: 84).

5   SC Res 384, 30 UN SCOR, Resolutions and Decisions 10, UN Doc. S/res/384 (1975); SC Res 389, 31 UN SCOR, Resolutions and Decisions 18, UN Doc S/Res/389 (1976) (the United States abstained on this resolution).

series of progressively diluted resolutions between 1976 and 1982.[6] Since then international law[7] and the world community has, until recently, steadfastly looked the other way.[8] This has occurred in the face of the repressive practices of the Indonesian military. Meanwhile, the efforts of East Timorese representatives at the United Nations and the hopeless but tenacious resistance of a small band of guerrillas in the hills of East Timor remained virtually unnoticed.[9]

Three events this decade have transformed this situation. First, on 12 November 1991, a group of East Timorese youths gathered at the Santa Cruz cemetery in Dili to mourn a young Timorese killed in a skirmish with the Indonesian authorities the previous month. Indonesian troops opened fire on the crowd killing hundreds.[10] This was not the first occasion on which force had been used against civilians in East Timor but it was the first time such an incident had been filmed.[11] The name 'Dili' was thus to take its place alongside other late-20th century outrages like Tiannanmen Square and Sharpeville.[12]

The second event occurred with the capture of East Timorese resistance leader Xanana Gusmao by the Indonesian authorities. While apparently a success for the Indonesian intelligence, Gusmao's capture brought in its wake increased media

---

6   See. for example, GA Res 3485 (XXX), 30 UN GAOR, Supp (No 34) 118, UN Doc A/10634 (1976); GA Res 34/40, 34 UN GAOR, Supp (No 46) 206, UN Doc A/34/46 (1979); GA Res 32/30, 37 UN GAOR, Supp (No 51) 227, UN Doc A/37/51 (1982). The resolutions became less damning because of intense Indonesian lobbying the eventual result of which was East Timor's complete removal from the agenda after 1982. See Jose Ramos Horta (1987).

7   There are some notable exceptions among international lawyers. See Clark (1980); Franck & Hoffman (1976).

8   The reasons for this neglect are not difficult to fathom. The United States had just been defeated by the Vietcong in Southeast Asia and regarded the Indonesians as potential allies in the region. Fretilin, the main East Timorese resistance force, was organised along Marxist lines and was therefore viewed with great suspicion by the Americans. The Australian position is set out in the fax sent by the then Australian Ambassador to Indonesia, Richard Woolcott in 1975 where he stated, 'we are all aware of the Australian defence interest in the Portuguese Timor situation. ... but I wonder whether the Department has ascertained the interest of the Minister of the Department of Minerals and Energy in the Timor situation. It would seem to me that this Department might well have an interest in closing the present gap in the agreed sea border *and this could more readily negotiated with Indonesia than with Portugal or independent Portuguese Timor* (my emphasis)' (Walsh, 1990: 90). It has even been suggested that the Indonesians were prepared to offer Australia generous terms on boundary limitation in the Timor Gap in exchange for recognition of the Indonesian invasion (Richardson, 1976).

9   For a discussion of the work of the East Timorese delegation at the United Nations, see Horta (1987). In recent years Portugal and Indonesia have had periodic discussions over the question of East Timor but, despite the encouragement of the United Nations, these have been marked by intransigence and inflexibility.

10   See, for example, The Age (1991a). Casualty figures vary. The Indonesian military initially put the figure at 19 but this was later revised to 50 by an official inquiry conducted by Indonesian authorities (The Age, 1991c). Witnesses estimate that upwards of 180 were killed that day and there were reports of mass killings of eye-witnesses subsequent to the shootings. See, Joint Letter from Members of the US Congress (1992). Accounts of the killing are contained in Tapol Bulletin (1991); Timor Link (1992); Inside Indonesia (1991).

11   Yorkshire Television's First Tuesday documentary team were in Dili at the time of the massacre. Their experiences are recounted in Stahl (1992).

12   Aid was suspended shortly after the massacre by Canada and the Netherlands (Age, 1991b).

focus on East Timor and a trial that has proved damaging to Indonesia's credibility and public image (Baker (1992); Washington Post (1991).[13]

These circumstances provide something of a context for a third development which forms the subject matter of this chapter. On 30 June 1995, the International Court of Justice (ICJ) or World Court held by a large majority of 14 votes to 2 that it could not adjudicate upon the dispute between Australia and Portugal because of the absence of an indispensable third party, Indonesia. In this chapter I explore some of the reasoning behind the decision, the implications of the judgment for East Timorese self-determination and the broader ramifications of the East Timorese dispute for our understandings of sovereignty and self-determination in international law.

The Portuguese and Australian Arguments: A Summary

On 22 February 1991, Portugal instituted proceedings against Australia in the East Timor case. Portugal claimed that Australia had breached its obligations to both Portugal and the East Timorese in entering into a treaty with Indonesia to exploit hydrocarbon resources in an area known as the Timor Gap. Portugal's case rested on three substantive grounds. First, the Portuguese argued that Australia had an obligation to conclude the treaty with Portugal rather than Indonesia since Portugal was the official administering power over East Timor. Secondly, Portugal maintained that Australia's failure to respect Portugal's position in turn gave rise to international responsibility towards the East Timorese on the basis of an infringement of the East Timorese right to self-determination. Finally, the Portuguese submission stated that Australia was in breach of both its obligation in international law not to recognise illegal acquisitions of territory and its obligation to carry out and respect Security Council Resolutions 384 and 389 condemning the Indonesian invasion of East Timor in 1975.

Portugal's difficulties in the case lay not in showing that there had been repeated breaches of international law but rather in demonstrating that these breaches were Australia's responsibility. Portugal had to convince the court that Australia was responsible for at least some of these illegal acts and that, importantly, a finding on Australia's duties and responsibilities did not depend on prior determinations regarding the legality of Indonesia's conduct.

Australia's defence in the case rested heavily on three main procedural arguments linked to these difficulties with the Portuguese claim. First, Australia argued that the court should decline to hear the case on the grounds that it offended judicial propriety or was 'removed from reality' (DFAT, 995: 1). Secondly, Australia claimed that Portugal lacked standing to bring the case to the court. According to Australia, Portugal had no legal interest in the Timor Gap matter because it was merely a colonial power who had withdrawn hastily from the region over 20 years ago. Finally, Australia argued that Indonesia's absence was fatal to Portugal's claims because of the long-standing rule that a court cannot determine the lawfulness of a third party's action in the absence of that third party. Each of

---

13 Gusmao was found guilty and given a life sentence. He went on hunger strike in 1993 (Guardian Weekly, 1993) and was visited in 1997 by President Nelson Mandela of South Africa. By May 1998 hopes for an early release were being expressed in the wake of the fall of Soeharto.

Portugal's substantive submissions, according to Australia, depended on preliminary findings as to the legality of Indonesia's conduct.

Australia's arguments on the merits included the observation that the Security Council resolutions relied on by Portugal had been adopted under Chapter VI (recommendatory) rather than Chapter VII (mandatory) of the United Nations Charter. These resolutions did not have the legal significance of, say, the Security Council's resolutions following Iraq's invasion of Kuwait. Australia also emphasised that it had no duty to negotiate with Portugal because Portugal's status as administering power was an anachronism. In addition, Australia noted Portugal's own poor colonial record during the period when East Timor was part of the Portuguese Empire. In relation to self-determination, Australia accepted East Timor's continuing right but argued that this position was not inconsistent with recognition of Indonesia's sovereignty over East Timor.

In the rest of this chapter I want to focus on only a few of these fascinating legal arguments.[14] In a brief first part I will comment briefly on the doctrine of absentee third parties. In the second part, the major body of the chapter, I will tease out the various meanings of sovereignty found in the text of the decision. This will involve an analysis of both the majority and dissenting judgments.

Absentee Third Parties

In its decision, the court found that it lacked jurisdiction to determine Australia's obligations towards Portugal because to do so would require a simultaneous or prior determination of the lawfulness of Indonesia's actions in invading Timor and entering into a treaty to exploit Timorese resources. This is the essence of the indispensable third party doctrine.

This doctrine grew out of a recognition that to adjudicate the claims of an absent third party in judicial proceedings would offend natural justice since that third party would be judged in its absence and without being able to provide a defence. Equally, it is impossible to bring a reluctant state before the court because the foundation of the World Court's jurisdiction is consensual. Ultimately, states can only be judged if they consent to such judgment.

The indispensable third party doctrine has developed over a series of cases, the earliest being the *Case of Monetary Gold Removed from Rome in 1943*.[15] This was a dispute between Italy and the United Kingdom over the ownership of Albanian Gold removed from Rome by the German army and later held by the Allies. The United Kingdom claimed the Albanian gold in satisfaction of the decision in its favour in the *Corfu Channel Case*[16] while the Italians asserted ownership as part

---

14 Space does not permit an examination of some key issues raised by Australia and discussed by the court. For example, the court dismissed Australia's argument that no dispute exists between itself and Portugal by pointing to the existence of certain legal facts about which there is disagreement between the two parties: '[I]t is clear the Parties are in disagreement, both on the law and on the facts, on the question of whether the conduct of Australia in negotiating, concluding and initiating performance of the 1989 Treaty was in breach of an obligation due by Australia to Portugal under international law', *Case Concerning East Timor (Portugal v Australia)*, ICJ Judgment, 30 June 1995 at para 22.

15 *Monetary Gold Removed from Rome in 1943* (Preliminary Question), Judgment of 15 June 1954, ICJ Reports, 1954, at 19.

16 *Corfu Channel Case*, ICJ Reports, 1949, 4.

compensation arising out of the nationalisation and expropriation of Italian banking assets in Albania. The court held that it could not adjudicate on Italy's claim without first determining the legality of Albania's actions in nationalising Italian assets. Since Albania was not present, the court declined to exercise jurisdiction in deference to the indispensable third party doctrine. The court however clarified the rule by stating that there would be a refusal to exercise jurisdiction only in cases where the interests of an absent state 'would not only be affected by a decision, *but would form the very subject matter of the decision*' (my italics).[17]

The court in the *East Timor Case* has applied what I take to be an anti-formalist reading of the indispensable third-party doctrine enunciated in Monetary Gold which may have interesting consequences for the rule of law in international relations. In a series of cases running from *Monetary Gold* through *Nicaragua v United States*[18] to the recent decision at the preliminary phase of the *Nauru*[19] proceedings, the court has developed a rather unusual and opaque version of the doctrine. In Nicaragua, the court held that it could determine the right of the United States to take action against Nicaragua in collective self-defence on behalf of El Salvador and Honduras without first determining whether those states themselves had suffered an armed attack capable of activating a right to unilateral self-defence. The court noted that neither Honduras nor El Salvador in that case were 'truly indispensable to the pursuance of the proceedings'.[20] The court also acknowledged that Arts 59 and 62 of the ICJ Statute tempered the application of the third parties doctrine: Art 59 by specifying that any decision is only binding on the parties to the case and Art 62 allowing intervention in the proceedings by an affected third party. The court recognised that these two Articles protected absent third parties in certain circumstances. In *Nauru*,[21] the court held that it was not barred from hearing the merits of Nauru's claim to compensation for damages caused by Australia as a member of the Administering Authority despite the absence of the other members of the Authority, New Zealand and the United Kingdom. The rights and duties of New Zealand and the United Kingdom were deemed not to form the very subject matter of the dispute in *Nauru*. Similarly, the right of self-defence held by Costa Rica, El Salvador and Honduras was not the very subject matter of the dispute in *Nicaragua*.

In the Nauru case, of course, the status of New Zealand and the United Kingdom as co-administrators was confirmed as a matter of United Nations Law and in the Trusteeship Agreement. In Nicaragua, El Salvador and Honduras possessed legal rights to self-defence that were found in the UN Charter and in customary international law. In neither of these case were the third parties thought to possess rights and duties central to the case. However, in the *East Timor Case*, Indonesia was held to have acquired third party rights through an act of invasion that was condemned by the Security Council and whose legality in customary international law is barely defensible.

Why did the court find that Indonesia's rights were implicated in this case more thoroughly that those of, say, New Zealand and the United Kingdom in the *Nauru* case? I argue that they did so by adopting an anti-formalist or realist approach to the

---

17   At 32.

18   *Military and Paramilitary Activities in and against Nicaragua (Nicaragua v United States)*, Jurisdiction and Admissibility, Judgment, ICJ Reports 1984, at 427.

19   *Certain Phosphate Lands in Nauru (Nauru v Australia)*, ICJ Reports 1992, at 240.

20   At 392.

21   At 240.

relationship between law and politics. In *Nauru*, though the formal, legal position of Australia, New Zealand and the United Kingdom was the same, the court was willing to find that their substantive positions varied dramatically. As a matter of fact more than law, Australia was the sole administering power. Australia had been committed to the task of physically administering Nauru. It had established infrastructure on the island, issued Australian currency as legal tender, and generally provided candidates for administrative positions. Thus, its rights and duties were deemed severable from those of New Zealand and the United Kingdom. Similarly, in the *Nicaragua* judgment the court recognised that, though the right to collective self-defence was one held jointly by Costa Rica, Honduras, El Salvador and the United States, in reality the dispute was a political one between Nicaragua and the United States. The United States interests were thus regarded as severable from those of the other third parties.

In the *East Timor Case,* despite Indonesia's lack of any formal status as a party to the dispute (compare New Zealand and the United Kingdom in *Nauru*), the political realities of its occupation of East Timor were recognised to be of over-whelming significance even in the face of formal statements declaring that occupation to be illegal.[22]

What are the implications of this sort of reasoning? The court seems to be moving towards a pragmatic approach to dispute resolution where it will take into account the interests of third parties if those interests are implicated on a continual and substantive basis. A formal instrument establishing that interest will be insufficient to vest rights and duties in third parties, for example, the administration agreements over Nauru where these agreements were unaccompanied by any political or economic links. The problem here is that this sort of legal reasoning skirts dangerously close to the mere confirmation of realpolitik. If Indonesia's legal interests ('established' by an illegal invasion) are regarded as having more legal effect than those of, say, New Zealand (in Nauru) (established by a United Nations Trusteeship Agreement) and are to be given more weight than successive United Nations Resolutions concerning East Timor itself then what price the rule of law? Surely, such a decision augurs well for future aggressors. If, for example, Iraq had remained in Kuwait following its invasion would it too have acquired third party interests in any future legal dispute over the territory?

Overlapping Sovereigns and Self-Determination

The opaqueness of sovereignty as an idea has hardly diminished its centrality as an organising principle of international relations. The various meanings and impli-cations of sovereignty were peculiarly resonant in the Timor Gap Case at both the procedural and substantive levels.[23] Indeed the outcome of the case very much depended on the degrees of sovereignty possessed by the various parties in different contexts. The political and legal disputes which provide a background to the case

---

22 See, for example, SC Res 384, UN SCOR, 30th Sess, 1869 mtg, at 10 (1975); SC Res 389, UN SCOR, 31st sess,1914th mtg at 18.

23 Unusually for an ICJ case, the parties agreed to join the procedural and substantive issues in argument. So, questions of jurisdiction and admissibility were heard within the framework of the pleadings on the merits. See Art 31, Rules of the Court.

revolve round a series of intersecting sovereignties which the court was obliged to arrange into some sort of hierarchical scheme.

First, there is the original dispute over the extent of Australia's, Portugal's and Indonesia's territorial sovereignties in the Timor Sea. Indonesia's sovereign writ is obviously questionable on a number of grounds but even in the absence of the East Timor issue a dispute was always likely to arise. This is because the Timor Gap is the area in which Indonesian and Australian territorial claims overlap.

Secondly, there are the competing sovereign claims of the East Timorese and the Indonesians. What degree of sovereignty does East Timor possess as a non-self-governing territory? Is permanent sovereignty over natural resources an element of territorial sovereignty? Is it a lesser degree of sovereignty? Can Indonesia's sovereign claims to East Timor rest on the annexation of 1975 or must it have firmer juridical foundations? What degree of sovereignty does Indonesia possess in East Timor? Is it full territorial sovereignty? Is it a sovereignty compromised and diminished by the manner of acquisition and the continuing international disapproval?

Thirdly, Australia's sovereignty is implicated in a number of ways. Is Australia's sovereign right to enter into treaties with other sovereign powers in any way limited by the rules of international law or by the moral claims of self-determination peoples? The degree to which Australia can exercise sovereignty in its external affairs is a factor in evaluating the legality of the Timor Gap Treaty and the legality of Australia's recognition of Indonesian sovereignty over East Timor.

Finally, there is the question of the extent of Indonesia's sovereign right to claim immunity from court proceedings in which its actions are at issue. The indispensability or otherwise of Indonesia rests on an assessment of the scope of its sovereignty. An analysis of this area has been undertaken in the previous section. As Judge Shahabuddeen acknowledges in his separate opinion in the *East Timor Case* the application of this particular doctrine is complicated by the fact of intersecting sovereignties. Such doctrines are likely to become increasingly important to the court because 'the increasingly complex character of international relations, legal disputes between states are rarely purely bilateral'.[24]

I would now like to turn in more detail to the first and second of these four areas in order to demonstrate just how complex this issue of overlapping sovereignties can be.

Overlapping Sovereigns: Portuguese and Australian Claims to the Timor Gap

Portugal's claim to possess exclusive treaty-making power on behalf of East Timor is challenged by both Australia and Indonesia. Indonesia, of course, argues that its sovereignty over East Timor and attached continental shelf areas is unlimited. Australia, meanwhile, argues that its sovereign rights to the Timor Gap do not depend on the legal status of East Timor but that as a matter of practicality it was obliged to treat with the party in effective sovereign control of the northern part of the Timor Gap, that is, Indonesia.

Portugal's sovereignty is based on a series of UN resolutions declaring it to be the administering power over East Timor. However, Portuguese sovereignty can be questioned on a number of grounds. First, there is the argument that Portugal

---

24   Shahabuddeen, Separate Opinion at 1.

abandoned East Timor in 1974. Secondly, there is the possibility that United Nations Security Council and General Assembly resolutions in 1975, 1976 and 1977 are implicit denials of continuing Portuguese sovereignty over East Timor.[25] Third, there is the argument that Portugal, because of its history of colonial rule in East Timor, is barred from taking any future interest in the dispute.

The argument that Portugal ceased to be the administering power when it abandoned East Timor in 1974 is difficult to sustain. The problem with this position is that it is based on the premise that administering powers have rights but not duties. The whole scheme of the trusteeship and non-self-governing territories system is directed at imposing obligations on the powers whose task it is to administer these territories. It would be strange if Portugal could repudiate a legal duty simply by abandoning the territory in question. It is surely the United Nations, the body in charge of administering the overall system, that determines the status and obligations of the administering power. Indeed, the facts hardly support the notion of abandonment anyway. The Portuguese retreated from East Timor under the twin threat of East Timorese social chaos and Indonesian military hegemony.

However, the Australians argued that the United Nations *had* implicitly terminated the administration arrangement in East Timor by failing to reiterate Portugal's status in Timor. This second argument is one endorsed in the Separate Opinion of Judge Oda. He notes that no UN General Assembly resolution since 1976 has mentioned Portugal's role as an administering power in East Timor and that, 'The United Nations when dealing with the problem of East Timor since 1976 has never indicated that Portugal should have right and the duty to administer this area as a Non-Self-Governing territory' (para 17). He then goes on to pointedly assert that Portugal entirely lacks standing in the present dispute because, 'it did not have any authority over the region of East Timor' (para 19). Thus, according to Oda, Portugal's sovereignty over East Timor has been completely extinguished since 1975.

There are several assumptions made in Oda's Separate Opinion that require scrutiny. The first is that the physical facts of control are somehow coterminous with the exercise of legitimate sovereignty. Simply because Portugal does not appear to be the coastal state north of Australia does not mean that it cannot enjoy the legal rights of administration. The second assumption, that UN Resolutions cease to have any legal effect with the passage of time, is equally flawed. Nowhere in the Charter or in customary law is there an indication that such resolutions lose their legal effect after a period of 20 years.[26] Security Council Resolutions imposing peace-keeping operations and calling for peaceful settlement of disputes continue to have effect years after they are adopted. Judge Oda's opinion that Portugal lacks standing is contradictory given his recognition that in 1982 the General Assembly called on all parties concerned (including Portugal) to begin exploring a settlement of the dispute. These consultations continue under UN auspices with Portugal playing a leading role.[27]

---

25 S/RES/389 (1976); A/RES/31/53 (1976); A/RES/32/34 (1977). See Judge Oda, Separate Opinion, at 2.

26 'The Status of East Timor ... is a status defined by the law of the United Nations. Unilateral acts – by Portugal during the dictatorship period, and now by Indonesia since 1975 and by the few States which grant recognition – have had and continue to have no primacy over that law', Judge Skubiszewski, Dissenting Judgment at para 116.

27 See, for example, UN Doc SG/SM/5519 of 9 January 1995.

If Portugal has 'no authority over the region (of East Timor)', one wonders why the United Nations continues to accept the credentials of this former European colonial power. It is surely much more likely that the initial resolutions on East Timor remain in force and with them Portugal's role as administering power. A number of UN General Assembly and Security Council Resolutions reject the claim that East Timor has been integrated into Indonesia. The United Nations cannot have meant to imply that both Indonesian and Portuguese involvement was illegal. This would leave an unprecedented vacuum of sovereignty in the territory.

Judge Oda's separate opinion, like the majority judgment on indispensable third parties, embodies a dangerous anti-formalist reading of international law. In this instance the replacement of the lawful administrator by an invading state creates a new legal situation. Thus, it is the facts of physical control that are deemed to have priority over legal instruments and relationships.

The third and final challenge to Portugal's sovereign rights relies on the facts of Portugal's own poor colonial record. According to this line of thought Portugal's maltreatment of the East Timorese throughout over three centuries of imperial domination precludes them from raising an action on behalf of the East Timorese as administering power. There is little doubt that Portugal's behaviour in East Timor before the Carnation Revolution in 1974 was reprehensible. However, it would be unfortunate if the East Timorese were made to suffer twice for this. Clearly, Portugal's actions on behalf of the East Timorese, providing they are made in good faith, cannot be impugned on the grounds that Portugal once exploited the East Timorese. Indeed, the Security Council accepted this argument in Security Council Resolution 384 when it censured Portuguese colonialism but continued to recognise its role as administering power. The relationship between the administering power and the non-self-governing territory is a fiduciary one.

Indonesia's sovereignty is discussed in the next section because of its obvious links to East Timor's claims to self-determination.

Degrees of Sovereignty: East Timor's Right to Self-Determination

The degree of sovereignty possessed by the East Timorese people has been the subject of much debate. Indeed, the history of East Timor is one in which sovereignty over the territory of East Timor has undergone a number of changes. The language of international law has both articulated these changes and legitimised them.

Before Portuguese conquest there are two ways of viewing the relationship between sovereignty and East Timor. The first perceives Timor through the lens of classical international law as a territory lacking government, legal system and social organisation. Timor is therefore terra nullius or unoccupied land. Crucially, the commencement of Portuguese colonisation is seen here as merely an occupation or discovery of empty land. A second, more historically accurate but legally questionable, view recognises the prior existence of a people on Timor prior to Portuguese invasion. The Portuguese occupation then becomes a conquest. According to this second view we have a transfer of sovereignty whereas the classical position imagines the introduction of sovereignty to hitherto uninhabited territory.

Regardless of the position taken above, there is no doubt that Portugal was regarded in international law as exercising full sovereignty over East Timor between the 16th century and 1960. In 1960, the United Nations General Assembly passed resolution 1542 which placed East Timor on the list of non-self-governing territories. At this point Portuguese sovereignty was modified. While Portugal retains the formal trappings of sovereignty as well as practical dominance in Timor itself, the East Timorese, for the first time, are given some recognition as a 'people' in international law. This can be conceived of as an acknowledgment of incipient East Timorese sovereignty over their own territory. The expectation of the United Nations in such cases is that, first, that the people come to exercise full sovereignty at some point in the future; and, secondly, that the present sovereign (in this case Portugal) prepare the territory for eventual independence.

When Portugal physically eventually left East Timor in 1974, there was a period in which the territory lacked an effective sovereign. It is important to recognise, however, that at no time during the period 1974-1975, nor since, has Portuguese sovereignty over East Timor been extinguished by the United Nations. It is arguable, however, that actual, effective control then passed to the East Timorese themselves or at least their representative government, Fretilin. A radical reading of the law of self-determination might indeed view the Fretilin government as the legitimate sovereign during the period after the departure of Portugal and before the Indonesian invasion.

The invasion itself was an attempt to impose a new sovereign over East Timor. The various arguments supporting this assertion of sovereignty are canvassed in more detail below. However, even if one accepts that the Indonesian occupation was lawful, there is room to argue that sovereignty rested with the East Timorese in the period immediately before and after the invasion. This is a point implicitly accepted by the Indonesians when they suggest that the East Timorese people had both requested the invasion and subsequently endorsed it as an act of self-determination.

The Australian position is different from this. There seems to be an acceptance of a continuing right of self-determination on the part of the East Timorese people. However, the conceptual flaw in the Australian Government's position (as expressed in the case at least) is that sovereignty and self-determination are seen as entirely discrete principles. According to this approach both Indonesian sovereignty and East Timorese self-determination are capable of existing side by side. Can this be the case? In order to understand the limitations of this approach one has to appreciate the complexities of the law of self-determination.

Self-determination is unquestionably a political phenomenon. Perhaps because of this it has lacked a definitive meaning in international law for some years now. This has in turn threatened the principle with obsolescence. While the ICJ has invoked the principle in some of its decisions the court has failed to arrest the principle's slide into legal indeterminacy.[28]

The ICJ has considered the issue of self-determination on several occasions in the past 25 years. The three major elements of the analysis here will concern respectively the existence of the right to self-determination; the potential beneficiaries of the right in international law;[29] and the possible qualifications on the exercise of that right.

---

28   For a general analysis of these issues, see Simpson (1996).

29   Closely associated with this second point is the legal relationship between a trust territory and an administering power no longer in physical possession of the territory. This is a matter of procedure rather than substance in that it goes to the *standing* of Portugal to bring the case on behalf of East Timor.

Existence of a Principle of Self-Determination

The question of whether the right to self-determination exists at international law is well settled. There are numerous ICJ decisions, United Nations declarations and human rights treaties confirming the existence of a right to self-determination.[30] In the *Namibia Advisory Opinion*,[31] where the ICJ first considered the issue, the court found that:

> [T]he subsequent development of international law in regard to non-self-governing territories, as enshrined in the Charter of the United Nations, made the principle of self-determination applicable to all Nations.[32]

This position was subsequently fortified in the *Western Sahara Case* where Judge Dillard recognised that:

> [A] norm of international law has emerged applicable to the decolonization of those non-self-governing territories which are under the aegis of the United Nations.[33]

Unfortunately, in the very case in which the ICJ discussed self-determination at greatest length, it arguably failed to advance the law. The most quoted phrase from the case is Judge Dillard's reminder that, 'it is for the people to decide the territory and not the territory the people'.[34] The epigrammatic appeal of this phrase is not matched by its utility. Any attempt to apply it to a concrete situation reveals its limitations immediately. It is unclear just how one would go about applying this formula in Krajina or Bosnia. In Toynbee's pithy phrase 'this is the statement of the problem not the solution' (Toynbee, 1925: 317).

In the more recent Frontier Dispute Case (*Burkino Faso v Mali*),[35] the ICJ again had cause to consider self-determination and, in particular, the relationship of self-determination to the right of states to their territorial integrity. In doing so, the court reaffirmed the existence of a principle of self-determination at international law but again declined to suggest limits on the exercise of such a right.

It is clear from these cases, reinforcing as they do a multitude of United Nations instruments, that arguments concerning the *status* of the principle have been laid to rest. This is confirmed by the weight of state practice during the period of decolonization when a billion people were liberated under the banner of self-determination. However, if its status is secure, the same cannot be said of the *scope* or potential application of the principle. Particularly problematic is its relationship

---

30 See, for example, Declaration on the Granting of Independence to Colonial Countries and Peoples, GA Res 1514, Dec 15, 1960, UN GAOR 15th Sess, Supp (No 16) at 66, UN Doc A/L323 (1960); GA Res 1541, UN GAOR, 15th Sess, Supp No 16. at 29, UN Doc A./4684 (1960) (Principles which should guide Members in determining whether or not an obligation exists to transmit the information called for under Art 73(e) of the Charter). The Declaration on Principles of International Law concerning Friendly Relations and Co-operation among States in accordance with the Charter of the United Nations GA Res 2625, UN GAOR, 25th Sess, Supp No 28 at 122, UN Doc.A/8028 (1970); The International Covenant on Civil and Political Rights, Dec 16, 1966, GA Res 2200A (XXI), 999 UNTS 171 [hereinafter ICCPR] and The International Covenant on Economic, Social and Cultural Rights, 16 December 1966, GA Res 2200A (XXI), 993 UNTS 3.

31 *Legal Consequences for States of the Continued Presence of South Africa in Namibia (South West Africa)*, Advisory Opinion, 1971, ICJ. 16.

32 At 31.

33 *Western Sahara*, ICJ Reports 1975, 39 at 122.

34 Judge Dillard, Separate Opinion, at 122.

35 *The Case Concerning the Frontier Dispute (Burkino Faso v Mali)*, 1986, 4 ICJ 554 at 566-67.

to other principles of international law with which it may come into conflict such as the norm requiring the maintenance of states' territorial integrity.

However, the most complex issue of all, and one that must be addressed next in relation to East Timor, can be encapsulated in one of the most frequently asked question in international law, namely, who is entitled to exercise the right to self-determination?

Beneficiaries of the Right to Self-determination

The question of beneficiaries or legitimate claimants to the right of self-determination has been a thorny one for the international community since Woodrow Wilson coined the term in the post-World War I reconstruction of Europe. The application of the principle has been notoriously selective and occasionally ill-fated (Yugoslavia was one of Wilson's early 'successes'). Somewhat prophetically, Lansing, Wilson's Secretary of State described self-determination as a principle 'loaded with dynamite' (Wells, 1963: 45).

Self-determination entered its most dynamic phase in the 1960s and 1970s when it became associated exclusively with the process of decolonization. As colonial empires crumbled, the right to self-determination ascended the normative scale in international law to the point where it was ascribed peremptory status by the international community (see Hannakainan, 1988: 381-84). However, when it became apparent that self-determination had become the favourite slogan of every self-respecting national liberation movement, the spectre of disintegration and secession was raised.

The problem of definition has dogged self-determination ever since.[36] The apparent absurdity of denying self-determination to the Biafrans while invoking it for the Palestinians has never been confronted. The most recent wave of self-determination claims (successful and unsuccessful) from South Ossetia to Slovenia and Quebec to Kazhakstan has served to reveal the ambiguity of the ideal as a legal norm. Successive attempts to delimit the application of the principle have in effect been exercises in damage control. Lansing's dynamite has threatened to explode our very notions of state sovereignty.

The right claimed by East Timor is, however, sui generis. There are complications but these can be considered in isolation from revolutionary chaos elsewhere in the world. A decision here may have few implications for secessionist claims in Europe or the rest of Asia. In common with most self-determination movements, but with significantly greater legal justification, the East Timorese regard themselves as exceptional. In contrast to those of Slovenia, Quebec, Bougainville and countless other secessionist entities, East Timor's right to self-determination has been confirmed by the United Nations both as part of the trusteeship process (it remains on the Decolonization Committee's list) and in the General Assembly Resolutions passed following the Indonesian invasion. In addition to this, the Security Council has passed two resolutions on the Indonesian invasion re-asserting East Timor's right to self-determination.[37]

---

36   For a critical analysis of these efforts, see Cass (1992: 21-40).

37   Security Council Resolutions are binding under Art 25 of the United Nations Charter.

The right to self-determination from colonial rule is a norm of *jus cogens* in international law. Its existence is undisputed. Indeed the problems associated with self-determination are related to the extension of the principle beyond the colonial context. Within the colonial context, its applicability has been relatively uncontroversial. On the face of it, the East Timorese issue falls squarely within this context. East Timor has been classified as a non-self-governing territory by the United Nations. Regardless of ambiguities in other areas of the law one facet of the principle is universally accepted, namely that non-self-governing peoples are entitled to a right of self-determination.

The questions then become: is this right qualified in any way by special circumstances (for example, the passage of time or the existence of other countervailing principles of international law) and what is the nature of the duty correlative to this right of self-determination?

These problems in turn raise a number of procedural and historical questions. For example, does a right of self-determination, once declared by the UN, continue indefinitely? Does the original colonial state retain its rights as the administering power? Have the East Timorese already exercised their right to self-determination and chosen integration with Indonesia, as the Indonesians claim? To further complicate matters some writers have argued that East Timor is merely a colonial enclave and that the Indonesians possess a right to reabsorb a small area of territory that is geographically contiguous to it (Fonteyne, 1991: 176).[38] Finally, there is the principle of *uti possidetis*.[39] Does it have any application to the present situation?

In discussing some of these issues I want to imagine three ways of conceptualising the East Timorese right to self-determination. In what might be termed the classic colonial paradigm where a people seeks self-determination from a European imperial power, the right to self-determination is unconditional. It is evident that East Timor fell squarely into this category in 1975. Nevertheless, the waters in the East Timor Case have been muddied by the replacement of the classic colonial ruler (Portugal) by the regional imperium (Indonesia). This raises several possibilities.

- First, it could be concluded that East Timor's legal status cannot have undergone a change simply by virtue of its occupation by a different alien power and that it remains a colony in the most restrictive and legally compelling sense. On this view, East Timor possesses a right to self-determination that parallels that of Nigeria's or Algeria's or Mozambique's during the 1950s and 60s.

- Alternatively, it might be argued that East Timor is no longer subject to 'colonial rule' since Indonesia is not a colonial empire. In legal terms, this would mean a denial that East Timor was subject to 'alien subjugation, domination and exploitation'.[40] Accordingly, East Timor would simply no longer possess a right to self-determination from colonial rule under customary international law (*lex lata*) and that what in fact the East Timorese are claiming is a right to secede from the Indonesian state. It is

---

38   See also, Crawford, (1979: 377-85) for a discussion of enclaves. He excludes East Timor from this category.

39   See *Frontier Dispute Case*, above. This meaning of this term and the implications of the doctrine are explained below.

40   The classic statement of this type of self-determination can be found in the *Declaration on the Granting of Independence to Colonial Peoples* (1960), GA Res 1514, above.

contended that this right is at best a right *de lege ferenda* and would never have been accepted by the ICJ given the absence of supporting state practice and the frequently explicit condemnation of secession within the international community.[41]

- Finally, there is the intermediate position which argues that East Timor retains a legitimate right *or claim* to self-determination but that this right must now be qualified by competing principles of international law, notably Indonesia's claim to its territorial integrity.

To return to the first position, the contention that East Timor's legal situation remains unchanged regardless of Indonesia's occupation is a powerful one. The United Nations and Security Council have passed numerous resolutions affirming East Timor's right to self-determination and condemning the Indonesian invasion. East Timor continues to be regarded as a non-self-governing territory at the United Nations and Portugal as the administering power for the purposes of Chapter XI of the United Nations Charter. Nonetheless, the international community's attitude has been modified over the years. While the Indonesian annexation has been recognised by few states (Australia is one of them) there has been a tacit recognition by many more states of Indonesia's sovereignty over East Timor. Whether these examples of realpolitik have been converted into a state practice possessing juridical significance is open to question.[42] In addition, the most recent UN General Assembly Resolution affirming East Timor's right to self-determination was in 1982.[43] It has been argued that this indicates a weakening of resolve on the issue and perhaps a recognition by the international community that other principles of international law have intervened with the passage of time. None of these arguments is particularly compelling but they serve to illustrate the complexities of the issue.

Ultimately, it would seem incontrovertible that East Timor possesses a right to self-determination of some description; and that this has legal implications greater than those of a political claim to secession. The United Nations has never accepted that East Timor is a secessionist dispute falling exclusively within Indonesia's domestic jurisdiction under Art 2(7) of the United Nations Charter. Therefore the second argument outlined above must necessarily fail.[44]

This leaves the third possibility that East Timor's right to self-determination has in some way been qualified by other principles of international law. Judge Petren, in a separate opinion in the Western Sahara Case, states:

> [A] veritable law of decolonization is in the course of taking shape ... [B]ut in certain specific cases, one must equally take into account the principle of national unity and integrity of states.[45]

---

41 The most famous example of this attitude can be found in a speech given by the then Secretary-General of the United Nations, U Thant, during the Biafran crisis in Nigeria in the late 1960s. See Nayar (1975: 330).

42 Most of the recognising states have been motivated by economic self-interest (the need to trade with Indonesia) or by the fear that their minorities might also agitate for secession.

43 GA Res 37/30 (1982).

44 It is probably the case that if the United Nations system is to operate in a meaningful way then there must be some method of distinguishing the two types of secession/self-determination.

45 *Western Sahara*, at 110.

Qualifications on the Right to Self-Determination

The three most likely, though still improbable, counterweights to the East Timorese right to self-determination are: first, Indonesia's right to territorial integrity (or a variation of the principle of *uti posseditis*); secondly, the proposition that East Timor represents an enclave at international law; and, finally, the argument that East Timor belongs to Indonesia by virtue of certain historical ties.[46]

Indonesia's Territorial Integrity, and the Principle of Uti Possidetis

Without doubt, the right of states to territorial integrity represents one of the fundamental norms of international law.[47] However, there are two conceptually discrete principles at work here. First, there is the standard doctrine of state sovereignty enunciated in Art 2(4) and (7) of the United Nations Charter. Each state within the international legal system is entitled to an area of exclusive or reserve jurisdiction under Art 2(7) and (4) no use of force is permitted 'against the territorial integrity or political independence' of a state.

This specific right to the fruits of statehood is merely the statement of a broader policy which informs the international legal system. International law is an inherently conservative system of rules dedicated to maintaining stability in the international order. The commitment to the maintenance of borders and territorial stability is native to the Charter system.[48] Hence the ambivalence towards the principle of self-determination. The need to preserve the integrity of states has proved a powerful counteracting force against the revolutionary and secessionist urges of individual groups. Whatever the moral or political claims of post-colonial self-determination movements, the law has been resolute in its rejection of them. The names make for a tragic and familiar litany to international lawyers working in this area: Kurdistan, Tibet, Aceh, Southern Sudan, Biafra. In the particular case of

---

46   The Indonesians also make two further arguments. First, they assert that the East Timorese have already exercised self-determination and that the integration of East Timor with Indonesia was in fact an expression of popular self-determination. Ali Alatas, the present Indonesian foreign minister argued this position forcefully at an address he gave to the Press Club in Washington DC in 1992. He stated 'Although the Indonesian people welcomed the expressed desire of the East Timorese people for integration, the Government declared that it would not accede to it until after a proper exercise of self-determination had been conducted. Hence, a provisional People's Assembly of East Timor was formed. ... In the capital city of Dili on May 31, 1976, this Assembly, in a public session ... formally cast its vote to choose independence through integration with the Republic of Indonesia' (Indonesian News, 1992: 20). President Soeharto himself has been quoted as saying 'Its the East Timorese themselves who *chose to be independent* (my emphasis) together with Indonesia. Hence we could not reject their plea' (The Age, 1992b). Professor Roger Clark (1980: 12-18) comprehensively disposes of these argument on the basis of historical evidence and United Nations practice and requirements in relation to acts of decolonization. Secondly, the Indonesians argue that East Timor is part of Indonesia by virtue of its close proximity with the Indonesian archipelago. This argument, sometimes called the right to retrocession, has virtually never been accepted by the United Nations or the world community, whether it be raised by the Argentinians in defence of their invasion of the Falklands in 1982 or Iraq in support of its claim to Kuwait in 1990. It is worth noting here that after the Dili massacre Indonesian President Soeharto made the remarkable claim that Indonesia never wanted East Timor in the first place (The Age, 1992a).

47   See, for example, United Nations Charter, Art 2(4); 1970 Declaration on Friendly Relations, GA Res 2625.

48   This explains the commitment shown by states towards ICJ adjudication in matters concerning border disputes and continental shelf delimitation.

Biafra, the position of the international community was clarified in 1970 by the United Nations Secretary-General at the time, U Thant who warned:

> As far as the question of secession is ... concerned, the United Nations' attitude is unequivocable [sic]. As an international organization, the United Nations has never accepted and does not accept and I do not believe it will ever accept the principle of secession of a part of its Member State (Nayar, 1975: 330).

This attitude was reflected in the prevarication surrounding the recognition of the republics of the former USSR and Yugoslavia. Nevertheless, new states have been recognised. Arguably, a new right to self-determination has arisen beyond the colonial context, one that can be applied to entitles as diverse as Slovenia, Georgia and Eritrea.[49]

East Timor's right to self-determination, of course, belongs to a different category from that of, say, the unsuccessful Biafran secession and the, ultimately, successful Slovenian independence movement. In particular, its relationship to Indonesia's territorial integrity is more complicated.

The ICJ has constantly reaffirmed the normative pre-eminence of the right to territorial integrity in international law most notably in the Nicaragua (Merits) decision. The relationship of territorial integrity to the principle of self-determination has also been explored. It is clear that the right to self-determination in the colonial context cannot be derogated from on the basis of a need to preserve territorial integrity, for example, it is absurd to suggest that Angola had no right to self-determination in, say, 1970 on the grounds that its exercise would fracture Portugal's territorial sovereignty.

However, Indonesia's claim to territorial integrity now may be much stronger than was Portugal's in 1970 simply by virtue of its proximity to East Timor and the fact that Indonesia is not a European power. Indonesia does not possess the typical indices of a colonial power and so is often not recognised as such. Portugal was a classic metropole, geographically distant and practising the form of exploitative colonialism distinctive to European powers. Indonesia, on the other hand, is often regarded as a champion of self-assertion in the developing world and a pathological enemy of imperialism. This has resulted in a marked reluctance to describe Indonesia using the unflattering dialect of anti-colonialism.

Nevertheless, I would suggest that the principle of *uti possidetis*, often associated with, and occasionally mistakenly thought to be synonymous with the principle of territorial integrity (see Franck, 1992: 25 note 53) in fact directs the ICJ to declare Indonesia's territorial integrity irrelevant in this particular case. *Uti possidetis* is the principle, articulated by the ICJ in the Frontier Dispute Case, whereby states become independent within existing colonial boundaries. It is often used as an argument for preserving the integrity of the newly independent colonial unit from further acts of self-determination, for example, Krajina from Croatia or, most notoriously, Biafra from Nigeria.

However, and this is the significant point for our purposes, the principle yields a duty correlative to this right. Newly created states while protected from secession must in return as Rosalyn Higgins (1992: 7) puts it, 'forfeit any historical claim they might aspire to regarding territories now held within old colonial boundaries'.

So, while *uti possidetis juris* may be an ally to Indonesia in its arguments against Aceh or Ambonese independence, it is wholly at odds with its absorption of East Timor into the Indonesian state. The principle already affirmed by the ICJ in

---

49   See Cass (1992).

the *Frontier Dispute Case* disbars Indonesia, a former Dutch colony, from laying claim to territories within the former Portuguese empire.

Enclaves in International Law

The arguments relating to enclaves and historical ties possess more ingenuity than they do merit. It is contended by some international lawyers that certain colonial entities are so small and insignificant that the United Nations will sanction their incorporation into a larger, usually contiguous, state.[50] The examples offered in support of this view are India's absorption of Goa and the Moroccan incorporation of Ifni.[51] In neither case, however, did the United Nations expressly condemn these actions. By contrast, both Security Council and the General Assembly have made it clear that East Timor is not an enclave but contains instead a people entitled to a right to self-determination. To suggest that East Timor belongs in this historically obscure category is to engage in academic sophistry.

Much the same can be said for historical ties.[52] In the *Western Sahara Case*, the ICJ investigated the existence of historical ties but even after having found them did not think they were of much relevance to Western Sahara's right to self-determination. Ultimately, it appears that East Timor's right to self-determination is unassailable.

This is indeed what the court concluded in a very carefully worded obiter which made it clear that East Timor continues to possess a right to self-determination as a non-self-governing territory. Interestingly, in a case which turned wholly on a technical procedural issue the court nevertheless takes care to affirm the East Timorese rights in the final paragraph of the judgment. It is critical to understand, then, that the court has neither validated Indonesia's invasion nor Australia's subsequent practice in relation to that invasion. Instead, it has issued a subtle reminder that this case represents neither the beginning nor the end of the East Timorese quest for meaningful self-determination.

Conclusion

So where does East Timorese self-determination go from here? In humanitarian terms the situation in East Timor remains grim. The United Nations Special

---

50   There is a further argument to the effect that East Timor is too small to be an independent state and furthermore lacks economic viability. The first limb of this argument is based on an erroneous reading of the Montevideo Convention on the Rights and Duties of States (1933) which establishes a definition of statehood that includes 'the capacity to enter into relations with other states' (Art 1(d)). Providing East Timor has independence and an effective government it will, according to principles of customary international law, possess sufficient capacity to meet the requirements of statehood. The absence of recognition in 1975 after the Declaration of Independence by The East Timorese Fretilin Government was a product of the perception that the Timorese lacked a government in effective control of the territory (Montevideo Convention Art 1(a)). In any event, East Timor is larger and more economically viable (especially if the hydrocarbon reserves in the Timor Gap are taken into account) than many existing states, for example, Nauru (pop 100,000), Micronesia and San Marino.

51   See Fonteyne (1991: 176)

52   The claims of the Indonesian Governments in this regard are outlined in Clark (1980: 20-21).

Rapporteur in 1994 remarked on 'the atmosphere of fear and suspicion currently prevailing in East Timor'.[53] On the other hand, there is sense that the Indonesian government would like to dislodge 'the stone in its shoe'. One suggestion is that East Timor may acquire special region status within Indonesia or *daerah istimewa*, a possibility reiterated recently by Indonesia's new President, Dr BJ Habibie and even increased to autonomy within the Republic. This option may, however, not be that useful given the unsatisfactory experience of the Aceh province under such an arrangement. Meanwhile, the UN Supervised Dialogue between Portugal, Indonesia and the various East Timorese groups trundles on.

Interestingly, the decision in the case may have benefited the East Timorese despite the apparently disappointing result. I predicted some time ago that:

> [A] defeat for Portugal in this case will be potentially traumatic for the East Timorese. Indonesia is likely to seize on such an outcome as a vindication of its policies in East Timor over the past eighteen years (Simpson, 1993: 347).

I was perhaps unduly pessimistic. The outcome of the World Court proceedings has certainly bruised some Portuguese egos but it seems to have heightened awareness in the Australian Government of the need to reach some sort of resolution in East Timor. Equally, the Timorese community has found plenty to cheer about in the judgment. Their rights to self-determination and sovereignty over natural resources are reaffirmed even if the enjoyment of these rights remains as distant a prospect as ever.

References

The Age, 1991a, '15 Minutes to Death', 16 November.

The Age, 1991b, 13 December.

The Age, 1991c, 'Conclusions of the Inquiry into The Dili Killings', 28 December.

The Age, 1992a, 'We never wanted Timor: Suharto', 11 January.

The Age, 1992b, 11 January.

The Age, 1993, 28 May.

Alatas, Ali, 1992, 'East Timor: De-Bunking The Myths Around a Process of Decolonization', *Indonesian News*, 20 March.

Australian Senate Standing Committee on Foreign Affairs and Defence, 1983, *Human Rights and the Condition of the People of East Timor*, AGPS, Canberra.

Baker, M, 1992, 'Timor rebellion is far from over', *Melbourne Age*, 14 December.

Cass, Deborah Z, 1992, 'Rethinking Self-Determination: A Critical Analysis', 18 *Syracuse Journal of International Law and Commerce*, vol 18: 21-40.

Clark, R, 1981, 'Does the Genocide Convention Go Far Enough? Some Thoughts on the Nature of Criminal Genocide in the Context of Indonesia's Invasion of East Timor', *Ohio Northern University Law Review*, vol 8: 321-28.

Clark, R, 1980, 'The "Decolonization" of East Timor and the United Nations Norms on Self-Determination and Aggression', *Yale Journal of World Public Order*, vol 7, no 1.

Crawford, J, 1979, *The Creation of States*, Clarendon Press, Oxford.

Department of Foreign Affairs and Trade, 1995, *Briefing Papers on Portugal v Australia*, Parliamentary and Media Branch, July.

Elliot, P, 1978, 'The East Timor Dispute', *International and Comparative Law Quarterly*, vol 27: 238-49.

Franck, T and Hoffman, P, 1976, 'The Right to Self-determination in Very Small Places', *New York Journal of Law and Politics*, vol 8: 331-86.

---

53   Report by the Special Rapporteur, Bacre Waly Ndiaye, on his mission to Indonesia and East Timor from 3 July to 13 July, I November, E/CN.4/1995/61/Add.1, I November 1994.

Franck, T, 1992, 'The Evolution of the Right to Self-Determination', Proceedings of the *Second Amsterdam International Law Conference on the Rights of Peoples and Minorities in International Law*, 18-20 June.

Fonteyne, JP, 1991, 'The Portuguese Timor Gap Litigation Before the International Court of Justice against Australia: A Brief Appraisal of Australia's Position', *Australian Journal of International Affairs*, 45: 170, 170-79.

Guardian Weekly, 1993, 6 June.

Hannakainan, 1988, *Peremptory Norms in International Law,* Finnish Lawyers Publishing Co.

Higgins, R, 1992, 'The Evolution of the Right to Self-Determination: Commentary on Professor Franck's Paper', *Proceedings of the Second Amsterdam International Law Conference on the Rights of Peoples and Minorities in International Law*, 18-20 June.

Horta, Jose Ramos, 1987, *Funu: The Unfinished Saga of East Timor*, copy in possession of the author.

Human Rights in East Timor and the Question of the Use of US Equipment by the Indonesian Armed Forces: Hearings Before the Subcommittee on International Organizations and on Asian and Pacific Affairs of the Committee on International Relations, 95th Cong, 1st Sess 1 (19 July 1977).

Inside Indonesia, 1991, no 29, December.

Joint Letter from Members of the US Congress and the Japanese Diet, Interparliamentary Human Rights Program, 1992.

Missing Peace, 1993, no 6, June

Nayar, K, 1975 'Self-determination Beyond the Colonial Context: Biafra in Retrospect', *Texas International Law Journal*, vol 10: 321-45.

Simpson, G, 1993, 'Judging the East Timor Dispute: Self-Determination at the World Court', *Hastings International and Comparative Law Review*, vol 17, no 3: 323-47.

Simpson, G, 1995a, 'Indispensable Sovereigns: Third and Fourth Parties in the Timor Gap Treaty Case at the World Court', *ILA, Marin House Papers* vol 4: 75-92.

Simpson, G, 1995b, 'The Timor Gap Treaty Case at the World Court', 28 *International Law News*: 43-49.

Simpson, G, 1996, 'The Diffusion of Sovereignty: Self-Determinations in the Post-Colonial Age', *Stanford Journal of International Law*, vol 32, no 2: 255-86.

Stahl, M, 1992, Procession of Death, *Observer*, 14 January.

Tapol Bulletin, 1991, no 108, December.

Testimony of Shepard Forman, Human Rights in East Timor, House of Reps, Subcommittee on International Organizations, Committee on International Relations, June 28, 1977.

Timor Link, 1992, no 22, February.

Toynbee, A, 1925, 'Self-determination', *The Quarterly Review*, vol 484: 317-38.

Walsh, P, 1990, 'Timor Gap: Oil Poured on Bloodied Waters', *Arena*, 90: 12-14.

Washington Post, 1991, 'A Wise Indonesia Would Deal With Mr Gusmao in a Political Process', 5 December.

Wells, B, 1963, *UN Decisions on Self-Determination*, University of Michigan, Microfiches.

Index

This index includes decided cases and international conventions.
References to all statutes may be found in the Table of Statutes on page xv
A glossary appears on page xxiii

A

Abbasids, 97
Abduh, Muhammad, 325
Abortion, at Islamic law, 167
ABRI (*Angkatan Bersenjata Republik Indonesia*), 197-198, 203-4, 206, 208, 213, 367, 370 (n 17), 375-79
    and administrative law, 224 (n 6)
    Dewan Kekaryaan, 212
    and *dwi fungsi*, 212, 226
    tensions with Soeharto, 212
Aceh, 2, 46 (n 11), 203, 208-9, 341, 344, 350, 395, 398
    election of governor of, 213-4
    independence of, 396
ACICA (Australian Centre for International Commercial Arbitration), 298
Adat, Chapters 4, 5, 12; 3-4, 6, 7, 12, 14, 34, 98, 99, 112, 114, 188-194, 231, 259, 342-3, 352, 364
    attitudes to, 47-49
    communities, 46-7
    concepts of land, 44-45
    Courts, 232
    and criminal law, Chapter 6
    definition, 42 (n 1)
    and developmentalism, 54-5
    and forest land, 62-4
    limits on, 51-4
    and nationalism, 49-51
    nature, 43-4
    and state land, 53-4
    See also *hak ulayat*; LAP
Adatrechtpolitiek, 232
Adatrechtskring, 125 (n 16)
Adi Agama, 116
Adil, Malikoel, 50
Adisumarta, RJ Kaptin, 253
Administrative Courts, Chapters 15 18 and 19; 161-72 (n 5), 179, 236 (n 16), 248 (n 10), 250
    interests protected by, 262
    natural justice in, 261-2
    procedural fairness in, 261-2
Administrative law, see Administrative Courts
Adultery, see *Zina*
Advocates, Chapter 16. See also *Peradin, Ikadin*
Africa, South, 383 (n 13)
Agreements, see Contracts
Agus, Abdul Latief, 334
Ahmad, Ziauddin, 331
Akhmadi, Heri, 195

Aksi sepihak, 52
Alatas, Ali, 395 (n 47)
Albania, 384
Al-Banna, Hasan, 324
Albrecht, JE, 35
Albright, Madelaine, 375
Alisjahbana, Sutan Takdir, 186, 189
Al-Mawat, 164
Al-Najjar, Sa'id, 326
Al-Namir, 'Abd al'Mun'im, 326
Al-Quff, Ibn, 161-2
Alternative dispute resolution, see Arbitration
Alting, JH Carpentier, 37
Al-Wadud, Abd, 161
Ambon, 45, 396
Anak daerah, 204, 206
Anas, Azwar, 334
Anderson, Benedict, 11, 235 (n 12)
Angkatan Bersenjata Republik Indonesia, see ABRI
An-Nai'm, A, 339, 352
Antara newspaper, 150
APEC, 279
Aqua case, 317
Arbitration, Chapter 21; 288. See also Convention
Argentina, 182
Aribowo, Tunky, 216
Aristotle, 161
Army, see ABRI
Artadi, I Ketut, 116
Arto, Soegih, 240
Asad, Muhammad, 326
Asas kekeluargaan, 18, 173, 180, 183, 259, 274
Asia Raya newspaper, 191
Asia Watch, 350, 375
Asian Law Centre, 282
ASPRI (Assisten Pribadi), 146
Astek, 376
Attamimi, Hamid S, 194
Australia, 280, 282, 288, 293 (n 9), 366
    and East Timor, Chapter 27
Aziz, M Amin, 334

B

Badan Koordinasi Bantuan Pemantapan Stabilitas Nasional, see BAKORSTANAS
Badan Pembinaan Hukum, see BPHN
Badan Pemerintah Harian, 207
Badan Peradilan Semu, 223
Badan Pertahanan Nasional, see BPN
Baduy, see Java, West
Bagus/Lily Ball case, 309 (n 31, 32)
Bahrain, 326
    Islamic Bank, 325
BAKORSTANAS, 180, 260, 350, 369, 370, 378
Bakrie, Abu Rizal, 334 (n 4) and see *Trading Corp of Pakistan* ...

Bali, 2, 45, 46 (n 11), 117 (n 19), 200, 341, 343
   adat, 114, 116
   Adi Agama, 116
Bandung, 5, 241
Bangladesh, 326
BANI (*Badan Arbitrase Naional Indonesia*), Chapter 21; 283
Banjarmasin, 98
Bank Muamalat Indonesia, Chapter 23
Bank Summa, 334
Bank, Mit Ghamr Savings, 325
Bank, Nasser Social, 325
Banking, Chapters 20, 23
Bappeda, 211
Bappenas, 54 (n 39), 215
Bastari, Captain, 148-156
Batak, 47, 91, 200
Batavia, 5
   Faculty of Law, 38
   See also, Jakarta
Basofi, 262
Batavian Republic, 222 (n 3)
Beamtenstaat, 171
Bekasi, 80
Benda-Beckmann, K von, 116 (n 16)
Berita Buana newspaper, 149
Berita Resmi Merek, 318
Berita Resmi Paten, 314
Berkeley Mafia, 8
Beschikkingsrecht, 45
Biafra, 396, 395
Bidara, Olden, 263
Biro Keuangan, 211
BKPM (*Badan Koordinasi Penanaman Modal*), 286
Blood, at Islamic law, 167-8
Bogor, 334, 370 (n 17)
   Declaration, 279
Bojonegoro, 149, 150
Bone, 206
BPHN, 129
BPN (*Badan Pertahanan Nasional*), 54 (text and n 39), 66, 68, 132 (n 62)
Brazil, 182
Budi Utomo, 5
Buku Putih, 146
Buleleng, 81
BULOG (*Badan Urusan Logistik) case*, 297 (text and n 24)
Bupati (Regent), 201, 202, 211-12
Burns, Peter, 342

C

Camat, 47, 201, 210
Cardin, Pierre, 315-6
Cassation, 104, 269, 275
Caturtunggal, 234
Censorship, see Chapter 19
Certainty, legal, 248-250

China, 33, 204
    Marriage Law, Chapter 3, esp 33, 36, 39-40
    People's Republic of (PRC), 285 (n 10), 287, 294
    Republic of, 33, 38
Chinese,
    business communities, 284
    colonial status of, Chapter 3
    trade marks, 316
Cianjur, 81
Cibogo, 236 (text and n 14)
Cirebon, 47
Clark, Roger, 395 (n 47)
Colombia, 182
Communism, 204 and see PKI
Company law, 286-7 (text and n 15-16)
Constitution
    1945, Chapters 11, 12; 6, 7, 15 (n 5), 16, 232-4, 259-60, 269, 283, 292 (n 5)
        foreign influences on, 18, Chapters11, 12, 15; 232-3
        and local autonomy, 201
        organs of government, Chapter 13
        social economy provisions, 18, 52
    1949 (federal), 6, 15 (n 5), 182, 201
    1950 (provisional), 6, 15 (n 5), 182
    See also, Federalism
Contraception, at Islamic law, 165-8
Contracts, Chapters 20 and 21
    joint venture, 282-3, 286-7
    technical Assistance, 282-3
    See also Franchising
Convention, International
    Berne, for the Protection of Literary and Artistic Works, 305
    Montevideo, on the Rights and Duties of States, 397 (n 51)
    New York, on the Recognition and Enforcement of Foreign Arbitral Awards, 288
    on the International Sale of Goods, 285 (n 11)
    Paris, for the Protection of Industrial Property, 1983, 305
    on the Political Rights of Women of 1958, 124
    of Rome, 1961, 307
    on the Settlement of Investment Disputes between States and Nationals of Other
        States (ICSID), 288 (n 21)
    on Trade-Related Aspects of Intellectual Property, 1993 (TRIPs), 305, 312, 316, 319
    WIPO (including Copyright and Trademark Treaties), 1979, 305
Copyright, Chapter 22
Corfu Channel case, 384 (text and n 16,
Corruption, judicial, Chapters 11, 16, 17, 18, 19, 24; 287-9, 293-4.
    See also Mafia pengadilan
Costa Rica, 385-6
Costa, da, Afonso Hendriques, 214
Council of Islamic Ideology, 328, 331
Courts, Chapters, 16, 17, 18 and 19; 288-9, 293-4
    Adat, see Adat
    Administrative, see Administrative Courts
    colonial, 231
    Islamic, see Syariah
    See also, Mahkamah Agung, Judiciary, Judicial Review
Criminal Law, Chapter 7, Chapters 24 and 25; 180, 238
Criminal procedure, Chapters 24 and 25

D

Daendles, Herman Willem, 3
Darul Islam, 203
Dawud, Abu, 164
Dayak, titles of, 55 (n 44) and see Kalimantan
Decentralisation, Chapters 14, 15
Desa, 47, 56, 201, 209
Detik magazine, 264, 272, 372
Detournement de pouvoir, 224
Development, 131; see also *Pembangunan*
Deventer, van, C Th, 37
Dewan Nasional, 204
Dewan Pemerintah Daerah, see DPD
Dewan Pers, Chapter 19
Dewan Perwakilan Rakyat, see DPR
Dewantara, Ki Hadjar, 259
Dewanto, 152
Dewi (murder victim), 145 (n 1), 154 (n 13)
Dharma Wanita, 131, 147-8
    Panca Dharma Wanita, 148
Dharsono, Lt Gen, 243
Dhukuh, 12, 56
Dietje, 153
Dili, 214, 382, 395 (n 47)
Dillard, Judge, 391
Diponegoro, 4
Dispute resolution, Chapters 20 and 21
District Court, see *Pengadilan negeri*
Djajadiningrat, Achmad, 40
Djaksanagoro, Sarwono, 193
Djokosutono, 192
Doughty, PL, 340
DPD (*Dewan Pemerintah Daerah*), Chapter 14
DPPD (*Dewan Penelitian Pengupahan Daerah*), 374
DPR (*Dewan Perwakilan Rakyat*), 19, 103, 122-3, 172 (text and n 4, 5), 173, 174, 179
    (ns 26, 27), 211 (n 36), 213 (n 41), 274, 374
    DPRD (*Dewan Perwakilan Rakyat Daerah*), Chapter 14
    structure and membership, Chapter 13; 223
Dubai Islamic bank, 325
Dunhill, Alfred, 315-6
Dwi fungsi, see ABRI

E

East Timor, see Timor
Economic growth, Introduction, Chapters 1 and 2; 291 (text and n 1)
Editor magazine, 264, 272, 372
Egypt, 169 (n 32), 326
Eigendom, 87
El Salvador, 182, 385-6
Elections, Chapter 13; 208-9
ELIPS project, 285 (n 11)
Embryo, at Islamic law, 169
Enlightenment, the, influence of, 186-195
ERA Hukum journal, 238, 242 (n 24)

Ethical policy, 4-5, 37 (text and n 6), 188
Execution of decisions, Chapter 17
Extra-marital sex, Chapter 6

F

Faisal Islamic Banks, 325
Falkland Islands, 395 (n 47)
Family planning, 165-66
Fasseur, Cees, 33-34 (notes), 37
Fatwa, 99, 105, 106, 139,
    in Malaysia, 164
    and medical science, see Chapter 10
FBSI (*Federasi Buruh Seluruh Indonesia*), 367-8
Federalism, Chapter 14
Fikh, 98, 99, 105-9, 122 (n 3), 125, 126, 129, 130 (n 49), 133, 139 (text and n 94), 140, 328
Fiqh, see *Fikh*
'Floating Mass' concept, 208
Flying Wheel case, 316 (n 61)
'Foreign orientals', Chapter 3; 4, 33
Forum Keadilan magazine, 238 (n 19)
Franchising, 286 (n 18)
Freeport, PT, 54
Freidman, Lawrence, 281
Fretilin, 390, 397 (n 51) and see generally, Chapter 27
Fromberg, PH, 37
Frontier Dispute case (Burkino Faso v Mali), 391, 393 (n 40)
Fruhling, F, 340
Fuehrer, see Germany
Furnivall, JS, 33-35

G

Gadjah Madah, 341
Gandasubrata, HR Purwoto S, 85, 240, 249, 253, 262
GATT (General Agreement on Tariffs and Trade), 305-6, 316, 319
Germany,
    influence on constitutional law, 174, Chapter 12
    and romanticism, Chapter 12
Gerwani (Gerakan Wanita Indonesia) 147
Gitosardjono, Sukamdani Sahid, 334 (n 4)
Globalisation and law, Chapter 20
Goa, 397
GOLKAR, 172 (ns 4, 5), 177 (text and n 18, 19), 212-15, 359
    and elections, Chapter 13, 208-9 (text and n 26), 212-15
Gotong-royong, 50, 52, 75, 192
Graaff, S de, 37
Graeff, ACD, 38, 39
Grafiti Pers, 273
Grimm, brothers, 187
    Jakob, 188, 192
Guatemala, 183
Guided Democracy (*Demokrasi Terpimpin*), 7, 175 (n 14), 176, 193, 205, 207, 229, 234, 235-6, 242, 357
Gusmao, Xanana, 382, 383 (n 13)
Gutto, Shadrack, 178

Index

H

Habibie, Dr Baharuddin Jusuf, 2, 9, 11, 16, 215, 219, 356, 362, 379, 398
    and ICMI, 334
    and Islamic banking, 323
    and *Tempo* case, 271-2
Hadith, 102, 166, 167
Hak milik, 49, 53, 88
Hak uji, see Judicial review
Hak Ulayat, Chapter 4, esp 45-6, 51 (n 30), 57-66, 67, 79, 86-7, 92
    definition of, 45
Hakam, 99
Hanafi, 99, 164
Hanbali, 99
Hanoch Hebe Ohee case, 251-3
Harahap, Tuti, 177 (n 18)
Haram, 165-6
Harmoko, 272-6
Harsono, Soni, 253
Hartarto, Hartini, 198
Hartato, 334 (n 4)
Hartono, General, 371
Hartono, Sunaryati, 285 (n 11)
Hasan, Mohamad (Bob), 334 (n 4)
Hasibuan, Albert, 177 (n 18)
Hatta, Mohammad, 5, 6, 191
Herzieningscommissie, 37
High Court, see *Pengadilan Tinggi*
Hills, Carla, 375
Himpunan Penasehat Hukum Indonesia (HPHI), 230 (text and n 4)
Hindu, Ibn, 161
Hoge Raad, 223-4
Homoud, Sami, 329
Honduras, 385-6
Hong Kong, 175, 285 (n 10), 294
Hoogerechtshof, 37
Hudud, 324
Hukum antargolongan, 4, 48(n 21)
Hukum dan Keadilian journal, 238 (n 19), 240 (n 23)
Hukum revolusi, 7, 233
Human rights, Chapters 24, 25, 26 and 27; 172, 273
Hurgronje, Snouke, 98
Hutomo Mandala Putra (Tommy), 334 (n 4). See also Timor, car

I

Ibrahim, Fauzi, 370
ICMI (*Ikatan Cendekiawan Muslim se-Indonesia*), 334
ICSID, see Convention
Idris, Fahmi, 373
Ijara, 330, 336
Ikadin (Ikatan Advokat Indonesia), 177, 238 (n 19), 242 (text and ns 24, 27), 243-5
Ikahi (Ikatan Hakim Indonesia), 177
Ikatan Cendekiawan Muslim se-Indonesia, see ICMI
Imam Mekah case, 317 (n 66)
IMF (International Monetary Fund), 9, 16, 17, 19, 379

India, 169 (n 32), 216, 397
Indische Staatsblad, 35
Indische Tjidschrift van het Recht, 40
Inlanders, 4, 5
Inpres, 103, 218
Insemination, 166-7
Instruksi Presiden, see *Inpres*
Integralist state, Chapters 11 and 12; 17, 186-195, 235 (n 13)
Integralistic Staatsidee, see Integralist state
Intel, 378
Intellectual property, Chapter 22
Interest, at Islamic law, Chapter 23
International Commission of Jurists, 173 (text and n 8), 350, 358
International Court of Justice, see World Court
International Islamic Bank for Investment and Development, 328, 330
International Labour Rights Education and Research Fund, 375
International Monetary Fund, see IMF
Internationalisation and law, Chapter 20
Intra Uterine Device, 166
IPHI (Ikatan Penasehat Hukum Indonesia), 242 (n 27)
Iran, 326
Iraq, 384
Irian Jaya, 2, 46 (n 46), 67 (n 82), 87, 91, 341
    Amungme people of, 54
    Hanoch Hebe Ohee case, 251-253
    Kamoro people of, 54
    Moi people of, 54,
    Sou people of, 54
Iskandar Muda, 119
Islam, Chapter 6, 8; 2-3, 5, 7, 16, 28
    and banking, Chapter 23
    Ideology, Council of, 328, 332
    and medical science, Chapter 10
    political suppression of, 126 (n 20)
    and politics, Chapters 6, 23, 209
    and regional rebellions, 203-4 (text and notes)
    revivalism, 323-4
    See also Muslim; and *Syariah*
Islamic Development Bank, 325-6
ITB *(Institut Teknologi Bandung)*, 146 (n 3)
Itjihad, 134 (n 73), 159 (n 1), 323-4

J

Jakarta, 5, 9, 11, 45, 81, 82, 92, 381
    North, Fisheries Office, 263 (n 7)
Jakarta Charter, 102, 126 (n 20)
Jakarta Heart Hospital, 165
Jakarta Post newspaper, 247 (n 9)
Jaksa, 104, 111-3, 363
Jakti, Kuntjoro, 177 (n 19)
Jama'at Islami, 324, 325
Japan. 40, 282, 286 (n 17), 294
    colonial status of, 35-6, 38
    corporate and contract culture, 291
    influence on constitutional law, 174, 191
    occupation of Indonesia by, 5-6, 17, 98

Jarsin, Julia, 145, 154 (n 13)
Java, 45, 98, 200, 341-2
    East, 376
    ideas of power in, 235(n 12)
    local government in, 202
    relationship with outer islands, Chapter 14, esp 203-204
    West, 46, 81; Baduy people of, 47; *Darul Islam* revolt, 203
'Javanism', 15, 16, 232-4
Jawa Pos newspaper, 247 (n 9)
Jayapura, 251-3
Jellinek, Georg, 188, 190
Jembatan Dua, 82
Jhering, Rudolf von, 188
Jim Willie/Swallow Brand case, 309 (n 31)
Joint venture agreements, Chapter 20
Judicial review, Chapter 15, 19; 174, 181--3, 238
Judiciary, 7, 13-14, 27
        independence of , Chapter 11, 16 and 19
Jurang Gupit, 148
Juru sita, 248

K

Kabupaten, 201, 202 (n 4)
Kacamatan, 47
KADIN (*Kamar Dagang dan Industri*), 265, 284, 298, 299
Kahin, AR, 200
Kalimantan, 45, 87, 91, 341
    Central, appointment of governor of, 213
    East, 54, 68, Sanggau, 55 (n 44)
    West, Dayak people of, 54
Kalurahan, 47
Kamaliyyat, 162
Kantor Urusan Agama, 100
Kantor Wilayah, 211
Kartasasmita, Ginandjar, 334 (n 4)
Kartini, Raden Adjeng, 124
Kasasi, see Cassation
Kawula-gusti, 174, 343
Kazhakstan, 392
Keboedajaan Timoer newspaper, 190
Kedung Ombo case, 14, 80, 82, 83-6, 87, 89, 92, 249-50 (text and n 21)
Kekeluargaan, see *Asas kekeluargaan*
Kekosongan hukum, 136
Kelurahan, 209
Kepala Daerah, 202, 205, 210-12, 214
Kepala desa, 80
Kesowo, Bambang, 308
Keterbukaan, 9, 215
KFM (*Kebutuhan Fisik Minimum*), 374
Khitab, 134
Khitabiyyah, 134 (n 73)
Kitab Kuning, 107
KKN (*Korupsi, Kolusi, Nepotisme*), 17 (text and n 17)
Kodim (Komando Distrik Militer), 369, 377-8
Koesomo, Joedo

Kollewijn, RD, 38, 39
Komando Operasi Pemulihan Keamanan dan Ketertiban, see KOPKAMTIB
Komisi Banding Paten, 314
KOMNASHAM (National Commission on Human Rights), 80, 358, 378-9
Kompas newspaper, 247 (n 9), 253, 271 (n 8)
Kompilasi Hukum Syariah, see *Syariah*
Kongres Perempuan Indonesia, 124 (n 10)
Kongres Wanita Indonesia (KOWANI), 147, 155
Konstituante, 6, 7, 18, 221 (text and n 1)
KOPKAMTIB, 180, 260. See also BAKORSTANAS
Koramil (Komando Rayon Militer), 369, 376-7
Korea, South, 175, 216, 240, 282, 285 (n 10), 294
KORPRI, 130, 178, 214, 254, 368
Kotamadya, 201
KOWANI, see *Kongres Wanita Indonesia*
Kowar, E, 334 (n 4)
Krismon (monetary crisis), 9, 16
KUHP, 128, 132
Kumpul kebol, 139
Kurdistan, 395
Kuwait, 326, 384, 386
    Finance House, 325

L

Labour law, Chapter 26
Land Administration Project, see LAP
Land redistribution, 15
Landraad, 33, 35, 40, 232
Lansing, 392
LAP (Land Administration Project), Chapter 4; 67
Latief, Abdul, 372
Law reform, Chapter 16
Lawyers, Chapters 16, 20
LBH (*Lembaga Bantuan Hukum*), 154, 230, 238, 241, 243, 378-9. See also *Peradin*
Leiden University, 188-9, 191, 342
Lembaga Bantuan Hukum, see LBH
Lev, Daniel, 175 (text and n 14), 259 (n 1)
Lex mercatoria, 30-1
Limburg-Stirum, van, 37
LP3ES, 138 (n 91, 92)
Lubis, Nur Achmad Fadhil, 139
Lubis, Todung Mulya, 343
Ludewijk, Mrs, see Supadmi
Lunca, I Ketut, Col, 214
Lurah, 80, 209
Luwu, 206
Lysol case, 317 (n 64)

M

Madura, 46, 98, 341-2
Mafia Pengadilan, 181; see also Corruption and Judicial independence
Mahkamah Agung, (Supreme Court), Chapters 16, 17 and 18; 7, 14, 50, 99, 104, 172
    (n 4, 5), 173 (n 9), 174, 175, 179, 181-3, 197, 346, 372, 378
    and arbitration, 294-7(text and n 15, 18, 19, 26), 300 (text and n 31)
    and execution of judgments, Chapter 17

Mahkamah Agung (cont)
    and Islamic law, Chapters 6 and 10
    and marriage, 113, 122, 124 (text and n 14), 127 (n 29), 128 (text and n 35), 129
        (text and ns 40, 42), 132 (n 60), 133, 135 (text and n 79), 136 , 137, 138, 139,
        140
    and right of review, Chapters 11 and 12
    *Surat Edaran (*Circular letter*)*, 7
    and *Tempo case*, 269, 272, 275-6
Mahkamah Islam Tinggi, (Islamic Court of Appeal), 101. See also Chapter 6
Mahmud, Syamsuddin, 214
Majelis Permusyawaratan Rakyat, see MPR
Majelis Pertimbangan Pajak, 223
Majelis Pertimbangan Penelitian Hakim (MPPH), 177
Majelis Ulama Indonesia, see MUI
Makasar, 145
Malang, 45
Malari Affair, 145
Malaysia, 105, 110, 164, 282, 294, 326
Malik, Adam, 381
Maliki, 99
Maluku, 202
Man, ED & F, (Sugar) Ltd v Yani Haranto case, see BULOG
Mandela, Nelson, 383 (n 13)
Mangkoedilaga, Benyamin, 253-4, 264, 272, 274-6 (text and n 18), 294 (n 10)
Manunggaling kawala lan gusti, 259
Marriage laws, Chapters 7, 8, esp 125 (n 19); see also China
Marshall, Chief Justice of the United States, 182
Marsinah, 363, 365-379
Maryadi, Eko, 372
Masik, Sumitro, 217
Maslahah mursalah, 162-3, 164
Masyumi, 203 (n 10)
Mawdudi, Abu al-A'ala, 324-5, 327
Mazhab, 99, 106
Medan, 113, 363, 371, 379
Medicine, medical science, and Islam. See Chapter 10
Memet, Yogie, 198, 211
Mentai, 117(n 19)
Merapi, Mt, 66 (n 81)
Milibrand, Ralph, 178
Military, see ABRI
Milk, at Islamic law, 168
Minahasa, 117(n 19)
Minangkabau, 46 (n 11), 48, 91, 200, 204, 341, 343. See also Sumatra, West
Ministry of Religion, 100
Moerdiono, 213 (n 41), 217
Moertopo, Ali, 193
Mohamad, Goenawan, 272-3 (text and n 15)
Molluccas, South, 203
Monarchy, Netherlands, 222 (text and n 3)
Monetary Gold Removed from Rome in 1943 case, 384 (text and n 15),
Monopolies
    anti-monopoly Law, 9, 16
Morocco, 397

MPR *(Majelis Permusyawaratan Rakyat)*, 17, 172, 183, 191, 215, 223, 259, 275, 355
- *Sementara* (MPRS), 101, 136 (text and n 81), 193
  on the hierarchy of laws, 269
  structure and membership, Chapter 13, 211 (n 36)
  See also *musyawarah*
Mudaraba, 328-336
Mudarib, 328-9, 333
Mudjono, 179, 240-1
Muhammad, Din, 274 (n 16)
Muhammad, Mar'ie, 271
MUI *(Majelis Ulama Islam)*, 163-6, 334
Muladi, 360-1
Muljoharjo, Ruslan, 204
Muqaddarat, 162
Murder, Chapter 9
Murtopo, Ali, 368
Musharaka, 328-31
Muslim
  Brotherhood, 324-5
  statistik, fanatik, 137, (n 90)
  See also, Islam, *Syariah*
Musyawarah, 51, 75, 77, 191,
  Musyawarah Pimimpin Daerah, 226
  and 'village republic', 191, 194
Mutlaq, 167
Muzaffar, Chandra, 324

N

Nahdlatul Ulama, 126 (n 20), 203 (n 10), 334
Nainggolan, Sahat, 177 (n 18)
Namibia Advisory Opinion case (Legal consequences for States of the Continued Presence of South Africa in Namibia (South West Africa), 391
Nanking, 39
Nasroen, Mohammad, 193
Nass, 163
Nasution, Dr Adnan Buyung, 243 (text and n 28, 29, 30)
Nasution, General, 192
National Commission on Human Rights, see KOMNASHAM
National Judicial Conference of 1993, 263
National Spatial Management Coordination Board, 68
Natural justice, 261-2. See also Chapter 15
Nauru v Australia case (Certain Phosphate Lands in Nauru), 385
Navigation Maritime Bulgare Varna v Pt Nizwar case, 296 (text and n 18)
Nazism, 174
Ne bis in idem, 114, 119, 120
Negara hukum, Chapters 1, 2, 11, 12 and 16; 8, 13-14, 17-20, 109, 171, 221-3, 227, 230, 231, 233, 235-8, 240, 247, 254, 258, 265-7.
Negara Islam, 102-3
New Order, 7-8, 13-19, 125, 126, 139, 147, 172, 173, 174, 177, 183, 193, 194, 208-9, 214, 219, 228, 230, 235-7, 258, 357. For summary, see Introduction
New York Agreement, 252. See also Convention, New York
NGOs, 240-1, 365, 373, 379
Nicaragua v United States case (Military and Paramilitary Activities in and against Nicaragua) 385 (text and n 18), 386
Nihin, 213
Noor, Zainulbahar, 334 (n 4)
Nusa Tenggara, 202, 341

O

Oda, Judge, 388-9
Oesman, Oetojo, 240
Oetama, Jacob, 272 (n 10)
Office of the Trade Representative (USA), 375
Ogushi, Toyo, 190
Old Order, 5-7, 13-14, 19, 172, 209, 214. For summary, see Introduction
OPEC, 306
Oppenheim, Jacques, 188
Organ transplants, 164-5
Ottomans, 97
Oudendijk, WJ, 39

P

P4P (*Panitia Penyelesaian Perselisahan Perburuhan Pusat*), 369
Pakistan, 326
Pakpahan, Muchtar, 19, 250 (n 22), 362-6, 372, 379
Pakpahan, Normin, 285 (n 11)
Palestine, 392
Paloh, Surya, 271
Pamong praja, 175 (n 14), 193, 203, 231
Pamungkas, Sri Bintang, 19, 358-361
Pancasila, 12, 82, 83, 86, 89, 92, 223, 237, 357 (text and n 5), 265
    and criminal law, 343, 349-51
    and industrial relations (*Hubungan Industrial Pancasila*), 368-70 (n 17), 372 (n 19), 373-5
    and Islam, 102-4, 106, 109, 126 (n 20), 129, 130, 137 (text and n 86)
    and *negara hukum*, 172 (n 4), 174, 180, 186, 193, 194, 197-9
Pangreh Praja, 231, 240
Panitera, 248
Panitia Pemeriksa Adat dan Tatanegara Dahoeloe, 191
Panitia Penyelesaian Perselisahan Perburuhan Pusat, 369
Papua New Guinea, 66
Parada, 214
Parliament, see DPR
Partai Demokrasi Indonesia, see PDI
Partai Komunis Indonesia, see PKI
Partai Nasional Indonesia, see PNI
Partai Persuatuan Pembangunan, see PPP
Partai Rakyat untuk Demokrasi, see PRD
Partai Uni Demokrasi Indonesia, see PUDI
Patents, Chapter 22
Patrimonialsim, Chapter 18
PDI (*Partai Demokrasi Indonesia*), 197-199, 214, 359, 361, 363, 372
Pegawai negeri, 178-9, 353
Peking, 38
Pembangunan, 131-2
Pemberontakan, 13
Pembreidelan, see Chapter 19
Pemerintah Revolusioner Republik Indonesia, see PRRI
Pemuda, 5, 13
Penembak misterius, see Petrus
Pengadilan
    Agama, see Religious Courts

Negeri (District Court), 101, 112, 135, 137 (n 89), 243 (n 30), 248, 249 (text and n 18), 252, 254, 296-7, 301, 309, 356, 378
   Tinggi (High Court), 135, 137 (n 89), 242 (n 27), 251
Penghulu, 133
Pengurus adat, 55
Peradin (Persatuan Advokat Indonesia), 177, 229 (n 3), 230, 234, 237-8, 240 (n 23), 241-2 (text and n 24), 244-5, 240 (n 23)-242 (text and n 24), 244-5
   Ikrar Peradin, 237
   and *negara hukum*, 237
   See also, *Ikadin*
Permesta, see PRRI
Persahi (Persatuan Sarjana Hukum Indonesia), 172
Persatuan Artis Indonesia (PARFI), 154
Persatuan Wartawan Indonesia (PWI), 153
Perwiranegara, Alamsyah Ratu, 334 (n 4)
Pesantren, 107
Petren, Judge, 394
Petrus (Penembak misterius), 194-5 (text and n 8), 239 (text and n 21, 22)
Philippines, 216, 285 (n 10), 294
Piagam Jakarta, see Jakarta Charter
PKI *(Partai Komunis Indonesia)* 5, 8, 81 (text and n 8), 180, 189 (n 4), 203 (n 10), 206
   and 1965 killings, 12, 13;
   and land redistribution, 15, 52 (n 31)
   and women, 147
Pluit Polder case, 82-3, 87, 89
Plumpang case, 80, 263 (n 7)
PNI *(Partai Nasional Indonesia)*, 5, 203 (n 10)
Pokrol bambu, 227-229, 242 (n 27)
Polisi, 369
Polres (Polisi Resort), 369, 376
Polygamy, Chapter 8
Porong, 376
Portugal
   Carnation Revolution, 389
   and East Timor, Chapter 27
Positivism, Chapter 12
PPP, 126 (n 20), 197-199, 358
PRD, 361
Press Council, Chapter 19
Press, law and the, Chapter 19
Prioritas case, 260, 271
Prit-Jigo, 146 (text and ns 2, 3)
Priyayi, 233
Probosutedjo, 334 (n 4)
Procedural fairness, 261
Profumo, John & Profumo affair, 149
Propinsi, 201
PRRI, 203 (text and n 9), 204
Public Prosecutor, see *Jaksa*
Puchta, Georg, 187
PUDI, 359
Pulo Mas, 92
Purwoto, see Gandasubrata

Q

Qard hasan, 335
Qatar Islamic Bank, 325
Qiyas, 164-5
Quebec, 392
Qur'an, 102, 105, 122, 126, 134 (n 72), 139, 159, 162 (n 10)-169, 324-7, 332, 336
Qutb, Sayyid, 327

R

Raad van Justitie, 33, 35
Raad *van Nederlandsch-Indie*, 37, 38, 40
Rabb al-mal, 328, 333
Raffles, Thomas Stamford, 3
Rahman, Fazlur, 326, 327
Rahmini, Siti, 152-3
Ramadan, 376
Rape, Chapter 6, esp 114-5, 119
Rashid Rida, Muhammad, 325
Rechtshoogeschool, 38
Rechtsstaat, Chapters 11, 12; 13, 227, 233, 234
Reformasi, 9, 12, 19-20
Regent, see *Bupati*
Regional government, Chapters 14, 15
Regional rebellions, Chapter 14
Religious Courts (*Pengadilan Agama*), Chapters 6, 8; 140
Repelita (Rencana Pembangunan Lima Tahun), 247
Republika newspaper, 247 (n 9)
Riba, Chapter 23
Robespierre, 187
Robison, Richard, 175
Romanticism, Chapter 12
Rome, 384
Rosenthal, Franz, 161-2
Rudini, General, 212
Rukun tetangga, 209 (n 28)
Rukun warga, 209 (n 28)
Rumah tangga, 202
Runggun, 91
Rusdi, E, 111
Rutgers, D, 38

S

Sachroni, Oman, 212
Sahid Jaya Hotel, 334
Said, Ali, 240, 241, 242-3(text and n 25), 244, 274 (n 17), 378
Saleh, Ismail, 175, 242-3 (text and n 29), 244, 262, 264
Salim, Amarullah, 262
Saljo, 177 (n 19)
Samola, Eric, 273
Santa Cruz cemetery, 382
Santoso, Amir, 212-3
Santoso, Hugeng Imam, 240
Sarekat Islam, 5
Sarf, 332
Sarumpaet, Ratna, 19, 355-58, 360

Saudi Arabia, 32-6
Savigny, Friedrich Karl von, 187-9
SBM (*Serikat Buruh Merdeka* – 'Solidarity'), 372
SBSI (*Serikat Buruh Sejahtera Indonesia*), Chapter 26; 19, 363, 371, 373
Schrieke, JJ, 38, 40
Secured transactions, 26, 287
Seidman, R & A, 92-4, 351, 353
Sekretariate Daerah, 211
Semarang, 83, 137 (n 89), 262
Semen, at Islamic law, 166-7
Sendang Pasir, 81
Senoaji, Oemar, 179
Separation of powers, 17-18, 28, 236, 259-60, 275-6
Serikat Buruh Sejahtera Indonesia, see SBSI
Serpara, JS, 253
Seven Up case, 316 (n 57), 317 (n 66)
Sexuality, Chapters 7, 8, 9
Shafi, 99, 106, 164
Shahabuddeen, Judge, 387 (text and n 24)
Shikak, 99, 108
Siahaan, Lintong Oloan, 262
Siddiqi, Muhamnmad, 327, 332
Sidoarjo, *Sistem Inteligine*, 378
Sinar Harapan newspaper, 146, 149
Singapore, 105, 110, 175, 285 (n 10), 294
Siregar, Arifin, 334 (n 4)
Siregar, Ashadi, 147 (n 5)
Siregar, Bismar, 113-4
Siregar, Syahrul Ralie, 334 (n 4)
SIT (*surat izin terbit*), 270
SIUPP (*surat izin usaha penerbitan pers*), see Chapter 19
Sjahrir, Sutan, 6, 192
Sjiqaq, see *shikak*
Skubiszewski, Judge, 388 (n 26)
Slovenia, 392
Soares, Abilio, 216
SOBSI (*Sentral Organisasi Buruh Seluruh Indonesia*), 367
Soedjana, FX, 177 (n 19)
Soegomo, 193
Soeharto, 11, 13-19, 23, 24, 138, 272, 284
    and administrative law, 258-60
    and anti-subversion laws, 355-9, 361-2, 365
    and East Timor, 383, 395 (n 47)
    and election, 198
    and Islamic banking, 323, 333-4
    and lawyers, 235, 239 (text and n 21),
    and *negara hukum*, 1 (text and n 2), 7-9, 183, 186, 193-195
    and regional government, 200, 212-13, 215, 216, 219
    and unionism, 367, 370, 379
Soekarno, 13-14, 15, 50, 101, 292 (n 50)
    and anti-subversion laws, 356, 357
    and lawyers, 233, 235, 258,
    and *negara hukum*, 1(n 2), 5, 6, 7, 172, 176, 182, 183 (n 30), 192, 193
    and regional government, 203, 204, 206
Soekarnoputri, Megawati, 359, 363
Soeparmanto, 213

Index

Soepomo, Raden, 7, 18, 173-4, 181-2, 183, 189-92, 194, 259, 274
    drafting of the 1945 Constitution, Chapter 12; 232-234, 235 (text and n 13)
Soerjono, 252
Soetomo, 13
Solidarity trade union, see SBM
Sonneveld, W, 37
Soviet Union, 97, 213 (text and n 41), 365, 396
Spit, HJ, 39
SPSI (*Serikat Pekerja Seluruh Indonesia*), Chapter 26
Staatsblad-Europeanen, 35
Sterilisation, 167
Strauss, Levi, 315-6
Strikes, see Trade Unions
Subardjo, 190
Subversion, Chapter 25; 183(n 30), 349-50, 356-360
Sudan, 325-6, 395
Sudharmono, 242 (n 25)
Sudomo, Admiral, 367-8, 372
Sudwikatmono, 334 (n 4)
Sukarsono, Imam, 179 (text and n 27)
Sukarton, 177 (n 19)
Sulawesi, 205, 341
    Central, 117
    local government, 202
    South, rebellion in, 203-4
Sumatra, 4, 202, 341, Nias, 341
    East, 45
    North, 209, 363, Batak people of, 47, 341, Karo Batak, 91; Sugapa people of, 54,
        see also Aceh
    rebellion in, 203-4
    West, 45, election of governor of, 214, see Minangkabau
Sunna, 324; see also Chapter 6
Suny, Ismail, Chapter 11
Supadmi, 148-156
Suparto, Malikus, 177 (n 18)
Supermi case, 317
Supersemar (Surat Perintah Sebelas Maret), 1 (n 2)
Supreme Court, see *Mahkamah Agung*
Surakarta, 131
Surat Edaran, see *Mahkamah Agung*
Surat nikah, 100
Surat sakti, 252-4
Sutrisno, Try, 372 (n 19)
Suwanda, Karna, 213
Suyono, 148-156
Syariah, 2, 3, 12, Chapters 6, 8, 10
    and banking, Chapter 23
    fasah, 105
    Kompilasi Hukum Syariah, 106-9, 130
Syarikat Takaful, 323
Syigag, 105
Syria, 169 (n 32)

T

Taiwan, 175, 285 (n 10), 287, 294
Talak, 105, 108-9

Taman Mini Indonesia Indah, 15
Tambuan, ASS, 177 (n 18)
Tanjung, Feisal, 370-1
Tapanuli, 203
Taqlid, 159 (n 1)
Tariffs, 284
Tasrif, Suardi, 182, 234, 238 (n 19), 240 (n 23)
Taufik, Ahmad, 372
Tax, 205 (text and n 16, 17), 218, 286
    Majelis Pertimbangan Pajak, 223
Teijin case, 317 (n 66)
Telek Pucung, 80
Temenggung, 55-6
Tempo magazine and case, Chapter 19; 111, 119, 215, 247 (n 9), 254, 264, 372
ter Haar, B, 38, 40, 43 (n 3), 53 (n 35)
Thailand, 216, 240, 285 (n 10), 294
Thamrin, MH, 38
Thant, U, 396
Tibet, 395
Timor,
    car, 16 (n 6)
    East, Chapter 27; 8, 11, 341, 344, 350, 365
        appointment of Regent in, 214
        Dili massacre, 382
        invasion of, Chapter 27, esp 381-2
    West, 381
Tjitrosubeno, Harjono, 242, 244
Tonang, A, 152
Trade and law, Chapters 1, 2, 20 and 21
Trade Marks, Chapter 22
Trade unions, 9, 16, 19, Chapter 26
Trading Corp of Pakistan v PT Bakrie Brothers case, 296 (text and n 19)
Transfusion, blood, 167-8
Trias Politika, 17
Tuan tanah, 87
Tubectomy, 166-7
Tunisia, 326

U
Ulama, 106, 108, 109, 130, 139, 140, 233-5
Umma/t, 324
UNCITRAL, 281, 283, 298, 299-301; see also Conventions
Undang-undang, 103
UNIDROIT, 281, Principles for International Commercial Contracts, 285 (n 11); see also
    Conventions
Unionism, see Trade Unions
United Arab Emirates, 325-6
United Nations, 6, 280, 358, 382 (n 9)
    and East Timor, Chapter 27
United States of America, 182, 204, 232, 280, 287, 375, 385-6
United States of Indonesia, 15 (n 5)
University of Indonesia, 192
University of Melbourne, 282
USSR, see Soviet Union

Utrecht
    Union of, 222 (n 3)
    University, 189
Uzair, Mohammad, 328

V

Vasectomy, 166
Vatikiotis, MR, 207
Venezuela, 182
Vereenigde Oost-Indische Compagnie, see VOC
Vietcong, 382 (n 8)
Vietnam, 286 (n 17)
Visman Commission, 40
Vivqueque, 214
VOC (*Vereenigde Oost-Indische Compagnie*), 3
Volksgeist, 187-8
Volksraad, 37, 38, 39
Vollenhoven, Cornelis van, 37, 43 (text and n 3), 44 (ns 5 and 6), 45, 46, 75, 188-190
    (text and notes)
Vonk Commission, 40

W

Wages, 374, Chapter 26
Wahyu, 43 (text and n 4)
Wakaf, 102, 104-5, 107, 130
Wakalah, 332
WALHI (*Wahana Lingkungan Hidup Indonesia*), 265
Walikota, 369
Weber, Max, 90, 260, 266-7
Wertheim, WF, Chapter 3, esp 33-4, 40
Western Sahara case, 394, 397
Wilson, Woodrow, 392
WIPO (World Intellectual Property Organisation), 305; see also Convention
Wiryohardjo, Soegyarti, 177 (n 18)
Women, Chapters 7, 8, 9. See also *Dharma Wanita*
Woolcott, Richard, 382 (n 8)
World Bank (ICJ – International court of Justice), 42, 279, 286 (text and n 17), 306
World Court, Chapter 27
World Intellectual Property Organisation, see WIPO
World War I, 392
World War II, 98
World Wildlife Fund, 68

Y

Yamin, Muhammad, 171, 232-3 (text and n 8), 235 (n 13)
Yap Thiam Hien, 234 (n 11)
Yayasan Amal Bhakti Muslim Pancasila, 334
Yayasan Lembaga Bantuan Hukum, see LBH
Yogyakarta, 45, 360
Yomn, Fistus C, 253
Yugoslavia, 213, 392, 396
Yurisprudensi, 99, 104, 105-6, 108-10, 129

Z

Zakat, 335
Zina/h, 115, 117